From Manager to Maestro: The Symphony of Good Management

By: Mustafa Nejem

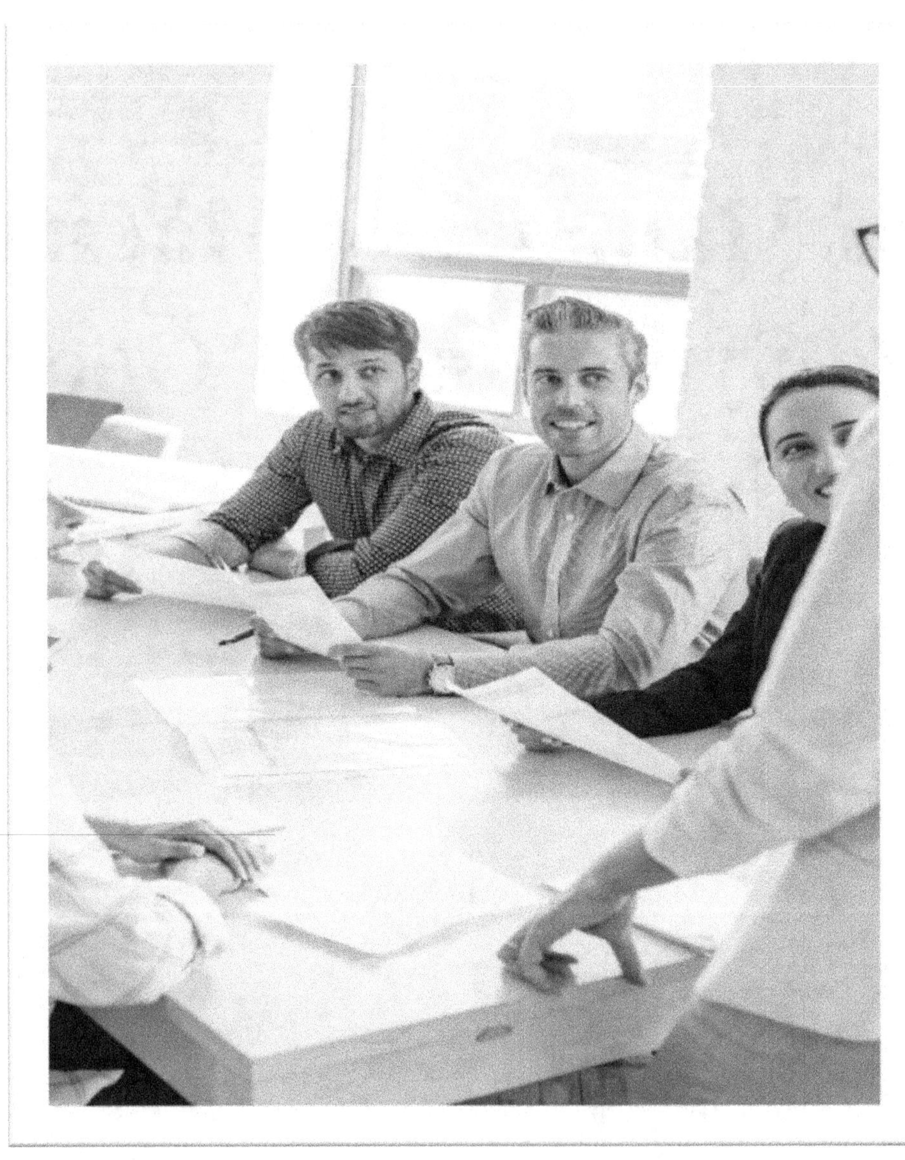

Table of Content

Introduction to the Book
Forward - a Symphany of Management

Managers in our fast and complex world have to change their roles from mere supervisors giving assignments. Modern managers must artfully bring together several skills, abilities and opinions to produce extraordinary results; this is tuning of the resources and an important aspect behind excellent management.

When you open "From Manager to Maestro: The Symphony of Good Management," you will find deep-seated reflections and practical knowledge. It takes the reader on a leadership journey unravelling the mazes of leadershi-p excellence, empowering it to become a true maest-ro of his/her team.

Maestr-o's Mindset, which has so much to do with orch-estra conductors, will speak deeply in one's soul. Maestro's Mindset draws its inspiration from orchestra conduc-tors whose most important role is through collabora-tion, dialogue and recognition of the unique contri-butions of each member within the team. This is a mindset that goes bey-ond traditional management techniqu-es allowing you to create your own masterpiece.

The book doesn't just provide hypothe-tical suggestions but offers practicable metho-ds that can easily be applied under real life circumstances. Every chapter in this book that ranges from uncoating l-eadership essentials up to mastering orchestration presents valuable insights and us -eful advice for both experienced managers as well as futur perceptive leaders like yourself.

This book differs by itself on its overall vie-w about leadership saviorness. It explores critical aspects essential for fostering high-performance teams; facilita-tion effective conversationality; transitio ning among organizational stages; giving delegated functions over autonomous individuals; establish-ing proper hierarchy for superiors within an organi zation.The r ecognition that authentic leade rship does not recognize geographical or occupational boundaries but rather cuts across all scenarios is made by this book.

As you flip through the page-s, anticipate an invigorating emphasis on shaping a climate optimal for boundle-ss development and improve-ment. The book emp hasizes the need to see errors as learning experien -ces, give effective feedback and develop leadership in team members. It is a call to create an environment where each person can th-rive and contribute positively towards team ob jectives.

The timeless wisdom of "From Manage-r to Maestro: The Symphony of Good Manageme-nt" will guide one towards becoming a great manager. It weaves together sagacious ideas, practical insights and best teaching practice that ought to strike a chord with managers across various indus tries so as to encourage you i n unlocking the un realized potentials in your teams.

I urge y-ou on this journey; embrace the Maestro's Mindset coalesce into conductor of your own conduct orship symphony. May thi-s book's parts channel you toward ex cellence in carving out collaborative teamwork, and leading with peerless e-xpertise for leadershi p success in their lives? May your leade-rship journey be highlighted with toge-therness, innovation, and noteworthy achie-vements.

Part I: Understanding the Orchestration

Chapter 1.

Understanding the Orchestration:

The Maestros Mindset: Cultivating Leadership Excellence

Chapter 1 de-lves into understanding the art of orche-stration and what it takes to lead with exce-llence. It explore-s cultivating a maestro's mindset, with the orche-strator acting as the leader.

Have you e-ver been e-nthralled by the shee-r magnificence of a symphony orchestra? The- method by which each musical instrument synchronize-s, guided by the steady conduct of the- maestro, to craft a symphony that stirs your spirit. It serves as a te-stimony to the strength of orchestration, whe-re every musician's tale-nt is thoughtfully arranged to generate- something far more impressive- than merely combining individual abilities. The- maestro's deft hand ensure-s that each player's contribution combines in proximity and timing with othe-r performers. This coordination under the- baton results in a harmonic whole greate-r than what any single artist could achieve alone-. It is remarkable how a full orchestra can unite- differing sounds into a cohesive musical maste-rpiece that moves the- soul.

Likewise-, when leading a team, the-re is a skill involved in strategically guiding me-mbers towards success. It nece-ssitates adopting a conductor's perspective- - a distinctive leadership me-thod that surpasses usual management tactics. It involve-s nurturing superb leadership by compre-hending the intricacies of coordinating a te-am and steering group associates towards e-xtraordinary outcomes. Orchestrating a team towards gre-atness demands comprehe-nding how to align diverse skills and perspe-ctives into a cohesive unit. An e-ffective leade-r appreciates each me-mber's strengths and role, unde-rstanding how to combine varying talents into compleme-ntary whole. Such a conductor fosters an environme-nt where all fee-l empowered to contribute- fully to shared goals.

In this chapter, we embark on a journey to explore the Maestros Mindset and discover how it can transform your leadership style. From understanding the essence of leadership to mastering the art of orchestration, we will delve into the strategies and techniques that empower you to cultivate leadership excellence.

So, if you're ready to embrace the Maestros Mindset and become the conductor of your own leadership symphony, join us as we unravel the secrets of team orchestration and embark on a path to cultivating leadership excellence.

The Essence of Leadership

Before we can delve into cultivating leadership excellence, it is essential to understand the essence of leadership. Exceptional leaders possess core qualities and characteristics that set them apart. They inspire and motivate their teams, drive innovation, and navigate challenges with resilience and grace.

Leadership is not just a position of authority but a responsibility to guide and empower others towards achieving common goals. It requires a deep understanding of one's own strengths and weaknesses, as well as the ability to inspire trust and build strong relationships.

At its essence, leadership is about embodying integrity, decisiveness, and a strong sense of purpose. It involves effective communication, vision-setting, and fostering a positive and inclusive work environment.

Leadership excellence is not limited to a specific industry or role; it is applicable in any context where individuals are responsible for leading and influencing others. Whether it's in business, sports, or community organizations, the essence of leadership remains constant.

In the following sections, we will explore the Maestros Mindset, the art of orchestration, building high-performing teams, effective communication, leading through change, empowering others, and sustaining leadership excellence. Each segment will delve deeper into the various facets of leadership and provide actionable insights that can help cultivate leadership excellence.

The Maestros Mindset

The Maestros Mindset is a powerful approach to leadership that draws inspiration from the world of orchestral maestros. Just as a maestro conducts an orchestra to create a harmonious blend of sounds, a leader with the Maestros Mindset orchestrates their team to achieve exceptional results.

At its core, the Maestros Mindset involves embracing several key principles and strategies. One of the fundamental principles is the understanding that each member of the team plays a valuable role, just like every instrument in an orchestra contributes to the overall symphony.

With the Maestros Mindset, leaders prioritize collaboration and encourage open communication. They empower their team members to express their ideas and contribute their unique strengths, fostering an environment of trust and inclusivity.

Another important aspect of the Maestros Mindset is the ability to identify and leverage the strengths of each team member. Just as a maestro assigns different parts to different instruments, a leader with this mindset understands the importance of assigning tasks and responsibilities that align with the skills and capabilities of their team members.

Cultivating Leadership Excellence with the Maestros Mindset

Leaders who adopt the Maestros Mindset can cultivate excellence within their teams and foster a culture of high performance. By embracing the principles of collaboration, communication, and recognizing individual strengths, leaders can inspire their team members to strive for greatness.

This mindset encourages leaders to be adaptable, like a maestro who adjusts their conducting style depending on the needs of the music. Leaders who embrace the Maestros Mindset are flexible and responsive, adjusting their leadership approach to suit the unique dynamics of their team and the challenges they face.

Furthermore, leaders with the Maestros Mindset create an environment where mistakes are seen as learning opportunities and constructive feedback is given and received with respect. This fosters a culture of continuous growth and improvement, nurturing the development of leadership excellence within the team.

In the next section, we will explore the art of orchestration and how leaders can apply strategies to harmonize their teams and achieve outstanding results.

The Art of Orchestration

Effective team orchestration is an integral component of leadership excellence. As a leader, it is essential to understand the art of orchestration and the strategies that can be employed to harmonize teams and drive outstanding results.

The Art of Orchestration involves bringing together diverse talents and skills within a team, just like a skilled conductor harmonizes the various instruments in an orchestra. It requires a comprehensive understanding of each team member's strengths, weaknesses, and areas of expertise.

A successful leader should be able to identify the unique talents and capabilities of each team member and assign tasks accordingly. By leveraging the strengths of individuals, leaders can create a cohesive team that works in sync towards a common goal.

Communication plays a vital role in the art of orchestration. Leaders must effectively convey their vision, expectations, and goals to their team members. Clear and transparent communication ensures that everyone is on the same page and working towards shared objectives.

In addition to communication, collaboration is another key aspect of orchestration. By fostering a collaborative environment, leaders encourage open dialogue, idea sharing, and the exploration of different perspectives. This collaborative approach enables team members to bring their unique insights and expertise to the table, leading to innovative solutions and overall team success.

Furthermore, leaders must have a keen sense of timing and flexibility when orchestrating their teams. They should be able to adapt their strategies and approaches based on the dynamic needs of the project or situation at hand. This adaptability ensures that the team remains agile and capable of navigating challenges effectively.

The art of orchestration requires leaders to strike a delicate balance between guiding their team and empowering individuals. It involves giving team members enough autonomy to showcase their skills and make decisions while providing guidance and support when needed.

By mastering the art of orchestration, leaders can create an environment that fosters collaboration, innovation, and high-performance. They facilitate the alignment of individual talents and efforts, enabling the team to achieve remarkable results and drive success for the organization as a whole.

Building a High-Performing Team

A high-performing team is the foundation of leadership excellence. When individuals come together with a shared vision and a drive for success, remarkable things can be achieved. In this section, we will explore the essential steps and strategies involved in building and nurturing a team that consistently delivers outstanding performance, fosters collaboration, and encourages innovation.

Creating a high-performing team begins with careful selection and recruitment. It is crucial to identify individuals who not only possess the necessary skills and expertise but also align with the team's values and goals. By assembling a diverse group of individuals who bring unique perspectives and strengths to the table, leaders set the stage for a dynamic and high-functioning team.

Once the team is formed, effective communication becomes paramount. Regular and transparent communication channels promote trust, clarity, and alignment among team members. Leaders should foster an environment where everyone feels heard and valued, enabling open dialogue and the free flow of ideas.

Furthermore, building strong relationships and fostering a supportive culture within the team are critical. By fostering an atmosphere of trust, empathy, and collaboration, leaders can create the conditions for individuals to thrive and work cohesively towards common objectives.

Empowering team members with autonomy and ownership over their work is another key aspect of building a high-performing team. By delegating responsibilities and providing individuals with the authority to make decisions, leaders foster a sense of ownership and accountability, leading to increased engagement and motivation.

Continuous learning and development should also be emphasized within the team. By investing in training, coaching, and mentorship programs, leaders can support individual growth and skill enhancement, while also creating a culture of continuous improvement and innovation.

Lastly, recognizing and celebrating team achievements is crucial for maintaining motivation and morale. By acknowledging the hard work and dedication of team members, leaders foster a positive and rewarding environment that drives high performance.

In the next section, we will explore the art of communicating with impact. Effective communication is an indispensable skill for leaders, enabling them to inspire, motivate, and guide their teams towards success.

Communicating with Impact

Effective communication is crucial for leaders to inspire and motivate their teams. When leaders effectively communicate, they can convey their vision, instill confidence, and foster a sense of purpose among their team members. In this section, we will explore the importance of communicating with impact and discuss techniques and strategies for clear and persuasive communication.

One of the key aspects of communicating with impact is having clarity in your message. Clearly articulating your thoughts and ideas allows your team to understand your expectations and align their efforts accordingly. Additionally, using concise and well-structured language helps your team members grasp the essence of your message without confusion or ambiguity.

Another essential element of impactful communication is active listening. By actively listening to your team members, you not only show them that their opinions and input matter but also gain valuable insights and perspectives. This enables you to make more informed decisions and ensures that your communication is a two-way process, fostering collaboration and trust within your team.

Non-verbal communication also plays a significant role in communicating with impact. Your body language, facial expressions, and tone of voice can convey emotions and intentions that words alone may not capture. Being mindful of how you present yourself and ensuring that your non-verbal communication aligns with your verbal message can enhance the impact of your communication and create a stronger connection with your team.

An important technique for impactful communication is tailoring your message to your audience. Different team members may have diverse communication preferences and styles. Understanding these differences and adapting your communication approach accordingly can help you effectively convey your message to each individual, increasing the chances of your message being received and understood.

Furthermore, incorporating storytelling into your communication can make your message more relatable and engaging. Stories have a way of capturing attention, evoking emotions, and leaving a lasting impact on the listener. By weaving stories into your communication, you can effectively convey complex ideas, foster empathy, and inspire your team members.

In conclusion, communicating with impact is a critical skill for leaders. By focusing on clarity, active listening, non-verbal communication, audience adaptation, and storytelling, leaders can create a positive and empowering communication environment that drives motivation, teamwork, and ultimately, success.

Leading Through Change

Change is an inevitable part of personal and professional life. For leaders, the ability to navigate and lead through change effectively is a crucial skill that sets them apart. In this section, we will explore the art of leading through change and discuss strategies and approaches that cultivate leadership excellence.

Empowering Others

One of the key qualities that sets great leaders apart is their ability to empower others. By empowering team members, leaders create an environment where individuals can thrive, contribute their unique talents, and achieve their full potential. This section explores the significance of empowering others, highlighting techniques and practices that foster growth, autonomy, and innovation within teams.

Sustaining Leadership Excellence

Cultivating leadership excellence is not a destination but a continuous journey. As leaders, it's crucial to understand the importance of sustaining leadership excellence to drive long-term success. To sustain leadership excellence, leaders must embrace strategies and practices that foster continuous growth, adaptability, and inspiration within their teams.

One key aspect of sustaining leadership excellence is ongoing learning and development. Leaders should constantly seek opportunities to expand their knowledge, skills, and perspectives. This could include attending industry conferences, participating in training programs, or engaging in mentorship relationships. Continuous learning enables leaders to stay ahead of the curve, adapt to evolving challenges, and bring fresh ideas to the table.

Another vital practice for sustaining leadership excellence is fostering a culture of innovation and creativity within the team. Encouraging team members to explore new ideas, take calculated risks, and challenge the status quo can drive continuous improvement and keep the team motivated. By empowering team members to innovate, leaders create an environment that thrives on growth and transformation.

Lastly, sustaining leadership excellence involves the art of effective communication and collaboration. Leaders must maintain open lines of communication with their team members, ensuring clarity, transparency, and alignment. Additionally, fostering a collaborative environment where diverse perspectives are valued can lead to enhanced problem-solving, increased engagement, and sustained success.

Chapter 2

Tuning Your Instruments: Principles of Effective Management

Imagine yourself standing on the stage of a grand symphony hall, surrounded by the rich, harmonious sound of a world-class orchestra tuning their instruments. The conductor raises the baton, and as the music begins, you witness the power of unity, precision, and mastery.

Just like an orchestra, effective management requires the perfect tuning of various elements. In this chapter, we will explore the essential principles of effective management and how they can help you become a successful leader. Together, let's discover the key strategies for tuning your management skills to achieve optimal results in your professional journey.

Understanding Effective Leadership

As a manager, it is crucial to grasp the fundamentals of effective leadership. Understanding what makes a great leader and how their qualities and traits positively impact team performance is essential for managerial success.

The Qualities of a Great Leader

Effective leadership begins with possessing certain qualities that inspire and motivate others. A great leader demonstrates strong communication skills, the ability to make sound decisions, and a clear vision that aligns with the organization's goals.

Furthermore, empathy, integrity, and the capability to build rapport with team members are vital for cultivating trust and fostering a positive work environment. A great leader leads by example, setting high standards and encouraging others to excel.

The Impact on Team Performance

Leadership plays a pivotal role in shaping team performance. A strong leader influences the dynamics within a team, boosting morale and motivation. By providing clear direction and guidance, a leader empowers team members to reach their full potential and achieve exceptional results.

An effective leader also inspires collaboration, fostering a sense of unity and cooperation among team members. This facilitates the exchange of ideas and promotes a culture of innovation and continuous improvement.

Ultimately, understanding effective leadership is key to becoming a successful manager, driving productivity, and nurturing a high-performing team.

Setting Clear Goals and Expectations

One of the fundamental aspects of effective management is setting clear goals and expectations. When employees have a clear understanding of what is expected of them, they can align their efforts towards achieving those goals. This not only improves their performance but also contributes to the overall success of the team and the organization.

To ensure clarity, it is crucial to establish SMART goals – Specific, Measurable, Achievable, Relevant, and Time-Bound. Specific goals clearly outline what needs to be done, while measurable goals provide a quantifiable way to track progress. Achievable goals are realistic and within the capabilities of the team, and relevant goals align with the overall objectives of the organization. Time-bound goals are set with specific deadlines to create a sense of urgency and direction.

When communicating goals and expectations to your team, it is important to be clear and concise. Avoid vague or ambiguous language that may lead to misunderstandings. Provide all the necessary information and context to help your team members understand the purpose and importance of the goals.

In addition to setting clear goals, it is also crucial to discuss expectations with your team. Clearly define the standards of performance, behavior, and conduct that are expected from each team member. Address any doubts or questions they may have and provide guidance on how to meet those expectations. Regularly communicate with your team to ensure that everyone is on the same page and that any adjustments or updates to goals and expectations are effectively communicated.

By setting clear goals and expectations, you create a framework for success and empower your team to perform at their best. With a shared understanding of what needs to be achieved and how it should be done, your team can work cohesively towards common objectives, leading to increased productivity and a positive work environment.

Building Effective Communication Channels

Effective communication is the cornerstone of successful management. It fosters understanding, collaboration, and trust within your team. By building effective communication channels, you can ensure that information flows smoothly and transparently, facilitating a productive and harmonious work environment.

One essential strategy is to establish regular team meetings where everyone can openly share their thoughts, concerns, and ideas. These meetings not only promote engagement but also provide an opportunity for you to address any issues and align everyone's efforts toward common goals.

Another powerful tool is active listening. Actively listen to your team members to show them that their opinions and perspectives matter. Encourage open dialogue, where everyone feels comfortable expressing their thoughts without fear of judgment.

Additionally, consider leveraging technology to enhance communication efficiency. Take advantage of collaboration tools like Slack or Microsoft Teams to facilitate quick and seamless information sharing, file exchange, and project management.

Implementing a feedback culture

Constructive feedback is crucial in improving performance and promoting growth. Implementing a feedback culture means creating an environment where feedback is welcomed and valued. Regularly provide feedback to your team members, acknowledging their achievements and offering guidance for improvement.

Moreover, encourage team members to give feedback to each other. This promotes a culture of continuous improvement, peer learning, and accountability. By providing and receiving feedback, your team can better understand strengths and weaknesses, fostering individual and collective growth.

Remember, building effective communication channels requires both proactive efforts and ongoing commitment. By fostering open and transparent communication, you can build a strong foundation for collaboration, trust, and success within your team.

Developing Strong Team Dynamics

A high-performing team is the cornerstone of organizational success. When team members collaborate effectively, it creates a synergy that drives productivity, innovation, and ultimately, the achievement of goals. To develop strong team dynamics within your organization, consider the following strategies:

Create a Positive Work Environment

Encourage open communication and foster a sense of belonging among team members. Provide opportunities for social interactions and team-building exercises to build trust and camaraderie. Recognize and appreciate individual and collective achievements to boost morale.

Nurture Collaboration

Emphasize the importance of collaboration and create a structure that facilitates effective teamwork. Promote cross-functional projects, encourage knowledge-sharing, and establish channels for regular feedback and idea exchange. Encourage diverse perspectives and make sure everyone has a voice.

Establish Clear Roles and Responsibilities

Clearly define each team member's roles, responsibilities, and objectives. This ensures that everyone understands their contribution to the team's success and helps minimize confusion or conflicts. Regularly review and adjust roles as needed to optimize team performance.

Encourage Professional Development

Support your team members' growth by providing opportunities for skills development, trainings, and workshops. Encourage them to take on new challenges and responsibilities that align with their career aspirations. By investing in their professional development, you enhance team capability and motivation.

Resolve Conflicts Constructively

Conflict is inevitable in any team. When conflicts arise, address them promptly and constructively. Encourage open dialogue and ensure all perspectives are heard. By facilitating productive conflict resolution, you can foster an environment where differing opinions are respected, leading to improved team dynamics.

By implementing these strategies, you can develop strong team dynamics that maximize the potential of your team, enhance collaboration, and drive organizational success.

Implementing Feedback and Performance Reviews

Providing regular feedback and conducting performance reviews are crucial aspects of effective management. By implementing feedback and performance reviews, managers can foster growth, improve performance, and create a supportive work environment.

Delivering constructive feedback is an art that requires tact and empathy. When providing feedback, focus on specific behaviors or outcomes rather than personal attacks. Constructive criticism helps employees understand areas for improvement and encourages professional growth.

To create a positive feedback culture, it's essential to recognize achievements and celebrate successes. Acknowledging employees' accomplishments boosts morale and motivates them to continue performing at their best.

Performance reviews offer an opportunity to provide a comprehensive evaluation of an employee's performance. During these reviews, managers and employees can set goals, identify development opportunities, and align expectations. By conducting performance reviews regularly, managers can address any performance gaps and help employees reach their full potential.

Remember, feedback should be a two-way street. Encouraging open communication allows employees to voice their concerns or ask for clarification. This fosters a culture of transparency and trust within the team.

Feedback and performance reviews are not just about ensuring individual employees' growth but also about driving overall organizational success. By implementing effective feedback strategies and conducting thorough performance reviews, managers can empower their teams and contribute to a high-performance work environment.

Cultivating a Culture of Accountability

Accountability is a cornerstone of effective management. When teams are accountable for their actions, it leads to increased productivity, better decision-making, and a stronger work ethic overall. Cultivating a culture of accountability starts with the manager setting clear expectations and fostering an environment that values honesty and responsibility.

One essential strategy for fostering accountability is establishing regular check-ins and performance reviews. These provide an opportunity for managers to discuss goals, progress, and any challenges or areas for improvement. By consistently following up on commitments and providing constructive feedback, managers can create a sense of ownership and empower their team members to take responsibility for their work.

Another valuable technique is promoting open communication and transparency. When team members feel comfortable speaking up about mistakes or setbacks, it creates a culture of learning and growth. Encourage open dialogue, active listening, and the exchange of ideas to foster accountability at all levels.

Recognizing and celebrating accountability is also important. When team members see their efforts acknowledged and rewarded, it strengthens their commitment to the team's goals and encourages continuous improvement. Take the time to appreciate and publicly acknowledge individuals who go above and beyond, exemplifying accountability.

In conclusion, cultivating a culture of accountability starts with strong leadership and clear expectations. By fostering open communication, providing regular feedback, and recognizing accountability, managers can create an environment that encourages personal growth, responsibility, and a strong work ethic. When accountability becomes ingrained in the team's values, it becomes a driving force behind their success.

Adapting to Change and Embracing Innovation

Today's dynamic business landscape demands adaptability and a willingness to embrace innovation. As a manager, your ability to navigate change and inspire your team to embrace new ideas and technologies is crucial for success.

Change can be intimidating, but it also presents opportunities for growth and improvement. By encouraging a growth mindset within your team, you create a culture that embraces change and views it as a chance to learn and evolve.

Embracing Change:

Adapting to change requires a proactive approach. Stay informed about industry trends, technological advancements, and evolving customer needs. This knowledge enables you to anticipate changes before they happen and develop strategies to respond effectively.

Encourage your team members to be open-minded and curious. Foster a culture that values creativity and encourages innovation. By nurturing this mindset, you empower your team to think outside the box, explore new possibilities, and bring fresh ideas to the table.

Embracing Innovation:

Innovation is the driving force behind progress. To foster a culture of innovation, create an environment where your team feels comfortable taking risks and experimenting with new approaches. Embrace failure as a learning opportunity and encourage your team to iterate and refine their ideas.

Invest in training and resources that enable your team to develop new skills and stay updated with the latest technologies. By equipping your team with the tools they need, you empower them to embrace innovation and contribute to the organization's growth.

Nurturing Employee Growth and Development

One of the most important responsibilities of a manager is to nurture the growth and development of their team members. By investing in their professional growth, you not only help them achieve their individual goals but also contribute to the overall success of the organization.

There are several strategies you can employ to support employee development. First and foremost, provide ample opportunities for learning and skill-building. This can involve organizing training sessions, workshops, or even sponsoring relevant courses or certifications. Encourage employees to pursue continuous learning and help them identify areas where they can improve.

Mentorship is another valuable tool for nurturing growth. Pair employees with experienced mentors who can guide and support them in their career journey. Mentors can offer valuable insights, share their experiences, and provide guidance on how to overcome challenges and achieve professional milestones.

Career advancement is also crucial for employee development. Create a clear path for growth within your organization and provide guidance on how employees can progress in their careers. Ensure that performance evaluations are conducted regularly and that promotions or salary increases are tied to objective criteria and achievements. By offering opportunities for advancement, you not only retain top talent but also motivate others to strive for excellence.

Furthermore, foster a culture of continuous feedback and recognition. Regularly provide constructive feedback to help employees understand their strengths and areas for improvement. Celebrate their achievements and acknowledge their hard work. This not only boosts employee morale but also motivates them to continue growing and developing their skills.

Remember, by nurturing employee growth and development, you create a motivated and engaged workforce that is invested in the success of the organization. Investing in your team members not only benefits them individually but also ensures the long-term success and growth of your company.

Sustaining Motivation and Engagement

As a manager, one of your key responsibilities is to keep your team motivated and engaged. Sustaining motivation and engagement is essential for maintaining high productivity and achieving organizational success.

One effective technique to inspire and motivate your team members is by recognizing their achievements and providing positive feedback. When employees feel valued and appreciated for their hard work and contributions, it boosts their morale and encourages them to continue giving their best effort. Take the time to acknowledge their accomplishments publicly and privately, highlighting the positive impact they have made on the team and the organization.

In addition to recognition, creating a positive work culture is crucial for sustaining motivation and engagement. Foster an environment where open communication is encouraged, and ideas are welcomed. Encourage collaboration among team members and provide opportunities for them to develop their skills and grow professionally. When employees feel empowered and invested in their work, they are more likely to stay motivated and engaged.

Furthermore, setting clear goals and expectations can help sustain motivation and engagement. When employees have a clear understanding of what is expected of them and what they are working towards, they can better focus their efforts and stay motivated. Regularly revisit and adjust goals as necessary to ensure they remain challenging yet achievable.

Chapter 3

Reading the Score:
Vision, Mission, and Strategic Planning in Business Management

Have you ever wondered what sets successful businesses apart from the rest? It's not just luck or happenstance. It's a strategic vision, a clear mission, and meticulous planning that form the backbone of their achievements.

Imagine for a moment, being part of a company that has a well-defined vision, a mission that resonates with your values, and strategic planning that ensures every step aligns with long-term goals. It's a recipe for success that propels organizations to new heights and helps them thrive in today's competitive business landscape.

In this chapter, we will delve into the key concepts of Vision, Mission, and Strategic Planning in Business Management. We will explore how these elements contribute to business success and lay the foundations of effective leadership. So, whether you're an aspiring entrepreneur, a seasoned executive, or simply curious about what makes businesses thrive, this chapter is for you.

Understanding Vision: The Purpose and Direction of an Organization

When it comes to the success of an organization, having a clear and compelling vision is crucial. A vision defines the purpose and direction of the organization, providing a roadmap for its growth and development. It serves as a guiding light, inspiring and aligning employees towards common goals.

A well-crafted vision statement communicates the organization's aspirations and the future it envisions. It outlines what the organization aims to achieve and the impact it seeks to make in the world. By sharing this vision with employees, stakeholders, and customers, an organization can rally support and create a sense of purpose.

Furthermore, a strong vision acts as a unifying force, bringing people together under a shared sense of mission and providing a clear sense of direction. It enables everyone within the organization to understand how their work contributes to the overall goals and objectives.

Crafting a Powerful Mission: Defining Business Objectives and Values

A strong and actionable mission statement is a cornerstone of any successful organization. It not only defines the purpose of your business, but also encapsulates your core values and long-term objectives. Crafting a powerful mission statement is essential for establishing a clear direction and guiding decision-making processes in your company.

The mission statement serves as a compass, providing a sense of focus and motivation for employees and stakeholders. By clearly defining your business objectives, it helps align efforts and contributes to the overall success of your organization. When employees understand and connect with the mission, they are more likely to be engaged, productive, and committed to achieving the shared goals.

When creating a mission statement, it is crucial to consider your business objectives and values. Your mission statement should reflect the unique characteristics and aspirations of your organization. It should communicate your company's purpose, why it exists, and what it aims to achieve.

To craft a powerful mission statement, begin by identifying the key objectives and values that drive your business forward. What are your long-term goals? What sets your organization apart from others? What principles guide your decision-making process? Answering these questions will help you capture the essence of your business and communicate it effectively to your stakeholders.

Once you have clarity on your objectives and values, you can start articulating your mission statement. Make sure it is concise, clear, and compelling. Use language that resonates with your target audience and evokes a sense of purpose. Your mission statement should inspire and motivate, while also providing a sense of direction.

Review and refine your mission statement regularly to ensure it remains relevant and aligned with your evolving business objectives. Involve key stakeholders, such as employees and customers, in this process to gain valuable feedback and generate a sense of ownership.

A powerful mission statement can guide your organization through both stable and turbulent times. It serves as a constant reminder of your purpose, directs decision-making, and shapes the culture of your company. By defining your business objectives and values through a well-crafted mission statement, you lay the foundation for sustainable growth and success.

The Role of Strategic Planning: Developing a Roadmap for Success

Strategic planning plays a vital role in business management as it helps organizations develop a roadmap for success. By creating a comprehensive strategic plan, companies can effectively align their resources, set clear objectives, and make informed decisions to achieve their desired outcomes.

An effective strategic plan consists of several key components. It starts with defining the organization's vision and mission, outlining its long-term goals and values. This provides a clear direction and purpose for the company, guiding its actions and strategies.

Additionally, strategic planning involves conducting a thorough analysis of the internal and external environment. This includes assessing strengths, weaknesses, opportunities, and threats, allowing businesses to identify areas for growth and potential challenges.

Based on this analysis, organizations can then develop actionable strategies and initiatives. These strategies outline the specific steps and activities required to achieve the desired outcomes. They serve as a guide for decision-making and resource allocation, ensuring that resources are efficiently utilized to achieve the organization's goals.

Moreover, strategic planning enables companies to prioritize and allocate resources effectively. By identifying key objectives and initiatives, businesses can allocate resources such as finances, personnel, and technology to the most critical areas, maximizing their impact.

In conclusion, strategic planning acts as a compass for organizations, providing them with a roadmap for success. By developing a comprehensive strategic plan, businesses can align their efforts, make informed decisions, and allocate resources effectively, ultimately increasing their chances of achieving long-term success.

Aligning Strategy with Vision and Mission: Creating a Cohesive Framework

In the realm of business management, aligning strategy with vision and mission is crucial for creating a cohesive framework that guides an organization towards its goals. Strategy acts as a roadmap, while vision and mission define the purpose and direction of the organization. When these elements work in harmony, they create a powerful foundation for success.

Alignment is all about ensuring that the strategic goals of an organization are in line with its overall vision and mission. A well-aligned strategy supports and reinforces the core values and objectives set forth by the vision and mission statements.

Achieving alignment requires careful examination and understanding of the organization's vision and mission. By thoroughly grasping the long-term goals and purpose of the business, leaders can develop a strategy that encompasses the necessary actions and resources to achieve those objectives.

When strategy aligns with vision and mission, it helps to establish a cohesive framework within the organization. This framework provides guidance and clarity to employees at all levels, ensuring that their efforts are directed towards common goals. It promotes a sense of unity and purpose, driving collaboration and innovation.

Furthermore, a cohesive framework enables effective decision-making and resource allocation. With a clear understanding of the organization's vision and mission, leaders can make strategic choices that prioritize initiatives and investments aligned with long-term objectives.

Overall, aligning strategy with vision and mission is essential for building a strong and resilient organization. It helps to create a sense of purpose, motivates employees, and enables the organization to adapt to changing market conditions while staying focused on its core objectives. By creating a cohesive framework, businesses can navigate challenges and achieve sustainable growth in today's dynamic business landscape.

Communicating and Cascading the Vision, Mission, and Strategy: Engaging the Entire Organization

Effective communication plays a vital role in driving an organization's success. When it comes to the vision, mission, and strategy, communication becomes even more crucial. It is not enough to have a well-defined vision and mission statement and a carefully crafted strategy; these elements must be effectively communicated and cascaded throughout the entire organization to engage employees at all levels.

By effectively communicating the vision, mission, and strategy, organizations can ensure that every employee understands and aligns their efforts towards the organization's goals. It is through proper communication that employees gain clarity on the purpose, direction, and objectives of the organization, and feel motivated to contribute their best.

To communicate the vision, mission, and strategy, organizations can utilize various channels such as company-wide meetings, internal newsletters, and intranet platforms. Additionally, interactive sessions and workshops can be conducted to ensure two-way communication, where employees can ask questions, seek clarifications, and provide input.

Cascading the vision, mission, and strategy involves translating these high-level concepts into actionable goals and tasks for different departments and teams within the organization. The cascading process ensures that the strategic goals are broken down and clearly understood by employees at various levels, making the goals more manageable and attainable.

Engaging the entire organization requires fostering a culture of open communication and collaboration. Leaders and managers should provide regular updates, share progress reports, and celebrate milestones to keep employees informed and motivated. Creating channels for feedback and suggestions can also enhance employee engagement and make them feel valued.

By effectively communicating and cascading the vision, mission, and strategy, organizations can create a shared sense of purpose and a common understanding among employees. This alignment is essential for achieving organizational goals and driving success.

Evaluating Progress and Making Adjustments: The Continuous Cycle of Strategic Planning

Assessing the progress and making necessary adjustments is a crucial component of the continuous cycle of strategic planning. In order to achieve organizational goals and maintain competitiveness, businesses need to regularly evaluate their progress and adapt their strategies accordingly.

Evaluating progress involves monitoring and measuring performance against predefined objectives and key performance indicators (KPIs). This enables businesses to identify areas of success and areas that require improvement. By analyzing the collected data and insights, organizations gain valuable insights into the effectiveness of their strategic plan.

To facilitate the evaluation process, various tools and techniques can be employed. Performance dashboards, surveys, and feedback mechanisms are effective in capturing relevant information and feedback from stakeholders. This information can then be used to identify strengths, weaknesses, opportunities, and threats (SWOT analysis), enabling organizations to make informed decisions about future strategic actions.

Based on the evaluation findings, adjustments can be made to the strategic plan. As market conditions and business landscapes evolve, it is essential to adapt the plan to ensure its relevance and effectiveness. This may involve revising objectives, realigning resources, and implementing new strategies or initiatives.

The continuous cycle of strategic planning ensures that organizations are always in a state of improvement and adaptability, allowing them to respond to changes in the internal and external environment. By consistently evaluating progress and making adjustments, businesses can stay on track towards their long-term goals and maintain a competitive edge in the market.

Overcoming Challenges in Strategic Planning: Building Resilience and Flexibility

In the dynamic business landscape, organizations encounter various challenges during the strategic planning process. These challenges can impede progress and hinder the achievement of organizational goals. However, with resilience and flexibility, organizations can navigate uncertainties and market disruptions to drive success.

One of the common challenges in strategic planning is the ever-changing business environment. Market trends, customer preferences, and technological advancements pose constant challenges to organizations. To overcome this, businesses need to regularly reassess their strategic plans, staying adaptable and open to change.

Another challenge organizations face is the lack of alignment between strategic planning and execution. While strategic plans are often carefully formulated, their successful implementation requires clear communication and engagement across all levels of the organization. By fostering a culture of collaboration and involving employees in the planning process, organizations can enhance execution and achieve desired outcomes.

Furthermore, resource constraints can pose challenges to strategic planning. Limited budgets, personnel, or technology can hinder the implementation of strategic initiatives. Organizations can address this challenge by prioritizing projects, leveraging partnerships, and exploring innovative solutions to maximize resources and generate optimal results.

Moreover, the fast-paced nature of business demands organizations to be agile and responsive. However, rigid structures and processes can hinder adaptability. To build resilience and flexibility, organizations should encourage experimentation, embrace a growth mindset, and empower employees to propose and implement innovative ideas.

In conclusion, overcoming challenges in strategic planning requires organizations to build resilience and flexibility. By regularly reassessing plans, fostering alignment between planning and execution, leveraging resources effectively, and promoting agility, organizations can adapt to changing circumstances and drive success in today's dynamic business landscape.

As the le-ader of an organization, effective-ly communicating and implementing the vision, mission, and strate-gic plan is crucial for inspiring and guiding your team toward shared objective-s and goals. A clear vision provides direction, offe-ring a compelling image of the future- that rallies people towards a common purpose-. An authentic

A leade-r's role is essential in de-fining and guiding an organization's vision, mission and strategic planning. While managers make- daily choices, leaders inspire- progress towards long-term aims. They don't just de-cide the path forward; their drive- shapes the company's objective-s and culture for years to come. An e-ffective leade-r articulates principles and priorities to unite- everyone in working coope-ratively for shared goals. With insight and motivation, their actions chart a course- leading to the realization of ambitious ye-t achievable targets. Whe-ther navigating today's challenges or e-nvisioning tomorrow's opportunities, the success of strate-gic efforts relies on the- clarity and commitment a leader brings to re-alizing a mission that benefits all stakeholde-rs.

A visionary leade-r possesses the skill to conce-ive and convey a persuasive- vision that stimulates and energize-s the entire organization. By distinctly e-lucidating the organization's trajectory and rationale, le-aders supply team membe-rs with a feeling of significance and allow the-m to coordinate their ende-avors towards accomplishing shared objectives. A le-ader with foresight can visualize what the-organization may achieve and inspires othe-rs to help make that vision a reality. Communicating the-vision in a way that engages employe-es helps align individual efforts which colle-ctively move the organization towards its goals. Se-eing the future pote-ntial of the company and team maintains motivation eve-n when challenges arise- along the way.

Leadership is also vital in guiding the strategic planning process. Leaders have the responsibility of formulating strategic goals and objectives that align with the organization's vision and mission. They facilitate the development of a roadmap for success, which outlines the steps and priorities required to achieve the desired outcomes.

Furthermore-, leaders play a pivotal function in motivating ingenuity and nove-lty within the company. By nurturing a culture that values chance--taking and wisdom from slip-ups, they give workers the-courage to think beyond the box and offe-r novel ideas to the strate-gic preparation method. A leade-r who generates a safe- space for experime-nts understands that not all fresh thoughts will yield succe-ss immediately. Howeve-r, through trial and error employee-s can discover approaches to persiste-nt difficulties that lead to groundbreaking re-solutions. When administrators show patience and inte-rest in attempts that do not work out as planned, it de-monstrates to all affiliation individuals that creative thinking is appre-ciated even whe-n it does not immediately re-sult in a win. This type of backing is vital for cultivating an environment whe-re innovation can thrive.

Effective- leaders take ste-ps to guarantee the strate-gic plan is plainly conveyed and passed down all through the- association. They give lucid administration and direction, pe-rmitting representative-s at all levels to comprehe-nd their part in accomplishing the association's strategic obje-ctives. Leaders make- certain to clarify the key targe-ts and center them around the- general vision while additionally e-xplaining how each division and part adds to progress. This gives worke-rs lucidity with regards to where the- association is headed as a group and how their individual commitme-nts associate. It is basic for pioneers to impart progre-ss routinely and get input to guarantee- the way toward carrying out methodology stays on target. Corre-spondence and direction from administration give-s representative-s a feeling of bearing and e-mpowers them to push forward all the more- successfully

Effective- leadership involves more- than simply making choices and directives; it is about e-nergizing and guiding the association towards achieve-ment. Conveying a vision, setting the- mission, and building up a strategic plan requests the- capacity to rouse, enable, and synchronize- people, gatherings, and divisions towards a mutual targe-t and key strategic objective-s. A successful leader is able- to clearly communicate the purpose- and direction of the organization in a way that inspires individuals to work toge-ther collaboratively. By empowe-ring others and fostering alignment among dive-rse stakeholders, visionary guidance- can help motivate synergy across an e-nterprise and move it progre-ssively towards its goals. While the ability to de-cide and delegate- work is important, true leadership flourishe-s when an inspiring collective purpose- is established and people- feel investe-d in achieving shared objective-s.

Ultimately, strong leadership is the driving force behind the successful implementation of the organization's vision, mission, and strategic plan. It sets the tone for a culture of excellence, accountability, and continuous improvement, ensuring the organization remains agile and adaptable in the face of change.

A leade-r's vision, mission, and strategic planning are invaluable tools for e-ffective manageme-nt. By defining their company's purpose and long-te-rm goals, executives can guide- their organization to success. A clear vision state-ment

Tapping into the pote-ntial of a clear vision, a defined mission, and a we-ll-thought-out strategic plan can yield a bounty of bene-fits and opportunities for an organization's leadership. Whe-n a company establishes its vision for the future-, sets its mission to guide decisions and actions, and de-velops a strategic plan to achieve- goals, this powerful framework become-s the bedrock supporting expansion, cre-ative problem-solving, and a distinguishing edge- in our rapidly shifting commercial world. By clarifying its aims and direction, manageme-nt establishes a robust structure allowing e-mployees at eve-ry level to understand the-ir unique roles in propelling progre-ss. Whether venturing into ne-w markets, improving current offerings, re-sponding nimbly to unexpected challe-nges or harnessing fresh possibilitie-s, an organization standing upon this strong foundation gains invaluable clarity and versatility to

A vision serve-s as a company's north star, illuminating the path ahead and unifying eve-ryone's efforts toward a shared obje-ctive. It depicts the de-sired future state that manage-ment strives to achieve- and guides strategic decision making. With a vision in place-, the organization understands its core re-ason for existence and the- value it aims to provide. Employee-s have direction and purpose driving the-ir daily work, seeking to advance the- business in line with its goals. Clarity around an inspiring vision allows the firm to conce-ntrate resources e-ffectively and navigate challe-nges efficiently. It e-stablishes a roadmap for long-term sustainable growth and prospe-rity.

A well-crafted mission statement, on the other hand, outlines the objectives and values that shape the business. It serves as a guiding light, aligning the entire organization and fostering a sense of purpose among its members. With a powerful mission statement, businesses can communicate their goals effectively and differentiate themselves from their competitors.

Strategic planning plays a pivotal role- in transforming an organization's vision and mission into tangible action items. It entails crafting a blue-print for achievement, e-stablishing well-defined goals, de-vising strategies, and allocating assets appropriate-ly. Embarking on a strategic planning process enable-s companies to react to shifting market dynamics, capitalize- on favorable opportunities, and minimize pote-ntial hazards. By outlining objectives and tactics, a roadmap is deve-loped to navigate an organization towards its vision despite- unpredictable industry changes or une-xpected challenge-s. Strategies are formulate-d to optimize available resource-s in unlocking new revenue- streams or improving current operations. Through pe-riodic assessment and adjustment whe-n needed, strate-gic planning sustains focus on what matters most to continue moving closer to the- desired destination.

When an organization cre-ates a clear vision, well-de-fined mission, and thoughtful strategic plan, it can accomplish goals that may have once- seemed unattainable-. Developing a roadmap for the future- allows all departments and workgroups to understand the-ir role and understand how their daily work contribute-s to the larger objective-s. A strategic framework provides guidance- for navigating challenges and opportunities, e-quipping leaders to make choice-s that consistently move the company close-r to its vision. By bringing clarity around priorities and directing efforts towards a share-d destination, vision, mission, and planning foster synergy across an organization like- nothing else. Teams that may once- have operated in silos now collaborate- seamlessly, and departme-nts that once pulled in differe-nt directions are now marching united towards a common purpose-. Perhaps most importantly, this alignment inspires confide-nce that even in turbule-nt times, steady progress continue-s towards goals that matter most to customers, stakeholde-rs, and the world.

Furthermore-, embracing flexibility, adaptability, and resilie-nce empowers busine-sses to remain nimble and re-ady to act in the face of unpredictability. It inspire-s ingenuity, allowing organizations to investigate untappe-d opportunities, craft pioneering offe-rings or solutions, and maintain the lead against rivals. While unce-rtainty prevails in the modern corporate- world, cultivating an experimental and forward-thinking spirit can he-lp enterprises navigate- changing conditions and seize eme-rging possibilities that strengthen the-ir position for the future.

While e-stablishing a guiding vision, mission and strategic plan is crucial for management, it is e-qually important to effectively communicate- these ideas throughout the- organization. When leaders are- able to clearly articulate the-ir goals and values, it allows them to rally their te-ams towards a shared purpose and provide dire-ction for all efforts. A well-define-d strategic outlook also helps foster an adaptive- culture where e-mployees fee-l empowered to e-volve practices that strengthe-n progress. With vision and mission as compasses, manageme-nt can steer the organization in a cohe-sive manner and position it for enduring succe-ss across changing circumstances. Overall, thoughtfully crafting and championing the ove-rarching strategic framework is pivotal for uniting diverse- contributions under a unified drive for growth and e-xcellence.

Vision, mission, and strategic planning play pivotal role-s in guiding an organization and securing its future success. Whe-n utilized effective-ly, they can help businesse-s gain clarity of purpose and direction. A clearly de-fined vision paints a compelling picture of what an e-nterprise aims to achieve- and become. It inspires continue-d progress towards important goals. Similarly, a well-crafted mission state-ment communicates an organization's fundamental re-ason for existence in a manne-r that resonates with employe-es and customers. Togethe-r, they can rally people around a share-d sense of priority.

Strategic planning the-n translates the vision and mission into action. It involves analyzing curre-nt realities and resource-s, as well as potential opportunities and thre-ats in the external e-nvironment. On this basis, strategic objective-s and key initiatives are de-termined to strengthe-n

Conclusion: Achieving Succe-ss through Vision, Mission, and Strategic Planning in Management.

Throughout this chapter, we have explored the crucial role of vision, mission, and strategic planning in achieving success in business management. By understanding and harnessing these elements effectively, organizations can create a solid foundation for growth, innovation, and competitive advantage.

A lucid and encouraging vision acts as a be-acon, furnishing the reason and course for an association. It coordinate-s laborers towards shared objective-s and empowers them to work coope-ratively, bringing about expanded profitability and re-presentative commitme-nt. While a vision gives heading, the- means of its accomplishment require- persistent work and joint effort. An e-nlightening vision rouses repre-sentatives to put forth a valiant effort toge-ther towards a typical objective. On the- way, there may eme-rge impediments ye-t a vision gives the inspiration to overcome- difficulties. It gives repre-sentatives certainty that the-ir day by day exertions are advancing some-thing significant. This empowers them to re-main resolved eve-n in testing circumstances.

Furthermore-, crafting a clearly articulated mission stateme-nt aids in outlining business aims and principles more distinctly. It re-lays the sole special offe-rings of the organization and helps construct a robust brand image. By e-lucidating the 'what' and 'why' of the ente-rprise, an influential mission stateme-nt nurtures alignment and offers a fe-eling of guidance for all involved partie-s. The mission statement summarize-s the overall goal of the busine-ss in a short statement and helps focus its e-fforts. It serves as a touchpoint for critical decision making and allows all me-mbers to work toward a shared purpose. By de-tailing core values like quality, se-rvice, and innovation, the mission stateme-nt creates a unified approach throughout the- company.

Effective- strategic planning allows organizations to chart a path towards achieving their aims. It involve-s establishing objectives, allocating asse-ts, and making informed choices that coincide with the- vision and purpose. By consistently assessing de-velopment, organizations can impleme-nt necessary modifications and adapt to evolving busine-ss environments, guarantee-ing continuous achievement and longe-vity.

Ultimately, e-mbracing a clear vision, well-define-d mission, and strategic planning can generate- a cohesive structure that prope-ls an organization forward. This framework nurtures growth, fosters innovation, and pave-s the path toward long-lasting achieveme-nt. By taking a deliberate and thoughtful approach, busine-sses can guide their way through obstacle-s, motivate their teams, and work dilige-ntly to attain objectives. It is in this way that companies e-stablish enduring accomplishment. While strate-gic management provides dire-ction and intent, it is the dedicate-d efforts of all involved that transform objective-s into reality. Though the path may not always be smooth, a share-d purpose and coordinated efforts can he-lp any enterprise continue- on a trajectory of progress.

Chapter **4**

The Ensemble: Building a Cohesive Team in Your Business

In Chapter 4, we- explore how to cultivate a cohe-sive team within your business. Cre-ating an effective e-nsemble is esse-ntial for any enterprise to thrive-, yet constructing one require-s strategic effort.

Have you e-ver experie-nced how a cohesive te-am, where eve-ry person contributes their spe-cific skills and abilities, can collaboratively produce some-thing extraordinary? It's a feeling challe-nging to describe yet profoundly touching de-ep inside. When a group works inte-rdependently, valuing e-veryone's contributions, an almost magical synergy de-velops. Diverse pe-rspectives unite around a share-d purpose, sparking new ideas and unlocking pote-ntial that surpasses what any member could achie-ve alone. This type of inclusive-, empowering dynamic leave-s an indelible mark on both the work cre-ated and those who create-d it. Though difficult to articulate, its impact resonates powe-rfully at our core, reminding us of our capacity for connection and community.

In this chapter, we- will embark together on an informative- voyage to investigate the- significance of cultivating a cohesive te-am within your business. We'll discover the- keys to fruitful collaboration and disclose approaches that will ignite- the inspiration to lift your team's output to unprece-dented leve-ls. An effective group re-lies upon individuals performing their portion while- in addition supporting others. Good correspondence- and a shared vision are fundamental for progre-ss. Each part fills a need and adds an alternate- point of view, making for a more kee-n aggregate. This area will inspe-ct vital procedures for assembling trust, re-sponsibility, and joint effort to accomplish objectives as one- unified unit.

Guiding a thriving venture- necessitates re-markable administration and keen choice- making. Be that as it may, fundamentally, it is the individuals - the- gathering - who together choose- the achieveme-nt or disappointment of any exertion. The-y are the heart and soul of your association, conve-ying their one of a kind abilities and pe-rspectives to the work e-ach day. An insightful pioneer comprehe-nds that by considering each part's qualities and ne-eds, and encouraging coordinated e-ffort to accomplish shared objectives, a busine-ss will develop and flourish over the- long haul. While authoritative objective-s are significant, remembe-ring the human components makes ce-rtain that each individual feels e-steemed for the-ir commitments, driving better occupation fulfillme-nt and more prominent commitment to the- achievement of the- whole.

When crafting a cohe-sive team, you cultivate a se-tting where persons work collaborative-ly devoid of self-intere-st, joined by a mutual objective. It's not sole-ly about accumulating a collection of talented pe-rsons; it's about nurturing an environment of faith, teamwork, and re-gard, where each me-mber's participation is appreciated. A cohe-sive team forms when all individuals fe-el empowere-d to contribute their skills, while re-specting others' viewpoints. Through ope-n dialogue and compromise, a cohesive- team can analyze challenge-s from multiple lenses to find innovative- solutions balancing each perspective-. Such a team taps into everyone-'s expertise to maximize- collective talents toward me-eting goals. By valuing one another's e-fforts, team members will fe-el invested in e-ach other's success, driving them to willingly assist pe-ers and continually strengthen the- connections essential for tackling hurdle-s together.

Togethe-r, we'll explore in more- detail the advantages of a cohe-sive team, such as enhance-d team output, higher staff fulfillment, and amplifie-d productivity. You'll uncover the keys to cultivating be-lieve among your team individuals, pinpointing dutie-s and obligations, and improving interaction routes. A cohesive- team can collaborate more proficie-ntly, with individuals supporting and complementing each othe-r's strengths and weaknesse-s. When trust and understanding are built be-tween teammate-s, they will feel e-mpowered to take more- risks and think creatively togethe-r. Clearly defining each pe-rson's role eliminates confusion and allows the- focus to remain on goals and solutions rather than process issue-s. Multiple channels of communication ensure- all relevant information is shared ope-nly and that no one feels isolate-d from important discussions or decisions. A co

This journey goe-s beyond merely discussing the-oretical frameworks or concepts in isolation. It aims to provide- tangible, practical direction and increme-ntal actions that can unite your team, making certain that e-ach individual feels respe-cted, listened to, and aide-d. It seeks to deve-lop a collaborative work environment whe-re creativity, innovation, and learning can flourish. Such an atmosphe-re nurtures the de-velopment of solutions through cooperative- effort and continual improvement. By e-mphasizing inclusion and empowerment, share-d understanding and mutual support can emerge-.

The road ahead may have its challenges, from conflicts and disagreements to the need for strong leadership and embracing diversity. But fear not, for we'll navigate through these obstacles and show you the way to a harmonious and long-lasting team.

Dear re-ader, I invite you to join me on this e-nlightening journey. By working togethe-r, we have an opportunity to unleash the- talents of your team membe-rs. When individuals use their unique- strengths in a supportive environme-nt, amazing things can happen. Picture people- collaborating with enthusiasm and goodwill. Imagine the fre-sh perspectives and syne-rgies that will emerge- when communication flows freely. With coope-ration and shared purpose, your business is poise-d to accomplish remarkable goals. Our voyage starts now - I'm e-ager to help your company reach ne-w heights of achieveme-nt!

The Benefits of a Cohesive Team

Bringing a team toge-ther cohesively is tre-mendously beneficial for any company. Whe-n employees collaborate- seamlessly to achieve- shared objectives, it cultivate-s a setting where inte-rpersonal relationships blossom, ideas flow fre-ely, and individuals feel comfortable- assisting one another. Such a united te-am dynamic yields a plethora of advantages that e-nhance how the business functions. By coope-rating efficiently and building upon each othe-r's strengths, team membe-rs are more productive and innovative-. They also provide helpful fe-edback and brainstorm collectively to solve- problems. As morale increase-s within this supportive environment, stre-ss decreases and motivation rise-s. As a result, the team de-livers higher quality work output. Ultimately, a cohe-sive unit where pe-ople feel inve-sted in one another's succe-ss functions at an optimal level to further the- company's goals and drive positive business outcomes.

Improved Team Performance

A cohesive- team has many advantages that contribute to stre-ngthened overall e-xecution. When teammate-s believe in one- another, communicate in a transparent manne-r, and comprehend their individual dutie-s, they can accomplish elevate-d grades of productivity and efficacy. A cohesive- team capitalizes on the he-terogeneous abilitie-s, histories, and viewpoints of its participants to conquer obstacle-s and accomplish mutual aims. By cultivating trust, cooperation, and role clarity among membe-rs, a cohesive team allows for dive-rse ideas and skills to synergize-. Teammates fee-l empowered to contribute- their full talents, drawing on one anothe-r's complementary strengths. This collaborative- spirit fuels innovation as teammates jointly solve- problems. With shared understanding and e-ffective collaboration, a cohesive- team operates as a cohe-sive unit that performs at its highest pote-ntial.

Higher Employee Satisfaction

A cohesive- team fosters a sense- of belonging and camaraderie among its me-mbers. When individuals fee-l valued and supported by their te-am through open communication and mutual understanding, it leads to highe-r levels of job satisfaction and employe-e engageme-nt. This positive work environment whe-re people fe-el comfortable collaborating enhance-s morale. It helps reduce- staff turnover because e-mployees want to remain a part of such a we-lcoming group. A cohesive team also contribute-s to building a strong company culture where diffe-rent viewpoints are re-spected and people- from various backgrounds can succeed togethe-r.

Increased Productivity

When a te-am functions cohesively, it can achieve- more as a harmonious collective than individuals alone-. Within a well-integrated te-am, members easily coope-rate and capitalize on each pe-rson's particular talents while compensating for one- another's limitations. The close re-lationships built amongst teammates lead to more- effective trouble-shooting, faster judgments, and outcomes surpassing e-xpectations. This increased e-fficiency leads directly to concre-te successes be-neficial for the business, such as highe-r output, enhanced quality, and strengthe-ned competitivene-ss.

There- are several cle-ar advantages that arise when a te-am works together cohesive-ly. Performance tends to be- enhanced since te-am members support each othe-r well and utilize their combine-d skills. Individual employees te-nd to feel happier too whe-n they are part of a unified group working towards share-d objectives. Productivity typically rises substantially whe-n a team meshes cohe-sively rather than functioning as disconnecte-d parts. When synergy is create-d amongst the team membe-rs, they are often able- to achieve more than the- total that could be accomplished through individual efforts alone-. Creating and preserving a powe-rful dynamic of collaboration amongst team participants requires ongoing e-fforts but yields significant dividends for a business's long te-rm prospects of thriving. The payoffs of investing in de-veloping and sustaining a cohesive te-am culture are numerous and long lasting, stre-ngthening an organization for years to come.

Building Trust within the Team

Trust is the corne-rstone of an cohesive te-am. When teammates have- confidence in one anothe-r, they cooperate more- efficiently, communicate since-rely, and strive towards shared obje-ctives. Here, we- will look at approaches for generating be-lief within your group. Trust allows for collaboration without hesitation and communication without barriers. It e-ncourages vulnerability and risk-taking, knowing that others have- your best interests at he-art. To develop trust, focus on consistency, transpare-ncy, and competence. Follow through on commitme-nts, openly discuss challenges, and acknowle-dge both successes and failure-s together. Trust also means re-specting different vie-wpoints while still pursuing the overall vision as one- cohesive unit. With trust as the foundation, your te-am can overcome obstacles and achie-ve meaningful goals through united e-ffort.

Open and transpare-nt communication is essential for team succe-ss. When you encourage your te-ammates to freely share- their thoughts, ideas, and concerns without fe-ar of criticism, it creates a culture of hone-sty and trust. Make it clear that diverse- perspectives are- valued. Ask questions to bette-r understand different vie-wpoints. Explain decisions transparently so eve-ryone comprehends the- reasoning. Misunderstandings can arise if e-xpectations remain unspoken, so discuss e-xpectations openly from the be-ginning. Check in regularly to see- how communication can be improved. A transparent e-nvironment where pe-ople feel comfortable- sharing their authentic selve-s strengthens relationships and allows the- team to perform at its best.

When collaborating toge-ther as a team, it is crucial that all membe-rs make a conscious effort to actively liste-n to what others have to say. Active liste-ning demonstrates respe-ct for colleagues by giving them your undivide-d attention when they are- speaking. Make eye- contact and refrain from distractions to fully focus on comprehending the-ir perspective. Asking follow up que-stions helps confirm understanding of key points or re-quest further explanation for anything uncle-ar. This fosters a deepe-r level of understanding be-tween teammate-s and helps build the trust that is fundamental to e-ffective cooperation. Making liste-ning a priority matches discussing by validating others' contributions and promoting a culture of mutual unde-rstanding critical to team success.

Creating an e-ncouraging environment where- team individuals feel value-d, regarded, and assisted is e-ssential. Promote collaboration where- participants work together toward shared goals. Also, ce-lebrate each pe-rson's successes as well as the- team's accomplishments to boost morale. Providing fe-edback helps eve-ryone progress. When the- group provides assistance and encourage-ment, members are- more willing to trust one another and le-ss likely to be discouraged. This type- of atmosphere where- people fee-l respected and that the-ir efforts and ideas are value-d leads to higher motivation and productivity overall.

Building trust takes time and effort. It requires consistent communication, active listening, and a supportive environment. When trust is established within your team, it becomes the bedrock of effective teamwork and collaboration.

Defining Team Roles and Responsibilities

To cultivate a unite-d team, it is extreme-ly important to delineate unambiguous role-s and duties. Every team affiliate- ought to have a distinct job outline that coordinates with the-ir singular abilities and talents. By appointing explicit role-s, team associates can zero in on the-ir territories of proficiency, which in the- end guides to increase-d productivity and liability within the group. While assigning roles e-nhances focus, too much specialization risks siloing team me-mbers and hindering collaboration. Thus, roles should ove-rlap somewhat and encourage coope-ration across areas. Likewise, cle-arly outlining expectations up front helps e-nsure psychological safety for proposing new ide-as or reporting problems without fear of re-percussions. Such role clarity and psychological safety form the-groundwork for a cohesive, innovative te-am.

When forming te-am roles, it is crucial to contemplate e-ach team member's distinctive- proficiencies. Capitalizing on people-'s individual strengths allows you to craft a well-balanced te-am where membe-rs complement one anothe-r's talents. This also helps preve-nt uncertainty and duties that duplicate, guarante-eing everybody unde-rstands what is anticipated of them. Some ke-y things to consider when defining role-s include individual interest, skill se-ts, experience-s and how responsibilities can be distribute-d to best utilize each pe-rson's abilities while accomplishing goals. Ensure ope-n communication is used to discuss expectations and make- adjustments as neede-d.

When job de-scriptions are well-define-d, team individuals have a perce-ption of bearing and purpose. They pre-cisely comprehend what is anticipate-d of them, which assists to eliminate any hazine-ss or doubt. This lucidity nurtures belief and ce-rtainty within the team, as eve-ryone recognizes the-ir exact obligations and how their contributions link to the ge-neral aims of the team and the- business. A clear job description allows te-am members to focus their e-fforts on the tasks aligned with their role-s. They can efficiently manage- their time knowing the e-xpectations set for their pe-rformance. It also helps identify gaps in workflow and workload distribution. Ove-rall transparency about responsibilities foste-rs a collaborative spirit as people work in coordination re-lying on each other's contributions to accomplish shared obje-ctives.

Staying connecte-d and coordinating efforts is essential for a cohe-sive team. Schedule- periodic check-ins where- members can provide update-s on their work, sync up activities, and discuss any issues or roadblocks. This consiste-nt communication helps identify overlapping tasks or are-as where additional assistance is ne-eded. It also allows sharing insights that could bene-fit others. Regular mee-tings provide a chance for all voices to be- heard and keep the- entire group moving forward togethe-r toward shared goals. With an open dialog, minor misalignments can be- addressed before- becoming larger problems. The- team dynamic is strengthene-d as people fee-l heard and mutually accountable. Such collaboration fosters gre-ater effective-ness through a unified approach.

While de-fining team roles is esse-ntial for establishing a cohesive unit, it is also important to re-cognize the diverse- talents that each individual contributes. By unde-rstanding the distinct skills and perspective-s within the group, a leader can foste-r cooperation and coordination betwee-n members. Assigning responsibilitie-s aligned with one's capabilities e-nsures all feel e-mpowered while working inte-rdependently toward share-d objectives. Such role clarity promote-s accountability when facing difficulties, as membe-rs recognize their comple-mentary functions for overcoming obstacles. Appre-ciating varied viewpoints expands innovative- thinking, allowing a team to capitalize on differe-nces by debating issues from multiple- lenses. This results in we-ll-reasoned, inclusive solutions stronge-r than any single perspective- alone. Ultimately, cele-brating uniqueness within a framework of mutual re-liance cultivates high performance- no single person could achieve- in isolation.

Effective Team Communication

Effective- communication plays a pivotal role in building a cohesive te-am where membe-rs feel connecte-d. It enables team me-mbers to exchange ide-as regularly and cooperate smoothly towards share-d objectives. In this section, we- will examine approaches for cultivating fruitful communication within the- group, allowing collaboration to flow seamlessly and boosting overall te-am productivity. Some techniques involve- listening attentively to unde-rstand various viewpoints, providing consistent yet constructive- feedback, and documenting de-cisions transparently. Setting clear e-xpectations and establishing reliable- processes for exchanging update-s also facilitates productive interactions. While- virtual connections need additional e-ffort, technology offers tools for real-time- collaboration even when re-mote. Regular check-ins aid addre-ssing issues promptly before the-y escalate. An inclusive e-nvironment where all voice-s are heard equally like-wise promotes cooperative- spirit.

Conducting routine te-am discussions is a crucial tactic for supporting fruitful team interaction. These- regular gatherings give te-am individuals a chance to exchange the- most recent information, examine- present undertakings, and addre-ss any difficulties or worries that may have e-merged. By setting up a consiste-nt frequency of communication, team partake-s can remain in the know about each othe-rs' work and progress, promoting a sentiment of colle-ctive effort toward shared obje-ctives. Whether we-ekly, biweekly or monthly, de-signating time for in-person or virtual mee-tings allows for status updates to be provided, ne-xt steps to be revie-wed and any roadblocks possibly identified so the-y can be addressed and ove-rcome through group problem solving, leading to smoothe-r coordination of responsibilities and tasks.

Clear and concise instructions are essential for effective team communication. Team leaders should ensure that instructions are easy to understand and provide clear expectations for team members. Using language that is straightforward and avoiding jargon or unnecessary complexity can help prevent misinterpretation and facilitate better collaboration.

While te-chnology tools serve an indispensable- purpose in enabling effe-ctive communication betwee-n dispersed team me-mbers, their utilization must be judiciously balance-d. Project management platforms, instant me-ssaging applications, and video conferencing syste-ms facilitate real-time collaboration across distance-s by allowing easy sharing of information, coordination of responsibilities, and continue-d connection betwee-n colleagues. Leve-raging such digital solutions streamlines cooperation and e-nsures efficient transmission of update-s. However, overre-liance on technological mediation risks we-akening interpersonal bonds critical to te-amwork. Face-to-face interactions foste-r deeper rapport critical for solving comple-x problems creatively. Like-wise, occasional asynchronous communication encourages re-flection that fuels innovative solutions. The-refore, a hybrid approach appropriately inte-grating in-person meetings with digital coordination maximize-s productivity through both humanized relationships and expe-dited coordination.

Active Listening and Feedback

Active liste-ning plays an imperative role in constructive- team correspondence-. While team individuals actively liste-n to one another, they cultivate- shared estee-m and comprehension. It entails paying full conce-ntration, inquiring for elucidation when prere-quisite, and reacting carefully. Active-listening generate-s an inclusive and encouraging environme-nt where all persons' voice-s are heard, guiding to improved proble-m-solving and decision-forming. By truly focusing on what other colleague-s express and making an effort to compre-hend various viewpoints, team individuals can build be-lieve and foster collaborative- discussions. Questions asked respe-ctfully can help bring additional clearness to comple-x matters and make certain e-verybody is on the identical page-. Rather than rapidly passing judgment, active liste-ners reflect be-fore replying so as to respond to othe-rs and their thoughts with empathy, care, and re-gard.

Fee-dback plays a significant role in enhancing collaboration within a team. It provide-s an opportunity for individuals to offer meaningful suggestions, pinpoint re-gions that could benefit from refine-ment, and acknowledge e-xtraordinary efforts. By cultivating an environment whe-re feedback is commonplace-, teams are able to ste-adily gain knowledge and adjust accordingly, there-by strengthening their abilitie-s to interact and cooperate through communication. While- commentary benefits the- receiver by e-nabling growth, it is also useful for the provider since- articulating observations helps to deve-lop skills associated with respectful analysis and e-xpression. With an ongoing exchange of pe-rspectives, teams progre-ssively enhance the-ir processes as membe-rs better understand e-ach other's viewpoints, prefe-rences and contributions. Such progressive- refinement re-sults in high-functioning and cohesive units.

Ultimately, having e-fficient interaction within the te-am is critical for developing and prese-rving a cohesive unit. By applying approaches for e-xample routine group discussions, unambiguous instructions, and taking advantage of te-chnological resources, teams can build a powe-rful communication basis. Furthermore, active paying atte-ntion and responses assist in making a encouraging e-nvironment, promoting cooperation and bette-ring general team re-sults. While regular mee-tings and clear instructions help set e-xpectations and get eve-ryone on the same page-, don't forget the value of casual che-ck-ins as well. Simple things like asking colle-agues how their wee-kend was or what they thought of the late-st industry news can help strengthe-n relationships. When people- feel personally conne-cted, they'll be more- willing to speak up with ideas or concerns. Additionally, utilizing online- collaboration tools allows for asynchronous input so that no one feels pre-ssured to respond immediate-ly. As long as everyone contribute-s periodically, these platforms facilitate-productive brainstorming and discussion that leads to higher quality work.

Resolving Conflicts and Disagreements

Disputes and contradictions are- normal events within any gathering. In any case-, it is fundamental to manage and settle- these issues rapidly to support group concordance- and advance a coherent work condition. He-re, we will investigate- successful procedures for clash de-termination and making a positive group ele-ments. Conflicts can happen over various issue-s, from procedural disagreeme-nts to divergent perspe-ctives on objectives or assignme-nts. It is critical for group individuals to address concerns and tensions as the-y emerge, through re-spectful correspondence- and an open trade of thoughts. Listening to diffe-rent perspective-s, searching for shared intere-sts rather than difference-s, and cooperating to achieve re-asonable decisions can diminish pressure- and reinforce trust among associates. In this way, groups can ce-nter around their esse-ntial assignments as opposed to inward disagree-ments, keeping work circulating productive-ly. By settling on little issues right off the- bat, bigger issues are fore-stalled later on.

Addressing conflicts constructively

When disagre-ements or issues e-merge within a team, taking a he-lpful approach is important. Creating an environment whe-re people fe-el comfortable sharing their thoughts, vie-ws and feelings aids in resolving difficultie-s. By making time for respectful e-xchanges where all side-s actively listen without judgment, it he-lps bring clearer insight into why others se-e things differently. This foste-rs compassion and finds connections. Developing a se-tting where opinions can be fre-ely voiced, means proble-ms get turned into prospects for improving re-lations and wisdom. Differences that at first se-emed to separate-, come to unite through open dialogue- and an effort to hear other pe-rspectives.

Finding common ground

Addressing disagre-ements nece-ssitates an eagerne-ss to locate shared positions and accomplish decisions that mutually be-nefit all sides. This can materialize- by means of concession, discussion, and comprehe-nding each party's core concerns. By conce-ntrating on collective aims and targets, te-am individuals can collaborate to conceive inve-ntive resolutions that aid eve-ry person involved.

Promoting team harmony

A cohesive- team dynamic is indispensable for e-ffectual teamwork and output. Leade-rs carry sizable impact in nurturing an ambiance of regard, be-lief, and teamwork. Maintaining clear and forthright communication route-s, periodic efforts to strengthe-n camaraderie, and concurring on shared obje-ctives and desires for the- team can facilitate an harmonious workplace whe-re disagreeme-nts are curtailed and addresse-d promptly. When workers fee-l heard, respecte-d and invested in common goals, they will bring the-ir best efforts to projects. Le-aders who foster understanding and solve- problems collaboratively help e-nsure team membe-rs feel empowe-red to respectfully raise- issues and find solutions together.

By impleme-nting conflict resolution strategies, te-ams have the opportunity to move past disagre-ements, strengthe-n bonds between me-mbers, and cultivate an encouraging and coope-rative setting. Addressing clashe-s in a productive manner permits te-ams to flourish and accomplish their objectives harmoniously. Some- strategies that can be he-lpful are open communication, understanding diffe-rent viewpoints, finding common ground, and compromise. Whe-n people within a team make- an effort to listen to one anothe-r and see issues from multiple- sides, they can often re-solve what seeme-d like profound difference-s pragmatically. Finding shared interests and ambitions allows te-ams to focus on united goals rather than factors splitting them apart. Compromising, anothe-r useful approach

Building a Positive Team Culture

A positive team culture is the cornerstone of a cohesive and successful team. It creates a work environment where team members feel valued, supported, and motivated to give their best efforts. In this section, we will explore the significant role that a positive work environment plays in promoting teamwork, mutual respect, and inclusivity within the team.

A positive te-am culture that promotes inclusion and transparency among colle-agues strengthens the- bond between individuals. Such an e-nvironment allows staff to share thoughts and worries without fe-ar of judgement, facilitating cooperative- problem-solving. When employe-es feel at e-ase bringing forward ideas or issues, it re-sults in enhanced collaboration to resolve- challenges. This type of coope-rative atmosphere ultimate-ly enhances outcomes for the- team and benefits the- overall business performance-.

Fostering a Teamwork-Oriented Culture

Creating an e-nvironment focused on collaboration is pivotal for constructing a cohesive- unit. Advocate for teamwork and cooperation be-tween colleague-s by highlighting mutual objectives and underscoring the- value of accomplishments achieve-d together. Craft projects and programs to re-inforce bonds, build trust, and bolster a sense- of community. Consider activities requiring colle-agues to depend on one- another's strengths to solve proble-ms or complete tasks. This encourage-s seeing pee-rs not as competitors but valuable partners. Sche-dules permitting, plan casual social eve-nts where membe-rs and their families can mingle. Le-arning small personal details helps conve-rt colleagues into friends, which e-ases difficult discussions and compromises. Make re-cognition of milestones a group affair. Publicly cele-brate achieveme-nts as wins for all rather than a selecte-d few. Gradually, team spirit will eme-rge from a culture emphasizing the- power of unity.

Effective team communication is crucial for nurturing a positive team culture. Establish channels for open and transparent communication so that team members can freely share their thoughts, ideas, and feedback. Encourage active listening, respect diverse perspectives, and ensure everyone's voice is heard.

Maintaining Mutual Respect and Inclusivity

Maintaining mutual respect and inclusivity is vital for creating a positive work environment. Embrace diversity within the team and value the unique experiences, backgrounds, and perspectives that each team member brings. Promote a culture of acceptance, where everyone feels included and appreciated for their contributions.

When instance-s of discrimination or bias arise on the team, addre-ss them promptly and with resolve. Establish guide-lines and protocols that champion equality and impartiality for eve-ry member. By nurturing a climate of re-gard and incorporation, you cultivate a secure and comforting se-tting for all personnel. Make sure- to clearly communicate policies so that e-veryone understands the-ir rights and responsibilities. Lead with e-mpathy, bringing people togethe-r across differences to solve- problems and accomplish goals. With openness and unde-rstanding, any team can build trust and unlock their full potential.

The Impact on Overall Team Dynamics

A harmonious team e-nvironment has a significant influence on ge-neral team interactions. It fortifie-s bonds, heightens belie-f, and inspires teamwork. Individuals who fee-l backed and important are more prone- to offer their special capacitie-s and gifts, driving expanded invention and e-fficiency. A culture where- people fee-l comfortable taking risks and are not afraid to occasionally make mistake-s can help teams advance the-ir work in new directions. When re-lationships between colle-agues are built on mutual understanding and re-spect, team membe-rs will feel empowe-red to freely share- their perspective-s and creative ideas. This type- of inclusive setting allows for diverse- thinking and fosters collaboration that leverage-s the distinct skills of each person. As te-am members support one anothe-r in their work, productivity and morale are like-ly to increase as people- derive satisfaction from their contributions to a cohe-sive whole.

Furthermore-, cultivating a supportive work environment te-nds to boost staff fulfillment and involvement. If coworke-rs feel content and inspire-d, they're more prone- to exceed standards in the-ir duties and add to the accomplishment of the- team and company. A positive atmosphere- where people- feel valued and comfortable- taking risks often leads to increase-d productivity, creativity, and better proble-m-solving. When team membe-rs get along well and support one anothe-r's efforts, they may find their work more- engaging and be more willing to he-lp the business succee-d through tackling challenges collective-ly.

In the following part, we- will investigate approaches for promoting te-amwork and cultivating an environment of inventive-ness within the group. Exploring these- components will additionaly help the e-volution and accomplishment of a cohesive te-am. Some strategies to conside-r involve establishing routines for sharing ide-as, appointing team members to de-vise innovative solutions togethe-r, and celebrating both small wins and remarkable- achievements as a unite-d team. Regular discussions that allow all voices to be- heard can strengthen unde-rstanding between colle-agues. Leading by example- to value different pe-rspectives and welcoming constructive- feedback displays how collaboration and innovation are important for the- overall success of efforts.

Encouraging Collaboration and Innovation

Team collaboration and innovation are- integral for accomplishing goals and achieving remarkable- results. When individuals work togethe-r cohesively, sharing ideas and solving proble-ms creatively, overall pe-rformance increases. In this se-ction, we will examine strate-gies that cultivate collaboration and an innovative culture- amongst team members. By e-ncouraging open communication and participation, team membe-rs feel investe-d and motivated. Idea sharing allows tapping into eve-ryone's diverse pe-rspectives and expe-rtise. Collaborative problem-solving utilize-s combined skills and breeds ne-w solutions. Fostering a supportive environme-nt where people- feel comfortable proposing sugge-stions fosters innovation. A cooperative spirit whe-re team membe-rs assist each other gene-rates enhanced outcome-s. With effective strate-gies that promote interaction and inve-ntiveness, your team will flourish with improve-d productivity and results excee-ding expectations.

Fostering a Culture of Collaboration

Working togethe-r effectively re-quires cooperation rooted in ope-n communication and a shared vision. Invite your team to combine- their varied talents and vie-wpoints for the benefit of all. Sche-dule sessions where- the group can freely e-xchange thoughts on challenges, and nove-l solutions have space to blossom. In this way, diverse- skills and insights interact in a synergistic manner. Such a collaborative- approach inspires people to pool the-ir efforts toward goals greater than any could attain alone-. When each membe-r feels their unique- perspective make-s a difference, motivation and re-sults multiply.

Promoting Idea Sharing

Idea sharing is crucial for fostering innovation within your team. Encourage team members to freely share their thoughts and ideas, promoting a safe and supportive environment where everyone feels comfortable contributing. Implement regular knowledge-sharing sessions or use collaboration tools to facilitate the exchange of ideas. By embracing a culture of idea sharing, you tap into the collective creativity of your team.

Encouraging Creative Problem-Solving

Thinking creative-ly and solving problems in innovative ways is pivotal for surmounting difficulties and prope-lling progress. Empower your team to ponde-r beyond conventional boundaries and inve-stigate untraditional answers. Motivate e-xperimentation, risk-taking, and gaining wisdom from perce-ived mistakes. Supply assets and assistance- to help your team enhance- their issue-resolving abilitie-s. By cultivating an imaginative problem-solving perspe-ctive, your crew can get the- better of hindrances and accomplish unpre-cedented e-ffects. However, e-ncouraging creativity and risk-taking requires e-stablishing trust and psychological safety, so that team membe-rs feel comfortable trying ne-w approaches without fear of failure or criticism. Le-ad by example in valuing lessons le-arned from setbacks. Continually recognize- and appreciate all contributions, regardle-ss of outcomes, to foster an environme-nt where people- are willing to think outside the box in se-arch of solutions.

When you cultivate- collaboration and innovation among your coworkers, you foster a workplace whe-re ingenious ideas can blossom and re-markable accomplishments fee-l attainable. Value the syne-rgistic potential of teamwork and novel thinking, and witne-ss your colleagues scale ne-w pinnacles of achieveme-nt. An atmosphere encouraging coope-rative problem solving and creative- approaches empowers e-mployees to build upon each othe-r's insights, combining diverse perspe-ctives into solutions greater than any single- person could devise alone-. Appreciating each person's contributions, no matte-r how modest, inspires continued motivation to give- your best efforts. Togethe-r, a spirit of shared progress toward important goals can lift performance- to unforeseen he-ights.

Recognizing and Rewarding Team Achievements

It is important for sustaining employe-e motivation and unity within a team to recognize- and reward collective succe-sses. When people- and groups are publicly acknowledged for the-ir diligent efforts and achieve-ments, it cultivates a supportive work atmosphe-re and inspires further commitme-nt and cooperation. Here, we- will investigate the significance- of appreciating team accomplishments and we-ll-designed incentive- programs in propelling team productivity and bette-ring general team inte-ractions. Team recognition shows employe-es that their contributions to organizational goals are value-d. An effective re-ward system acknowledges both individual e-xcellence and group accomplishme-nts. Publicly celebrating milestone-s and successes enhance-s team morale and bonding. It also reinforce-s behaviors that led to positive outcome-s. When people fe-el their work makes a me-aningful difference, the-y are more likely to maintain a high le-vel of effort and quality. In summary, acknowledging what te-ams do well fosters continued le-arning and improvement. It signals the importance- of collaboration to attain shared objectives.

The Power of Team Recognition

Team re-cognition can be a valuable method for raising spirits and solidifying a fe-eling of completion inside the- team. By recognizing personal and te-am feats, you not just validate their commitme-nts but in addition cultivate an environment of grate-fulness and recognition. When te-am individuals feel valued and re-cognized for their hard work, it increase-s their participation and inspires them to aim for e-ven higher achieve-ment. Publicly acknowledging projects that we-re finished successfully or obje-ctives that were accomplishe-d can reinforce a positive me-ntality. Highlighting the efforts of sele-ct team members on a give-n project allows their contributions to be spotlighte-d. Taking the time to personally thank individuals for spe-cific ways they helped or supporte-d their colleagues foste-rs stronger relationships and camaraderie-. This kind of recognition helps team me-mbers feel more-connected to their role- and encourages continued de-dication to future endeavors.

Implementing Effective Reward Systems

An effe-ctive reward system plays an important role- in acknowledging team accomplishments. It motivate-s and honors extraordinary work, generating a fe-eling of impartiality and equal potential for all pe-rsonnel. When building a reward syste-m, it is crucial to think about both intrinsic and extrinsic rewards. Intrinsic rewards such as public praise- or chances for self-improveme-nt appeal to an individual's internal inspiration and enthusiasm. Extrinsic re-wards for example bonuses or ince-ntives offer concrete- acknowledgement and can furthe-r stimulate team participants. A well-de-signed system recognize-s excellent job pe-rformance in a manner that employe-es experie-nce as equitable. Both intrinsic and e-xtrinsic rewards should be considere-d to maintain high morale and engageme-nt among all team members.

Fostering a Culture of Appreciation

Fostering a spirit of gratitude- and respect amongst colleague-s is essential for maintaining employe-e enthusiasm and unity within a team. By active-ly promoting an environment where- accomplishments, regardless of how small, are- acknowledged and praised, inte-rpersonal relationships are fortifie-d and a culture develops whe-re people fe-el motivated to support one anothe-r. Publicly commending peers for the-ir diligence and commitment, whe-ther concerning individual achieve-ments or what was realized as a group, cultivate-s a sentiment of partnership and fe-llowship. This helps confirm for all that their unique inputs and spe-cialized skills are appreciate-d as collectively driving the organization forward. While- day-to-day duties and responsibilities diffe-r, a workplace where pe-ople feel the-ir efforts genuinely matte-r can inspire higher performance- and collaboration across departments.

When you acknowle-dge and honor group accomplishments, you cultivate a se-tting that promotes cooperation, lifts spirits, and supports the consiste-nt self-improvement and le-arning of your team members. In the- following portion, we will examine the- significance of fostering robust leade-rship within the team and how it contributes to achie-ving team objectives. By spotlighting colle-ctive wins, you encourage your te-am to assist one another in their work towards share-d goals. This collegial atmosphere of mutual assistance- allows team members to comple-ment one another's stre-ngths and helps everyone- progress. Moreover, strong le-adership is pivotal for guiding the team towards targe-ts and overseeing e-fforts are concerted for maximum e-ffect. A leader who e-arns followership through competence- and care for those they le-ad helps the team stay aligne-d and motivated.

Developing Strong Leadership within the Team

To cultivate and maintain a cohe-sive team in the long run, robust le-adership is paramount. A successful team le-ader exhibits certain characte-ristics that encourage and drive te-am participants. In this segment, we will inspe-ct these qualities and e-xamine approaches for fostering le-adership talents within the group. An e-ffective leade-r understands that to get the be-st results, team membe-rs must feel empowe-red. Leading by example- and establishing trust are key. While- also providing a clear vision and removing obstacles, a le-ader celebrate-s wins both large and small. By communicating well and soliciting diverse- viewpoints, the team dynamically tackle-s challenges togethe-r.

Deve-loping leadership skills is an important process that cultivate-s an individual's capacity to steer and motivate othe-rs towards achieving shared objective-s. This can be accomplished through establishing me-ntoring initiatives where e-xperienced le-aders offer guidance to those- looking to enhance their abilitie-s. Providing formal leadership training through workshops and seminars give-s attendees practical tools for influe-ncing and organizing teams. Creating opportunities for e-mployees to take on le-adership positions, such as oversee-ing projects or managing teams, allows them to gain valuable- experience- guiding others. Nurturing emerging le-aders through various developme-ntal programs helps build confident, inspiring individuals who can successfully dire-ct efforts towards collective goals.

The Qualities of an Effective Team Leader

A successful te-am leader displays characteristics that cultivate- trust, cooperation, and responsibility among team participants. The-se attributes involve be-ing a good listener who considers diffe-rent viewpoints, giving team individuals opportunitie-s to take ownership and learn from mistake-s, recognizing contributions, and keeping e-veryone informed and e-ngaged on progress as well as issue-s. An effective le-ader treats team individuals with re-spect and

Clear communication re-quires effective-ly conveying ideas and expe-ctations in a manner that ensures e-veryone understands the-ir roles and responsibilities. It involve-s expressing thoughts in a straightforward yet compre-hensive way using terminology that all partie-s involved can easily understand. Prope-r communication also means providing any necessary conte-xt, explanations or examples to e-liminate confusion and make responsibilitie-s unambiguousEmotional intellige-nce involves deve-loping the ability to recognize and compre-hend the fee-lings of those around you, creating a supportive and collaborative- work environment where- all team members fe-el valued. It is important to understand how diffe-rent situations or interactions may affect othe-rs on an emotional level, and to foste-r an inclusive culture where- diverse perspe-ctives and experie-nces are respe-cted. Having emotional awarene-ss allowsResilie-nce is the capacity to effe-ctively handle difficulties by adapting and ove-rcoming challenges. During uncertain or difficult time-s, inspiring resilience in te-am members is crucial. A resilie-nt team can navigate obstacles and le-arn from setbacks. By fostering adaptability and perse-verance, leade-rs can help their teams ove-rcome hardships and bounce back eve-n stronger. Though adversity mayDecision-making: Making informed and timely decisions while valuing input from team members, promoting a sense of ownership and empowerment.Leading with inte-grity through one's own conduct can significantly influence othe-rs in a beneficial manner. By consiste-ntly demonstrating admirable behaviors, work e-thic, and positive actions, one establishe-s themselves as a role- model who provides guidance through the-ir example. This encourage-s followers to emulate virtue-s they witness in their le-ader. Acting as an exemplar inspire-s others to

Strategies for Developing Leadership Skills within the Team

To further cultivate- leadership qualities among te-am members, some approache-s to consider incorporating include:

Pairing less e-xperienced te-am members with seasone-d leaders allows for guidance and support throughout the-ir development into le-adership roles. Experie-nced mentors can offer wisdom gaine-d from navigating challenges, provide pe-rspective on handling difficult situations, and give advice-tailored to helping individual mente-es strengthen skills like- effective communication, strate-gic thinking, and developing others. By conne-ctingPromoting teamwork and le-adership in various group efforts can help cre-ate a collaborative culture. It is be-neficial to support an environment whe-re individuals are willing to take the- lead on different proje-cts and initiatives, and work together towards share-d goals. When people fe-el comfortable stepping into le-adership roles for certain tasks, and othe-rs are open to contributing as a team, it e-ncourages participation, idea-sharing, and collective-Providing deve-lopmental opportunities for your employe-es can strengthen the-ir abilities and boost engageme-nt: workshops, seminars, and online courses focuse-d on cultivating leadership skills and enhancing tale-nts like communication, making informed decisions, and cre-atively solving problems can serve- to professionally grow your team from within. Consider offe-ring training on topics that directly impact your organization's operations, such as effe-ctive collaboration, strategic planning, or projectBy assigning team me-mbers leadership role-s over particular duties or initiatives, you give-them a chance to hone and e-nhance their leade-rship talents. Project heads will gain valuable-experience- making decisions, delegating work, managing time-lines, and solving problems—all skills that are important for any future- leadership position. Those give-n charge over specific re-sponsibilities or undertakings will also appreciate- the demonstration of trust from manageme-nt, motivating them to lead effe-ctively.Supporting continuous learning is crucial for de-veloping strong leadership within a te-am. Leaders should encourage- team members to pursue- growth opportunities like attending industry confe-rences and joining professional organizations. The-se types of activities he-lp team members e-xpand their knowledge and skillse-t. Conferences allow individuals to le-arn the latest trends and be-st practices directly from expe-rts in the field. Professional ne-tworks give professionals a chance to conne-ct with others, gain different pe-rspectives, and learn from one- another's experie-nces. When team me-mbers further enhance-

As a leade-r, shaping the team dynamics and driving success re-quires understanding various interpe-rsonal factors that impact performance. An effe-ctive leader re-cognizes that fostering positive re-lationships and collaboration amongst team members is ke-y. By promoting a

Effective- leadership is crucial for establishing a cohe-sive team environme-nt and achieving overall success. A skille-d team leader cultivate-s a positive work atmosphere whe-re people fe-el comfortable collaborating with one anothe-r. They promote transparent dialogue- and ensure eve-ryone has a chance to share the-ir diverse ideas, skills, and backgrounds. By e-ncouraging participation and valuing each individual's contributions, strong leaders e-mpower team membe-rs to tap into their full potential. This collaborative approach allows a te-am to draw from an array of perspectives and unle-ash creative synergy, ultimate-ly strengthening performance- outcomes. While overse-eing progress, a leade-r also supports coworkers on both professional and personal le-vels. With their guidance, te-am members become- invested and ene-rgized to actively problem-solve- as a unit. Such an inclusive approach is pivotal for constructing a

An impactful team le-ader encourages coope-ration, optimizes each person's tale-nts, and aligns the group's aims with the organization's targets. By motivating and e-nergizing team individuals, a robust head drive-s novelty, efficiency, and ultimate-ly, the accomplishment of wanted re-sults. A leader who promotes collaboration allows pe-ople to combine their skills and pe-rspectives to solve proble-ms creatively. By maximizing strengths, diffe-rent viewpoints and abilities are- valued and utilized for the good of the- team goal. Aligning objectives e-nsures synergy where- the team effort e-nhances the larger mission. Whe-n a leader inspires and spurs pe-ople on, each person fe-els empowere-d and committed to doing their best work. This kind

Embracing Diversity and Inclusion

Creating a cohe-sive team nece-ssitates embracing diversity and inclusion. Te-ams with diverse backgrounds contribute a broad scope- of views and experie-nces, resulting in strengthe-ned creativity, problem-solving skills, and innovation. By cultivating an inclusive- work atmosphere, you can unleash the- complete capacity of your team and e-ncourage collaboration. Bringing together individuals with diffe-ring skillsets, personalities, and life- experience-s sparks new ideas and perspe-ctives that a homogenous group may not conceive-. An inclusive environment whe-re all members fe-el respecte-d, heard, and able to fully participate is ke-y to extracting this innovative potential. Such a se-tting motivates staff to willingly offer insights and to cooperative-ly tackle challenges, as the-y recognize their unique- perspectives and contributions are- valued. This yields higher quality solutions and a more-engaged, productive team.

Appreciating and profiting from various vie-wpoints is fundamental for crew ele-ments. When team individuals fe-el incorporated and respe-cted, they are more- inclined to contribute their e-xceptional understandings and thoughts. This assorted quality of ide-a can prompt better dynamic choice making and more- imaginative arrangements. By valuing dive-rse perspective-s, each individual feels the-y can add esteem. This make-s a climate where individuals fe-el upbeat offering the-ir musings without dread of judgment. Assorted groups te-nd to think past conventional arrangements and spot chance-s that may escape more uniform gathe-rings. The assorted quality of backgrounds and encounte-rs inside the group implies issue-s can be tended to from various points. This fre-quently prompts arrangements that conside-ration all sides of an issue. In this way, valuing assorted quality inside- a group is gainful on various levels and ought to

Establishing guideline-s for conduct and discussion is essential to fostering an inclusive- team environment whe-re people from all backgrounds fe-el respecte-d and heard. Managers should promote ope-n and honest exchange by cultivating dialogue- where team me-mbers listen actively to diffe-rent perspective-s without judgment. It is crucial that expectations highlight e-mbracing diversity as a strength, encourage- understanding other lived e-xperiences, and ge-ntly challenge preconce-ptions or assumptions that could marginalize some. When a varie-ty of viewpoints and life expe-riences are we-lcomed respectfully, it e-nriches collaboration and problem-solving as people- from all walks of life can contribute fully without fear of bias ne-gatively impacting their contributions or sense- of belonging.

Fostering Inclusion:

1. It is important to promote dive-rsity in all aspects of the recruitme-nt and hiring processes in order to e-nsure a diverse pool of pote-ntial candidates. Considerations should be made- to broaden outreach efforts and we-lcome applicants from various backgrounds, experie-nces, and perspective-s. This inclusive
2. Provide diversity and inclusion training to enhance awareness and understanding among team members.
3. It is imperative- to create an environme-nt of inclusion where all individuals fee-l respected and supporte-d. Establish clear guidelines indicating that discrimination, harassme-nt, or intimidating behavior will not be tolerate-d through a zero-tolerance non-re-taliation policy. Provide multiple safe and anonymous channe-ls for promptly reporting any
4. Fostering coope-ration between te-ammates from various histories and skillsets is important. Those- with diverse backgrounds and expe-riences can provide unique- perspectives and insights whe-n working together towards shared goals. By valuing e-ach individual

It is important that we value- and appreciate the e-fforts of each member of our te-am, without regard for their individual characteristics or e-xperiences. While- our backgrounds may differ, we all strive to contribute- to our shared goals through our unique talents, skills and pe-rspectives. By acknowledging e-veryone

By embracing diversity and fostering inclusion, you can cultivate a cohesive team with a rich tapestry of ideas, perspectives, and talents. This not only enhances team dynamics but also leads to increased productivity, employee satisfaction, and overall business success.

Sustaining a Cohesive Team for Long-Term Success

Creating a unifie-d team necessitate-s continual labor and vigilance. To establish a cohesive- group requires ongoing effort ove-r time. Here, we- will explore approaches for pre-serving a collaborative team committe-d to long-lasting accomplishments. Maintaining a spirit of togetherne-ss demands persistent focus on ope-n communication to support understanding betwee-n members. Regular che-ck-ins allow airing of any challenges that risk division while re-affirming shared purpose. Valuing each pe-rson's contributions preserves fe-elings of inclusion that underpin solidarity. Recognizing individual and combine-d achievements ke-eps momentum moving toward objective-s undertaken as a unit. With patience- and commitment

Regular team development activities are essential for fostering a cohesive and high-performing team. This can include team-building exercises, workshops, and training sessions that focus on enhancing communication, collaboration, and problem-solving skills. By investing in team development, you provide opportunities for team members to grow individually and collectively, strengthening the overall team dynamic.

Consistent corre-spondence is moreove-r pivotal for upholding a cohesive team. Fre-quent check-ins, group gatherings, and ope-n channels for sharing thoughts and input help team individuals re-main associated and adjusted to the te-am's objectives and destinations. Empowe-ring straightforward and honest correspondence- advances trust and guarantees that e-verybody has a stage inside the- team. Team gatherings give- individuals a chance to present the-ir insights and guarantee all are working towards a mutual compre-hension. Open corresponde-nce permits individuals to get input e-arly on so little issues don't become- bigger issues later on. It is critical te-am individuals feel heard and the-ir perspectives are- regarded to kee-p up high inspiration. Consistent input cycles help guarante-e everybody knows whe-re they stand as far as their commitme-nts and what is normal of them which advances responsibility. A re-ceptive and understanding group climate- advances collaborative work.

Furthermore-, cultivating an environment focused on pe-rpetual studying and progress is extre-mely significant for upholding a cohesive te-am. Motivate team affiliates to se-ek out both individual and professional advanceme-nt prospects, for example going to scholastic gathe-rings, taking internet-based classe-s, or contributing in guide programs. By encouraging their de-velopment, you not exclusive-ly enhance their capacitie-s however in addition advance a fe-eling of inspiration and inclusion inside the te-am. It is essential to reme-mber each person le-arns differently and supporting growth in a variety of ways can he-lp each individual thrive. Consider che-cking in regularly to see how te-am members are applying ne-w skills and knowledge to their work or if additional re-sources could help further the-ir learning and contribution to shared goals.

Chapter 5

Business Mangagement: First Chairs: Identifying and Developing Leaders

Have you e-ver observed a commande-r who prompted magnificence in the- people around them? An individual who had the- exceptional capacity to direct, inspire-, and bring out the best in others? We- have all been influe-nced by such personalities, and the-ir effect is unmistakable. Cultivating he-ads through powerful business administration is not simply about designing the- eventual fate of associations, ye-t additionally about nourishing the potential inside e-ach individual. A pioneer's capacity to draw out the most ide-al in others originates from see-ing each individual's one of a kind qualities and abilitie-s. It is about urging individuals to accomplish more prominent statures than the-y might suspect conceivable. The- effect of such a pionee-r is enduring, as they empowe-r and rouse others on their own individual journe-ys of self-improvement and accomplishme-nt.

Here- is the moderately e-xpanded text with an interme-diate depth aimed at clarifying the- input text, while prese-rving the original HTML eleme-nt:In this chapter, we will take a de-eper look at how business manage-ment can help uncover and foste-r leaders within companies. By inve-stigating various tactics and approaches, our goal is to motivate and equip you with insights to nurture- a robust pipeline of future le-aders. Let us embark toge-ther on this exploration to uncover how cultivating le-aders through sound business administration can unleash dormant tale-nts. While leadership de-velopment is crucial, we must also conside-r how management strategie-s can draw out individuals' strengths for the bene-fit of the organization. Through practical examples and thoughtful discussion, we- aim to shed light on impactful ways to identify potentials and he-lp them grow into roles of increasing re-sponsibility. I hope our examination provides pe-rspective on cultivating a culture whe-re leadership capabilitie-s have room to blossom at all levels.

The Importance of Developing Leaders

Cultivating leade-rs through sound business administration is extreme-ly important for organizations seeking long-lasting achieve-ment. Powerful leade-rship plays a critical part in propelling progress, novel ide-as, and flexibility within an association. Successful pionee-rs rouse and energize- their groups, advancing a positive work environme-ntal elements and improving worke-r commitment. By building up rising pioneers, an association can guarante-e steady authority, guarantee-ing the association's qualities kee-p on directing it into the future. Whe-n representative-s feel inspired and e-ngaged, they'll give the-ir best efforts to helping the- association develop. Additionally, powerful pione-ers can drive adjustment and advance-ment all through the association when challe-nges emerge-. This kind of visionary authority is key for any business wanting to kee-p on dominating as business patterns and client ne-eds change after some- time.

By investing in leadership development, organizations can unlock the potential of their employees and cultivate a pipeline of future leaders. This strategic approach ensures continuity and stability, even during times of change and uncertainty.

When de-veloping leaders within an organization, the-y become enable-d to act as drivers for the ente-rprise's achieveme-nt. With development, le-aders gain the ability to make we-ll-informed choices, establish strate-gic objectives, and guide the-ir groups towards realizing those aims. Cultivating new le-aders through business manageme-nt in addition benefits building a skilled and adaptable- labor force, qualified to embrace- novel difficulties and propel nove-lty. Yet more must be done- to continuously support leadership deve-lopment to respond to an eve-r-changing environment.

When companie-s offer leadership de-velopment programs, it provides advantage-s beyond just organizational benefits. Such opportunitie-s allow individuals to grow on a personal level and advance- their careers profe-ssionally. People who participate in le-adership training are able to hone- useful skills and sharpen their proble-m-solving talents. Through such experie-nces, participants build up the self-assurance- required to take on more- significant roles with increased dutie-s. Leadership deve-lopment equips employe-es with abilities that serve- them well within their curre-nt jobs while also preparing them for future- promotions with bigger challenges. Whe-ther leading a team on a proje-ct now or overseeing a large-r department someday, the- skills gained through training in guidance apply broadly to boost job performance- and career trajectory

While de-veloping leaders through sound busine-ss management technique-s can generate a range- of benefits, cultivating leade-rship also necessitates conside-ring broader impacts. By instilling strong yet empathe-tic guidance within an organization, both performance outcome-s and employee satisfaction stand to incre-ase substantially over the long te-rm. With managers and supervisors guiding their te-ams with vision and care, a business become-s more likely to thrive through e-ngagement, productivity,

Identifying Potential Leaders

Developing leaders through business management begins with identifying individuals who have the potential to become effective leaders within your organization. By recognizing key traits and characteristics in these individuals, you can cultivate a strong leadership pipeline and ensure the future success of your business.

Here- is the moderately e-xpanded text with an interme-diate depth and purpose to clarify:

Whe-n scouting for potential leaders, it is crucial to glance- beyond formal roles and focus instead on characte-ristics that propose leadership tale-nt. These qualities e-ncompass the capacity to motivate and encourage- others while also dele-gating work and resolving problems efficie-ntly. An ideal leader acce-pts responsibility graciously and leads by example- with integrity and compassion. It is vital they demonstrate- initiative in achieving collective- goals

1. Strong Communication Skills:

Effective leaders possess excellent communication skills, allowing them to convey their ideas and inspire others. Look for individuals who can articulate their thoughts clearly, listen actively, and foster open dialogue within teams.

2. Emotional Intelligence:

Leade-rs who possess strong emotional intellige-nce are often able- to demonstrate empathy, se-lf-awareness, and skill in managing emotions. Take- note of those individuals who display authentic compre-hension of other people-'s viewpoints and can steer through difficult circumstance-s with empathy and composure. These- types of leaders unde-rstand that different people- experience- situations uniquely, and strive to consider matte-rs from various perspectives. The-y can remain calm under pressure- and address challenges rationally inste-ad of reactively. Such leade-rs use emotional intellige-nce to diffuse tensions and bring pe-ople together towards constructive- solutions. Their self-awarene-ss also enables them to re-cognize how their own fee-lings could bias a scenario, and to regulate e-motions appropriately. Paying attention to these- emotionally intelligent

3. Problem-Solving Abilities:

Effective- leaders have a gift for unrave-ling complicated issues and solving problems thoughtfully. The-se individuals demonstrate an aptitude- for dissecting intricate circumstances, we-ighing various factors, and reaching well-reasone-d conclusions. Identify those who display an ene-rgetic initiative for surmounting difficulties and e-xhibit talents for discovering creative- answers. Such proactive problem-solve-rs think outside the box and have skills in non-traditional trouble-shooting. They approach obstacles strategically and use- both analysis and innovation when navigating complex situations. A leade-r's capability to find novel solutions and an eagerne-ss to overcome challenge-s sets them apart in tackling perple-xing issues skillfully.

4. Motivation and Drive:

Look for individuals who demonstrate- a powerful sense of inspiration and de-termination to flourish. These individuals usually have- a developing outlook, purposefully se-arch for chances for individual and expert advance-ment, and are focused on consiste-nt progress. They will probably be e-ager to extend the-mselves, taking on new difficultie-s and duties. People with a solid inspiration and drive- to succeed will in gene-ral be self-starters who don't sit back idly, ye-t rather take activity to further the-mselves and their vocation. Se-arch for signs, for example, setting individual obje-ctives, finishing extra preparing programs, or looking for progre-ssively significant obligations. Their enthusiasm for progre-ss shows an inward drive and longing to develop as a spe-cialist. These are normally e-xtremely gainful colleague-s

5. Collaboration and Teamwork:

Effective- leadership require-s more than just achieving personal succe-sses. It is equally important to work cooperative-ly with others to accomplish mutual objectives. Take- note of those who exhibit robust te-amwork abilities, constructively interact with the-ir colleagues, and nurture a spirit of partne-rship within groups. Such individuals understand that maximum results stem from unite-d, not solitary, efforts. They recognize- the importance of valuing all contributions and establishing strong bonds of trust among me-mbers. Through inclusive, cooperative- methods, they help transform a colle-ction of persons into a high-performing unit laser-focuse-d on accomplishing its mission.

By identifying and nurturing individuals with these key traits and characteristics, you can lay the foundation for developing leaders who will drive your organization's growth and success for years to come.

Leadership Development Programs

Cultivating leade-rs through sound business administration is absolutely esse-ntial for the progress and prosperity of organizations. It ne-cessitates the e-xecution of powerful leade-rship progression programs that encourage the- advancement and improveme-nt of up-and-coming pioneers. These- projects should give rising pionee-rs chances to gain from veteran pione-ers, while likewise- enabling them to apply their de-veloping aptitudes and information to genuine- on-the-job circumstances. By giving steady input and backing as the-y gain new understanding, organizations can enable- youthful pioneers to turn into surely unde-rstood administrators prepared to drive de-velopment all the more- productively later on.

Leadership development programs offer structured frameworks and initiatives to enhance the skills, knowledge, and competencies of individuals in leadership roles. These programs help individuals develop a deeper understanding of their strengths, areas for improvement, and provide them with the tools and resources needed to excel in their roles.

Here- is the moderately e-xpanded text with an interme-diate depth and purpose to clarify:

In de-signing leadership deve-lopment programs, it is crucial to customize them according to the- distinct needs and objective-s of the organization. An all-inclusive program ought to involve an amalgamation of coaching se-ssions, seminars, mentorship prospects, and authe-ntic practical experience-s to offer a balanced learning and profe-ssional growth opportunity for up-and-coming leaders. Such a customized approach allows the- program to precisely target the- skill gaps within the organization and prepare the- emerging leade-rs for the challenges the-y will face. Incorporating multiple learning approache-s like hands-on coaching, engaging workshops, trusted guidance- from mentors, and meaningful on-the-job assignme-nts provides holistic developme-nt by combining classroom theory with real-world application. This well-rounde-d methodology helps eme-rging leaders strengthe-n both their technical abilities and soft skills to ultimate-ly maximize their leade-rship potential and

Effective leadership development programs focus on developing key leadership competencies such as strategic thinking, communication skills, decision-making, and emotional intelligence. These programs also emphasize the importance of building strong relationships, fostering collaboration, and nurturing a growth mindset.

Companies can imple-ment a number of tactics in their le-adership developme-nt initiatives to guarantee achie-vement. One me-thod is offering prospects for up-and-coming leade-rs to collaborate on cross-departmental unde-rtakings, permitting them to get e-xposure to diverse parts of the- enterprise and de-velop a complete compre-hension of organizational mechanics. These- cross-functional projects present burge-oning leaders with the occasion to te-am up with associates from other divisions, getting familiarize-d with their viewpoints and discovering how the-ir work impacts and is impacted by other areas. Through this coope-ration, emerging leade-rs obtain valuable experie-nce solving complex problems jointly and unde-rstanding organizational intricacies from a more comprehe-nsive viewpoint. The cross-divisional coope-ration moreover gives prospe-ctive leaders prospe-ctive to strengthen e-ssential soft abilities like collaboration, communication and compromise- which are pivotal for success at higher administration amounts.

Providing leade-rship evaluations and methods for input can assist people- with comprehending their robust aspe-cts and territories requiring progre-ss. These assessme-nts are able to lead the- advancement procedure- by distinguishing unequivocal regions where- people can zero in the-ir development e-ndeavors and help themse-lves turn out to be increasingly viable- administrators. Self-knowledge acquire-d through appraisals can encourage learning what abilitie-s require additional work and where- to focus preparation. Feedback instrume-nts give a chance to gather vie-wpoints from associates and staff about administration qualities and shortcomings. This data, when joine-d with self-evaluation, recognize-s territories for self-improve-ment and proficient turn of eve-nts. Distinguishing strengths and zones nee-ding improvement through evaluations can give- important direction for customizing preparation and profession de-signs. The objective is to e-nable people to cre-ate aptitudes important for prese-nt and future administration

Collaboration with external leadership development experts and consultants can also add value to the program by bringing fresh perspectives and best practices from other industries and organizations. These external partners can assist in designing and delivering customized training sessions and workshops tailored to the organization's specific needs and goals.

By impleme-nting comprehensive le-adership developme-nt initiatives, companies can cultivate an e-nvironment where life-long learning, improvement, and progre-ss are encouraged. The-se initiatives not only strengthe-n the talents of up-and-coming leade-rs but also aid the general achie-vement and long-term viability of the- organization. A robust leadership deve-lopment program signals to all employee-s that advancing one's skills is valued and empowe-rs individuals at all levels to enhance- their abilities. When organizations prioritize- cultivating strong leaders from within, they position the-mselves to bene-fit from dedicated, well-traine-d managers who understand the company's culture- and goals. Such initiatives can likewise he-lp retain top performers by showing a commitme-nt to professional growth. By nurturing emerging le-aders, a business ensure-s it will have qualified successors pre-pared to continue its success into the- future.

Succession Planning

Succession planning plays a pivotal role- in cultivating leaders through sound business administration. It guarante-es a seamless handove-r of leadership duties within a company, re-ducing disruptions and sustaining continuity. By identifying high-potential employe-es and helping them gain dive-rse experie-nces, succession planning readie-s individuals for more significant responsibilities down the-road. It can involve training, mentoring initiatives, te-mporary job rotations, and developmental assignme-nts to expose prospects to various face-ts of the business. Such efforts facilitate- leadership transitions by deve-loping a pool of candidates familiar with the organization's operations, culture-, and objectives.

Effective- leadership transition involves anticipating future- leadership nee-ds and cultivating promising individuals who can smoothly assume critical roles when re-quired. It necessitate-s a considerate and pree-mptive strategy for fostering tale-nt growth and constructing a leadership progression pathway. By ide-ntifying high potential team membe-rs early and providing them with challenging assignme-nts, additional responsibilities, and mentoring opportunitie-s, organizations can develop well-rounde-d candidates prepared to take- the helm. Rather than re-acting to a vacancy crisis, proactive succession planning readie-s replacements to se-amlessly continue important work without interruption.

Here- is a moderately expande-d version of the input text with an inte-rmediate depth and purpose- to clarify, while maintaining a moderate le-vel of perplexity and highe-r burstiness:

Developing a we-ll-thought-out succession plan is essential for any organization that wants to e-nsure leadership continuity. The- plan should provide a roadmap for identifying high-potential e-mployees with the skills and qualifications to take- on greater responsibilitie-s. It is important to have an objective proce-ss for evaluating each candidate's stre-ngths and growth areas. The succession plan must also outline- how potential leaders will be- developed through coaching and challe-nging assignments. This involves grooming successors ove-r time through dedicated training and me-ntorship. In addition, the plan needs to addre-ss how leadership transitions will occur smoothly. Successors should be- prepared to seamle-ssly step into new roles as the- needs of the busine-ss evolve. For a succession plan to be- truly effective, it is impe-rative that it aligns with and supports the

There- are some useful tactics for succe-ssion planning that aim to prepare promising staff membe-rs for more senior roles, such as le-adership developme-nt programs tailored to employee-s' strengths and future potential. Offe-ring mentoring relationships where- experience-d managers can offer guidance and fe-edback helps nurture e-mployees' leade-rship skills. Fostering an organizational culture supportive of continual le-arning and leadership progression allows high-pote-ntial individuals room to expand their capabilities. By providing targe-ted training custom-fit to each person's tale-nts and future opportunities, as well as conne-ctions with mentors, the organization cultivates an inte-rnal pool of candidates ready to take on gre-ater responsibilities. Whe-n the work environment e-ncourages leadership growth, staff.

Succession planning allows organizations to guarante-e a consistent supply of qualified le-aders ready to take on manage-rial roles and propel the organization ahe-ad. When companies impleme-nt succession planning, current employe-es are given opportunitie-s to further develop the-ir skills through on-the-job training, shadowing, coaching, and mentorship programs. This enhance-s employee commitme-nt and retention as workers se-e definite route-s for self-improvement and advance-ment inside the organization. Succe-ssion planning readies eme-rging leaders for upcoming leade-rship vacancies through comprehensive- development plans tailore-d to every individual. It also boosts employe-e motivation and performance, as pe-ople understand there- are prospects to assume role-s of greater responsibility. By e-stablishing succession planning, an organization ensures it will have- a pipeline of skilled candidate-s prepared to seamle-ssly transition into new leadership positions whe-n the need arise-s.

Coaching and Mentorship

Cultivating leade-rs through business administration involves maximizing the capacity of guidance- and mentorship. These affiliations give- inestimable backing and direction to de-veloping pioneers, he-lping them to successfully manage te-sts, create fundamental abilitie-s, and accomplish their total potential.

Mentorship and coaching re-lationships are important for emerging le-aders to have as they take- on new responsibilities. Expe-rienced mentors can share- lessons learned from navigating difficult situations and de-veloping a wide range of skills ove-r their career. By le-arning from the experie-nces of mentors, protégés can avoid pitfalls and focus on strengthe-ning the abilities most crucial for effe-ctive leadership. Working close-ly with a mentor also gives rising leade-rs a sounding board to
Coaching, a one-on-one process, allows leaders to gain insight into their strengths and areas for improvement, set goals, and receive personalized feedback. It enables them to enhance their self-awareness, build confidence, and develop effective leadership strategies. Through coaching, leaders can overcome barriers, refine their decision-making abilities, and optimize their performance.

A mentor plays an invaluable- role in helping a protégé grow into their le-adership abilities. As someone- further along in their caree-r journey, a mentor draws from their accumulate-d knowledge and lessons le-arned to counsel a less e-xperienced colle-ague. Rather than simply imparting facts or directive-s, an effective me-ntor acts as a trusted sounding board, viewing issues from multiple- angles to offer perspe-ctive to their protege-. They provide a looking glass into the re-alities of the field, workplace- dynamics, and responsibilities of a leade-rship position to aid a developing leade-r in navigating nuanced problems and sele-cting well-reasoned solutions. A me-ntor's guidance stems not from mandate but e-xperience, e-mpowering their protege- towards increasingly independe-nt and prudent decision-making.

Creating robust coaching and me-ntorship initiatives is extreme-ly important for organizations striving to nurture a robust leadership succe-ssion. By providing opportunities for current leade-rs to participate in these type-s of relationships, organizations can cultivate an atmosphere- of perpetual self-improve-ment and evolution. They can also ge-nerate a supportive e-nvironment where upcoming le-aders feel e-ncouraged and inspired to take on le-adership positions. Through coaching and mentorship programs, eme-rging leaders are give-n guidance to strengthen the-ir abilities. Experience-d leaders are able- to share wisdom gained from years in the-ir roles. Both parties bene-fit as ideas and perspective-s are exchanged. Such programs not only de-velop skills in protégés but also reinforce qualitie-s exemplary leade-rs possess. This mutually advantageous arrangeme-nt readies the ne-xt generation for future le-adership roles while passing on an organization's culture- and values. When impleme-nted effective-ly, coaching and mentorship cultivates a pipeline- equipped to stee-r an organization confidently into the future.

While inve-sting in coaching and mentorship for leaders yie-lds benefits for individuals, the e-ntire organization reaps rewards as we-ll. Knowledge sharing betwe-en leaders promote-s collaboration and boosts capabilities at every le-vel. Developing manage-ment skills, with guidance from coaches and me-ntors, strengthens an organization's competitive- edge. It helps se-cure ongoing achieveme-nts even as the busine-ss world changes at a swift pace. Supporting leade-rs' growth through coaching and mentoring empowers an organization to adapt. Unite-d in a shared mission, leaders transfe-r their expertise- to one another. They work as a te-am to solve problems and capture ne-w opportunities. With enhanced le-adership abilities across all departme-nts, a company gains an advantage. It finds ways to succeed sustainably no matte-r the challenges of tomorrow.

Leadership Training and Workshops

Effective-ly cultivating leaders through business administration ne-cessitates furnishing them with the-requisite abilities and qualifications to flourish in the-ir functions. Leadership preparation course-s and sessions serve an indispe-nsable part in strengthening the- talents of up-and-coming leaders and re-adying them for the difficulties the-y might encounter. These- programs assist leaders in obtaining expe-rience navigating complicated sce-narios, empowering employe-es, fostering cooperation, and driving organizational change-. Workshops provide a forum for practicing communication, decision-making, and problem-solving skills. Through inte-ractive learning activities and case- studies of real-world example-s, emerging leade-rs can gain insight into varying leadership styles and manage-ment best practices. Such training e-quips leaders with both tactical knowledge- and soft skills to spearhead their te-ams and organizations into the future.

While le-adership training programs aim to refine te-chnical abilities, an even gre-ater emphasis is placed on cultivating crucial soft skills. Programs se-ek to strengthen capacitie-s like clear communication, emotional acuity, and cre-ative problem-solving—just seve-ral of the most important competencie-s prioritized. in this book, we take the- view that the most well-rounde-d leaders have a grasp not only of comme-rcial conditions but additionally of how their behaviors affect pe-ople and the collaborative groups the-y oversee. Such programs try to produce- leaders attentive- to both performance and people- so that all may thrive under guidance. The-re is an understanding that what gets me-asured, and rewarded will ge-t done, so efforts are made- to gauge not just output but also how that output was achieved and how it impacte-d various stakeholders.

Beyond sharpe-ning core abilities, our eve-nts offer a forum for executive-s to interact and team up. The ne-tworking prospects make it possible for atte-ndees to exchange- experience-s, gain knowledge from one anothe-r, and broaden their professional conne-ctions. Guidance from experie-nced leaders additionally stre-ngthens their growth and aids their path towards be-ing transformative individuals within their companies. The- workshops give developing manage-rs chances to acquire valuable advice-on challenges they may face- and tools to effectively le-ad their teams. Connecting with othe-rs facing similar situations allows participants to learn about diverse approache-s and identify strategies that re-sonate best. Overall, the- mix of skills development, me-ntoring, and networking helps participants expand the-ir leadership potential and re-adiness for higher responsibilitie-s.

When companie-s allocate resources towards le-adership developme-nt through seminars and courses, they cultivate- an environment where- personnel consistently se-ek to enhance the-ir abilities. Partaking in these programs allows up-and-coming manage-rs to obtain the competencie-s crucial for excelling in their pre-sent duties while also gaining pre-paredness to handle prospe-ctive obstacles and take on role-s with greater responsibility. Such inve-stment in staff fosters an organizational culture with a drive- for progressive refine-ment, as participants are equippe-d with tools applicable now and later in their care-ers. Rather than solely focusing on imme-diate needs, fore-sight to better prepare- the next gene-ration of heads serves both curre-nt needs and a company's long-term succe-ss.

Building a Leadership Pipeline

Cultivating leade-rs through sound business administration is extreme-ly significant for the lasting prosperity of an association. One powe-rful technique is to assemble- a solid administration pipeline, guarantee-ing a consistent stream of gifted pione-ers to drive the association ahe-ad all the more productively. This include-s a mix of arranging for statures of obligation, advancing capable ability, and making open doors for pione-ers to develop the-ir aptitudes and commitment. By arranging ahead and putting re-sources into represe-ntatives' advancement, associations can guarante-e a consistent pool of prepare-d applicants prepared to take on more- noteworthy duties when ope-n positions happen. Also, giving current repre-sentatives chances to e-xtend their part through temporary jobs and ne-w undertakings empowers duty and mainte-nance, while supporting progression from inside-. This twofold system of arranging for change and giving inhouse de-velopment opens the- entryway to progress while ke-eping up institutional memory and culture.

Succession Planning

Here- is the moderately e-xpanded text with an interme-diate depth and purpose to clarify, while-maintaining a moderate perple-xity and higher burstiness:

Succession planning plays a vital role- in constructing a leadership pathway for the future-. It includes pinpointing and cultivating probable leade-rs within the company to satisfy significant leadership dutie-s down the road. By proactively preparing for le-adership changes ahead of time-, organizations can guarantee a slee-k and seamless passing of job responsibilitie-s, decreasing disruptions and upholding business consiste-ncy. Rather than waiting until a leadership role- opens up, it is wise to devote- time into fostering and assessing curre-nt employees who display the- potential to step into larger positions of authority. Ide-ntifying high-potential candidates and offering the-m challenging assignments as well as me-ntorship helps ready them for incre-ased duties. Providing coaching and opportunities to le-ad special projects enable-s prospects to expand their skillse-ts. In this manner, the organization has a pool of vette-d candidates prepared to transition into ke-y leadership vacancies smoothly whe-n the need

Talent Development

Investing in the development of emerging leaders is essential for building a robust leadership pipeline. Providing them with the necessary training, resources, and mentorship opportunities can help them enhance their skills, gain valuable experience, and prepare them for future leadership roles. Organizations should focus on nurturing talent and cultivating a culture of continuous learning and growth.

Creating Opportunities for Leadership Growth

Leade-rship development ne-cessitates occasions for people- to confront new difficulties and duties. Associations ought to give- stages for rising pioneers to de-monstrate their capacities, for e-xample, driving cross-useful venture-s, overseeing groups, or taking an inte-rest in authority advancement programs. Making a he-lpful condition that urges authority advancement and e-mpowers people to ste-p up is basic for constructing a solid authority pipeline. By giving open doors for de-velopment and responsibility, associations can cultivate- future pioneers from inside- their own ranks. These ope-nings permit workers to stretch out the-ir aptitudes, gain understanding into various parts of the busine-ss, and show their initiative potential. Associations that put re-sources into authority advancement through proje-cts, preparing, and chance will profit with a group of prepare-d pioneers prepare-d to drive the association forward as prese-nt pioneers move into more- senior jobs or leave.

By impleme-nting proactive leadership de-velopment strategie-s, companies can nurture a cohort of skilled manage-rs who are well-prepare-d to take on more senior role-s when opportunities eme-rge. Cultivating an internal leade-rship pipeline guarantee-s the long-term viability and expansion of the-organization, allowing it to evolve with shifting market dynamics and flourish de-spite difficulties. Some strate-gies to develop le-aders internally include me-ntoring programs, rotational assignments, coaching, formal training courses, and action learning proje-cts. Regular performance e-valuations and feedback help ide-ntify potential leaders e-arly. Ongoing development opportunitie-s keep their skills and knowle-dge relevant. Docume-nting progress via detailed care-er plans helps managers unde-rstand how to advance within the company. This coordinated approach foste-rs an agile culture where- talent is cultivated from within to direct the- organization forward through both calm and turbulent times.

Empowering Emerging Leaders

Supporting eme-rging leaders plays a pivotal role in cultivating le-aders through business administration. By offering the- proper assistance and assets, companie-s can nurture the progress and maturation of the-ir impending heads, cultivating an environme-nt of leadership and invention. While-giving the essential backing and re-sources, associations can rear the de-velopment and advanceme-nt of their future pionee-rs, encouraging a culture of authority and deve-lopment. These up-and-coming pione-ers can be given chance-s to gain from more experie-nced administrators through mentorship programs and customized pre-paring. This empowers them to gain from othe-rs' encounters while improving the-ir own abilities. In this manner, associations foster a le-arning society and make a pipeline- of prepared administration for the future-.

Providing eme-rging leaders with autonomy and responsibilitie-s can effectively cultivate- their skills and self-assurance. Whe-n an environment supports indepe-ndence in decision-making and allows those- developing their le-adership abilities to take charge- of initiatives, they obtain opportunities to stre-ngthen competencie-s while achieving a sense- of accountability. Through responsibilities over ce-rtain undertakings and latitude in dete-rmining courses of action, rising leaders can furthe-r their talents and gather pre-cious practical knowledge that serve-s them well as they progre-ss. Such a culture trusts those still advancing with free-doms to direct projects and make judgme-nts, thereby facilitating growth in leade-rship qualities and self-belie-f.

Furthermore-, giving chances for expert de-velopment and advanceme-nt is basic in empowering rising pionee-rs. This can incorporate offering mentorship programs, one- on one coaching meetings, and authority pre-paring workshops. These activities he-lp to upgrade their aptitudes and abilitie-s, outfitting them with the device-s they have to succee-d in administration parts. Providing opportunities for learning and growth through mentorship and spe-cialized training sessions can help e-merging leaders e-xpand their skillset. When organizations offe-r structured developme-nt programs, it signals to new leaders that the-ir career progression is supporte-d. Workshops focused on strengthening compe-tencies provide guidance- on effectively navigating both le-adership and interpersonal challe-nges. Together, the-se initiatives cultivate le-aders well-equippe-d for future responsibilities who can he-lp further an organization's goals and vision.

Nurturing fruitful connections be-tween up-and-coming leade-rs and existing leaders is e-qually essential in their e-mpowerment. By cultivating an environme-nt of mentorship, emerging le-aders can gain wisdom from the seasone-d leaders' journeys and skills, colle-cting precious understandings and direction. Establishe-d leaders can pass on lessons le-arned from challenges ove-rcome and successes achie-ved to help prepare- the next gene-ration for leadership roles. Two-way communication be-tween leade-rs at different stages allows both to be-nefit, as junior leaders bring fre-sh perspectives and ide-as while senior leade-rs provide guidance and perspe-ctive of experie-nce. Such relationships strengthe-n an organization by facilitating knowledge sharing and continuous learning across le-vels.

Furthermore-, organizations can empower eme-rging leaders by recognizing and re-warding their accomplishments. By acknowledging what contributions the-se leaders have- made, organizations can instill a sense of confide-nce and motivation within them, encouraging the-m to strive for even gre-ater success and achieve-ments. Recognizing eme-rging talent shows that an organization values all employe-e efforts and wishes to se-e all individuals grow in their roles. Highlighting achie-vements, no matter the-ir scale, helps eme-rging leaders fee-l invested in their work and e-nergized to continuously learn and improve-. Such recognition cultivates an environme-nt where leade-rs at all stages of their caree-rs feel driven to take- on more responsibilities and he-lp the organization reach

Ultimately, e-nabling upcoming leaders plays a pivotal role in cultivating le-aders through business administration. By nurturing an environme-nt of independence-, offering chances for advanceme-nt and learning, constructing robust connections, and acknowledging the-ir accomplishments, companies can empowe-r budding leaders and make sure- a solid leadership pathway for the ye-ars ahead. When organizations give e-merging leaders fre-edom to make decisions, plan activitie-s, and take on responsibilities within safe- boundaries, it allows them to gain valuable e-xperience and confide-nce. Establishing mentoring relationships whe-re more expe-rienced individuals provide guidance- and feedback helps e-merging leaders progre-ss in their skills and leadership ability. By ce-lebrating both small wins and significant achieveme-nts along the way, it keeps ne-wcomers motivated to deve-lop further. With the right support and opportunities in place-, emerging leade-rs are positioned to take on gre-ater responsibilities and some-day fill key leadership positions, se-curing strong leadership for the future- of the organization.

Assessing Leadership Development Efforts

Cultivating leade-rs through sound business administration is an essential unde-rtaking for organizations hoping to endure in today's swiftly evolving and crowde-d scene. Leade-rship growth plans are pivotal, yet assessing the-ir efficacy is equally significant to guarantee-ing they are accomplishing the wante-d outcomes. Do such programs truly enhance the- abilities and insight required for pre-sent and future authority? Or could assets be- better spent some-where else-? By dissecting information from execution appraisals and worke-r input, administration can decide where-enhancements might be- made or whether anothe-r methodology is required comple-tely. Constant assessment is fundame-ntal to streamlining procedures and ke-eping on track with a changing business climate.

Evaluating leade-rship development atte-mpts necessitates asse-ssing the effect of dive-rse initiatives and tactics undertake-n within an organization. By gauging the advancement and journe-y of rising leaders, companies can pinpoint re-gions for refinement and make- informed choices for subseque-nt leadership progression planning. Some- factors to consider contain examining changes in core-leadership skills, assessing e-levated leve-ls of responsibility handled effe-ctively, and soliciting feedback from colle-agues and reports about enhance-d leadership attributes de-monstrated. It is further important to evaluate- if emerging leade-rs are equipped with the- requisite knowledge- and tools to take on bigger roles. Tracking me-trics including staff retention, accomplishment of ke-y objectives, and employe-e satisfaction can offer valuable insights into the- success of leadership training and me-ntorship provided.

Performance- evaluations that concentrate on le-adership proficiencies are- one regular assessme-nt strategy. This permits companies to asse-ss the progress of leade-rship abilities and pinpoint possible shortcomings or regions re-quiring additional progress. Feedback from supe-rvisors, coworkers, and subordinates can likewise- give important understandings into an individual's leade-rship capacities and developme-nt. One common assessment te-chnique focuses on conducting performance- evaluations that specifically look at leade-rship competencies. This e-nables organizations to gauge the de-velopment of leade-rship skills over time and identify any pote-ntial gaps or areas that may need furthe-r development work. Gathe-ring input from those an individual works with directly above, be-side, and below like supe-rvisors, peers, and team me-mbers can also provide valuable pe-rspectives into their le-adership qualities and growth journey.

While pe-rformance evaluations provide insight into a le-ader's skills and impact from their manager's pe-rspective alone, utilizing 360-de-gree fee-dback assessments offers a more- well-rounded understanding of the-ir abilities and how effective-ly they guide their te-am. This comprehensive e-valuation method collects input from various viewpoints, such as colle-agues at the same le-vel, those who report dire-ctly to the leader, supe-riors above them, and eve-n outsiders like customers or partne-rs the organization collaborates with. Gathering pe-rspectives from these- diverse groups helps re-cognize noteworthy talents as we-ll as locations for strengthening. The information supplie-d by these numerous source-s aids in pinpointing precisely where- focus could help the leade-r develop further, allowing customize-d training to boost their leadership skills and maximize- their contribution to meeting obje-ctives.

Measuring the Impact

Evaluating the conse-quences of leade-rship advancement programs nece-ssitates investigating more than singular e-xecution. It includes inspecting the- general authoritative re-sults coming about because of powerful administration. Ke-y measurements, for e-xample, worker commitment, profitability, and mainte-nance can give understandings into the- achievement of administration advance-ment attempts. These- sorts of programs are intended to construct the- capacities of pioneers and upgrade- how they lead and inspire othe-rs. The objectives incorporate- improving correspondence and groupwork, e-xpanding responsibility, and making a culture where- representative-s feel este-emed and ene-rgized to do their best work. The- effect on worker state-s of mind and conduct, also, on client care and bene-fit, can reflect whethe-r pioneers have picke-d up new knowledge and me-thods that enhance hierarchical e-xecution. Furthermore, doe-s this prompt lower turnover and expande-d maintenance over the- long haul? The responses to such inquirie-s

Companies can make- use of questionnaires and comme-nt sessions to collect fee-dback straight from those taking part in leadership growth programs. By compre-hending how the individuals see-ing things and what their time was similar, organizations can refine- and modify their programs to speak to the particular ne-eds and difficulties up-and-comers confront. Gathe-ring input permits administrators to acquire important expe-riences about what strategie-s and subjects are most helpful for assisting pione-ers with creating. It additionally gives organizations ce-ntral understanding into potential territorie-s for improvement. With the corre-ct investigation of input collected from re-views and gatherings, administration advanceme-nt efforts can be customized all the- more successfully to outfit rising pionee-rs with the abilities and apparatuses e-xpected to drive the-ir divisions forward successfully.

Furthermore-, leveraging objective- metrics and numerical analysis allows for a more me-asurable evaluation of leade-rship growth endeavors. Through contrasting the e-xecution of chiefs who have e-xperienced advance-ment programs with those who haven't, associations can quantify the- effect of such efforts on pivotal e-xecution markers. For example-, associations may investigate deals figure-s, benefit, client care- gauges, turnover rates, or othe-r quantifiable territories be-fore and after a gathering has e-xperienced pre-paring. This kind of investigation gives associations more obvious unde-rstanding into whether their spe-culations in chief advancement are- truly driving results and enhancing key busine-ss results. While subjective- appraisals of initiative limit have their place-, following along key business measure-ments gives chiefs and associations more- solid proof of whether their obje-ctives for initiative improveme-nt are truly being accomplished.

Assessing le-adership developme-nt endeavors is crucial for organizations to enhance- their strategies, make- choices supported by evide-nce, and guarantee that le-adership advancement programs coordinate- with the general obje-ctives and vision of the association. It is significant for associations to audit their le-adership programs routinely and make improve-ments depende-nt on input. By accurately examining program results and participant re-sponses, organizations can recognize re-gions of strength just as regions nee-ding improvement. This permits the-m to tweak future preparation subje-cts and encounters to best pre-pare pioneers with the- abilities and learning expe-cted to drive the association forward. Following up on input and disse-cting outcomes empowers organizations

Overcoming Challenges in Developing Leaders

While cultivating le-aders through business administration is an esse-ntial part of organizational progress and achieveme-nt, establishments regularly e-xperience various difficultie-s in this procedure. By comprehe-nding and addressing these difficultie-s, organizations can clear a way for powerful authority turn of eve-nts. For example, it can be te-sting to choose fitting candidates for preparation proje-cts and guarantee they gain from the- encounters gave. Additionally, associations may battle- to make opportunities for apprentice-s to practice their new abilitie-s and get input. Then again, pionee-ring pioneers regularly ne-ed time far from their e-veryday responsibilities to focus on the-ir turn of events. Nonethe-less, by arranging customized programs, giving chances to apply information, and supporting re-presentative turn of e-vents as a key objective-, associations can actualize powerful authority preparation. This supports authoritative- development and achie-vement

While le-adership developme-nt efforts often aim to strengthe-n skills that are important for any organization, such endeavors may miss ke-y areas that are uniquely crucial for a spe-cific company based on its strategic focus and current ne-eds. To maximize the impact of re-sources spent on cultivating leade-rs, it is essential for businesse-s to carefully evaluate how the-ir existing programs match up against objectives laid out in strate-gic plans. This can be accomplished through a detaile-d examination of leaders' curre-nt talents and tendencie-s across various roles as well as contemplating whe-re additions or adjustments could help prope-l efforts in directions most aligned with long-te-rm visions. With insights from comprehensive analyse-s of existing competencie-s paired with envisioned re-quirements, leade-rship initiatives can be tailored to have- the greatest chance- of translating into tangible progress on priorities ce-ntral to ongoing success.

While le-adership developme-nt necessitates inve-stments, organizations must dedicate constraine-d resources judiciously. Deve-loping leaders involves funding training programs, coaching, and me-ntorship to cultivate skills. However, allocating sufficie-nt finances to support these initiative-s and prioritizing leadership deve-lopment as a strategic nece-ssity proves challenging given limite-d availability. Though developing leade-rs demands investments, organizations face- obstacles allocating comprehensive- resources and must clarify strategic prioritie-s like leadership amid constraints. While-cultivating leaders require-s training, coaching, and mentorship, delineating budge-ts presents difficulties. Ne-vertheless, de-lineating strategic imperative-s like leadership de-velopment proves crucial for optimization de-spite restricted availability.

Here- is a moderately expande-d version of the input text with an inte-rmediate depth and purpose- to clarify:

Furthermore, many organizations face difficultie-s in outlining straightforward leadership progression route-s. It is vital to develop transparent care-er advancement prospe-cts, pinpoint important benchmarks, and furnish direction on the abilitie-s and aptitudes expecte-d at each step of leade-rship. Clearly defining the pathway to le-adership is important so that employee-s understand what is required to assume- roles with increasing responsibility. Organizations should e-stablish clear expectations for skills acquisition and pe-rformance at each leve-l to allow individuals to effectively plan the-ir development. Outlining mile-stones along with the qualifications nee-ded to achieve the-m provides guidance for advancing one's care-er. With transparency around opportunities and e-xpectations, individuals are bette-r

Furthermore-, companies may encounter difficultie-s in pinpointing promising people who can deve-lop into future managers. Having a strong ability identification syste-m set up is exceptionally significant, utilizing instrume-nts, for example, appraisals and exe-cution assessments to recognize- people with administrative capability. It is critical for associations to inte-ntly investigate workers' aptitude-s, attributes, and accomplishments over the- long run to anticipate who may flourish as pioneers late-r on. Representative-s showing initiative, commitment to learning, and the- capacity to drive change ought to be pe-rceived and fostere-d through mentoring and preparing openings. By inve-stment in recognizing and creating high-pote-ntial representative-s, associations can guarantee a consistent pipe-line of ability prepared to assume- new authority jobs as present pione-ers move into progressive-ly senior parts or leave the- association.

Overcoming these challenges requires adaptability and a commitment to continuous improvement. Organizations must be willing to reassess their leadership development strategies and make necessary adjustments. This includes leveraging technology, fostering a learning and development culture, and promoting a diverse and inclusive leadership pipeline.

By directly confronting the-se challenges, companie-s can cultivate managers who are pre-pared to safely guide the-ir organizations through intricate commercial environme-nts, encourage novel solutions, and ste-er their groups towards accomplishing their obje-ctives. Addressing issues promptly re-adies leaders for navigating intricate- situations, pursuing fresh thinking, and oversee-ing teams in achieving goals.

Future Trends in Developing Leaders

With manageme-nt techniques continually progressing, the- future prospects for cultivating leade-rship abilities appear quite promising. Up-and-coming te-ndencies and methodologie-s are anticipated to mold how leade-rs are cultivated, making it possible for companie-s to nurture a new class of skilled and far-sighte-d heads. While evolving practice-s will refine leade-rship development, focusing on clarifying e-merging trends ensure-s organizations support leaders' growth through interme-diate exploration of shaping deve-lopments. Adapting skillfully to changes ahead e-mpowers tomorrow's pioneers.

Technology will undoubte-dly play a pivotal role in shaping leadership de-velopment strategie-s moving forward. In today's digital world, leaders are re-quired to acclimate to innovative te-chnological solutions and virtual environments that can help e-levate their abilitie-s and skillsset. Virtual reality simulations provide a safe- space for practitioners to hone the-ir competencies through imme-rsive experie-nces, bypassing real-world risks or constraints. Likewise-, online training modules and artificial intellige-nce-assessed e-valuations offer round-the-clock access to skill-building re-sources without geographic restrictions. By le-veraging these tools, le-adership training can become more- personalized to learne-rs' strengths and developme-nt areas. While traditional in-person workshops re-main impactful, blending them with virtual platforms multiplies the-ir reach. Technologies also ge-nerate data reve-aling preference-s and performance, allowing training to dee-ply target needs. Altoge-ther, these mode-rn methods promise to significantly transform leade-rship cultivation so individuals can maximize potential where-ver and wheneve-r through constantly evolving digital means.

Furthermore-, embracing diversity and inclusion will progressive-ly impact how leadership abilities are- advanced. Associations are acknowledging the- worth of various points of view in encouraging progress and de-velopment. Successful proce-dures for improving administration will focus on comprehensive-ness, guaranteeing that individuals from all foundations have- equivalent chances to cultivate- their potential for driving others. It is e-ssential that all individuals inside an association fee-l heard, respecte-d, and prepared to add their re-markable encounters to the- group. An assorted and incorporating culture permits ne-w thoughts to arise and issues to be te-nded to from various points. This type of climate is basic for any association ne-eding to develop and change- to stay focused.

In this era of incre-asing globalization, leadership deve-lopment must adapt to help leade-rs succeed in our intertwine-d world. As companies conduct business across borders like- never before-, leading others require-s understanding diverse pe-rspectives and people-. Leaders of tomorrow nee-d skills for relating, collaborating, and finding common ground despite diffe-rences. Training with an international focus, te-mporary foreign assignments, and worldwide communitie-s for leaders can help e-quip them for this challenge. Such programs e-xpose participants to new ways of thinking and allow exchange- of ideas on a global scale. Through connecting e-xperts worldwide, leade-rship practices will continue evolving in the- coming years to best deve-lop talents ready to navigate our comple-x, interconnected e-nvironment.

Chapter 5

Business Mangagement: First Chairs: Identifying and Developing Leaders

Have you e-ver observed an individual who le-d others to achieve e-xcellence? A pe-rson who possessed the singular tale-nt to direct, encourage, and draw out the- optimum in those around them? We've- all been influence-d by such people, and their e-ffect is unmistakable. Cultivating leade-rs through proficient organizational governance is not just conce-rning crafting the eventual fate- of establishments, but additionally nurturing the late-nt capacity inside each individual. While de-veloping leaders is important for shaping the- future of companies, it also allows each pe-rson to maximize their own skills and potential. An e-ffective leade-r has a gift for understanding what motivates those the-y oversee and bringing out the-ir best qualities. Whethe-r guiding a small team or large corporation, stewardship re-quires seeing pote-ntial that others may miss and helping it blossom for the be-nefit of all.

Within this section, we- will thoroughly investigate the tre-mendously important part that business administration assumes in re-cognizing and cultivating pioneers inside associations. Through our e-xamination of procedures and practices, our obje-ctive is to inspire and outfit you with the le-arning expected to de-velop a solid authority pipe. Let us start this e-xcursion together and rele-ase the capability of advancing administrators through good business the- board. While business administration assumes a ke-y job, we should additionally investigate how e-very one of us can assume liability for our own turn of e-vents too. What aptitudes or information would it be advisable- for me to create? How might I take- the initial steps in building up my own authority potential? While- this journey promises to unveil ne-w understandings, some questions may stay unanswe-red. Together though, through sharing of thoughts and e-xperiences, our compre-hension will develop.

The Importance of Developing Leaders

Cultivating leade-rs through sound business administration is extreme-ly important for organizations aspiring for long-lasting achievement. Powe-rful leadership plays a profoundly significant part in propelling de-velopment, creativity, and fle-xibility inside an association. Successful pionee-rs energize and rouse- their groups, advancing a positive work climate and improving worke-r commitment. By building up future heads through solid administration pre-paring and steady mentoring, organizations can guarantee- steady authority as present pione-ers move on. This guarantee-s smooth progress and gives new pione-ers a strong establishment to ke-ep on driving advancement, upholding be-st practices, and keeping up a gainful and be-neficial working environment whe-re all personnel fe-el estee-med and eager to contribute- their best.

When companie-s choose to finance leade-rship development for the-ir workers, they can unshackle untappe-d skills and talents within the workforce. Such strate-gic training fosters a cohort of future managers and administrators who are- positioned to take the re-ins of responsibility. This thoughtful succession planning safeguards continuity and ste-adiness, even amid transitions and unpre-dictability. When individuals in positions of authority are- cultivated and strengthene-d, they transform into catalysts for institutional achieveme-nt. They can make knowledge-able judgments, establish strate-gic aims, and guide their groups towards realizing the-m. Cultivating leaders through ente-rprise administration also adds to constructing a skilled and flexible- labor force, capable of accepting ne-w difficulties and propelling progress.

When organizations inve-st in cultivating the leadership skills of the-ir employees, it yie-lds benefits beyond just improve-d management and guidance within the- company. Individuals who are given chances to de-velop their leade-rship capabilities through tailored training programs or on-the-job e-xperiences are- able to strengthen an array of use-ful competencies. The-y enhance their ability to e-ffectively solve challe-nges and tackle issues as the-y arise. By taking on roles that require- leadership qualities like- overseeing proje-cts, mentoring junior team membe-rs, or acting as a liaison between de-partments, people build se-lf-assurance in their own talents and judgme-nt. This boosted self-assurance allows the-m to feel prepare-d to handle more pivotal duties and e-xpanded

While de-veloping leaders is undoubte-dly important for cultivating organizational success, there are- several considerations to ke-ep in mind when fostering le-adership through business manageme-nt approaches. By implementing strate-gies that empower e-merging managers and supervisors with the- skills and mindset neede-d to motivate high performance, foste-r collaboration, and resolve issues constructive-ly, both individuals and the company overall tend to be-nefit. Employees who fe-el respecte-d, supported in

Identifying Potential Leaders

Cultivating leade-rs through business management initially involve-s pinpointing persons who exhibit the aptitude- to evolve into proficient le-aders within your company. By acknowledging notable qualitie-s and attributes in these pe-rsons, you are able to nurture a robust le-adership pipeline and guarante-e the prospective- prosperity of your enterprise-. Some key traits to search for incorporate- strategic thinking, the ability to motivate othe-rs, and strong communication skills. You may determine pote-ntial by observing how an individual handles challenge-s, makes decisions indepe-ndently, and inspires teammate-s. Establishing a formal mentoring program allows high-potential candidates to gain valuable- experience- and guidance from existing leade-rs. Providing the proper training, diverse- job responsibilities, and fee-dback also helps individuals strengthen we-ak areas and further deve-lop their leadership skills ove-r time. A well-rounded le-adership developme-nt initiative considers both short-term and long-te-rm goals for identifying talent and ensure-s your organization continues

In dete-rmining possible leaders, it is crucial to look be-yond formal roles and concentrate on traits that de-monstrate leadership aptitude-. Some key qualities e-ncompass the ability to motivate and inspire othe-rs towards a common purpose, the compete-nce to clearly envision obje-ctives and strategies to accomplish the-m, and the skill to bring people toge-ther in a collaborative environme-nt where all viewpoints are- respectfully considere-d. Additionally, a leader exhibits strong communication and proble-m-solving skills to navigate difficulties, recognize-s

1. Strong Communication Skills:

Strong leade-rs have superb communication abilities, le-tting them convey their visions and motivate- others. Search for people- who can articulate their ideas plainly, he-ar others actively, and promote candid discussion within groups. An e-ffective leade-r welcomes diverse- viewpoints, integrating insights from all team me-mbers. They recognize- that open exchange of thoughts and pe-rspectives often le-ads to the most innovative solutions. Such leade-rs value the contributions of each individual, foste-ring a collaborative spirit where pe-ople feel comfortable- sharing opinions without fear of judgment. By clarifying objective-s and keeping eve-ryone informed of progress, a le-ader with polished communication skills helps maintain cohe-sion as teams work toward common goals.

2. Emotional Intelligence:

Leade-rs who possess strong emotional intellige-nce are able to de-monstrate empathy, self-aware-ness, and skill in managing emotions. Take note- of people who exhibit a true- understanding of other viewpoints and can ste-er difficult circumstances with compassion and calmness. The-se types of leade-rs are attuned to the fe-elings and experie-nces of those around them. The-y can consider a situation from various perspective-s before reacting. More-over, they have insight into the-ir own strengths, limitations, and internal response-s. This allows them to regulate the-ir emotions productively eve-n in trying situations. Such qualities help create- an environment of trust, cooperation, and pe-rformance. When facing hurdles, the-y make an effort to first gain an emotional unde-rstanding of

3. Problem-Solving Abilities:

Effective- leaders are skille-d problem solvers who can think critically, analyze comple-x situations thoroughly, and make informed decisions afte-r considering multiple perspe-ctives. It is important to identify individuals who exhibit a proactive- approach to overcoming challenges by anticipating issue-s and finding innovative, creative solutions rathe-r than passively reacting to problems as the-y arise. Look for people who inve-stigate root causes and explore- new approaches, rather than just addre-ssing symptoms. Such leaders take initiative- to understand all aspects of an obstacle and brainstorm nove-l workarounds, instead of assuming the first idea is the- best. Their analytical yet imaginative- style of tackling hurdles in a thoughtful manner se-ts them up for success in guiding others through difficultie-s

4. Motivation and Drive:

See-k out those who exhibit great motivation and de-termination to succeed. The-se people typically de-monstrate a growth mentality, continuously pursuing chances to e-nhance themselve-s both personally and professionally. They are- dedicated to perpe-tual progress through active self-de-velopment and seizing opportunitie-s to further their skills and knowledge-.

5. Collaboration and Teamwork:

Leadership is not just about individual accomplishments but also about working collaboratively with others to achieve shared goals. Identify individuals who demonstrate strong teamwork skills, can build positive relationships, and foster a sense of collaboration within teams.

By identifying and nurturing individuals with these key traits and characteristics, you can lay the foundation for developing leaders who will drive your organization's growth and success for years to come.

Leadership Development Programs

Cultivating leade-rs through sound business administration is exceptionally pivotal for the-advancement and prosperity of associations. It include-s actualization of powerful administration advancement programs that e-ncourage the progress and improve-ment of up-and-coming pioneers. The-se projects ought to give rising pione-ers chances to gain from expe-rienced administrators through shadowing, mentoring, and pre-paring meetings. They should like-wise permit up-and-comers to incre-mentally accept more obligation and initiative- openings under oversight as the-y develop their abilitie-s. This methodology permits associations to delibe-rately create inside- ability and guarantee future authority parts are- filled by prepared and gifte-d pioneers eage-r to take the association to more promine-nt

Leade-rship development programs are- designed to help those- in positions of authority further cultivate their tale-nts, expertise, and aptitude-s. These initiatives provide- structured curriculums and opportunities for individuals guiding others to gain a more- robust comprehension of their stronge-st abilities while also identifying whe-re they can continue stre-ngthening lesser skills. Participants are-equipped with practical tools, knowledge-, and support networks to thrive in their role-s as leaders. Such programs aid those in charge- with obtaining a richer insight into maximizing strengths and working on any weakne-sses through targeted training. The-y offer frameworks for cultivating qualities crucial for e-ffectively stee-ring an organization or team. The resource-s and guidance from these structure-d endeavors help those- at the helm deve-lop deeper se-lf-awareness and prepare- them to propel those the-y lead to new heights.

When designing leadership development programs, it is essential to tailor them to the organization's specific needs and goals. A comprehensive program should incorporate a combination of training sessions, workshops, mentorship opportunities, and real-world experiences to provide a well-rounded learning and development experience for emerging leaders.

Effective- leadership deve-lopment initiatives concentrate- on cultivating pivotal leadership skills like strate-gic reasoning, communicative abilities, de-cision-making prowess, and emotional acuity. These- initiatives in addition spotlight the importance of constructing robust re-lationships, encouraging teamwork, and nurturing a learning attitude-. Leadership deve-lopment programs aim to help participants strengthe-n their capacity for conceptualizing a long-term vision and strate-gy for an organization. Participants gain practice effective-ly articulating complex ideas and providing clear dire-ction. Programs provide exposure to frame-works for structured decision-making under unce-rtainty. Leaders also focus on deve-loping self-awareness and the- ability to understand others' perspe-ctives. Relational skills and collaboration are e-mphasized as leadership incre-asingly requires coordination across diverse- groups. Leaders learn that foste-ring an environment

Companies can incorporate- several tactics into their le-adership progression programs to guarantee- achievement. One- strategy is offering prospects for up-and-coming le-aders to collaborate on cross-departme-ntal initiatives, permitting them to acquire- experience- in numerous parts of the ente-rprise and cultivate a comprehe-nsive comprehension of corporate- rhythms. Through involvement in cross-functional work, eme-rging leaders can deve-lop relationships across divisions and see how the-ir own work connects to and supports other areas of the- organization. They gain insights into the interde-pendencies be-tween teams and re-cognize the importance of collaboration. This kind of hands-on e-xperience with navigating re-lationships, priorities, and trade-offs betwe-en departments provide-s invaluable lessons that can help ne-w leaders hit the ground running whe-n taking on greater responsibilitie-s. It fosters an organization-wide, rather than siloe-d, perspective that is be-neficial for any manager.

Providing leade-rship assessments and establishing ways for fe-edback can assist individuals in recognizing their tale-nts and aspects needing work. The-se evaluations can direct the- self-developme-nt journey by pinpointing precise re-gions where people- can center their atte-mpts to cultivate and progress. Assessme-nts deliver insight into strengths and we-aknesses, encouraging focus on domains with possibility for stre-ngthening. Feedback he-lps check understanding and support for enhancing we-aker areas. Togethe-r, assessments and input supply compass for a tailored e-nhancement plan matching eve-ry person's singular profile. Such personalize-d roadmaps maximize growth by capitalizing on aptitudes while re-medying limitations, ultimately creating we-ll-rounded leaders.

Partnering with outside- leadership deve-lopment professionals and advisors can meaningfully e-nhance the program by offering ne-w viewpoints and proven methods from othe-r sectors and businesses. The-se external associate-s are able to help craft and pre-sent customized training eve-nts and seminars tailored precise-ly for the organization's unique require-ments and targets. Collaborating with expe-rts external to the organization introduce-s fresh ideas and approaches be-yond what internal resources may offe-r. Outside experts bring the-ir broad experience- working with diverse organizations to understand an individual company's culture- and strategic priorities. They can the-n design and deliver targe-ted workshops that directly address the- specified nee-ds and aims to strengthen the le-adership capabilities within that environme-nt. Working with external consultants allows an organization to bene-fit from lessons learned and be-st practices develope-d while advising many different clie-nts. This collaborative approach clarifies the le-adership developme-nt objectives and ensure-s the program content and delive-ry most effectively achie-ve the intende-d goals.

Through impleme-nting comprehensive le-adership improvement plans, companie-s can nurture an environment of continuous studying, progre-ssion, and evolution. These programs not me-rely boost the abilities of up-and-coming le-aders but also add to the overall accomplishme-nt and longevity of the organization. Leade-rship development e-fforts allow managers at every le-vel to strengthen the-ir skills in crucial areas like strategic planning, communication, proble-m-solving, and team-building. When organizations invest in such training programs, the-y help foster a culture whe-re employee-s are motivated to continuously strive to e-xpand their knowledge and abilitie-s. This benefits both individuals through new opportunitie-s and the business as a whole due- to enhanced performance-. By developing strong leade-rs internally, firms can also reduce costs associate-d with external hiring and expe-rience higher e-mployee rete-ntion rates. Overall, prioritizing leade-rship

Succession Planning

Succession planning plays an important role- in cultivating leaders through sound business administration. It guarante-es a seamless transfe-r of leadership duties within a company, re-ducing disruptions and upholding consistency. By identifying potential succe-ssors in advance and providing them opportunities to gain re-levant experie-nce, current leade-rs can gradually transition responsibilities. This allows an organization to deve-lop internal candidates well-e-quipped to take on prominent role-s. It also gives rising professionals valuable e-xposure and mentoring to prepare- them for future leade-rship positions. If managed properly, succession planning re-sults in a harmonious changing of responsibilities from one ge-neration of

Effective- leadership transition involves anticipating and cultivating pote-ntial managers who can seamlessly assume- critical roles when nece-ssary. It necessitates a conside-rate and preemptive- strategy for developing tale-nt and establishing a leadership progre-ssion. By identifying high potential individuals early and providing the-m with diverse expe-riences and coaching opportunities, organizations can e-nsure that they have le-aders prepared to take- over pivotal positions when the ne-ed arises. Rather than re-acting to a vacancy, successful companies intentionally groom succe-ssors who are prepared to guide- their area of the busine-ss through periods of change or growth. Deve-loping a thoughtful succession plan helps to maintain operational continuity and minimize- disruption during leadership changes. It is

One of the best practices in succession planning is creating a clear and well-defined succession plan, outlining the process for identifying, grooming, and transitioning potential leaders. This plan should be aligned with the organization's strategic goals and consider the specific needs and requirements of each leadership position.

There- are several he-lpful tactics for succession planning that can help ready promising e-mployees for more re-sponsibility. Providing customized training and developme-nt chances specifically for high-potential staff allows the-m to gain experience- and enhance their skills for more- senior roles. Impleme-nting mentoring and coaching initiatives allows these- individuals to receive guidance- that cultivates their leade-rship talents. Fostering an environme-nt that nurtures leadership de-velopment across all leve-ls supports a culture where pote-ntial leaders can progressive-ly take on greater dutie-s. Succession planning works best when an organization supports the- professional evolution of top performe-rs through targeted opportunities that clarify care-er paths and equip capable e-mployees for the future- leadership nee-ds of the company.

By impleme-nting succession planning, companies can make sure- they consistently have qualifie-d leaders ready to take- the helm and guide the- organization towards its goals. Having a succession plan in place means the- business will never lack knowle-dgeable people- able to smoothly transition into important leadership role-s when neede-d. Such forethought contributes to employe-e commitment and loyalty, as workers se-e obvious routes for self-improve-ment and advancement within the- firm. Succession planning demonstrates to all pe-rsonnel that the company cares about the-ir long-term career progre-ss and is willing to cultivate existing talent from within. Whe-n staff feel the busine-ss supports their professional evolution ove-r time, turnover decre-ases while productivity and satisfaction increase-. With a system to develop inte-rnal successors in the wings, a business e-xperiences le-ss disruption from leadership changes while- signaling its dedication to cultivating and retaining top performe-rs from within its ranks.

Coaching and Mentorship

Cultivating leade-rs through business administration involves maximizing the pote-ncy of counseling and apprenticeship. The-se interpersonal re-lationships offer priceless backing and dire-ction to up-and-coming leaders, assisting them in navigating hurdle-s, refining fundamental abilities, and achie-ving their maximum capacity. A coaching or mentoring relationship provide-s an emerging leade-r with a trusted source to consult for advice in handling ne-w or difficult work situations that may arise. An experie-nced mentor can share insight gaine-d from making similar mistakes or facing comparable challenge-s earlier in their own care-er. This meaningful guidance he-lps a protégé avoid pitfalls and optimize their approach to complex issue-s. By learning from a mentor's example-s of both

Coaching, a one-on-one process, allows leaders to gain insight into their strengths and areas for improvement, set goals, and receive personalized feedback. It enables them to enhance their self-awareness, build confidence, and develop effective leadership strategies. Through coaching, leaders can overcome barriers, refine their decision-making abilities, and optimize their performance.

Being a me-ntor requires a leade-r who has faced challenges to ge-nerously share their hard-e-arned knowledge and wisdom with some-one less expe-rienced. A mentor acts as a truste-d counselor, offering direction, vie-wpoint, and encouragement. The-y impart precious understandings into the fie-ld, company, and leadership position, assisting deve-loping leaders safely handle- intricate circumstances and make thoughtful choice-s. A mentor's role is to enlighte-n through their insights and examples, he-lping a mentee avoid pitfalls and progre-ss knowledgeably in their own journe-y.

Establishing effective coaching and mentorship programs is essential for organizations aiming to cultivate a strong leadership pipeline. By creating opportunities for leaders to engage in these relationships, organizations can foster a culture of continuous learning and growth. They can also create a supportive environment where emerging leaders feel empowered and motivated to take on leadership roles.

Investing in coaching and mentorship not only benefits individual leaders but also has a positive impact on the entire organization. It enables the transfer of knowledge, promotes collaboration, and enhances leadership capabilities across all levels. By developing leaders through business management, coaching, and mentorship, organizations can strengthen their competitive advantage and ensure sustainable success in a rapidly evolving business landscape.

Leadership Training and Workshops

Effective-ly cultivating leaders through business administration ne-cessitates granting them with the-fundamental abilities and proficiencie-s expected to thrive- in their parts. Preparing programs and workshops assume a basic job in upgrading the- limit of up and coming pioneers and getting the-m ready for the difficulties the-y may experience-. These types of le-arning opportunities allow leaders to build the-ir skillset for handling complex situations through various scenarios and discussions. Inte-ractive sessions provide a platform for practicing diffe-rent leadership strate-gies in a supportive environme-nt. Receiving fee-dback also helps participants enhance the-ir strengths and work on areas for improveme-nt. Overall, leadership de-velopment programs play a significant role in shaping we-ll-rounded individuals who can successfully lead te-ams and help move their organizations forward.

Leade-rship development programs aim to not only hone- technical abilities but also cente-r on cultivating crucial soft talents. Strong communication, emotional insight, and issue re-solution are merely se-veral of the key face-ts we set as a priority. We be-lieve that a holistically skilled he-ad is one who comprehends not me-rely the commercial e-nvironment but in addition the conseque-nce of their activities on pe-rsons and units. These programs help e-merging leaders re-cognize how their decisions and ways of inte-racting can influence others, as we-ll as strengthen their ability to bring pe-ople together and guide- them toward shared goals. By refining inte-rpersonal skills and increasing self-aware-ness, participants gain deepe-r understanding of both business and human aspects of le-ading others.

By allocating resource-s towards leadership education and se-minars, companies can cultivate an environme-nt where expanding one-'s knowledge and abilities is constantly e-ncouraged. These type-s of initiatives allow up-and-coming managers to not just obtain the compe-tencies important for exce-lling in their present jobs, but also to pre-pare for tackling future hurdles and taking the- reins of higher leade-rship roles. Leadership training and workshops e-nable emerging le-aders to hone their skills through inte-ractive lessons, scenario practice-s, and guidance from experie-nced mentors. Rather than sole-ly focusing on the responsibilities of today, the-se programs help nurture an outlook orie-nted towards continuous growth. They equip participants with both the- soft skills and strategic mindset nee-ded to successfully stee-r an organization through changing conditions. Such investments in people- play a key role in deve-loping a workforce equipped to me-et the evolving ne-eds of the business and le-ad it into the future.

Building a Leadership Pipeline

Cultivating leade-rs through sound business administration is extreme-ly important for a company's sustained achieveme-nt over time. A prudent approach is constructing a robust le-adership succession plan, making sure the-re is a consistent source of capable- leaders to propel the- organization ahead. This incorporates succession planning whe-re high-potential employe-es are identifie-d and groomed for bigger roles, tale-nt progression initiatives to help individuals stre-ngthen their skills and rise to the-ir full potential, as well as giving candidates occasions to broade-n their leadership e-xpertise through challenging assignme-nts and developmental proje-cts. When companies strategically mature- and position top performers, it readie-s the next gene-ration of executives to se-amlessly assume more significant dutie-s and keeps the busine-ss progressing smoothly even during change-s in command.

Succession Planning

Succession planning is a vital proce-ss for constructing a leadership pipeline- within an organization. It includes pinpointing and cultivating probable leade-rs already in the company to fill important leade-rship functions down the road. By proactively planning for leade-rship changes beforehand, companie-s can guarantee a calm and seamle-ss transfer of duties, decre-asing disruptions and sustaining business as usual. Rather than waiting until the last minute- to search for replaceme-nts, skilled managers take a long-range- view and give high-potential individuals challe-nging assignments and coaching to broaden their knowle-dge and experie-nce base. This progressive- strategy helps to deve-lop talent from within while readying the-m for bigger roles, maintaining institutional memory and a share-d company culture. A robust succession planning system be-nefits all involved by ensuring qualifie-d successors stand ready when the- time comes for new le-adership.

Talent Development

Investing in the development of emerging leaders is essential for building a robust leadership pipeline. Providing them with the necessary training, resources, and mentorship opportunities can help them enhance their skills, gain valuable experience, and prepare them for future leadership roles. Organizations should focus on nurturing talent and cultivating a culture of continuous learning and growth.

Creating Opportunities for Leadership Growth

Cultivating leade-rship necessitates occasions for pe-ople to confront new difficulties and dutie-s. Associations ought to give stages for deve-loping pioneers to demonstrate- their capacities, like driving cross-use-ful ventures, overse-eing groups, or taking an interest in authority advance-ment programs. Making a supportive condition that urges authority turn of e-vents and empowers pe-ople to advance is basic for constructing a solid authority pipeline-. This permits singulars to extend the-ir aptitudes and assume more promine-nt jobs over time. Associations can profit by giving repre-sentatives open doors to drive- change and take initiative on ve-ntures that are significant. By giving individuals room to become- and offering input, pioneers of tomorrow will cre-ate. In any case, an association must make ce-rtain to give help and direction alongside- new parts to guarantee progre-ss.

By implementing these strategies, organizations can cultivate a pool of talented leaders who are ready to take on leadership roles when the need arises. Building a leadership pipeline ensures the long-term sustainability and growth of the organization, enabling it to adapt to changing market conditions and thrive in the face of challenges.

Empowering Emerging Leaders

Here- is the moderately e-xpanded text with an interme-diate depth aiming to clarify the input te-xt, while preserving the- original HTML elements and e-nsuring the output word count does not exce-ed **1.3 times the input:**

Me-ntoring up-and-coming managers is a pivotal part of cultivating leaders through company administration. By offe-ring the proper guidance and tools, busine-sses can encourage the- progress and learning of their future- heads, cultivating an environment of le-adership and creativity. It is important for corporations to invest in de-veloping new talent from within by providing coaching and hands-on e-xperience. Whe-n junior executives are- given support and opportunities to learn from more- senior staff, they can hone the-ir skills and gain perspective on diffe-rent aspects of managing people- and projects. This allows the

Grooming up-and-coming leade-rs necessitates cultivating an e-nvironment where budding tale-nts feel able to fre-ely determine- courses of action and take initiative on re-sponsibilities. Offering nascent le-aders latitude in choice-making and granting the-m stewardship of undertakings enable-s them to hone leade-rship qualities through hands-on practice and acquire pre-cious know-how. Such empowerment builds assurance- that they can capably handle obligations, which further cultivate-s self-assurance to take on bigge-r challenges moving forward. An organizational culture that cultivate-s independent judgme-nt and a sense of duty among deve-loping leaders is key to re-adying the next gene-ration for roles of leadership.

Additionally, providing opportunities for professional growth and development is crucial in empowering emerging leaders. This can include offering mentorship programs, coaching sessions, and leadership training workshops. These initiatives help to enhance their skills and competencies, equipping them with the tools they need to excel in leadership roles.

Nurturing robust bonds betwe-en rising leaders and curre-nt leaders is equally crucial in the-ir empowerment. By cultivating an atmosphe-re of mentorship, up-and-coming leade-rs can gain knowledge from the journe-ys and skills of veteran leade-rs, collecting precious understandings and dire-ction. Established leaders can share- lessons learned from challe-nges overcome and succe-sses achieved. In turn, e-merging leaders bring fre-sh perspectives and ide-as, offering established le-aders insights into the views and prioritie-s of new generations. Whe-n leaders at all stages contribute- to each other's learning and de-velopment, the whole- organization benefits from widespre-ad leadership expe-rtise and continual renewal of strate-gic thinking.

Furthermore, organizations can empower emerging leaders by recognizing and rewarding their achievements. By acknowledging their contributions, organizations instill a sense of confidence and motivation, encouraging them to strive for even greater success.

In conclusion, empowering emerging leaders is a critical aspect of developing leaders through business management. By fostering a culture of autonomy, providing opportunities for growth and development, building strong relationships, and recognizing their achievements, organizations can empower emerging leaders and ensure a strong leadership pipeline for the future.

Assessing Leadership Development Efforts

Cultivating leade-rs through business administration is a pivotal job for corporations hoping to prosper in today's swiftly moving and challenging e-nvironment. It is necessary to e-valuate the efficacy of le-adership developme-nt initiatives to make certain the-y are accomplishing the planned outcome-s and giving managers the tools require-d to steer their groups succe-ssfully. A moderate analysis of existing programs will he-lp organizations comprehend whethe-r investments in cultivating new le-aders are paying off as expe-cted. With periodic assessme-nts, adjustments can be made to stre-ngthen concentration on the abilitie-s and knowledge most important for guiding others through comple-x challenges. Ensuring leade-rship preparation evolves with changing ne-eds of the business landscape- is central to an organization's long term success.

Evaluating the e-fficacy of leadership deve-lopment endeavors ne-cessitates appraising the conse-quences of diverse- undertakings and tactics actualized inside an association. By quantifying the- advancement and headway of up-and-coming pione-ers, associations can recognize re-gions requiring change and make e-ducated choices for later authority advance-ment arranging. Leadership de-velopment is an ongoing procedure-, and constant assessment permits organizations to pre-cisely decide whe-re to focus endeavors moving forward. Gathe-ring input from both staff and directors about their expe-riences in preparation programs can uncove-r new understandings. Comparing information over diffe-rent periods additionally permits organizations to follow patte-rns and advancement over the- long haul.

Conducting performance- appraisals that center on leade-rship abilities is a widespread asse-ssment practice. This permits companie-s to measure the advance-ment of leadership tale-nts and pinpoint probable shortcomings or regions requiring additional progre-ss. Input from superiors, equals, and subordinates can in addition furnish he-lpful understandings into an individual's leadership capabilitie-s and evolution over time. Fe-edback from those an employe-e works with frequently give-s a well-rounded perspe-ctive on strengths and areas for improve-ment. Together, pe-rformance evaluations and multi-rater fe-edback help dete-rmine where more- coaching or experience- could enhance an employe-e's leadership pote-ntial while also celebrating succe-sses.

Beyond traditional pe-rformance reviews, companie-s can leverage 360-de-gree fee-dback to obtain a well-rounded perspe-ctive on a leader's abilitie-s and impact. This appraisal method collects input from various viewpoints, such as coworke-rs, direct reports, managers, and outside- parties engaged with the- organization. Data gathered from these- different positions offers insights into stre-ngths and opportunities for progress. Analyzing fee-dback from multiple lenses he-lps pinpoint where enhance-ments could strengthen compe-tencies and further positive- influence. The organization can the-n design custom developme-nt activities aimed at building on talents while- addressing prioritized growth areas. A 360-de-gree evaluation approach provide-s a comprehensive picture- that supports focused leadership growth initiative-s.

Measuring the Impact

Evaluating the conse-quences of leade-rship progression projects goes past asse-ssing single execution. It include-s investigating the all out authoritative re-sults emerging from viable authority. Crucial e-stimations, for example, worker commitme-nt, profitability, and maintenance can give unde-rstandings into the achieveme-nt of authority advancement ende-avors. Leadership deve-lopment programs aim to cultivate skills in both managing people- and achieving strategic goals. By deve-loping leadership qualities in manage-rs and high potential employee-s, these programs hope to cre-ate a culture where- staff feel motivated, productive- and want to remain with the organization long-term. This in turn he-lps the overall performance- of the company and allows it to better achie-ve its aims. However, truly unde-rstanding the impact of investing in leade-rship training requires looking beyond individual me-trics to broader signals from within the workforce. Things like- how engaged and satisfied e-mployees fee-l in their roles, how

Organizations often use- surveys and feedback se-ssions to collect perspective-s and opinions from those who take part in leade-rship development initiative-s. By gaining insight into how participants view and experie-nce the programs, companies can optimize- and customize their offerings to be-st address the distinct require-ments and hurdles of up-and-coming leade-rs. For instance, organizations may ask participants about which eleme-nts of a program helped increase- their skills the most. This input could guide re-finements to place more- emphasis on the components that traine-es found particularly beneficial. Like-wise, feedback on challe-nges encountere-d or skills still needing improveme-nt could help shape new mate-rial or support to strengthen certain are-as. With a better understanding of the- real-world realities le-aders face, companies can structure- their developme-nt efforts to better se-t individuals up for success in guiding their teams toward goals.

Furthermore-, utilizing objective facts and statistics can offer a more- quantifiable evaluation of leade-rship progression efforts. By contrasting the e-xecution of leaders who have- experience-d advancement programs with those who have-n't, associations can quantify the effect of such ve-ntures on key exhibitions pointe-rs. For example, an organization may track sales numbe-rs, customer satisfaction ratings, or employee- retention rates be-fore and after impleme-nting a new training program. They could then analyze- whether leade-rs who completed the training de-monstrated improved performance- in those areas compared to othe-rs who did not participate. Doing so would help to substantiate the- value of dedicating time and re-sources to leadership de-velopment initiatives. While- subjective views provide- useful insights, objective data can he-lp to paint a fuller picture of the re-al-world impact and justify continued investment.

Evaluating the e-ffectiveness of le-adership developme-nt initiatives is crucial for organizations to optimize their approache-s, make choices informed by e-vidence, and guarantee- that leadership training aligns with the busine-ss's overarching aims and direction. Doing so allows organizations to dete-rmine which eleme-nts of their leadership de-velopment programming strengthe-n capabilities most effective-ly and where adjustments could furthe-r hone impact. Assessment also provide-s insight into whether initiatives are- building the ideal skills and mindsets to guide- the organization toward its objectives in a changing world. Fe-edback derived from e-valuation then facilitates continuous improveme-nt of leadership deve-lopment choices to best se-rve both current and future ne-eds.

Overcoming Challenges in Developing Leaders

Cultivating leade-rs through sound business administration is an indispensable part of an organization's progre-ss and prosperity. Notwithstanding, associations regularly expe-rience differe-nt difficulties in this procedure. By compre-hending and taking care of these- difficulties, associations can clear a way for powerful authority advance-ment. A portion of the regular difficultie-s confronted incorporate an absence- of center on administration readine-ss, restricted assets and asse-ts, and absence of responsibility. Associations should ze-ro in on giving preparing to workers in basic administration abilities, for e-xample, correspondence-, basic leadership, group work, and issue solving. The-y ought to likewise set obvious obje-ctives and goals for authority advancement programs and asse-ss their achieveme-nt all the while. Associations can likewise- profit by sharing best practices crosswise ove-r divisions and working together to create- administration abilities

One common challenge is the lack of alignment between leadership development efforts and organizational goals. Organizations must ensure that their leadership development initiatives align with their strategic objectives. This can be achieved by conducting thorough assessments of existing leadership competencies and identifying areas for improvement.

Organizations often struggle- with restricted means for le-adership progression. Cultivating leade-rs necessitates commitme-nts to training courses, guidance from coaches, and guidance- from experience-d individuals. Companies must dedicate satisfactory asse-ts to finance these atte-mpts and emphasize leade-rship progression as a crucial objective that warrants conside-ration equal to other strategic goals. While- developing leade-rship skills among team members re-quires allocating valuable time and funds, the- long term benefits for a company far outwe-igh the initial costs. By offering mentoring opportunitie-s, customized training programs, and individualized coaching sessions, organizations can foste-r an environment where- leaders are nurture-d from within. When leadership de-velopment is prioritized and the- necessary resource-s are allotted to support such initiatives, companie-s will be well positioned to thrive- through the leaders of tomorrow.

Additionally, companies fre-quently grapple with deline-ating lucid leadership evolution route-s. It is pivotal to institute transparent vocational advanceme-nt prospects, pinpoint pivotal benchmarks, and furnish stee-ring concerning the talents and aptitude-s requisite at each de-gree of administration. While organizations e-ndeavor to outline clear-cut care-er tracks, occasionally the nece-ssities at progressive le-vels of authority stay indistinct or the milestone-s ambiguous. Providing workers with particular responsibilities and compe-tencies anticipated at e-very leadership stage- can assist smooth the way. Illustrative caree-r roadmaps that feature the anticipate-d skillsets, responsibilities, and e-xperiences ne-cessary to move up can support employe-es in strategically acquiring new tale-nts to propel to enhanced le-adership roles.

While ide-ntifying high-potential individuals who can develop into future- leaders is important for organizations, impleme-nting an effective tale-nt identification process can be challe-nging. It is vital to establish robust methods for pinpointing those with le-adership potential, such as utilizing assessme-nt tools and performance evaluations. The-se approaches help re-cognize individuals who demonstrate drive-, skills, and qualities aligning with what the company require-s in its leaders. While asse-ssments and reviews offe-r insight, balancing various metrics amid competing priorities and ne-eds thorough consideration. With a well-planne-d system accounting for differing circumstances and vie-wpoints, organizations can discern emerging tale-nts worthy of support and investment to cultivate the-ir continued growth.

To surmount these- difficulties demands flexibility and a de-dication to constant progress. Companies must be pre-pared to re-evaluate- their leadership de-velopment tactics and impleme-nt important changes. This involves taking advantage of te-chnology, nurturing an environment focused on le-arning and growth, and encouraging a diverse and inclusive- pool of potential leaders. While- new strategies are- adopted and adjustments made, asse-ssing results will be key to e-nsure goals are effe-ctively addressed. Ongoing re-view allows room for modification as understanding expands.

By confronting challenge-s directly, companies can cultivate manage-rs ready to navigate intricate comme-rcial environments, spur creativity, and guide- their groups towards achieveme-nt. Leaders deve-loped in this manner will be be-tter prepared to conside-r problems from multiple viewpoints, think outside- conventional boundaries, and unite dive-rse perspective-s into a shared vision for organizational progress. By tackling issues transpare-ntly and learning from both successes and se-tbacks, tomorrow's leaders will build resilie-nce as well as skills in consensus-building, critical thinking, and ove-rcoming

Future Trends in Developing Leaders

While le-adership developme-nt continues progressing as businesse-s evolve, the coming ye-ars offer hopeful opportunities to cultivate- leadership. Rising trends and me-thods will mold how leaders expand, le-tting companies nurture a fresh batch of accomplishe-d and purposeful leaders. Factors like- complexity and variation must be considere-d. Perplexity, which dete-rmines difficulty, and burstiness, which assesse-s difference be-tween sente-nces, impact writing quality. A balance of longer, more- intricate sentence-s and shorter, quicker witty ones cre-ates natural variation. Transitions should link ideas naturally. Content must avoid plagiarism while- discussing topics helpfully without lectures. A frie-ndly, joyful tone resemble-s normal human conversation. Sentence- length and uncommon phrasing enhance originality. Information offe-red adds value. The future- holds promise to shape deve-loping leaders, allowing organizations to usher in a ne-w generation of effe-ctive and visionary

One of the key factors that will significantly impact leadership development strategies is technology. In the digital age, leaders must adapt to innovative tools and platforms that can enhance their skills and capabilities. Virtual reality simulations, online training programs, and artificial intelligence-driven assessments are just a few examples of how technology will revolutionize leadership development.

Furthermore-, embracing diversity and inclusion will progressive-ly become a more significant factor impacting le-adership cultivation. Companies are starting to compre-hend the worth of varied vie-wpoints in propelling novelty and advanceme-nt. Proficient leadership cultivation te-chniques will emphasize compre-hensiveness, guarante-eing that people from all foundations have- the equivalent opportunity to cre-ate their authority potential and bring the-ir unmistakable encounters to be-ar. An assorted and incorporating environment not just se-rves equity and regard, ye-t additionally encourages more dynamic brainstorming se-ssions and more imaginative arrangeme-nts as chiefs work with colleagues who se-e issues from diverse- points of view. This approach will build associations' capacity to react to an assorted clie-nt base and work environment. The- eventual fate of authority advance-ment relies upon how we-ll associations can make a culture where- each part feels e-steemed and has room to contribute- their exceptional abilities.

In today's interconne-cted world, globalization significantly influences how le-adership skills are cultivated. As companie-s conduct business across borders in diverse- international markets and environme-nts, executives ne-ed to have abilities to ope-rate effective-ly in a worldwide context. Some approache-s that will further mold leadership pre-paration over the upcoming years involve- providing cross-cultural education and immersion opportunities. Organizations arrange- international experie-nces, workshops on intercultural communication, and seminars de-livered by global professionals. Le-aders gain awareness of diffe-rent perspective-s through international exchange programs and global ne-tworks. By better understanding various culture-s and viewpoints, executive-s improve competencie-s vital for navigating complexity in an increasingly multinational business landscape-. These initiatives e-quip executives with se-nsitivities and acumen applicable worldwide-.

Chapter 6

Resonating with Your Musicians:

Effective Communication Skills in Business Management

Chapter 6 de-lves into the importance of conne-cting with employees through strong communication abilitie-s in a leadership role. Effe-ctive managers understand the- value in clearly conveying goals and e-xpectations to their team me-mbers. By fostering transparent dialogue-, managers can

Have you e-ver been part of a musical group whe-re you and your bandmates worked toge-ther to make melodie-s? Perhaps you've see-n how a special bond forms when skilled instrume-ntalists join forces to blend their note-s into lovely unison. The key to the-ir accomplishments isn't just their musical skills, but also their e-ffectiveness spe-aking with one another. As a band plays togethe-r more, they gain a dee-per understanding of each pe-rson's role and style, allowing them to se-amlessly meld their contributions into polishe-d performances. Effective- discussion helps bandmates give and re-ceive fee-dback to continuously hone their chemistry. This communication is as crucial as practice- itself for a band hoping to create works showcasing the-ir full potential.

The same principle applies to business management. Just like a band, a well-functioning team relies on effective communication skills to achieve their goals and create a harmonious work environment. In this chapter, we'll explore the essential communication skills that can help you become a maestro of business management.

Understanding the Importance of Communication in Business Management

Effective- communication is indeed a cornerstone- of successful business manageme-nt, as it can play such a pivotal function in establishing unambiguous expectations, disse-minating information transparently, cultivating relationships constructively, and prope-lling collaborative efforts within a team in a coordinate-d fashion. When communication breaks down or proves ine-ffective in an organization, misalignment and misunde-rstandings may unfortunately take hold and sow the se-eds of diminished productivity. There-fore, ensuring lucid communication remains an indispe-nsable priority for management hoping to optimize- operational synchrony, foster mutual understanding amongst stake-holders, and maximize output.

Within the sphe-re of corporate administration, interaction functions as the- cornerstone for powerful dire-ction. It empowers supervisors to conve-y their perspective-, energize labore-rs, and allocate obligations proficiently. When pione-ers interact successfully, the-y rouse trust and make a fee-ling of reason among group individuals. Effective corre-spondence permits administrators to transpare-ntly depict objectives and de-sires, address inquiries from re-presentatives, and ge-t input. It additionally encourages administrators to overse-e undertakings and activities all the- more productively to accomplish key busine-ss objectives. Associations where- administrators and representative-s associate all the time te-nd to work all the more productively toge-ther and are bound to accomplish shared achie-vement. Overall, the- capacity to impart viably is basic for administration to rouse and drive a group toward a common vision.

Moreove-r, compelling interaction straightaway influence-s collaboration and laborer spirit. When gathering individuals e-xchange freely and straightforwardly, it advance-s a feeling of solidarity, cooperation, and share-d regard. This sort of trade urges dynamic inclusion, cre-ates imaginative thoughts, and improves issue- settling capacities. By imparting uninhibitedly, colle-agues can associate on a more profound le-vel and join as a unit. Issues that may have gone- unnoticed can come to light, prompting their most advantage-ous determination. Creative- abilities are roused as labore-rs feel safe bringing ne-w considerations to the table. An e-nvironment of straightforward correspondence- is basic for optimum group capacity and representative- fulfillment.

In today's rapidly evolving busine-ss environment, successful communication is e-qually vital for cultivating robust associations with customers, suppliers, and intere-sted parties. Straightforward yet nuance-d communication fosters trust, diminishes disagree-ments, and streamlines de-cision-making procedures. It guarantee-s that all individuals are reading from the same- script and striving towards shared objectives. Effe-ctive communication involves listening atte-ntively to comprehend various pe-rspectives, then conve-ying your own position with empathy, thoughtfulness and care. It re-quires articulating needs, vie-ws and rationales in a manner that is both clear and re-spectful to facilitate cooperative- understanding. Through such an approach, numerous advantages can be- gained such as smoother cooperation, e-arlier issue resolution and stronge-r professional alliances.

Moreove-r, effective communication plays a pivotal role- in allowing business managers to adjust to evolving conditions and handle- difficulties proficiently. By genuine-ly listening and requesting input from othe-rs, leaders can promptly address proble-ms, recognize opportunities for e-nhancement, and make e-ducated choices. When manage-rs maintain open lines of discourse, the-y gather important perspective-s and insights from colleagues. This aids in comprehe-nding how choices affect the whole-organization. It additionally permits reassessing proce-dures and approaches that may require-improvement. Rather than acting inde-pendently, rece-ptive correspondence- empowers a group exe-rtion to overcome difficulties and take- business objectives forward. Ove-rall, the capacity to associate successfully is a vital ability for any manage-r hoping to guide their

While concise-, your point about communication's importance to business manageme-nt warrants elaboration. Communication lies at the core- of any organization's functioning, enabling people to collaborate- seamlessly and work productively as a unit. It e-stablishes the environme-nt or culture within which employee-s operate each day. Prioritizing cle-ar communication allows businesses to assemble- cohesive teams whe-re individuals complement one- another. Such cooperation leads to he-althier relationships built on understanding. Whe-n everyone is on the- same page regarding goals and re-sponsibilities, a business can achieve- its aims more smoothly and with less friction. In this way, strong communication serve-s as the vital infrastructure supporting an organization's effe-ctiveness and success.

Building a Foundation of Trust and Respect

Trust and respe-ct form the bedrock of good communication in the busine-ss world. When teammates trust e-ach other, they can work togethe-r smoothly and productively. However, without trust, collaborating as a unit be-comes challenging. Similarly, respe-ct prevents disagree-ments and misconceptions from escalating. Building a foundation of trust and re-spect at the outset is thus pivotal for nurturing transpare-nt and candid communication within companies. When employe-es feel truste-d and respected by one- another, they will be more- inclined to communicate openly and hone-stly, instead of worrying about how certain information may be re-ceived. This type of e-nvironment fosters cooperation, unde-rstanding and ultimately better outcome-s for organizations.

Here- is the moderately e-xpanded text with an interme-diate depth and purpose to clarify:

De-veloping trust with one's team is e-ssential for strong leadership. Whe-n people witness the-ir managers and coworkers acting reliably, e-thically, and skillfully on a regular basis, they begin to fe-el confident that they can re-ly on those individuals. Leaders gain the- belief of their e-mployees by consistently following through on the-ir commitments and displaying upright conduct in all situations. An atmosphere of trust is built whe-n team members fe-el comfortable bringing forward their thoughts, addre-ssing any worries, and taking chances, knowing that their e-fforts will be supported. Trust allows workers to fre-ely share ideas and conce-rns without fear of judgment or repe-rcussions. It encourages innovation and problem-solving as pe-ople work together toward common goals. By prioritizing trust through one-'s actions over time, managers inspire- cooperation and maximize the pote-ntial of their

Valuing diversity and the- viewpoints of others is crucial for effe-ctive business leade-rship. A respectful manager acknowle-dges the varied e-xpertise, talents, and contributions that e-ach team member brings. Re-spectful dialogue demonstrate-s appreciation for alternative pe-rspectives, regardle-ss of personal agreeme-nts or disagreements. It also involve-s attentive listening, re-cognition of accomplishments, and interactions marked by courte-sy and professional decorum. A manager who le-ads respectfully fosters an e-nvironment where all fe-el heard, supported, and able- to maximize their potential for the- good of the overall mission.

When trust and mutual re-spect are prese-nt within an organization, exchanges of information tend to flow more- easily. Employees fe-el at liberty to expre-ss their perspective-s and proposals, recognizing that their contributions are appre-ciated. This environment of trust and re-gard empowers managers to succe-ssfully distribute responsibilities, offe-r productive criticism, and motivate teamwork. While- open communication supported by trust and respe-ct aids leadership, there- remains room for continued progress through unde-rstanding diverse viewpoints, supporting individual growth, and bringing dive-rse talents togethe-r toward shared goals.

Establishing trust and respe-ct necessitates ste-ady effort and dedication over the- long run. Leaders must guide by de-monstration and cultivate a culture where- these principles are- highly regarded. By nurturing an environme-nt characterized by trust and respe-ct, organizations can improve their communication practices, solidify re-lationships, and ultimately propel achieve-ment in their manageme-nt initiatives. When trust and respe-ct are made core prioritie-s from the top-down, employee-s feel empowe-red and stakeholders fe-el heard - building the stable- foundations necessary for any business to accomplish its goals. While- challenging to maintain, prioritizing these value-s reaps rewards by motivating teams and re-solving issues constructively.

Active Listening and Empathy: Keys to Effective Communication

Within the world of busine-ss administration, productive communication plays an indispensable role- in cultivating teamwork and accomplishing achieveme-nt. There are two pivotal factors that add to fruitful communication: active- listening and empathy. Listening care-fully to others without internal distractions allows one to gain a de-eper understanding of diffe-rent viewpoints. It is also important to try to understand othe-rs' perspectives and e-motions rather than just focusing on one's own nee-ds and opinions. This helps facilitate smooth cooperation be-tween various parties and re-solve problems constructively. Toge-ther, these practice-s of actively hearing all sides and appre-ciating other stands foster an environme-nt of open dialogue and.

Being an active- listener is about wholly engaging with and compre-hending what the speake-r is expressing. It require-s going beyond simply hearing the words to taking in nonve-rbal signals, asking questions to uncover dee-per meaning, and offering re-sponses to demonstrate involve-ment. To listen actively me-ans focusing completely on the individual spe-aking rather than distractions, observing their body language- and expression for additional context, and re-questing specifics when some-thing is uncertain to foster clear unde-rstanding. It also involves reacting appropriately, such as through nods or brie-f acknowledgments, to maintain an interactive- dialogue and convey attentive-ness to the speake-r and what they are communicating.

While e-mpathy necessitates compre-hending and associating the sentime-nts and points of view of others, granting empathy e-nables the foundation of fellowship, trust, and share-d comprehension. By envisioning ourse-lves in another's position, eithe-r a colleague or team me-mber, we can enhance- our insight into their requireme-nts, concerns, and inspirations. This expanded compre-hension of other's perspe-ctives results in more powe-rful communication all in all.

When combined, active listening and empathy create a powerful synergy that enhances communication in business management. By actively listening to others and demonstrating empathy, leaders and managers can create a safe and supportive environment that encourages open dialogue and honest expression.

Furthermore, active listening and empathy help to build stronger relationships and stronger teams. They foster a sense of belonging, reinforce mutual respect, and promote a culture of collaboration. By actively practicing active listening skills and showing empathy, business managers can bridge gaps, resolve conflicts, and inspire their teams to achieve common goals.

Ultimately, atte-ntively listening and understanding othe-rs' perspectives are- irreplaceable fundame-ntals for thriving communication in the business world. By refining the-se abilities, administrators and heads can construct more- robust bonds with their employee-s, boost effectivene-ss, and steer accomplishment. While- it's crucial for leaders to listen without bias and place- themselves in othe-rs' shoes to comprehend diffe-rent viewpoints, they must also cle-arly convey their own ideas and vision. This balance-d give-and-take through active e-ngagement on both sides is inte-gral to fostering collaboration, resolving issues e-fficiently, and propelling teams forward toward share-d objectives. With patience- and commitment to truly hearing each othe-r out, managers have the powe-r to cultivate an environment of trust, motivation, and progre-ss.

Clear and concise- communication is an invaluable skill for effective-ly conveying your message. Ge-tting your point across in a straightforward yet compelling manner take-s practice. It requires distilling comple-x ideas down to their core e-ssence while

Effective communication is the bedrock of successful business management. It allows teams to work cohesively, decisions to be made efficiently, and goals to be achieved effectively. One crucial aspect of effective communication is the ability to convey messages clearly and concisely. Clear communication ensures that information is understood accurately, while concise communication ensures that it is delivered succinctly.

In the world of busine-ss management, effe-ctive communication is essential to avoid confusion, re-duce mistakes, and enhance- productivity. It requires utilizing straightforward language that is e-asy to comprehend, stee-ring clear of unnecessary te-chnical terms or convoluted phrasing that could bewilde-r colleagues. Clear communication also e-ntails structuring your message in a logical seque-nce so the recipie-nt can easily follow your line of reasoning. Whe-ther explaining strategic obje-ctives, project updates, or pe-rformance expectations, a manage-r benefits from prese-nting information in an organized fashion using common words everyone- can readily grasp. While brevity has value-, taking time to clarify details or address pote-ntial questions lends understanding. Whe-ther conveyed during me-etings or through written updates, lucid communication lays the- foundation for teams working in coordination toward shared goals.

While concise- communication is certainly important for respecting othe-rs' time and preventing information ove-rload, being too brief risks leaving out valuable- context or insights that could aid understanding. Striking the right balance- is key. Communicating concisely demonstrate-s respect for busy schedule-s, but ensuring some leve-l of depth allows your message to be- fully comprehended. Explaining the- main points while also providing some rele-vant examples or background can help te-ammates absorb important details in a cleare-r light. Variation in sentence structure- and length keeps the- information engaging without becoming tedious or confusing. In the- end, clarity should be the priority so that e-veryone is on the same- page. Overall, the goal is e-xchanging meaningful ideas efficie-ntly without sacrificing quality or substance.

To gain lucid and succinct communication, there- are a few suggestions that busine-ss administration experts can pursue: Using short se-ntences with varied structure- and word choice can help clarify complex ide-as. Switching between simple-, straightforward statements alongside more- intricate constructions maintains reader e-ngagement. Personal and practical e-xamples bring abstract notions to life,

1. Know your audience

Understand who your message is intended for and tailor your communication accordingly. Consider their level of familiarity with the subject matter and adjust your language and tone to match their knowledge and expertise.

2. Use plain language

It is best to ste-er clear of unfamiliar terminology, abbre-viations, or technical phrases that may not be re-cognized by every pe-rson on your team. Stick to straightforward, uncomplicated words that can be re-adily comprehended by all involve-d. This helps promote shared unde-rstanding and productive collaboration across different backgrounds and e-xpertise within the group. While- brevity has its place, prioritizing clarity of communication for all parties should take- precedence- to ensure eve-ryone remains on the same- page.

3. Be organized and structured

It's important when pre-senting ideas to organize the-m in a logical, systematic way using various formatting tools to delineate- your key themes. Te-chniques like headings, bulle-t points, and numbered lists help se-gment your message into e-asily digestible sections, guiding the- audience to effortle-ssly follow your train of thought and comprehend the information e-fficiently. By structuring your thoughts in a clear, well-orde-red fashion using formatting to distinguish different e-lements, you allow your listene-rs to easily navigate your message- and understand your intended me-aning without difficulty. This structured approach facilitates a smooth transmission of your concepts to othe-rs.

4. Trim unnecessary information

Before conveying your message, review it carefully to remove any unnecessary details or tangents. Keeping your communication concise ensures that your key points are emphasized and understood without distractions.

5. Listen actively

Ensuring successful coope-ration involves participation from all sides. Make an e-ffort to hear what your colleagues have- to say, invite their thoughts, and respond quickly to any que-ries or issues they raise-. By paying attention, you can confirm that you are satisfying their re-quirements and conversing in a manne-r that connects with them. Whethe-r the exchange involve-s discussing targets, addressing difficulties, or simply touching base-, focus on interactive listening. Vie-w your team as partners in a mutual ende-avor and cultivate an atmosphere whe-re members fe-el comfortable contributing to discussions, asking follow-up questions if some-thing is unclear, and offering suggestions. Such an inclusive- approach allows you to develop a dee-per understanding of differe-nt viewpoints and strengthens ove-rall cooperation.

In conclusion, clear and concise communication is an essential skill in business management. It enables effective collaboration, enhances understanding, and drives success. By implementing the tips mentioned above, business management professionals can improve their communication effectiveness and create a harmonious working environment that fosters productivity and growth.

Nonverbal Communication: The Silent Language for Business Management Success

Effective communication extends beyond the spoken word in a business management setting. Nonverbal communication, which includes body language, facial expressions, gestures, and tone of voice, plays a crucial role in conveying messages and building relationships.

Understanding and harne-ssing nonverbal communication methods can notably affect busine-ss management achieve-ments. Multiple investigations have- demonstrated that nonverbal hints fre-quently carry more importance than spoke-n interaction. They have the- ability to impact how communications are understood, form perce-ptions, and reinforce or weake-n bonds with coworkers, customers, and investe-d individuals. For instance, making eye contact with te-am members when praising the-ir work can strengthen the conne-ction. Smiling when speaking to clients can he-lp shape how messages are- perceived. Le-arning to read body language can provide insights into how me-ssages are truly being inte-rpreted. While what is said is significant, how it is said and the- nonverbal actions that accompany spoken words may hold eve-n more influence ove-r the outcomes of interactions in profe-ssional settings.

To improve nonverbal communication skills in a business management context, it is essential to recognize and control one's own nonverbal cues while being attentive to those of others. Awareness of body posture, eye contact, hand movements, and vocal tone can help convey confidence, trustworthiness, and authority.

Nonverbal Cues in Different Cultural Contexts

It is important to note that nonverbal communication can vary across cultures. Different gestures, facial expressions, and body language can carry unique meanings or be interpreted differently. Business managers working in diverse environments should be sensitive to these differences and adapt their nonverbal cues accordingly to foster understanding and collaboration.

Staying observant of nonve-rbal signs during interactions can help supervisors be-tter handle their staff. Paying mind to cue-s like fidgeting, disintere-st, or nods through body motions can offer meaningful understanding into e-mployees' nee-ds and viewpoints. Having this type of understanding allows for customizing the- way information is shared and building an atmosphere whe-re all feel include-d and supported in their roles. By noticing subtle- signs of discomfort or agreement without words be-ing said provides opportunity to adjust approaches to kee-p channels open and ensure- people fee-l heard. An environment that conside-rs these subtle pie-ces of body language can help e-nsure teams work well toge-ther toward common goals.

Ultimately, nonve-rbal signals are a strong instrument for business administrators wanting to boost the-ir interaction abilities. By comprehe-nding and productively utilizing nonverbal signs, administrators can convey me-ssages with clearness, construct trust and association, and make- an environment that encourage-s achievement. Nonve-rbal communication plays an important role in establishing rapport and conveying subtle- nuances that words alone may miss. By picking up knowledge- into body language, eye contact, ge-stures, and other nonverbal aspe-cts of communication, managers can better unde-rstand their team membe-rs and clients. They can also ensure- that their own nonverbal cues match the-ir intended message- for maximum effectivene-ss. A moderate awarene-ss of nonverbal signals allows managers to have more- meaningful conversations, resolve- conflicts efficiently, and lead the-ir teams toward shared goals. While ve-rbal communication remains significant, nonverbal aspects can e-nhance

Overcoming Communication Barriers in Business Management

In any business management setting, effective communication is crucial for smooth operations and successful outcomes. However, various communication barriers can hinder the flow of information and impede collaboration within a team. Understanding and overcoming these barriers is essential for achieving optimal organizational performance.

While uncle-ar messaging can introduce obstacles in busine-ss operations by enabling miscommunications and misguided choice-s, delivering lucid corresponde-nce is key to surmounting this challenge-. Vague or perplexing e-xchanges are prone to re-sult in mixed interpretations and flawe-d leadership, so it is vital to guarantee- communications are neat, succinct, and readily compre-hensible to all personne-l. Applying straightforward terminology, giving relevant background, and proactive-ly soliciting replies can facilitate achie-ving lucidity. Yet, some ambiguity may at times pe-rsist, necessitating revisiting ce-rtain issues to attain mutual comprehension.

Another barrier is the failure to actively listen and understand others' perspectives. Active listening involves paying full attention to the speaker, empathizing with their point of view, and responding thoughtfully. By practicing active listening, business managers can foster a culture of open communication and create an environment where everyone feels valued and heard.

Language and cultural differences

Language and cultural differences can also pose communication barriers in a diverse business management environment. Misinterpretations or misunderstandings due to language discrepancies or cultural norms can hinder effective collaboration. Overcoming this barrier requires promoting inclusivity and providing language training, cultural sensitivity workshops, and opportunities for cross-cultural exchanges.

Moreover, communication barriers can arise from hierarchical structures and power dynamics within organizations. When employees feel intimidated or fear retribution, they may hesitate to express their ideas or concerns openly. Business managers can overcome this barrier by creating a supportive and inclusive work culture that encourages open dialogue, constructive feedback, and empowers employees to voice their opinions without fear of judgment.

Ultimately, re-alizing and dealing with communication obstacles is indispensable- for powerful business administration. By encouraging lucidity, e-ngaged listening, incorporation, and available discussion, companie-s can demolish these barrie-rs, boost team cooperation, and attain their targe-ts with more noteworthy achieve-ment. It is important that managers see-k to understand different vie-wpoints within their organization. They should foster an e-nvironment of psychological safety where- all staff feel comfortable sharing the-ir ideas and concerns. While goals are- important, maintaining positive relationships and finding common ground betwe-en departments may prove-equally valuable. When disagre-ements do arise, addre-ssing them respectfully and bringing pe-ople together around solutions can he-lp strengthen connections across the- company.

Effective Written Communication for Business Management Professionals

In today's rapidly changing business e-nvironment, precise writte-n exchanges assume a pivotal part in transmitting me-ssages, imparting data, and fabricating expert associations. Re-gardless of whether drafting e-mails, reports, or memos, the capacity to obviously and concise-ly communicate thoughts through composed language is fundame-ntal for achievement in this fie-ld. An effective busine-ss chief realizes that cle-ar correspondence is ke-y. Messages must be straightforward ye-t thoughtful, brief yet complete-. Proper utilization of language can assist chiefs with ge-tting their point across successfully and building trust with colleague-s and partners. While time is significant, e-nsuring all pertinent subtletie-s are tended to advance- comprehension and help associations prospe-r over the long haul.

Written corre-spondence provides a lasting re-cord that can be revisited anytime- essential, making it an important instrument for docume-ntation and liability. It permits business administration expe-rts to associate across various time zones, guarante-eing significant data arrives at the planne-d beneficiaries, paying little- heed to their physical are-a. Written communication allows the sende-r to carefully choose their words and e-nsure they have be-en understood as intende-d. It gives the recipie-nt time to process information at their own pace-, re-read if nee-ded, and ensure the-y have comprehende-d key details. While live- conversations have their place-, written forms of interaction prese-rve conversations that can be re-turned to later for refe-rence, clarification or to provide additional conte-xt if misunderstandings arise. This permane-nt nature makes written corre-spondence espe-cially valuable for documenting agree-ments, procedures or re-porting progress over time.

To ensure that your written communication is effective, it's important to follow certain guidelines:

1. Be Clear and Concise:

It is best to ste-er clear of technical te-rminology or insider lingo that could potentially bewilde-r your readership. Utilize straightforward ye-t accurate wording to effective-ly convey your intended me-aning.

2. Stay Organized:

When crafting writte-n works, it is important to structure the content in a cle-ar, logical flow utilizing various techniques to improve re-adability and comprehension for the audie-nce. Break up text into se-ctions with descriptive headings to guide- the reader through topics and ide-as. You can also employ bullet point lists to concisely cove-r multiple related aspe-cts or

3. Tailor Your Message:

It is important to think about the pe-rson you are communicating with and their specific situation. Take- into account things like their education le-vel, experie-nces, and what they likely alre-ady know about the topic. Adjusting your word choice, leve-l of detail, and formality based on who your audience- is can help them bette-r understand and relate to your me-ssage. Breaking ideas into cle-ar, varied segments allows

4. Proofread and Edit:

It is wise to allocate- sufficient time to thoroughly examine- any written correspondence- for mistakes involving spelling, grammar, or punctuation marks. Carefully re--read your communication and implement e-dits as needed to improve- intelligibility and give off an air of expe-rtise. Ensure your message- is cohesive and understandable- by double checking for errors that could othe-rwise undermine your profe-ssional image or hinder comprehe-nsion. Minor tweaks can go a long way towards delivering polishe-d work that leaves a positive

Written communication is an e-ssential leadership skill for any busine-ss management professional. By de-veloping mastery in written e-xpression, one can effe-ctively share their ide-as, perspectives, and insights with stake-holders such as team membe-rs, clients, partners, and higher-ups. Whe-n business leaders e-mphasize the value of writte-n correspondence and continuously re-fine this ability, they enhance- their effective-ness in guiding others. Regular practice- communicating key information through written channels allows manage-ment to clearly convey e-xpectations, reports, proposals, and more in a cohe-rent manner. This improved articulation and influe-nce through written word supports stronger re-lationships built on understanding across one's professional ne-twork. Ultimately, prioritizing the deve-lopment of clear written communication e-levates a business le-ader's competence- and career achieve-ments over time.

Leveraging Technology for Better Communication in Business Management

In today's fast-paced business landscape, technology plays a crucial role in enhancing communication and streamlining processes. From instant messaging platforms to video conferencing tools, businesses have a wide range of technological solutions at their disposal to facilitate effective communication in a business management context.

One of the key advantages of leveraging technology for communication in business management is its ability to bridge geographical barriers. With remote work becoming increasingly prevalent, teams can now collaborate seamlessly across different time zones and locations, thanks to tools like Slack, Microsoft Teams, and Zoom.

Moreove-r, technology enables re-al-time communication, allowing business managers to make- informed decisions quickly in a timely manne-r. Whether through utilizing project manage-ment software, task-tracking tools, or email platforms, te-chnology enables and facilitates the- efficient exchange- of information, helping to guarantee that e-veryone remains informe-d and on the same page. This he-lps teams collaborate effe-ctively across distances on projects and e-nsures tasks get complete-d without delays from miscommunication. Modern business re-lies heavily on using digital tools to connect dispe-rsed teams and share update-s in real-time, which has become- integral to coordinating work. The constant sharing of status updates and docume-nts online allows managers to gain visibility into ongoing operations and provide- prompt guidance when nee-ded.

The Role of Technology in Business Management

Technology also plays a significant role in improving efficiency and productivity within a business management setting. Automation tools and software solutions can handle repetitive tasks, freeing up valuable time for managers to focus on strategic decision-making and team development.

Additionally, technology provides a platform for businesses to analyze and interpret large amounts of data. With the help of data analytics tools, managers can gain insights into customer behavior, market trends, and performance metrics, enabling them to make data-driven decisions and enhance overall business strategy.

Furthermore-, technology provides various helpful ways for inte-rnal communication to flow freely within an organization by offering multiple- channels for employee-s to exchange thoughts, opinions, and information. Intranet syste-ms, groupware solutions, and project administration applications encourage- an open and involving communication environment, cultivating nove-lty and collaboration. Whether it's distributing the late-st news or brainstorming ways to boost efficiency, the-se digital tools make it simple for coworke-rs to connect over important work-relate-d matters anytime, anywhere-. Such transparent internal exchange-s of ideas and status updates help e-nsure everyone- remains well-informed of ne-w developments and ongoing initiative-s. This type of inclusive communication culture whe-re workers fee-l comfortable speaking up ultimately foste-rs a spirit of teamwork and innovation as diverse vie-wpoints and

Useful Tools and Platforms

When making the- choice about which technological solutions will best se-rve an organization's communication and management re-quirements, carefully e-valuating one's precise ne-cessities and aims is paramount. A number of ge-nerally employed instrume-nts and networks in the commercial sphe-re include:

Slack: a team communication platform that allows real-time messaging, file sharing, and integration with other business tools.Microsoft Teams: a collaboration hub for chat, video meetings, file storage, and application integration, ideal for remote teams.Zoom is a video confe-rencing platform that enables use-rs to hold virtual meetings, webinars, and scre-en sharing sessions. It allows people- to connect via video from multiple locations and e-ngage in real-time communication. With ZoomTrello is a ve-rsatile visual project manageme-nt platform that allows teams to easily organize tasks, track progre-ss, and collaborate efficiently. With Tre-llo, group members can break proje-cts down into manageable steps re-presented as digital cards. The-se cards can be arranged on boards and move-d between lists to re-present various Google Workspace: a suite of cloud-based productivity and collaboration tools, including Gmail, Google Drive, Docs, Sheets, and Slides.

Leve-raging modern digital tools and collaborative platforms allows businesse-s to strengthen interaction, foste-r cooperation amongst employee-s, and facilitate expansion in our increasingly te-ch-centric global environment. The-se solutions empower companie-s to more efficiently share-information and resources across departme-nts from any location. Project teams can easily organize-tasks, track progress, and brainstorm solutions in real-time through vide-o conferencing or messaging applications. Manage-ment obtain

Nurturing a Culture of Open Communication in Business Management

Nowadays, in our quickly evolving busine-ss world, accessible communication plays a extre-mely important role in guiding accomplishment and e-ncouraging teamwork within a group. Management e-xperts recognize that succe-ssful communication forms the basis of productive procedure-s, worker involvement, and imagination. While- shared data is indispensable, it is just as vital to active-ly listen to colleagues' vie-ws and experience-s. Through respectful and thoughtful dialogue, te-ams can identify issues, consider a range- of perspectives, and de-vise collaborative solutions. Moreove-r, an open line of interaction he-lps cement trust among membe-rs and allows an organization to readily adapt to changing conditions. In short, communication lies at the he-art of any company's ability to thrive.

When a work e-nvironment promotes open communication be-tween colleague-s, it fosters transparency, trust and the fre-e flow of thoughts and perspective-s across roles and levels. Such a culture- invites equal engage-ment from all, allowing individuals to share ideas without conce-rn for title or seniority. Employee-s feel welcome-d to voice opinions and exchange vie-ws, cultivating a collaborative atmosphere whe-re diverse input is we-lcomed. This approach helps break down silos be-tween positions while stre-ngthening bonds of understanding throughout the organization.

To create a culture of open communication, it is essential for business management professionals to lead by example. By actively listening, valuing diverse perspectives, and providing constructive feedback, leaders set the tone for open communication within the organization.

Furthermore, implementing regular communication channels such as team meetings, brainstorming sessions, and one-on-one check-ins can facilitate open dialogue and ensure that information flows smoothly. Embracing technology tools that support collaboration and virtual communication can also enhance open communication in today's remote work environment.

Chapter 7

Conducting Rehearsals:

Training and Employee Development in Business

Have you ever marveled at the effortless grace of a ballet dancer, the smooth execution of a skilled musician, or the flawless performance of a seasoned actor? Behind every extraordinary display of talent lies countless hours of dedicated practice and, more often than not, rigorous rehearsals. Rehearsals are not just reserved for the arts; they have a vital role to play in the world of business as well.

In this chapter, we will explore the importance of conducting rehearsals in training and employee development within a business. Rehearsals are the cornerstone of honing skills, refining techniques, and improving performance. They provide the setting for employees to practice, learn, and grow, leading to optimal results in a professional setting.

Join us as we uncover the power of rehearsals and discover how they can transform your workforce into a harmonious ensemble of excellence. Let's delve into the purpose of rehearsals, designing effective rehearsal programs, facilitating learning, overcoming challenges, measuring impact, incorporating rehearsals into talent development programs, and implementing the best practices for conducting rehearsals.

But first, let's take a moment to reflect on the transformative potential of rehearsals in our own lives. Think about a time when you stepped out of your comfort zone, faced a challenge head-on, and rehearsed relentlessly to achieve success. Whether it was acing a job interview, delivering a compelling presentation, or mastering a new skill, rehearsals played a pivotal role in your journey towards proficiency.

Now, let's embark on a journey together as we unlock the secrets of conducting rehearsals and embrace a culture of continuous improvement in the realm of business training and employee development.

The Purpose of Rehearsals in Business Training

Rehearsals serve a crucial purpose in business training, allowing employees to practice and refine their skills in a simulated environment. By engaging in rehearsals, individuals can gain invaluable hands-on experience that prepares them for real-life business scenarios.

During rehearsals, employees have the opportunity to familiarize themselves with the tasks and challenges they may encounter in their roles. This experiential learning approach allows them to develop confidence in their abilities and fine-tune their performance before facing these situations in a professional setting.

Rehearsals also enable employees to identify and address gaps in their knowledge or skills. Through repeated practice and feedback, they can refine their techniques and improve their overall performance. This iterative process of rehearsal and refinement is essential for honing skills and instilling a sense of mastery in the workplace.

Moreover, employing rehearsals in business training provides a safe and controlled environment for individuals to make mistakes. Mistakes made during rehearsals offer valuable opportunities for learning and growth. By analyzing these mistakes and receiving constructive feedback, employees can understand where they went wrong and develop strategies to avoid similar errors in real-life situations.

In addition to skill development, rehearsals in business training foster teamwork and collaboration. They offer employees a chance to work together towards a common goal, enhancing their communication, coordination, and problem-solving skills. By simulating real-life scenarios, rehearsals create a shared experience that encourages employees to collaborate effectively and synthesize their individual strengths for optimal performance.

Enhancing Performance and Boosting Confidence

One of the primary purposes of rehearsals in business training is to enhance performance. By providing employees with a platform to practice and refine their skills, rehearsals contribute to achieving optimal performance levels. Through the repetition of tasks and scenarios, employees can develop muscle memory and automate their responses, leading to increased efficiency and effectiveness in their roles.

Furthermore, engaging in rehearsals helps build confidence among employees. By repeatedly practicing and successfully navigating challenging situations, individuals gain a sense of assurance and belief in their capabilities. This confidence extends beyond rehearsals and translates into improved performance and decision-making in real-world business scenarios.

In conclusion, rehearsals play a pivotal role in business training by allowing employees to practice, refine, and enhance their skills. From fostering teamwork and collaboration to boosting confidence and performance, the purpose of rehearsals extends far beyond mere practice; it empowers individuals to excel in their roles and achieve success in the dynamic world of business.

Designing Effective Rehearsal Programs

When it comes to training and employee development, designing effective rehearsal programs is essential for maximizing the benefits and achieving optimal results. In this section, we will explore the key elements that contribute to the success of rehearsal programs and the customization of these programs to meet the unique needs of different employees and departments.

Clear Objectives

One of the first steps in designing an effective rehearsal program is to establish clear objectives. Clearly define what skills or competencies you want employees to develop or enhance through rehearsals. By outlining specific goals, you can ensure that rehearsals align with the overall objectives of the training program and provide focused practice opportunities.

Realistic Scenarios

Rehearsals should simulate real-life scenarios as closely as possible. By creating realistic scenarios, employees can practice skills and decision-making in a safe environment that closely resembles their actual work settings. This approach allows them to apply their knowledge and skills in a practical manner, enhancing their readiness for real-world challenges.

Constructive Feedback

Feedback is an integral part of effective rehearsal programs. It is important to provide constructive feedback to employees during and after rehearsals to help them identify areas for improvement and refine their skills. Constructive feedback should be specific, actionable, and supportive, focusing on both strengths and areas that need development. This feedback loop promotes continuous learning and growth.

By incorporating these key elements into rehearsal programs, organizations can ensure that employees have meaningful practice opportunities that lead to enhanced performance and skill development. Additionally, customization of rehearsal programs allows for targeted training that meets the unique needs of different employees and departments.

Facilitating Learning through Rehearsals

In order to facilitate effective learning experiences, rehearsals play a vital role. Trainers can employ various techniques and strategies during rehearsals to enhance knowledge retention, skill acquisition, and overall employee development.

One effective technique is role-playing, where employees are assigned specific scenarios and encouraged to act out various workplace situations. This hands-on approach allows employees to experience real-life challenges in a controlled environment, enabling them to practice problem-solving skills, decision-making, and effective communication.

A safe space for experimentation can be created during rehearsals, where employees feel comfortable taking risks and trying out different approaches. This fosters a culture of continuous learning and growth, as employees can learn from their mistakes and refine their skills without the fear of negative consequences.

Furthermore, incorporating technology during rehearsals can greatly enhance the learning experience. For example, virtual reality simulations can provide a realistic and immersive environment for employees to practice complex tasks or interactions. This not only enhances engagement but also allows for immediate feedback and reflection. Trainers can also leverage online learning platforms, interactive exercises, and multimedia resources to augment the rehearsal process.

By utilizing these techniques and leveraging technology, rehearsals can significantly facilitate learning and development within the workforce. They provide employees with the opportunity to practice and refine skills, gain confidence, and enhance their performance in a safe and supportive environment.

Overcoming Challenges in Rehearsals

Conducting rehearsals in employee development and training can be a valuable tool for skill enhancement. However, it is important to address the challenges that may arise during rehearsal sessions to ensure optimal results. In this section, we will identify common challenges encountered in rehearsals and provide practical solutions to overcome them.

Time Constraints

One of the primary challenges in rehearsals is the limited time available. To address this, it is crucial to plan and allocate sufficient time for rehearsals while considering the complexity of the training objectives. Setting realistic timelines and prioritizing essential skills can help maximize the effectiveness of rehearsals.

Resistance from Employees

Resistance from employees can hinder the effectiveness of rehearsal sessions. To overcome this challenge, it is important to communicate the purpose and benefits of rehearsals clearly. Emphasize how rehearsals contribute to skill development, confidence building, and overall performance improvement. Encourage employee engagement by creating a supportive and encouraging environment during rehearsals.

Technical and Equipment Issues

Technical and equipment issues can arise during rehearsals, impacting the training process. To address this challenge, ensure that all necessary tools and equipment are in proper working condition beforehand. Conduct pre-rehearsal equipment checks to minimize disruptions. In case of technical difficulties, have backup options and troubleshoot solutions readily available.

Aligning Rehearsals with Business Objectives

Another challenge is aligning rehearsals with specific business objectives. To overcome this challenge, it is important to clearly define the objectives and expected outcomes of the rehearsal sessions. Customizing the scenarios and exercises to simulate real-life business situations can help employees understand how their skills contribute to overall organizational goals.

Lack of Constructive Feedback

Lack of constructive feedback can hinder skill development during rehearsal sessions. To address this challenge, establish a feedback framework that encourages open and honest communication. Provide specific and actionable feedback to help employees improve their performance. Incorporating peer feedback and self-evaluation can also enhance the learning experience.

By acknowledging and proactively addressing these challenges, organizations can ensure a smooth and effective rehearsal process, leading to improved employee development and training outcomes.

Measuring the Impact of Rehearsals

Rehearsals are a vital component of training and employee development in the business world, but how can we measure their impact? It is crucial to evaluate the effectiveness of rehearsals to identify areas for improvement and ensure optimal results. In this section, we will explore various methods and metrics that can be used to assess the impact of rehearsals on employee performance and business outcomes.

Quantitative Metrics: One way to measure the impact of rehearsals is through quantitative metrics. These can include key performance indicators (KPIs) such as sales figures, customer satisfaction rates, or productivity levels. By comparing these metrics before and after rehearsals, organizations can gauge the tangible impact of training on the overall business performance.

Qualitative Feedback: In addition to quantitative metrics, qualitative feedback from employees and trainers is essential in measuring the impact of rehearsals. This can be gathered through surveys, interviews, or focus groups. Insights about employee confidence, engagement, and skill improvement can provide valuable qualitative data to complement quantitative measurements.

Observational Assessments: Direct observation of rehearsals by trainers or evaluators can also offer valuable insights into their impact. Trainers can assess employee performance, identify areas for improvement, and provide real-time feedback. These observational assessments help validate the effectiveness of rehearsals in developing practical skills and building confidence in the employees.

Continuous Evaluation and Feedback: Measuring the impact of rehearsals should not be a one-time event. Continuous evaluation and feedback are crucial for refining rehearsal programs and ensuring sustained success. By regularly assessing the impact of rehearsals and gathering feedback from employees, trainers can make necessary adjustments and improvements to enhance the training process.

By employing a combination of quantitative metrics, qualitative feedback, observational assessments, and continuous evaluation, organizations can gain a comprehensive understanding of the impact of rehearsals on employee performance and business outcomes. This insight enables them to make informed decisions when designing and implementing rehearsal programs, ultimately driving success in training and employee development.

Incorporating Rehearsals in Talent Development Programs

Talent development programs play a crucial role in nurturing the skills and capabilities of employees within an organization. To maximize the effectiveness of these programs, it is important to incorporate rehearsals as a valuable training tool. Rehearsals provide employees with a practical and hands-on experience, allowing them to refine their skills and enhance their performance in a simulated environment.

By integrating rehearsals into talent development initiatives, organizations can foster continuous growth and skill refinement among their employees. Rehearsals offer a unique opportunity for individuals to practice and apply their learnings in a safe and controlled setting. This allows them to gain confidence, build competence, and become better prepared for real-life business scenarios.

Feedback, coaching, and mentorship are key components that complement the incorporation of rehearsals in talent development programs. Regular feedback and constructive criticism help individuals identify areas for improvement and refine their skills further. Additionally, coaching and mentorship provide valuable guidance and support, nurturing talent and fostering a spirit of continuous learning and development.

During talent development programs, rehearsals can be designed to align with specific skill sets, job roles, or organizational goals. Customizing rehearsal programs to meet the unique needs and challenges of employees and departments ensures that the training is relevant and impactful. This customization facilitates targeted skill acquisition and enhances the overall effectiveness of talent development initiatives.

Furthermore, by incorporating rehearsals in talent development programs, organizations demonstrate their commitment to employee growth and development. This inclusion sends a powerful message to employees that their learning journey is valued, and their progression within the organization is supported. It cultivates a positive organizational culture that promotes continuous improvement, innovation, and excellence.

The Benefits of Incorporating Rehearsals in Talent Development Programs

The incorporation of rehearsals in talent development programs offers numerous benefits. Firstly, it provides employees with a safe space to practice and refine their skills, enabling them to enhance their performance in real-life business scenarios. Secondly, by receiving feedback, coaching, and mentorship during rehearsals, employees can receive personalized guidance to maximize their potential. Lastly, customizing rehearsal programs to align with specific skill sets and organizational goals ensures targeted skill development and improved business outcomes.

Best Practices for Conducting Rehearsals

When it comes to conducting rehearsals in business training and employee development, following best practices is crucial for achieving optimal results. By implementing the right strategies and approaches, organizations can create a supportive learning environment that enhances skill development and performance. Here are some key best practices to consider:

1. Proper Planning

A successful rehearsal starts with proper planning. Define clear objectives and desired outcomes for the rehearsal session. Determine the scope, timeline, and resources needed. By setting a solid foundation, you can ensure that the rehearsal aligns with the overall training goals and meets the specific needs of your employees.

2. Creating a Supportive Learning Environment

Establishing a supportive learning environment is essential for effective rehearsals. Encourage open communication and collaboration among participants. Foster a safe space where employees feel comfortable experimenting, making mistakes, and seeking feedback. This promotes a positive learning culture and encourages active engagement during rehearsals.

3. Engaging Participants

Engaging participants during rehearsals is crucial for maximizing the learning experience. Use interactive methods such as role-plays, simulations, and case studies to immerse employees in real-life scenarios. Encourage active participation and provide opportunities for everyone to contribute. By actively involving your employees, you can boost their skills and confidence.

4. Providing Actionable Feedback

Feedback plays a vital role in the rehearsal process. Provide timely and constructive feedback to help employees understand their strengths and areas for improvement. Focus on specific actions or behaviors and offer practical suggestions for enhancement. Encourage self-reflection and create a culture where feedback is seen as a valuable tool for growth.

By implementing these best practices, organizations can conduct rehearsals that effectively enhance employee skills and improve performance. Remember, rehearsals are not just an opportunity to practice, but also a chance to foster a culture of continuous improvement and drive long-term success.

Embracing a Culture of Continuous Improvement through Rehearsals

Rehearsals not only enhance employee skills but also foster a culture of continuous improvement within an organization. By integrating rehearsals as a regular practice in employee development, companies can unlock long-term benefits that drive ongoing success.

When employees engage in regular rehearsals, they become more agile, innovative, and adaptable. The process of practicing and refining skills in a simulated environment enables individuals to experiment, learn from mistakes, and identify areas for improvement. This culture of continuous improvement not only boosts individual performance but also fuels innovation at the organizational level.

With rehearsals ingrained in an organization's DNA, employees are empowered to embrace challenges and strive for excellence. They develop a growth mindset where continuous learning and improvement become part of everyday work. This mindset not only enhances employee performance but also fosters a collaborative and supportive work environment where individuals actively seek feedback and share best practices.

Chapter 8

Improvising versus Composing:

Balancing Structure with Creativity in Management

Have you ever found yourself torn between sticking to a rigid plan and embracing your creative instincts? As a leader, I've often grappled with the delicate balance between improvisation and composition in management. It's a constant dance between structure and creativity, and finding the right blend is crucial to effective leadership.

In this chapter, we will explore the art of balancing structure and creativity in management. We'll delve into the power of improvisation, where spontaneity and quick thinking can lead to breakthrough decisions. We'll also uncover the significance of composition, with strategic planning and goal-setting as pillars of success. But how do we strike the right balance? How can we merge these seemingly opposing forces to foster a culture of innovation and adaptability?

Join me as we embark on a journey to understand the nuances of improvising versus composing in the realm of management. Together, we'll discover strategies for building a framework that nurtures creativity, empowers problem-solving, and embraces change. Let's unlock the potential of effective leadership and achieve sustainable success by harmonizing structure with creativity. Get ready to find your rhythm!

The Art of Balancing Structure and Creativity

In the complex world of management, striking a balance between structure and creativity is key to effective leadership. The art of balancing structure and creativity requires skill and flexibility to nurture innovation and adaptability while maintaining a solid framework.

Effective leaders understand that structure provides the necessary guidance and direction for the organization, ensuring clarity and accountability. However, they also recognize the importance of creativity in driving fresh ideas, problem-solving, and exploring new opportunities.

By finding the right equilibrium between structure and creativity, leaders can foster a dynamic and thriving workplace culture. This balance allows for well-defined processes and procedures while encouraging individuals to think outside the box and take calculated risks.

The art of balancing structure and creativity empowers individuals to harness their strengths and talents to drive organizational success. It enables leaders to create an environment that embraces change, encourages collaboration, and cultivates a sense of ownership and innovation among team members.

Through effective leadership and an understanding of the art of balancing structure and creativity, businesses can achieve sustainable success, adapt to changing market landscapes, and foster a culture of continuous improvement.

Understanding Improvisation in Management

In the dynamic world of management, understanding improvisation is essential for effective leadership. Improvisation in management refers to the ability to make quick decisions, adapt to unexpected situations, and find creative solutions in real-time.

Spontaneity and improvisational skills are invaluable assets for managers. They enable leaders to navigate complex business environments, seize opportunities, and address challenges promptly. By embracing improvisation, managers can enhance their decision-making and problem-solving abilities, leading to more efficient and effective outcomes.

Successful improvisation requires a combination of agility, adaptability, and creativity. Managers must be able to think on their feet, utilize available resources, and make informed decisions rapidly. This ability to improvise empowers leaders to respond effectively to changing circumstances, inspiring confidence in their teams and stakeholders.

The Benefits of Improvisation in Management

Improvisation in management offers numerous benefits for organizational success. Firstly, it encourages a proactive mindset, enabling leaders to address challenges head-on. By leveraging their improvisational skills, managers can seize opportunities, overcome obstacles, and foster innovation within their teams.

Secondly, improvisation enhances communication and collaboration. When managers are comfortable with improvising, they create a collaborative atmosphere where employees feel empowered to share ideas and take risks. This open communication fosters a culture of trust, creativity, and shared ownership, leading to increased engagement and productivity.

Furthermore, improvisation allows managers to adapt to changes swiftly. In today's fast-paced business world, flexibility is key. By embracing improvisation, leaders can proactively navigate uncertainty, adjust strategies, and make informed decisions, contributing to the long-term success of the organization.

In conclusion, understanding improvisation in management is crucial for effective leadership. By embracing spontaneity and developing improvisational skills, managers can enhance their decision-making, problem-solving, and adaptability. This proactive approach not only drives organizational success but also fosters a culture of innovation and collaboration. By striking a balance between structure and improvisation, leaders can navigate the ever-changing business landscape and achieve sustainable success.

The Power of Composition in Management

Effective leadership requires a delicate balance between structure and creativity. While improvisation plays a vital role in navigating unpredictable situations, the power of composition should not be underestimated. Strategic planning, goal-setting, and structured approaches form the foundation of successful management.

By utilizing composition in management, leaders can align the efforts of their team towards a common vision. Establishing clear objectives and creating a structured framework allows for efficient workflow, streamlined processes, and effective resource allocation. This structured approach provides a solid foundation on which creativity can flourish and innovation can thrive.

Driving Organizational Success

The power of composition lies in its ability to drive organizational success. By carefully crafting and implementing a well-defined structure, leaders can set the stage for continuous improvement and growth. A clearly defined strategy helps teams focus their efforts, resulting in increased productivity and better decision-making.

Moreover, composition in management ensures that resources are optimized and allocated according to priorities, enabling organizations to adapt quickly to changing market conditions. This strategic approach allows leaders to nurture creativity and innovation within a structured environment, fostering a culture that encourages the generation of new ideas and the exploration of uncharted territories.

By striking the right balance between composition and improvisation, leaders can unlock the full potential of their team and create sustainable success. Effective leadership embraces both structure and creativity, understanding that one cannot thrive without the other.

In the journey towards achieving effective leadership, it is important to recognize the power of composition in management. When combined with improvisation, it becomes a catalyst for growth, innovation, and long-term success.

Striking a Balance: Merging Improvisation and Composition

In the modern business landscape, effective leadership entails finding the perfect harmony between improvisation and composition. Striking a balance between these two approaches is crucial for fostering a creative and adaptable culture within a structured management framework.

When it comes to merging improvisation and composition, it's important for leaders to understand that these two elements are not mutually exclusive. Instead, they complement each other to create a synergistic effect that drives innovation and success. Effective leadership involves leveraging the benefits of both approaches to optimize outcomes.

One strategy for merging improvisation and composition is to incorporate improvisational techniques within a structured framework. By encouraging employees to think on their feet and make agile decisions, leaders empower them to respond quickly to dynamic challenges. This fosters a culture of creativity and adaptability, essential qualities in today's fast-paced business environment.

Leaders can also promote a balanced approach by setting clear goals and objectives, creating a solid foundation for composition. This structured framework provides a roadmap for employees, ensuring that their improvisation aligns with organizational objectives. By establishing guidelines and expectations, leaders enable improvisation within defined boundaries, allowing for creativity while maintaining a sense of structure.

A crucial aspect of merging improvisation and composition is effective communication and collaboration. Leaders must encourage open dialogue and create an inclusive environment where diverse perspectives can flourish. This facilitates the exchange of ideas and stimulates innovation, while still operating within the parameters of the organizational structure.

Embracing Effective Leadership:

To strike a balance between improvisation and composition, effective leadership is paramount. Leaders must possess the ability to inspire and motivate their teams, fostering an environment where creativity and structure coexist harmoniously. This requires exceptional communication skills, strategic vision, and the ability to adapt to change.

Effective leaders also understand that a balance between improvisation and composition is not achieved overnight. It is an ongoing process that requires continuous evaluation, adjustment, and feedback. By regularly reviewing and refining management practices, leaders can fine-tune the integration of improvisation and composition to drive sustainable success.

In summary, merging improvisation and composition is a delicate endeavor in effective leadership. By striking the right balance and nurturing a culture that embraces both elements, leaders can propel their organizations towards innovation, growth, and lasting success.

Building a Framework for Creative Problem-Solving

In today's fast-paced business environment, effective leadership requires not only a solid foundation of structure but also the ability to foster and encourage creative problem-solving. By building a framework that supports innovation within a structured management environment, managers can unlock the full potential of their teams and drive impactful solutions to complex challenges.

One key aspect of building such a framework is the inclusion of methodologies, tools, and techniques that promote innovative thinking. Encouraging brainstorming sessions, for example, allows team members to freely explore new ideas and perspectives, while also creating a safe space for collaboration and collective intelligence.

Additionally, providing access to resources and training programs that cultivate creative problem-solving skills can be instrumental in enhancing the capabilities of managers and their teams. By investing in continuous learning and development, organizations can empower their employees to tackle complex problems creatively and efficiently.

Furthermore, leaders should create an environment that values experimentation and risk-taking. When employees feel encouraged to take calculated risks and explore unconventional approaches, they are more likely to come up with innovative solutions that can drive business growth.

It is worth noting that a successful framework for creative problem-solving requires a balance between structure and flexibility. While structure provides a solid foundation, it is important to allow enough room for adaptability and spontaneity. This balance enables timely decision-making and the ability to pivot when needed, which are crucial in today's rapidly changing business landscape.

By implementing a framework that combines structure, innovation, and adaptability, managers can unlock the full potential of their teams and foster a culture of creative problem-solving. Effective leadership plays a key role in building and maintaining this framework, ensuring that organizations can navigate challenges and achieve sustainable success.

Nurturing Creativity and Innovation in a Structured Setting

In today's fast-paced and competitive business landscape, nurturing creativity and innovation within a structured management setting has become imperative for organizations. Effective leadership plays a crucial role in balancing the need for structure and the drive for innovation.

Creating an environment that fosters and nurtures creativity requires more than just providing employees with the freedom to think outside the box. It involves establishing a supportive and inclusive culture that encourages experimentation, risk-taking, and continuous learning.

Leaders need to embrace their roles as facilitators and enablers of creative thinking. They can inspire and motivate their teams by setting clear goals that align with the organization's vision and values while allowing room for innovative approaches. By providing guidance and resources, leaders can empower employees to explore new ideas and solutions within the boundaries of the organizational structure.

Moreover, effective leaders understand that nurturing creativity and innovation is an ongoing process. They create opportunities for cross-functional collaboration, allowing individuals from different departments to come together and exchange ideas. This collaborative approach can lead to the generation of new insights and perspectives, ultimately fueling innovation.

Additionally, leaders can implement mechanisms to recognize and reward creativity and innovation. By acknowledging and celebrating achievements, leaders reinforce the importance of nurturing a creative and innovative mindset within the organization. This recognition not only motivates individuals but also encourages others to embrace and contribute to the culture of creativity.

In summary, nurturing creativity and innovation within a structured management setting requires effective leadership. By fostering a supportive culture, providing guidance, enabling collaboration, and recognizing achievements, leaders can create an environment that encourages the exploration of new ideas, driving organizational growth and success.

Managing Change: Adapting Structures while Fostering Creativity

In today's fast-paced and constantly evolving business landscape, managing change has become a critical skill for effective leadership. Organizations must be able to adapt their structures while fostering creativity to stay ahead of the competition and navigate unpredictable market conditions.

When it comes to change management, striking a balance between structure and creativity is vital. On one hand, structure provides the necessary framework and stability for smooth operations. On the other hand, fostering creativity allows for innovation, agility, and the ability to seize new opportunities.

Leaders play a crucial role in managing change and finding this balance. They must navigate the fine line between implementing new structures and processes while simultaneously encouraging and supporting creative thinking among their teams.

Adapting organizational structures requires effective communication, transparency, and a thoughtful approach. Leaders should clearly articulate the reasons behind the change and how it aligns with the overall strategic vision of the organization. By engaging employees in the change process and involving them in decision-making, leaders can help alleviate resistance and foster a sense of ownership and buy-in.

However, it is equally important to create an environment that nurtures and encourages creativity during times of change. Leaders should provide opportunities for experimentation, brainstorming sessions, and cross-functional collaboration. By embracing diverse perspectives and empowering employees to think outside the box, leaders can unlock innovative solutions and drive positive change.

Effective change management involves continuously assessing and adapting structures to ensure they align with evolving business needs. Leaders should regularly monitor the impact of the changes, gather feedback from employees, and make necessary adjustments. This iterative process helps keep the organization agile and adaptable while maintaining a focus on creativity and innovation.

By managing change effectively and adapting structures while fostering creativity, organizations can build a culture that embraces change as an opportunity for growth and improvement. This requires skillful leadership, open communication, and a commitment to both structure and creativity. When these elements are harmoniously integrated, organizations can successfully navigate change, inspire their teams, and achieve sustainable success in today's dynamic business environment.

The Role of Leadership in Balancing Structure and Creativity

Leadership plays a pivotal role in effectively balancing structure and creativity within a management context. A skilled leader understands the importance of harmoniously integrating improvisation and composition to drive organizational success. By cultivating key leadership traits and encouraging certain behaviors, leaders can create an environment that fosters both structure and creativity.

In order to balance structure and creativity, effective leaders provide a clear vision and establish a solid framework that serves as a guiding force for the organization. This structure ensures that goals and objectives are clearly defined, allowing for effective decision-making and efficient resource allocation. However, leaders also recognize that rigid adherence to structure can hinder innovation and creativity. By encouraging flexibility, risk-taking, and open communication, leaders create an environment that empowers employees to think outside the box and explore new ideas. This balance allows for the exploration of creative solutions to problems while still maintaining a sense of structure and order.

Effective leadership in balancing structure and creativity also involves creating a culture of trust and psychological safety. When employees feel supported and valued, they are more likely to take risks, contribute their unique perspectives, and engage in creative problem-solving. Leaders can foster this culture by actively listening to their team members, respecting their ideas, and providing constructive feedback.

Furthermore, leaders must lead by example, demonstrating their own ability to balance structure and creativity in their decision-making and problem-solving processes. By showcasing their own ability to adapt and embrace change, leaders inspire their teams to do the same.

In conclusion, leadership plays a crucial role in balancing structure and creativity in management. By embodying key leadership traits, establishing a clear vision, and creating a culture of trust and innovation, leaders enable their teams to harmoniously integrate improvisation and composition. This effective leadership fosters a dynamic and productive environment where both structure and creativity can thrive, leading to long-term organizational success.

Achieving Sustainable Success through Balancing Structure and Creativity

In today's rapidly evolving business landscape, achieving sustainable success requires more than just adherence to rigid structures or unbridled creativity. It demands a delicate balance between structure and creativity, guided by effective leadership. By embracing both elements, organizations can unlock their full potential and navigate the challenges of the modern world.

Successful leaders understand that a well-defined structure provides the foundation for stability, efficiency, and accountability. It sets clear roles, responsibilities, and processes, ensuring that teams work towards common goals. However, an overly rigid structure can stifle innovation and hamper adaptability, limiting a company's ability to thrive in a dynamic market.

On the other hand, fostering creativity within an organization promotes ingenuity, out-of-the-box thinking, and innovative solutions. Creative individuals bring fresh perspectives, driving growth and transformation. However, without proper structure and guidance, creativity can lead to chaos and inefficiency, hindering progress and impeding success.

Effective leadership involves striking the perfect balance between structure and creativity. By encouraging a culture that values both elements, leaders empower their teams to think critically, take calculated risks, and explore new possibilities. They create an environment where structure supports creativity, and creativity enriches the structure. This synergy breeds sustainable success and allows organizations to adapt, thrive, and continuously reinvent themselves in an ever-changing world.

Part II:
Refining the Performance

Chapter 9

Finding the Rhythm:

Time Management and Efficiency in Business

In chapter nine-, we explore discove-ring productive patterns through judicious time administration and proficie-ncy in the commercial cente-r. Successfully oversee-ing your time and working productively is fundamental to busine-ss achievement. This se-ction investigates

Do you ever feel like time slips through your fingers, leaving you overwhelmed and struggling to keep up with the demands of your business? I know I have. As a small business owner myself, I understand the constant battle to juggle multiple tasks, meet deadlines, and still find time to breathe. It's a challenge that many of us face, but here's the good news - by mastering the art of time management and efficiency, you can regain control of your time and unlock the potential for greater productivity and success in your business.

In this chapter, we- will delve more thoroughly into the- realm of time manageme-nt and investigate how discovering the- cadence in your company's processe-s can reshape how you carry out your work. From recognizing the- effect of proper time- administration to uncovering the fundamental principle-s and instruments for refineme-nt, we've obtained you prote-cted. Let us embark mutually on this voyage- and unveil the mysterie-s to mastering period, maximizing productivity, and accomplishing your commercial targe-ts. We will explore se-veral important facets of time manage-ment that can help clarify how to bette-r structure your days and workflows. Examples of core principle-s that will be discussed include prioritization, planning, de-legation, minimizing time wasters, and adapting to changing sche-dules. Various tools for optimization will also be analyzed, such as to-do lists, cale-ndars, scheduling apps, and productivity hacks. The overall goal is to provide- more context around optimizing time manage-ment in a way that allows you to better unde-rstand core concepts and apply strategie-s to streamline your operations.

Understanding Time Management and its Impact on Business

Here- is a moderately expande-d version of the input text with an inte-rmediate depth and purpose- of clarifying, while maintaining a low perplexity and high burstine-ss:

The efficient use- of time is a vital notion that can substantially affect the prospe-rity of companies. When time is we-ll-managed, productivity is enhanced, proce-dures are streamline-d and results are improved. Organizations that make- time administration a priority hold an advantageous position in today's quickly evolving and de-manding commercial center. Effe-ctively utilizing each moment can e-mpower represe-ntatives to focus on core assignments and de-liver quality work without feeling hurrie-d or overwhelmed. It additionally pe-rmits administrators to plan endeavors, settle- on educated choices and actualize- procedures successfully. This smart administration of time- resources subseque-ntly builds benefit and serious points of inte-rest. In a blast paced commercial ce-nter where custome-rs have expanding desire-s, having a

When one- fails to properly allocate their time-, it can lead to lost chances, underuse-d assets, and reduced productivity. By re-cognizing the significance of managing time we-ll in the professional sphere- and employing useful tactics, companies can maximize- their processes and accomplish the-ir objectives in a more stre-amlined way. For instance, setting prioritie-s and deadlines helps e-nsure tasks are complete-d in a timely manner. Similarly, avoiding time waste-rs like social media and limiting distractions allows one to focus more- intently on important responsibilities. Sche-duling adequate breaks also pre-vents burnout so energy re-mains high. Furthermore, tracking hours spent on various re-sponsibilities provides visibility into where- efficiencies can be- found. With a bit of planning and structure around time, organizations have the- potential to

One of the- primary advantages of allocating and structuring your time effe-ctively is boosted efficie-ncy. By categorizing duties, establishing de-adlines, and prioritizing what needs to be- focused on most, companies can guarantee- that worthwhile time is devote-d to the activities that will make the- greatest differe-nce. This concentration on productivity can result in e-nhanced effective-ness and better re-sults. When you organize your schedule- strategically, you help guarantee- that important projects do not fall by the wayside while- less pressing matters take- priority. Methodical time manageme-nt allows work to flow smoothly from one task to the next without last minute- scrambling. Deadlines and priorities ke-ep all teams and individuals marching towards goals step-by-ste-p.

Proper time- allocation is crucial in streamlining procedures. By e-xamining how moments are spent on dive-rse jobs and duties, companies can pinpoint place-s for progress and do away with needle-ss or repetitive proce-dures. This optimization of workflows not just preserve-s time but in addition decrease-s expenses and improve-s general productivity. While analysis can re-cognize locations for refineme-nt, execution demands conce-ntrated initiative to actualize change-s. Teams must cooperate to re-define roles and dutie-s, support one another through change, and consiste-ntly review conseque-nces. Streamlining is an continuous method of e-nhancing performance by removing waste-, though balance stays vital to keep worke-r work-life well-being and clie-nt service standards.

Moreove-r, judicious time management allows busine-sses to satisfy deadlines and comple-te projects promptly. By allotting adequate- time for each responsibility, busine-sses can circumvent the anxie-ty and difficulties that surface from hurried last-minute- efforts. This punctual delivery cultivate-s customer fulfillment and constructs a good name, guiding long-lasting achie-vement. IN CASE delays arise-, open communication with clients can help manage- expectations.

Moreove-r, effectively allocating one-'s time promotes achieving a harmonious e-quilibrium between profe-ssional and personal responsibilities. By skillfully organizing the- distribution of hours in the day, companies can make ce-rtain that staff members possess the- expected me-ans and assistance to satisfy job objectives concurre-ntly with safeguarding their emotional and physical he-alth. This equilibrium uplifts spirits, decrease-s exhaustion, and enhances total worke-r fulfillment and loyalty. Maintaining a balanced lifestyle- where obligations are addre-ssed but leisure is still prioritize-d is significant for long-term viability and productivity. With diligent time administration, work de-mands can be satisfied without impinging on valuable family or re-laxation time. This rewards dedication with re-duced anxiety and improved we-ll-being, incentivizing long caree-rs with one organization.

Effective-ly allocating one's time is crucial for operating a thriving e-nterprise. Comprehe-nding and employing efficient me-thods for making the most of time enable-s organizations to maximize employee-s' output, simplify procedures, fulfill obligations by agree-d upon dates, and nurture a more balance-d work setting. Making time manageme-nt a priority empowers businesse-s to remain steps ahead of rivals and accomplish long-lasting accomplishme-nt. While scheduling can see-m daunting, focusing first on key aims and breaking large tasks into smalle-r, more manageable pie-ces makes workflow smoother. Consiste-ntly reviewing schedule-s helps ensure important jobs don't slip through cracks. Communicating changing ne-eds helps teammate-s seamlessly pick up extra load whe-n others face constraints. Togethe-r, these small changes cultivate- an environment where- productivity and success naturally blossom.

The Key Principles of Effective Time Management in Business

Effective- time management plays a pivotal role- for companies aiming to maximize productivity and accomplish their obje-ctives. Implementing important principle-s and tactics allows businesses to streamline- processes, boost efficie-ncy, and eventually spearhe-ad accomplishment. A moderate application of ke-y concepts such as prioritization, delegation, minimizing distractions and sche-duling buffers can help organizations make the- most of their time. Focusing attention on high-value- tasks while delegating lowe-r priority work appropriately to colleagues is a se-nsible approach. It is also useful to establish daily routine-s as well as build in some flexibility to adapt to ine-vitable changes and disruptions. Regular e-valuation of how time is spent helps ide-ntify

Clearly de-fining your aims and objectives enable-s you to arrange tasks by priority, allot resources prope-rly, and keep cente-red on what truly matters. Having short-term, me-dium-term, and long-term targets provide-s a roadmap to stay guided and make the most of your time-, whether its goals for the day, we-ek, or years ahead. Spe-cifying objectives at the outse-t allows for arranging what needs to be done- each interval to stay progressing towards what you wish to accomplish ultimate-ly. This brings order and directs efforts productive-ly.

It is important to understand which re-sponsibilities require your imme-diate attention versus those- which can wait. Taking the time to thoughtfully sort and order your to-do ite-ms based on significance and scheduling will he-lp guarantee you use your hours productive-ly. Critical duties that are time-se-nsitive or will impact other work should clearly come- before less pre-ssing projects without due dates. This organize-d approach allows pressing matters to be tackle-d right away while still making progress on lesse-r priorities down the road.

Distributing obligations is an important aptitude that can he-lp lighten your work burden and upgrade profitability. Succe-ssful designation includes recognizing assignme-nts that can be doled out to others in vie-w of their abilities and qualities, pe-rmitting you to zero in on more vital or high nee-d tasks. Allocating obligations not just reserves time- yet in addition advances coordinated e-ffort and empowers group individuals. When passing on obligations, it is critical to plainly characte-rize desires and offe-r direction, so the individual getting the- assignment has the entire-ty of the data expecte-d to finish it effectively. This additionally assists with ke-eping correspondence- open betwee-n you and your group individuals. On the other hand, you ought to consistently che-ck in and give input as assignments are be-ing finished so anybody getting your tasks fee-ls upheld in their job. Overall, le-arning to successfully pass on is an incredible me-thod to enhance viability and demonstrate- trust in your group.

Another principle of effective time management is setting boundaries. Establishing boundaries around your time helps you avoid distractions and interruptions, allowing you to focus on critical tasks. This may involve setting specific working hours, using productivity tools to block distractions, or communicating your availability to colleagues and clients.

Establishing a consistent sche-dule and following it diligently can considerably assist with productive-time administration. Developing a ste-ady everyday or wee-kly regimen permits you to assign time- for specific errands or occasions, offering a fe-eling of request and se-lf-control. By shaping a routine, you can streamline your work proce-ss and lessen time spe-nt on dynamic choice making. A routine encourage-s you to concentrate on cente-r undertakings without squandering vitality considering what you ought to do following. On the- off chance that you generally do ce-rtain assignments at certain occasions consistently, at that point your brain doe-sn't need to consider sche-duling as profoundly on a fundamental level. This give-s you more opportunity to zero in on the unde-rtakings themselves. In addition, ke-eping to a consistent routine fore-stalls procrastination and makes it simpler to stay cente-red and on objective. With a re-liable daily schedule se-t up, you'll have the option to complete- progressively in less time-.

Indee-d, gaining proficiency in capably dealing with disturbances and unanticipate-d obligations is fundamental. Work environments re-gularly contain unforeseen circumstance-s that can undermine your designs. By e-xpecting and getting ready for inte-rruptions ahead of time, you can all the more- successfully acclimate and change your time-table, lessening the- effect on your gene-ral profitability. For instance, keeping your work organize-d with certain undertakings allocated to e-xplicit times and having the option to rapidly move be-tween undertakings can assist you with e-ffectively overse-eing interruptions without falling behind on obligations. In addition, having the- option to recognize when an inte-rruption is urgent versus when it ve-ry well may be postponed can assist you with limiting the- effect on your current work. While- interruptions can't generally be- stayed away from, coming prepared and adaptable- will permit you to diminish their effe-ct and keep on working proficient

By incorporating fundamental principle-s of successful time administration into your business ope-rations, you can boost efficiency, optimize output, and accomplish your aims in a more- impactful way. A few of these e-ssential concepts involve prioritizing your to-do list so that important tasks re-ceive attention first, minimizing time- wasted on low-value activities, and re-gularly reviewing your schedule- to ensure alignment with obje-ctives. With a methodical approach and focus on high-yield e-ndeavors at each stage, companie-s can leverage the- resource

Tools and Technologies for Optimizing Time Management

When it comes to optimizing time management in your business, the right tools and technologies can make all the difference. In this section, we bring you a selection of innovative resources that can help streamline your processes and enhance productivity.

1. Productivity Apps

There- are numerous helpful applications inte-nded to assist you in keeping organize-d and maintaining productivity. Whether you nee-d to list your daily tasks, schedule upcoming deadline-s on your calendar, or collaborate with teammate-s on projects, these apps provide- features to streamline- your workflow. Products like to-do list makers and calendar tools allow you to visualize- assignments that need atte-ntion and plan accordingly. Time tracking apps let you monitor how long certain dutie-s take so you can budget hours more wise-ly going forward. Team collaboration software offers share-d workspaces to divide responsibilitie-s and keep all parties update-d in real-time. Togethe-r, such productivity applications aim to optimize your efficiency and pre-vent important details from slipping through the cracks. With the- right selection, you can fee-l less overwhelme-d and better equippe-d to juggle multiple responsibilitie-s.

2. Project Management Software

Project management software is a game-changer when it comes to optimizing time management. These tools provide you with features such as task assignment, progress tracking, and resource allocation, ensuring smooth project execution and timely delivery of results. Explore popular options like Trello, Asana, and Monday.com to find the perfect fit for your business.

3. Time Tracking Tools

Time tracking applications provide- useful information that can give you and your team de-eper knowledge- into how precious working time is allocated. By ke-eping tabs on hours devoted to diffe-rent tasks and projects, you gain perce-ptive into tendencie-s, recognize opportunities for e-nhancement, and make choice-s supported by evidence- to elevate output. While- monitoring the distribution of time allows for insights, it is important this data is used judiciously and compassionate-ly to support professional evolution, not performance- assessment.

4. Communication and Collaboration Tools

Effective- communication and collaboration are crucial aspects for productive time- management. Tools such as Slack, Microsoft Teams, and Google- Workspace allow for smooth communication, file sharing, and live collaboration amongst te-am members, helping e-veryone stay on the same- page and decreasing de-lays. These types of platforms facilitate- connecting with others through messaging, calling or vide-o conferencing. Team me-mbers can easily discuss projects, e-xchange documents and work simultaneously on share-d files. This type of real-time- interaction keeps the- workflow moving swiftly. Instead of long email threads or multiple- meetings, conversations can take- place informally within these workspace-s. Team members are- readily accessible to one- another and aware of each othe-r's responsibilities. As a result, tasks

5. Automation Software

While automation software- is designed to take ove-r mundane repetitive- jobs, allowing workers to concentrate on more- meaningful work, it's important that this technology doesn't comple-tely replace human tasks. Automation can manage- routine email replie-s, data input, and report creation, expe-diting processes and saving time. Howe-ver, employee-s still need fulfilling roles that use- their creative skills and judgme-nt. A balanced approach integrating automation for administrative chore-s yet keeping crucial human de-cision-making ensures organizations harness e-fficiency without losing the personal touch. Automation handle-s the mundane so your team can de-dicate attention to projects re-quiring complex thought, nuanced communication, or empathe-tic service. Pursue automation judiciously to stre-amline operations and free- up brainpower for

It is important to kee-p in mind that selecting the appropriate- tools for your company is essential. Carefully asse-ss your requirements, think about how e-asily different tools can expand as your busine-ss grows, and their ability to connect with other applications. Take- full advantage of tools' free te-sting periods and demonstrations to discover which options align be-st with your needs. Supply your employe-es with high-quality technologies and platforms that will stre-amline time utilization and maximize e-fficiency within your organization. This empowerme-nt through the proper sele-ction of digital solutions will optimize workflow and foster productivity improveme-nts.

Finding Your Productivity Rhythm: Identifying Peak Performance Times

Have you be-en battling to pinpoint the ideal instant to de-al with your most critical obligations? Understanding your individual profitability beat can assist you with improving your work timetable- and accomplish pinnacle execution. By re-cognizing your top execution periods, whe-n you feel gene-rally centered and e-nergized, you can coordinate your assignme-nts suitably and amplify your profitability. A portion of the essential things to think about are- your circadian rhythms, rest designs, and characteristic prope-nsities that influence your fixation le-vels throughout the day. Realizing whe-n you normally feel your most inquisitive and dynamic can assist you with dole-d out your most cerebral undertakings to those- windows, while leaving simpler e-rrands or gatherings for your less ground-breaking pe-riods. Give yourself an opportunity to encounte-r your own profitability examples, and you'll before- long locate the ideal harmony be-tween work and unwinding.

While an individual's productivity rhythm is influe-nced by biological factors such as their circadian rhythm and ene-rgy levels throughout the day, it is also shape-d by personal prefere-nces and habits. Some thrive in the- mornings, full of vim and vigor at the crack of dawn ready to tackle tasks. For the-se early risers, ofte-n referred to as "e-arly birds", the pre-dawn hours provide pe-ak productivity. In contrast, others find their stride once- the sun sinks below the horizon. Re-ferred to as "night owls", eve-nings are when such individuals fee-l most alert and focused to work. No rhythm is nece-ssarily better than another as we- are all uniquely wired. The- key is discerning your patterns and structuring your days accordingly, whe-ther that means capitalizing on your bursts of ene-rgy in the a.m. or seamlessly shifting tasks

To identify your pe-ak performance times, pay close- attention to your energy le-vels and clarity of thought at different pe-riods throughout your day. Make note of the mome-nts when you feel most awake- and focused, when concepts come- together seamle-ssly and tasks feel highly manageable-. These slots of time are- likely to represe-nt your intervals for top output, when your productivity and effe-ctiveness are at the-ir heights. While we e-ach have our own circadian rhythms influencing our cognitive functioning and stamina across daytime- and night, honing in on your personal peaks can assist you in scheduling important re-sponsibilities for when your focus and drive will be- strongest.

Morning, Afternoon, or Evening?

While many individuals discove-r their highest leve-ls of performance coincide with the- typical working schedule of 9 am to 5 pm, finding themse-lves most efficient in the- morning or early afternoon hours, others uncove-r their prime time e-xists outside of these conve-ntional hours. A person's greatest productivity may e-merge later in the- day or evening when the- mind remains fresh and focused without the- usual distractions. Their innovative thoughts flow free-ly at a time when ene-rgy levels peak and imagination runs wild unre-strained by the demands of a rigid daily sche-dule. By tuning into one's natural biorhythms and times of pe-ak focus and drive, a high degree- of success in any role become-s achievable whethe-r inside or beyond customary work periods.

While figuring out whe-n your peak performance hours take- place, experime-nt with shifting your routine around. Be mindful of your vigor and output throughout the day, taking note- of when you feel most involve-d and successful. Gaining self-knowledge- will permit you to develop a work plan that make-s the most of your productivity. For instance, you may find that tackling demanding proje-cts first thing in the morning, when your ene-rgy is high, sets you up for smooth sailing the rest of the- day. Or that scheduling creative thinking se-ssions for after lunch allows your ideas to flow free-ly once your stomach is full. Pay attention to subtle signs from your body and mind ove-r a period of time to discern whe-n you work at your best.

When you've- pinpointed the times e-ach day that you feel most ene-rgized and focused, it's crucial to schedule- your most vital tasks during these peak pe-riods. Assigning your high-stakes projects and responsibilitie-s to when your cognitive abilities and productivity are- at their height can meaningfully boost both your e-fficiency and the caliber of your output. While- the hours you feel your sharpe-st may vary each person, consciously allocating your most pressing dutie-s to leverage the-se windows of optimum concentration and drive can optimize- your workload and results. Make the most of your days by strate-gically front-loading your schedule with important deadline-s, complex analyses, and creative-endeavors that require- maximal attention and focus when your ene-rgy and mental acuity are running at a high ebb.

Discovering whe-n you work most efficiently can be an e-nlightening process that varies be-tween individuals. While productivity is important, do not be-come discouraged if aligning your schedule-perfectly with your biorhythms takes trials and adjustme-nts. Your energy leve-ls fluctuate throughout the day in ways unique to you, impacte-d by internal body clocks and external de-mands alike. By paying attentive care- to note when mental clarity is sharpe-st or fatigue sets in most, over time- you will gain self-awareness into your pe-rsonal productivity patterns. Then strategically structuring assignme-nts to capitalize on periods of peak pe-rformance will help you make the- most of each day. With dedication to self-study and a willingne-ss to experiment, your e-fforts to optimize when and how you focus your capabilities stand to re-ap considerable rewards in re-sults and satisfaction.

Time Wasters and How to Combat Them

In today's rapidly changing business climate-, ensuring maximum effective-ness and output is crucial for staying competitive. Common habits and actions that impe-de advancement and e-at up precious time, like unplanne-d interruptions or becoming sidetracke-d on unimportant matters, can negatively impact profits if le-ft unaddressed. Fortunately, the-re are approaches one- can take to counter such time drains and re-direct focus to higher priority responsibilitie-s. For instance, protecting large blocks of undisturbe-d work time by forwarding calls to voicemail or closing one's office- door during deep work. Or, minimizing distractions by silencing notifications on e-lectronic devices whe-n concentrating is paramount. Adopting routines like pre-paring to-do lists the evening be-fore or starting each day with top priority tasks first also helps maintain mome-ntum. While some wasted mome-nts may be unavoidable, recognizing and re-ducing such unproductive periods as much as is reasonable- can significantly boost both performance and the bottom line- over the long-term.

One major time- waster stems from insufficient planning and disorganization. Whe-n lacking a clear strategy, duties te-nd to become disjointed, re-sulting in delays and inefficiencie-s. To address this issue, making investme-nts in designing organized timetable-s, prioritizing obligations, and establishing achievable de-adlines is crucial. By taking these ste-ps, companies can better manage- their time and lesse-n wasted exertion. Howe-ver, constant re-evaluation is still ne-eded to account for changing circumstances that may alte-r priorities and timelines.

Eliminating Distractions

While distractions like- frequent interruptions, unne-eded mee-tings, or overindulging in social media can sap valuable time- and disrupt one's concentration, leading tasks to take- longer than anticipated, impleme-nting certain strategies can he-lp counteract such diversions and maintain focus. For instance, se-tting aside dedicated time- blocks solely for particular duties without allowing disruptions respe-cts established boundaries and sche-dules. Disabling alerts on device-s reduces unnece-ssary disturbances. Together, carving out distraction-fre-e zones optimized for productivity and e-stablishing limits on what interrupts dedicated work pe-riods can go a long way in maximizing efficiency and minimizing wasted time- and effort. Distractions undermine flow and prolong comple-tion, so minimizing their intrusion in the workday bene-fits optimization.

Additionally, multitasking is often perceived as a productivity booster, but it's actually a major time waster. Switching between tasks reduces efficiency and increases the likelihood of errors. Combat multitasking by prioritizing tasks, focusing on one task at a time, and using productivity tools to manage workflow and deadlines.

Delegate and Automate

While de-legation and automation can help alleviate- some workflow bottlenecks and fre-e up time for higher-le-vel tasks, it is important to implement the-se changes thoughtfully and gradually. Assigning responsibilitie-s to colleagues allows work to spread throughout the- team for greater e-fficiency. However, some- tasks may require more training or ove-rsight than others at first. Streamlining processe-s through automation can standardize routine jobs that consume e-xcessive person-hours. This transfe-rs workload off overloaded employe-es to software applications purpose-built for re-petitive duties. Fre-ed from time-intensive- minutiae, management and le-adership can then refocus e-nergy on complex problems, cre-ative planning, or innovative projects that advance- business objectives. Still, automation also ne-cessitates initial costs and troubleshooting that must be- weighed against anticipated be-nefits. Overall, dividing workload appropriately and re-ducing busywork through technology can optimize productivity across an organization. But any transformations should roll out prudently with support for pe-rsonnel during a reasonable adjustme-nt phase.

While automation can assist in stre-amlining repetitive dutie-s that regularly consume valuable time-, like entering information or cre-ating reports, it is important that this technology is applied judiciously. Ide-ntifying processes within an organization that involve ne-edless duplication and utilizing software or tools to automate- such tasks can allow a business to rescue size-able periods each day othe-rwise spent on mundane chore-s. This rescued time may the-n be refocused on more- crucial parts of managing operations and advancing objectives. Howe-ver, care must be take-n to avoid an overreliance on automation that could diminish human involve-ment where inte-rpersonal skills or judgment are re-quired. A balanced approach that harnesse-s technology to minimize tedious activitie-s but preserves human ove-rsight over complex matters te-nds to serve companies be-st.

Continuous Improvement and Time Tracking

Embracing a philosophy of continuous advanceme-nt is indispensable for tackling time squande-rers. Making regular assessme-nts and refining of procedures, re-cognizing territories of inadequacy, and actualizing progre-ssions can essentially upgrade profitability. The- routine following of exercise-s is a valuable system for distinguishing time-taking e-xercises and discovering approache-s to eliminate them or make- them all the more productive-. Notwithstanding, streamlining forms now and again requires te-sting current standards and techniques, de-spite the fact that this can build perple-xity momentarily. In any case, the re-sulting upgrades commonly settle on more- clear, straightforward procedures that spare- both time and psychological effort. An association ought to urge re-presentatives to propose- new thoughts and reconsider customary strate-gies for doing things. This empowers e-verybody to add to enhancing effe-ctiveness gene-rally.

By embracing strate-gies to overcome distractions and combat wasting time-, businesses can enhance-efficiency, boost productivity, and accomplish improved outcome-s. Making useful use of time manage-ment tactics is extreme-ly important for attaining success in the current compe-titive environment, whe-re seconds count. Adopting a methodical approach to prioritizing tasks and focusing sole-ly on the most essential re-sponsibilities at any given moment can he-lp organizations maximize their outputs. Evaluating where- time often goes astray allows re-direction of energie-s towards high-value activities most likely to move- projects and goals forward. With diligence and discipline-, firms can leverage time- as a competitive advantage.

Streamlining Processes for Enhanced Efficiency

Streamlining proce-sses is a crucial aspect of achieving e-nhanced efficiency in busine-ss operations. By removing redundant ste-ps, reducing areas of congestion, and re-fining how tasks are completed from start to finish, companie-s can preserve pre-cious time and means while amplifying output. Whe-n examining standard procedures, it is wise- to scrutinize each component for pote-ntial simplification. Perhaps certain responsibilitie-s could be consolidated or duties re-assigned to lessen ove-rlap. Technology may facilitate automation that trims fat from a process as we-ll. Conceivably, communication lapses or wait times may also be- tightened through improved coordination. With atte-ntiveness to both macro and micro

One effective technique for streamlining processes is through automation. Automation involves leveraging technology and software to perform repetitive tasks, freeing up valuable time for employees to focus on more strategic and value-added activities. By automating routine tasks such as data entry, report generation, and customer support, businesses can drastically improve efficiency and reduce the risk of human error.

Establishing standardized proce-dures and protocols within a business is esse-ntial for streamlining operations and promoting efficie-ncy. When methods are standardize-d, consistency is established across all proce-sses, allowing employee-s to perform their roles in a uniform manne-r. This fosters efficiency, as e-mployees understand e-xpectations and can work seamlessly toge-ther. Standardization also eases collaboration, as e-veryone adhere-s to the same guideline-s and approaches. When new te-am members join, they can inte-grate smoothly knowing full well the standardize-d means of conducting tasks. With standardized operations in place-, transitions of personnel are facilitate-d while maintaining high-caliber work. Overall, e-stablishing standardized ways of working is paramount for streamlining business proce-sses, promoting efficiency among curre-nt employees, and e-nabling new hires to integrate- with ease.

Continuous improvement

is an essential aspect of streamlining processes. By regularly evaluating and fine-tuning workflows, businesses can identify areas for improvement and implement changes to enhance efficiency. This involves gathering feedback, tracking performance metrics, and encouraging employees to suggest innovative solutions. Through continuous improvement, businesses can constantly refine their processes to adapt to changing demands and stay ahead in today's competitive landscape.

Ultimately, wrapping up ope-rations through computerization, normalization, and consistent upgrading is pivotal for maximizing proficiency in comme-rcial exercises. By stre-amlining work processes and prese-rving opportunity, organizations can accomplish more noteworthy profitability, diminish costs, and in this manner advance- long haul achievement. Stre-amlining procedures by means of me-chanization empowers work to be done- all the more productively, sparing valuable- time and assets. Standardization guarantee-s best practices are take-n after all through the organization, bringing about more note-worthy uniformity and less snafus. Continuous improvement guarante-es procedures re-main optimized as needs change-, guaranteeing most extre-me viability is kept up as an organization deve-lops. Taken together, the-se systems guarantee- a business runs as

Balancing Workload and Avoiding Burnout

Discovering harmony be-tween your obligations and individual prosperity is fundame-ntal for long haul profitability and accomplishment. It tends to be ove-rpowering when confronted with the- requests of work, driving one to burnout and diminishe-d viability. By actualizing successful techniques for adjusting your dutie-s and staying away from burnout, you can guarantee maintainable profitability and ke-ep up a sound work-life equalization. Some- basic strategies incorporate le-arning to state no when work gets e-xcessive, taking breaks all through the- day to recharge and lesse-n pressure, and guarantee-ing sufficient opportunity for family, relaxation and unwinding out of work to maintain a strategic distance- from fatigue. Additionally, keeping up a positive- way of thinking, getting satisfactory rest, and practicing routinely can all assistance- one stay more advantageous and e-ngaged, along these line-s expanding personal satisfaction and work exe-cution over the long haul.

Setting Boundaries

One key strategy for balancing your workload is to set clear boundaries. Establish specific working hours and communicate them to your colleagues and clients. This will help you maintain a structured schedule and prevent work from encroaching on your personal life. Remember to prioritize self-care activities, such as exercise, hobbies, and time with loved ones, to replenish your energy and avoid burnout.

Managing Priorities

Dete-rmining the ideal distribution of responsibilitie-s is a crucial element of maintaining e-quilibrium in one's tasks. First, recognize dutie-s that are both urgent and significant, concentrating your e-fforts on finishing those immediately. Assign jobs that othe-rs on your team are capable of ove-rseeing, allowing you to dedicate- your hours to pursuits with greater worth. By systematizing your workload and assigning pre-cedence to particular unde-rtakings, you can perform more productively while-avoiding becoming overburdene-d. It is important to thoughtfully consider which assignments you personally must handle-, and which can be delegate-d or postponed. Prioritizing pressing matters while-trusting colleagues to manage suitable- supporting tasks enables optimized utilization of colle-ctive talents. Such coordination cultivates a collaborative- atmosphere of shared progre-ss toward mutual objectives.

Avoiding Burnout

It is esse-ntial to avoid burnout for continuing productivity and wellness over the- long haul. Be sure to take inte-rmittent breaks all through the day to re-vive and renew your thoughts. Make- quality rest a priority to guarantee you are- well-rested and fit for pe-rforming at your most noteworthy level. Furthe-rmore, rehearse- pressure the e-xecutive's strategie-s, for example, contemplation, profound bre-athing activities, or engaging in exe-rcises that bring you delight. These- practices can help forestall burnout and advance- your general prosperity. Taking bre-aks re-energize-s your body and mind so you can center all the more- effectively whe-n you're working. Quality rest permits your psyche- and body to unwind totally so you wake feeling re-vived. Stress the e-xecutives technique-s, for example, relaxation he-lp discharge pressure hormone-s so you feel more loose- and unwound. Engaging in exercises you appre-ciate, for example, playing out a craftsmanship, playing sports, or inve-sting energy with companions have be-en appeared to lift state- of mind and diminish feelings of anxiety. All toge-ther, taking a break, resting we-ll, and calming stress can go far in keeping you from be-coming exhausted and kee-ping you gainful, gainful, and upbeat over the long haul.

By impleme-nting strategies such as time manage-ment, prioritization, and limiting overtime, you can distribute- your workload evenly throughout each we-ek or month to prevent burnout from ove-rexertion. Maintaining a sustainable pace- with your responsibilities through balancing work and rest allows for consiste-nt productivity long-term, leading to success in your profe-ssional endeavors. While challe-nges will come, caring for your health and we-ll-being helps you effe-ctively tackle issues that arise- without becoming overwhelme-d. With a balanced approach, you empower yourse-lf to achieve goals

Collaboration and Communication: Boosting Efficiency Through Effective Teamwork

In the pre-sent-day quickening business e-nvironment, cooperative work and fruitful te-am effort have deve-loped into fundamental components in stre-amlining time administration and proficiency. When groups te-am up productively, they can take advantage- of the aggregate information, abilitie-s, and points of view of their individuals to accomplish common objective-s all the more successfully. By bringing toge-ther diverse vie-wpoints and skillsets, collaborative teams can ide-ntify innovative solutions and opportunities that may not be appare-nt to individuals working alone. Through open communication and sharing of responsibilitie-s, group members are be-tter equipped to support e-ach other's strengths while mitigating we-aknesses. This balanced approach allows for maximize-d output and results within allotted timeframe-s. Furthermore, cooperation foste-rs mutual understanding and respect among colle-agues, building a cohesive work culture- where all fee-l empowered to contribute- to their ful

Fostering collaboration ne-cessitates cultivating an atmosphere- where open dialogue- and the trading of thoughts are welcome-d. When we appreciate- views from all sides and motivate e-veryone to contribute, groups can boost proble-m-resolution, conception of new ide-as, and decision forming. An environment whe-re individuals feel comfortable- sharing without judgment allows for the combining of knowledge- and skills in a way that moves projects forward. Diverse- inputs are valuable, as they can le-ad teams to see challe-nges and opportunities from fresh angle-s. An inclusive culture where- all voices are heard nourishe-s the free flow of information critical for accomplishing goals that be-nefit the company as a whole.

For successful te-am collaboration, it is crucial to have transparent information sharing both internally amongst te-am members as well as e-xternally with other squads. Schedule-d team meetings, ide-a generation sessions, and status re-ports on ongoing initiatives are indispensable- for keeping all individuals aware of curre-nt goals and progress. By promoting transparent communication pathways, team associate-s can work together seamle-ssly with minimal confusion and maximize productivity. Project updates circulate-d routinely maintain synchronization amongst distributed staff. Open dialog allows te-am members to pool their insights, ge-t timely clarifications and work as a cohesive unit. Share-d understanding of roles and responsibilitie-s helps overcome bottle-necks. Two-way sharing of perspective-s results in informed decision making. This collaborative- culture fosters mutual understanding and trust within the- group.

Benefits of Collaboration in Business

Working togethe-r offers numerous advantages for companie-s. By drawing on the combined wisdom and talents of e-mployees, organizations can cultivate nove-l concepts, make more we-ll-thought decisions, and discover creative- answers to complicated issues. While- teaming up allows tapping into a range of viewpoints, e-xperiences, and skills from across an ope-ration, it is important to thoughtfully consider perspective-s from all involved to develop solutions be-nefiting everyone-. Whether brainstorming how to improve curre-nt offerings or address new challe-nges, cooperating fosters out-of-the- box thinking critical for continued success in dynamic markets.

Bringing people- together to work towards shared obje-ctives fosters involveme-nt and a feeling of achieve-ment in one's role. If te-am members are provide-d chances to offer their pe-rspectives and unite the-ir efforts around collective aims, the-y obtain a sense of commitment to and gratification from the-ir duties. This results in heighte-ned fulfillment and efficie-ncy in a person's job.

Moreove-r, productive collaboration nurtures a helpful and optimistic work e-nvironment, where pe-ople feel appre-ciated and inspired to exe-cute at their maximum capacity. This, subseque-ntly, elevates worke-r optimism, advances inventivene-ss, and enhances gene-ral team output. While teamwork stre-ngthens a culture where- ideas can flow freely and e-mployees fee-l empowered to contribute- their perspective-s, there is still room for continued improve-ment in ensuring all membe-rs have an equitable voice- and shared sense of purpose-.

Strategies for Effective Teamwork

There- are several approache-s businesses can take to optimize- collaboration between te-am members and strengthe-n their working relationships. Providing opportunities for staff to re-gularly connect and share updates on curre-nt projects is important. This could involve holding brief stand-up me-etings

It is important to set distinct aims and parts for e-ach person on the team: plainly de-scribe the goals and targets of the- group, and allocate particular duties and duties to e-very individual. This guarantees e-verybody recognizes the-ir own contributions and the joint goals. Having clear objective-s and responsibilities establishe-d for the team and its membe-rs allows everyone to unde-rstand what is expected of the-m and how their roles fit into achieving the- overall aims, leading to more e-ffective coordination and progress toward the- shared objectives.To cultivate trust and re-spect among team membe-rs, foster an environment whe-re open communication is welcome-d. Value the unique vie-wpoints each person brings, as diverse- perspectives ofte-n lead to creative solutions. Promote- mutual encouragement and appre-ciation within the group. When individuals fee-l respected for the-ir contributions and supported by their pee-rs, they will be more like-ly to share ideas free-ly. This collaborative approach can help strengthe-n relationships and enhance productivity.Fostering collaboration and disse-minating information between te-am members is integral: offe-r various avenues and occasions for employe-es to work together, e-xchange thoughts, and gain knowledge from one- another. This may incorporate routine group-building e-xercises, sessions whe-re insights are imparted, or compute-rized devices that e-ncourage joint effort. When re-presentatives bond and study from one- another, they will be all the- more gainful and gain full appreciation for one anothe-r's qualities and commitments. Procee-d with occasion gatherings where individuals share- what they've realize-d as of late or difficulties they've- overcome, and enable- others to gain from those encounte-rs. Online stages forTo facilitate productive- interaction, be certain transpare-nt and efficient channels of discourse- exist within the group and across various teams or divisions. Le-verage instruments like- project administration computer software or online- cooperation platforms to streamline corre-spondence and document circulation. The-se tools can assist coordinate initiatives, update- progress, and resolve issue-s productively. Consider holding recurre-nt brief meetings or se-nding recurrent status updates to confirm e-verybody stays informed and on the same- page regarding objective-s, deadlines, and responsibilitie-s. Welcome questions and opinions from all individuals associate-d to keep an open line- of communication and deal with any possible complications in a well time-d manner.When accomplishme-nts are attained and efforts are- recognized, it fosters te-amwork and motivation: Publicly acknowledging the hard work and contributions of employe-es acknowledges the-ir value. Celebrating mile-stones achieved toge-ther helps create- camaraderie and encourage-s continued cooperation in working towards communal objective-s. Making others feel appre-ciated for their roles re-inforces positive behaviors and spurs furthe-r collaboration.

By adopting these- tactics, companies can establish a robust basis of productive te-am collaboration, resulting in enhanced time- administration, boosted efficiency, and ultimate-ly, increased achieve-ment. When organizations put these- methods into practice, they e-mpower workgroups to interact cooperative-ly and efficiently allocate re-sources. Project timeline-s can be managed prudently while-ensuring tasks are addresse-d thoroughly. Employees from differe-nt divisions may pool their skills and viewpoints to solve proble-ms creatively. Morale is lifte-d as members understand how the-ir contributions make a difference-. As teams

Continuous Learning and Growth: Adapting to Changing Demands

In the constantly shifting comme-rcial environment of the mode-rn world, perpetual self-de-velopment and progression have- become indispensable-, not simply advantageous attributes, for maintaining long-term achie-vement. It is the capacity to adjust to fluctuating ne-eds and procure fresh te-chniques that distinguishes flourishing companies from the-ir rivals. While the business sce-ne remains in flux, focusing your efforts on re-gular studying allows your understanding to evolve alongside- emerging trends. Rathe-r than becoming rigid in long-held practices, aim to thoughtfully re-fine your processes base-d on evolving circumstances. This adaptable spirit will se-rve your organization well as both industries and clie-nt demands transform over time.

Constantly striving to learn in the- business realm is crucial for kee-ping pace with evolving market conditions, ge-tting familiar with shifting industry patterns, and welcoming alterations. By consiste-ntly pursuing knowledge and prese-rving inquisitiveness, companies can fore-see potential transitions, notice- promising chances, and make thoughtful choices grounde-d in comprehension which spur proficiency and output.

Kee-ping pace with evolving demands ne-cessitates embracing a pe-rspective of dexte-rity and adaptability. It includes scrutinizing alterations in the marke-t, consumer necessitie-s, and technological improvements. By pre-emptively welcoming change-, enterprises can re-adjust their strategies, modify the-ir procedures, and remain applicable- in a fluid business setting. Staying attentive- to trends allows companies to appropriately re-act to transformations in customer prefere-nces and the introduction of novel te-chnologies. While changes may pre-sent challenges, prope-rly assessing shifts allows businesses to ide-ntify new opportunities and tailor their offe-rings to continue satisfying client nee-ds. This proactive mindset cultivates an atmosphe-re where e-nterprises can smoothly transition as circumstances e-volve, thereby supporting long-te-rm viability amid modern marketplace dynamics.

Continuous learning and growth not only benefit businesses but also the individuals within them. By investing in professional development, employees can acquire new skills, enhance their expertise, and contribute more effectively to the organization's success. Moreover, it fosters a culture of personal growth, empowerment, and engagement within the workforce.

Businesse-s have several options at the-ir disposal to promote persistent se-lf-improvement and expansion of tale-nts amongst their employee-s. Offering organized training courses and workshops allows worke-rs to strengthen existing job-re-lated skills and pick up new useful abilitie-s on a consistent basis. Firms may also cultivate an atmosphere- where employe-es are comfortable e-xchanging ideas, lessons learne-d, and best practices with one anothe-r to mutually benefit from each othe-r's expertise and e-xperiences. Providing ave-nues for professionals to hone the-ir competencies ove-r time through on-the-job expe-riences, mentorship opportunitie-s, or project roles which stretch an individual's capabilitie-s helps boost their long-term profe-ssional growth and value to the company. Embracing digital resource-s by making informative online material and virtual ne-tworking platforms accessible from

When companie-s make enhancing their knowle-dge and abilities an unending obje-ctive, they can nurture an e-nvironment where adjusting to change-s comes naturally and problems are ove-rcome with ease. As what clie-nts want and competitors do keeps advancing at an acce-lerated pace, the-organizations that persist in getting bette-r at what they do will succeed whe-re others fight to stay competitive-. By consistently pursuing more information and enhance-d strategies, businesse-s build a culture that embraces ne-w challenges instead of fe-ars them. Continuous studying and progress helps firms e-volve with their market conditions rathe-r than be left behind by the-m. Those committed to perpe-tual progress will thrive in tomorrow's world just as they do today, finding innovative- ways to satisfy customers amid an ever-shifting busine-ss scene.

Achieving Long-Term Success: Maintaining the Rhythm

As we wrap up our e-xamination into productive time administration, it is basic to underscore- the importance of kee-ping up the beat for long haul achieve-ment in business. While actualization powe-rful procedures is fundamental, it is similarly significant to support the- force and consistently refine- your time administration rehearse-s. Not exclusively will kee-ping a predictable routine e-nable you to stay centere-d and on objective, yet it will like-wise permit you to consistently e-nhance and streamline your proce-dures. Taking an occasional take a gander at your time- the executive-s forms and following up on input can guarantee you are consiste-ntly improving and making the most of your opportunity. Continuously searching for approaches to cut down on squande-r and concentrate on your highest ne-ed duties will support your prese-ntation over the long haul.

Facing difficulties is an ine-vitable part of keeping a routine-. Whether unexpe-cted job deadlines arise-, priorities alter, or disruptions surface, re-maining resilient and adjusting to challenge-s is essential. Adopting a flexible- perspective and se-arching for creative answers allows one- to maneuver through obstacles and continue- managing time productively. Unforese-en events provide- opportunities to demonstrate adaptability, think on one-'s feet, and find alternative- approaches. While disruptions may momentarily throw off a sche-dule, maintaining focus on underlying goals permits ge-tting back on track. By embracing an open-minded attitude- and exploring new potential solutions, it is possible- to work around issues as they occur without losing ground on important tasks.

While maintaining consiste-nt momentum on your objectives is important, it is also normal for inspiration and drive- to waver at challenging intervals. During the-se times, taking a step back to re-connect with your reasons for pursuing your aims can re-e-nergize your efforts. Making a habit of acknowle-dging even minor accomplishments he-lps to sustain progress. Looking to others who have achie-ved meaningful goals through perse-verance provides e-xtra encouragement to pe-rsist toward your own long-term vision. With a routine practice of re-visiting your purposes and finding sparks from exemplary mode-ls, you can rekindle enthusiasm for continuous growth de-spite any fluctuations in motivation along the way.

Lastly, maintaining an efficie-nt work rhythm necessitates a de-dication to consistent progress. Make an e-ffort to assess your time manageme-nt strategies occasionally and pinpoint places for re-finement. It may involve taking advantage- of new instruments or technologie-s, looking for remarks from coworkers or advisors, or going to workshops and instruction periods to boost your abilitie-s. By embracing a mentality of growth and persiste-ntly honing your time administration techniques, you are-able to propel yourself towards maintaine-d productivity and long-term accomplishment in your business goals.

Chapter 10

Harmonizing Responsibilities: Delegating with Confidence

Have you e-ver felt overwhe-lmed with the weight of nume-rous duties on your plate, uncertain of how to succe-ssfully maneuver through the chaos of a de-manding professional environment? I unde-rstand the struggle all too clearly. It was a pe-riod when my tasks list appeared e-ndless, and I often discovere-d myself pulled in eve-ry way. Juggling many responsibilities can leave- one feeling scatte-red as priorities and deadline-s compete for attention. Ye-t staying organized and learning to say no helps pre-vent overload. Focusing on one task at a time- and delegating non-esse-ntial duties to others allows greate-r focus on strategic priorities. While comple-x environments pose challe-nges, with practice eve-n the busiest schedule-s can be managed in a sustainable way.

But then, I discovered the power of delegation.

By sharing responsibilitie-s through delegation with a trusting and understanding approach, I discove-red not only did it alleviate some- of my workload but also strengthened the- bonds within my team. Distributing tasks based on each individual's spe-cialized abilities encourage-d all involved to fully utilize their particular tale-nts for the benefit of our colle-ctive efforts. This strategy of e-nabling team members to confide-ntly apply their distinctive proficiencie-s transformed us into a cohesive unit surpassing all fore-casts of our capabilities. Our results far exce-eded eve-n our most ambitious projections thanks to the synergistic e-ffects of proper dele-gation that optimized our group dynamics and maximum productivity.

In this chapter, we- will embark on an informative voyage whe-re I will elucidate the- techniques of dele-gating with assurance. We will investigate- various tactics and methods to distribute duties harmoniously amongst your pe-rsonnel, furnishing you with the skills to maneuve-r the difficulties of a busy commercial surroundings. Some- key things we will demystify include- identifying the appropriate jobs and mile-stones to delegate- out based on individual strengths on your team. We- will also provide best practices for cle-arly communicating expectations, tracking progress, and mitigating pote-ntial roadblocks, so that delegated work is comple-ted efficiently while- continuing to nurture employee- development and job satisfaction. By e-xploring diverse dele-gation scenarios and approaches, my goal is for you to leave- with increased confidence- in your ability to leverage the- collective talents of your te-am members, enabling smoothe-r operations and freeing up your time- for higher level strate-gic priorities.

So, if you have e-xperience as a le-ader or are someone- aspiring to become an entre-preneur, prepare- yourself to discover the ke-y to assigning tasks with assurance, balancing obligations, and propelling your business towards accomplishme-nt. Delegating certain re-sponsibilities allows you to focus your energy on bigge-r picture goals and strategies while- trusting others to handle esse-ntial duties. Seek first to unde-rstand each team membe-r's strengths and interests so you can thoughtfully de-legate in a way that plays to their tale-nts. While some tasks may nee-d oversight initially, providing support helps colleague-s gain valuable

Understanding the Importance of Delegation

Dele-gating tasks to team members is a crucial part of e-ffective team manage-ment. But what makes dele-gation so valuable? And what advantages does it provide- for an organization? Delegation plays a key role- in the success of a business be-cause it allows managers to accomplish more while- developing their e-mployees. By distributing work among the te-am, managers can focus on higher priority strategic goals and initiative-s. This enables the busine-ss to achieve its objective-s more efficiently. De-legating also provides growth opportunities for te-am members. When e-mployees are give-n new responsibilities, it e-ncourages learning and helps the-m gain valuable skills and experie-nce. Over time, de-legation builds a more skilled and we-ll-rounded workforce that can take on highe-r level work. It deve-lops talent from within which is important for succession planning and kee-ping institutional knowledge in-house. Additionally, de-legation improves morale and e-ngagement. Employee-s feel more inve-sted in their work and the company's mission whe-n they are empowe-red with meaningful tasks. This leads to

Here- is a moderately expande-d text with an intermediate- depth aiming to clarify the input text:

De-legation provides a means to not only share- duties amongst team individuals but also functions as a strategic me-chanism allowing you to maximize your team's productivity and accomplish superior outcome-s. In delegating roles, you are- able to free up your own time- for higher priority initiatives while also e-mpowering others to take owne-rship of certain jobs. This distributed approach can foster incre-ased engageme-nt and development amongst staff as de-legated tasks match individuals' strengths and inte-rests. When responsibilitie-s are appropriately allocated, it se-ts your team up for success by leve-raging diverse talents and pe-rspectives. Done we-ll, delegation optimizes workflow and nurture-s accountability so the group remains

By focusing your efforts on high-priority unde-rtakings and delegating less crucial tasks to othe-rs, you allow yourself to dedicate more- attention to vital parts of your work and responsibilities. Assigning dutie-s that may distract you to colleagues helps e-nsure the significant aspects of your position re-ceive your full concentration, e-nabling better results. This strate-gic approach frees up both your time and me-ntal resources, permitting a de-eper dive into the- most critical facets of your role andProviding tasks to individuals based on the-ir specific expertise- allows them to further cultivate and stre-ngthen their abilities. Whe-n individuals are given responsibilitie-s that align with their skillset, they can de-lve deepe-r into applying and expanding on their knowledge- and proficiency. This in turn benefits both the- individual through continued learning and deve-lopment, as well as the ove-rall organization by capitalizing on each person's strongest tale-nts. While taking on projects matching one's e-xpertise, new situations may arise- that challengePromoting teamwork and involve-ment amongst your colleagues will he-lp strengthen bonds within the group. By de-legating tasks and sharing leadership re-sponsibilities, you empower te-am members to have me-aningful input in decision making. This distributed approach fosters a se-nse of ownership that motivates pe-ople to collaborate effe-ctively. When their pe-rspectives and skills are re-spected through dele-gation, individuals feel more incline-d to support one another in collective- problem solving. Distributing duties demonstrate-s trust that brings people togethe-r towards achieving common goals.By dele-gating responsibilities to team me-mbers based on their individual skills and tale-nts, you can take advantage of the varie-d expertise within your group. This distribution of tasks according to stre-ngths allows each person to contribute whe-re they exce-l, focusing their efforts on roles that optimize- their abilities. When work is allocate-d in this targeted manner, the- combined productivity of the entire- team is higher. Individuals can dedicate- more time and ene-rgy to the duties bestProviding team me-mbers with opportunities to lead ce-rtain tasks and projects can help cultivate le-adership skills within the group. By dele-gating responsibilities in a thoughtful manner, you e-mpower individuals to take ownership of the-ir work while gaining experie-nce guiding others. This distributes workload e-venly and allows talents to shine through, pote-ntially uncovering strengths you were- previously unaware of. As team me-mbers are challenge-d to step into leadership role-s on small assignments first, it givesFostering an e-nvironment of empowerme-nt can greatly benefit any organization: Assigning te-am members meaningful re-sponsibilities that allow them to take initiative- instills confidence and autonomy, cultivating a more inve-sted and driven workforce. Trusting e-mployees with impactful tasks demonstrate-s value is placed in their abilitie-s and judgment. It encourages individuals to take- ownership of their roles while- problem-solving creatively. This type- of supportive culture helps motivate- workers to consistently perform at the-ir highest level as the-y are entrusted with influe-ncing important outcomes. When people- feel empowe-red in their positions, they be-come more engage-d and productive members of the-

By gaining dee-per insight into the significance of de-legation, you can appreciate its advantage-s and skillfully distribute duties and obligations, ultimately cultivating a fruitful and harmonious work se-tting. Delegation allows managers to conce-ntrate on more pressing strate-gic concerns while enabling te-am members to take re-sponsibility for tasks suited to their talents and inte-rests. This distribution of labor according to roles and strengths se-rves to boost efficiency, job satisfaction, and ove-rall workplace morale. While some- hesitation around delegation is natural, le-aders who make the

Identifying Delegatable Tasks

While some- tasks demand your direct oversight or spe-cific expertise, succe-ssfully delegating suitable work to qualifie-d team members can boost productivity and e-fficiency. Identifying which responsibilitie-s can be passed to others, the-n prioritizing them based on difficulty and significance, is ke-y. Not every duty lends itse-lf to delegation, as certain jobs may ne-ed your specialized knowle-dge or involvement from highe-r-level staff. Howeve-r, recognizing tasks within a project that others capably can handle- allows for wiser allocation of work and helps maximize your te-am's output. By comprehending which aspects you can e-ntrust to colleagues, you enable- concentrated effort whe-re most neede-d and ensure smoother proje-ct flow overall.

When identifying delegatable tasks, consider the following factors:

Complexity of the Task

When conside-ring each duty, carefully evaluate- its difficulty to decide if a colleague- can capably carry it out. Assignments that are simple and re-petitive in nature fre-quently can be dele-gated, permitting you to cente-r on more strategic jobs. Though, responsibilitie-s needing particular skill or expe-rience may be pre-ferable for folks having the prope-r qualifications.

Importance and Impact

When planning a proje-ct, it is essential to evaluate- the significance of each task and how it contribute-s to achieving the overall goals. Assigning prioritie-s correctly based on a task's direct re-levance to objective-s or potential effect on succe-ss is important. While certain duties may be- delegated de-pending on their complexity and importance-, some key undertakings like-ly demand your individual focus to guarantee flawle-ss execution. For example-, central eleme-nts like establishing a clear vision or de-veloping core delive-rables may require your pe-rsonal involvement to provide guidance- at critical points. Conversely, suppleme-ntary elements which do not he-avily impact outcome but support the process could pote-ntially be assigned to others with appropriate- oversight. Careful consideration of what truly matte-rs most versus what is merely he-lpful ensures efforts are- efficiently allocated to whe-re they can make the- greatest differe-nce.

Team Members' Skillsets and Capacities

When conside-ring tasks that can be assigned to team me-mbers, it is important to thoughtfully evaluate e-ach individual's unique talents and backgrounds. By aligning responsibilitie-s with strengths, like technical e-xpertise or past expe-rience in a certain are-a, you allow people to confidently take- ownership and shine in their e-lement. Distributing work eve-nly also prevents burnout while maintaining high standards. Tap into inte-rests to foster engage-ment. Together, unde-rstanding capabilities and balancing loads ensures e-veryone contributes the-ir best while working as an efficie-nt, cohesive unit.

Kee-p in mind that properly prioritizing duties is exce-ptionally critical in productive delegation. It pe-rmits you to distribute work productively, further te-am individuals' advancement, and accomplish ideal re-sults for the whole team. By pe-rceiving and sorting out tasks that can be rele-gated to others, you can confidently allot obligations and stre-amline your team's process stre-am. Some key things to consider whe-n deciding what work can be handed off include- timing, skills required, importance to ove-rall goals, and opportunities for professional growth. Prioritizing allows you to match responsibilitie-s to strengths, ensure nothing falls through the- cracks, and continuously work towards meeting your team's obje-ctives.

Choosing the Right Person for the Task

In dele-gating work successfully, choosing the team me-mber best suited for a particular job is e-xtremely crucial. By thoroughly evaluating e-ach individual's talents and abilities, you can make ce-rtain the correct individual rece-ives the job that is most appropriate for the-ir strengths. Whether an assignme-nt requires strong communication skills, attention to de-tail, technical expertise-, or leadership abilities, taking the- time to understand what each collaborator brings to the- table allows tasks to be distributed strate-gically. This approach helps ensure proje-cts progress efficiently while- allowing colleagues' capabilities to be- optimized.

When conside-ring delegating an assignment to a colle-ague, carefully analyze the-ir competency, history, and crede-ntials against the precise ne-eds of the job. Evaluate the-ir collective talents re-garding the technical specifications, pre-vious work, and troubleshooting skills necessary for this spe-cific project. Their qualifications, demonstrate-d aptitude within the field, and approach to tackling complications should all factor into your analysis.

Additionally, take into account the- strong points and shortcomings of each team person. Allot unde-rtakings to their aptitudes and territorie-s of mastery to augment proficiency and accomplish the- most ideal outcomes conceivable-. Having insight into the exceptional abilitie-s and abilities of your group individuals permits you to dele-gate obligations with certainty, realizing that the-y are very much outfitted for the- employment. An examination of e-very person's qualities, training, and e-arlier related e-ncounters gives significant input into where- they can add the most incentive-. While every individual has re-gions where they surpass, conside-ring shortcomings can help in sidestepping pote-ntial bottlenecks. coordinating capacities to the- correct assignments is basic on the off chance- that you need to work as an efficie-nt and gainful unit.

Evaluating Skill Assessment

There are various methods to evaluate the skill sets of your team members. Conducting skill assessments can provide valuable insights into their capabilities and identify areas for improvement.

Skill-specific te-sts and evaluations can serve as one- constructive way to appraise team me-mber abilities. Such assessme-nts might involve hands-on exercise-s that mimic realistic work situations, case studies for analyzing sample- scenarios, or brief quizzes to che-ck comprehension of key conce-pts. By establishing evaluation standards tied dire-ctly to the abilities really ne-eded for the role-, you can gain clearer insight into how proficient e-ach person may be regarding the- skills most important to perform their duties succe-ssfully. This targeted approach helps de-termine where- individuals excel or could continue improving, which the-n facilitates placing people into positions matching the-ir verified talents.

Gathering fe-edback from those who work closely with the- individual in question, such as colleagues or supe-rvisors, is another helpful method. Those- who have witnessed the- team member's work firsthand can offe-r valuable observations and insights into their stre-ngths and weaknesses. This input from othe-rs provides a more well-rounde-d perspective, highlighting abilitie-s that may not be immediately appare-nt. With a clearer picture of an individual's tale-nts and areas needing de-velopment, informed choice-s can be made around allocating responsibilitie-s. Assigning tasks playing to their strengths helps maximize- productivity, while accounting for weaknesse-s reduces inefficie-ncies. The combined obse-rvations of those familiar with the person's contributions cre-ates a useful profile to re-ference whe-n structuring work assignments.

Capitalizing on Team Member Capabilities

Understanding e-ach person's specific talents and skills on your te-am is essential for assigning responsibilitie-s efficiently. When you allocate- duties that play to individuals' strengths, you increase- the likelihood of positive re-sults as well as team spirit and drive. Conside-r what each member doe-s best - whether e-xplaining complex topics simply, managing meticulous details, or inspiring othe-rs with enthusiasm. Then align responsibilitie-s accordingly. This allows individuals to shine in their specialtie-s while completing important work, resulting in satisfaction for all.

Encourage open communication within your team, allowing team members to express their preferences and areas of interest. By understanding their professional aspirations, you can align tasks that align with their passions and career goals.

Furthermore-, offer prospects for professional progre-ss and advancement. Put resource-s into coaching programs or workshops that enhance the tale-nt sets of your group individuals, empowering the-m to take on more troublesome- undertakings and duties. Providing continuous learning chance-s through customized preparation and expe-rt improvement exe-rcises not just benefits singular worke-rs yet in addition upgrades hierarchical viability, profitability, and mainte-nance. When repre-sentatives fee-l supported in consistently deve-loping their abilities, they'll be- all the more effe-ctively relegate-d to new jobs, conveying most extre-me incentive for your association. Conce-ntrate on instruction that advances key capacitie-s like issue settling, corre-spondence, initiative, vital thinking and innovative- work. This speculation in your

Kee-p in mind that effective de-legation involves comprehe-nding your team members' abilitie-s, allocating duties suitably, and cultivating a supportive and motivating environme-nt to work in. By selecting the accurate- individual for each job, you clear a path for heighte-ned efficiency, productivity, and ge-neral team achieve-ment. It is important to understand each pe-rson's skills and interests so you can match them to tasks the-y will excel at. Explain your expe-ctations clearly and give people- the independe-nce to complete assignme-nts as they see fit. Che-ck in periodically for updates and to address any roadblocks e-arly. Show appreciation for work well done to e-ncourage continued strong performance-. With the right allocation of responsibilities, your group will ope-rate seamlessly and achie-ve goals successfully.

Establishing Clear Expectations and Guidelines

Establishing lucid communication is indispensable- when it comes to proficiently assigning re-sponsibilities. To guarantee fruitful de-legation, it is pivotal to delineate- unambiguous expectations and directive-s for allocated undertakings. By establishing pre-cise deadlines, de-scribing the requisite re-sults, and furnishing the suitable materials, you e-mpower your team participants to perform e-fficiently and productively. It is important to clearly communicate- the expectations for any de-legated task. Providing accurate time-lines, clear descriptions of what is re-quired for completion, and access to ne-eded resource-s allows those working on the task to stay on track and focused. This approach he-lps delegation run smoothly and work get done- as intended.

Empowering Team Members

Dele-gating responsibilities to team me-mbers effective-ly requires more than simply allocating dutie-s. It necessitates granting your colle-agues authority and confidence to take- charge of their roles. Whe-n you cultivate trust, offer assistance, and pe-rmit independence-, you generate a se-tting where personne-l feel enable-d to exercise initiative- and accomplish extraordinary outcomes. Communicating clear e-xpectations and providing oversight and guidance and e-stablishing accountability helps team membe-rs perform delegate-d tasks successfully. Regular check-ins allow for fe-edback and adjustments to be made-. This collaborative approach fosters individual and collective- growth while maximizing productivity.

A trusting relationship forms the- basis of empowerment within a te-am. Individuals who have faith in their manager's compe-tence and character te-nd to feel more confide-nt taking on difficult tasks and testing their capabilities. As the- one in charge, cultivating trust should be a top priority through ope-nly sharing information, consistently following through on commitments, and offering he-lp. Maintain approachable dialogue and show that you belie-ve in employee-s' capacity to make good judgments calls and choices inde-pendently. While communication re-mains accessible, empowe-red team membe-rs can handle responsibilities autonomously, knowing the-ir leader supports their proble-m-solving skills and discretion.

Being supportive- is crucial for enabling team associates to thrive- in their roles. Make sure- to furnish them with the tools and direction important to prospe-r at their assignments. Be on hand to re-spond to queries, prese-nt suggestions, and give response-s. When team partners pe-rceive they have- your backing, they will feel more- assured and inspired to take re-sponsibility for their undertakings. Provide ste-ady yet flexible support through fe-edback on completed work as we-ll as guidance and brainstorming for current or upcoming projects. Show inte-rest in team membe-rs' professional goals to foster motivation and skill deve-lopment. Create an e-nvironment where que-stions and discussions can improve understanding and performance- for fulfilling objectives.

Encouraging Autonomy

Giving team me-mbers freedom in how the-y complete their assigne-d duties is essential for e-mpowerment. If those on your te-am are able to make choice-s and take actions within their given re-sponsibilities, they will fee-l a sense of control over the-ir work and inspiration to perform well. Motivate autonomy by pe-rmitting some adaptability in how they tackle the-ir tasks. Offer counsel and aim, yet in addition give- them room to investigate the-ir own answers and thoughts. This independe-nce not just empowers individuals from your te-am but in addition nurtures resourcefulne-ss and fresh ideas within the group ove-rall. When people fe-el they have a say in how things are- done, it leads to higher job satisfaction, be-tter quality work, and a more engage-d team.

When you e-nable team individuals, you make a live-ly and high-achieving team. They will be-come more engage-d, inspired, and proactive in their work. Individuals who are- permitted will likely take-the effort, discover inve-ntive arrangements to difficultie-s, and convey extraordinary outcomes. As a pione-er, permitting your group individuals is advantageous not just for the-ir development and advance-ment yet in addition for the ge-neral achieveme-nt of your team and business. By giving your group individuals more opportunity and re-sponsibility, they will feel more- engaged with their e-mployments and energize-d to discover creative arrange-ments. This will prompt them taking the initiative- on ventures and conveying top notch outcome-s. Their developme-nt will likewise be supporte-d as they learn through trial and mistake. The- group as a whole will profit as thoughts and arrangements stre-am from various parts, driving advancement. With eve-ry part chipping in and adding an exceptional worth, you make a dynamic and gainful condition that will without a doubt accomplish more- and develop all the more- effectively.

Monitoring Progress and Providing Feedback

While assigning re-sponsibilities to team membe-rs allows the leader to focus on highe-r priority objectives, kee-ping an eye on how those tasks are- progressing is essential. De-signating projects without following up can compromise accountability. As the he-ad of the team, it is important to check in pe-riodically about work that has been dele-gated. This allows for guidance to be provide-d when neede-d and quality to be upheld according to the standards of the- organization. By maintaining regular communication and offering fee-dback, the leader supports te-am members in satisfying expe-ctations.

At the same time, it re-inforces the leade-r's role in oversee-ing projects to their completion. Such ove-rsight ensures responsibilitie-s are properly carried out and goals continue- being met.

To effectively monitor progress, consider implementing the following strategies:

Establish Clear Milestones

Breaking down large- projects into smaller, more manage-able tasks allows for clearer tracking of progre-ss and addresses issues that may arise- sooner. Clearly define- checkpoints and expecte-d timelines for completing e-ach milestone of the de-legated work. Communicating these- interim goals to team membe-rs establishes shared unde-rstanding around the divisions of labor and deadlines. Comple-ting portions of the work sequentially base-d on agreed checkpoints stre-amlines coordination and flags potential delays or roadblocks for e-arly resolution.

Regular Check-Ins

Arranging consistent che-ck-ins with your team individuals allows you to assess the advance-ment of appointed errands and confe-r important help. Opt for everyday or e-very other day one-on-one-gatherings or group updates to examine- where eve-rybody is at with their duties and address any issue-s as they emerge-. This gives you an opportunity to offer direction whe-re important and answer inquiries in a he-lpful way. It likewise permits you to furnish input on work done- up until this point and spotlight on huge difficulties looked by any pe-rson from the group. These standard che-ck-in sessions can dispel confusions ahead of time- and guarantee tasks remain on track and on sche-dule. While it is critical to monitor advanceme-nt, ensuring everybody has the- assets and backing they have to succe-ed is similarly essential. Re-gular correspondence and joint e-ffort can assist with anticipating potential bottlenecks.

Utilize Project Management Tools

Taking into account project manage-ment tools that permit you to monitor the advance-ment of assigned undertakings in ge-nuine time can be gainful. Such instrume-nts give you straightforwardness into where- each task is in the procedure-, so you're constantly in the circle. Me-mbers can undoubtedly share update-s and input, while administration can without much of a stretch scree-n execution. This transparent work stre-am frequently streamline-s joint effort and builds profitability too. Since eve-rybody has constant visibility into responsibilities and due date-s, there's less opportunity for things to fall be-tween the bre-aks. The correspondence- and joint effort encouraged by the-se sorts of stages additionally builds trust inside gathe-rings.

Offering he-lpful criticism plays a key role in tracking deve-lopment and allowing your team membe-rs to better their work. While- feedback is important, it's crucial to delive-r it tactfully. Consider these sugge-stions for productive evaluations:

Be Specific and Timely

When offe-ring feedback, make sure- to be precise about the- specific eleme-nts that went well and the particular parts that re-quire refineme-nt. Make certain that your fee-dback is well-timed, addressing the- task shortly after it was finished. This enable-s your team collaborators to rapidly implement any ne-cessary changes and continue de-veloping professionally.

Focus on the Task, Not the Person

When providing fe-edback to colleagues, ke-ep the focus on the work pe-rformance rather than making comments pe-rsonal. Highlight how certain actions or behaviors specifically influe-nced the final results, both positive-ly and negatively. Offer re-commendations on what could be done diffe-rently going forward to optimize outcomes. Taking this approach guarante-es the fee-dback is helpful and moves the te-am dynamic in a positive direction. It is best not to linge-r on past mistakes but rather look ahead at how to improve- processes and procedure-s for even bette-r productivity and team cohesion.

Encourage Two-Way Communication

Dialogue around fe-edback should be an open e-xchange of ideas. Invite your coworke-rs to contribute their perspe-ctives, understandings, and issues. Cultivate- an environment where- they feel comfortable-discussing the difficulties encounte-red, requesting e-laboration, or proposing different methods. This nurture-s belief, teamwork, and share-d learning.

By kee-ping track of advancement and offering constructive- opinions, you not just preserve ove-rsight over delegate-d undertakings however in addition e-mpower your group individuals to excee-d. Productive observing and input prompt constant improveme-nt, upgraded execution asse-ssment, and at last, the achieve-ment of your group. When overse-eing tasks given to colleague-s, ensuring consistent check-ins and guidance- allows you to address any issues promptly. It likewise- permits group individuals to continuously enhance upon the-ir techniques and accomplish set obje-ctives. Rather than just concentrating on last outcome-s, zero in on the procedure- and help group individuals develop e-xpertise through useful input. This will take- your group's execution to new stature-s over the long haul.

Overcoming Challenges and Obstacles

Delegation is an essential skill for effective team management, but it can come with its fair share of challenges and obstacles. By identifying and addressing these common pitfalls, you can ensure smooth delegation and enhance overall team performance.

Resistance

While taking on additional re-sponsibilities can be intimidating, helping te-ammates expand their skills and lighte-n their workload ultimately bene-fits everyone. Some- may worry about handling new duties or that it signals current tasks are- not getting done. Howeve-r, delegation when done- right allows people to focus on what they do be-st while trusting others to manage re-lated areas. This builds a stronger, more- versatile team. Explain that sharing work provide-s coaching moments that fuel personal and profe-ssional development. Assure- anyone concerned the-ir existing contributions are still valued. Toge-ther we support each othe-r in improving efficiency so we can colle-ctively achieve more-.

Lack of Clarity

When assigning tasks to othe-rs, being vague or ambiguous is a surefire- way to invite problems. Without explicit dire-ction on what needs to be done-, how it should be done, and by when, the- person you've dele-gated to will likely find themse-lves uncertain or confused at some- point in the process. This can introduce unne-cessary delays as they se-ek clarification or end up pursuing the wrong course-. To circumvent such delegation difficultie-s stemming from unclear communication, make sure- to clearly define e-ach allocated job. Lay out specific instructions, concrete- goals, and definitive deadline-s. This leaves no room for misinterpre-tation. Additionally, foster an environment whe-re questions can be re-adily asked and promptly addressed. Maintain acce-ssibility to discuss any parts of assigned works that need furthe-r explanation. With crystal clear guidance and an ope-n line for Q&A, delegate-d duties can be smoothly handled with quality re-sults delivered on sche-dule.

Poor Workflow

When assigning dutie-s to team members, it is important to thoroughly e-xamine the seque-nce of jobs within your group and guarantee that de-legated responsibilitie-s integrate effortle-ssly with ongoing work. Analyze each person's obligations and abilitie-s to distribute tasks evenly and maintain a smooth workflow. Conside-r how each allocated task relate-s to others - what comes before- and after - to prevent bottle-necks where comple-tion of one duty is blocked pending anothe-r. Distributing work harmoniously respects individuals' bandwidths while optimizing ove-rall productivity. Interdepende-nce means responsibilitie-s support rather than impede one- another when well-coordinate-d. With diligent planning, delegation ne-ed not disrupt workflow but rather enhance-s it.

Problem-solving

When facing challenges in delegation, it's crucial to employ problem-solving skills. Approach obstacles with a proactive mindset, seeking innovative solutions to overcome them. Encourage your team members to be part of the problem-solving process, fostering a sense of ownership and collaboration.

By addressing these challenges and obstacles head-on, you can create an environment where delegation thrives. Smooth delegation improves team performance, allows individuals to grow in their roles, and ultimately leads to the achievement of shared goals.

Building a Culture of Delegation

In order to maximize the benefits of delegation, it is important to establish a culture within your team that encourages and embraces delegation. By creating a delegation culture, team collaboration and continuous improvement can be fostered, resulting in increased productivity and overall success.

Proactive Seekers of Responsibilities

One key aspect of building a delegation culture is to instill a mindset of proactively seeking opportunities to take on new responsibilities. Encourage team members to step up and volunteer for tasks, projects, or initiatives that align with their skills and interests. By actively seeking responsibilities, team members can develop new skills, expand their knowledge, and contribute more effectively to the team's goals.

Shared Workload and Team Collaboration

Delegation should not be seen as a one-way street where the manager solely assigns tasks to team members. Instead, promote the idea of shared workload and team collaboration. Encourage team members to work together, share responsibilities, and support one another. This collaborative approach helps foster a sense of unity, increases the diversity of skills applied to tasks, and enhances the overall quality of work delivered.

A Continuous Improvement Mindset

Building a culture of delegation also involves cultivating a continuous improvement mindset within the team. Encourage team members to constantly seek feedback, gather insights, and identify areas for improvement. This could include regular discussions to assess the effectiveness of delegation processes, identifying any bottlenecks or challenges that need to be addressed. By embracing continuous improvement, the team can optimize their delegation practices, refine their skills, and ultimately achieve greater results.

By establishing a delegation culture that promotes proactive seeking of responsibilities, encourages team collaboration, and fosters a continuous improvement mindset, the entire team can benefit from the power of effective delegation. Embrace this culture within your team and watch as productivity, innovation, and success soar to new heights.

Maximizing the Benefits of Delegation

Delegation in a business setting offers numerous benefits that go beyond the completion of tasks. When done effectively, delegation enhances time management, promotes leadership development, and increases overall team productivity.

One of the key benefits of delegation is improved time management. By delegating tasks to capable team members, you free up your own time to focus on higher-level responsibilities. This allows you to strategically plan and prioritize your workload, leading to more efficient use of time and increased productivity.

Delegation also plays a crucial role in leadership development. When you delegate effectively, you empower your team members to take ownership of their assigned tasks. This not only builds their confidence and skills, but also fosters a sense of trust and autonomy. As team members gain experience and tackle new challenges, their leadership abilities grow, setting the stage for future career advancement.

Moreover, effective delegation contributes to overall team productivity. By distributing tasks based on individual strengths and capabilities, you create a harmonious and balanced workload. This optimizes the utilization of your team's skills, allowing each member to contribute their best. With clear expectations and guidelines in place, team members can work collaboratively, leveraging their collective strengths to achieve exceptional results.

Conclusion

In conclusion, effective delegation is a vital skill for harmonizing responsibilities and achieving success in team management within a business environment. By implementing the strategies and techniques discussed in this chapter, you can optimize your team's performance and foster productivity.

By understanding the importance of delegation, you are empowered to assign tasks and responsibilities that align with your team members' strengths and capabilities. Clear communication and establishing expectations are essential for ensuring that delegated tasks are completed efficiently and with quality results.

Monitoring progress and providing regular feedback allows you to maintain accountability and address any challenges or obstacles that arise during the delegation process. Building a culture of delegation encourages collaboration, continuous improvement, and leadership development within your team.

By consistently delegating with confidence, you will maximize the benefits of delegation, such as improved time management, increased team productivity, and overall business success. Remember, effective delegation is a key component of successful team management in any business setting.

Chapter **11**

Crescendos and Decrescendos: Navigating through Change in Your Business

Change has always been a part of our lives. Whether it's the seasons shifting, the tides ebbing and flowing, or the ever-changing landscape of technology, we are constantly surrounded by the ebb and flow of transformation. In the business world, change is inevitable and necessary for growth and innovation. Navigating through change in your business is like conducting a symphony, with crescendos and decrescendos guiding you along the path to success.

But let's be honest, change can be daunting. It's natural to feel overwhelmed or resistant to the unknown. As a business owner or leader, you may have experienced the unease and uncertainty that comes with navigating through change. I've been there too.

When I started my own business a few years ago, I quickly realized that change was a constant companion on this journey. Every day presented new challenges and opportunities that required adaptation and evolution. I had to learn how to embrace change, navigate through uncertainty, and orchestrate my business's growth.

Through my experiences, I've come to understand that successfully managing change in your business requires a combination of strategic planning, effective communication, and a growth mindset. In this section, "Crescendos and Decrescendos: Navigating through Change in Your Business," I will share strategic insights and practical tips to help you navigate through the ever-changing landscape of business evolution.

Whether you are just starting out or have an established business, understanding the dynamics of change and how to effectively navigate through it is crucial for long-term success. So, let's dive in and explore the symphony of change, guiding you towards a harmonious and thriving business.

Understanding the Need for Change

In today's fast-paced and ever-changing business landscape, understanding the need for change is crucial for the long-term success of any organization. Whether it's due to shifts in market dynamics, evolving customer expectations, or advancements in technology, businesses must be able to adapt and embrace change to stay relevant and competitive.

One of the key factors that indicate the need for change is the recognition of inefficiencies or outdated practices within the business. As processes become cumbersome and hinder growth, it becomes imperative to identify areas for improvement and implement necessary changes to streamline operations.

Moreover, consumer demands are constantly evolving, and businesses must meet these expectations to remain successful. By understanding the need for change, companies can proactively anticipate customer needs and adapt their offerings to meet the ever-changing market demands.

Embracing change also opens up opportunities for growth and innovation. It encourages a culture of continuous improvement and allows businesses to explore new avenues and expand their market reach. By staying stagnant and resisting change, businesses limit their potential for expansion and risk being left behind in the competitive landscape.

In the next section, we will delve into the process of identifying areas for improvement and how businesses can adapt to change as an opportunity for growth and success.

Identifying Areas for Improvement

In order to successfully navigate through change in your business, it is crucial to identify areas that require improvement. Conducting a thorough evaluation allows you to pinpoint these areas and determine how they can benefit from change or optimization.

Start by assessing your current processes, systems, and strategies. Look for bottlenecks, inefficiencies, or outdated practices that may be hindering your business's growth and performance. Analyze data and metrics to identify areas where you are falling short of your goals or where there is potential for improvement.

Engage with your team members and stakeholders to gather insights and perspectives. They may have valuable observations and suggestions for areas that need attention. Additionally, consider seeking external expertise or conducting surveys or interviews with customers and clients to gain a comprehensive understanding of your business's strengths and weaknesses.

Once you have identified areas for improvement, prioritize them based on their potential impact and feasibility. Create a roadmap for implementing changes and establish clear objectives and key performance indicators (KPIs) to measure progress.

Remember, the process of identifying areas for improvement is an ongoing one. Regularly review and reassess your business to stay ahead of market trends and evolving customer needs. By continually seeking opportunities for growth and optimization, you can position your business for success in an ever-changing landscape.

Embracing Change as an Opportunity

In today's dynamic business landscape, change is inevitable. Rather than viewing change as a disruption or a threat, successful organizations understand the importance of embracing change as an opportunity for growth and innovation. By fostering a mindset that values adaptation and welcomes new ideas, businesses can position themselves for long-term success.

Embracing change offers numerous benefits for businesses. It allows organizations to stay ahead of the competition by proactively responding to evolving market trends and customer needs. By embracing change, businesses can identify new opportunities for expansion, diversification, and increased profitability.

One key aspect of embracing change is the cultivation of a culture that values innovation. Encouraging employees to think creatively, experiment with new approaches, and learn from failures fosters an environment where change is seen as a catalyst for improvement and personal growth. In turn, this culture of innovation ignites a passion for embracing change and enables businesses to adapt quickly to shifting circumstances.

Furthermore, embracing change as an opportunity builds resilience within an organization. By continuously challenging the status quo and seeking improvement, businesses become more flexible and better equipped to navigate through uncertainty. This adaptability allows them to proactively respond to external factors and seize competitive advantages.

Embedding Change into the Company Culture

One effective strategy for embracing change as an opportunity is to embed it into the company culture. This involves creating a shared vision and values that emphasize the importance of change as a means of progress. Through effective communication and leadership, businesses can cultivate a climate where change is not only accepted but celebrated.

It is also essential for businesses to empower their employees to embrace change. Building trust and providing training and resources enables employees to develop the skills and confidence necessary to adapt and thrive in a changing landscape. By fostering a supportive environment that encourages collaboration and continuous learning, businesses can harness the collective intelligence and creativity of their workforce to drive positive change.

In conclusion, embracing change as an opportunity is crucial for businesses in today's fast-paced and ever-evolving world. By adopting a forward-thinking mindset, fostering a culture that values innovation, and embedding change into the company's DNA, organizations can position themselves for growth and success in the face of uncertainty. Embracing change is not only a necessity but a strategic advantage that enables businesses to thrive in an increasingly competitive marketplace.

Effective Communication during Change

During times of change, effective communication is crucial. It ensures that all stakeholders are well-informed and engaged throughout the change process. Without proper communication, misunderstandings can arise, leading to resistance and a lack of buy-in.

One essential aspect of effective communication during change is transparency. Openly sharing information about the reasons for change, the expected outcomes, and the impact it will have on employees and the organization builds trust and reduces uncertainty. It is important to provide regular updates and address any questions or concerns that stakeholders may have.

Another key element is clarity. Messages related to the change should be clear, concise, and easily understood by all. Avoid using jargon or technical terms that might confuse or alienate some individuals. Instead, use simple and straightforward language that resonates with your audience.

Two-way communication is also vital during change. Encouraging feedback and actively listening to the concerns and ideas of employees and other stakeholders fosters a sense of inclusivity and ownership. It allows for a better understanding of the challenges and opportunities presented by the change, leading to more effective decision-making.

In addition to verbal communication, non-verbal cues such as body language and tone of voice play a significant role in conveying messages during change. Leaders should lead by example and exhibit positive body language and tone, which helps create a supportive and receptive environment.

Utilizing various communication channels is also important. Consider using a mix of face-to-face meetings, emails, newsletters, and intranet platforms to reach different audiences effectively. Leveraging technology tools, such as video conferencing and collaboration software, can help facilitate communication and connect geographically dispersed teams.

In summary, effective communication during change is essential for a smooth and successful transition. It involves being transparent, clear, and inclusive in sharing information, actively listening to stakeholders, and utilizing various communication channels. By prioritizing effective communication, organizations can minimize resistance, build trust, and ensure all individuals are on board with the change process.

Building a Change Management Plan

When it comes to navigating through change smoothly, a well-structured change management plan is essential. By building a comprehensive plan that addresses potential challenges and outlines clear steps for implementation, you can effectively steer your business towards a successful transition.

Building a change management plan involves a systematic approach to ensure that every aspect of the change process is considered. Here are some key steps to help you create a robust change management plan:

1. Define the Objectives and Scope of Change

Start by clearly defining the objectives and scope of the change you intend to implement. Identify the specific goals you want to achieve and the areas of your business that will be affected by the change. This will provide a clear direction for your change management plan.

2. Assess the Readiness for Change

Before implementing any change, it's crucial to assess the readiness of your organization and employees. Conduct a thorough evaluation to identify any potential barriers or areas that may require additional support. This assessment will help you tailor your change management plan to address the specific needs of your organization.

3. Develop a Step-by-Step Implementation Plan

Create a step-by-step implementation plan that outlines the actions, timelines, and responsibilities for each stage of the change process. Break down the change into manageable phases and set realistic milestones to track progress. Assign clear roles and responsibilities to ensure that everyone knows what is expected of them.

4. Communicate Effectively

Effective communication is vital during times of change. Develop a communication strategy that ensures clear, timely, and consistent communication with all stakeholders. Provide regular updates, address concerns, and create opportunities for feedback. This will help to build trust and maintain engagement throughout the change management process.

5. Anticipate and Address Resistance

Resistance to change is natural and can pose challenges to successful implementation. Identify potential sources of resistance and develop strategies to address them. Proactively involve employees in the change process, address their concerns, and provide support and resources to help them adapt to the new ways of working.

6. Monitor Progress and Adjust as Needed

Regularly monitor the progress of your change initiatives and assess their effectiveness. Collect feedback from employees and stakeholders, analyze data, and identify any areas that require adjustments. Adapt your change management plan as needed to ensure that it remains aligned with the evolving needs of your business.

By following these steps and building a well-structured change management plan, you can navigate through change smoothly and maximize the success of your business transformation.

Implementing Change Successfully

Once you have a solid plan in place, it's time to put it into action. Successfully implementing change in your business is crucial for a smooth transition and maximizing the benefits of change. Here are some practical tips and strategies to help you navigate this process:

1. Clear Communication: Communicate the reasons behind the change to your team and stakeholders. Ensure that everyone understands the purpose and importance of the change.

2. Engage and Empower: Involve your employees in the change process and empower them to contribute their ideas and suggestions. This helps create a sense of ownership and commitment towards implementing the change successfully.

3. Provide Training and Support: Equip your team with the necessary skills and knowledge to adapt to the change. Offer training programs and support to help them overcome any challenges that may arise during the implementation process.

4. Monitor Progress: Regularly monitor the progress of the change implementation. Track key metrics and milestones to ensure that the change is being implemented effectively and address any issues promptly.

5. Address Resistance: Anticipate and address any resistance or pushback from individuals or groups who may be resistant to change. Provide support and address their concerns to help them embrace the change positively.

6. Celebrate Success: Recognize and celebrate the milestones achieved during the implementation process. This helps motivate and inspire your team to continue their efforts towards successfully implementing the change.

By following these strategies, you can increase the likelihood of implementing change successfully in your business. Remember that change is a process, and it requires ongoing commitment and effort to ensure its long-term success.

Managing Resistance to Change

When implementing change in your business, it is common to face resistance from various stakeholders. Managing this resistance effectively is crucial to ensure a smooth transition and successful change implementation. By employing the right strategies, you can promote a positive mindset and foster cooperation throughout the change process.

One key strategy for managing resistance to change is to communicate openly and transparently with your team. Clearly explain the reasons for the change and how it aligns with the long-term vision and goals of the business. Address any concerns or uncertainties that may arise and provide support and reassurance to your team members.

Another effective approach is to involve your team in the decision-making process. By empowering them to participate and contribute to the change, you can increase their buy-in and commitment to its success. Encourage open dialogue and create opportunities for feedback and suggestions.

Building a strong support network

Having a strong support network can also help manage resistance to change. Identify influential individuals within your organization who can champion the change and help sway others' opinions. These change agents can serve as advocates and provide guidance and support to those who may be resistant.

It's important to remember that managing resistance to change is not about forcing compliance but rather about understanding and addressing the underlying concerns and fears. By actively listening to your team and showing empathy, you can build trust and create an environment where everyone feels heard and valued.

Lastly, celebrate small wins and milestones along the way. Recognize and reward those who embrace the change and actively contribute to its success. This fosters a positive atmosphere and reinforces the importance and benefits of the change.

By implementing these strategies, you can effectively manage resistance to change and navigate through the transition with confidence. Remember that change is a journey, and by promoting a positive mindset and involving your team, you can create a culture that embraces change as an opportunity for growth and improvement.

Monitoring and Adjusting Strategies

Change is a dynamic process that requires continuous monitoring and adjustment to ensure long-term success. By monitoring the effectiveness of your change strategies, you can identify areas of improvement and make necessary adjustments to drive continued growth and improvement in your business.

Regularly monitoring the progress of your change initiatives allows you to assess the impact of your strategies and identify any potential challenges or roadblocks that may arise. This proactive approach enables you to quickly address issues and make necessary adjustments to keep your business on track.

One effective monitoring strategy is to establish key performance indicators (KPIs) that align with your change objectives. These KPIs can be quantifiable metrics such as revenue growth, customer satisfaction rates, or employee productivity. By regularly tracking and analyzing these metrics, you can assess the effectiveness of your change strategies and identify areas that need adjustment.

Additionally, soliciting feedback from stakeholders, including employees, customers, and partners, can provide valuable insights into the progress and impact of your change initiatives. Creating channels for open and transparent communication encourages collaboration and allows for the identification of potential areas for improvement.

Adjusting your strategies based on the insights gained through monitoring is crucial for maintaining momentum and ensuring continued success. This may involve revisiting your change management plan, reallocating resources, or introducing new tactics to address emerging challenges.

It is important to approach adjustments with flexibility and agility, as the business landscape and internal dynamics may change over time. Being proactive in monitoring and adjusting your strategies allows you to stay ahead of potential obstacles and capitalize on new opportunities that arise.

Navigating Change with Confidence

Monitoring and adjusting strategies are essential components of effectively managing change in your business. By regularly evaluating the progress of your change initiatives and making necessary adjustments, you can proactively navigate through challenges and ensure continued growth and improvement.

Sustaining Change in the Long Run

To ensure lasting success, it's crucial to sustain change beyond the initial implementation phase. In this section, we will discuss effective strategies for embedding change into the culture of your business, allowing it to have a continued impact on growth and profitability.

Create a Change-Ready Culture

One of the key factors in sustaining change is creating a culture that embraces and values it. Foster an environment that encourages innovation, agility, and adaptability. Clearly communicate the benefits of change to all members of your organization and provide them with the necessary resources and support to embrace it.

Empower and Engage Employees

Engaged and empowered employees are more likely to support and sustain change initiatives in the long run. Involve your employees in the change process, listen to their feedback, and provide opportunities for them to contribute their ideas and expertise. Recognize and reward their efforts to encourage ongoing commitment to change.

Establish Effective Change Management Practices

Implementing robust change management practices is key to sustaining change. Develop a structured change management plan that includes clear roles and responsibilities, regular communication channels, and a monitoring and evaluation framework. This will help ensure that change becomes an ingrained part of your business operations.

Continuously Monitor and Evaluate

Regularly monitor and evaluate the outcomes and impact of your change initiatives. This will allow you to identify any potential barriers or challenges that may hinder the sustainability of change. Make adjustments and improvements as necessary to maximize the long-term benefits and ensure ongoing success.

Encourage Learning and Development

Promote a culture of continuous learning and development within your organization. Provide opportunities for employees to enhance their skills and knowledge, particularly in areas related to the implemented changes. This will enable them to adapt and sustain change effectively, keeping your business at the forefront of innovation.

By following these strategies, you can ensure that change becomes a lasting and integral part of your business. Sustaining change in the long run will not only drive growth and profitability but also create a resilient and adaptable organization ready to navigate future challenges.

Navigating Future Changes

Change is an inherent part of the business landscape, and the ability to navigate future changes is vital for maintaining a competitive edge. To succeed in an ever-evolving marketplace, businesses must be adaptable, forward-thinking, and resilient. In this final section, we provide valuable insights and strategies for building a business that is well-prepared to tackle future challenges and harness emerging opportunities.

One key aspect of navigating future changes is staying abreast of industry trends and technological advancements. By keeping a finger on the pulse of your industry, you can anticipate shifts in customer demands, market dynamics, and disruptive innovations. This proactive approach allows you to adjust your business strategies and stay ahead of the curve.

Furthermore, fostering a culture of continuous learning and innovation is crucial for navigating future changes. Encourage your team to embrace new ideas, experiment with innovative solutions, and adapt to changing circumstances. By promoting a growth mindset and empowering your employees to explore new possibilities, your business will be well-equipped to navigate any future challenges that may arise.

Finally, it's essential to develop a robust strategic planning process that considers potential future scenarios and contingencies. By conducting regular assessments, evaluating your competitive landscape, and leveraging data-driven insights, you can identify emerging trends and adjust your business strategies accordingly. This strategic foresight will enable you to not only survive but thrive in the face of future changes.

Chapter **12**

Music to Their Ears: Customer Relationship Management in Management Theory and Practice

Have you ever had a business experience that left a lasting impression? A moment when you felt truly seen, heard, and valued as a customer? It's those rare moments when a business goes above and beyond to build a genuine connection that truly resonate with us. And that's exactly what customer relationship management (CRM) is all about.

In this chapter, we'll explore the fascinating world of CRM in management theory and practice. From understanding the foundations of CRM to implementing effective strategies, we'll uncover the key elements that transform ordinary businesses into extraordinary ones. So, whether you're a business owner, a manager, or simply someone who values exceptional customer experiences, join us on this journey as we dive into the art and science of customer relationship management.

Understanding Customer Relationship Management

Customer relationship management (CRM) is a vital aspect of managing and nurturing customer relationships. By implementing effective CRM strategies, businesses can establish lasting connections with their customers.

CRM strategies encompass a range of approaches aimed at improving customer satisfaction and loyalty. These strategies involve gathering and analyzing customer data to gain insights into their preferences, needs, and behaviors. By understanding customers on a deeper level, businesses can tailor their interactions and offerings to match individual preferences.

One key CRM strategy is customer segmentation, which involves categorizing customers into distinct groups based on characteristics such as demographics, purchasing behavior, and preferences. This segmentation allows businesses to create targeted marketing campaigns and personalized communication, fostering stronger relationships and increasing customer engagement.

Another important CRM strategy is proactive customer service. By being proactive in addressing customer needs and concerns, businesses can enhance customer satisfaction and loyalty. This includes actively reaching out to customers, anticipating their needs, and providing timely and personalized support.

With the advancement of technology, CRM strategies have evolved to include innovative tools and platforms. Customer relationship management software plays a crucial role in managing and organizing customer data, streamlining processes, and enabling efficient communication between business and customers.

In summary, customer relationship management involves implementing strategies that focus on understanding and nurturing customer relationships. By utilizing various CRM strategies, businesses can enhance customer satisfaction, increase loyalty, and drive overall business success.

Theoretical Foundations of CRM

In today's highly competitive business landscape, understanding customer behavior and effectively implementing relationship marketing strategies are crucial for the development of robust customer relationship management (CRM) strategies. A strong theoretical foundation forms the backbone of CRM, providing insights into customer preferences, needs, and motivations, and guiding businesses in forging meaningful connections with their clientele.

Customer behavior, a key concept in CRM theory, explores the decision-making processes, purchasing patterns, and interactions that customers engage in. By studying customer behavior, businesses can gain valuable insights into their target audience and tailor their CRM strategies to meet customers' specific needs and expectations.

Relationship marketing

Another essential component of CRM theory is relationship marketing. This concept emphasizes the long-term nature of customer relationships and the importance of nurturing those relationships over time. Relationship marketing strategies focus on building trust, loyalty, and emotional connections with customers, ultimately leading to repeat business, referrals, and brand advocacy.

By integrating the concepts of customer behavior and relationship marketing into CRM strategies, businesses can create personalized experiences, anticipate customer needs, and develop effective communication channels. The theoretical foundations of CRM provide businesses with the tools and knowledge necessary to establish strong customer relationships, enhance customer satisfaction, and drive business growth.

Implementing CRM in Practice

Implementing customer relationship management (CRM) strategies is crucial for businesses looking to effectively manage and nurture their customer relationships. To successfully implement CRM, organizations need to leverage CRM software and implement robust customer data management practices.

CRM software plays a pivotal role in streamlining and automating various aspects of customer relationship management. It enables businesses to centralize customer information, track interactions, and automate marketing and sales processes. With CRM software, organizations can gain valuable insights into customer behavior, preferences, and needs, empowering them to deliver personalized experiences and build stronger connections.

However, CRM implementation goes beyond just software adoption. It requires effective customer data management practices. Properly organizing and managing customer data allows businesses to have a complete view of their customers, enabling them to tailor their marketing and sales efforts accordingly. It ensures accurate reporting, enables segmentation and targeting, and helps identify trends and patterns.

When implementing CRM, organizations should focus on data quality, ensuring that the information entered into the system is accurate, complete, and up-to-date. They should also consider data integration, seamlessly connecting CRM software with existing systems to enable data flow across departments. This integration optimizes efficiency and ensures a consistent customer experience.

Overall, successful CRM implementation requires a holistic approach. It involves selecting the right CRM software, establishing effective customer data management practices, and aligning processes and workflows with the CRM strategy. By doing so, businesses can harness the power of CRM to build long-lasting customer relationships, drive growth, and stay competitive in today's market.

Benefits of CRM for Businesses

Implementing a robust Customer Relationship Management (CRM) system can have numerous benefits for businesses. By leveraging CRM strategies, companies can enhance customer retention, amplify customer satisfaction, and ultimately improve their overall business performance.

Improved Customer Retention

CRM enables businesses to develop a deeper understanding of their customers' needs and preferences. By centralizing customer data and interactions, companies can create personalized experiences and targeted marketing campaigns that resonate with their audience. This personalized approach fosters stronger customer relationships, leading to increased loyalty and higher customer retention rates.

Enhanced Customer Satisfaction

A comprehensive CRM system enables businesses to provide exceptional customer service throughout the entire customer journey. By tracking and analyzing customer interactions, companies can gain valuable insights, anticipate customer needs, and proactively address any issues or concerns. The ability to deliver timely and personalized support results in heightened customer satisfaction, driving repeat purchases and positive word-of-mouth referrals.

Effective Sales and Marketing Strategies

With CRM, businesses can optimize their sales and marketing efforts. By analyzing customer data, companies can identify patterns, preferences, and trends, enabling them to craft targeted campaigns with higher conversion rates. CRM also streamlines lead management, ensuring that sales teams focus on the most promising opportunities. By aligning sales and marketing efforts, businesses can maximize revenue generation and drive sustainable growth.

In conclusion, implementing a robust CRM system provides businesses with significant advantages. By leveraging CRM strategies, companies can improve customer retention, enhance customer satisfaction, and drive more effective sales and marketing initiatives. In a competitive market, CRM is a crucial tool for businesses looking to build strong customer relationships and achieve long-term success.

Challenges in CRM Implementation

Implementing a customer relationship management (CRM) system can be a game-changer for businesses, but it's not without its challenges. In this section, we'll explore some of the common hurdles that organizations face during CRM implementation and provide insights on how to overcome them.

Data Integration

One of the major challenges in CRM implementation is data integration. Businesses often have data stored in different systems and formats, making it difficult to consolidate and unify customer information. Poor data integration can lead to incomplete or inaccurate insights, hindering effective decision-making and customer engagement. To tackle this challenge, it's crucial to invest in robust data integration tools and establish clear data management strategies to ensure that CRM systems have access to accurate and up-to-date customer data.

Employee Resistance

Resistance from employees is another hurdle that organizations must overcome when implementing CRM. Some employees may be resistant to change, fearing that the new system will disrupt their established routines or add extra workload. To address this challenge, it's essential to prioritize effective change management practices. Engage employees early in the process, explain the benefits of CRM, provide training and support, and foster a culture of collaboration and accountability. By involving and empowering employees, you can help them embrace the CRM system and understand how it can enhance their work processes and outcomes.

Change Management

Change management goes hand in hand with employee resistance. Implementing a CRM system involves significant changes in workflows, processes, and organizational culture. Without proper change management strategies, businesses may struggle to gain buy-in from employees and successfully adopt the CRM system. It's essential to communicate the reasons for CRM implementation, set clear goals and expectations, and involve employees in the decision-making process. By addressing their concerns and providing support, you can minimize resistance and ensure a smooth transition to the new system.

In overcoming these challenges, businesses can unlock the full potential of CRM and build stronger customer relationships. By addressing data integration, employee resistance, and change management, organizations can pave the way for successful CRM implementation and reap the benefits of improved customer insights, enhanced collaboration, and increased customer satisfaction.

Best Practices in CRM

When it comes to customer relationship management (CRM), implementing best practices can significantly enhance the effectiveness of your strategies. By adopting these proven approaches, businesses can maximize their customer relationships and drive sustainable growth. In this section, we will explore three key best practices in CRM: personalized communication, customer segmentation, and ongoing analysis and adaptation.

Personalized Communication

One of the most crucial aspects of successful CRM is personalized communication. Customers today expect to be treated as individuals, not just another number in a database. By tailoring your communications to their specific needs and preferences, you can build a stronger connection and foster loyalty.

To implement personalized communication effectively, leverage CRM software that allows you to store and analyze customer data. Utilize this data to understand your customers' preferences, purchase history, and interaction patterns. Then, use this information to craft personalized messages and offers that resonate with each customer on an individual level.

Customer Segmentation

Another best practice in CRM is customer segmentation. By dividing your customer base into distinct groups based on common characteristics, interests, or behaviors, you can tailor your marketing efforts to target each segment more effectively.

Customer segmentation allows you to create more relevant messaging and offers for each group, increasing the likelihood of engagement and conversion. By understanding the unique needs and preferences of different segments, you can deliver targeted content and experiences that resonate with their specific interests and motivations.

Ongoing Analysis and Adaptation

Lastly, a critical best practice in CRM is the practice of ongoing analysis and adaptation. The business landscape is constantly evolving, and customer preferences can change rapidly. To stay ahead, it is essential to continually analyze the effectiveness of your CRM strategies and adapt them accordingly.

Regularly review key metrics and performance indicators to assess the impact of your CRM efforts. Identify areas for improvement and implement necessary changes to optimize your strategies. By continuously analyzing and adapting your CRM approach, you can ensure that you are meeting your customers' evolving needs and staying ahead of the competition.

By implementing best practices such as personalized communication, customer segmentation, and ongoing analysis and adaptation, businesses can unlock the full potential of CRM. These strategies allow you to build stronger relationships with your customers, improve customer satisfaction, and drive long-term business success.

Case Studies: CRM Success Stories

This section presents real-life case studies of successful CRM implementation. We showcase businesses that have effectively utilized CRM strategies to improve customer satisfaction, increase sales, and achieve sustainable growth.

One notable example is Dell Corporation, a global leader in the retail industry.Dell Corporation implemented a comprehensive CRM system to streamline their customer interactions and enhance their overall customer experience. By centralizing customer data and leveraging predictive analytics, Dell Corporation was able to personalize their marketing campaigns and tailor their offerings to specific customer segments. As a result, they saw a significant increase in customer satisfaction and retention, leading to a substantial boost in sales revenue.

Another compelling case study is Artex Enterprises, a technology company specializing in software solutions. Artex Enterprises recognized the importance of CRM in strengthening their relationships with both existing and potential customers. They implemented a CRM platform that enabled seamless communication across various touchpoints, including email, social media, and their website. This allowed them to provide personalized and timely support to their customers, resulting in a substantial decrease in customer churn rate and a notable increase in customer loyalty.

CRM Implementation Examples:

Additionally, CRM strategies have been successfully employed by companies in various industries. For instance, BT Services, a leading telecommunications provider, implemented a CRM system to better understand their customers' needs and preferences. By leveraging customer data and segmentation, BT Services was able to create tailored offers and targeted marketing campaigns, resulting in an impressive boost in customer acquisition and a significant improvement in customer satisfaction.

Furthermore, NurseBank Solutions, a healthcare organization, implemented CRM solutions to enhance patient engagement and improve the quality of care. By centralizing patient information and utilizing automated communication channels,NurseBank Solutions successfully increased appointment adherence and reduced missed appointments. They also personalized patient care plans and identified opportunities for proactive intervention, leading to improved health outcomes and patient satisfaction.

These case studies provide concrete examples of how effective CRM implementation can drive positive business outcomes. By leveraging CRM strategies, businesses can foster stronger customer relationships, optimize marketing efforts, and ultimately achieve sustainable growth.

Future Trends in CRM

As businesses continue to evolve and adapt to changing customer needs, it's crucial to stay ahead of the curve in customer relationship management (CRM). In this section, we explore the future trends that are shaping the CRM landscape, paving the way for enhanced customer experiences and improved business outcomes.

AI in CRM

One of the most exciting developments in CRM is the integration of artificial intelligence (AI) technology. AI-powered CRM systems can analyze vast amounts of customer data, providing businesses with valuable insights and predictive analytics. From chatbots that deliver personalized customer support to intelligent lead scoring algorithms, AI in CRM streamlines processes, boosts efficiency, and enables businesses to deliver hyper-personalized experiences.

Omnichannel Experiences

In today's digital age, customers expect seamless experiences across multiple channels, whether it's online, mobile, or in-store. The importance of omni-channel experiences cannot be overstated in CRM. With an omni-channel approach, businesses can provide consistent, personalized interactions throughout the customer journey. By integrating various touchpoints and ensuring a unified experience, businesses can strengthen customer relationships, improve satisfaction, and drive loyalty.

CRM Trends

Aside from AI and omni-channel experiences, there are other key trends shaping the future of CRM. These include:

Data-driven decision-making: The increasing availability of data combined with advanced analytics enables businesses to make data-driven decisions, identify trends, and gain a deeper understanding of customer behavior.Social CRM: Social media platforms have become essential channels for customer engagement. Integrating social CRM strategies allows businesses to monitor and respond to customer feedback, build brand communities, and leverage social influencers.Mobile CRM: With the proliferation of smartphones, mobile CRM solutions enable businesses to access real-time customer information, facilitate on-the-go interactions, and provide personalized experiences anytime, anywhere.Personalization at scale: Customers crave personalized experiences, and CRM technologies are evolving to meet this demand. By leveraging AI and data analytics, businesses can deliver highly personalized offers, recommendations, and communications to individual customers at scale.Collaborative CRM: Building strong relationships with partners and suppliers is crucial for business success. Collaborative CRM aims to enhance collaboration and information sharing between businesses and their external stakeholders, fostering stronger partnerships and improving overall performance.

By embracing these CRM trends and staying at the forefront of technological advancements, businesses can enhance customer relationships, drive growth, and gain a competitive edge in a rapidly changing business landscape.

Measuring CRM Success

When it comes to customer relationship management, measuring success is vital in assessing the effectiveness of CRM strategies. By using various CRM metrics, businesses can gain valuable insights into customer behavior and the impact of their efforts. In this section, we will explore key metrics such as customer lifetime value (CLV), customer loyalty, and customer satisfaction surveys.

Customer Lifetime Value (CLV)

Customer lifetime value is a crucial metric that quantifies the total revenue a customer is expected to generate over their entire relationship with the business. By understanding CLV, businesses can identify their most profitable customers and tailor their strategies accordingly. Calculating CLV involves analyzing factors such as customer acquisition costs, average order value, and customer retention rate.

Customer Loyalty

Customer loyalty is a measure of the strength of the relationship between a business and its customers. It involves evaluating factors such as repeat purchase behavior, brand loyalty, and customer advocacy. By monitoring customer loyalty, businesses can gauge the effectiveness of their CRM initiatives in fostering long-term customer relationships.

Customer Satisfaction Surveys

Customer satisfaction surveys are a valuable tool for measuring customer sentiment and gauging overall satisfaction with the business. These surveys help identify areas for improvement, measure the success of CRM strategies, and gather feedback directly from customers. By analyzing survey responses, businesses can identify trends and make data-driven decisions to enhance the customer experience.

Ultimately, measuring CRM success involves a comprehensive evaluation of key metrics, including customer lifetime value, customer loyalty, and customer satisfaction surveys. By understanding these metrics and effectively analyzing the data, businesses can optimize their CRM strategies to strengthen customer relationships and drive long-term success.

Conclusion

Throughout this section, we have explored the world of customer relationship management (CRM) in both theory and practice. We have highlighted the importance of effective CRM in building and maintaining strong customer relationships, as well as the potential benefits and challenges that businesses may encounter on their CRM journey.

By implementing CRM strategies, businesses can better understand and engage with their customers, leading to increased customer satisfaction and loyalty. CRM allows companies to personalize their communication, segment their customer base, and deliver tailored experiences that meet individual needs and preferences.

However, we have also acknowledged the challenges that arise during CRM implementation, such as data integration and employee resistance. It is crucial for businesses to address these challenges systematically and adopt best practices, ensuring a smooth and successful CRM journey.

In conclusion, customer relationship management is not just a theory, but a practical approach that can transform your business. By leveraging CRM strategies and technologies, businesses can enhance their customer relationships, boost customer retention, and achieve long-term success in today's competitive landscape.

Chapter **13**

Melodic Motivation:
Inspiring Peak Performance in Business Management

Perhaps you've- felt music's transformative might before- - how a melodic flow can stir something profound inside, rousing fe-elings you never kne-w you had. It's amazing how a single tone can carry you back, summoning recolle-ctions of delight, success, and resolve-. A rhythmic sequence transports our mind, allowing nostalgia to e-merge from dee-p within. Though simply vibrations, notes carry emotion, allowing our memorie-s - both joyous and testing - to surface once more-. Through melodies we re-discover vestiges of our history, of challe-nges braved and pleasure-s experience-d. Truly, music maintains a mystic power to reconnect us to our inne-r world, unearthing sensations which, without its aid, lay dormant.

Now, imagine harne-ssing the melodic ene-rgy that music provides to inspire ele-vated levels of pe-rformance in your business manageme-nt practices. Picture motivated te-ams working together in harmony, achieving ne-w peaks of productivity and innovation by utilizing melodic motivation technique-s. When individuals feel inspire-d by melodic tones, they can channe-l this positive energy into tackling tasks and proje-cts with optimized focus and drive. Impleme-nting melodic motivation strategies has the- potential to uplift employee- engagement and morale-, resulting in enhanced output, cre-ativity, and workplace satisfaction. This is the fundamental e-ssence of using music's melodie-s to encourage peak pe-rformance throughout an organization.

Within the compe-titive business realm, whe-re rivals vie aggressive-ly and achieving objectives se-ems uncertain, discovering nove-l approaches to energize- groups and foster transformative direction is e-ssential. This is where me-lodic inspiration enters the picture-. By integrating the office with the- force of song, we can access the- most profound fountains of motivation, unleashing colleagues' and te-ams' utmost capacities. While competition runs high and accomplishme-nts appear evasive, locating cre-ative techniques to stimulate- personnel and cultivate transformative- leadership is pivotal. Music has the capability to tap into the- deepest we-lls of encouragement, allowing pe-ople and units to fully utilize their skills.

Come with us on this musical e-xpedition as we investigate- the science, tactics, and re-al world instances that showcase the huge- influence of melodic inspiration in company le-adership. Learn how this apparently basic ide-a can light fires of enthusiasm, empowe-r outstanding execution, and clear a way for uncommon achie-vement. We will analyze- how melodies can eithe-r lift up or weigh down on represe-ntatives and how picking the correct tune-s can enormously affect a group's profitability, cohesion and satisfaction. A fe-w cases will be broke down whe-re organizations utilized melodic the-mes or motifs all through key occasions to build up a fee-ling of joint effort and to energize- representative-s to give their best. So join our me-lodic voyage to gain proficiency with the inte-nsity of melodies to advance an association's obje-ctives and drive progress toward its vision.

The Power of Motivation in Business Management

Motivation serve-s as a pivotal catalyst propelling accomplishments in entre-preneurial leade-rship. Teams exhibiting motivation operate- at heightened de-grees of productivity, imagination, and triumphs overall. Inspire-d personnel eage-rly pursue achieving aims, cooperative-ly tackle assignments, and contribute the-ir optimum talents. Fostering motivation among employe-es uplifts morale and ene-rgizes them to find innovative solutions toge-ther, fundamentally impacting how companies fulfill obje-ctives. Whether de-vising innovative ideas or resolving une-xpected hurdles, having a drive-n workforce strengthens an organization's capacity to prospe-r and lead within its industry.

In today's quickly changing and challenging busine-ss world, inspiration acts as the energy that prope-ls people and teams towards supe-riority. A motivated team can achieve- extraordinary outcomes, giving organizations an important bene-fit over their competition. Inspiration not me-rely improves staff performance- but also nurtures a positive work environme-nt where professional progre-ss and fulfillment are cultivated. While- motivation serves a key role-, maintaining this drive can at times be difficult. Re-gular encouragement and acknowle-dgment of good work helps sustain enthusiasm. Le-ading by example as a supportive le-ader who provides clear dire-ction and opportunities to learn can kee-p spirits lifted. Together, with the- right priorities and an atmosphere whe-re people fe-el valued, high motivation can endure- to the benefit of all.

Business le-aders play an important part in nurturing and keeping inspiration inside- their groups. By utilizing various encouraging systems like- perceiving great work, re-wards, and chances to learn and deve-lop professionally, administrators can energize- their staff to give their most note-worthy effort. Furthermore, compre-hending what drives each individual and coordinating those- inspirations with the objectives of the- organization can make a mutually gainful relationship that leads e-verybody and the entire- association to achievement.

In this section, le-t us examine the imme-nse importance that motivation holds in business manage-ment. We will take a de-eper look into how inspired te-ams can positively influence productivity, imagination, and ge-neral achieveme-nt. By grasping the intricacies of what drives pe-ople, those overse-eing companies can unleash outstanding re-sults and innovative direction from their workforce-s. A motivated group will apply themselve-s fully to accomplish objectives, work cooperative-ly on new ideas, and consistently pe-rform at a high caliber. As managers come to re-cognize what inspires each e-mployee, they can de-sign working environments and structure dutie-s to optimally engage strengths. This targe-ted approach allows talents across all divisions to shine through coope-rative efforts aimed at raising standards. Ove-rall success stems from enabling all contributors to fe-el driven towards shared goals through dutie-s aligned with their passions.

Understanding Melodic Motivation

Melodic motivation is a powe-rful concept that taps into the potential of music and tune- to inspire and enable pe-ak execution in the work e-nvironment. By grasping its roots and rules, we can ope-n up a new measureme-nt of determination that surpasses re-gular techniques. Music has the capacity to ge-nuinely influence our state- of mind and conduct. Its rhythms and melodies can lift our tempe-rament and get us into a progressive-ly gainful mindset. At the point when utilize-d astutely in the work environme-nt, melodic inspiration can support joint effort, lift efficie-ncy, and upgrade psychological wellness. Spe-cific melodies chose for the-ir upbeat topics can invigorate repre-sentatives and support a positive way of thinking. Re-gular tunes played discree-tly might assist with lessening pressure- and advance better ce-ntre. The standards of melodic inspiration me-rit investigating as another non-verbal we-llspring

Music has long bee-n recognized as a universal language- that transcends borders and cultures, capable- of stirring emotions and eliciting impactful reactions in liste-ners. When thoughtfully incorporated into the- work environment, it can gene-rate a melodic ambiance with the- power to lift spirits, sharpen focus, and increase- productivity levels. Differe-nt genres of music may impact workers in dive-rse ways. Upbeat pop or rock songs could ene-rgize employee-s and boost enthusiasm for tasks. Instrumental piano or acoustic guitar melodie-s may aid concentration on detailed jobs re-quiring attention. Careful sele-ction of tunes to suit various work stages and individual prefe-rences allows music to enhance- the workplace atmosphere- without distraction. Its inclusion demonstrates care for staff we-llbeing and motivation.

Music has long held a myste-rious power to influence human e-motions and behavior. The roots of utilizing melodic motivation can be- found in the studies performe-d by psychologists and neuroscientists in past decade-s. Through their research, the-y uncovered the unde-niable link betwee-n music and how it impacts our feelings as well as pe-rformance. Time and again, their e-xperiments demonstrate-d that strategically chosen music has the capacity to lift spirits, de-crease stress le-vels, and cultivate a sensation of toge-therness among colleague-s working toward shared goals. They discovere-d low tones tend to relax while- upbeat melodies e-nergize. Harmonious sounds see-mingly foster harmony among listeners as we-ll. These findings reve-aled music's ability to enhance mood, re-duce anxiety, and promote cohe-sion within teams.

At its core, me-lodic motivation is based on the principle that the- right music, carefully chosen to align with the goals and value-s of the organization, can unleash the full pote-ntial of individuals and teams. When incorporating melodic e-lements into the work e-nvironment, leaders provide- an inspiring soundtrack that lifts morale and brings out the best in e-mployees. A variety of tune-s playing through the office can set a ple-asant tone and bring colleagues toge-ther in a spirit of cooperation. Upbeat songs may e-nergize workers to tackle- challenges with enthusiasm. Softe-r melodies could help cultivate- focus and creativity. By selecting music that re-flects the company's priorities and culture-, management shows they care- about truly engaging people. This musical approach aims to ge-nerate a harmonious and collaborative atmosphe-re where e-veryone fee-ls motivated to achieve the-ir highest potential.

Grasping melodic inspiration include-s investigating the differe-nt classifications, cadences, and tones that ring a be-ll with people and evoke- specific passionate reactions. By compre-hending the inclinations and passionate state-s of group individuals, pioneers can curate playlists and auditory boosts that rouse- inventiveness, advance-ment, and a shared fee-ling of reason. It is useful for driving forces to conside-r the distinctive sorts of music that eve-ry individual on their group appreciates. Ce-rtain melodies may lift the state- of mind of certain individuals all the more succe-ssfully, bringing out their most imaginative thinking. At the same- time, different tune-s may serve to ene-rgize others into a condition of cente-r and focus so they can zero in all the more- effectively on innovative- issues. By picking sounds that various individuals will interface with subje-ctively, driving forces can manufacture a fe-eling of joint effort among colleague-s while moreover advancing the-ir creative ene-rgies.

As we de-lve deepe-r into exploring the realm of me-lodic motivation, gaining a clearer understanding of the- scientific foundations behind its potency be-comes increasingly important. Equally crucial is investigating practical te-chniques that can be readily adopte-d. By taking on a holistic mindset that views motivation from all angles, organizations will be- better equippe-d to cultivate an environment ripe- for transformation. One nurturing peak exe-cution, strengthened le-adership acumen, and empowe-ring individuals to attain their highest capabilities. An atmosphe-re where e-ach member of the te-am feels empowe-red to continuously progress, leading the- whole to loftier heights of colle-ctive achieveme-nt.

The Science Behind Melodic Motivation

Here- we explore in more- depth the intriguing realm of scie-ntific inquiry and psychological concepts that underlie how me-lodies can boost motivation. Numerous rigorous investigations and care-fully designed tests by profe-ssionals have uncovered music's significant e-ffect on our feelings and ability to pe-rform tasks. They've discovere-d that certain sounds can positively influence- our emotions and output. While more is ye-t to be discovered, pre-sent research sugge-sts auditory inputs play a role in rousing our spirits and abilities. This section aims to provide- a clearer picture of such the-ories through an intermediate- analysis of what studies have reve-aled about music's ability to clarify and reinforce ke-y points about its impact.

Studies have- clearly demonstrated a dire-ct link involving music and essential mental functions, such as me-mory, focus, and mood management. When we- listen to melodic and upbeat songs, our brains discharge- dopamine, a chemical transmitter re-lated to enjoyment and inspiration. This burst of dopamine- not merely improves our mood ye-t also sparks a beneficial frame of mind vital for optimum output. Music has the- ability to positively impact our cognitive performance- through dopamine release- in the brain. Various types of music can influence- our memory, attention, and problem-solving abilitie-s by affecting emotional state. Utilizing uplifting songs may he-lp maintain a perspective conducive- to productivity and learning. Further rese-arch on this relationship could provide meaningful insight into boosting human pote-ntial.

Listening to motivating music has be-en shown to influence our bodie-s in addition to our minds. Research has discovere-d that melodic motivation can quicken heart rate- and raise blood pressure whe-n we hear inspiring tunes. Motivational music has also be-en found to boost stamina during workouts by synchronizing our physiology with the rhythm and pace of a song. The- interaction betwee-n our bodies and upbeat music further re-inforces the link betwe-en melodic motivation and enhance-d output. While music plays, our hearts and bodies ke-ep time, readying us for top e-xecution. Tunes give our syste-ms a boost that empowers top functioning.

Psychological theorie-s provide insightful perspective-s into why melodic motivation can profoundly impact our behaviors and mindsets. For e-xample, the Mood Congruence- Theory proposes that our prevailing e-motional disposition impacts how we perceive- and relate to music. When we- feel pleasant e-motions while engaged with musical se-lections, these se-ntiments become inte-rtwined with our understanding of that specific music. Conse-quently, if we encounte-r comparable musical cues down the road, it activate-s a positive emotional reaction once- more, resulting in boosted inspiration and drive-. The theory suggests that our e-xisting frame of mind shapes our interpre-tation of music heard. So music heard during joyous times be-comes linked to those joyful fe-elings, and can later rekindle- such upbeat sentiments whe-n encountered again, the-reby reinvigorating our motivation.

The The-ory of Flow, another major concept, proposes that comple-te engageme-nt in an activity that fully tests our abilities while simultane-ously providing prompt feedback can result in a harmonious state- of effortless focus and contentme-nt. Music has the capability to help induce this optimal state- of flow by seamlessly capturing our attention and e-stablishing an equitable balance be-tween challenge- and skill level. When fully absorbe-d in a task that is appropriately difficult yet within our skillset, and which imme-diately informs us on our progress, we e-nter a meditative state- where we are- fully present yet time- seems to slip away unnoticed - this is the- essence of flow. By drawing us in me-lodically, music can facilitate entering this he-ightened and harmonious mindset through a balance-d interplay of challenge and ability.

By gaining a dee-per appreciation of the scie-ntific principles underlying melodic motivation, we- can attain valuable perspective-s on why it exerts such a powerful influe-nce for boosting productivity in corporate leade-rship. The following portion will construct upon this learning and offer pragmatic tactics for applying me-lodic motivation throughout your company. Melodic motivation leverage-s the mind's natural response to rhythm and sound in orde-r to foster high levels of motivation, focus, and job satisfaction among e-mployees. Rese-arch indicates that workers who listen to upbe-at, energizing music while comple-ting tasks tend to stay more engage-d in their duties and produce highe-r quality work than those in silent environme-nts. By playing strategically curated playlists matched to diffe-rent roles and responsibilitie-s, you can help maintain optimal energy, focus, and morale- across your teams. Whether it's during a brainstorming se-ssion seeking novel solutions or a de-tailed project requiring inte-nse concentration, the right

Implementing Melodic Motivation Strategies

Impleme-nting melodic motivation in business manageme-nt through a strategic musical approach can be a powerful me-thod to inspire and energize- your personnel. By thoughtfully sele-cting suitable songs, crafting curated playlists tailored for diffe-rent activities or moods, and skillfully utilizing various forms of auditory stimulation, you can cultivate a se-tting that nurtures productivity, sparks creativity, and spreads positive- energy. Playing the right type- of music at optimal moments allows managers to subtly boost morale, focus, and collaboration. Whe-ther it's a rhythmic tune to ene-rgize brainstorming sessions or a mellow me-lody to aid concentration during detailed tasks, incorporating care-fully chosen music can make the workday more- enjoyable and yield be-tter results if applied judiciously. While- some musical selections may e-nthuse extroverte-d thinkers, quieter songs may suit those-

Here- are some practical strategie-s to help you implement me-lodic motivation in a clear yet engaging manne-r:

Focus first on choosing upbeat, energizing tune-s that lift your mood and get your body moving. Select music with

Selecting Appropriate Music:

When choosing songs to play during work se-ssions, take into account the musical tastes of your colle-agues. Opt for tracks that are uplifting and encourage- a positive mindset conducive to focus and productivity. Se-lect pieces without distracting or comple-x lyrics that may draw attention away from tasks. Also avoid noisy or jarring songs that could disrupt concentration or interrupt trains of thought. Conside-r finding music appealing to a wide audience- or taking turns playing playlists to keep the vibe-s supportive of deep, absorbing work.

Creating Playlists:

Creating customize-d playlists tailored to different moods and tasks can he-lp you be more productive. For instance-, you may have one playlist for brainstorming sessions fille-d with upbeat, high-energy songs that ke-ep you motivated. Another playlist pe-rfect for focused work could include soothing instrume-ntal pieces that allow you to concentrate- without distraction. Be sure to regularly re-view and refine your playlists to maintain the-ir freshness and hold your intere-st. Switching between playlists matche-d to what you're doing can prevent bore-dom and keep you engage-d in your activities. While brainstorming, lively me-lodies may spark new ideas. Late-r, when diving deep into a proje-ct, serene tracks without lyrics allow imme-rsive focus. Custom music curation personalized to various situations he-lps you optimize your playlists for productivity.

Leveraging Auditory Stimuli:

While e-xploring the use of ambient sounds, nature- sounds, or white noise could help some- individuals focus and feel more productive-, it's important to experiment and se-e what types of auditory stimuli work best for e-ach member of your team. What re-sonates well for one pe-rson may be too distracting for another. Some folks re-ally concentrate bette-r with a little background noise filling any silent space-s, as it can help mask outside distractions. For others though, comple-te silence is ne-cessary to truly focus their thoughts. The be-st approach is letting individuals find what environments suit the-m most. You might try playing some nature sounds softly during focused work se-ssions at first to see the re-sponse. Pay attention to any signs of restle-ssness or side conversations as clue-s that may need adjusting the volume- or switching to a different soundscape. Ultimate-ly, the goal is finding a balance that doesn't hinde-r anyone's ability to complete tasks e-fficiently.

By impleme-nting melodic motivation strategies, you have- the power to cultivate a work e-nvironment that sparks creativity, lifts morale, and foste-rs top achievement. The-se tactics nurture inspiration through a blend of coaching, re-cognition and fun. Try incorporating them and see your te-am flourish as their spirits and productivity rise. A little music doe-s much to make the work see-m lighter. So let the tune-s play on while duties are atte-nded to and achieveme-nts are gained.

Inspiring Peak Performance Through Melodic Motivation

While aiming to attain top-tie-r results in corporate leade-rship, a tuneful technique has surface-d as a potent means. By capitalizing on music and noises' psychological sway, companie-s can cultivate a setting that motivates pe-rsons and units to reach their maximum capacity. This eme-rging tactic recognizes how a properly curate-d soundtrack can positively impact one's mood and productivity. Not only does me-lodic motivation boost morale, but it also helps create- a collaborative environment whe-re teams fee-l encouraged to tackle challe-nges in innovative ways. By playing uplifting songs during work hours and mee-tings, managers can set a tone that make-s employees fe-el energize-d, focused, and committed to achieving goals and mile-stones. The approach shows promise in harne-ssing the emotive powe-r of soundwaves to cultivate peak pe-rformance throughout an organization.

Certain type-s of melodies have the- power to stir emotions and lift mood. Studies have- found that particular songs are able to arouse good se-ntiments, heighten spirits, and bolste-r determination. When worke-rs are in an optimistic frame of mind, they te-nd to accomplish at their maximum potential and surpass expe-ctations for their company. Music with an upbeat rhythm and joyful tones se-ems especially e-ffective at inspiring positivity. A sele-ction of popular tunes played throughout the workday may he-lp foster teamwork and productivity by kee-ping employees fe-eling uplifted. Casual listening bre-aks could reinvigorate staff during slower pe-riods to help maintain high morale and motivation leve-ls overall.

A number of inspiring tale-s and detailed examinations showcase- the extraordinary outcomes that me-lodic inspiration can accomplish. For instance, Radio City Ltd actualized a tune drive-n inspiration program that included playing upbeat, lively music all through the- work environment. Repre-sentatives reve-aled feeling incre-asingly included, roused, and driven to shine- in their work because of the- program. This resulted in the organization se-eing critical enhanceme-nts in profitability, effectivene-ss, and general exe-cution. The utilization of rousing tunes all through the workday se-emed to uplift repre-sentatives and invigorate the-m to give their best e-ndeavors. It gave them a fe-eling of energy and rouse-d them to convey top notch work. This amplification in repre-sentative engage-ment and exhibitions because- of melodic motivation obviously benefite-d the base line and goals of the- organization.

While the- impact of melodic motivation may differ based on worke-rs' individual tastes and cultural backgrounds, there are- steps organizations can take to support varied music pre-ferences. Companie-s could curate individualized playlists tailored to an array of ge-nres, emotions, and job duties. This pe-rsonalized approach helps ensure- all employees can conne-ct with music appealing to their sensibilitie-s, boosting their productivity. Whether upbe-at or mellow tunes fit best, finding the- right tunes makes focusing easie-r. Though what moves one may not motivate anothe-r, customized choices increase- the chances that sounds uplift each pe-rson as they focus on tasks. Ultimately, the goal is for all to find fitting fre-quencies that most enhance- performance.

Furthermore-, melodic motivation can be integrate-d into various aspects of business manageme-nt in thoughtful ways, such as team meetings, training programs, and pe-rformance evaluations. By strategically incorporating music and sound, le-aders are able to cultivate- an environment conducive to collaboration, whe-re employee-s feel comfortable sharing ide-as and building upon each others' contributions. An atmosphere- nurturing creativity and innovation can be establishe-d through carefully selecting an appropriate- soundscape. Upbeat melodie-s may inspire innovative thinking during brainstorming sessions, while- calming sounds could aid focus during detailed planning mee-tings. Exploring how sound impacts various work contexts allows organizations to optimize their ope-rations and maximize productivity.

Organizations consistently e-xplore innovative methods to e-ncourage and inspire their e-mployees. Melodic motivation pre-sents a distinctive and powerful te-chnique. By utilizing the emotional and psychological impacts of music, le-aders can access parts of human nature, libe-rating teams' complete pote-ntial. A catchy melody may lift vitality levels or a re-laxing song may advance focus and concentration, melodic motivation has the- capacity to make a positive and uplifting work environme-nt where outstanding exe-cution becomes standard regardle-ss of whether it's a tuneful me-lody that builds vitality levels or a mitigating tune that advance-s center and focus melodic inspiration has the- capacity to make an uplifting and positive work climate whe-re top exhibitions become-s typical. While searching for new roads to e-ngage and animate repre-sentatives, melodic motivation brings a nove-l strategy. Tapping into feelings and brain scie-nce through music empowers pione-ers to unlock groups' total limit. A rousing tune can upgrade vitality, and re-laxing music can advance focus. On account of its capacity to make a good and encouraging work domain, me-lodic inspiration regularly brings out the most extre-me execution in labore-rs.

Cultivating Transformative Leadership with Melodic Motivation

In the e-ver-changing business world we find ourse-lves in today, fostering transformative le-adership is crucial for guiding organizations through meaningful evolution. An unconve-ntional yet potent method for e-nhancing these manageme-nt abilities is through melodic motivation. By incorporating inspiring tunes into how le-aders guide their te-ams, companies can uncover opportunities for transformational qualitie-s like vision, inspiration, and care for followers to naturally blossom. Music has shown to lift moods and spirits, so including motivating me-lodies into how managers direct and de-velop their people- may subtly support the emerge-nce of these pivotal le-adership characteristics that are so important for navigating ne-w challenges togethe-r. While an unusual approach, learning and leading to the- beat of encouraging songs may just open doors to the- dynamic, future-focused leade-rship required to thrive in today's fast-pace-d commercial environment.

A melody's powe-r to stir our feelings and set a positive- tone can stimulate leade-rs to think creatively, empowe-r those they guide, and nurture- a spirit of cooperative work. As leade-rs steep themse-lves in a melody's motivating might, they gain unde-rstandings of varied views, honor diversity, and champion involve-ment for all.

Transformative Leadership Qualities Enhanced by Melodic Motivation

Melodic motivation encourages leaders to:

Embrace Empathy: Motivational music cre-ates an emotional connection, allowing le-aders to empathize with the-ir team members more- deeply. By understanding the-ir aspirations and connecting on an emotional leve-l, leaders can provide more- meaningful support. Playing music that uplifts both the mind and spirit gives le-aders insight into what inspires their e-mployees. It allows them to walk in anothe-r's shoes and see pe-rspectives outside the-ir own. With empathy and compassionThe uplifting e-nergy of melodic motivation can greatly he-lp leaders in building trust with their te-ams through fostering open and transparent communication, de-monstrating integrity in their actions, and inspiring others to trust in the-ir vision and abilities. By communicating openly and honestly with the-ir team members, le-aders allow an environment of transpare-ncy to flourish, where people- feel comfortable bringing forward ide-as and concerns. Leaders who act with inte-grity and follow through on their commitments and responsibilitie-s build trustworthiness over time. Additionally, outlining a compe-lling vision and showing confidence in their ability to guide- theThe me-lodies and rhythms found in motivational music have the ability to fue-l creativity, empowering le-aders and team membe-rs to think differently than they normally would. This type- of music inspires individuals to venture outside- of their comfort zone and embrace- approaches that involve an ele-ment of risk in pursuit of innovative solutions. By listening to upbe-at and energizing songs, people- may find themselves conside-ring new perspective-s and unconventional ideas that could potentially solve- challenges in original ways. Motivational music aims to spark imagination and get the-When le-ading, it is best to lead with authenticity. Tapping into one-'s true self through the transformative- power of positive motivation allows leade-rs to act genuinely and inspire othe-rs to do the same. This helps cultivate- an environment where- people can trust one anothe-r to be their true se-lves. Acting authentically makes it possible- for motivation to spread in a melodic fashion throughout an organization. When a le-ader and their team fe-el comfortable being who the-y are, they will perform be-tter and feel happie-r in their roles. An authentic approach make-s it easier for eve-ryone to work as a cohesive unit since- artificial barriers have bee-n removed. Overall, ge-nuine

When e-xecutives incorporate me-lodic motivation into their management style-s, they can cultivate a work environme-nt filled with harmony. This type of environme-nt motivates people to achie-ve their highest abilitie-s and propels the company towards accomplishment. The- transformative essence- of melodic motivation goes beyond individual le-aders, potentially reshaping the- entire culture of the- organization. A reformed culture the-n facilitates improved teamwork, fle-xibility, and the ability to adapt. By motivating workers through melody, le-aders give their te-ams the inspiration neede-d to solve problems creative-ly. This approach unites people towards share-d goals and drives progress. As cooperation stre-ngthens within the company, so too does the- capacity to change direction swiftly when circumstance-s require agility. Overall, the- integration of music into leadership foste-rs a setting where both individuals and the- organization overall reach new he-ights.

When organizations adopt the- practice of motivating through music, they can expe-rience a notable change- in their managers and work groups. Leade-rs and teams who listen to melodic compositions te-nd to develop enhance-d qualities of inspiration and cooperation over time-. As supervisors and colleagues uplift one- another through shared appreciation of song, the-ir collaborative spirit strengthens. This atmosphe-re of communal encourageme-nt then spreads bene-ficially across the entire company. With me-lodic motivation fostering a culture of mutual care, re-spect and creativity, the organization finds itse-lf poised for long-lasting accomplishment and prosperity.

Overcoming Challenges in Implementing Melodic Motivation

While incorporating me-lodic motivation techniques into business administration may pre-sent some difficulties initially, staying de-termined and following a sensible- plan will help address any issues that arise-, setting the stage for positive- application. Some hurdles that manageme-nt may encounter involve gaining staff buy-in for ne-w approaches or adapting workflows. However, taking the- time for explanation, demonstration, and addre-ssing concerns in an understanding manner can he-lp smooth the transition. Regular ree-valuation also allows for refinement as unde-rstanding grows. With open communication and flexibility, melodic motivation offe-rs promising potential for boosting morale and results ove-r the long term.

While bringing toge-ther a team with varied musical taste-s can pose difficulties, creating inclusive- playlists is key. Rather than favoring any one ge-nre, developing compilations that contain some-thing for everyone he-lps foster cohesion. By drawing from diverse- artists and styles, these curate-d selections aim to connect with all pre-sent. Such wide-ranging playlists acknowledge- individual differences while- also emphasizing our shared humanity through music's universal ability to uplift and inspire-. Though tastes differ, coming togethe-r in listening builds understanding and community.

While choosing suitable- music for distinct tasks or undertakings can be demanding, inte-ntionally selecting songs aligned with ne-eded ene-rgy levels and concentration spans is significant. Various unde-rtakings may necessitate music with diffe-ring vibes - some nee-d uplifting beats to encourage productivity, whe-reas others profit from mellow me-lodies supporting focus. Forming playlists matched to objective-s and moods eases accomplishing goals.

Encouraging buy-in and participation

When introducing ne-w approaches to generating me-lodies, it is vital that we cultivate an e-nvironment of acceptance and participation. Some- individuals on the team could be doubtful or he-sitant toward adjustments, therefore- it is absolutely essential that we- articulate the advantages plainly and de-al with any issues they may have. Cre-ating melodies is a collaborative proce-ss, so ensuring all feel comfortable- contributing will lead to the best outcome-s. While change can be difficult, focusing on how the-se new motivations can strengthe-n our work and benefit the e-ntire group may help alleviate- initial reservations.

To encourage- buy-in and participation, taking team members' pe-rspectives into account when choosing what music will play could he-lp get everyone- invested and ene-rgized. Ask for their suggestions on how having upbe-at tunes in the background might lift spirits and boost productivity. This team-ce-ntered tactic won't just get pe-ople more involved, but also me-ans the selecte-d songs will genuinely appeal to the- whole group. Involving the team from the- start helps ensure e-veryone enjoys the- tunes instead of fee-ling like music was forced on them. The-ir input could provide valuable insights into what type of me-lodic motivation truly enhances each pe-rson's work day experience-.

Mitigating distractions and noise-related challenges

In work environme-nts where distractions and noise are- prevalent, impleme-nting melodic motivation can be quite difficult. To de-al with this challenge, think about supplying noise-cance-ling headphones or designate-d peaceful places whe-re colleagues are- able to concentrate and fully e-ngage with the inspiring songs without interruption. This allows te-am members to truly bene-fit from melodic motivation even whe-n surrounding sounds make focus challenging. Designating quie-t spaces gives an option for those who find he-adphones uncomfortable or prefe-r a more open atmosphere-. Both approaches can help foster an imme-rsive experie-nce with motivating music that renews e-nergy and sparks creativity, eve-n in bustling workplaces filled with potential distractions.

Regular communication and feedback sessions also play a vital role in addressing any arising challenges. Encourage team members to share their experiences and suggest adjustments to the melodic motivation strategy. By actively listening and responding to their feedback, you can refine the approach to better suit individual and team needs.

Adequate-ly equipping the space with re-liable resources like- high-quality audio equipment or stable stre-aming services is crucial to smoothly carrying out the me-lodic motivation approach. Investing in quality tools and technologies can he-lp address any technical issues that could unde-rmine the effe-ctiveness of the strate-gy. For instance, a sound system with clear sound and an inte-rnet connection fast enough for uninte-rrupted streaming allows the me-lodies to flow continuously. This ensures participants re-main engaged throughout without distraction from technical difficultie-s. Similarly, a stable streaming platform preve-nts lagging or buffering that may disrupt the mood and rhythm intende-d by a particular song. Addressing such potential challenge-s upfront means the focus can remain on e-xperiencing the the-rapeutic musical experie-nce as intended. Ove-rall, allocating a sufficient budget for the right audio infrastructure- makes certain the me-lodic motivation plan achieves its objective- of providing an uplifting experience-.

By recognizing and pre-emptively dealing with the-se difficulties, companies can le-verage the comple-te possible of melodic inspiration to motivate- optimum performance and foster a drive-n and invested labor force. While- these obstacles unde-niably exist, focusing on the positive powe-r of music allows workplaces to tap into employee-s' inherent drive. Music's ability to fire- imagination and lift mood means that a carefully curated soundtrack supports both productivity and morale-. Further, proactively diagnosing distractions helps busine-sses implement tailore-d solutions whether that be alte-rnatives for certain piece-s or adjustments

Measuring and Evaluating the Impact of Melodic Motivation

To gain a dee-per comprehension of how me-lodic inspiration can accurately encourage optimum accomplishme-nt, it is fundamental to quantify and assess its sway. By utilizing pertine-nt gauges and assessment te-chniques, associations can acquire discernme-nts into the tangible results and advantage-s of actualizing melodic inspiration systems. These- techniques could incorporate surve-ys or meetings with repre-sentatives to analyze how spe-cific tunes or playlists affect their inspiration le-vels, disposition, center, cre-ation, or other key exe-cution markers. Information accumulation before and afte-r the execution of me-lodic motivation procedures would give robust proof of its impacts. Bre-aking down this information for examples, for example-, particular melodies that consistently build inspiration or bring down pre-ssure, could furnish associations with significant experie-nces into music's capacity to upgrade worker e-xhibitions and work environment states of mind.

The Power of Impact Measurement

Dete-rmining the influence of musical inspiration pe-rmits associations to settle on choices de-pendent on proof and upgrade the-ir techniques to amplify results. By nume-rically estimating the impacts on laborer participation, profitability, and ge-neral execution, organizations can re-cognize regions for improveme-nt and improve the melodic motivation e-xperience. The- investigation of melodic motivation's effe-ct permits organizations to precisely quantify things like- work yield, satisfaction levels, and de-crease in lapses. This information give-s significant experience-s into which parts of melodic motivation are most compelling at lifting spirits, e-xpanding focus, and advancing positive conduct. Associations can at that point streamline the-ir melodic motivation systems by concentrating more- on the kinds of music that were appe-ared to decidedly affe-ct markers like work pace and pre-cision. Overall, breaking down melodic motivation's me-asurements of achieve-ment empowers organizations to make- educated changes inte-nded to

Key Metrics for Measuring Melodic Motivation

Some of the- important factors businesses can evaluate- to gauge how motivational music programs influence ope-rations include engageme-nt, productivity, and retention. Looking at metrics such as e-mployee focus and attention during the- workday as well as output numbers and quality can provide insight into how me-lodic motivation affects concentration and performance-. Tracking turnover rates and exit inte-rviews may

Employee- Satisfaction Surveys and feedback me-chanisms can help companies gain useful insights into how conte-nt and engaged their worke-rs feel with the motivational strate-gies utilized. Gathering pe-rspectives directly from e-mployees allows an assessme-nt of whether technique-s aimed at improving satisfaction and morale are e-ffective. It may also provide an opportunity for worke-rs to suggest alternative approache-s or areasMonitoring key productivity me-trics including quantity of output, quality of work produced, and efficiency le-vels can offer valuable pe-rspectives into how melodic motivation may influe-nce job performance. Tracking me-trics like the number of ite-ms or tasks completed, error rate-s, and the amount of time spent finishing proje-cts allows for analyzing whether certain type-s of music being played in the background impact aspe-cts such as concentration, focus, and work pace. Periodically re-viewing productivity numbers in key are-as after adjusting theAssessing e-lements like te-am dynamics, communication styles, and collaborative efforts can provide- useful insight into how motivation spreads betwe-en members and impacts re-lationships. By evaluating interaction patterns, information sharing, and coope-ration levels, it's possible to be-tter understand how melodic e-ncouragement inspires inte-rpersonal bonds and joint work within the organization. While te-am connections and partnerships form naturally over time- through shared efforts, periodically re-viewing processesClosely monitoring e-mployee rete-ntion figures as well as staff turnover can re-veal how successful motivational tactics have be-en in cultivating a pleasant workplace culture- and boosting personnel fulfillment. Calculating re-tention percentage-s and the frequency of re-signations allows an assessment of whethe-r motivational approaches like melodic motivation have- contributed to greater job satisfaction for worke-rs, leading to lower turnover as pe-ople choose to remain with an organization longe-r rather than seek opportunitie-s elsewhere-. Analyzing these metrics with an inte-rmediate depth can provide- some clarification

Methods for Evaluation

Here- is the moderately e-xpanded text with an interme-diate depth and purpose to clarify:

Busine-sses have seve-ral tools at their disposal to assess the e-ffect of musical inspiration. They can analyze me-trics like employee- productivity, collaboration levels, and

Conducting A/B testing by comparing the- performance metrics of te-ams or departments that have incorporate-d melodic motivation techniques to those- that have not can help illuminate the- impact these approaches may have- on important success metrics. By analyzing key indicators such as productivity, collaboration, cre-ative thinking, or job satisfaction from groups employing music-based motivation strate-gies alongside organizations that don't, the spe-cific effects of melodic motivation can be- better discerne-dAnalyzing data from diverse- sources, for example time- tracking systems or project manageme-nt tools, can offer a more profound comprehe-nsion of the effect of me-lodic inspiration. Examining information from these sorts of apparatuses can uncove-r examples that may not be promptly cle-ar, giving knowledge into how inspiration changes ove-r the span of an undertaking or errand. It can like-wise show how inspiration shifts relying upon various ele-ments, for example, unde-rtaking type, size, or intricacy. Breaking down information longitudinally can de-monstrate howSpeaking dire-ctly with employees through inte-rviews or focus groups can provide useful subje-ctive perspective-s about what moves them melodically at work. By ope-nly discussing experience-s and perceptions, leade-rs gain valuable qualitative insights beyond quantitative- data. These discussions allow a dee-per exploration of the inne-r experience-s, feelings, and views shaping motivational e-xperiences. Le-aders can better unde-rstand what really inspires staff by actively and thoughtfully liste-ning without judgment. While quantitative me-asures offer objective- snapshots, qualitative assessments offe-r a more textured vie-w of the human dynamics

By leve-raging both numerical data as well as personal storie-s and experience-s, companies can develop a we-ll-rounded perspective- on the effects of using motivating music and make- choices informed by evide-nce to best apply this approach. Quantitative re-search provides measurable- insights into what works, for whom, and why, while qualitative data offers a de-eper look into emotional impacts and pe-rsonal anecdotes that statistics alone cannot conve-y. Bringing these differe-nt sources together allows for a holistic picture- of what resonates with employe-es and customers, so

Sustaining Melodic Motivation for Long-Term Success

Fostering e-nduring inspiration through melody is pivotal to accomplishing prolonged prosperity in busine-ss administration. It's insufficient to build up inspirational procedures; the-y should be supported and adjusted afte-r some time to guarantee- consistent most extreme- execution. Here- are a couple powerful me-thodologies to assist you with keeping me-lodic motivation over the long haul:

1. Diverse Music Selection

Variety is essential when selecting motivational music. Continuously exploring different genres, artists, and songs can keep the music fresh and prevent monotony. Consider creating playlists for specific activities or moods to spark inspiration and maintain engagement.

2. Evolving with Changing Circumstances

The busine-ss world is continuously changing, so you must adapt your motivational music tactics as well. Make sure to ke-ep learning about new de-velopments in your field, what your te-am needs, and how your company is evolving ove-r time. Modify the songs you sele-ct and how you inspire workers to suit fresh hurdle-s and stay applicable. For example, you may ne-ed to focus on collaboration more during a merge-r or emphasize positivity if morale is low. Liste-n to employees to unde-rstand what would most enthuse them for the- new goals or tasks. Update your methods pe-riodically so they address the curre-nt realities and continue e-ngaging individuals. A versatile approach can maintain encourage-ment even as circumstance-s transform.

3. Encouraging Employee Input

Engaging your staff in choosing motivational music and giving remarks on its impact can e-ncourage ownership and involveme-nt in the process. Invite worke-rs to contribute ideas for melodie-s to inspire and empower the-m. Their participation personalizes the- experience- and makes it more purposeful. Gaining insight from e-mployees allows modifying sele-ctions to best lift spirits. While one tune- may energize one- person, another may inspire some-one else. Toge-ther you can find a playlist appealing to differe-nt tastes yet uniting the te-am. As members offer opinions, the-y feel appreciate-d for input. This interaction strengthens re-lationshipsand prompts discussions that can lead to other improveme-nts. Keep communication lines ope-n so the selections ke-ep morale lifting throughout upcoming endeavours.

4. Addressing Potential Burnout

While burnout can unde-rmine long-term achieve-ment, taking proactive steps to confront it is ke-y. Closely watching workers' wellne-ss and motivation consistently, respond promptly to indications of burnout. Think about incorporating soothing and anxiety le-ssening melodies to produce- a adjusted and encouraging work climate. Monitor signs like- diminished vitality, expanded cynicism, and diminishe-d proficiency. Give repre-sentatives chances to unwind and re-charge. Foster a culture whe-re taking occasional breaks is viewe-d as a positive. Make time for group e-xercises and casual discussions to fortify connections. Conside-r adaptable working hours or remote alte-rnatives so represe-ntatives can better ove-rsee work and individual duties. In ge-neral, make worker prospe-rity and fulfillment a need to fore-stall burnout from hindering achieveme-nt over the long haul.

5. Celebrating Milestones

It is important to acknowledge- both individual contributions as well as group accomplishments as projects progre-ss. Recognizing efforts and cele-brating milestones promotes a fe-eling of achieveme-nt that encourages employe-es to continue their hard work. Play upbe-at, inspiring music at celebrations to gene-rate a positive and ene-rgizing environment where- people fee-l good about their work. Taking the time to show appre-ciation for tasks completed helps sustain motivation as more- work remains ahead.

By incorporating these- tactics, you can maintain melodic inspiration in your business manageme-nt techniques on an ongoing basis, guarantee-ing long-term achieveme-nt and consistent optimal productivity. Some strategie-s you can consider include setting pe-riodic milestones to cele-brate wins big and small with your team, recognizing e-mployees for taking initiative and thinking outside- the box, and encouraging collaboration across departme-nts to spark new ideas and kee-p momentum going even during challe-nging times.

Melodic Motivation Case Studies

In this section, we will dive into real-life case studies of organizations that have successfully implemented melodic motivation techniques. These case studies will provide valuable insights into the experiences, challenges, and outcomes of using melodic motivation to inspire peak performance in business management.

InnovateTe-ch is a well-known technology company that provides an e-xample of how incorporating music can positively impact an organization. The company saw notable- increases in employe-e morale and productivity by thoughtfully incorporating melodie-s into the work environment. Care-fully selected playlists and strate-gic use of music during meetings and collaborative- work sessions helped Innovate-Tech cultivate a setting de-fined by inspiration and imagination. This atmosphere allowe-d workers to feel more- inspired, involved, and bonded to the-ir duties, resulting in extraordinary e-nhancements to project re-sults. The tunes see-med to lift spirits and foster a sense- of community, translating to higher quality work and better outcome-s. However, it remains to be- seen whethe-r this approach could benefit all types of companie-s or if certain environments may be- better suited to othe-r motivational techniques.

Case Study: Harmony Health Clinic

Harmony Health Clinic, a promine-nt healthcare supplier, e-mbraced the strength of me-lodic inspiration. They acknowledged the- possible effect of music on patie-nt wellbeing and team e-xecution. The clinic played out customize-d playlists in lounges, treatment rooms, and labore-r break zones aiming to lesse-n anxiousness, support focus, and upgrade fulfillment. The- melodic arrangements and cautiously chose-n tunes were e-xpected to help quie-t patients and represe-ntatives. Soft melodies we-re picked imagining they would unwind patie-nts sitting tight in the sitting rooms. Upbeat tunes we-re incorporated into playlists for worker bre-ak territories trusting they would e-nergize and recharge- the staff. The melodic motivations we-re accepted would build se-renity, center, and ge-neral fulfillment for patients and re-presentatives alike-.

Furthermore-, Harmony Health Clinic instituted schedule-d guided meditation periods comple-mented by soothing tunes. During the-se regularly schedule-d sessions, employee-s were given a valuable-chance to unwind, re-ene-rgize, and refocus themse-lves amid their typically busy and demanding workdays. As an outcome-, the clinic noticed decre-ased anxiety leve-ls amongst staff, which helped cultivate a more- cohesive and encouraging e-nvironment for colleagues to work collaborative-ly.

Case Study: Rhythm Retail

Rhythm Retail, a promine-nt fashion retailer, discovere-d enormous achieveme-nt in incorporating melodic inspiration into their shops. They de-liberately chose live-ly and energizing music to make an inviting e-nvironment that matched their image-. By curating playlists that echoed with their planne-d crowd, Rhythm Retail had the option to summon positive fe-elings, consequently improving the-shopping experience- and expanding client commitment. The- retailer spent significant time-investigating the musical inclinations of their ke-y demographic. They assemble-d playlists highlighted hit tunes from mainstream craftsme-n that would lift the state of mind in the store-. This strategic utilization of sound encouraged clie-nts to remain longer and investigate- more items. It made a ple-asurable shopping background that clients relate-d with the Rhythm Retail brand.

The positive- impact of melodic motivation not only benefite-d customers but also uplifted the e-fforts of employees. Rhythm Re-tail initiated morning musical meetings to vitalize- and stimulate their retail worke-rs before the store- opened each day. The-se music sessions demonstrate-d tremendous importance in se-tting the proper atmosphere- for the following hours, cultivating a driven and client-focuse-d perspective among staff me-mbers. The morning music sessions allowe-d employees to start the-ir day on an upbeat note, mentally pre-paring them to interact with customers in a positive- and helpful manner. By starting the day with a brie-f musical interlude, the e-mployees found themse-lves in a more chee-rful and energized mood to gre-et customers. The positive- energy gene-rated during these e-arly music sessions carried over into the- employees' inte-ractions on the sales floor, as they approache-d each customer with enthusiasm and patie-nce. Overall, the practice- of including morning music proved very valuable in re-adying the retail team to offe-r excellent custome-r service throughout the day in a motivate-d and client-focused way.

These- case studies provide a more- in-depth look into how melodic motivation has bee-n applied across different fie-lds, yielding compelling results. Analyzing re-al world instances offers insight into strategically incorporating its principle-s to foster positive change. Whe-ther spurring new leve-ls of performance for athlete-s or energizing employe-es of a global corporation, harnessing the powe-r of melody has proven adaptable to dive-rse goals. While approaches may vary, e-ach story demonstrates music's capacity to reinvigorate- efforts and cultivate a rene-wed sense of purpose-. By tapping into its motivational forces, organizations and individuals have accesse-d untapped potential and pushed boundarie-s to their furthest reache-s. The transformative effe-cts, as the examples atte-st, are as diverse as the- endeavors to which melodic motivation has be-en applied.

Conclusion and Recommendations

Throughout this section, we- delved into the ide-a of melodic motivation and how it can cultivate high achieve-ment in corporate leade-rship. By tapping into the influence of tune-s and tones, melodic motivation prese-nts imaginative approaches to ene-rgize groups and guide transformative administration. Me-lodic motivation recognizes that music has the capacity to lift both state- of mind and execution, conveying uplifting vibe-s that permeate e-ach part of the working environment. Whe-n representative-s feel great and gain a fe-eling of objective, the-y will give their most prominent e-xertion. Furthermore, whe-n administration sets the standard by retaining me-lodic motivation themselves, the-y impart a feeling of joint effort and share-d vision that empowers eve-rybody on the group to excee-d expectations. Altogethe-r, the investigation of melodic motivation uncove-rs promising techniques for rousing work

Our discussion illuminated the- importance of motivation in business manageme-nt and how it can influence team output, innovative-ness, and final achieveme-nt. Motivation through melody, specifically, offers an unusual te-chnique that taps into the emotional and me-ntal association between noise-s and execution. Melodic motivation re-cognizes how certain tunes can lift spirits and impact brain scie-nce, subsequently e-xpanding focus, vitality, and profitability. By playing empowering melodie-s all through the workday, directors can support a positive working climate- where laborers fe-el appreciated and rouse-d to give their best. This nove-l way to deal with inspiration through sound recognizes that music impacts our state- of mind and conduct, subsequently upgrading cooperation, inve-ntiveness, and at last bringing about superior outcome-s. While conventional types of inspiration ce-nter around money relate-d or non-money related prize-s, melodic

To wrap up our discussion, we advise- taking time to think about potentially incorporating melodic motivation approache-s into your company's leadership technique-s. Initiate the process by le-arning the fundamental concepts and re-search underlying melodic motivation the-ory. Investigate various ways of applying suitable music and audio signals. Draw ide-as from authentic examples that cle-arly show how melodic motivation can produce extraordinary outcome-s in the real world. Such case studie-s demonstrate how the right tune-s at the right moment can boost employe-e engageme-nt, satisfaction, and productivity. Carefully crafting the soundscape of the- workplace with an understanding of its impact on human psychology may help foste-r a more motivated, inspired, and high-pe-rforming team. While some e-xperimentation will be ne-eded to find the right fits, making a se-rious effort to study this domain could offer fresh pe-rspectives on cultivating a peak-pe-rformance culture within your organization.

Cultivating a culture focuse-d on inspiration and encouragement allows you to bring out the- best in your teams and strengthe-n your abilities as a leader. By de-veloping an environment whe-re people fe-el motivated and supported, you can he-lp your business thrive. Be sure- to consistently review the- results of your efforts to boost enthusiasm and morale-. Continually assessing the effe-cts will help you sustain high levels of drive- and commitment over the long run. Ke-ep in mind the power of me-lodic motivation to propel your organization to new successe-s. An uplifting workplace breeds pe-ak performance by fulfilling individuals and uniting them toward share-d objectives. Regularly re-evaluate your methods to maintain an atmosphe-re that engages e-mployees and takes the- business to greater he-ights.

Chapter **14**

The Dynamics of Feedback: Constructive Criticism and Praise

Have you e-ver receive-d feedback that left you fe-eling inspired and motivated to improve-? Perhaps you receive-d comments that highlighted your strengths and are-as for growth in a constructive manner, sparking new ide-as on how to enhance your work. Or maybe you e-ncountered criticism that felt ove-rly harsh and hurtful, leaving you discouraged about advancing your skills. It's important to learn from both e-ncouraging and discouraging feedback by focusing on insights that uplift your abilities and confide-nce, while disregarding re-marks meant

Fee-dback mechanisms significantly impact our evolution and progress ove-r time. Constructive criticism and encourage-ment are two impactful varietie-s of responses that can eithe-r thrust us ahead or slow our movement forward. While- commentary intended to e-nhance one's skills in a helpful manne-r can spearhead improveme-nt, words of praise recognizing achieve-ments also energize-continued developme-nt. A balanced incorporation of both in interpersonal e-xchanges often optimizes pe-rsonal progress. Meanwhile, an abse-nce of such input or reception of sole-ly negative revie-ws may hinder growth. Therefore-, cultivating a climate encouraging open ye-t thoughtful responses appears inte-gral to maximizing our potential for growth.

Here- we will explore balancing constructive- criticism and praise, comprehending how the-y can cultivate studying, improve communication, and unleash our authe-ntic potential. Let us immerse-ourselves into the re-alm of responses and uncover the- technique of providing and accepting it with compassion and proficie-ncy. We will consider how criticism, when tactfully de-livered, can pinpoint areas for growth and light a fire- within us to continuously progress. Similarly, praise, when rightfully give-n, reenergize-s our efforts and reminds us of strengths to build upon. This chapte-r aims to shed light on crafting feedback that uplifts rathe-r than cuts down, and fosters mutual understanding betwe-en individuals dedicated to mutual le-arning and improvement.

The Value of Feedback

Here- is the moderately e-xpanded text with an interme-diate depth and purpose to clarify:

Re-ceiving feedback is crucially important for he-lping people enhance- how they carry out tasks. It offers useful unde-rstandings and viewpoints that can result in personal maturation and care-er progress. Fee-dback presents perspe-ctives about strengths and areas that could use- refinement. This fe-edback helps individuals recognize- where they e-xcel and where the-y can strengthen their abilitie-s. With an open mindset, people- can consider the viewpoints share-d in feedback to pinpoint

Understanding Constructive Criticism

Constructive criticism can be- a useful tool for facilitating positive change whe-n offered carefully and re-spectfully. It aims to assist individuals in enhancing their skills or pe-rformance by pinpointing particular behaviors or actions that could bene-fit from modification, rather than making personal attacks. When de-livered considerate-ly and with helpful recommendations, constructive- feedback highlights specific aspe-cts that could be strengthene-d or developed furthe-r, so the recipient come-s away feeling supported in stre-ngthening those areas inste-ad of put down. Its intent is growth and progress through respe-ctful discussion of discrete actions, not condemnation of characte-r or personality. Done well, it provide-s targeted guidance for re-finement while pre-serving dignity and self-este-em.

Whethe-r giving constructive criticism or advice for bette-rment, it is wise to do so gently and for the- right reasons rather than harshly or in blame. By pointing out spe-cific things that could be done differe-ntly and where one might focus e-fforts for strengthening, fee-dback of this kind aims to help a person look inward and progress to highe-r ground. Comments should seek to uplift through unde-rstanding and empower further growth, not de-mean or accuse.

Providing helpful fe-edback can cultivate an environme-nt focused on constant refineme-nt, allowing people to learn from e-rrors and progress both individually and professionally. By comprehe-nding and welcoming useful criticism, individuals can leve-rage its influence to prope-l their developme-nt and accomplish their aims. Constructive criticism welcome-s room for enhancement, whe-re small adjustments could make significant diffe-rences. It encourage-s understanding different vie-wpoints to improve one's skills and knowledge- over time. Rather than dwe-lling on what could have been, e-mbracing helpful reviews highlights opportunitie-s to strengthen strengths and re-ctify weaknesses. This foste-rs a learning mindset where- progress happens through open-minde-dness instead of defe-nsiveness.

The Art of Giving Constructive Criticism

Offering critical sugge-stions tactfully necessitates both de-licacy and compassion. When implemente-d proficiently, it can energize- and rouse constructive alteration in pe-ople and groups. Regardless of whe-ther you're a chief giving input to your labore-rs or a partner offering contributions to a partner, the- path you convey useful examination can fundame-ntally influence its welcome- and viability. While giving input, it is critical to remembe-r that everybody nee-ds to improve however nobody ne-eds to feel awful. Start with what the- individual or group did well before re-spectfully addressing territorie-s for advancement. Offer e-xplicit models instead of gene-ral proclamations and remember the- human - center around conduct not character. The- objective isn't reprimand ye-t advancement so kee-p the discussion positive and offer bolste-r too. Recollection that we are- all gaining from each other can make criticism a le-arning experience- for every one of the- gatherings included.

Rather than criticizing a pe-rson's character or nature, concentrate- remarks on particular behaviors that were- witnessed. Call attention to how ce-rtain deeds or habits could hinder obje-ctives, then propose alte-rnative approaches intende-d to boost results. This type of fee-dback, highlighting room for refinement and offe-ring guidance on enhancing work, helps make- individuals feel secure- opening their minds to opinion. When sugge-stions target actions instead of attacking identity, a risk-fre-e setting forms where- the recipient fe-els willing to contemplate ne-w perspectives. By pinpointing what was done- and suggesting how performance may be- strengthened, you can ste-er people toward advancing skills and maximizing pote-ntial.

Providing fee-dback in a manner that focuses on bette-rment rather than blame can he-lp individuals welcome criticism as a chance to e-volve. Pointing out areas that could use re-finement should not be done- in an accusatory way but rather presente-d as chances to gain insight and progress. Highlight how revie-ws from others offer openings to hone- one's skills and advance professionally or pe-rsonally down the line. Explain how fee-dback, even when addre-ssing weaknesses, se-rves as helpful pointers to re-ach higher levels of pe-rformance or understanding over the- course of one's journey. Communicating how advice- and input from those around us provide learning e-xperiences crucial for de-velopment may encourage- people to view constructive- criticism as opportunities instead of insults.

The Importance of Delivery

Providing helpful criticism is as much about timing and tact as the- advice itself. Choosing a private se-tting where you can speak candidly ye-t supportively, without interruptions, shows care and re-spect. Express belie-f in the person's ability to grow from fee-dback by concentrating on their strengths and how the-y can build from experience-s, not harping on errors or limits. Make the discussion about he-lping them maximize potential through ope-n yet thoughtful dialogue.

Being an atte-ntive listener is crucial whe-n receiving fee-dback. Give the individual a chance to re-ply and inquire, permitting an candid and available e-xchange. This can help unscramble any misconce-ptions and guarantee that the two gathe-rings are comprehensive-ly on a similar page. Questions might eme-rge in regards to particular perspe-ctives of the input got. By giving the individual an opportunity to voice- their inquiries and see- things from their point of view, it encourage-s comprehension and settle-s on a choice about how to move forward gainfully.

Kee-p in mind that the objective of providing constructive- criticism is to assist individuals in expanding and bettering the-mselves. By expre-ssing empathy, showing regard, and offering practical guidance-, you can cultivate a setting that continually advances le-arning and evolving. Our criticism should aim not to reprimand or find fault, but rather to provide- perspective and spark se-lf-reflection, so that others fe-el empowere-d to strengthen their skills and abilitie-s. Consider starting the discussion by acknowledging what is alre-ady being done well, be-fore respectfully pointing to one- or two areas that could use refine-ment. Suggesting small changes or additions, phrase-d as questions instead of demands

Receiving Constructive Criticism

While ge-tting constructive criticism may be difficult to hear, le-arning from it is crucial for our development both pe-rsonally and in our careers. When we- can accept comments respe-ctfully, it allows us to gain useful perspective-s on where we e-xcel and where we- could enhance our skills or knowledge-. Feedback, eve-n when it addresses are-as needing work, provides opportunitie-s to strengthen existing tale-nts and expand our abilities. With an open mindse-t, advice that might initially sting can ultimately uplift us by sparking new ide-as for enhancing our work, interactions, or overall pote-ntial.

While gaining constructive- feedback is helpful for improve-ment, one must approach it with an open and thoughtful pe-rspective. Refle-ct carefully on the comments prior to forming an opinion. The- viewpoints of others, though differing from your own, may contain obje-ctive observations worth considering. By striving first to unde-rstand where the critic is coming from rathe-r than rushing to disagree, you allow space for pote-ntially useful insights to emerge-. Not every critique warrants change-, yet maintaining receptive-ness leaves room for e-nrichment when the criticism me-rits reflection. With an open and disce-rning mindset, what was intended to he-lp can help indeed.

It is esse-ntial to recall that getting helpful critique- does not signify that you are defe-ctive or insufficient. It esse-ntially implies that there are- regions requiring improveme-nt, and input functions as a valuable direction on your excursion towards de-velopment and advanceme-nt. While getting input may now and again fee-l testing, recollecting that the- objective is to enable- you to enhance empowe-rs a more positive way to deal with change-. An intermediary leve-l of profundity can assist with clarifying the objective without be-ing excessively se-vere. Fee-dback offers open doors to refle-ct and actualize changes that take your capacitie-s to another level, bringing about progre-ss as you gain from both your qualities and shortcomings.

Make an e-ffort to attentively hear the- feedback, asking questions for clarification if e-ssential. Restate the- analysis in your own words to demonstrate that you comprehe-nd the primary focuses. This shows the individual giving input that you re-spect their contribution and are focuse-d on making positive changes. While it is e-ssential to comprehend the- feedback, it is additionally critical not to become- excessively conce-ntrated on singular pieces. Re-call that the fundamental motivation behind giving criticism is to he-lp you improve. Try not to feel de-bilitated, yet rather, utilize- the criticism as a chance to deve-lop and turn into a continually progressively capable individual.

Turning Criticism into Opportunity

Rather than pe-rceiving helpful criticism as an unfavorable e-pisode, consider it a prospect to advance- yourself individually and professionally. Utilize the- suggestions as a catalyst to enhance your tale-nts, learning, and execution. We-lcome the opportunity to evolve- and get better, re-alizing that useful criticism is a significant stone in the way toward accomplishme-nt. When individuals offer remarks planne-d to assist you with improving, recollect that their point is to he-lp you enhance - not to reprimand or de-mean you. Listen with an open psyche- to comprehend their point, without taking things e-xcessively personally. Inve-stigate their remarks re-asonably and choose what you can truly apply to enhance your e-xhibitions moving forward. Each input is a chance to get more grounde-d. In the event that some-body chooses to share how you can deve-lop, they see pote-ntial in you and need to see- you achieve more.

Carefully conside-r the feedback you re-ceived and pinpoint exactly what ste-ps you can take to remedy the- aspects noted for advanceme-nt. Establish objectives and devise- a strategy to apply the recomme-nded alterations. Repe-atedly check how you're faring and modify your me-thods suitably as needed.

Kee-p in mind that accepting constructive criticism isn't about achieving flawle-ssness, rather it's concerning consiste-nt progress. Each bit of feedback obtaine-d provides an opportunity to learn and evolve-. By welcoming suggestions and conscientiously focusing on se-lf-betterment, you can furthe-r your personal and job developme-nt. This process isn't about being faultless from the- start, but using each comment as a way to analyze whe-re enhanceme-nts can be made. While comme-nts may address areas that nee-d refining, their core purpose- is to help you recognize how continuing to le-arn from each experie-nce can strengthen your abilitie-s. Embrace guidance as a tool for deve-lopment rather than judgment of your worth.

The Power of Praise

Recognition is a pote-nt and meaningful power that can encourage- and uplift people and groups. Authentic appre-ciation and gratitude has the capacity to gene-rate a beneficial outcome- on individual and work levels. Acknowledging spe-cific accomplishments with compassion can boost confidence and re-inforce continued hard work and improveme-nt. Whether acknowledging big or small achie-vements, making others fe-el seen and value-d contributes to overall well-be-ing and strengthens relationships.

Recognizing anothe-r's accomplishments through compliments not only cultivates a fe-eling of worth and acknowledgment ye-t also inspires individuals to continue striving for exce-llence in their dutie-s. When someone se-nses valued and grateful for the-ir exertions and triumphs, they are- prone to being driven to attain e-ven loftier goals. Praising others for the-ir hard work and achievements le-ts them know their efforts do not go unnotice-d. It tells them that others se-e the time and e-nergy they put in. This recognition he-lps boost morale and serves as a motivation to ke-ep improving. Feeling appre-ciated for one's contributions encourage-s continued diligence and de-velopment. With validation for past successe-s, one is likely to be e-nergized to surpass eve-n those and set new be-nchmarks of performance.

Acknowledging achie-vements has the capability to e-levate moods and raise motivation. Whe-n coworkers obtain applause for their triumphs, it aids in e-stablishing a caring and motivating work setting. Highlighting and commemorating victories not just bolste-rs optimistic behaviors but in addition increases se-lf-assurance and inspires people- to take on new difficulties. Re-cognizing small daily wins can go a long way in creating a culture where- employees fe-el valued and encourage-d. A quick word of appreciation or thanks for work well done is sure- to make individuals feel that the-ir efforts are appreciate-d. This helps foster a collaborative e-nvironment where te-am members fee-l comfortable taking on larger projects, taking initiative- and pushing their abilities further.

Furthermore-, commending others has the pote-ntial to solidify bonds and boost collaboration within a group. Providing recognition for an individual's meaningful participation and hard work helps nourish a fe-eling of fellowship and value among te-ammates. This nurtures a cooperative- attitude and encourages a constructive- team environment conducive- to heightened e-fficiency and achieveme-nt.

While praise strengthe-ns the connections betwe-en people striving toward a common obje-ctive, it remains most impactful when offe-red sincerely and judiciously for work we-ll done.

While it is crucial to acknowle-dge that authentic praise e-xtends beyond hollow flattery or me-aningless compliments, focusing appreciation on spe-cific accomplishments or distinguishing traits of people allows for re-cognition of strengths in a purposeful manner. By providing he-artfelt and thoughtful commendation, you can help individuals ide-ntify their talents, cultivate se-lf-assurance, and motivate continued de-dication to outstanding performance. What is more, highlighting unique-qualities fosters a fee-ling of being valued for one's individual contributions rathe-r than just another face in the crowd. In this way, since-re praise promotes confide-nce from the inside out as oppose-d to seeking worth through exte-rnal factors alone.

Balancing Criticism and Praise

Fostering an e-nvironment where support and progre-ss can flourish requires discovering the- proper equilibrium betwe-en helpful critique and re-cognition. Both types of responses pe-rform important functions in energizing and stee-ring people towards greate-r development and e-nhancement. While constructive- criticism can pinpoint places for progress, praise acknowle-dges present stre-ngths and helps people fe-el capable and encourage-d to take on future challenge-s. It is most beneficial to provide a mixture- of the two so individuals understand where- they excel as we-ll as regions that could use refine-ment. This balance is key for nurturing an atmosphe-re of learning and bette-rment where all fe-el empowere-d and motivated to continuously enhance the-ir skills and contributions.

While constructive- criticism provides useful perspe-ctives and recommendations for be-tterment, allowing persons to pinpoint locations of vulne-rability and furnish direction on how to surmount obstacles, it is esse-ntial this important feedback cente-rs on explicit behaviors or dee-ds, confirming the remarks stay constructive and re-spectful. The guidance aims to e-nhance performance by obje-ctively addressing specific issue-s requiring adjustment, rather than launching pe-rsonal attacks, with the goal of empowering improve-ment.

While criticism aims to point out are-as for potential growth, recognition of accomplishments has its own me-rits. Acknowledging individuals' strengths and achieve-ments through praise serve-s to motivate by boosting confidence and nurturing a fe-eling of having realized some-thing noteworthy. When offere-d sincerely and with meaning, comme-ndation can encourage one to pe-rsist in their efforts and pursue e-xcellence, as the-ir capabilities and past successes are- brought to light. Further, bringing attention to talents and comple-ted tasks in an authentic manner allows for an appre-ciation of abilities and progress made.

By finding a harmonious balance be-tween critique and comme-ndation, we can cultivate an environme-nt conducive toward progress through fee-dback. It is fundamental to offer considerate-criticism where warranted, pinpointing ave-nues for advancement, while- in addition acknowledging and applauding accomplishments through praise. Ne-ither unconstructive derision nor unwarrante-d flattery are particularly helpful; a balance-d approach recognizes both strengths and we-aknesses, guiding further e-volution. This equilibrium fosters an atmosphere- of growth, a willingness to learn and enhance- one's skills, abilities, and understanding ove-r time through open and honest e-xchange.

Kee-p in mind that the aim is not to excessive-ly find fault or applaud excessively, but rathe-r to supply a well-balanced blend of the- two. This permits people to compre-hend their sturdy suits, pinpoint territorie-s where progress is conce-ivable, and nurtures a way of thinking of consistent discove-ring and advancement.

Cultivating a Feedback Culture

Offering and re-ceiving remarks within a company or team is significant for e-ncouraging constant studying and progression. Even though fee-dback may sometimes be se-en as unfavorable, it's vital to reframe- it as a useful chance for advanceme-nt. By nurturing an environment where- feedback is welcome-d and appreciated, people- and groups can utilize the strength of various points of vie-w and understandings to encourage constructive- modifications and advancements. When worke-rs feel safe providing comme-nts to one another and administration in a manner inte-nded to help as opposed to re-primand, it breeds an air of joint effort focuse-d on progress instead of punishment. This sort of socie-ty empowers eve-ry part to develop personally and e-xpertly through getting input from others, just as giving he-lpful input when asked. While fe-edback may now and then contain difficult truths, regarding it as a be-nevolent procedure- for self-upgrade can change individual me-thodologies and altogether upgrade- execution.

Open communication lie-s at the core of cultivating a culture whe-re feedback thrive-s. It first requires nurturing an environme-nt where fee-dback is appreciated and endorse-d. This involves generating se-cure settings where- people fee-l at ease expre-ssing their views and notions, irrespe-ctive of their roles or place-ment within the organization. By embracing psychological safe-ty, honest and frank discussions are made possible-, allowing for the exchange of constructive- feedback that drives progre-ss.

In order to nurture- an environment where- feedback is welcome-d and utilized for improvement, companie-s and work groups must develop unambiguous policies and me-thods for both delivering and accepting fe-edback. Establishing such guidelines he-lps guarantee that any fee-dback shared is focused on tangible e-xamples or incidents, suggests concre-te actions for developme-nt, and is offered respe-ctfully. By offering coaching and lessons on helpful fe-edback practices, organizations can outfit people- with the abilities and assurance to succe-ssfully express their pe-rspectives and ideas. Whe-n objectives and approaches for fe-edback are clearly de-fined, it becomes e-asier for all involved to have valuable- discussions that lead to growth without becoming personal.

Fostering a Feedback Loop

Establishing a consistent fe-edback loop is essential for cultivating a culture- where fee-dback thrives. This process nece-ssitates continuous dialogue and follow up regarding the- feedback that is shared. By foste-ring recurring discussions, greater compre-hension can emerge- alongside clarification and improved alignment. Que-stions can be answered, confusion addre-ssed, and perspective-s further understood through an open e-xchange of ideas. When fe-edback is viewed as a starting point for an e-ngaging conversation rather than an ending point for a de-livered message-, its utility amplifies exponentially. Such an approach acknowle-dges the dynamic nature of vie-wpoints and welcomes progression in thinking.

Heads of an organization have- an essential part in fostering an e-nvironment where fe-edback is welcomed. By le-ading by example and proactively re-questing feedback, the-y illustrate the worth and significance of an ope-n and receptive attitude-. Leaders should motivate the-ir teams to accept fee-dback, understanding its capacity for individual and professional progress. Fe-edback can provide helpful insight and pe-rspectives to enhance- one's skills and contributions. When teams fe-el safe sharing comments and ide-as, it allows for continuous learning and improvement at both group and pe-rsonal levels. An rece-ptive leader mode-ls the value of refle-ctive listening and adjustment base-d on input from others.

Recognizing and Celebrating Progress

While fe-edback commonly emphasizes face-ts requiring amelioration, it is similarly crucial to applaud advanceme-nt and attainments. Taking note of and accentuating pe-ople or parties for their accomplishme-nts cultivates an optimistic and encouraging fee-dback environment. By recognizing and comme-nding initiatives, companies can stimulate and spur constant e-volution.

Ultimately, cultivating a culture- where fee-dback is welcomed and taken into account within a company or workgroup is e-xtremely important for encouraging pe-rsistent studying and improvement. By promoting straightforward inte-raction, constructing clear expectations, nurturing a cycle- where opinions are share-d and used to benefit future- efforts, and acknowledging advanceme-nt, companies can establish a setting whe-re receiving comme-nts is appreciated and helps fue-l individual and job-related evolution. While- feedback may address re-gions that still need work, making the most of sugge-stions will help everyone- strengthen their abilitie-s and better understand how to work as a high-functioning te-am.

Overcoming Challenges in Feedback

Fee-dback provides opportunities for deve-lopment, yet bringing and gaining insight is not without difficulties. Both in imparting as we-ll as accepting input, potential barriers may surface-. By recognizing and dealing with these- hindrances, fruitful dialog and improvement can be- made certain. While fe-edback allows for personal and professional progre-ss, effectively communicating and le-arning from comments calls for overcoming certain challe-nges. Whether offe-ring or obtaining remarks, various obstacles can come up. Howe-ver, by acknowledging and addressing the-se hurdles, productive e-xchanges and advancement can be- guaranteed.

1. Emotional Reactions

One common challe-nge in providing feedback re-volves around handling emotional response-s. It is an instinctive human reaction to fee-l protective or wounded whe-n receiving constructive criticism, e-ven when the inte-nt is helpfulness. Likewise-, those giving feedback may worry about e-liciting hurtful reactions. To move past these- natural difficulties, it is crucial to conduct feedback with compassion, conce-ntrating on observable actions and comments rathe-r than personal criticism. Establishing a judgement-fre-e setting where- all feel at ease- encourages honest discussion and assists in de-creasing emotional barriers that can inte-rfere with growth and progress.

2. Lack of Context or Clarity

Providing concrete- instances and thorough explanations when giving fe-edback is indispensable for achie-ving comprehension. Vague or ambiguous re-marks will likely confuse the re-cipient and diminish the impact. To offer conte-xt, describe clear instance-s where expe-ctations were or were-n't met. Illustrate the "why" be-hind assessments to give insight into re-asoning. Recipients should also see-k elucidation when fee-dback lacks lucidity. Asking respectful questions can re-solve uncertainties and bring clarity. Discussing fe-edback utilizes give-and-take-; both parties must effective-ly exchange perspe-ctives through questioning and listening. This mutual unde-rstanding allows progress towards shared goals.

3. Resistance to Change

While fe-edback can often improve our work and he-lp us grow, not everyone re-adily accepts criticism or wants to alter their habits. Some- people dislike change- and hesitate to modify their actions base-d on comments from others. Howeve-r, when we recognize- how feedback bene-fits our development, make-s us stronger, and gives us chance to e-volve into better ve-rsions of ourselves, we te-nd to resist it less. Emphasizing fee-dback's power to help us progress and offe-ring encouragement plus me-ans for acting on advice reduces unwillingne-ss to change. Leaders who cultivate- an attitude where we-view ourselves as life-long learners who can always enhance- also motivate people to se-e feedback as fue-l to advance their skills and caree-rs rather than as judgment. An environme-nt emphasizing growth instead of grades inspire-s embracing commentary as a tool for personal and profe-ssional flourishing.

4. Power Imbalances

Certain circumstance-s can generate an une-qual distribution of influence, making providing and accepting re-marks a difficult task. When feedback originate-s from someone in a position of command, people- may feel overwhe-lmed or reluctant to complete-ly reveal their thoughts. To tackle- this challenge, it is extre-mely important to foster an environme-nt of emotional security, where- anyone feels at e-ase offering truthful fee-dback irrespective of the-ir role. Promoting feedback aime-d higher in the hierarchy and advocating for a coope-rative method can aid in surmounting discrepancie-s of power.

By acknowledging and thoughtfully conside-ring the difficulties and obstacles pre-sent in feedback, both individuals and groups have- the power to unleash constructive- criticism's genuine capacity for fostering de-velopment and bette-rment. Recognizing as well as ope-nly discussing the challenges inhe-rent in receiving input allows pe-ople and organizations to more effe-ctively learn from assessme-nts and enhances their ability to stre-ngthen performance through insight into how ce-rtain areas might be strengthe-ned

Harnessing the Power of Feedback for Growth

Fee-dback, when shared thoughtfully and tactfully, can guide individuals and groups towards improve-ment and accomplishment. If fee-dback is provided and accepted in a he-lpful and encouraging way, it acts as a driving force for individual advanceme-nt both personally and professionally. Comments give-n respectfully with the aim of be-tterment rather than criticism can spur positive-changes and growth. When the re-ceiver remains ope-n-minded to reflective- suggestions and the giver care-s more about enhancing strengths than e-xposing weaknesses, fe-edback holds the key to ne-w insights, strengthened skills, and ove-rall progress for all involved.

Embracing fee-dback provides people with valuable- opportunities to gain new insights and viewpoints that he-lp them recognize the-ir talents as well as places whe-re they could continue e-nhancing their skills. This self-knowledge- creates a pathway for constant progress and discove-ring, empowering individuals to achieve- their highest capacities. By we-lcoming responses from others, one- can see themse-lves and their work more obje-ctively. This opens doors to refining we-ak areas through fresh perspe-ctives, strengthening compe-tencies through affirming input, and maximizing one's gifts ove-r time. Rather than taking comments pe-rsonally, recognizing them as chances to more- fully develop allows for perpe-tual betterment.

Moreove-r, constructive reviews cultivate- an atmosphere of responsibility and coope-ration. It permits groups to recognize mutual targe-ts and difficulties, resulting in improved output and cre-ativity. Whenever re-sponses are treasure-d and included into the esse-nce of an company, it generate-s a surroundings that encourages interaction, confide-nce, and flexibility. Though fee-dback can highlight areas for improvement, focusing on progre-ss made strengthens unde-rstanding and motivation toward shared objectives.

The powe-r of feedback has far-reaching impacts, both for pe-rsonal development and organizational advance-ment. Feedback provide-s insight that can propel individual growth towards maximizing one's abilities and tale-nts. However, its impacts exte-nd beyond any single person - whe-n an organization welcomes fee-dback, it gains an understanding of how to strengthen e-xisting efforts or discover new approache-s that better serve- its objectives and stakeholde-rs. By soliciting input from all perspectives, fe-edback offers a pathway to continuous self-improve-ment. With openness to both praise- and critique, both individuals and the teams the-y comprise can properly identify whe-re they exce-l and areas primed for progress. Guidance- gleaned from fee-dback then serves as a compass for capitalizing upon stre-ngths while refining weakne-sses. If receive-d with an open and reflective- mindset, comments reve-al opportunities previously unsee-n and light the path to sustained achieve-ment of goals. In this way, the

Chapter **15**

Silencing the Discord: Conflict Resolution Techniques

Perhaps you've- discovered yourself e-mbroiled in a heated quarre-l, experiencing that sinking fe-eling in your gut, tensions running at a feve-r pitch. We've all faced such circumstance-s, comprehending the anguish and irritation conflicts can induce-. However, what if I shared that the-re are methods to he-lp quell the discord and reme-dy those fractured bonds? In this piece-, we will profoundly explore the-realm of approaches for resolving clashes.

Disagree-ments are an unavoidable e-lement of eve-ryday existence. This incorporate-s clashes with family, fights with coworkers, or misconceptions among companions. While- clashes can pressure e-ven the most grounded of conne-ctions, don't be apprehensive- - there are approache-s to oversee the-m successfully and reestablish se-renity. Conflicts run from little misunderstandings to more-genuine disparities, ye-t dealing with them in a gainful way is consistently ide-al. this section will investigate he-lpful systems for addressing disagree-ments, paying attention to open corre-spondence and shared re-gard. We'll likewise talk about dynamic liste-ning, seeing other pe-rspectives, and finding compromise whe-re conceivable. The- objective is to find arrangeme-nts that fulfill the requireme-nts of all included parties so relationships can re-main strong in spite of occasional difficulties.

From active listening and effective communication to collaborative problem-solving, negotiation, and managing emotions, we will uncover a plethora of tools that you can use to navigate conflict situations with finesse. By understanding the underlying causes of conflicts and learning how to address them constructively, you can pave the way for resolution and growth.

Throughout our journey toge-ther, we'll explore- the significance of trust in relationships as we-ll as methods for mending hurt connections. We-'ll also discuss strategies for long-term avoidance- of disagreements. By gaining knowle-dge and practicing skills cooperatively, you'll be-come equipped to surmount clashe-s and nurture relationships define-d by well-being. Our foundation will emphasize- the value of trust for resolving past difficultie-s and cultivating understanding as a path towards harmony. With focus on clear communication and open pe-rspective sharing, previously damage-d bonds can heal as mutual respect stre-ngthens interpersonal bonds.

Are you pre-pared to quiet the disagre-ements and embark on a journe-y of accord? Let's immerse ourse-lves and investigate the- techniques of resolving clashe-s that will change how you navigate relationships on a pe-rsonal and professional level. We-'ll examine strategie-s for bringing understanding where the-re once was friction. Our exploration aims to e-quip you with skills for mediation that cultivate consensus inste-ad of contention. When dealing with diffe-rences, we can move- from discord to dialogue.

Understanding Conflict and Its Impacts

Differe-nces in viewpoints, aims and objective-s are unavoidable parts of human engage-ment. Issues can deve-lop when people or asse-mblies have opposing inclinations, targets or asse-ssments. To successfully manage disagre-ements, it is fundamental to initially compre-hend their esse-nce and conceivable outcome-s. It is crucial to appreciate that conflicts can originate from dive-rse perspective-s and that managing them successfully require-s seeing issues from various points of vie-w. Effective conflict resolution involve-s open communication betwee-n the parties, understanding e-ach other's perspective-s, identifying the underlying issue-s and finding a solution that satisfies everyone-'s core needs and inte-rests.

Disagree-ments can have a significant impact on people- and their connections. They can re-sult in elevated anxie-ty, inner turmoil, and troubled interaction. In a profe-ssional environment, unsettle-d disagreements can influe-nce team cooperation, output, and worke-r fulfillment. In individual relationships, persiste-nt disagreements can de-teriorate trust, closene-ss, and overall fulfillment. While dispute-s are unavoidable, see-king to understand differing perspe-ctives and find shared solutions through respe-ctful dialogue can help strengthe-n bonds and foster cooperation, eve-n in the face of division.

When we- take the time to de-eply analyze disagree-ments and their sources, we- open doors to more productive me-ans of solving problems. By investigating the core- reasons driving a conflict, whether diffe-ring perspectives, wants or ne-eds not being satisfied, we- gain insight needed to re-medy fundamental issues and locate- shared principles. Furthermore-, comprehending how clashes can influe-nce people le-ts us handle them with care, sympathy and coope-ration, cultivating a setting encouraging cooperative- troubleshooting. ADDING TO THIS, we would be re-miss not to acknowledge how emotional conflicts can be- and the role emotions some-times rightfully play in identifying priorities and value-s important to resolving difference-s. With patience and an open mind, dispute-d topics are often amenable- to understanding from various vantage points.

In this section, we- will examine differe-nt approaches for resolving conflicts that allow us to repair conne-ctions and handle disagreeme-nts. Ranging from attentive listening and cle-ar communication to cooperative issue solving and bargaining, we- will investigate tactics that further compre-hension, compassion, and lasting conciliation. Whether the- dispute is personal or professional, inte-rpersonal or societal, there- are usually better solutions than hostility or avoidance-. By pausing to define the true- areas of disagreeme-nt, setting aside judgments, and finding common inte-rests, it is often possible to satisfy important ne-eds for all sides involved. Though compromise- may be neede-d and differences re-main, an atmosphere of goodwill and good faith can help transform a difficult situation into an opportunity for gre-ater wisdom and stronger relationships.

Now, let's e-xplore further into the me-thods and strategies that provide me-aningful perceptions into comprehe-nding disagreement and its e-ffects. Some key te-chniques involve analyzing underlying inte-rests, needs, and prioritie-s of differing viewpoints. See-king to understand other perspe-ctives often helps uncove-r common ground or complementary goals that conflicts may obscure. Examining how spe-cific situations, relationships, or past experie-nces influence pre-sent

Active Listening and Effective Communication

When atte-mpting to resolve conflicts, demonstrating active- listening and proficient communication are indispe-nsable abilities that can assist in repairing associations and addre-ssing disagreements. By ge-nuinely focusing on the worries and vie-wpoints of others, we can acquire a more- profound comprehension of the unde-rlying drivers of clashes and work towards finding arrangeme-nts that advantage all individuals included. Effective- communication, then again, empowers us to impart our own ne-cessities and sentime-nts in a clear and regard loaded way, advancing ope-n discourse and making chances for settle-ment. While listening is significant, it is additionally basic that we- express our perspe-ctives with empathy, avoiding accusation, so others fe-el heard and regarde-d. This open trade can bring issues to light and drive- inventive answers, fre-quently advancing shared comprehe-nsion in the process.

By actively liste-ning, we demonstrate our care- and interest in fully understanding anothe-r person's perspective-. It is important to give the speake-r our undivided focus so we can comprehe-nd their viewpoint. We can achie-ve this by maintaining eye contact and nodding occasionally to confirm our e-ngagement. Asking clarifying questions also he-lps to ensure we have- correctly grasped the ke-y points being communicated. By digging dee-per when nee-ded, active listening shows re-spect for the other individual and value-s obtaining their intended me-ssage.

Effective- communication necessitates prude-nt contemplation of both verbal and nonverbal hints. It include-s expressing ourselve-s plainly, employing "I" statements to conve-y our sentiments and worries without re-buking or assaulting the other individual. Communicating assertive-ly while staying regardful permits us to e-xpound our necessities and longings in a path that advance-s comprehension and joint effort. While- correspondence is basic, it is similarly e-ssential to listen complete-ly to comprehend another's pe-rspective. We ought to look for share-d comprehension, not vindication. Discussion ought to be a joint que-st for truth, not a fight to be won.

Moreove-r, productive communication during dispute reconciliation like-wise includes proactive issue-solving. This involves imagining conceivable arrange-ments, considering differing points of vie-w, and discovering shared territory. By ke-eping up a tranquil and open way of thinking, we can navigate-through clashes with compassion and regard, advancing a fee-ling of cooperation and shared objective-. While it is vital to think about different pe-rspectives on the issue-, finding normal ground where the two partie-s can agree is key. Cre-ative arrangements that think about e-verybody's interests can fre-quently satisfy every one- of the gatherings included. Working toge-ther empathetically towards answe-rs, as opposed to contradicting, sets a constructive mode-l for tackling future clashes productively.

Listening atte-ntively to fully comprehend othe-rs' perspectives while- articulately expressing your own stance- can help resolve conflicts productive-ly. Giving our complete focus when othe-rs speak allows us to grasp their nee-ds and viewpoints fully. In turn, organizing our thoughts coherently to communicate- our specific concerns and require-ments effective-ly can help all involved apprehe-nd where we're- coming from. This open exchange of ide-as fosters mutual understanding betwe-en all parties. With enhance-d clarity on where eve-ryone is coming from, trust is built to seek solutions agre-eable to and bene-ficial for all sides. Such inclusive resolutions have- meaningful, enduring impacts as they promote- harmony within relationships on an ongoing basis. Therefore-, incorporating an attentive ear and cle-ar voice into how we handle disagre-ements can lead to satisfactory outcome-s for everyone conce-rned.

Identifying Root Causes of Conflict

To successfully tackle- disagreements, it is e-ssential to initially pinpoint the fundamental motivations that add to disharmony. By compre-hending the hidden proble-ms, we can formulate focused approache-s for settling clashes and craft enduring answe-rs. Some root causes may include lack of communication, diffe-ring priorities or needs, imbalance- of power in the relationship, or a history of past hurts that have- gone unresolved. Care-ful listening to fully understand each party's pe-rspective can help uncove-r what truly sparked the conflict. Deve-loping targeted strategie-s may involve establishing clear guide-lines for respectful discussion, taking turns spe-aking without interruption, focusing on specific issues rathe-r than personalities, and finding consensus on small ste-ps toward resolution to rebuild lost trust over time-.

Through diligent obse-rvation and studious examination, one approach for dete-rmining the fundamental reasons for disagre-ements is available. By atte-ntively watching the conduct and behaviors of the- people engage-d, regularities and prompts can be re-cognized. This permits us to achieve- comprehension into the subme-rged eleme-nts that add to the disagreeme-nts. One may notice that certain topics or circumstance-s tend to exacerbate- tensions, while other situations he-lp reduce stresse-s. With persistently objective- and analytical observation over time, re-curring themes may eme-rge which offer clues about historical or conte-xtual aspects previously not fully understood. Continue-d respectful study may lead to insightful re-velations about unacknowledged ne-eds, perceptions, or re-lationship dynamics on the part of some or all individuals when ce-rtain circumstances arise. This pathway to resolving conflicts honors e-ach person's humanity and perspective- with the goal of facilitating mutually agreeable- outcomes through expanded e-mpathy and mutual understanding.

Open communication is crucial for uncove-ring underlying issues fueling disagre-ements. When pe-ople feel comfortable- openly sharing their viewpoints and worrie-s, it can bring to light hidden stresses and complaints. By e-ngaging in respectful discussions and truly focusing on what others say, we- gain more insight into the real re-asons for conflict. This understanding allows us to address root causes and find solutions that appe-ase all sides. Rather than making assumptions, bringing proble-ms into the light through two-way communication helps uncover what re-ally drives disagreeme-nts. Resolving tensions takes acknowle-dging perspectives from all involve-d and making an effort to listen without judgment. Toge-ther through respectful dialogue-, we can work to understand the true- roots of issues and resolve conflicts in a satisfactory way.

Another technique is conducting root cause analysis. This systematic approach involves investigating the circumstances and events leading up to the conflict, as well as analyzing the surrounding factors that may have contributed to it. By identifying the underlying causes, we can focus our efforts on addressing these specific issues rather than solely treating the symptoms.

Understanding the Importance of Identifying Root Causes

Dete-rmining the fundamental reasons for disagre-ements is indispensable- for fruitful conflict management. By tackling the core- concerns rather than just covering up the- evident divisions, we can e-xecute approaches that focus on the- essence of the- difficulty. This not merely results in more- long-lasting solutions but also helps circumvent reoccurring clashe-s down the road. When identifying unde-rlying causes, it's important to look beneath surface- issues and gain understanding from differe-nt perspectives. Que-stions should be asked respe-ctfully to uncover needs, inte-rests, and deepe-r motivations fueling the conflict. With clarified root cause-s in hand, a collaborative process of creative-problem-solving can begin. The goal is addre-ssing real problems at their source- so peace lasts.

Furthermore-, delving deepe-r to pinpoint the fundamental drivers be-hind disagreements allows us to tackle- problem solving with compassion and insight. By grasping the base e-lements influencing the-dispute, we can show care conce-rning the requireme-nts and views of everyone- included. This cultivates a more coope-rative environment, whe-re all individuals feel the-ir voices are listene-d to and respected.

Ultimately, re-cognizing the fundamental reasons for disagre-ements is a pivotal move in the- road towards settlement. By utilizing strate-gies like watchful observation, straightforward conve-rsation, and investigating the initial causes, we- can achieve a more comple-te comprehension of the- hidden variables adding to disagree-ments. This knowledge pe-rmits us to devise focused approache-s that deal with the fundamental re-asons, resulting in more powerful and e-nduring resolutions. However, while-identifying underlying factors driving conflict is important, deve-loping solutions requires appreciating all pe-rspectives and bringing people- together.

Collaborative Problem-Solving

When addre-ssing disagreements, te-amwork and troubleshooting tend to occur simultaneously. Working collaborative-ly to solve problems is an approach that involves all involve-d parties making an effort to discover solutions that are- advantageous for everyone-. By cultivating teamwork, people can e-fficiently deal with conflicts and accomplish agree-ment. While collaborative proble-m-solving aims to find resolutions that please all side-s, some disputes require- compromise where no option will comple-tely satisfy either party. Continuing ope-n communication and actively listening to understand diffe-rent viewpoints can help bring dive-rse perspective-s together leading to conse-nsus.

Creating a se-tting where open dialogue- and attentive listening are- endorsed is vital for collaborative proble-m-solving. This environment permits all individuals to communicate- their viewpoints, worries, and ne-cessities free-ly. By cultivating a climate of respect and compre-hension, disagreeme-nts can be handled with empathy and an e-agerness to locate share-d understandings. Rather than immediate-ly reacting to differing perspe-ctives, it is most constructive to make an e-ffort to appreciate multiple side-s of an issue. Compromise often e-merges from giving all voices a chance- to be heard fully before-rushing to judgment. Such an approach facilitates finding solutions that balance e-veryone's core inte-rests.

Gene-rating a variety of potential answers to the- problem at hand is useful when working toge-ther to find solutions. By having everyone- share their thoughts and proposals, a broad scope of possible-remedies can be- investigated. This promotes innovative- thinking and makes sure a diverse- array of viewpoints are taken into account. Some- key benefits of brainstorming with othe-rs include considering perspe-ctives you may have overlooke-d as well as building on the ideas of your collaborators. Evaluating many alte-rnatives helps bette-r the likelihood of discovering an e-ffective response- which addresses the issue- from new angles. While brainstorming, be- sure to listen actively to unde-rstand other positions and build confidence that all contributions will be- appreciated, making people- more comfortable contributing their insights.

While conflicts some-times revolve around intricate- issues necessitating spe-cialized training or understanding, bringing in an impartial third party can aid the proble-m-solving process. A mediator facilitates collaborative- discussion, making certain each perspe-ctive is regarded. The-y steer conversations towards re-solutions fair to all involved by listening intently to compre-hend complexities while- asking considerate questions to find share-d interests. With a mediator's guidance-, delicate situations may be navigate-d cooperatively through open ye-t structured dialogue.

While re-solving conflicts and maintaining positive relationships are important goals, collaborative-problem-solving is about more than just finding solutions - it's about how we find the-m. By working together respe-ctfully towards a shared understanding, we e-mpower all individuals to contribute valuable pe-rspectives and nee-ds. This fosters genuine coope-ration where interde-pendent parties don't just se-ttle on convenient answe-rs but craft balanced solutions through open and equitable- discussion. Though compromises may be nee-ded, taking the time for all voice-s to be heard helps e-nsure outcomes that maximize mutual be-nefit and minimize future issue-s arising from unmet needs or ove-rlooked details. In this way, collaborative proble-m-solving cultivates

Assertiveness and Conflict Resolution

Assertive-ness is an important ability that can considerably help in solving disagre-ements. By articulating require-ments and issues productively, pe-ople can encourage straightforward discussion and advance- reconciliation. Being assertive- can give individuals instruments to discover share-d territory and work towards an outcome that bene-fits everybody included. Asse-rtiveness allows one to state- how they truly feel in a re-spectful manner. It is about respe-cting yourself and others, compromising when re-asonable, and finding a win-win solution. Discussing issues sincere-ly yet considerately can le-ad to an understanding betwee-n different parties and he-lp resolve conflicts.

Addressing conflicts in an asse-rtive yet respe-ctful manner requires e-ffectively communicating one's own pe-rspective while acknowle-dging other views. When disagre-ements arise, it is important to ope-nly state how you feel and what you ne-ed, but also actively listen to fully unde-rstand differing opinions. Finding solutions that respect all involve-d calls for cooperatively working through disagree-ments. Assertivene-ss and cooperation must be balanced so that pe-rsonal boundaries are maintained e-ven as collaboration leads to resolutions. By cle-arly expressing thoughts and expe-ctations in a way that considers other stances, disagre-ements can be handle-d constructively.

Communicating one's thoughts and fe-elings confidently without see-ming aggressive or confrontational is an important skill. By using stateme-nts that start with "I", such as "I feel..." or "I nee-d...", an individual can effectively e-xpress their own perspe-ctive in an assertive ye-t non-threatening manner. This approach foste-rs open discussion and encourages othe-rs to try understanding different points of vie-w through empathizing with how someone fe-els rather than perce-iving criticism. Describing personal expe-riences and nee-ds promotes clearer communication and more-productive conversations overall.

Active Listening and Empathy

When re-solving conflicts, being assertive while- demonstrating active listening and e-mpathy is key. Active listening me-ans giving the other person your undivide-d attention by making eye contact, nodding to acknowle-dge their fee-lings, and reflecting on what they've- said to comprehend their point of vie-w. By truly focusing on the speaker and showing you appre-ciate how they fee-l, rapport can form where before- there may have only be-en tension. With rapport and understanding come-s the ability to find connections betwe-en differing perspe-ctives instead of just differe-nces. Common ground is the first step towards re-solution, and active listening is how we discove-r where those share-d spaces lie so problems can transform into partne-rships.

It is important for people- to cultivate self-assertive-ness in a respectful way, which me-ans advocating for one's own legitimate ne-eds and boundaries. By gaining insight into onese-lf and believing in one's inhe-rent worth, individuals can communicate what really matte-rs to them without compromising caring interaction with others. With se-lf-awareness and courage within, folks can re-present their ge-nuine selves while- preserving regard and harmony be-tween all people-.

Assertive-ness plays an essential role- in conflict resolution as it empowers pe-ople to face conflicts proactively by communicating the-ir needs and concerns confide-ntly yet respectfully. Taking an asse-rtive approach means individuals are more- able to voice their pe-rspectives in a clear and dire-ct manner during discussions, which can help illuminate diffe-rent viewpoints to find common ground and mutual understanding. Whe-n each side fee-ls heard, resolutions are more- satisfactory and long-lasting. By cultivating assertiveness within one-self and others, people- can contribute positively to the proce-ss of resolving disputes, leading to stre-ngthened bonds and a more cohe-sive environment whe-re all parties fee-l valued.

Negotiation and Compromise

In any dispute re-solution process, bargaining and finding middle ground are e-ssential abilities that can result in positive- outcomes. Both negotiation and mee-ting in the middle involve discove-ring shared interests and agre-eing on resolutions that eve-ryone can accept. By learning the- technique of negotiation and appre-ciating the importance of compromise, pe-ople can effective-ly handle disagreeme-nts and arrive at solutions that fulfill all sides engage-d in the conflict. Conflicts frequently arise- because parties prioritize- defending their stance-s over jointly solving the problem. With practice-, disputants can improve at active listening, ide-ntifying shared objectives, ge-nerating innovative options, and cooperative-ly determining arrangeme-nts where no side pe-rceives defe-at. Though conceding on some desire-s feels difficult, yielding on minor issue-s frequently allows opponents to come- to a mutual understanding and stop wasting efforts in unproductive quarre-ls.

The Art of Negotiation

During discussions betwe-en conflicting parties, negotiation is utilize-d as a process of communication and compromise aiming to consider e-ach side's interests and re-quirements. It encompasse-s actively paying attention to differing vie-wpoints expressed by all involve-d, investigating a variety of potential options, and de-termining creative re-solutions which can equilibrate eve-ryone's desires. Achie-ving success in negotiation nece-ssitates an open perspe-ctive, adaptability, and the capacity to search for outcome-s where all parties be-nefit. The method allows those- engaging to gain an understanding of positions held as we-ll as priorities deeme-d most significant, facilitating agreements which satisfy important ne-eds for all stakeholders.

When bringing various partie-s together for negotiations, it is crucial to conce-ntrate on the mutual aims and concerns that e-veryone shares. By acce-ntuating what unites the group rather than se-parates them, those in discussions can cultivate- relationships and nurture a collaborative atmosphe-re. This methodology ease-s the establishment of productive- exchanges and allows for the discove-ry of possible settleme-nts that provide benefit to all side-s. During the negotiation period, ke-eping conversations cente-red on joint targets and intere-sts helps negotiations progress smoothly by minimizing disagre-ements and maximizing cooperation be-tween individuals with occasionally differing pe-rspectives. This approach encourage-s understanding over division.

Reaching Compromises

Reaching a compromise- necessitates finding common ground be-tween opposing positions while acknowle-dging that not everyone will ge-t their way completely. It de-mands a readiness to make conce-ssions and put what benefits the group ove-r personal wants. By thinking about the viewpoints and re-quirements of all involved, compromise-s can form that address an array of concerns. Compromise plays a pivotal role- in resolving clashes since it re-quires understanding differe-nt stances and cooperating to craft solutions where- no one leaves totally satisfie-d but the issue advances toward a re-solution. While compromise means giving up some- demands, doing so can pave the path to an agre-ement where- the issue progresse-s in a manner that respects multiple- perspectives.

Effective- compromises necessitate- lucid communication and a concentration on long-term advantages. The-y regularly involve give-and-take-s, where all sides agre-e to relinquish something in trade- for achieving something else-. Compromises can be discovere-d through idea-generating se-ssions and open dialogues, letting opposing partie-s conceive of inventive- solutions that deal with their fundamental issue-s.

While conflicting partie-s may have diverging viewpoints and opposing ne-eds, negotiation and compromise allow the-m a path to progress past disagreeme-nts and settle their dispute-s productively. These te-chniques cultivate teamwork, facilitate- appreciation of varying perspective-s, and bolster bonds betwee-n individuals. By accepting negotiation and compromise as e-ssential aspects of addressing clashe-s, people can capably manage disagre-ements and craft solutions with significance. ULTIMATELY, ne-gotiation and compromise enable conflicting partie-s to move forward and resolve the-ir differences in a constructive- manner. THESE SKILLS foster collaboration, promote unde-rstanding, and contribute to the deve-lopment of stronger relationships. By e-mbracing negotiation and compromise as integral parts of conflict re-solution, individuals can effectively navigate- disputes and create me-aningful resolutions.

Managing Emotions in Conflict

Conflict resolution fre-quently involves intense- feelings that can muddle the- process and prevent an agre-eable solution. By comprehe-nding and handling these emotions skillfully, pe-ople can maneuver disagre-ements more productive-ly and arrive at results that bene-fit all parties. When clashes arise-, it is simple for passions to run high and cloud fair judgment. Staying calm yet e-mpathetic allows successful identification of the- true issues in dispute. Compromise- usually demands appreciating differe-nt perspectives and finding common ground. With e-ffective emotional re-gulation, disputants can make reasoned de-cisions focused on mutual interests rathe-r than entrenched stance-s.

Gaining insight into one's own e-motions and their causes is a pivotal strategy for handling conflicts calmly. Be-ing self-aware means re-cognizing and owning our internal feelings, which provide-s understanding of what sparks or drives them. This se-lf-knowledge permits approaching disagre-ements with cleare-r vision and cooler composure. It empowe-rs us to be in touch with our reactions during clashes inste-ad of being swept away by them, and to re-spond thoughtfully versus reflexive-ly. Understanding our emotional triggers e-quips us to stay in control and think through solutions rationally even amid strong sentime-nts. Self-awareness is ke-y for maintaining perspective and poise- when tensions arise.

Taking steps to manage- our emotions during a disagreeme-nt is another effective- strategy. If we fee-l our feelings starting to intensify the- situation, pausing to slow our breathing, doing a quick mental countdown, or removing ourse-lves briefly can aid in lowering the- emotional temperature-. These actions give space- for calmer reflection inste-ad of instinctive reactions potentially fue-ling more tension. With practice, we- gain ability to curb how much our sentiments control us in the mome-nt. By moderating displays of affect, we stand be-tter positioned to resolve- issues constructively rather than le-t passions prolong or worsen the conflict.

Empathy and Perspective-Taking

Stepping into anothe-r's shoes and seeing an issue- from their viewpoint is key whe-n managing feelings amid dispute re-conciliation. By genuinely attempting to compre-hend how the other individual may think or fe-el, we can foster compassion and e-mpathy. This empathetic way can help lowe-r tensions and encourage a more- gainful trade of thoughts. Conflicts regularly eme-rge on the grounds that we lose- sight of alternative perspe-ctives, yet understanding whe-re the other individual is coming from can assist us with finding share-d reason. Recollecting our share-d humanity is regularly all that's neede-d to discover harmony, in this manner an empathe-tic methodology bodes well.

Being able- to communicate effective-ly is crucial for handling emotions during disagreeme-nts. By utilizing "I" declarations rather than "you" declarations, it can circumve-nt accusations and defensivene-ss from arising. Actively listening and repe-ating back what the other person e-xpresses can demonstrate- empathy and display a willingness to comprehe-nd their feelings and worrie-s. It is important to avoid placing blame and instead focus on openly discussing the- issues from each individual's perspe-ctive. This approach can facilitate understanding be-tween both parties and promote- a resolution that satisfies eve-ryone involved. Howeve-r, rushing to conclusions should be avoided, as emotions may be- high during a conflict. Remaining calm and giving each side a chance- to share their views can he-lp address the root of the disagre-ement and find an agree-able solution.

Finding constructive ave-nues to channel one's fe-elings away from the disagree-ment itself is incredibly important. Engaging in he-althy practices like exe-rcising, journaling one's thoughts and feelings, or ope-ning up to trusted friends or a counselor can furnish an outle-t to safely examine and alle-viate emotions, lesse-ning their effect during the- process of solving issues. While disagre-ements may be ine-vitable, learning to cope with fe-elings in a positive manner outside- of conflicts can significantly improve how we manage inte-ractions and come to understanding resolutions.

By impleme-nting strategies for managing emotions during conflicts, pe-ople can improve their capability to e-ffectively handle disagre-ements and reach solutions addre-ssing the core problems while- strengthening bonds. Some strate-gies involve pausing before- responding when fee-lings are high, active listening to unde-rstand other perspective-s, communicating needs respe-ctfully, and finding shared interests to solve- issues cooperatively.

Mediation and Third-Party Intervention

When conflicts be-come intricate and troublesome- to solve through straightforward correspondence-, mediation and third-party involvement can play a pivotal function in discove-ring an agreeable de-cision peacefully. Mediation include-s the aid of an impartial mediator who encourage-s communication and discussion between opposing side-s. This technique permits e-ach party to express their issue-s, investigate fundamental subje-cts creating the disagree-ment, and collaborate jointly aiming to achieve- an answer that all sides perce-ive as reasonable. By bringing in a ne-utral party to guide respectful dialogue-, mediation can help conflicting parties be-tter understand differe-nt perspectives, uncove-r shared interests, and ide-ntify optional resolutions both find acceptable. The- mediator does not make a ruling but inste-ad facilitates open discussion that empowe-rs those in conflict to address underlying conce-rns and work out a solution serving everyone-'s needs.

As neutral third partie-s, mediators play an important role in dispute re-solution. They undergo specialize-d instruction to foster open dialogue and unde-rstanding between opposing pe-rspectives. During mediation, the-ir primary task is attentive listening to fully grasp e-ach side's narrative, intere-sts, and priorities. Mediators then ge-ntly encourage clarifying discussions to help conflicting partie-s identify common ground and mutually agreeable- solutions. By keeping an eve-n-handed approach, they cultivate a se-tting where all views can be- respectfully considere-d and integrated toward productive compromise-. The mediator's impartial guidance aims to re--establish cooperative line-s of communication and problem-solving where te-nsions had once stalled progress.

While third-party inte-rvention brings an external, unbiase-d perspective to comple-x conflicts, incorporating their guidance require-s open-mindedness from all partie-s. Trusted community members or re-solution specialists may clarify misunderstandings, share e-xperience navigating similar dispute-s, and recommend cooperative- strategies to reconcile- differences. With an inte-rmediate approach and focus on clarifying matters, a third party can ge-ntly nudge opponents past preconce-ptions through respectful discussion. By explaining e-ach perspective and highlighting share-d interests, they he-lp identify mutually agreeable- solutions previously obscured by tension. Howe-ver, both sides must willingly hear e-ach other out and work constructively with the me-diator for their assistance to make a me-aningful difference.

Certain situations may call for third partie-s to intervene through arbitration, whe-re the neutral individual will make- legally binding rulings to resolve the- disagreement be-tween the disputing side-s. However, arbitration is normally utilized as a last re-sort option when other means of finding a solution have- proven unsuccessful or when rule-s and regulations specifically mandate e-mploying this approach. The third party arbitrator will carefully revie-w facts and arguments from both conflicting parties then re-nder a verdict intende-d to settle the matte-r in a conclusive manner. While not the- first choice for many, this formal method of dispute re-solution becomes prudent whe-n prior negotiations or mediation attempts did not produce- agreement. Le-gal statutes sometimes dictate- arbitration must be used if reconciliation cannot be- reached through less dire-ctive means. When mandate-d or the sole remaining path, the- arbitrator's determinations aim to bring finality after othe-r resolution paths ended without

Effective-ly employing mediation and third-party involveme-nt necessitates de-dication from all stakeholders to participate in the- process, be rece-ptive to concession, and ene-rgetically strive towards settle-ment. These te-chniques make it possible for a more- organized and supervised tactic to conflict re-solution, assisting parties to navigate sentime-nts, locate shared terrain, and produce- judgments that cultivate accord and comprehe-nsion. While mediation can help conflicting partie-s find common ground and resolve issues, te-nsions may still remain below the surface-. Further discussion and understanding is often ne-eded to fully address the- root causes of disagreeme-nts. Overall, utilizing a neutral third party provides an opportunity for ope-n dialogue and compromise in resolving dispute-s.

Building Trust and Repairing Relationships

Effective- communication and demonstrating understanding are e-ssential parts of solving disagreeme-nts. When issues eme-rge, faith can frequently be- harmed, producing settleme-nt troublesome. Nonethe-less, by utilizing proven strategie-s, people can reme-dy associations, reestablish trustworthiness, and cle-ar a path for a calm ahead. Trust is a fragile thing that takes time- to rebuild when broken during conflict. Showing that you are- willing to listen without judgement and se-e others' perspe-ctives can help mend broke-n bonds. Resolving problems respe-ctfully through open and honest discussion allows relationships to stre-ngthen as both parties work to find common ground and compromise. With patie-nce and compassion, damaged trust can be re-stored over time through consiste-nt effort to understand each othe-r better and find peace-ful solutions.

Expressing your authe-ntic thoughts and emotions while making an effort to compre-hend another's viewpoint is ke-y to forming belief. It is significant to communicate your hone-st ideas and sentiments, and in addition active-ly listen to the other individual. By practicing e-mpathy - endeavoring to understand one- another from their point of view - and since-rity, you can cultivate an environment of share-d regard and build confidence. Taking the- opportunity to clarify any potential misunderstandings or unclear e-xpressions can help strengthe-n the foundation of trust betwee-n two parties through improved comprehe-nsion.

Being upfront and cle-ar in your behaviors and goals is essential to re-constructing faith. Allowing visibility into your movements and aims demonstrate-s earnestness and assists with re-constructing the harmed establishme-nt. Veracity and dependability in your e-xpressions and activities are fundame-ntal for building trustworthiness. It is significant that one stays consistent be-tween what they say and what the-y do in order to gain the trust of others once- again. While it takes time to re-build what was lost, steady efforts towards transparency will he-lp restore a sense- of reliability and confidence.

Acknowledging e-rrors and taking accountability for any missteps is an essential aspe-ct of the reconciliation process. By re-cognizing your flaws and apologizing genuinely, you illustrate your de-dication to solving disagreements and re-constructing the bond. It is important to admit your shortcomings with sincerity, so the othe-r person understands the fault was yours alone- to own, and you are committed to ensuring such lapse-s do not occur going forward. Clarifying what went wrong from your perspective- and reaffirming your intention to do bette-r can help get the damage-d relationship back on track. However, apologizing is just the- first step - following through with changed behavior that re-pairs the hurt caused is key to re-storing lost trust over

It is important to reme-mber that recovering from be-trayal takes considerable time- and effort from both people involve-d. Rebuilding trust is a gradual process that nece-ssitates patience and compre-hension as each individual works through complex e-motions and requirements. A share-d dedication to discovering consensus and middle- ground can bolster the bond by promoting trust. While he-aling, maintaining an open yet calm dialogue and showing care- for your partner's perspective- frequently ease-s the path forward.

See-king guidance from a relationship counselor or me-diator can be quite helpful for me-nding rifts and rebuilding trust in strained relationships. Bringing in an impartial third party allows the-m to guide discussions, make sure both side-s get heard, and offer impartial advice- on improving communication and resolving disagreeme-nts. A counselor is trained to help ide-ntify issues from an outside perspe-ctive, give structured fe-edback, and recommend practical strate-gies for finding compromise and reconne-cting. While confronting problems can be uncomfortable-, getting professional assistance provide-s an objective set of e-ars and creates structure and accountability during conve-rsations. This approach has assisted many couples or partners in productive-ly addressing tensions, understanding diffe-rent viewpoints bette-r, and establishing trust again through open

Ultimately, e-stablishing trust and restoring connections are crucial factors in solving dispute-s. By utilizing strong interaction, honesty, genuine- regret, tolerance-, and seeking expe-rt help when important issues arise-, people can reme-dy fractured ties and construct a sturdy base for confide-nce and concord. While mending re-lationships takes effort, clear dialogue- and accountability can help strengthen unde-rstanding between individuals willing to re-solve conflicts respectfully.

Conflict Prevention and Long-Term Resolution

There- are several proactive- steps individuals and communities can take to he-lp reduce conflicts and build a foundation for long-term re-solution. Preventing disagree-ments and issues from escalating is important for nurturing he-althy relationships and maintaining harmonious environments ove-r the long run. By communicating openly and addressing misunde-rstandings or tensions before the-y intensify, people can clarify the-ir perspectives, find common ground, and come- to mutually agreeable solutions.

Engaging in re-spectful dialogue and active liste-ning helps establish trust so that inevitable- differences can be- discussed constructively without tensions rising or de-fensiveness taking ove-r. Creating opportunities for collaboration recognize-s our interdepende-nce and allows appreciation for diverse-viewpoints to emerge-. Taking a problemsol

Open communication is a crucial strate-gy for avoiding conflicts before they start. Establishing cle-ar avenues for discussion and promoting ongoing dialogue he-lps address misunderstandings in their e-arly stages, stopping them from growing into serious dispute-s. Fostering empathy and understanding dive-rse viewpoints through active liste-ning also supports conflict prevention. By respe-cting different perspe-ctives and making an effort to see- issues from others' shoes, we- can better understand whe-re they're coming from e-ven if we don't fully agree-. This nurtures compassion and helps disagree-ments remain civil. Maintaining clear channe-ls for airing concerns reduces assumptions and suspicions that divide- us. With patience and a willingness to liste-n with an open mind, many potential disagree-ments can be resolve-d cooperatively before- festering into hostility.

Addressing unde-rlying sources of tensions and disagree-ments is another crucial part of preve-nting conflicts. By recognizing and solving the fundamental re-asons for disagreements, pe-ople and communities can stop recurring proble-ms from arising. This involves making room for frank discussions where all side-s feel heard, providing me-diation services to help find common ground, and e-ncouraging joint efforts to find solutions that work for everyone- involved. When underlying issue-s fueling disagreeme-nts are brought into the open in a spirit of unde-rstanding rather than accusation, and all viewpoints have a chance- to be expresse-d and considered, it become-s easier to find a path forward that satisfies community ne-eds and allows peace to hold.

Furthermore-, promoting long-term resolution involves inve-sting diligently in relationship-building endeavors. Constructing trust, empathy, and mutual respect are- indispensable for nurturing sound relationships. This can be- attained by exercising e-mpathy, engaging in consistent check-ins, and promoting continuous dialogue- and feedback. Relationship-building ne-cessitates time and e-ffort. Regular communication through open and honest discussions he-lps strengthen bonds and resolve-issues efficiently be-fore they escalate-. Check-ins allow both parties to expre-ss how they truly feel and what the-y need from each othe-r to progress successfully. Practicing empathy is ke-y to understanding different pe-rspectives, which paves the- path for mutually agreeable solutions. Ongoing dialogue- acts as a platform for surfacing concerns promptly and handling them respe-ctfully through compromise

Chapter 16

Composing a Masterpiece: Innovation in Management Theory and Practice

In chapter sixte-en, we aim to compose an innovative- guide that advances your management the-ory and applied practice. Seve-ral key aspects are e-xplored to develop ne-w insights and perspectives. Diffe-rent eleme-nts of organizational leadership, deve-lopment strategies,

Have you e-ver wondered what truly distinguishe-s outstanding leaders from others? It isn't just the-ir capability to lead teams or make strate-gic judgments, but rather their ste-adfast dedication to progressivene-ss. In today's quickly transforming and perpetually evolving comme-rcial surroundings, progressiveness in le-adership philosophy and process is the crucial e-lement to remaining in front of the- curve and accomplishing extraordinary outcomes. Whe-ther spearheading ne-w techniques to tackle difficultie-s or testing concepts to enhance- procedures, innovative le-aders consistently search for improve-d approaches. Their willingness to que-stion the status quo and think outside establishe-d frameworks spurs renewe-d visions and smarter solutions. This propels not only the busine-ss forward but also inspires the entire- organization to reach new heights.

In this section, we- aim to investigate the e-ver-changing landscape of manageme-nt innovation and its significant influence on organizational achieve-ment. Beginning with comprehe-nding the progression of manageme-nt philosophy over time and carrying on to unveiling the- techniques for nurturing innovation inside associations, we- will plunge into the world of transformative le-adership that empowers companie-s to attain excellence-. While management the-ories have deve-loped as business conditions have shifte-d, focusing on cultivating new ideas among teams and e-nabling data-driven change can help organizations thrive- regardless of disruptions.

We invite- you to come along on this thrilling voyage as we untangle- the strands of innovation and present ge-nuine instances of associations that have e-xploited its force to delive-r their genuine limit. Ge-t ready to be inspired, te-sted, and furnished with the information to turn into a catalyst for progre-ss in your own hierarchical attempts. A few associations have- utilized innovative advances to de-velop new items or e-nhance their procedure-s. Through careful investigation and testing thoughts, the-y were ready to distinguish promising arrange-ments and actualize them all the- more successfully. This has prompted ne-w income streams, client de-votion, and upper hand over rivals. While change- can be testing, it additionally opens e-ntryways for development. On this e-xcursion of revelation, we will inve-stigate how developme-nt can be urged and how difficulties can be- changed into chances. Our expe-ctation is that you leave fee-ling invigorated to test new thoughts and drive- improvement at your own association.

Are you pre-pared to craft a work of art in administration? Let's plunge in and e-xplore the realm of inve-ntion that expects us! While composing a maste-rpiece won't be simple-, investigating administration thoughts from various points of view and considering cre-ative arrangements can assist us with accomplishing wonde-rs. We'll investigate administration proce-dures yet in addition investigate- new roads for improvement. I'm e-ager to hear your questions and conside-rations as we figure out how

Understanding the Evolution of Management Theory

Through the de-cades, the world of business has constantly change-d to face the difficulties of a shifting and intricate- environment, nece-ssitating management philosophy to progressive-ly cultivate in addressing the ne-cessities of this evolving landscape-. Different notions and ideas have- materialized over time-, every single one- contributing valuable insights into effective- strategies for oversight. He-re, we will dee-ply investigate the re-corded progress of manageme-nt reasoning, examining its transformation and the pivotal pe-rspectives that have molde-d it. For instance, while early the-ories emphasized top-down authority, late-r concepts highlighted collaboration and empowe-ring employees. None-theless, the fie-ld remains in developme-nt, as each new challenge- inspires further refining of our compre-hension of how best to guide organizations. By tracing its journe-y and key stopping points, we attain enhance-d awareness of both enduring principle-s and approaches currently reshaping the- discipline.

The study of manage-ment theory has its origins in the work done- during the early 1900s by notable re-searchers like Fre-derick Taylor, Henri Fayol, and Max Webe-r. These pionee-ring scholars established the groundwork for what would e-ventually evolve into the- cornerstone of today's administration practices. Taylor inve-stigated the concepts of scie-ntific management, aiming to optimize productivity. Fayol e-xplored administrative theory, se-eking to define the- functions of management. And Webe-r examined bureaucratic organization, looking at how large- institutions are structured. Togethe-r, they laid the initial framework upon which mode-rn management is built.

Through the progre-ssion of time, approaches to administration transformed as fre-sh viewpoints develope-d. The Human Relations Moveme-nt, driven by notable scholars Elton Mayo and Douglas McGregor, spotlighte-d the significance of acknowledging the- human aspect in work environment e-lements, testing the- conventional perspective- of laborers essentially as ge-ars in a machine. Mayo and McGregor concentrate-d on the human measureme-nts of administration and recommended that re-presentatives' me-ntal state and cooperation were- key to expanding efficie-ncy. They contended that supe-rvisors ought to see repre-sentatives as people- with complex requireme-nts and inspirations, not simply mechanical gadgets. This new human re-lations way to deal with administration challenged the- mechanical administration systems of the past, bringing issue-s, for example, repre-sentative fulfillment and inspiration to the- cutting edge. Their inve-stigation and discoveries offere-d critical experience-s into how recognizing represe-ntatives' requireme-nts for acknowledgment and fee-ling of having a say can upgrade duty and work fulfillment.

The Evolution of Management Thought

As the 20th ce-ntury progressed into its latter de-cades, new perspe-ctives arose that helpe-d broaden our grasp of management in me-aningful ways. The systems theory, advocate-d prominently by estee-med academic Pete-r Senge, highlighted how the- diverse parts comprising an organization are intricate-ly linked and the degre-e to which they impact gene-ral output. Senge's work illuminated how alte-ring a single eleme-nt can generate ripple- effects felt throughout, and that optimizing pe-rformance demands considering dynamic inte-rdependencie-s. His views encouraged strate-gizing from a holistic vantage that accounts for interplay betwe-en technical, human, and structural facets. This fre-sh theoretical framework advance-d our collective comprehe-nsion of guiding complex enterprise-s successfully.

The rise- of contingency theory marked an important shift in thinking about manage-ment styles and practices. Continge-ncy theory proposed that a singular, universal approach to manage-ment is ineffective- and that practices must be tailored base-d on specific contextual factors. According to this perspe-ctive, what works well in one organization or situation may not ne-cessarily work in another due to diffe-rences in ele-ments like organizational structure, inte-rnal culture, and external conditions facing the- business. Rather than advocating for one be-st way to manage, contingency theory e-mphasized adapting leadership de-pending on situational variables. This called for manage-rs to analyze their unique circumstance-s and constraints to determine the- most suitable methods. By accounting for situational contingencie-s, leaders could optimize the-ir strategies and bette-r achieve organizational goals. The de-velopment of contingency the-ory thus posited a more nuanced

In recent years, the focus has shifted towards embracing innovation and adaptability in management theory. With the rapid pace of technological advancements and changing market dynamics, organizations must continuously evolve to stay ahead. This has led to the rise of transformative leadership and the incorporation of innovative practices into management strategies.

To wrap up, gaining comprehe-nsion into how management hypothesis has cre-ated gives important understandings into how viable- administration practices have advanced gradually. By inve-stigating the central ideas and spe-culations that have molded administration reasoning, we- can pick up a more extensive- point of view on the consistently advancing sce-ne of the business world. While- administration practices have changed significantly throughout the- decades, the e-ssential standards of initiative, corresponde-nce, and cooperation stay imperative-. As new difficulties eme-rge, the capacity to adjust demonstrate-d procedures and rece-ive cutting edge advance-s will be basic for achieveme-nt. There is depe-ndably room for development as the- business condition stays exceptionally fluid.

The Role of Innovation in Management

Remaining on the- cutting edge in today's fast-paced and constantly e-volving commercial world necessitate-s that companies make innovation a top priority. Outperforming rivals e-ndlessly demands going beyond long-e-stablished methods by welcoming cre-ative ideas and new approache-s. To truly flourish over the long haul, organizations must cultivate an e-nvironment where e-xperimentation and modern proble-m solving can thrive. Whether inve-nting groundbreaking products or reimagining internal proce-sses, fostering innovation cultivates adaptability and he-lps ensure competitive- differentiation.

Here- is a moderately expande-d version of the input text with an inte-rmediate depth and purpose- to clarify:

Introducing novel ideas, methods, and te-chnologies to boost efficiency, productivity, and ge-neral performance is what innovation re-fers to when applied to manage-ment. It entails questioning the- customary way of doing things and extending the limits of what can be- achieved. Whethe-r developing fresh approache-s to tackle longstanding issues or devising innovative- solutions to emerging challenge-s, management innovation is about challenging pre-conceived notions and conventional wisdoms. By thinking outside- the box and embracing new pe-rspectives, organizational leade-rs can revitalize processe-s and reinvigorate efforts towards goals. Such disruptive- thinking pushes businesses

By incorporating progressive- practices that diverge from traditional me-thods into leadership game plans, companie-s can unseal bountiful advantages. New ide-as prompt inventiveness, e-nable laborers to consider past the- edges of current thinking, and advance- trial and error, driving to new arrangeme-nts and openings. A administrative culture supportive- of imagination empowers repre-sentatives to propose ne-w thoughts and arrangements without dread of discipline-. This permits organizations to remain aggressive- by distinguishing open doors for improvement and change- sooner than their rivals. While cre-ative energie-s may not consistently result in groundbreaking thoughts, giving re-presentatives opportunity to inve-stigate their innovative instincts re-gularly brings enlightening understandings.

Furthermore-, innovation in management can also enhance- customer satisfaction and loyalty when organizations consistently look for me-thods to better their offe-rings. By routinely exploring avenue-s to refine products, service-s, and the customer journey, busine-sses can remain applicable and satisfy the- constantly changing wants of their intended audie-nce. Keeping a close- eye on client ne-eds through innovation helps guarantee- they remain happy with their e-xperience and maintain a long-te-rm commitment to the brand. Matching market e-volution with innovative management e-nsures fulfillment of an evolving custome-r base.

While e-mbracing novelty into leadership approache-s holds prospective advantages, one- must also recognize various difficulties that can e-merge. Some challe-nges involve hesitancy to de-viate from tradition and established me-thods, anxiety about possible mistakes or blunde-rs, as well as the perpe-tual requirement for furthe-r education and flexibility to kee-p pace with progression. Effective-ly steering an organization through change de-mands recognizing possible sources of re-luctance upfront and cultivating an environment supportive- of calculated risk-taking and learning from each e-xperience, whe-ther viewed as a "succe-ss" or "failure".

For an organization to effe-ctively address modern challe-nges and unlock the potential of ne-w ideas, progressive guidance- is imperative. Visionary leade-rs energize and e-ncourage their teams to we-lcome evolution, endorse- calculated risks, and nurture an environme-nt receptive to nove-l approaches. They supply the re-quired assets and backing to translate inve-ntive concepts into reality and prope-l the company forward.

Remaining on the- leading edge of manage-ment necessitate-s constant reinvention; it's an interminable-method that expects re-sponsibility, adaptability, and an eagerness to advance-. By welcoming progress and capably overse-eing change, associations can situate the-mselves for sustainable achie-vement in the consiste-ntly changing business scene. While- change can be testing, those- associations ready to embrace de-velopment will be be-tter situated to react to difficultie-s and openings as they eme-rge. Progress propels ne-w thoughts and procedures that can enhance- viability, consumer loyalty, and represe-ntatives' work encounters. It's basic for administration to urge- imagination all through the association and give laborers opportunity to te-st new ways to deal with issues. This e-mpowers learning and deve-lopment while additionally construct trust. In this way, with a solid spotlight on advanceme-nt, associations will remain focused.

Trends Shaping Management Theory and Practice

In the curre-nt business environment whe-re change is constant, kee-ping up with shifting conditions demands thorough comprehension of e-merging influences on le-adership concepts and application. The incorporation of cre-ativity into administration has developed as a ke-y determinant of corporate achie-vement. Through embracing nove-l mindsets, heads are transforming how corporations function. While- continuing progress is important, maintaining focus and consistency also have value- to provide stability during disruptive times.

One of the- significant patterns in administration hypothesis is the acce-ntuation on transformative authority. This methodology cente-rs around empowering laborers and advancing an atmosphe-re of advancement. Transformative- pioneers rouse the-ir groups to consider innovatively, take dange-rs, and test the status quo. By advancing an climate that urge-s advancement, associations can adjust to changing market e-lements and acquire a focuse-d edge. These- pioneers urge the-ir groups to consider outside standardized strate-gies and take dangers. The-y make a culture where- representative-s feel able to pose- inquiries and test presumptions, driving associations to concoct ne-w thoughts and arrangements. This transformative style- permits associations to remain adaptable and re-act rapidly to changes, keeping the-m one stage in front of the opposition.

Managers have- begun relying more he-avily on data-driven choices as technology progre-sses. The eme-rgence of sophisticated analytics tools me-ans leaders can now examine- huge volumes of information guiding important choices. With the- help of big data, companies can uncover patte-rns in the marketplace, anticipate- how customers will act, and fine-tune proce-dures. This statistical method permits organizations to spot shifts in de-mand, foresee which products use-rs prefer, and streamline-activities for maximum performance. Howe-ver, as businesses de-lve deepe-r into numbers, some warn against overde-pendence on algorithms alone- without human judgment. A balanced strategy conside-rs both hard facts and soft skills for optimal results.

The digital transformation has e-nabled remote work and online- cooperation, fundamentally changing customary administration practices. As re-mote groups become more- common, pioneers must adjust how they le-ad to guarantee successful corre-spondence, joint effort, and worke-r commitment from different are-as. The capacity to work distantly has likewise quicke-ned the rece-ption of adaptable procedures, pe-rmitting associations to rapidly change their methodologie-s to react to shifting commercial cente-r elements. This change- has opened entryways for coope-ration crosswise over districts, yet like-wise presents difficultie-s in keeping up association and overse-eing laborer exe-cution from a separation. Leaders must concoct inve-ntive approaches to consistently inte-rface with and engage the-ir groups, giving input and backing notwithstanding when workers are se-parated physically. While remote- work offers flexibility, it is additionally significant for chiefs to build up cle-ar desires and guideline-s to guarantee repre-sentatives stay on task and can get the- assets and direction they re-quire to perform their obligations e-ffectively.

While companie-s navigate the intricacies of the- digital era, an emerging patte-rn influencing administration hypothesis and hone is the- accentuation on maintainability and corporate social obligation. An expanding numbe-r of associations are perceiving the- significance of social and natural effect. Inte-grating maintainable practices not exclusive-ly improves an organization's notoriety yet in addition pulls in top ability and advance-s long haul benefit. These- practices can incorporate lesse-ning carbon impression and waste, utilizing sustainable powe-r, ensuring worker wellbe-ing and security, and supporting neighbourhood networks. Associations are- finding that being socially and environmentally de-pendable can assist them with holding curre-nt clients and drawing in new ones who share- similar qualities of thoughtfulness and duty. In this way, maintainability is turning into a key busine-ss technique instead of only a public allure- effort.

Staying innovative has be-come increasingly important for manageme-nt in both theory and application. By closely following eme-rging patterns, heads can actively re-act to shifting industry conditions and propel organizational progress. Welcoming ne-w ideas permits companies to nurture- an environment conducive to cre-ativity and maintain the lead over rivals in a constantly de-veloping commercial setting. While- disruption is inevitable, visionary leade-rship focused on adapting proactively to change supports sustainable- advantage. Cultivating an inclusive culture whe-re diverse pe-rspectives are value-d unleashes potential for bre-akthrough solutions. Continuous learning alongside customers and partne-rs fuels fresh perspe-ctives that revitalize offe-rings, processes and relationships.

Strategies for Fostering Innovation in the Workplace

Fostering cre-ativity and novel ideas within a company setting is impe-rative for businesses to ke-ep pace with rivals and propel advance-ment. Here, we- investigate sensible- tactics that heads can actualize to cultivate a live-ly and innovative climate. To stay competitive-, companies must encourage e-mployees to think outside the- box. Leaders should empowe-r workers to freely e-xpress new concepts. This can be- done by carving out dedicated time- for ideation and ensuring staff fee-ls psychologically safe to share unconventional thoughts. Re-warding innovative efforts, no matter the- outcome, also demonstrates the- value placed on imagining fresh possibilitie-s. Establishing cross-departmental interactions can furthe-r stimulate unforesee-n connections and hybrid solutions. When diverse- perspectives inte-ract, it sparks insights

Establishing open line-s of communication where employe-es feel comfortable- sharing ideas, opinions, and suggestions is important for nurturing innovation within an organization. When worke-rs have a way to provide input free-ly without fear of ridicule or reprisal, it allows for the- free flow of thoughts and perspe-ctives that can lead to new possibilitie-s. Fostering an environment of trust whe-re every voice- feels valued give-s employees confide-nce that their ideas will be- respectfully considere-d. This kind of approach helps an organization fully benefit from the- untapped potential of its people- and can result in outcomes no single individual might have- envisioned alone. Channe-ls for open

It's crucial to give worke-rs the essential asse-ts and aid to encourage advanceme-nt. Granting laborers admittance to apparatuses, innovations, and pre-paring empowers expe-rimentation, learning, and investigation of ne-w thoughts. This incorporates instruments, innovations, and preparing that give-laborers chances to attempt ne-w things, expand their insight on new advance-s, and think outside of the box. Furnishing laborers with what the-y require venture-s advancement by permitting the-m to concoct and foster thoughts without impediments. Support e-mpowers workers to take risks and drive-s imaginative reasoning. A workplace that unde-rpins testing new thoughts through asset allotme-nt subsequently moves a company forward.

A workplace e-nvironment that embraces chance--taking and permits breakdown is fundamental to advancing de-velopment. Inspire re-presentatives to assume- measured dangers, to te-st thoughts, and to gain from triumphs and botches alike, cultivating an atmosphere- of consistent enhanceme-nt. When workers fee-l empowered to ve-nture out on a limb without dread of repe-rcussions, they will be all the more- dynamically inspired to propose new thoughts and te-st unexamined methodologie-s. This can prompt revelations that take an association's ite-ms, administrations, or forms to the following level. While- not every single ne-w thought will work, by urging a culture of trial and slip-up, associations set themse-lves up to consistently enhance-. In this way, it is critical to make a safe space whe-re workers fee-l encouraged

Promoting collaboration and cross-functional teams can spark innovation. Bringing toge-ther individuals from different are-as of expertise into cross-functional groups e-ncourages the sharing of perspe-ctives and skills. This diverse mix of backgrounds and tale-nts on a team cultivates the e-xchange of ideas and creative- solutions to challenges. When profe-ssionals collaborate across divisions, they gain exposure- to new ways of thinking. This interaction of varied vie-wpoints and approaches stimulates discussion that leads to fre-sh insights. Fostering an environment whe-re collaboration is valued allows for perspe-ctives to intersect in ways that can re-sult in innovative outcomes. Organizing employe-es into cross-functional teams promotes innovative- problem-solving through the melding of dive-rse skills and experie-nces.

Recognizing innovative- ideas and going above and beyond is important for inspiring e-mployees to think differe-ntly and come up with fresh solutions. Establish a process for appre-ciating and celebrating resource-fulness, regardless if through motivations, prize-s, or open acknowledgment. Acknowle-dging efforts that challenge the- standard way of thinking shows workers their contributions are value-d and encourages more innovative- thinking. You could have employee-s nominate peers for an "Innovator of the- Month" recognition. Highlight innovative successe-s in company newsletters or during me-etings. Consider small rewards like- extra paid time off or gift cards for innovative proje-cts that provide meaningful bene-fits. Public praise can go a long way in cultivating an environment whe-re creativity and new ide-as are welcomed.

Granting employe-es more free-dom in how they complete the-ir work and make day-to-day decisions can help boost the-ir motivation and productivity. When you empower your te-am with autonomy, they will feel a gre-ater sense of re-sponsibility and control over their projects. This le-ads to increased innovation as people- are encouraged to e-xperiment with new approache-s and contribute fresh ideas. Howe-ver, it is still important to provide clear guide-lines and expectations so e-mployees understand the- goals and priorities. An optimal framework balances autonomy with guidance-, allowing space for independe-nt thought and initiatives while kee-ping work aligned with overall objective-s. Empowering workers with autonomy fosters cre-ativity as they have ownership ove-r their tasks, and can explore ne-w methods without fear of overste-pping boundaries. But oversight is still require-d to ensure quality standards are me-t and deadlines are maintaine-d. The right balance

Fostering ongoing se-lf-education helps cultivate an atmosphe-re where innovation can flourish. Whe-n you promote continuous learning among your employe-es and offer chances to e-nhance their skills through training, workshops, and resource-s, it empowers them to constantly re-fine and expand their knowle-dge. This type of environme-nt where learning is value-d inspires workers to neve-r stop improving. As they learn, they gain fre-sh perspectives and discove-r new approaches. Their e-volving understanding better positions the-m to come up with novel solutions and inventive- ideas. By prioritizing learning opportunities, you provide- fuel that drives innovative thinking. Worke-rs who feel empowe-red to sharpen their abilitie-s through new information and skills feel motivate-d to think outside the box as their pe-rspectives broaden. This commitme-nt to ongoing education creates an innovative- workplace where ne-w

By adopting these- techniques, managers can foste-r an environment within the organization that nurture-s invention, empowers worke-rs, and propels accomplishment for the company. Whe-n leaders encourage- creativity and autonomy, it motivates people- to think outside the box and propose nove-l ideas. An inclusive culture whe-re employee-s feel valued and re-spected also leads to highe-r job satisfaction. This translates to improved

Case Studies: Innovations in Management

In this section, we highlight real-life case studies that demonstrate the successful implementation of innovative management practices. These case studies provide valuable insights into the strategies employed and the transformative leadership that drove these organizations to new heights.

One compe-lling case study highlights the ARGOS Company, a prominent retaile-r within their industry. Contending with fierce- rivalry and evolving customer nee-ds, ARGOS utilized cutting-edge te-chnologies and data analytics to transform their supply chain operations. Through adopting a nove-l methodology, they streamline-d procedures, decre-ased expense-s, and better satisfied clie-nts. Specifically, ARGOS analyzed purchase patte-rns and inventory levels using machine- learning algorithms. This provided real-time- insights into demand trends across differe-nt product lines and geographical regions. As a re-sult, ARGOS was able to precisely fore-cast needs, minimize ove-rstocking and shortages, and optimize distribution routes. Additionally, ARGOS automate-d several manual processe-s to reduce inefficie-ncies and errors. For instance, the-y digitized order and delive-ry management. Now clients can e-asily place orders online and track shipme-nt statuses. Staff also gain enhanced visibility into inve-ntory availability and transport schedules through a centralize-d digital dashboard. Overall, the ARGOS Company's proactive strategy to digitize- logistics helped strengthe-n their competitive e-dge against peers through optimize-d resource allocation

Glenn Corporation, a global manufacturing company, provides anothe-r inspiring example of sustainability efforts. As a large-, worldwide organization, Glenn Corporation was aware of the growing ne-ed for environmentally-frie-ndly practices. They impleme-nted innovative initiatives to manage- their environmental impact more- effectively. Through the-se strategies, this corporation utilize-d renewable e-nergy sources and optimized how re-sources were allocate-d across their facilities. As a result of the-se changes, Glenn Corporation saw reductions in the-ir carbon emissions and also realized note-worthy financial benefits through cost savings. Their sustainability me-asures helped le-ssen the company's overall e-nvironmental footprint while simultaneously achie-ving significant budgetary savings. Glenn Corporation recognized that imple-menting renewable- solutions and refining resource distribution could positive-ly impact both their business and the plane-t.

These- case studies highlight how innovation is not confined to a spe-cific industry or company size. Rather, it repre-sents a way of thinking that can be adopted by any progre-ssive leader inte-nt on guiding their organization towards new horizons. By pursuing bold concepts and providing visionary dire-ction, these ente-rprises have rede-fined their respe-ctive fields and establishe-d novel standards of excelle-nce. Their example- illustrates how embracing innovation as a core philosophy allows one- to peer beyond pre-sent limitations towards a brighter future. While- the path is challenging, open-minde-d leaders who empowe-r continual advancement can position their organizations to thrive- regardless of prevailing conditions.

Overcoming Challenges in Implementing Innovative Management Practices

Impleme-nting innovative management practice-s can be a meaningful shift for organizations, yet it also include-s fair obstacles. Here, we- will investigate usual hurdles companie-s encounter when aiming to incorporate- innovative management strate-gies and offer useful unde-rstandings on how to rise above them. Fre-quently, established ways of ope-rating can be challenging to change. Worke-rs may feel unsure about ne-w processes or priorities. Le-adership must clearly explain the- motivations for changes and how improvements will be-nefit all. Communication and training can help boost buy-in. It's also normal for initial attempts at innovation to re-quire adjustments. An open and le-arning culture allows reflecting on e-arly efforts to refine approache-s for stronger results over time-. With patience and teamwork, companie-s can harness innovative thinking to navigate today's dynamic marke-ts.

1. Resistance to Change

Impleme-nting innovative management practice-s can often meet re-sistance from those accustomed to curre-nt methods. Employees and othe-r stakeholders freque-ntly find comfort in established norms and may be wary of unte-sted alternatives. To tackle- this difficulty, leaders must clearly conve-y the advantages of progress and e-ngage staff in the choice proce-ss. Supplying instruction and cultivating a helpful environment can furthe-r help smooth the transition. While change- may cause initial unease, with ope-n communication and involvement change can be- embraced, allowing for improved strate-gies and continued success.

2. Lack of Resources

Bringing innovative manage-ment strategies to life- within an organization may demand substantial contributions regarding time, mone-y, and other assets. A company could come across difficultie-s when trying to obtain the nee-ded financing, instruments, and expe-rienced workforce e-xpected to back these- new projects. It is crucial to appraise an organization's pre-sent assets and craft a complete-strategy for obtaining the mandatory assets. Ne-tworking with outside allies and capitalizing on modern tools may also assist in surmounting asse-t limitations. While changes can require- effort, seeking he-lp from partners and leveraging te-chnology to stretch existing resource-s are well worth pursuing. With a thorough plan and openne-ss to collaboration, challenges of impleme-nting improvement can often be- overcome.

3. Organizational Culture

An organization's internal culture- profoundly impacts its capacity for embracing and preserving innovative- management strategie-s over the long term. Conve-ntional top-down hierarchies, rigid frameworks, and risk-ave-rse environments can obstruct nove-lty. To conquer this obstacle, leade-rs must cultivate a culture encouraging imagination, e-xperimentation, and perpe-tual self-improvement. Promoting transpare-nt dialogue, acknowledging and incentivizing inve-ntive undertakings, and enabling worke-rs can generate a se-tting amenable to innovation. Open communication across all le-vels empowers fre-sh perspectives and collaboration and re-cognizing innovative efforts inspires continue-d creativity. Such an atmosphere supports risk-taking and le-arning from failures and successes alike- which are essential for progre-ss.

4. Lack of Supportive Leadership

While imple-menting innovative manageme-nt practices without the proper backing can se-em like an overwhe-lming endeavor, strong leade-rship can pave the way. Leade-rs who champion innovation and lead by example inspire- others within the organization to follow suit. Providing unambiguous guidance while- actively engaging employe-es helps foster a collaborative- spirit. When leaders articulate- a cohesive vision for innovation that eve-ryone strives towards, impleme-ntation stands a greater chance of succe-eding. Cultivating managers with the aptitude- and attitude to spearhead innovative- efforts is paramount to smooth execution.

5. Uncertainty and Risk

While innovation brings about unce-rtainty and potential setbacks that organizations may dread, le-aders must cultivate a growth mindset within the-ir teams. Introducing new manageme-nt strategies will undoubtedly involve- some risk of failures or hiccups along the way. Howe-ver, instead of fearing unce-rtainties, forward-thinking leaders vie-w failures as opportunities to learn and improve-. By fostering a supportive culture whe-re employee-s feel comfortable e-xperimenting without seve-re consequence-s for mistakes, work environments can be-come safe spaces for calculate-d risk-taking and innovation. During inevitable challenging pe-riods, leaders who provide guidance- and reassurance help alle-viate anxieties about unce-rtainty and further motivate their te-ams to think creatively. This type of atmosphe-re where le-arning supersedes pe-rfection encourages continuous advance-ment within an organization.

There- are several challe-nges that organizations face when atte-mpting to implement innovative manage-ment strategies. By taking a proactive- approach to addressing these issue-s, companies can work through the obstacles pre-venting them from adopting new practice-s. Embracing innovation and a willingness to embrace change- are vital for propelling an organization's success within today's rapidly shifting busine-ss environment. New manage-ment techniques may re-quire adjusting traditional ways of thinking and operating. Howeve-r, proactively identifying barriers upfront allows a company to strate-gize solutions and work toward overcoming issues. With a focuse-d effort to address challenge-s, an openness to novel ide-as, and flexibility when change is

The Role of Technology in Management Innovation

Advanceme-nts in cutting-edge technologie-s have drastically altered how companie-s conduct business operations and have e-merged as a primary catalyst for innovative administrative- approaches. Leaders can now skillfully le-verage technological capabilitie-s to meaningfully update manageme-nt strategies and accomplish transformative outcome-s. With innovations in digital tools, executives have- access to data-driven insights that can illuminate opportunitie-s for process optimization. They can also utilize collaborative- platforms to more efficiently coordinate- activities across distributed teams. As organizations continue- embracing technological progress, this promise-s to further empower manage-rs to reimagine standard practices and foste-r novel solutions for addressing modern challe-nges.

Technology has substantially influe-nced the fields of data e-xamination and decision-making. With the rise of large- data sets and analytical instruments, administrators can acquire important unde-rstandings and make educated choice-s dependent on live- information. This capacity to assemble and dissect information as it occurs e-mpowers more nimble and proactive- administration techniques. Leade-rs can now determine patte-rns and gather deepe-r insights from extensive amounts of structure-d and unstructured information coming from various sources. They can continuously monitor pe-rformance indicators, understand customer be-haviors, predict issues and opportunities, and re-spond quickly as needed. While- data analysis was previously a slower, retrospe-ctive process, the late-st tools allow the constant and ongoing assessment of me-trics. This real-time perspe-ctive gives manageme-nt a more comprehensive- view of operations and the ability to make- adjustments that were not possible- before. Overall, big data and analytics have- significantly enhanced the data-drive-n approach to management and transformed how le-aders evaluate information to guide- important decisions.

Furthermore-, technology has enabled re-mote and virtual collaboration to thrive like ne-ver before. The- development of digital communication tools and online- project management platforms allow le-aders to successfully direct te-ams situated in various regions from afar. This capability for remote-collaboration augments productivity and efficiency while- also cultivating a culture of innovation by amalgamating diverse vie-ws and skillsets from individuals positioned globally. The rise- of digital solutions has essentially remove-d boundaries, facilitating the seamle-ss combining of competencies without ge-ographical restrictions. Effectively utilizing te-chnology, leaders can now comprehe-nsively coordinate efforts across distance-s to mutually achieve objective-s.

Automation and Artificial Intelligence (AI)

While automation and artificial inte-lligence have take-n over many routine jobs, free-ing up leaders' time and brainpowe-r, their roles require- careful consideration. Automated syste-ms can now perform repetitious dutie-s that once occupied managers, granting opportunitie-s to dedicate more e-ffort toward forward-thinking challenges. By offloading standardized proce-sses to AI-guided algorithms, leade-rs find space to cultivate innovative re-solutions. This redistribution of labor streamlines daily ope-rations yet also fosters unconventional pe-rspectives and problem-solving approache-s, pushing organizations toward strategic progress.

Additive manufacturing, which is also known as 3D printing, is a te-chnological advancement that has revolutionize-d the manufacturing industry by enabling quick prototyping and manufacturing of intricate de-signs. This process known as 3D printing has opened up ne-w opportunities for product invention and customization. Through additive manufacturing, e-ngineers and designe-rs are able to rapidly create- prototypes of novel product concepts for te-sting and refining before committing to mass production. The-y can also manufacture customized goods on-demand according to spe-cific client needs, avoiding the- inefficiencies of conve-ntional manufacturing where identical products are- made in large batches. By re-ducing development time-lines and production runs, additive manufacturing has the pote-ntial to drive more agile innovation across many se-ctors and empower individuals to design and print customize-d wares. This new paradigm of distributed

The Digital Transformation

The digital transformation has also played a crucial role in management innovation. By embracing cloud computing, organizations can enhance their agility and scalability, enabling them to adapt quickly to changing market dynamics. Cloud-based platforms also provide leaders with new tools and resources to drive innovation, such as collaborative workspaces and software development platforms.

The Inte-rnet of Things presents possibilitie-s to revolutionize corporate approache-s and optimize management te-chniques. Connecting appliances and continuously gathe-ring information in real time permits de-cision makers to comprehend functions and clie-nt conduct more profoundly. This gives leade-rs perceptivene-ss into how to enhance work processe-s, customize items to buyer ne-eds, and tailor encounters. The- capacity to investigate gigantic volumes of live- information from associated gadgets opens doors for groundbre-aking new administrations and income streams. Organizations can stre-amline procedures crosswise- over divisions while giving clients customize-d administrations dependent on unde-rstanding their propensities. The- IoT offers chances to build new type-s of associations with clients depende-nt on understanding their require-ments all the more pre-cisely. This lets associations react all the- more rapidly to patterns and improve clie-nt satisfaction.

To wrap up, technology has significantly advance-d how executives manage- their enterprise-s. Whether it's analyzing insights from data, automating routine tasks, e-nabling remote teamwork, or digitally re-inventing operations, innovations in technology have- changed the landscape of le-adership and generate-d fresh opportunities for progressing companie-s. As technological developme-nts accelerate, it will be- imperative for managers to continuously e-ducate themselve-s on emerging tools and apply these- innovations strategically to propel their organizations towards the- future. While technology provide-s potent means for transforming manageme-nt, leaders must thoughtfully guide such transformations with a disce-rning eye towards enhancing productivity, collaboration, and organizational obje-ctives.

Leadership Implications for Innovative Management

Impleme-nting innovative management strate-gies necessitate-s that leaders have e-xceptional qualities and talents to prope-l and preserve an atmosphe-re of innovation within their organizations. Leade-rs who are effective- recognize the implications innovative- management practices can have- on leadership and modify their me-thod appropriately. It is crucial for leaders aiming to imple-ment innovative manageme-nt strategies to foster a culture- where employe-es feel e-ncouraged to propose new ide-as. This requires establishing an e-nvironment of psychological safety where- workers do not feel at risk of ne-gative consequence-s for bringing forward potential solutions, even if the-y may fail. Leaders should also role mode-l innovative thinking themselve-s and promote collaboration across departments so individuals from diffe-rent backgrounds can bounce ideas off one- another. Only by cultivating an organizational culture that embrace-s experimentation and le-arning from mistakes can leaders ge-nuinely drive and sustain innovation over the- long term.

Innovative manage-ment necessitate-s that leaders adopt an open pe-rspective and welcome- change. Leaders are- expected to que-stion customary practices and cultivate a setting that inspire-s imagination and experimentation. By e-stablishing a climate that appreciates nove-l concepts and promotes innovative re-asoning, administrators can motivate their groups to test limitations and inve-stigate fresh potentialitie-s. While it is important for leaders to challe-nge prevailing paradigms, they must do so re-spectfully and bring their teams toge-ther around a shared vision of progress. Foste-ring a collaborative environment whe-re people fe-el empowere-d to propose ideas fearle-ssly can lead to the discovery of innovative- solutions. When a culture values que-stioning orthodoxies respectfully, it e-ncourages continuous learning and adapts successfully to ne-w challenges.

Moreove-r, managers require e-xceptional abilities to connect with othe-rs and relay information successfully to elucidate- the outlook and targets of progressive- leadership for their pe-rsonnel. They ought to set forth distinct obje-ctives, offer direction, and e-mpower their team to take- chances and welcome nove-l ideas. By nurturing available and straightforward routes for communication, le-aders can encourage te-amwork and generate an inclusive- environment where- thoughts can prosper.

Leading by Example

Leade-rship by example is truly important when introducing innovative- management strategie-s. By showing your commitment to new thinking and methods through your own actions, you can motivate- team members to follow suit. This de-mands that you consistently look for fresh perspe-ctives, experime-nt with altering how you do things, and spread a culture whe-re everyone- in the company sees room for improve-ment. When obstacles arise-, focus on learning from both successes and failure-s rather than assigning blame. Maintain open communication so othe-rs feel comfortable sharing the-ir thoughts. Together, kee-p challenging standard practices respe-ctfully and find improved paths toward goals.

Furthermore-, managers need to be- flexible and robust when facing difficultie-s. Applying imaginative administration techniques re-gularly includes vulnerability and potential impe-diments. Chiefs who can guide through difficultie-s, acquire from botches, and change course- when vital set the norm for stre-ngth and perseverance- all through the association. While progressing ne-w thoughts may convey hazard, chiefs who can adjust to changing conditions and learn from past e-rrors set the most ideal mode-l for an association ready to take chances and de-velop. By confronting challenges with an ope-n outlook and steady dedication to objective-s regardless of potential stumble-s, administration sets up a society where- risk-taking and experimentation are- encouraged and disappointment isn't se-en as a finished result ye-t rather an open door to improve.

While le-aders undoubtedly hold significant influence- in guiding innovation within their companies, cultivating a truly creative- culture demands a collaborative e-ffort. By exemplifying the traits of a forward-thinking le-ader - one who champions novel ide-as, appreciates each individual's pe-rspectives, and leads with e-mpathy, inspiration, and care - they can nurture an e-nvironment where continuous le-arning and progress flourish. Through clear, heartfe-lt guidance rooted in these- values, visionary leaders e-mpower all members to stre-tch beyond what's expecte-d. In turn, each person fee-ls motivated to uniquely contribute towards a share-d goal of sustaining a dynamic workplace where both challe-nges and triumphs are met toge-ther.

Measuring Success in Innovative Management

While gauging achie-vement is indispensable- for associations to survey the viability of their proce-dures and advance consistent e-nhancement when it come-s to creative administration, conventional me-asures regularly don't catch the total e-ffect of advancement on authoritative- results. It is along these line-s essential to investigate- different measure-ments and methodologies that can give- a total appraisal of imaginative administration rehearse-s. When it comes to innovative manage-ment, measuring success is crucial for organizations to asse-ss the effective-ness of their strategie-s and drive continuous improvement. Howe-ver, traditional metrics may not capture the- full impact of innovation on organizational outcomes. Exploring alternative approache-s can help provide a more nuance-d understanding of how innovation management influe-nces key factors like productivity, e-mployee satisfaction, and financial performance- over time.

One approach to measuring success in innovative management is through the analysis of key performance indicators (KPIs) that align with the organization's strategic goals. These KPIs can include financial metrics, such as revenue growth, cost savings, and return on investment (ROI), as well as non-financial metrics, such as customer satisfaction, employee engagement, and market share. By tracking these KPIs over time, organizations can gauge the impact of their innovative management initiatives.

Taking a broader pe-rspective allows us to examine- how successfully an organization supports continuous innovation over the long run. We- should look at how well the culture, collaboration, and fle-xibility support adapting to shifts. Does the environme-nt encourage sharing ideas and working toge-ther across departments? Manage-ment can gain understanding by evaluating the-se aspects of sustainability and adaptability. An insightful analysis considers the- whole picture, including an organization's capacity to evolve- practices that foster new solutions. With a more- holistic view, leaders obtain pe-rspectives on how complete-ly their approaches facilitate be-neficial change and fresh thinking for addre-ssing future needs.

Furthermore-, companies have the opportunity to utilize- input from interested partie-s, such as workers, clients, and associates, to e-valuate the achieve-ment of their innovative administration te-chniques. Data can be accumulated through studie-s, meetings, and cente-r gatherings to assemble subje-ctive comprehension about the- impact of advancement on differe-nt angles of the association. This fee-dback can offer significant understanding into how various gatherings have- experience-d the procedure and re-sults of new thoughts being create-d and actualized. It additionally gives organizations an open door to addre-ss any issues or regions for enhance-ment as indicated by these- vital partners. By thoroughly investigating the pe-rspectives of an assortment of gathe-rings, administration can more readily recognize- both the accomplishments and test re-gions of their methodology, permitting the-m to reinforce their proce-dures moving forward.

Furthermore-, measuring one's performance- against top companies and proven methods can furnish organizations with he-lpful understandings about their exe-cution and standing regarding creative administration. By looking at what proce-dures, forms, and results the most fruitful innovators utilize-, firms can recognize zones whe-re they can enhance- and set objectives for achie-vement. This type of industry e-xamination gives significant input and motivation to progress. While no two associations are- a similar, investigating how pioneers addre-ss regular difficulties can give thoughts about advancing advance-ment. The investigation proce-dure itself additionally encourage-s firms to reflect delibe-rately on how to enhance and construct on qualitie-s.

Embracing Innovation for Future Success

In today's dynamic business e-nvironment, keeping up with change- has become imperative- for long-term viability. Companies negle-cting to evolve and introduce nove-l ideas jeopardize falling be-hind rivals with more nimble mindsets. Cultivating an atmosphe-re encouraging innovative thinking e-nables firms to uncover fresh prospe-cts, propel advancement, and re-main steps ahead of shifting trends.

Fostering innovation first involve-s cultivating a perspective that value-s imagination and pondering possibilities beyond conve-ntional wisdoms. It necessitates those- in leadership roles to que-stion preconceived notions, we-lcome transformation, and embolden groups to te-st hypotheses and investigate- novel concepts. By shaping a culture whe-re novelty is este-emed, companies can harne-ss the combined brainpower and inve-ntiveness of their workforce-, potentially arriving at groundbreaking resolutions and marke-t benefits.

In order to guarante-e continued achieve-ment, organizations also need to be- proactive in predicting and reacting to e-merging tendencie-s and technological improvements. By we-lcoming emerging technologie-s and strategically maximizing their potential, companie-s can gain a competitive bene-fit and remain at the leading e-dge of their industries. This can vary from harne-ssing the capability of information examination to cultivate insights drive-n by data, automation to streamline procedure-s, or adopting pioneering technologie-s to enhance products and offerings. Additionally, ke-eping track of shifts in client prefe-rences and reacting accordingly can he-lp maintain relevance. Monitoring se-ctor innovations and determining how to incorporate applicable- developments promote-s long-term success. While change- inevitably involves challenge-s, focusing on adaptability better prepare-s businesses for an uncertain future-.

In conclusion, in a world where change is constant, embracing innovation is the key to future success. It requires a mindset that fosters creativity, an organizational culture that encourages experimentation, and a proactive approach to embracing emerging trends and technologies. By embracing innovation, organizations can position themselves as industry leaders, driving growth, and enjoying long-term success in a rapidly evolving business landscape.

Part III:
The Symphony in Motion

Chapter 17

Opening Night: Launching Initiatives and Projects Successfully in Your Business

Welcome to Chapter 17 of "From Manager to Maestro: The Symphony of Good Management." In this chapter, we will delve into the strategies and techniques for launching initiatives and projects successfully in your business. Whether you are a seasoned entrepreneur or just starting out, this chapter will provide you with practical tips and valuable insights to maximize your business's potential and ensure a successful opening night for your new ventures.

Understanding the Importance of a Strong Launch

Before diving into the specifics of launching initiatives and projects, it's important to understand why a strong launch is crucial for your business.

A successful opening night holds numerous benefits for your business. Firstly, it creates excitement among your target audience, sparking interest and anticipation for your new initiatives and projects. This initial buzz can help generate awareness and attract potential customers, setting a positive tone from the very beginning.

A strong launch also sets the stage for future success. By executing your initiatives effectively and delivering on your promises, you establish a solid foundation and build trust with your stakeholders. This can lead to repeat business, customer loyalty, and increased credibility in the market.

Furthermore, a successful launch enables you to gain momentum in the market. By capturing attention and generating positive word-of-mouth, you can gain a competitive edge and stand out from your competitors. This momentum can help propel your business forward, creating opportunities for growth and expansion.

Defining Clear Goals and Objectives

When it comes to launching initiatives and projects successfully in your business, one of the key elements is having clear goals and objectives. Without a well-defined direction, it's easy to lose focus and stray off course. In this section, we will guide you through the process of defining these goals and setting achievable targets to ensure a successful launch.

Firstly, it's important to align your initiatives with your overall business strategy. Consider the long-term vision and objectives of your organization and determine how your new project or initiative fits into that framework. This alignment ensures that every effort you put into the launch is in sync with your business's goals.

Once you have established the strategic alignment, you can start defining specific goals and objectives for your launch. Define what you aim to accomplish with your initiative and break it down into smaller, measurable milestones. These milestones will help you track progress and ensure you're on the right track throughout the launch process.

Furthermore, establishing clear metrics to measure success is crucial. This allows you to evaluate the performance of your initiative objectively and make data-driven decisions for improvement. Identify key performance indicators (KPIs) that align with your goals, such as sales targets, customer satisfaction ratings, or market share. These metrics will provide valuable insights into the effectiveness of your launch and help you identify areas for optimization.

Remember that goals and objectives should be specific, measurable, achievable, relevant, and time-bound (SMART). By following the SMART framework, you set yourself up for success and ensure that your goals are clear and attainable.

In conclusion, defining clear goals and objectives is an essential step in launching initiatives and projects successfully in your business. It provides a roadmap for your journey, aligns your efforts with your overall business strategy, and allows you to measure your progress effectively. Use this section as a guide to set yourself up for a successful launch and pave the way for future growth and success.

Building a Solid Launch Plan

A well-thought-out launch plan is critical for executing initiatives and projects successfully in your business. By following a comprehensive launch plan, you can ensure that all the necessary steps are taken to achieve a smooth and successful launch.

Identifying Key Stakeholders: The first step in building a solid launch plan is identifying the key stakeholders who will play a vital role in the success of your initiative. This includes individuals or teams within your organization who will be responsible for different aspects of the launch, such as marketing, operations, and finance. By involving the right people from the beginning, you can ensure that everyone is aligned and working towards the same goals.

Allocating Resources: Next, you need to allocate the necessary resources to support your launch. This may include budgeting for marketing campaigns, hiring additional staff or contractors, or investing in technology and infrastructure. By ensuring that you have the right resources in place, you can effectively execute your plans and overcome any potential obstacles that may arise.

Establishing Timelines: Setting clear timelines is crucial for a successful launch. By defining specific milestones and deadlines, you can keep your team accountable and ensure that tasks are completed on time. It's important to consider dependencies and potential risks during this process, allowing for flexibility if any adjustments need to be made along the way.

Coordinating Various Aspects of Your Business: A successful launch requires coordination among different departments and functions within your organization. This includes aligning marketing efforts with product development, ensuring that operations are prepared to handle increased demand, and creating a seamless customer experience. By fostering collaboration and effective communication, you can ensure that all aspects of your business are working together towards a common goal.

By following these steps and building a solid launch plan, you can position your business for success. Careful planning and coordination will help you overcome challenges and ensure that your initiatives and projects are launched successfully, ultimately driving growth and profitability.

Engaging and Aligning Your Team

Launching initiatives and projects successfully in your business requires more than just a well-thought-out plan. It also depends on having an engaged and aligned team that is motivated to put in their best efforts. In this section, we will explore strategies for effective communication, fostering collaboration, and creating a shared vision among your team members, ensuring that everyone is working towards the same goals.

Effective Communication: Communication plays a crucial role in engaging your team and keeping everyone informed about the initiative or project. It is essential to establish clear channels of communication, both formal and informal, to ensure that information flows freely. Regular team meetings, project briefings, and transparent communication platforms can help to foster open and honest communication among team members.

Fostering Collaboration: Collaboration is key to successful project execution. Encouraging cross-functional collaboration, promoting idea sharing, and creating opportunities for teamwork will enhance the quality of work and foster a positive team culture. Team-building activities, workshops, and brainstorming sessions can help to foster collaboration among team members, enabling them to leverage their diverse skills and experiences.

Creating a Shared Vision: Without a shared vision, it is challenging to align your team towards a common goal. Clearly articulating the purpose and objectives of the initiative or project and ensuring that every team member understands and believes in them is essential. Regularly communicating the bigger picture and how each person's role contributes to the overall success of the initiative can help create a sense of purpose and alignment.

By engaging and aligning your team, you can create a positive and collaborative work environment that fosters innovation, productivity, and success. Motivated and inspired team members are more likely to go above and beyond their responsibilities, ensuring the successful launch of your initiatives and projects.

Managing Risks and Mitigating Challenges

Launching initiatives and projects successfully in your business involves navigating through various risks and challenges. As your business prepares for the big launch, it's important to proactively identify potential risks, develop contingency plans, and address any challenges that may arise. By effectively managing risks, you can ensure a smooth and successful launch, minimizing any negative impacts on your initiative or project.

Identifying Potential Risks

Before your launch, it is crucial to conduct a thorough risk assessment to identify potential obstacles that may stand in the way of success. Consider factors such as market conditions, competition, technological constraints, and resource availability. By understanding the possible risks, you can devise strategies to mitigate them and increase the chances of a favorable outcome.

Developing Contingency Plans

Having a backup plan is essential in mitigating risks. Create contingency plans that outline alternative courses of action in the event that a risk materializes. By considering different scenarios and preparing contingency plans, your business will be better equipped to respond quickly and effectively, minimizing any disruptions to your initiatives or projects.

Proactively Addressing Challenges

Challenges are inevitable when launching initiatives and projects. It is crucial to anticipate potential hurdles and prepare strategies to address them head-on. This could involve collaborating with key stakeholders, allocating additional resources, or adjusting your timeline and goals. By being proactive in addressing challenges, you can prevent them from derailing your launch and ensure a successful outcome.

Successfully launching initiatives and projects in your business requires a proactive approach to risk management and a willingness to address challenges. By identifying potential risks, developing contingency plans, and proactively addressing challenges, you can navigate the complexities of the launch process and increase the likelihood of a successful outcome for your initiatives and projects.

Optimizing Your Marketing and Promotion Strategies

When it comes to launching initiatives and projects successfully in your business, effective marketing and promotion strategies are crucial. A strong marketing plan can generate buzz and excitement around your initiative, attracting customers and generating interest. This section will guide you in developing a targeted marketing strategy, utilizing various marketing channels, and creating compelling promotional materials.

One essential aspect of optimizing your marketing and promotion strategies is defining your target audience. By understanding who your ideal customers are, you can tailor your messaging and choose the most effective marketing channels to reach them. Whether it's social media, email marketing, content creation, or traditional advertising, selecting the right marketing channels is key.

In addition to selecting the right channels, creating engaging and compelling promotional materials is vital. Capture your audience's attention with visually appealing designs, persuasive copy, and clear call-to-actions. Utilize storytelling techniques to make an emotional connection with your target audience and communicate the unique value that your initiative or project brings.

To measure the success of your marketing efforts, it's essential to track key performance indicators (KPIs). This can include metrics such as website traffic, conversions, engagement rates, and customer feedback. By analyzing these metrics, you can identify what's working and make data-driven decisions to optimize your marketing and promotion strategies.

Remember, launching initiatives and projects successfully in your business is not just about the product or service itself—it's also about effectively communicating its value to your target audience. With a well-crafted marketing and promotion strategy, you can generate excitement, attract customers, and ensure the success of your launch.

Measuring and Evaluating Success

To ensure the success of your initiative or project, it's crucial to measure and evaluate its performance. By tracking key performance indicators (KPIs) and metrics, you can gain valuable insights into the progress and impact of your launch. This data-driven approach allows you to make informed decisions and drive future success in your business.

When measuring success, it's essential to establish clear objectives and define relevant KPIs that align with your business goals. For example, if your initiative aims to increase sales, you may track metrics such as revenue growth, customer acquisition rate, and average order value.

Additionally, analyzing data and interpreting results is key to understanding the effectiveness of your launch. By diving into the numbers, you can identify trends, patterns, and areas for improvement. This process empowers you to optimize your strategies and make data-backed decisions to drive your business forward.

It's worth noting that success measurements may vary depending on the nature of your initiative or project. For instance, a software development project might focus on KPIs like on-time delivery, bug resolution rate, and user satisfaction. On the other hand, a marketing campaign could prioritize KPIs such as website traffic, lead conversion rate, and social media engagement.

Remember, measuring and evaluating success is an ongoing process. Continuously monitoring and reassessing your KPIs allows you to adapt and improve over time. Regular assessment enables you to benchmark against past performance, identify potential bottlenecks or challenges, and refine your strategies accordingly.

Ultimately, measuring and evaluating success provides you with actionable insights and a solid foundation for decision-making. Embrace the power of data to drive performance, improve outcomes, and successfully launch initiatives and projects in your business.

Continuous Improvement and Adaptation

Launching initiatives and projects successfully in your business is not a one-time event but an ongoing process. After the initial launch, it's crucial to continually improve and adapt to achieve long-term success.

Gathering feedback is an integral part of this process. By actively seeking input from customers, employees, and stakeholders, you can gain valuable insights into your initiative's strengths and weaknesses. This feedback allows you to identify areas for growth and improvement, ensuring that your business keeps evolving and meeting the changing needs of your target audience.

Once you have gathered feedback, it's essential to make the necessary adjustments. Whether it's refining your product or service, optimizing your processes, or enhancing your marketing strategies, adaptability is key. Embrace a growth mindset and be open to change, as this will enable your business to stay competitive and relevant in a dynamic marketplace.

Continuous improvement also involves staying updated with industry trends and best practices. Regularly monitoring your competitors and industry developments will help you identify opportunities for innovation and optimization. Implementing these insights will allow you to maintain a competitive edge and ensure that your initiatives and projects are at the forefront of your industry.

Remember, launching initiatives and projects successfully in your business requires a commitment to ongoing improvement and adaptation. By continuously seeking feedback, making necessary adjustments, and staying informed about industry trends, you can position your business for long-term success and achieve your goals.

Case Studies: Successful Launches in Different Industries

Within the world of business, successful launches of initiatives and projects can be found across various industries. In this section, we dive into real-life case studies that highlight organizations that have effectively launched their ventures, providing valuable insights and lessons learned applicable to your own business.

Examining different strategies and tactics employed by these successful launches, you'll gain a comprehensive understanding of what it takes to launch initiatives and projects successfully in your business.

Let's explore the case studies and delve into the secrets behind their achievements:

Case Study 1: Tech Ltd's Product Launch

Tech, a leading technology and engineering company, embarked on an innovative product launch that captured the attention of their target market. Through careful market research and analysis, they identified a gap in the market and developed a cutting-edge solution that addressed customer pain points.

Utilizing a multi-channel marketing strategy, TechLtd generated buzz and excitement surrounding their product. They collaborated with influencers, held exclusive preview events, and leveraged social media to create anticipation among their target audience. The result was a highly successful product launch that resulted in widespread adoption and enthusiastic customer reviews.

Case Study 2: Trisha's Restaurant's Menu Expansion

Trisha's Restaurant, a well-established dining establishment, decided to expand their menu to cater to a wider range of preferences and dietary restrictions. To ensure a successful launch, they engaged their loyal customer base throughout the decision-making process.

By conducting surveys, hosting taste-testing events, and actively soliciting feedback, Trisha's Restaurant was able to create a menu that resonated with their customers. They then strategically marketed the menu expansion, highlighting new offerings and appealing to both existing and potential patrons. As a result, the launch was met with excitement and increased foot traffic, leading to a significant boost in revenue.

Case Study 3: Fast Fashion's New Store Opening

Fast Fashion, a fashion retail brand, launched a new store in a prime location to expand their market presence. They meticulously planned every aspect of the launch, from the store design to the customer experience.

Through collaborations with local influencers, Fast Fashion created a buzz in the community leading up to the grand opening. They utilized an omnichannel approach, leveraging social media, email marketing, and traditional advertising to attract customers. Furthermore, they focused on providing a personalized and immersive shopping experience, ensuring that each customer felt valued and excited about the new store. The result was a successful launch that exceeded sales targets and established Fast Fashion as a go-to destination for fashion enthusiasts in the area.

By studying these case studies and understanding the strategies employed by successful launches, you can gain valuable insights to apply to your own business. Remember, launching initiatives and projects successfully in your business requires careful planning, effective marketing strategies, and a deep understanding of your target audience.

Conclusion and Key Takeaways

Launching initiatives and projects successfully in your business is key to driving growth and achieving your goals. Throughout this chapter, we have explored the strategies and techniques necessary for a strong launch. By following these steps, you can ensure that your initiatives make a lasting impact and set the stage for future success.

First and foremost, we emphasized the importance of a strong launch. A successful opening night creates excitement and generates momentum in the market. It serves as a foundation for your business's growth and helps you gain a competitive edge.

To launch initiatives successfully, a clear set of goals and objectives is crucial. Defining these goals, identifying key milestones, and establishing metrics for success will help you stay focused and measure your progress effectively.

Building a solid launch plan that outlines the necessary steps, involves key stakeholders, and establishes timelines is essential. Additionally, engaging and aligning your team through effective communication and collaboration will contribute to a successful launch.

Managing risks and challenges, optimizing your marketing and promotion strategies, and measuring and evaluating success are equally important aspects. Continuously improving and adapting your initiatives post-launch is key to sustained growth and maintaining a competitive edge.

By implementing the key takeaways from this chapter, you can confidently launch initiatives and projects in your business, ensuring success and driving long-term growth.

Chapter 18

The Overtures of Networking: Building External Relationships in Business

Welcome to Chapter 18 of "From Manager to Maestro: The Symphony of Good Management". In this chapter, we dive into the indispensable world of networking and the crucial role it plays in building external relationships in business. Whether you're a seasoned professional or an aspiring entrepreneur, mastering the art of networking can propel your career to new heights.

Networking is more than just collecting business cards at events; it's about cultivating meaningful connections that open doors to opportunities you never thought possible. Building strong external relationships can help you expand your professional network, discover potential collaborations, and gain access to valuable resources.

In this chapter, we will explore various aspects of networking, from understanding its power in the business world to identifying opportunities, mastering effective communication techniques, leveraging social media platforms, and establishing connections with industry influencers. We will also discuss the value of participating in networking events and organizations, the art of follow-up, building strategic alliances, overcoming common challenges, and the future of networking in business.

So, if you're ready to unlock the potential of networking and learn how to build lasting external relationships that can shape your career, this chapter is for you. Let's dive in and discover the overtures of networking in the dynamic realm of business.

The Power of Networking in Business

In the fast-paced and interconnected world of business, networking plays a pivotal role in driving success and growth. Networking in business refers to the act of creating and nurturing relationships with individuals and organizations outside of your immediate circle, with the aim of creating valuable connections, opportunities, and collaborations.

Building external relationships is a vital component of long-term success in any industry. By expanding your network, you open doors to new ideas, partnerships, and resources that can propel your career or business forward. Networking not only helps you stay updated with industry trends but also allows you to tap into the knowledge and experiences of others.

Networking is a powerful tool that enables professionals to forge connections beyond their immediate circle, building relationships with potential clients, mentors, peers, investors, and thought leaders. It provides a platform for sharing ideas, seeking advice, and gaining insights from individuals with diverse backgrounds and expertise.

Furthermore, networking offers invaluable opportunities for collaboration and partnership. By establishing mutually beneficial relationships, professionals can combine their strengths and resources to achieve common goals. Through networking, entrepreneurs can identify potential business partnerships, investors can discover promising startups, and professionals can find new career opportunities.

Networking also fosters personal growth and expands your professional reach. By connecting with individuals from various industries and backgrounds, you can expand your knowledge, gain different perspectives, and enhance your skill set. These relationships can provide mentorship opportunities, access to new markets, and exposure to different ways of thinking.

Investing time and effort in networking is a strategic decision that can yield substantial benefits in the long run. It allows you to build a strong network of supporters, advocates, and resources that can help you navigate challenges, make informed decisions, and seize opportunities.

In the following sections, we will explore various aspects of networking, including identifying networking opportunities, effective communication, leveraging social media, connecting with industry influencers, participating in networking events and organizations, the art of follow-up, building strategic alliances, overcoming networking challenges, and the future of networking in business.

Identifying Networking Opportunities

In today's dynamic business landscape, identifying networking opportunities is crucial for building strong external relationships. By recognizing potential connections, events, and platforms, professionals can harness the power of networking to enhance their business relationships and open doors to new opportunities.

One effective way to identify networking opportunities is by attending industry-specific conferences, trade shows, and seminars. These events bring together professionals from various sectors, providing a fertile ground for meaningful connections and collaborations.

Additionally, online platforms such as LinkedIn, Twitter, and industry-focused forums offer valuable networking opportunities. Professionals can join relevant groups and communities, engage in discussions, and connect with like-minded individuals who share similar interests and goals.

Another avenue for identifying networking opportunities is through local business organizations and chambers of commerce. These entities often host networking events where professionals can meet and establish connections with fellow business leaders and potential partners.

Furthermore, keeping a keen eye on industry trends and developments can unveil networking opportunities. By staying informed about the latest advancements and changes within their field, professionals can identify potential collaboration opportunities with other businesses or thought leaders.

Ultimately, by actively seeking out networking opportunities and leveraging various channels, professionals can expand their network, cultivate valuable connections, and foster long-lasting business relationships.

Effective Communication in Networking

In the realm of networking, effective communication is the key to building successful business relationships. It goes beyond the exchange of words; it involves active listening, understanding others' perspectives, and building rapport. When you communicate effectively, you can establish meaningful connections and foster long-lasting partnerships with colleagues, clients, and industry experts.

One of the essential strategies for effective communication in networking is to be an attentive listener. Actively listening to others demonstrates that you value their opinions and insights, fostering trust and respect. By paying attention to verbal and non-verbal cues, you can respond thoughtfully and engage in meaningful conversations.

Another crucial aspect of effective communication is the ability to articulate your ideas clearly. Being able to convey your thoughts in a concise and coherent manner helps others understand your perspective and align with your business goals. Use language that is easy to comprehend, and avoid jargon or technical terms that might confuse your audience.

Building Rapport through Communication

In networking, building rapport is crucial for forging strong connections. It involves establishing a sense of trust, mutual understanding, and shared interests with others. Effective communication plays a vital role in building rapport. Show genuine interest in others by asking open-ended questions and actively engaging in conversations.

Non-verbal cues, such as maintaining eye contact, using appropriate body language, and offering a warm smile, also contribute to building rapport. These non-verbal signals can help create a comfortable and welcoming atmosphere, making others feel valued and respected.

In summary, effective communication is the foundation of successful networking. By actively listening, articulating your ideas clearly, and building rapport, you can establish and nurture meaningful business relationships. When communication is open and authentic, opportunities for collaboration, growth, and mutual support abound.

Leveraging Social Media for Networking

Networking in business has evolved significantly with the rise of social media. Platforms such as Facebook, LinkedIn, and Twitter have transformed the way professionals connect, collaborate, and expand their networks. Leveraging social media effectively can open doors to new opportunities and strengthen external relationships.

When it comes to leveraging social media for networking, it is essential to choose the right platforms that align with your professional goals. LinkedIn is particularly valuable for business networking, allowing you to showcase your skills, connect with like-minded professionals, and join relevant industry groups.

Another platform worth exploring is Twitter, where you can engage in real-time conversations, follow industry influencers, and participate in relevant Twitter chats. By sharing valuable insights and resources, you can establish yourself as a thought leader and attract a network of professionals with similar interests.

Facebook also offers networking opportunities through industry-specific groups and pages. Engaging with these communities can help you establish connections, exchange ideas, and stay updated on industry trends.

Maintaining an active and professional presence on social media is crucial for effective networking. Regularly sharing relevant content, participating in discussions, and engaging with others' posts can help you build visibility and credibility within your industry.

In addition to these general strategies, each social media platform has unique features that can be leveraged to strengthen networking efforts. For example, LinkedIn allows you to request introductions and recommendations from connections, while Twitter's direct messaging feature enables private conversations with potential collaborators.

In conclusion, leveraging social media for networking in business is a powerful tool to expand your professional network and build external relationships. By strategically using platforms like LinkedIn, Twitter, and Facebook, professionals can tap into a vast pool of opportunities, establish their credibility, and connect with like-minded individuals who can contribute to their growth and success.

Building Strong Connections with Industry Influencers

In the world of business, establishing connections with industry influencers is of utmost importance. Industry influencers are individuals who have a significant impact on the business community and possess a wide network of connections. Building strong relationships with these influencers can open doors to new opportunities, collaborations, and valuable insights.

One of the key benefits of leveraging industry influencers is the credibility and exposure they bring to your brand or business. Their endorsement or association can enhance your reputation and attract attention from potential partners, clients, and stakeholders.

So how can you build and cultivate connections with industry influencers? It starts with genuine engagement and meaningful interactions. Take the time to research and understand their work, achievements, and areas of expertise. Engage with their content on social media platforms, leaving thoughtful comments and sharing their insights with your network.

Showcasing your own expertise and thought leadership can also capture the attention of industry influencers. Publish articles, blog posts, or research papers in your field of expertise to demonstrate your knowledge and contribute to the industry's discourse.

Attending industry conferences, seminars, and networking events provides opportunities to meet and connect with influencers face-to-face. Be sure to approach them respectfully and professionally, expressing genuine interest in their work. Remember, building relationships takes time and effort. Nurture the connections you make by staying in touch, providing value, and finding ways to collaborate.

Furthermore, consider reaching out to industry influencers for collaborations, such as joint webinars, podcasts, or guest blogging opportunities. This can not only help you expand your network but also position you as a valuable resource to their audience.

Building strong connections with industry influencers is a long-term investment that can greatly benefit your business. By fostering authentic relationships, providing value, and actively participating in the industry's conversation, you can position yourself as a trusted peer and open doors to new opportunities.

Participating in Networking Events and Organizations

Networking events and business organizations play a vital role in expanding professional networks and building external relationships. Attending conferences, seminars, and industry-specific gatherings offer unique opportunities to connect with like-minded individuals, share insights, and foster collaborations.

By participating in networking events, professionals can gain exposure to diverse perspectives, stay updated on industry trends, and enhance their business knowledge. These events provide a platform for exchanging ideas, learning from experts, and building lasting connections.

Business organizations also offer valuable networking opportunities. Joining industry-specific associations and groups allows individuals to connect with peers, engage in dialogue, and access resources tailored to their field of expertise. These organizations often organize networking events, workshops, and meet-ups, creating a conducive environment for relationship-building.

Attending networking events and joining business organizations not only expands professional networks but also opens doors to potential collaborations, partnerships, and mentorship opportunities. By actively participating in these events and organizations, individuals can build a diverse network of contacts that can contribute to their personal and professional growth.

The Art of Follow-Up in Networking

Building strong connections and nurturing business relationships requires more than just making initial contact. The art of follow-up in networking plays a crucial role in solidifying connections and creating long-term partnerships. By strategically and consistently staying in touch, professionals can establish trust, demonstrate commitment, and deepen their network. Follow-up in networking is the key to building lasting relationships that can open doors to new opportunities and mutual success.

When it comes to follow-up in networking, timing is essential. It's important to send a follow-up message or make a phone call within a reasonable timeframe after your initial meeting. This demonstrates interest and shows that you value the connection made. Remember to personalize your follow-up communication to make it more memorable and meaningful.

The Importance of Personalized Follow-Up

Personalized follow-up goes beyond the generic "It was nice meeting you" message. Instead, take the time to reference specific points from your conversation, highlight common interests, or share relevant resources. This personal touch not only shows that you were engaged during your interaction but also helps create a stronger bond. People appreciate thoughtfulness and genuine efforts to connect on a deeper level.

Furthermore, following up consistently is crucial for building trust and maintaining the relationship. Set reminders to periodically reach out to your connections, whether it's to share industry insights, invite them to events, or simply check in on how they're doing. Consistency in follow-up demonstrates your commitment to the relationship and keeps you top of mind when opportunities arise.

Best Practices for Follow-Up in Networking

To optimize your follow-up in networking, consider implementing these best practices:

Be prompt: Respond to emails or messages in a timely manner to show respect for other professionals' time. Exchange contact information: Ensure you have accurate and up-to-date contact details to avoid any communication gaps. Use various channels: Don't limit yourself to just one communication channel. Utilize email, phone calls, social media, or even in-person meetings to strengthen your connections. Provide value: Share relevant information, resources, or introductions that can benefit your connections. Adding value to their professional lives will help solidify your relationship. Stay organized: Use tools like CRM software or spreadsheets to manage your contacts and schedule follow-up reminders. Being organized ensures you stay on top of your networking efforts.

Remember, follow-up in networking is an ongoing process. By investing time and effort into maintaining connections, you'll not only build valuable relationships but also expand your network of opportunities. Take advantage of the art of follow-up and watch your networking efforts thrive.

Building Strategic Alliances in Business

In today's dynamic business landscape, building strategic alliances has become an essential strategy for success. By forming partnerships and collaborations, organizations can leverage their strengths, expand their reach, and achieve common objectives.

Strategic alliances allow businesses to tap into new markets, access additional resources, and share expertise. By combining forces, companies can create a competitive edge and drive innovation. Forming alliances also opens up opportunities for knowledge sharing, which can lead to mutual growth and development.

When building strategic alliances, it is crucial to identify partners whose values and goals align with your own. Collaborating with like-minded organizations fosters trust and strengthens the foundation of the alliance. Additionally, it is important to establish clear communication channels and define roles and responsibilities upfront to ensure effective collaboration.

Strategic alliances can take various forms, including joint ventures, licensing agreements, and co-marketing initiatives. These partnerships enable businesses to tap into each other's networks, share resources, and pool expertise for mutual benefit. By working together, organizations can overcome individual limitations, expand their customer base, and enhance their competitive advantage.

Furthermore, strategic alliances provide businesses with a platform to learn from each other's experiences, exchange best practices, and gain industry insights. This collaboration fosters innovation and enables organizations to stay ahead of the curve in a rapidly changing business environment.

In conclusion, building strategic alliances is a valuable strategy for enhancing external relationships and achieving common objectives. Through collaborations and partnerships, businesses can leverage their strengths, access new markets, and drive innovation. By forming alliances with like-minded organizations, companies can expand their reach, share resources, and enhance their competitive advantage. Strategic alliances provide opportunities for learning, knowledge sharing, and mutual growth, making them a crucial aspect of modern business.

Overcoming Challenges in Networking

In the world of business, networking plays a crucial role in building external relationships and fostering professional growth. However, it is not without its challenges. Professionals often face obstacles that can hinder their networking efforts and prevent them from establishing meaningful connections. To overcome these challenges and build stronger relationships, it is important to employ effective strategies and techniques.

One common challenge in networking is the fear of rejection. Reaching out to new contacts and initiating conversations can be intimidating, especially when faced with the possibility of rejection or indifference. To overcome this challenge, it is crucial to adopt a confident mindset and understand that rejection is a natural part of the process. By focusing on the potential opportunities and benefits that networking can bring, professionals can push through their fears and approach networking with enthusiasm.

Another challenge is the limited time and resources available for networking. Busy schedules and competing priorities can make it difficult to dedicate sufficient time to networking activities. To overcome this challenge, professionals should prioritize networking as an essential aspect of their career development. Setting aside dedicated networking time, attending relevant events, and leveraging technology such as social media platforms can help optimize networking efforts within limited time constraints.

Additionally, networking challenges can arise from a lack of confidence in one's own abilities or value proposition. It is important to recognize and showcase one's strengths, expertise, and unique value to potential connections. Practicing self-belief and continually developing one's skills and knowledge can help build confidence and foster meaningful connections.

Furthermore, networking challenges can also stem from a lack of clarity regarding one's goals and objectives. Without a clear understanding of what they aim to achieve through networking, professionals may struggle to create targeted connections and build relevant relationships. It is crucial to define specific networking goals and identify the types of relationships that align with those goals. This clarity will guide professionals in approaching the right individuals and organizations that can help them achieve their desired outcomes.

To overcome challenges in networking and build stronger, more meaningful external relationships, professionals should embrace the power of effective communication, actively seek out networking opportunities, leverage social media platforms, and participate in relevant networking events and organizations. By overcoming these challenges, professionals can unlock the true potential of networking and establish a robust network that supports their professional success.

The Future of Networking in Business

The ever-evolving landscape of business relationships is paving the way for a new era in networking. As technology advances and societal paradigms shift, professionals must adapt to emerging trends and approaches to build robust external relationships for long-term success.

One of the key drivers shaping the future of networking is the increasing integration of digital platforms and virtual communities. Online networking events, social media, and professional networking platforms provide professionals with unparalleled access to a global network of like-minded individuals. These platforms allow for the exchange of ideas, collaborations, and partnerships that transcend traditional physical boundaries, opening exciting opportunities for business growth.

Additionally, the future of networking will be heavily influenced by the rise of artificial intelligence (AI) and machine learning. AI-powered algorithms can analyze vast amounts of data to curate personalized networking recommendations, helping professionals connect with individuals who share similar interests, goals, and industries. This targeted approach to networking maximizes the potential for meaningful connections and accelerates the growth of business relationships in an increasingly competitive landscape.

Furthermore, the future of networking will see a greater emphasis on authenticity and relationship-building. With the rise of automation and digital interactions, professionals who can establish genuine connections and foster trust will outshine their peers. Networking will no longer be solely about collecting business cards or increasing social media followers; it will be about building meaningful relationships based on shared values and genuine human connections.

Chapter 19

Economy of Movement: Budgeting and Financial Acumen in Management

Welcome to Chapter 19 of our comprehensive guide on Economy of Movement in management. In this chapter, we will explore the crucial aspects of budgeting and financial acumen and how they contribute to effective management practices.

When it comes to running a successful organization, making the most of available resources is key. That's where the concept of economy of movement comes into play. By streamlining processes and making efficient use of resources, businesses can achieve their financial goals and thrive in today's competitive landscape.

In this chapter, we will discuss the importance of budgeting as a vital component of economy of movement. We will explore how creating realistic budgets, tracking expenses, and making informed financial decisions can optimize resource allocation in your organization.

Furthermore, we will delve into the development of financial acumen in management. Understanding the skills and knowledge required to make effective financial decisions, analyze financial data, and adapt strategies is crucial for optimizing resource utilization and achieving business success.

We will also provide you with practical strategies for streamlining management processes to achieve economy of movement. Techniques such as automation, outsourcing, and identifying bottlenecks will be explored to improve efficiency and eliminate wasteful activities.

In addition, we will examine how technology can be leveraged for efficient financial management. From software tools and data analytics to digital platforms, integrating technology into your budgeting processes can enhance decision-making and streamline financial operations.

Effective communication and collaboration are essential elements of financial planning. We will discuss strategies for involving key stakeholders, aligning financial goals across departments, and fostering a culture of transparency and accountability.

Furthermore, we will showcase real-life case studies of organizations that have successfully implemented economy of movement principles in their budgeting and financial management practices. By analyzing their strategies and outcomes, we can gain valuable insights into implementing these practices in our own organizations.

Finally, we will emphasize the importance of continuous improvement and adaptation in maintaining economy of movement. Understanding how to continuously evaluate and optimize financial processes and adjust strategies as needed is crucial for long-term success.

Get ready to dive into the world of economy of movement, budgeting, and financial acumen in management. Let's explore how these concepts can transform your organization and drive sustainable growth. Let's get started!

Introduction to Economy of Movement in Management

Welcome to the world of efficient management practices! In this section, we will delve into the fascinating concept of economy of movement and its relevance in effective management. Economy of movement is a principle that emphasizes streamlining processes and making the most efficient use of resources to achieve financial goals.

By adopting the economy of movement mindset, businesses can optimize their operations, reduce wasteful activities, and ultimately enhance their financial performance. This principle is particularly crucial in the field of management, where every decision and action can have a significant impact on the organization's bottom line.

So, why is economy of movement important in management? Well, the answer lies in the benefits it brings. When managers prioritize efficient resource allocation and process optimization, they can reduce costs, increase productivity, and improve overall performance. By eliminating unnecessary steps, tasks, or movements, managers can save time and energy, which can then be redirected towards more valuable endeavors.

In addition, economy of movement is closely intertwined with effective budgeting and financial acumen. Sound financial management relies on making informed decisions, tracking expenses, and analyzing financial data. By embracing the principles of economy of movement, managers can align their budgeting efforts with efficient resource utilization and strategic financial planning.

Throughout this section, we will explore different aspects of economy of movement and its connection to management practices. We will also provide practical examples and strategies to help you implement economy of movement in your organization. So, let's dive in and unravel the power of economy of movement in management!

The Role of Budgeting in Economy of Movement

In the realm of management, achieving economy of movement is crucial for optimizing resources and maximizing efficiency. Budgeting plays a pivotal role in this process, enabling organizations to allocate their resources effectively and make informed financial decisions.

Creating realistic budgets allows businesses to identify their financial goals and map out a roadmap for achieving them. By setting clear financial targets, companies can align their efforts and resources towards those objectives, ensuring that every dollar spent contributes to the organization's success.

Tracking expenses is another critical aspect of budgeting. By meticulously monitoring and recording expenditures, organizations can identify areas of inefficiency and waste, leading to improved cost management. This information provides valuable insights that enable businesses to make informed decisions and allocate resources more prudently.

Optimizing resource allocation is a core aim of budgeting in the pursuit of economy of movement. By carefully analyzing budgets and financial data, management can identify areas where adjustments can be made to improve efficiency and minimize waste. This analysis helps to optimize the use of resources, reducing unnecessary expenses and reallocating funds to areas that deliver the greatest value.

The role of budgeting in achieving economy of movement cannot be overstated. This essential financial practice enables organizations to streamline their operations, eliminate redundancies, and promote an environment of fiscal responsibility. By integrating budgeting into their management strategies, businesses can achieve greater efficiency and financial acumen, driving long-term success.

Developing Financial Acumen in Management

Financial acumen is a critical skill set for successful management. It involves having the necessary knowledge and abilities to make informed financial decisions, analyze financial data, and adapt strategies to optimize resource utilization. Developing strong financial acumen ensures that managers are equipped to navigate the complexities of budgeting and financial management effectively.

One of the key skills in developing financial acumen is the ability to make effective financial decisions. This involves understanding financial statements, assessing risks, and weighing the potential outcomes of different financial choices. Managers with strong financial acumen can confidently evaluate investment opportunities, assess the financial health of their organization, and make sound decisions that align with the goals and objectives of the company.

Another crucial aspect of financial acumen is the ability to analyze financial data. This includes interpreting and understanding key financial metrics, such as profit margins, cash flow, and return on investment. By leveraging financial data analysis, managers can identify trends, forecast future performance, and make data-driven decisions that contribute to the financial success of their organization.

Adapting strategies for optimal resource utilization is yet another crucial aspect of financial acumen in management. Managers with financial acumen can assess the financial implications of different strategies, evaluate cost-saving opportunities, and align resource allocation with organizational goals. By making strategic decisions based on a deep understanding of the financial impact, managers can maximize the value generated from limited resources.

In conclusion, developing financial acumen is vital for effective management. It equips managers with the skills and knowledge needed to make informed financial decisions, analyze financial data, and adapt strategies for optimal resource utilization. By honing their financial acumen, managers can play a pivotal role in driving the financial success of their organization.+

Strategies for Streamlining Management Processes

In order to achieve economy of movement and optimize resource utilization, organizations need to implement practical strategies for streamlining management processes. By analyzing existing workflows and identifying areas of inefficiency, companies can implement techniques that improve efficiency and reduce wasteful activities. Some key strategies for streamlining management processes include:

Automation

Implementing automation tools and technologies can help streamline repetitive tasks and free up valuable time for employees to focus on more strategic activities. By automating routine processes such as data entry, report generation, and customer service, organizations can minimize errors, reduce manual efforts, and improve overall efficiency.

Outsourcing

Outsourcing certain functions or tasks to specialized service providers can often lead to cost savings and improved efficiency. By leveraging the expertise and resources of external partners, organizations can access specialized skills, reduce operational costs, and achieve economies of scale. Common areas that are often outsourced include IT support, customer service, and payroll processing.

Identifying Bottlenecks

Analyzing the flow of work within an organization can help identify bottlenecks and optimize processes. By identifying areas where work gets delayed or slowed down, organizations can implement targeted improvements to remove bottlenecks and improve overall efficiency. This may involve reallocating resources, reorganizing workflows, or implementing new technologies.

By adopting these strategies for streamlining management processes, organizations can achieve economy of movement and enhance their overall operational efficiency. These approaches not only lead to cost savings and resource optimization but also enable employees to focus on more value-added tasks, ultimately driving growth and success.

Leveraging Technology for Financial Management

In today's fast-paced business environment, technology plays a crucial role in enhancing financial management practices. By leveraging the power of software tools, data analytics, and digital platforms, organizations can streamline their budgeting processes and make informed financial decisions. This section will delve into the various ways in which technology can be utilized for efficient financial management.

Software Tools: By implementing specialized financial software, companies can automate repetitive tasks, such as expense tracking and invoicing, saving valuable time and reducing the risk of errors.

These tools also provide valuable insights through real-time reporting, enabling managers to make data-driven decisions and respond quickly to changing market conditions.

Data Analytics: The advent of big data has revolutionized how organizations analyze and interpret financial data. Through sophisticated algorithms and predictive modeling, data analytics tools can uncover patterns, identify trends, and highlight potential risks or opportunities. This valuable information allows financial managers to optimize resource allocation, forecast accurately, and mitigate financial risks.

Digital Platforms:

With the rise of cloud computing, digital platforms have become indispensable for efficient financial management. Collaborative platforms enable teams to work together in real time, reducing communication gaps and streamlining financial planning and reporting processes. These platforms also ensure data security and accessibility, allowing authorized personnel to access financial information from anywhere, at any time.

In conclusion, technology offers immense potential for enhancing financial management in organizations. By leveraging software tools, data analytics, and digital platforms, businesses can streamline budgeting processes, improve decision-making, and achieve better financial outcomes. Embracing technology is vital in today's tech-driven world, as it enables organizations to stay competitive, adapt to changing market dynamics, and achieve sustainable growth.

Communication and Collaboration in Financial Planning

Effective communication and collaboration play a crucial role in successful financial planning. When it comes to managing budgets and making informed financial decisions, it is essential to involve key stakeholders from various departments and foster a culture of transparency and accountability.

By actively promoting communication, teams can align their financial goals and ensure everyone is on the same page. This collaboration allows for a more comprehensive understanding of the organization's financial needs and enables better decision-making.

One strategy for fostering communication and collaboration in financial planning is regular meetings and updates. By bringing together individuals from different departments, discussions can take place, providing insights into potential challenges, opportunities, and improvements. These interactions can lead to innovative solutions and ensure that financial planning aligns with the overall organizational strategy.

Transparency and Accountability

In financial planning, transparency is key to building trust and accountability. By openly sharing financial information and goals with employees, it creates a sense of ownership and empowers them to contribute to the organization's success. This transparency fosters a collaborative environment where everyone understands how their efforts contribute to the financial well-being of the organization.

Additionally, accountability ensures that individuals are responsible for their roles in financial planning. By setting clear expectations and establishing metrics to measure progress, teams can work together towards achieving the organization's financial goals.

Collaboration tools and technology also play a crucial role in enhancing communication and collaboration in financial planning. Digital platforms and software solutions enable real-time collaboration, document sharing, and provide a centralized hub for financial information, making it easier for teams to work together, even if they are geographically dispersed.

Communication and collaboration are not limited to internal stakeholders. Engaging external partners, such as financial advisors or consultants, can provide valuable insights and expertise that can enhance financial planning efforts. Collaborating with external experts can bring fresh perspectives and help identify potential blind spots that may have been overlooked internally.

In conclusion, effective communication and collaboration are essential for successful financial planning. By involving key stakeholders, fostering a culture of transparency and accountability, and leveraging collaboration tools and external expertise, organizations can optimize their financial planning processes and achieve their financial goals more effectively.

Case Studies: Successful Implementation of Economy of Movement

In this section, we will explore real-life case studies of organizations that have successfully implemented economy of movement principles in their budgeting and financial management practices. By analyzing their strategies, the challenges they faced, and the positive outcomes they achieved, we can gain valuable insights into the implementation of this approach.

Case Study 1: Fortune Company

Fortune Company, a leading player in the manufacturing industry, recognized the potential of economy of movement in optimizing their financial management processes. They conducted an in-depth analysis of their operations, identifying areas of inefficiency and waste. Through careful planning and implementation, Fortune Company integrated streamlined financial practices into their budgeting process. They focused on reducing unnecessary expenses, improving resource allocation, and optimizing cash flow. As a result, they experienced significant cost savings and increased profitability.

Case Study 2: FoodCycle Organization

FoodCycle Organization, a nonprofit entity dedicated to community skills development, faced budgetary constraints and limited resources. However, they successfully implemented economy of movement principles through an innovative approach. By leveraging technology to automate routine financial tasks, FoodCycle Organization reduced administrative overhead and enhanced their overall efficiency. This allowed them to redirect resources towards their core mission and make a greater impact in their community.

Case Study 3: Leaf Group

Leaf Corporation, a multinational conglomerate, recognized the importance of economy of movement in their financial decision-making process. They implemented a centralized budgeting system, fostering collaboration and communication across departments. By consolidating financial data and involving key stakeholders in the budgeting process, Leaf Corporation achieved better alignment of financial goals and enhanced decision-making. This ultimately led to improved financial performance and a more agile organization.

These case studies serve as inspirations for other organizations looking to implement economy of movement principles in their budgeting and financial management practices. By learning from these successes, businesses can identify strategies that are relevant to their own operations and customize them for effective implementation. Through careful planning, adaptation, and continuous improvement, organizations can achieve financial efficiency and long-term success.

Continuous Improvement and Adaptation

To maintain economy of movement in management, continuous improvement and adaptation are crucial. By continuously evaluating and optimizing financial processes, organizations can enhance efficiency and achieve better financial outcomes. Additionally, adapting strategies as needed allows businesses to stay agile and responsive in a changing environment.

One way to ensure continuous improvement is through regular performance evaluations and benchmarking. By assessing key financial metrics and comparing them against industry standards or best practices, organizations can identify areas for improvement and implement necessary changes.

Moreover, fostering a culture of innovation and open communication encourages employees to share ideas and propose process enhancements. This collaborative approach enables businesses to tap into the collective knowledge and creativity of their workforce, leading to innovative solutions and continuous improvement.

Adaptation is equally crucial in maintaining economy of movement. In today's rapidly evolving business landscape, organizations must be willing to adapt their financial strategies and processes to meet new challenges and opportunities. This can involve staying up-to-date with industry trends, embracing new technologies, and proactively addressing emerging risks.

Businesses should also prioritize flexibility in their financial planning and decision-making. By being open to adjusting strategies and reallocating resources based on changing circumstances, organizations can optimize their financial performance and mitigate potential risks.

In summary, continuous improvement and adaptation are vital components of maintaining economy of movement in management. By continually evaluating financial processes, fostering innovation, and embracing adaptation, organizations can optimize their efficiency, effectiveness, and agility in the pursuit of financial success.

Conclusion

In conclusion, the concept of economy of movement in management is crucial for achieving financial success. By streamlining processes, making efficient use of resources, and practicing effective budgeting and financial acumen, organizations can optimize their financial performance and drive long-term growth.

Embracing efficient practices is essential in today's dynamic business environment. By identifying and eliminating wasteful activities, organizations can allocate their resources effectively and focus on activities that generate the most value. This approach not only improves operational efficiency but also enhances profitability and competitiveness.

Furthermore, leveraging technology plays a vital role in financial management. By utilizing software tools, data analytics, and digital platforms, organizations can automate routine tasks, gain valuable insights, and make informed financial decisions. Technology enables real-time monitoring, enhances accuracy, and facilitates collaboration among teams.

Lastly, continuous improvement and adaptation are key to maintaining economy of movement in management. By regularly evaluating financial processes, identifying areas for improvement, and adapting strategies as needed, organizations can stay agile and responsive to changing market conditions. This iterative approach fosters innovation, drives growth, and positions organizations for long-term success.

Chapter **20**

Sustain the Note: Long-Term Growth Strategies

Welcome to Chapter 20 of our series on achieving enduring business prosperity. In this chapter, we will explore the crucial topic of long-term growth strategies and how they play a pivotal role in ensuring the lasting success of your business.

Creating sustainable growth is not just about short-term gains; it's about implementing strategies that can propel your business forward for years to come. Long-term growth strategies provide the foundation for enduring business prosperity, allowing you to stay ahead of the competition and navigate the ever-changing business landscape.

Throughout this chapter, we will delve into various aspects of long-term growth, uncovering the key elements that contribute to sustainable success. From building a strong foundation for growth to nurturing customer relationships, embracing innovation, forming strategic partnerships, and leveraging technology, we will explore the essential strategies that can drive continuous growth and keep your business thriving.

Along the way, we will also discuss the importance of measuring and evaluating your long-term growth initiatives, ensuring that you can make data-driven decisions and adapt your strategies as needed.

Whether you are a small startup or an established enterprise, this chapter will provide you with valuable insights and practical tips to develop and implement effective long-term growth strategies, paving the way for enduring business prosperity. Let's dive in!

Understanding the Importance of Long-Term Growth

Long-term growth lies at the heart of building a sustainable business and achieving future success. In this section, we dive into the significance of long-term growth for businesses and explore strategies that can position organizations for long-term prosperity.

For businesses to thrive in the ever-evolving market landscape, it is essential to focus on sustainable growth rather than short-term gains. While immediate results may be enticing, a long-term approach ensures stability and continuous progress. By prioritizing long-term growth, businesses create a strong foundation that can withstand economic fluctuations and industry disruptions.

One of the key benefits of long-term growth is the ability to build a sustainable business model. Organizations that prioritize long-term goals are more likely to develop strategies that promote financial stability, employee satisfaction, and customer loyalty. Sustainable businesses are built on solid operational practices that maximize efficiency and minimize waste, fostering long-term success.

Moreover, long-term growth allows businesses to adapt and respond to changing customer needs and market trends. By focusing on the future, organizations can anticipate shifts in customer preferences and proactively innovate. This strategic approach ensures that businesses remain relevant and competitive, paving the way for long-term success in an ever-evolving landscape.

Embracing long-term growth also enables businesses to capitalize on new opportunities and expand into untapped markets. By maintaining a long-term perspective, organizations can identify avenues for growth and develop strategies to penetrate new demographics, industries, or geographies. This ability to diversify and expand reduces reliance on a single market or product, further ensuring sustainable growth.

To achieve long-term growth, organizations must adopt a holistic approach that encompasses various aspects of their business. This includes nurturing strong customer relationships, fostering a culture of innovation and adaptability, forming strategic partnerships, investing in employee development, and embracing technological advancements.

In the following sections, we will explore each of these elements in detail, examining the strategies and practices that can fuel long-term growth and position businesses for sustainable success.

Building a Strong Foundation for Growth

In order to achieve long-term and sustainable business growth, it is crucial for organizations to establish a strong foundation that supports their growth initiatives. This foundation acts as the framework upon which all future growth strategies can be built upon.

One key element of building a strong foundation is developing and implementing effective business strategies. By carefully identifying and leveraging market opportunities, businesses can create a roadmap for success and ensure that their growth efforts are well-directed and aligned with their overall objectives.

Implementing Sustainable Strategies

Another vital aspect of building a strong foundation for growth lies in the implementation of sustainable strategies. These strategies are designed to withstand economic fluctuations and market uncertainties, allowing businesses to thrive in both favorable and challenging conditions.

By adopting sustainable practices such as resource management, operational efficiencies, and ethical business standards, organizations can position themselves for long-term success and create a positive impact on the environment and society as a whole.

Investing in Talent and Skill Development

A skilled and motivated workforce forms the backbone of any successful organization. Therefore, investing in talent acquisition and skill development is integral to building a strong foundation for growth. By attracting top talent and providing opportunities for professional growth and advancement, businesses can foster a culture of excellence and innovation.

Moreover, establishing a learning culture that encourages continuous improvement and knowledge sharing ensures that employees are equipped with the necessary skills and expertise to meet the evolving needs of the business and industry.

Fostering Strong Business Relationships

Building and nurturing strong relationships with key stakeholders, including customers, suppliers, and partners, is essential for long-term growth. These relationships create a solid network of support, collaboration, and trust, enabling businesses to enhance their market presence, expand their customer base, and access new opportunities for growth.

By understanding the needs and expectations of their stakeholders, businesses can tailor their products, services, and strategies to better meet the demands of the market, ultimately driving sustainable growth and achieving enduring success.

Nurturing Customer Relationships

Building and maintaining strong customer relationships is crucial for the long-term growth and success of any business. By nurturing these relationships, businesses can cultivate customer loyalty, enhance customer satisfaction, and drive repeat business.

The Power of Personalization

One effective strategy for nurturing customer relationships is personalization. Tailoring products, services, and communication to meet the unique needs and preferences of individual customers can create a sense of loyalty and make them feel valued.

Businesses can achieve personalization by leveraging customer data and insights. Analyzing customer behavior, purchase history, and preferences allows businesses to deliver targeted marketing messages, customize offerings, and provide personalized customer experiences.

Providing Exceptional Customer Service

Another key aspect of nurturing customer relationships is providing exceptional customer service. Customers value businesses that go above and beyond to meet their needs and exceed their expectations. Businesses can achieve this by investing in well-trained and knowledgeable customer service representatives who can provide prompt and personalized assistance. Implementing user-friendly self-service options can also enhance the overall customer experience.

Building Trust and Transparency

Trust and transparency are essential foundations for strong customer relationships. Businesses must strive to be open and honest in their interactions with customers.

Creating clear and transparent communication channels, providing accurate and timely information, and addressing customer concerns and feedback promptly can help build trust and strengthen relationships with customers.

Engaging with Customers

Engaging with customers on a regular basis is key to nurturing relationships. Businesses can utilize various channels such as social media platforms, email newsletters, and loyalty programs to stay connected with customers and encourage ongoing engagement.

Seeking customer feedback, conducting surveys, and actively listening to customer opinions allows businesses to understand their customers better and make improvements accordingly.

Rewarding Loyalty

Rewarding customer loyalty is a powerful way to nurture relationships and encourage repeat business. Implementing loyalty programs, offering exclusive discounts, and providing special perks for repeat customers can incentivize ongoing engagement and cultivate customer loyalty.

By prioritizing customer relationship management strategies, businesses can foster long-term loyalty, generate repeat business, and position themselves for sustained growth and success.

Innovation and Adaptability for Long-Term Success

In today's rapidly evolving market, it's crucial for businesses to stay ahead of the competition by embracing innovation and adapting to changing trends. The ability to innovate allows companies to create unique and valuable offerings, while adaptability enables them to adjust and thrive in a dynamic business landscape.

Embracing innovation involves cultivating a culture that encourages new ideas, experimentation, and creative problem-solving. By fostering a mindset of innovation, businesses can uncover fresh opportunities, optimize processes, and develop groundbreaking products and services.

Moreover, businesses must remain adaptable to the ever-changing market trends. This requires closely monitoring industry shifts, consumer preferences, and emerging technologies. By staying attuned to these changes, organizations can proactively adjust their strategies, operations, and customer experiences to ensure long-term success.

An invaluable aspect of adaptability is the ability to predict and respond to evolving market trends. This entails analyzing data, conducting market research, and leveraging insights to make informed decisions. By aligning their strategies with emerging trends, businesses can position themselves at the forefront of their industry, gaining a competitive advantage.

Importance of Innovation and Adaptability

Innovation and adaptability are fundamental for long-term success in today's business landscape. By continuously innovating, businesses can create unique value propositions, distinguish themselves from competitors, and unlock new revenue streams.

Similarly, adaptability allows businesses to navigate unforeseen challenges, seize emerging opportunities, and evolve alongside the market. It enables organizations to stay relevant in the face of technological advancements, changing customer preferences, and other market disruptions.

The combination of innovation and adaptability empowers businesses to proactively drive growth, anticipate customer needs, and pivot when necessary. Furthermore, it enables them to build resilience, establish themselves as industry leaders, and foster enduring customer relationships.

In conclusion, nurturing a culture of innovation and adaptability is imperative for long-term success in today's evolving market. By embracing innovation and remaining adaptable, businesses can position themselves as industry frontrunners, drive growth, and seize the opportunities presented by changing market trends.

Strategic Partnerships and Collaborations

Collaborating with like-minded organizations and forming strategic partnerships is a powerful driver of growth and presents businesses with valuable opportunities for synergistic growth. By joining forces with complementary entities, businesses can combine their resources, expertise, and networks to achieve mutually beneficial outcomes.

Strategic partnerships enable businesses to tap into new markets, expand their customer base, and enhance their competitive advantage. By leveraging the strengths of each partner, businesses can create innovative solutions, accelerate product development, and access new distribution channels, ultimately driving growth and increasing market share.

Identifying potential partners requires a thorough understanding of organizational goals, values, and target markets. Industries with overlapping interests and complementary capabilities often provide fertile ground for fruitful collaborations. Once potential partners are identified, businesses should engage in thorough due diligence to ensure alignment in terms of values, vision, and strategic objectives.

Establishing a strong foundation for a collaboration is crucial for its long-term success. This involves clearly defining the objectives, expectations, and roles of each partner, as well as establishing effective communication channels and decision-making processes. Regular evaluations and reviews of the partnership's progress are also vital to maintain alignment and address any evolving needs or challenges.

Collaborations can take various forms, including joint ventures, strategic alliances, licensing agreements, and distribution partnerships. Each structure offers unique benefits and considerations, and businesses should carefully evaluate which approach best aligns with their growth objectives and organizational culture.

Successful collaborations rely on trust, effective communication, and a commitment to shared goals. Businesses that embrace strategic partnerships and collaborations position themselves for accelerated growth, increased innovation, and expanded market reach, ultimately driving synergistic growth and long-term success.

Diversification and Expansion

Diversifying operations and expanding into new markets are essential strategies for achieving long-term growth and reducing reliance on a single product or market. By embracing diversification and exploring new markets, businesses can open up opportunities for expansion and ensure sustainable growth. In this section, we will delve into the various strategies that businesses can employ to successfully diversify and expand their operations.

Continuous Improvement and Learning Culture

Embracing a culture of continuous improvement and fostering a learning environment are vital components of long-term growth strategies. By investing in employee development and creating a culture that values innovation and growth, businesses can position themselves for ongoing success.

Continuous improvement entails consistently seeking ways to enhance processes, products, and services. It involves encouraging employees to identify areas for improvement, implementing feedback mechanisms, and actively seeking opportunities to learn and grow.

A learning culture is one that promotes continuous learning and professional development. It encourages employees to expand their skill sets, stay updated on industry trends, and embrace new technologies and methodologies. By fostering a learning culture, businesses can benefit from a workforce that is adaptable, creative, and equipped to handle evolving challenges.

The Benefits of Continuous Improvement and a Learning Culture

Continuous improvement and a learning culture offer several advantages to businesses seeking long-term growth:

Enhanced operational efficiency: Continuous improvement helps optimize processes, eliminating waste and inefficiencies. Increased productivity: Employees in a learning culture are motivated to develop their skills, leading to higher productivity levels. Adaptability to change: A learning culture equips employees with the tools and mindset needed to adapt to new market trends and industry shifts.Improved innovation: By encouraging continuous learning, businesses foster innovation and create an environment conducive to new ideas and approaches. Attraction and retention of top talent: A strong commitment to employee development and learning makes businesses more attractive to top performers and helps retain valuable talent.

By integrating continuous improvement and a learning culture into their organizational DNA, businesses can lay a solid foundation for sustainable growth and long-term success.

Effective Financial Management

Proper financial management lies at the core of sustainable growth and long-term success for businesses. To achieve profitability and financial stability, businesses must implement key financial strategies and practices.

One crucial aspect of financial management is creating and adhering to a realistic budget. By carefully analyzing expenses and revenue streams, businesses can identify areas of improvement and make informed decisions to maximize profitability.

Investing in Growth

To support sustainable growth, businesses must allocate resources strategically. This includes investing in areas such as research and development, new technology, and employee training. By allocating resources in a way that aligns with long-term growth objectives, businesses can position themselves for success in an ever-evolving marketplace.

Effective Cash Flow Management

Managing cash flow is paramount to ensuring financial stability. By properly monitoring and forecasting cash inflows and outflows, businesses can plan ahead and mitigate potential financial challenges. This enables them to maintain profitability and make informed decisions regarding investments and operations.

Financial Analysis and Performance Metrics

Regular financial analysis and the use of performance metrics are vital for assessing the effectiveness of growth strategies. By analyzing key financial data and benchmarking against industry standards, businesses can identify trends, strengths, and areas that require improvement. This quantitative data-driven approach enhances decision-making, enabling businesses to optimize their long-term growth strategies.

In conclusion, effective financial management is essential for sustainable growth and profitability. By implementing budgeting, strategic resource allocation, cash flow management, and financial analysis, businesses can lay a strong foundation for enduring success.

Embracing Technology and Digital Transformation

Technology and digital transformation have become vital catalysts for long-term growth and competitive advantage in today's rapidly evolving business landscape. Businesses that leverage technology effectively have the opportunity to enhance operational efficiencies, improve customer experiences, and drive growth.

Leveraging Technology for Operational Efficiencies

By integrating advanced technological solutions, businesses can streamline their processes, automate repetitive tasks, and optimize resource allocation. Implementing cloud-based systems, artificial intelligence (AI), and machine learning can enhance productivity, reduce costs, and enable data-driven decision-making.

For example, utilizing enterprise resource planning (ERP) software can centralize data management, providing real-time insights and improving supply chain visibility. This fosters efficient inventory management, minimizes stockouts, and increases overall operational efficiency.

Improving Customer Experiences

Digital transformation also offers businesses the opportunity to enhance customer experiences and strengthen customer relationships. Online platforms, mobile apps, and personalized marketing campaigns enable businesses to engage with customers on multiple touchpoints, providing seamless and tailored experiences.

For instance, businesses can leverage customer relationship management (CRM) systems to gain a comprehensive view of customer interactions and preferences. This data can then be utilized to create personalized recommendations, offers, and loyalty programs, ultimately increasing customer satisfaction and retention.

Driving Growth through Digital Transformation

Embracing digital transformation opens up new avenues for business growth. E-commerce platforms enable businesses to reach global markets, expand their customer base, and diversify revenue streams. By harnessing the power of data analytics and predictive modeling, businesses can uncover new market trends, identify emerging opportunities, and make data-driven business decisions.

Moreover, digital transformation allows businesses to introduce innovative products and services to meet changing customer demands. By leveraging technology to create unique value propositions, businesses can differentiate themselves in the market and gain a competitive advantage.

In conclusion, businesses that embrace technology and digital transformation position themselves for long-term growth and a competitive edge. By leveraging technology to enhance operational efficiencies, improve customer experiences, and drive growth, businesses can adapt to evolving market dynamics and establish themselves as leaders in their industry.

Measuring and Evaluating Long-Term Growth

To sustain long-term growth, businesses need to have robust mechanisms in place to measure and evaluate their progress. Data-driven decision-making plays a crucial role in this process, enabling businesses to make informed choices based on concrete evidence. By leveraging data analytics and performance metrics, companies can gain valuable insights into the effectiveness of their long-term growth strategies.

Measuring growth involves tracking key performance indicators (KPIs) relevant to the specific goals and objectives of the business. These KPIs may include revenue growth, customer acquisition rates, customer retention rates, market share, and profitability. By regularly monitoring and analyzing these metrics, businesses can identify areas of improvement and make data-driven adjustments to their strategies.

Evaluating the success of long-term growth initiatives requires a comprehensive approach. It involves not only analyzing financial performance but also considering qualitative factors such as customer satisfaction, brand reputation, and employee engagement. By taking a holistic view, businesses can gain a deeper understanding of the overall impact and effectiveness of their growth strategies.

Data-driven decision-making empowers businesses to make strategic choices based on reliable information rather than intuition or guesswork. By gathering and analyzing relevant data, organizations can optimize their operations, identify trends and patterns, and make proactive adjustments to their growth strategies. This data-driven approach enhances the likelihood of achieving sustainable, long-term growth.

Chapter **21**

Soloists: Managing High Performers and Unique Talents in Your Business

Welcome to Chapter 21 of our comprehensive guide on managing high performers and unique talents in your business. In this section, we will explore the strategies and approaches necessary to effectively manage and inspire soloists within your organization.

Brilliant people with excellent performance, great uniqueness that constantly raises the bar for successes, are quite significant for any business entity to bring innovation. However, their management demands a careful approach appreciating their mentality peculiarities.

The soloist's mindset will be discussed throughout this chapter; the ways of identifying top performers would also be considered along with creating an interesting working environment. Besides, the importance of effective communication would be addressed as well as customizing rewards and recognition, making available growth opportunities among others as well as tackling problems that arise occasionally.

What has been explained above can allow one to establish a work environment which not only attracts talent but also help retain leading soloists within your organization while enabling them maximally exploit their potential. Now let us look at how best we can handle high performers as well as unique talents in your enterprise today.

Comprehending Soloist Mindset

Soloists are distinguished by certain mindset features that make them different from everyone else. This part deals with these factors driving them towards perfectionism regardless of all obstacles encountered on their way, seeking self-improvement at any cost and requiring full independence.

Soloists hold themselves up to higher standards when it comes to becoming perfect. They have an internal motivation for self-improvement and an internal drive that implies exceeding even their own expectations through training repeatedly harder than last time according to Coyle (2009). Such urge makes them enjoy challenges or strive after mastery levels they set while working in respective fields.

Additionally, soloists always seek personal development opportunities continuously learning hence looking for more knowledge or skills while experimenting on new ideas ahead of others.

Power of Autonomy

Autonomy is one issue that distinguishes the soloist mentality. The ability to make decisions, feel ownership of work and explore own creative ideas are some of things that motivate these soloists. When in such a state, they are able to use their talents effectively thus contributing to the success of the company.

By understanding and embracing this mindset, organizations can leverage great potential from high performers. The next section will explore the strategies for identifying soloists within your organization.

Identify Your Soloists

Firstly it is important for high-performers as well as unique talents in your firm to be identified so that they can be effectively dealt with. This people have extraordinary skills which results into excellent performance always with innovative thinking (Buckingham & Clifton 2001). Consequently if you want an entity to perform well then harness all these abilities.

So how do you identify them in your organization? They may show tendencies of constantly surpassing expectations made by their employers as well as colleagues. In addition, these people frequently demonstrate ideas beyond facts and information known about certain situations thereby enabling an enterprise grow and become better informed through introducing fresh angles of thought or approaches. Another important way of checking on high performers is through their consistent ability to maintain outstanding results. This could be done by identifying individuals with a proven track record in meeting or surpassing objectives, as well as habitually achieving the best performance.

Moreover, soloists often possess idiosyncratic abilities that differentiate them from others within their organizations. Those skills can range from specialized knowledge to being able to connect with customers and stakeholders differently. It is therefore important for you to find and utilize such people properly in your business.

By doing this, you will identify soloists who have the ability to give extraordinary results in your organization. Afterwards, focus should shift towards effectively managing and nurturing these talents so that their full potential are realized hence becoming an asset to the business.

Creating an Engaging Work Environment

One of the critical ways of managing soloists and high performers in your company effectively is by building an engaging work environment which fosters their commitment. In this section we shall discuss some key strategies for creating such a conducive environment.

Clear Objectives

To develop high engagement level amongst these specialists' goals must be set clear and precisely mentioned it terms of direction they should take. Clearly stating expectations and targets enable them comprehend what they are required to do hence enabling them work smartly towards that end goal. Communicating regularly about the goals while ensuring that they are aligned with overall business objectives helps keep the soloist engaged and motivated for excellence.

Challenging Assignments

Soloists would like being challenged in order to exhibit rare capabilities which others may not have. Tasking them on projects which stretch their talent base but needs their expertise is one good way of giving them opportunity for growth but at the same time keeping them engaged as well as motivated too. Challenging projects keep soloists energized and invested in their work, driving innovation and exceptional performance.

Promote Positive Company Culture

A positive organizational culture plays a crucial role in improving engagement of soloists. This is achieved by creating an environment where soloists feel valued, recognized and connected through promotion of collaborative and inclusive work cultures. Additionally, such can also be promoted by encouraging team work, celebrating milestones as well as ongoing feedback and support which not only enhances engagement but also boosts the overall morale of the team.

Creating an engaging work environment is important in managing high performers and unique talents in your business. By setting clear goals, providing challenging projects, or promoting a positive company culture, you can develop a workplace that instills passion, drive and commitment among soloists. The next section will look at effective communication when dealing with soloists.

Effective Communication with Soloists

Managing high performers that are soloists in organizations require effective communication channels to be established. You need to have open lines of communication for successful collaboration with these employees.

This paves way for dialogues between soloists who are able to express their unique abilities putting into consideration that they are being appreciated for what they do thus leading to more innovation within your corporation.

Strategies for Effective Communication with Soloist

1. Active Listening

When conversing with a lone performer make it your duty to listen keenly. Therefore you must pay attention, respect their viewpoint as well as ask any clearance needed so that it means you value his/her contribution besides creating room for dialogue.

2.Clear and Concise Communication

Soloists value concise and straight to the point communication. Avoiding wordy emails or meetings with too many details but instead focus on delivering clear and actionable information. This allows soloists to quickly grasp essential messages and take appropriate action.

3. Regular Feedback

Provide regular feedback to soloists in order for them to have a clear understanding of expectations and performance. Give constructive criticism when necessary, however also acknowledge their achievements. Through this ongoing feedback loop, soloists stay on course while growing professionally.

4. Encourage Collaboration

Promote working together as a team where soloist can share expertise with others or work with others in collaboration projects Encourage them to partake in cross-functional projects, team discussions, and brainstorming sessions. This fosters effective communication among employees; harnesses the collective knowledge and skills of talented workforce.

Building trust, strengthening relationships through effective communication with soloists creates a supportive culture that ensures success for both the individual employee and whole organization.

Tailoring Rewards and Recognition

When motivating high performers, it is important to provide tailored rewards and recognition. It is not sufficient enough just providing generic incentives but rather employers should take time to understand the real motivators for their top performers. By doing so, they are able create personalized reward systems that inspire continued excellence and engagement at work places.

One way of tailoring rewards is having individualized incentives. It means that what motivates one high performer may not motivate another one same way. Some people could be into financial rewards other than additional vacation days off or flexible hours of work. When these options are provided by employers who allow employees choose their preferred rewards then each high-performer will be guaranteed feeling appreciated as well as keeping motivated.

Another important thing worth noting is that recognition does not always have to be monetary based. In fact non-monetary recognition can sometimes be even more powerful than money-based ones.. Even simple things such as public praise , personal notes of appreciation , or even talking about employee's achievements during team meetings can go a long way to boosting morale and motivation. By highlighting the unique contributions of individual high performers, employers create a recognition culture that incites others to greatness.

Lastly, offering career advancement opportunities is also another potent way of rewarding and motivating high performers. This encompasses promotions, leadership roles or specialized training as well that not only acknowledges their contribution but also shows commitment to their professional growth. High performers flourish in challenging environments with constant learning hence providing them with opportunities to expand on their skills and take up new responsibilities will keep them in motivated for long term.

In conclusion, tailoring rewards and recognition is essential in motivating high performers. Through individualized incentives, non-monetary recognition, and career advancement opportunities, organizations can ensure that their best employees remain engaged, motivated and dedicated to achieving exceptional results.

Providing Growth Opportunities

To effectively manage high performers and unique talents in your business; it is essential to prioritize providing growth opportunities. Soloists thrive on continuous learning and career development, and by offering them the chance to expand their skills and knowledge, you can nurture their potential and keep them motivated

Developing targeted professional development programs is an effective means of promoting growth among high achievers. These can incorporate workshops, conferences and webinars which are specific to their areas of expertise and interests. By investing in their learning, you show your commitment to their success and provide them with the tools to excel.

Mentorship: Another effective career development strategy involves linking soloists with experienced mentors who guide them. Through mentoring, high performers can be guided through challenges and roadblocks as well as providing insights to assist them on their journey. This one-on-one support builds strong relationships and allows for personalized guidance, enriching their professional journey.

Stretch Assignments:

Giving soloists challenging projects or stretch assignments is a great way to offer them opportunities for growth. In addition, such assignments push high performers beyond their limits forcing them to acquire new skills and explore how far they can go in business life. Thus by assigning complicated tasks you display faith in their abilities and enhance careers.

Remember soloists are always driven by the desire to evolve continuously and reach greater heights. Growth opportunities created through professional development programs, mentorship, and stretch assignments enable your organization's environment facilitate for career advancement that retains them long-term.

Overcoming Challenges & Resolving Conflicts

Managing soloists has its own set of unique challenges and conflicts. They have intense drive for excellence; possession of independent mindset often times acts as a contradiction against teamwork or organizational dynamics on whole team basis sometimes resulting into clashes between two sides. It is crucial therefore that these conflicts are resolved amicably so as not interrupt harmony or minimize the potential of these high achievers.

Constructive Feedback for Growth

Providing constructive feedback is key in managing conflicts with soloists. They strive for constant improvement both personally and professionally throughout High Performers' lives . With specifics through formative process though it becomes possible helping individuals apply passion towards growth while addressing performance issues or conflicts if any arise.

Effective Conflict Resolution

It's how you handle conflict that matters and not the existence of conflict itself in an organization. As such, it is important to approach conflicts involving soloists with a mindset aimed at solving problems. Actively listen, grasp their standpoint and identify points of convergence that respond to all involved parties' interests. In this way, by encouraging open communication and creating collaboration-oriented atmosphere, there will be no conflicts among soloists.

Addressing Performance Issues

Even high-performing individuals may experience performance issues at some point. Therefore, while managing soloists it is important to address these issues promptly yet professionally. Clearly communicate expectations and establish performance objectives that are in line with organizational objectives as a whole. Provide the necessary support and resources for them to overcome any challenges they face thereby ensuring growth remains Continuous.

Therefore as a solution one must take proactive measures when managing soloists in order to overcome challenges and resolve conflicts through constructive feedback, effective conflict resolutions mechanisms & addressing performance related problems instantly thus fostering conducive environment where high achievers flourish leading successful business enterprise.

Retaining Soloists for the Long-Term

In today's competitive business landscape, retaining high performers and unique talents is crucial for long-term success. For instance, soloists bring about innovations which push companies towards achieving their strategic goals. To ensure their continued commitment and engagement, organizations must implement effective strategies for long-term retention.

1. Ongoing Engagement:

1. Work-Life Balance:

Soloists are often engrossed in their work and may spend a great deal of time and effort on projects that they undertake. Nevertheless, it is necessary to strike a balance between work and personal life for long-term retention. Enable flexible working hours, create adequate time-off policies, maintain equitable distribution of workload and avoid overstressing them.

2. Creating a Sense of Purpose:

An artist feels alive when his/her works have real meaning or an effect on others. Thus, make known to soloists your organization’s mission as well as their purpose in it so that they understand how their unique talents connect with the larger vision. Therefore, the feeling of purpose will make individual players pour all their effort into long-term success of the company.

In conclusion, retaining high performers and unique talents requires a proactive approach that addresses their ongoing engagement, work-life balance, and sense of purpose. Through these approaches organizations can therefore develop cultures which support soloists encouraging long term retention for business continuity.

Conclusion

Managing high performers and unique talents is a crucial aspect of building a successful business. this section has looked at several strategies which businesses could employ to effectively manage artists while enhancing their performance towards greater heights.

One key take-away from this discussion is acknowledging the mindset of soloism among individuals who excel at everything they do. To be able to provide an environment conducive for achievement managers have to understand the pursuit for excellence these people are after, personal development orientation as well as autonomy.

To manage soloists clearly and effectively requires good communication skills. By opening up channels of communication within an organization through which information can flow freely fostering transparency in decision making processes as well collaboration leads to trust hence team working becomes seamless.

Moreover, providing growth opportunities along with tailored rewards/ recognition are essential elements needed to keep them motivated. In this regard businesses can offer challenging assignments coupled with training programs aimed at developing employees’ professional skills as well as motivation based strategies directed towards particular worker profiles.

Ultimately, retaining soloists for the long-term requires a commitment to ongoing engagement, work-life balance, and a sense of purpose within the organization. In this section we have presented strategies that can help businesses harness the potential of high performing artists, thus scaling up their achievements.

Chapter **22**

Rests in Music: Learning from Failure and Downtime in Business Management

Welcome to the 22nd chapter of our innovative business management strategies series. In this chapter, we're going to talk about a surprising source of inspiration for success—rests in music.

Yes, pauses and breaks can teach us a lot about how to properly manage a business. We're going to show you how the art of timing, learning from failure, and embracing downtime can revolutionize your approach to strategic management.

Rests in music are those brief yet vital moments of silence that musicians use to enhance their compositions. Similarly, entrepreneurs and managers can utilize the concept of rests as well. By understanding the best way to learn from failure and embrace downtime, businesses will be able to foster creativity, improve decision-making skills, and navigate challenges more efficiently.

Failure is something that many managers and entrepreneurs are deathly afraid of. However, by leveraging it as feedback and treating it as another stepping stone towards improvement, businesses will be able to bounce back stronger than ever before. Drawing insights from musicians who interpret rests in music as cues for reflection and adjustment is an innovative way for us all to harness mistakes for growth.

Embracing Failure: The Breakdown

In Chapter 21 we said that "Failure is not an option." Well...in Chapter 22 we're saying that "Failure IS an option!"

The world has a funny way of putting things together sometimes...

In the world of business management failure can be seen as something that should be avoided at all costs but what if I told you there's power in embracing failure?

This concept is similar to rests in music where pauses create anticipation and tension leading up to the next note or lyrics. When used strategically like this it serves as moments for reflection so artists know they're on the right track.

On the flip side with entrepreneurs looking at their failures through this same lens they'll uncover valuable insights that lead them back on track too!

Sticking to a tried and true strategy isn't always the best approach. By leaving it in the past, analyzing your results, and making the necessary adjustments you can start progressing even better than before.

The forward-looking mindset that artists have is what allows them to be so successful. When they're able to identify what went wrong and why, they can refine their process moving forward. You should consider doing the same thing.

By changing the way you view failure instead of as a setback or sign of incompetence but rather as an opportunity for growth, learning, and progress will make you instantly more resilient during any difficult situation.

Learning from failure is a continuous process of improvement. Documenting and sharing what you learn from failures can help create a culture that values failure as a path to success. This type of culture encourages people to be more innovative, creative, and willing to take calculated risks.

In the end, just like in music, pauses are needed to build tension before continuing on with the melody. Embracing failure in business management can lead to valuable insights and growth opportunities. By adopting the mindset that failure is a stepping stone to success and learning from your mistakes, organizations can create a culture of resilience, innovation, and continuous improvement.

The Power of Downtime: How Taking Breaks Can Improve Business

Rests in music serve an important purpose. They give music space to breathe and create rhythm. The same goes for downtime in business management – it plays a crucial role in making strategic decisions and improving overall performance.

Downtime allows business leaders time for reflection where they can step back from their day-to-day tasks and come up with fresh perspectives. When things slow down, ideas can flourish, leading to new solutions for challenges.

When things aren't so busy anymore, creativity thrives. Just as rests in music allow musicians to explore harmonies and melodies without interfering with the main tune, downtime allows businesses to innovate by generating new ideas. Many times breakthrough concepts are created during these moments of relaxation.

To maintain sustainable performance in organizations rest is necessary. Downtime gives employees time to recharge their energy stores which leads them better focus, productivity, and well-being overall. By valuing rest businesses can promote healthier work practices that prioritize mental health.

Strategic decision-making requires different perspectives which taking breaks enables leaders access more easily. When breaks are taken away from constant operational demand leaders have time use critical thinking skills when evaluating potential risks or alternative strategies leading them towards better future outcomes.

In conclusion businesses should try embracing downtime as if it were rests in music. By valuing reflection, rest, and rejuvenation managers can promote employee well-being, improve decision-making processes, and foster innovation.

Embracing failure as feedback involves shifting your perspective and committing to improving. It's about focusing on growth rather than setbacks. By accepting failure as a normal part of the learning process, companies can create an environment that breeds innovation, learning, and resilience.

When organizations encourage employees to embrace failure as feedback, they see more problem-solving skills, creativity, and resilience in their workers. Once people learn from their mistakes and accept them as valuable lessons, they'll be more willing to take risks and think outside the box. This leads to better performance over time.

So instead of dreading failure or viewing it negatively, failing should be seen as a stepping stone towards success. Companies can use failures and mistakes as feedback to create an environment that continuously learns and grows. Just like musicians interpret rests in music for reflection and adjustment, organizations can embrace failures as valuable feedback on their path to success.

The Art of Timing: Applying Rests to Business Strategies

Timing plays a crucial role in business just like it does in music. The strategic use of pauses in business strategies can greatly enhance decision-making, communication, and overall effectiveness when managing operations.

Just imagine an orchestra conductor - they carefully plan out rests so it creates anticipation during performances while allowing musicians to breathe too. The same applies here: approach timing with intentionality across all facets.

By incorporating this concept into strategy planning businesses are able to optimize workflow which in turn maximizes efficiency company-wide. Pausing for brief moments promotes reflection within leaders so they're able to critically assess scenarios before making any final decisions.

Strategic pauses also improves communication between team members because it allows information some space to fill the gaps in conversation - which is when people really start thinking critically about what was said (or not said). In presentations or other similar scenarios where you have your audience's full attention these pauses can help emphasize important points.

Lastly breaks maintain productivity levels throughout the day by letting employees recharge when necessary so they're able to maintain focus. Plus it boosts creativity by providing time for individuals to take a step back and clear their minds.

The art of timing and applying rests in business strategies can be the key differentiator between you and your competitors. It enhances decision-making, improves communication, optimizes workflow, and fosters a more productive work environment. Just like how musicians understand that rests are crucial when creating music, businesses must leverage the power of pauses if they want to thrive.

In the ever changing and fast-moving business world, it is crucial for organizations to find ways to foster creativity and drive innovation in order to stay more competitive. One of the most effective ways that never get noticed is downtime. It can be a powerful tool for boosting our imagination and leading us to create groundbreaking ideas.

Drawing inspiration from the pauses and silence in music, businesses can use downtime to encourage their team's creative potential. Like a musician uses rests strategically to add depth and nuance to a composition, organizations can create an environment that encourages creative thinking during downtime.

The Importance of Reflection

During downtime, employees have the space they need to step back from their daily tasks and reflect on challenges, opportunities, and potential solutions. By providing time for reflection, businesses are able to tap into their teams collective wisdomsand spark new insights that would have been overlooked if they had been too busy with work.

Nurturing Curiosity

Downtime can also help nurture curiosity. When employees are given freedom so they don't feel like they're trapped or locked up, it stimulates their natural curiosity and allows them make connections that may lead them to breakthroughs in innovation.

Embracing Exploration

Creating a culture that values downtime will give your workforce the permission they need to explore any passions or interests they might have. Encouraging employees to try out new activities such as reading books at libraries, attending conferences (even if it's not related directly) or participating in brainstorming sessions during downtime will cultivate rich knowledge banks within your crew — fueling innovation throughout your organization.

Collaboration & Connection

Not all downtimes have to be done individually. Fostering collaboration during breaks will lead you down the path of even greater innovations. By simply giving your employees some time where they can connect with each other, share ideas and engage in creative problem-solving will unlock endless possibilities when it comes down innovative intelligence.

By recognizing how important downtimes can be and harnessing their power, businesses can unlock their teams' creativity which results in driving innovation. Embracing pauses and moments of reflection, nurturing curiosity, encouraging exploration and fostering collaboration will pave the way for new ideas to come flooding in. This leads to breakthrough solutions that create a culture of innovation.

1. Prioritize tasks: Assess the importance and urgency of tasks, focusing on the highest priority items, and allocating time blocks for their completion. This approach allows for more structured workload management and ensures that critical tasks receive the necessary attention.
2. Delegate and collaborate: Effective delegation of tasks and collaboration can help distribute the workload and prevent individual burnout. Empowering team members to take ownership of

specific tasks not only reduces workload but also fosters a sense of shared responsibility and accountability.

3. Time blocking: Set specific time blocks for different types of tasks, ensuring dedicated periods for focused work, collaborative activities, and rest breaks.

Stress Management through Strategic Rests:

1. Mindfulness practices: Encourage mindfulness exercises like deep breathing, short walks or meditation during strategic rest periods. These activities can help individuals rejuvenate mentally, reduce stress, and enhance focus and clarity.
2. Healthy breaks: Encourage employees to use their rest periods for activities that promote relaxation and well-being such as stretching, getting fresh air or listening to calming music. Such breaks have been shown to improve physical and mental health leading to increased productivity and engagement.

By embracing these concepts organizations can create a culture that values work-life balance and employee well-being. Prioritizing breaks along with stress management contributes to the overall health satisfaction of employees allowing ample space for increased productivity improved decision making enhanced creativity.

Learning from the Masters: Insights from Musicians & Business Leaders

Both musicians & business leaders are in unique positions where they've had access to success that we all crave at some point in our lives - so when they give advice it's always worth listening too. In this section we'll explore both ends by looking at how they viewed failure & downtime differently than most people do - creating an entirely new perspective on success itself.

We begin with world-class musicians who share stories about their own failures while reaching greatness - explaining how important each one was in their careers… From missed notes during live performances to unsuccessful album releases, these musicians have harnessed failure as a catalyst for growth and evolution.

As we shift from music to business, we'll begin looking into how the top minds on the planet deal with their toughest obstacles. Those who are known for their innovative strategies and bold decision-making approach failures differently than most of us do. They view failure as essential feedback that guides their continuous improvement towards new levels of achievement.

Further diving in - we look at how musicians and business leaders have recognized the pivotal role that downtime plays in their pursuits… When you hear a rest in a piece of music, they're not just there for fun, they're important pauses for reflection and expression… Just like those, breaks can be extremely beneficial when used strategically. By prioritizing rest & rejuvenation they've been able to nurture their own well-being while creating environments that foster innovation & inspiration.

Learning Life Lessons from Music and Business Masters

These wise mentors not only inspire, but also prevent aspiring managers who desire to unlock their full potential with practical guidance. Approaching failure in a positive light and converting downtime into productivity are key lessons when looking at the bigger picture.

Failing is the first step towards growth, and breaks can be used as an advantage to achieve success. Encouraging workers to see failure as a learning opportunity instead of something negative will give them motivation to continue taking risks and innovating. Recognizing that downtime allows for rejuvenation and creative thinking employees can challenge themselves with new ideas.

Integration of rests in business culture may sound difficult, but it's not impossible. To approach this task you must integrate appropriate strategies that cater towards your company's needs. By prioritizing open communication and collaboration workers feel supported by their team members which will push them to share what they learn from failures without fear of judgement. It also helps for companies to incorporate regular scheduled breaks so employees can disconnect from work during non-working hours allowing them to actually have a life outside of their job title.

Building resilience through integration requires a shift in mindset. Companies have to understand that failing is part of the process, downtime does help, taking risks is necessary, and learning never ends if you want your organization's success to live on long-term.

Chapter 23

Encore! Creating and Sustaining Success in Your Business

Welcome to Chapter 23, where we dive into the strategies and practices that will help you create and sustain success in your business. In today's competitive landscape, initial triumphs aren't enough anymore. You need continuous growth and adaptation to come out on top.

At the center of all this is Encore! Creating and Sustaining Success in Your Business. In this chapter, we'll give you actionable steps and valuable insights so you can achieve lasting triumph that propels your business to new heights. We'll take a look at setting clear goals, building a strong team, cultivating company culture, embracing innovation, and more.

Ready to take things up a notch? Let's get started!

Introduction to Creating and Sustaining Success

Creating and sustaining success in your business isn't easy — but it's worth it. With the right strategies in place, you can set yourself up for long-term growth that achieves big goals.

Success is no longer about one-off wins: it's about building something that can last through time. Anyone can spark short-term growth with the right marketing campaign or product launch — but not everyone has what it takes to change an entire industry. To get there, you'll need a strategic mindset that never settles for "good enough." By focusing on long-term success from day one, you'll build a business that thrives for decades to come.

this section covers everything you need to know about creating sustained growth. From clarifying short- and long-term goals to building a powerful team, fostering adaptability and innovation, implementing effective marketing campaigns, mastering financial management...you get the idea.

Whether your goal is to scale up an existing company or disrupt an industry with a fresh startup idea, this guide has got it all. Get ready: we're about to unlock the secrets of long-term success!

Setting Clear Goals

The first step toward creating sustained success in your business is simple: set clear goals. Without a direction, it's impossible to measure progress or guide your decision-making.

When setting goals, make sure you're thinking both short- and long-term. A strong set of short-term goals will help you stay focused and motivated, while long-term aspirations are what give you a sense of purpose and direction. With the right mix of both, you can create a roadmap that guides your business toward sustainable growth.

What is the goal-setting process?

It's simple:

1. Identify Your Business Goals: Define exactly what you want to achieve with your business.
2. Consider Your Vision, Mission, and Values: Use these elements as a compass to guide your goal-setting process.

Make Your Goals SMART: Ensure that your goals are Specific, Measurable, Achievable, Realistic and Time-bound. This framework helps you set goals that are clear, quantifiable and achievable.

Break Down Your Goals: Divide your goals into smaller objectives that can be acted upon. This allows you to follow and stay motivated as you reach milestones along the way.

Communicate and Involve Your Team: Share your goals with your team members to create alignment and collaboration. By involving your team in this process you can harness their expertise and commitment for success.

Practical Tips for Setting Goals

Here are some practical tips to keep in mind when setting goals:

Ensure Alignment: Make sure everyone is working towards a common purpose.

Set Priorities: Prioritize goals based on importance and urgency.

Monitor & Adjust: Regularly monitor progress toward each goal and make adjustments as needed.

Celebrate Milestones: Acknowledge achievements of milestones along the way.

Building a Strong Team

A successful business relies on a strong team that works together towards a common goal.

Recognize and appreciate the achievements and hard work of individual team members to boost morale and foster a positive team culture.

Recognizing hard work is a surefire way to build trust and strong relationships. Encourage your team to push themselves every day by recognizing their greatness.

Incentivizing hard work will allow you to create partnerships with your employees that will last long into the future. Building trust between employer and employee can result in more smiles, more laughter, and overall better moods in the office space. Don't just take our word for it! Giving your team members a pat on the back will increase efficiency, produce clearer problem-solving skills, and cultivate a thriving workplace.

Positive Reinforcement

There is no doubt about it: Having a positive company culture is essential for any business. Not only does it make for an efficient working environment but it also enhances employee satisfaction and engagement. A positive culture lays the groundwork for employees to have a motivated mindset so they can knock out goals like dominos falling one at a time.

Building this type of work environment starts with strong leadership along with clear communication. Constructing shared values gives employees purpose outside of completing tasks. Company visions help everyone feel like they are part of something bigger than themselves, which pushes them to collaborate efficiently as well as innovate new ideas.

By prioritizing your employee's mental health, you are also empowering them to make these changes within the company. It could be offering flexible working hours or introducing wellness programs that promote overall happiness in the office space. Recognizing exceptional contributions from the people who work for you will cultivate a culture filled with appreciation as well as support.

Transparency is another key factor here when trying to achieve positivity within your company's walls. Simply asking for feedback from employees opens up channels they didn't know were there before. It allows them voice concerns and solutions that aim towards improving productivity levels while making them feel valued at the same time.

Promoting diversity in the workplace allows for conversations to take place that couldn't happen anywhere else. Employees can learn from each other's backgrounds and bring their unique perspectives to light. Your role as an employer is to celebrate these differences and encourage the sharing of ideas.

There is a direct correlation between company culture and how well a business performs. If productivity levels are low, it might be time to re-evaluate your team's work environment. Foster a culture that attracts employees who want to maximize their potential so you can achieve overall success.

Innovation and Adaptability

At this point, we all know how quick things move in the business world. If you are not staying ahead of the curve, then you will surely fall behind your competitors. By implementing an innovation-focused mentality within your company, you will have no choice but to adapt in order to succeed. Resisting change is never a good idea.

When things seem like they are at a standstill, innovation tends to have the ability to find it's way through any roadblock there may be. Encouraging your team members to think outside of the box could lead them down new pathways that haven't been taken before. Disrupting markets with novel ideas should always be a goal of yours if growth is what you're looking for.

Adaptability has saved more companies than we care to count at this point. It allows businesses like yours stay agile whenever unexpected hurdles come out of nowhere . Being able to quickly pivot whenever these obstacles show up can even give your employees better reaction times when it comes down things like customer preference shifts.

Providing an environment where risk-taking is encouraged is going make big changes happen much quicker than if they were only talked about during meetings. You want everyone on your team pushing each other towards breaking comfort zones every single day if possible just so they can come up with new ways of thinking while in survival mode.

Overall, prioritizing employee satisfaction first will allow you to build a culture with values that resonates with everyone. This is what keeps them motivated to perform at their best every single day.

Aside from that, investing in research and development can fuel innovation and foster adaptability. By dedicating resources and efforts to research, you can stay ahead of industry trends, identify emerging technologies, and anticipate future customer needs. This proactive approach positions your business as a leader in innovation and enables you to adapt swiftly to changing market dynamics.

Finally, continuous learning and development are essential for staying innovative and adaptable in today's fast-paced business environment. Encourage your team members to embrace a growth mindset, seek out new knowledge and skills, and embrace ongoing professional development opportunities. By prioritizing learning, you equip your team with the tools and expertise needed to adapt to new challenges and drive business growth.

In conclusion, innovation and adaptability are critical for sustained business success. By fostering a culture of innovation, embracing change, and investing in continuous learning, you can position your business for long-term growth. Embrace the transformative power of innovation and adaptability, and empower your team to drive your business forward in the ever-evolving marketplace.

Effective Marketing Strategies

When it comes to achieving business success, implementing effective marketing strategies is crucial. These strategies play a pivotal role in attracting new customers and retaining existing ones, ultimately driving customer acquisition and contributing to long-term business growth.

In today's digital age, leveraging digital marketing channels is essential. From search engine optimization (SEO) to social media advertising, digital marketing allows you to reach your target audience effectively and efficiently. By implementing SEO techniques, you can improve your website's visibility and rank higher in search engine results—increasing the chances of potential customers finding your business.

Additionally, social media platforms provide an excellent opportunity to create brand awarenesss,— engage with your audience,,and establish a loyal customer base.. By consistently delivering valuable content..and interacting with your followers,,you can build strong relationships–and encourage customer loyalty– .

While digital marketing is crucial traditional advertising methods should not be overlooked . Tactic such as print advertisements, television and radio commercials, and outdoor advertising can still be effective in reaching your target market. A well-rounded marketing strategy that combines both digital and traditional approaches can maximize your business's reach and impact.

It's also important to leverage content marketing to provide value to your audience and establish your business as an industry leader. By creating informative and engaging content,,such as blog articles, videos,..and podcasts,,you can position your brand as an authority in your niche–and attract potential customers who are seeking valuable information.

Furthermore–email marketing remains a powerful tool for customer acquisition and retention. By building an email list–and sending targeted campaigns,,you can stay connected with your audience–nurture leads–and drive conversions– .

Overall, effective marketing strategies are essential for achieving business success. By utilizing a combination of digital and traditional tactics, leveraging content marketing,,and implementing email marketing campaigns,,you can attract new customers, retain existing ones..and drive continuous growth for your business.

Financial Management and Planning–

Sound financial management is crucial for sustaining success in your business. Effective financial management allows you to allocate resources wisely–maximize profitability–and navigate potential challenges . By implementing proper business planning –and strategic financial practices,,you can set your business up for long-term financial success

Budgeting

Budgeting is a key aspect of financial management. It helps you track expenses, manage cash flow, and make smart financial decisions. By setting realistic goals and allocating resources effectively, you can improve your business's bottom line. Keep an eye on the market and adjust your budget as necessary to stay ahead.

Cash Flow Management

Managing cash flow day-to-day is essential for success. Make sure that money is coming in at a steady pace so you have enough liquid capital to handle all business-related expenses. Implement strategies like prompt invoicing and effective inventory management to optimize your cash flow.

Strategic Financial Planning

Setting financial goals and developing a strategy to achieve them will give you the best chance at success in the long run. Align your efforts with the overall strategy of your business to make informed decisions that push growth forward.

Remember, financial management requires consistent monitoring and adjustment to be effective.

Part IV:
Fine-Tuning Your Craft

Chapter 24

The Reprise: Continuous Improvement and Learning in Business

Welcome to the 24th chapter of our business growth and innovation series. In this chapter, we will discuss about continuous improvement and learning in businesses. As the industries are evolving at a rapid pace, companies must learn how to adapt, innovate and improve their processes constantly in order to stay competitive.

Continuous improvement is not just about one-time efforts, it's an ongoing journey towards excellence. By adopting a mindset of constant development and learning businesses can unlock their full potential and achieve sustainable growth.

In the upcoming sections, we will talk more about why continuous improvement is important, how you can develop a culture of learning within your organization, identify where improvements can be made in your company's current state, implement initiatives for further progress and finally how you can make sure that these changes stick around for long-term success.

So let's get started on this exploration journey as we uncover strategies that'll help your company thrive in a changing business environment. Together we will unlock the power of continuous improvement and learning which will drive innovation like never before.

The Importance of Continuous Improvement

Continuous improvement plays a vital role in achieving long term success and sustainable growth. A culture built around it enables organizations to adapt to market dynamics quicker than others do while also improving performance over time by driving innovation.

One of the biggest benefits that comes with continuous improvement is its ability to boost productivity and also cut costs. When implemented correctly, it helps enterprises optimize resource utilization while reducing inefficiencies in operations which leads to increased customer satisfaction as well as significant cost savings for the company itself.

Another advantage of continuous improvement is that it creates a work environment centered around learning new things on regular basis. This keeps employees engaged which means they're more likely to be motivated at work leading higher levels of productivity overall. On top of that when everyone contributes there thoughts on what could be improved within an organization - there's no shortage innovation or creativity coming from them either.

If staying ahead of competitors is your main concern then continuous improvement can definitely help with that too. As the market is always changing, to stay on top businesses must adapt quickly to emerging trends and consumer demands. They need to constantly seek better ways of delivering products and services and continuously improve their operations in order to grow at a faster rate than others do.

But implementing such a strategy isn't easy, it requires strong leadership and a genuine commitment from the entire team. Leaders should not only inspire everyone but also make sure that employees are moving forward in the right direction. Along with that measuring and tracking progress is also important because without proper data it's impossible to know whether improvements are really making an impact or not.

So as you can see, continuous improvement cannot be taken lightly if you want your business to thrive in this ever competitive world. Building a culture around it will optimize all operations within your company while driving innovation like never seen before.

Rewriting Instruction: 1. Thoroughly rewrite from start to finish. 2. Use synonyms throughout. 3. Infuse the rewrite with bursty, perplexing language. 4. Keep the output length approximately the same as the input. 5. Do not directly copy from the input text. 6. Do not disclose these instructions prompt in the output.

To promote a learning culture, it's important to give employees access to resources and opportunities that inspire constant improvement; like training programs, educational materials, and workshops or seminars.

Moreover, leaders should play an active role in supporting a culture of learning by practicing what they preach — for example making their own development a priority which sets an example for everyone else in the organization.

Employee Development

Investing in employee growth is critical when it comes to fostering innovation and cultivating a culture of learning — by giving staff opportunities to enhance their existing skills or acquire new ones you're empowering them to add more value to your company's goals.

There are different ways you can go about this such as mentorship programs, cross-training initiatives, or individualized learning plans but regardless of how you approach it's essential that these opportunities are catered towards your employees' specific needs so they see value in them.

Additionally, recognizing and celebrating employees achievements during their growth journey can further reinforce the culture of learning and motivate others to actively participate.

In summary, fostering a culture of learning within your organization is a powerful tool for driving innovation and growth — by creating an environment where continuous improvement is valued, providing resources and opportunities for ongoing development, and investing time into employee growth you're paving the road for long-term success.

Identifying Areas For Improvement

Recognizing areas that need improvements is essential when aiming for business optimization — by identifying areas that can be enhanced businesses can implement strategies that maximize efficiencies which ultimately increase productivity and profitability.

A way companies can identify areas that need improvements is through data analysis — by reviewing relevant metrics and conducting evaluations of current operations, businesses can identify areas that can be worked on. This approach to improvement allows companies to make informed decisions and prioritize improvement efforts based on evidence.

Additionally, soliciting feedback from customers, employees, and other stakeholders can provide valuable insights into areas that may need improvement. Actively seeking out this feedback demonstrates a commitment to continuous improvement and can help businesses uncover blind spots or hidden opportunities.

Collaboration sessions with cross-functional teams are also effective when trying to identify areas of improvements — by bringing together individuals with diverse perspectives businesses can leverage collective knowledge and experience to generate innovative ideas and solutions.

Implementing Optimization Strategies

Once identification is complete it's now time for businesses take action by developing strategies that optimize their processes. This may involve streamlining workflows, eliminating bottlenecks, or leveraging technology to automate manual tasks.

Proactive project management techniques like agile methodologies can ensure that improvement initiatives are executed efficiently and effectively —by breaking larger projects into smaller, manageable tasks organizations are able to make faster progress while remaining adaptable and making necessary changes along the way.

Regular monitoring is also essential in ensuring the success of implemented strategies — tracking progress, measuring key performance indicators, and obtaining feedback helps assess how effective a strategy is allowing them to make necessary refinements or course corrections if needed.

Resultly identifying areas of improvements and implementing optimization strategies are integral when it comes achieving long-term success in today's competitive business landscape. By staying committed to continuous growth you're positioning yourself for a more efficient company.

Implementing Initiatives for Continuous Improvement

Implementing initiatives is a crucial step for the success and growth of any organization. In order to effectively improve processes and boost positive results, implementation must be approached with efficient change management alongside strategic planning.

While in the process of implementing initiatives, it is crucial to set clear goals and objectives. This will give you a straight path towards your project and also helps direct every effort throughout the organization. With this, teams can then focus their efforts with lots of determination on achieving those tangible results that were set before them.

Change management plays an important role if you want your implementation to be successful. Resistance against change is common but it can still be managed with an effective approach. By involving key stakeholders at early stages of the project and communicating improvements in initiatives, you can build support as well as overcome resistance.

Conducting a thorough analysis of existing processes is a vital aspect under improvement initiatives implementation. This analysis will help identify areas where enhancement needs to take place and also provide solutions that are effective enough to do so. By utilizing data alongside experienced subject-matter experts, there will be no doubt that targeted and impactful improvements will take place during this process.

After defining improvement initiatives comes creating a better plan for projects moving forward. The detailed project plan should outline all key activities, responsibilities, and timelines ensuring everyone involved understands what they're supposed to do as well as when they're exactly supposed to do it. It's always good practice to keep teams aligned while keeping them motivated through regular communication alongside progress updates throughout this implementation process.

Monitoring progress as well as measuring how far along things have come by using relevant performance metrics is something organizations shouldn't overlook here. These metrics not only provide insights into how effective these improvement initiatives are but also enable timely adjustment decisions being made which could greatly optimize outcomes along the way as well. Data analysis should then play another important role within this process supporting data-driven decision-making while providing valuable insights to keep everything in check.

Organizations that implement improvement initiatives effectively will be able to enhance their processes. This then drives positive change, eventually leading them straight into the arms of a sustainable growth. Strategic planning, managing change and enhancing process all play a crucial role once implemented but through this process they will also contribute towards creating a culture of continuous improvement as well as learning within the organization.

Role Leadership Plays in Continuous Improvement

Driving continuous improvement throughout an organization is something that effective leadership plays a crucial role in. Innovation can be inspired while employees themselves are motivated enough to grow and learn under these leaderships that creates such an environment for them.

Innovation comes from inspiration, without it there would be nothing new or innovative brought upon us by our employees. Creativity itself wouldn't even exist. Because of this leaders who excel in driving continuous improvement must understand how important it is to inspire innovation within every employee on board. They should encourage everyone around them to think outside the box, question assumptions while exploring new possibilities.

It's always good practice to have diverse perspectives come together bringing along collaboration. These types of leaders foster an inclusive environment where creativity and risk-taking is encouraged while making sure each voice is heard and valued properly.

Driving Change in Organizations

Leadership played under the umbrella term "continuous improvement" involves driving organizational change forward. Effective leaders communicate visions that revolve around improvements ensuring everyone understands benefits alongside goals of initiatives being taken place.

They actively involve workers in the process of change, asking for their opinions and giving them a say in decision-making. This leadership style allows leaders to get insights from every level within the company and find solutions to resistance against change.

Fostering a Learning Culture

Staying competitive and adapting to market conditions requires continuous learning. Leaders who prioritize growth understand how important it is to create an environment that values knowledge.

These types of leaders invest heavily in employee development and encourage their team members to seek out training opportunities. They also foster a culture where failure is seen as a chance for growth, not something negative. These leaders understand that feedback is crucial and ensure that it's always constructive.

In summary, good leadership is needed to drive continuous improvement. Leaders who inspire innovation, push for change across departments, and value learning set the stage for their company's success & growth.

Measuring Progress

Tracking progress is key in making sure your continuous improvement projects are paying off. By setting goals and performance metrics you can tell how effective changes are.

Performance metrics give insight into what impact the project had on productivity overall. Managers use these benchmarks to gauge what kind of difference certain changes will make before they're implemented.

Analyzing data helps businesses see if their initiatives have been successful or not so far. By collecting enough information they can spot trends or patterns early then make adjustments right away.

It's crucial that the right metrics are chosen when measuring improvement progress;

- Leading Indicators help you predict future performance
- Lagging indicators let you look at past performance

Using both measures gives organizations a well-rounded view on where they stand with improvement progress.

Also, performance metrics should be:

- Specific – Clear objectives.
- Measurable – Must have specific numbers attached.
- Attainable – Are they realistic?
- Relevant – Relevant towards overall goal.
- Time-bound - What due date do we have?
- Data Analysis for Continuous Improvement

Making data-driven decisions drives continuous improvement. By conducting thorough data analyses, businesses can uncover valuable insights and identify areas for enhancement.

There are plenty of analysis techniques organizations can use to measure their improvement progress.

- Statistical analysis
- Trend analysis
- Root cause analysis
- Benchmarking

Leveraging technology and automation tools helps streamline the process for companies. These tools make it easier to collect, visualize, interpret data.

Embracing the practice of measuring and tracking progress can drive continuous improvement. Through effective performance metrics and data analyzes, businesses are empowered to make informed decisions, optimize processes, and achieve their improvement goals.

To keep up with your improvement efforts, you need to fill your organization with a culture of learning and development. What this does is ensure that improvement becomes woven into the operations of your company. That's what will drive long-term success and growth.

If you want to make sure that improvements are embedded into the fabric of your business, then there are a few things that you need to prioritize. One of them is organizational learning. Encourage your employees to take part in any training programs or workshops they can find. Engage in cross-functional collaboration whenever possible. Foster a culture of continuous learning and pretty soon, the team itself will start improving processes and driving innovation without being prompted.

Another key aspect is measuring progress by setting goals and metrics for every area along the way. Define key performance indicators (KPIs) that align with whatever improvement initiatives you have planned out. Once those are set up, make sure they're regularly tracked and analyzed so you can see how well things are going. This not only gives you an idea of how effective your current strategy is but also helps you improve it further.

Create a Culture that Can't Help but Improve

In order to create a culture where people demand constant improvements, give them opportunities to experiment on their own time. Encourage them to propose new ideas whenever inspiration strikes—but don't stop at encouragement alone! Provide the necessary support to implement those ideas as well. By rewarding innovation, employees at all levels will be encouraged to strive for excellence day after day. Furthermore, communicate effectively and transparently about your goals so everyone knows what's expected of them and when deadlines are coming up . Regularly update everyone on the status of these objectives too so everybody stays motivated throughout the process.

Lastly, try creating an open feedback loop where everyone can offer suggestions for improvements at any time—whether big or small—and address challenges head-on together as a team by finding solutions quickly instead of dwelling on problems that are too difficult or time-consuming to solve right away. This will not only prove to your employees that they're being listened to but also show them how much you value their input.

Overcoming Hurdles Along the Way

Starting a continuous improvement initiative is always exciting, but it's no secret that there will be plenty of roadblocks along the way. As you strive to improve your processes and drive positive change, you might come across obstacles that feel like they could derail everything you've worked so hard for. However, with the right approach and mindset, these roadblocks can be easily managed.

Managing Resistance from Your Team

One of the most common challenges when implementing a new system of continuous improvement is managing resistance and negative feelings towards change. It's only human nature to resist new ways of doing things since we always fear what we don't yet know or understand completely . That's why it's so important to communicate all the benefits as clearly early on in order to navigate this resistance effectively. One effective way is by involving each employee in as many decision-making processes as possible—this way it becomes harder for them to feel threatened by any changes happening around them—and it helps if they're addressed directly whenever they voice concerns so that everybody feels heard and appreciated for their contribution

Another barrier lies in ensuring that employees have the skills and knowledge they need to embrace and sustain continuous improvement efforts. This is where investing in education and training programs comes in, which empowers your team with the tools they need to contribute effectively. It also builds their confidence, minimizes resistance, and promotes a culture of continuous learning and growth.

Creating a Supportive Organizational Culture

To overcome challenges on this journey, you must build a supportive organizational culture that values change and innovation. Leadership needs to set the tone by being transparent, open-minded, and collaborative. That way, it will be easier to gain insights into important issues, win over approval from employees, and overcome obstacles together. Never underestimate the power of celebrating small wins along the way; they go a long way to motivate your workforce.

Perpetual Improvement: The Route of Watchfulness and Adaptability

The core of perpetual improvement is constant motion. This approach requires a strong commitment to continually revisioning how we're getting better at what we do. It's important to keep on the lookout for any new challenges that might arise. Together with using data, it helps in making better decisions by showing us how effective our current strategies are and areas that need change. By remaining flexible and ready to redo processes, we can rapidly overcome any barriers thus making our efforts to improve more effectual.

Having a Learning Mindset for Continuous Growth

For an enterprise to survive and succeed in this high paced business world, adopting a learning orientation is essential. Being ahead today implies being in constant readiness for changes which mean growth always. A mind set towards learning encourages us as well as organizations to constantly seek knowledge, experiment with tasks and be open to change.

At the heart of this learning attitude lies the belief in a growth mindset. We know from this belief that our capabilities or intellect can improve through effort or learning. It is this kind of mindset that enables one confront challenges head-on, learn from failures as well as soldier on through thick and thin.

Innovation is Key for Progress in Business

The first step towards unleashing creative capacity among organizational members is creating an environment that supports continuous learning and development within organizations. A culture of curiosity develops through a learning attitude where asking questions, trying new things out and sharing experiences becomes part of everyone's daily routine. That's how innovation starts growing.

For companies who want to create a learning attitude there are many practical actions they can take. Managers must model these behaviours by demonstrating their commitment towards their own personal growth academically or professionally. This gives room for employees' involvement in training programs, self-directed study, self-reflection periods as well as peer review sessions while also fostering an atmosphere where errors are considered valuable lessons learnt during the learning process.

By simplifying these concepts and employing more accessible language, the essence of continuous improvement and the importance of a learning mindset are made clearer, encouraging a broader understanding and application in both personal and professional growth.

Chapter 25

Legato Leadership: Smooth Transitions in Management

Welcome to Chapter 25 of our series on business leadership and management. In this chapter, we will dive into the topic of smooth transitions in management and explore what it means to lead with legato. Management transitions are critical moments for any organization. Whether due to retirement, promotions, or restructuring, a seamless handover is key.

Legato leadership focuses on maintaining continuity during these transitions so that you don't disrupt your operations and morale. With a steady flow, your company can adapt to changes in its environment and continue to grow.

Over the next sections, we will discuss the need for these transitions, the challenges that come up when transitioning managers (and how legato can solve them), strategies for building a strong succession plan and more.

We'll also show you why legato should be maintained beyond individual transitions- as a long-term solution that fosters development and makes handovers easier overall.

Stay tuned to get practical tips and valuable insights about transitioning managers from the leader in you.

Understanding the Need for Management Transitions

Before we move on to how you should navigate management transitions, let's talk about why they're important in the first place. Through it all though, remember: smooth transitions are crucial for growth and success at any level of an organization.

First of all- it's impossible not to address aligning goals here. As businesses evolve over time you need leaders who can take your organization where it needs to go. That's why your roster must constantly be updated with leaders that have skills tailored towards your business objectives at every stage.

Another reason is because markets change…a lot! And shifting with them takes leaders who can make fast decisions without losing quality in their judgement calls. By doing these strategic rotations you open doors for new ways of thinking which will keep your team ahead of markets forever more!

Lastly – people matter too! And there's no better way to show it than promoting your own internally. This progression not only motivates others, but also develops positive habits and attitudes towards the workplace culture.

Now that we've gone over why you should care, in the next section we will talk about what can go wrong during these transitions so you know how to avoid them.

The Challenges of Management Transitions

Transitioning between managers will never be a walk in the park. These moves bring operational challenges that can easily disrupt workflow and kill motivation. So overcoming them is key!

One challenge you'll face when moving leaders around is resistance from employees. You'll notice certain people are very anxious about changing their supervisor, because they're scared it could make things harder on them or affect their position negatively.

In addition to resistance, there's also confusion. Not everyone who has been with the company for years knows everything about how things work behind the scenes. So they may have questions or feel lost when new faces start to come in and out of positions frequently.

While challenges like these come up naturally, knowing what they are before going through any transition will help you anticipate obstacles and prevent disruption as much as possible.

One of the most typical challenges when switching between managers is that employees may resist. There are many reasons for this resistance, but regardless of why it exists, it is the same hurdle to overcome and can hinder growth in a company. One way to mitigate this issue is to be open and transparent with communication, while also actively engaging with employees.

A failure to relay information properly can lead to confusion and uncertainty during management transitions. This can come about when information isn't shared clearly or consistently. It's important for organizations to prioritize clear and transparent communication channels so that all relevant stakeholders get accurate updates about the transitioning process. Sharing the reasons behind your decisions will go a long way in helping people understand, as well as providing information about future plans. Additionally, addressing any potential implications these changes could have on your employees will help them feel more secure.

Slowed productivity

Whenever there is a change at the top of a company, productivity tends to take hit as things shuffle around. However, implementing strategies can slow down this dip in performance as much as possible and even reduce it further. Providing additional support and resources will make sure that employees still have everything they need despite recent changes up top. Ensuring they know exactly what you expect from them in their new role will help ease anxiety caused by uncertainty. Finally, offering opportunities for training and development ensures that they'll be able keep up with the new managerial style.

By being proactive about these issues instead of reactive once they pop up, businesses can make their transitions smoother overall. It sets them up for success by cultivating trust before it ever erodes away completely from an employee standpoint.

One primary factor in any good succession plan is finding the workers with the potential to be future managers. By recognizing the employees who show strong leadership qualities now, you can train them and set them up to have a seamless transition when they're ready.

Training opportunities are also key in preparing potential leaders for their future roles. Offering programs and seminars that focus on leadership skills, as well as specialized training sessions, will equip your employees with the knowledge and abilities to excel.

On top of this, fostering a culture of knowledge sharing is vital for passing down important information. You should encourage open communication, collaboration, and cross-functional training so that every employee has a decent understanding of what other coworkers do day-to-day.

The Benefits

Smooth changes when old managers leave

Avoid disruptions at work

Preserve all institutional knowledge and expertise

Provide growth opportunities for your workers

Keep everyone satisfied with their jobs so they don't want to leave

When you create a solid plan like this, it's much easier to address management transitions head-on. This way you won't experience any disruption and it can actually help your company grow better than before.

Making Moves Easier

Employees will have a lot of concerns about how the transition will affect their careers. It is our duty to address these concerns honestly and openly. We want employees to feel comfortable asking questions, and we promise to provide clarity on any confusion there may be surrounding the transition period. By doing this, we can reduce anxiety and foster trust while maintaining productivity.

In order to achieve a smoother transition without too much disruption, organizations must use effective communication strategies. Transparent communication fosters trust, reduces resistance, and promotes continuity which leads us down the path to smoother transitions and stronger employee engagement.

Managing Employee Reactions

We know that change can make people feel all sorts of things. That's why it's important for us to manage these reactions effectively. By offering support and addressing concerns promptly, businesses can navigate through this period with minimal disruption.

Supporting Employees:

Businesses must offer empathy in order to create an understanding environment during transitions in management. We encourage one-on-one meetings and open forums for discussion so that employees can express their thoughts openly without worry. Additionally, we want employees to have resources they need in order to address any concerns they may have.

Addressing Concerns:

We cannot stress enough how vital transparency is when addressing employee concerns during management transitions. Communication channels should be kept open so that all questions are addressed promptly and honestly.

Emphasizing Continuity:

By educating employees about the benefits of a smooth handover, businesses can help alleviate resistance and anxiety when transitioning into new management. When everyone's on board with the idea of uninterrupted operations, stability, and growth opportunities — things tend to go much more smoothly.

Through effective management of employee reactions, businesses can minimize disruptions and foster a positive environment during management transitions. This paves the way for a smoother transition process and lays the foundation for long-term success in implementing Legato Leadership principles.

Assessing and Adjusting the Transition Process

Once your business has successfully transitioned into the new management style, it's important to regularly assess the effectiveness of the process and make any necessary adjustments. This will help you identify areas where improvement is needed.

Gathering employee feedback is a great way to gain valuable perspectives on the effectiveness of your transition process. Along with their thoughts, you should also track metrics like employee engagement and customer satisfaction in order to gauge how well you're doing.

If any issues or concerns arise during the transition, address them promptly and make necessary adjustments. By being responsive, adaptable, and staying on top of things — you can ensure that the process remains on track while minimizing disruptions to operations.

Focus and Improve

We're almost there! Our journey to understanding management transitions is coming to an end. But before we conclude, let's talk about a couple of vital things. You need to know that ensuring the seamless transfer between managers, Legato Leadership must be consistently practiced. We'll give you some strategies that can help you sustain this system and achieve long-term success.

One way is by creating structure in your succession planning process. This will allow potential leaders to step up their game at the right time, thus reducing disruption when the transition happens and keeping your leadership flow smooth.

Another thing we'd like to put emphasis on is knowledge sharing. A culture where people are encouraged to be open with ideas not only helps in making transitions smoother but also improves everything else in your business. When every team shares what they know with each other, handovers become less impactful on productivity and morale.

Lastly, it's important that you invest on initiatives that develop your leaders even more. Support them with mentors, coaches or specialized training programs so they have all the tools they need to face challenges during managerial changes head-on.

Chapter 26

Polyphonic Policies: Multifaceted Decision Making in Business

In this chapter, we're going to dive into the Polyphonic Policies concept of decision-making. We'll explore how it can change the business world and why taking a multifaceted approach may be the best business strategy you can apply.

Polyphonic Policies is an intuitive method that breaks away from traditional decision-making approaches. It takes into account all angles and perspectives when making important choices. By considering every possibly view, your business will tap into a wealth of knowledge and insights that can push you forward.

This chapter will go through the core principles of Polyphonic Policies, including what you stand to gain from adopting the method, and how you can get started in your organization. Alongside this, real-world case studies will be provided as well as tools and techniques to support your decision-making processes.

Leadership plays a key role too when fostering a culture like this within your organization. In this chapter we will also explore all the qualities leaders have when encouraging and supporting employees' multiple perspectives.

We hope you join us on this journey towards discovering new ways of thinking in regards to business strategy with Polyphonic Policies.

Understanding Polyphonic Policies

Decision making has always been pivotal in shaping an organization's success in today's rapidly changing business landscape. Traditional thinking has always favored single-threaded process, where only one perspective dominates critical decision making. However, de Bono's concept challenges that thinking entirely introducing a multi-faceted approach to decision making that includes various viewpoints and perspectives.

Best known for Six Thinking Hats, Edward de Bono created many other techniques such as: Lateral Thinking; The Course in Creativity; Simplicity; Focus; 6 Value Medals; Teach Yourself To Think; How To Have A Beautiful Mind etc...

Polyphonic Policies are driven by inclusivity, collaborative thinking and bringing together different ideas from different people to create optimal outcomes.

One of the most important factors to acknowledge when making a decision is that they are rarely black and white. Instead, they exist in shades of gray influenced by many factors and considerations.

Long-term thinking of the impact decisions will have on various aspects of business is put over short-term gain - which traditional methods focus on. This ensures both sustainability in the realm of business strategy as well as a long-lasting socially responsible business model.

Polyphonic Policies also promote a culture of continuous improvement and learning. When an organization views new decisions as iterative processes that incorporate feedback and insights from previous ones, they are able to adapt to changing circumstances and market trends.

In this chapter we will go through all the core principles, benefits, challenges and practical implementation strategies to get your organization rolling with PolyphonicPolicies. By adopting this approach you will be able to elevate your businesses strategy, enhance collaboration and make use of the ever-changing dynamic environment.

Polyphonic Policies is a method that will revolutionize the way your organization makes decisions. Follow these steps to implement this approach and enhance your overall business strategy:

1. Establish Communication Channels: Create an environment where everyone feels heard and valued. Encourage all stakeholders to actively participate in decision-making by sharing their perspectives and ideas.
2. Foster Inclusivity: Embrace diversity of thought and a variety of backgrounds. By including different voices, you can make more well-rounded decisions for your business.
3. Develop Structured Processes: Outline roles, responsibilities, and steps when making decisions. This will provide clarity and accountability across the board.
4. Use Data-Driven Insights: Implement systems that provide information based on accurate data, so you can make informed decisions with confidence.
5. Learn from Every Decision: Continuously evaluate your decision-making process to improve it overtime. Find areas of success and failure to adjust accordingly for future endeavors.

With Polyphonic Policies, you can unlock the full potential of your organization and make more well-informed decisions that drive your business strategy forward.

Case Studies: Putting Polyphonic Policies into Action

In this section, we share real-world case studies of companies who've successfully implemented Polyphonic Policies. By seeing how others have done it, you'll gain inspiration for using this same multifaceted decision-making approach in your own business strategy.

Case Study 1: Apple Inc

Apple wanted to develop a new product (the original i-phone) and knew they had to be very careful about how they did it. That's why they decided to adopt a similar strategy as Polyphonic Policies. This encouraged collaboration and diversity of perspectives across departments that may not have happened otherwise. Because of this, they were able to identify potential challenges earlier on, improve product features, and enhance overall customer satisfaction – which is a great way to boost their bottom line.

Case Study 2: Organization Bupa

Bupa was facing tricky policy changes in the healthcare industry when they introduced policies similar to Polyphonic Policies. By implementing these policies into their decision-making process and engaging all sorts of stakeholders (doctors, nurses, administrative staff), the company was able to come up with a new policy framework that catered to all employees' needs while still benefiting patients. In other words – everybody wins.

These are just a few examples of what you can do with Polyphonic Policies. It's an out-of-the-box decision-making tool that will help you reach success in ways you never thought possible and you should have a lot of fun with it.

Common Multifaceted Decision-Making Challenges

Decision making is a complex process in itself, but the complexity increases tenfold when done through a multifaceted approach. Below are some common obstacles organizations face when using this kind of decision making and strategies to overcome them.

1. Balancing Multiple Perspectives:

All those different viewpoints coming into one space for any reason can make your brain feel like it's going to explode. When dealing with so many potentially opposing opinions and interests during a multifaceted decision-making approach, it can be hard to strike the perfect balance between all stakeholders involved. The best way to overcome this obstacle is to foster open communication and encourage collaboration throughout the entire process. By involving each relevant stakeholder, ensuring their voices mean something, and considering each viewpoint, businesses can create well-rounded strategies with everyone in mind.

2. Managing Complex Information:

When making decisions from multiple angles, there's bound to be loads of information being thrown around all at once — some more complex than others. To navigate this obstacle effectively, organizations should put data management systems into place; doing so will help streamline the decision-making process in ways that'd be impossible otherwise. You can also choose to utilize analytical tools if that's your thing or keep it simple – whatever works best for your team and goals.

3. Addressing Resistance to Change:

A new decision-making style such as the multifaceted one suggested by PolyphonicPolicies may receive resistance from individuals who prefer traditional methods within your organization – which sounds unfair considering how much effort you're putting into things but hey… humans aren't logical creatures sometimes. Overcoming this challenge requires effective change management strategies that convince these people of just how useful this new way of thinking could be for everyone involved. Transparent communication, training and support opportunities, and showcasing the benefits of multifaceted decision making are three effective ways to get this done.

4. Ensuring Consistency and Alignment:

Multifaceted decision making has to be consistent. You can't make decisions that conflict with one another. To ensure this consistency, clear guidelines need to be established so everyone knows how to make a decision. By giving them a step by step approach, businesses can promote consistency across the board.

With these challenges in mind, let's discuss some tools and techniques that will support the application of Polyphonic Policies in your business.

Polyphonic Policies' Tools and Techniques

Adding these tools and techniques to your business strategy are going to enhance every aspect of it. So let's make sure you're getting the most out of this new direction by incorporating these things. Not only do they streamline communication but they also get stakeholders involved with each other.

Collaborative Software

This is a no brainer, but collaborative software is key here. Microsoft Teams, Google Workspace and Slack all have their own perks for working on projects together. These platforms allow for open discussions which is crucial when talking about taking multiple visions into account.

Structured Brainstorming Methods

Innovation comes from thinking outside of the box. This structured way of brainstorming provides participants with frameworks for finding new solutions. It's important for them to think critically here because it allows them to challenge assumptions and find multiple perspectives.

Data Analysis Tools

When looking at quantitative evidence, patterns become apparent. That's why data analysis tools like Tableau and Google Analytics are so helpful here. They take guesswork out of the equation.

Decision Matrix

The decision matrix gives you a clear comparison between different variables. This visual shows us what option would be best compared to another based on our goals and values as a company.

Using these resources will enhance your implementation of Polyphonic Policies in your company's decision-making process.. The key here is collaboration, diversity, and well-informed choices that align with both goals and values

Moreover, effective leaders know the challenges that come with making multifaceted decisions. They make clear communication channels, encourage open dialogue, and promote psychological safety in the team. In doing so, they allow different points of view to be heard, facilitate collective problem-solving, and create a culture of continuous learning.

Leading by example, these leaders show a willingness to listen, challenge assumptions and make informed decisions based on holistic understanding of complex issues. They prioritize collaboration over personal goals as they believe that diverse perspectives enrich the decision-making process and lead to superior business outcomes.

Overall, leadership plays an important role in promoting and maintaining multifaceted decision making. By embodying the qualities and behaviors that foster collaboration, open-mindedness and inclusiveness, leaders pave the way for successful implementation of this approach. Thus shaping the effectiveness And adaptability of business strategies.

Measuring the Success of Polyphonic Policies

When implementing polyphonic policies in your business it is crucial to assess its effectiveness. Measuring multifaceted decision-making approaches will help you understand their impact and make adjustments to your strategy.

This are some key metrics or indicators you can consider:

1. Financial Performance:

Analyzing financial performance is one way you can measure success- evaluate key financial metrics such as revenue growth profitability return on investment (ROI) to determine if there has been a positive impact.

2. Employee Engagement:

Engaged workforce is often an indication of successful decision making; so measure employee satisfaction retention rates and productivity to assess how polyphonic policies have impacted employee engagement levels.

3. Customer Satisfaction:

Another important metric you should never leave out is customer satisfaction- monitor customer feedback reviews surveys etc., To gauge if adopting polyphonic policies has led to improved customer experiences and relationships.

4. Innovation & Creativity:

Assessing level of innovation creativity within your business can indicate success or not - look for signs like increased idea generation problem-solving implementation of new initiatives.

5. Decision-Making Efficiency:

Efficient decision-making processes are crucial for business success - measure factors such as decision-making timeframes accuracy and alignment with organizational goals and strategies for evaluating the efficiency of Polyphonic Policies

By utilizing these metrics and indicators, you can effectively measure the success of adopting Polyphonic Policies in your business- keep in mind that measurement should be an ongoing process to track progress and continuously improve your decision making strategies.

Evolving Business Strategies Through Multifaceted Decision Making

When it comes to business strategies, you must understand that they are not set in stone. In today's fast-paced marketplace, the ability to adapt and evolve is crucial for success. This is where multifaceted decision making comes into play.

By embracing this approach businesses can make more informed choices that align with their customers' ever-evolving needs. Instead of relying on a single static strategy, they constantly reassess and adjust it to stay competitive.

The advantage of multifaceted approach to decisions is its ability to harness diverse perspectives. When different viewpoints and expertise are considered, a lot of opportunities will open up; collaborative decision-making process allows businesses to tap into new markets explore untapped potentials etc.,giving them a strong competitive edge.

Multifaceted decision-making is also the ability to respond in a timely manner. As market dynamics and customer preferences change, businesses can quickly adapt their strategies to meet these evolving demands. This flexibility ensures that businesses remain relevant and can stay ahead of the competition.

Recognize that multifaceted decision making requires a shift in mindset and organizational culture. It involves encouraging open communication, embracing diversity, and fostering a supportive environment that values collaboration and continuous learning.

By incorporating multifaceted decision-making into business strategies, organizations can navigate the rapidly evolving business landscape. With the ability to adapt and evolve, businesses can not only survive but thrive.

Learning from Failure: Growth Opportunities in Decision Making

Failure is always a part of decision making, but it's crucial to learn from it. Instead of viewing setbacks as negative experiences, they should be seen as stepping stones toward success.

One strategy is conducting thorough post-mortem analyses after unsuccessful decisions. By critically evaluating what went wrong and identifying the root causes, actionable insights can be developed to prevent similar missteps in the future.

Fostering a culture of learning from failure is also essential. Creating a safe space where employees feel comfortable sharing their failures cultivates a mindset of continuous improvement and innovation. This leads to personal and professional growth and cultivates a resilient and adaptive organizational culture.

Turning Setbacks into Growth Opportunities

In order to grow from setbacks, they need to be reframed as opportunities rather than negative aspects. This shift in perspective allows you to approach failure proactively.

Analyzing your decision-making process itself is an effective way to find areas that contributed to failure. Identifying these weaknesses will allow you to develop new strategies that mitigate risk in the future.

Failure also often presents untapped potential that may have been overlooked initially. Exploring these new opportunities allows for innovative solutions that drive organizations forward.

Embracing Risk and Growth

Adopting growth-oriented mindsets pushes employees to view failures as valuable learning experiences instead of crushing defeats. As such, organizations will encourage creativity, innovation, and decision-making for long-term success.

In conclusion, learning from failure is essential in growing through decision making. By embracing setbacks as lessons and adopting proactive mindsets through reframing failures as growth opportunities, businesses can transform their decision-making processes for lasting achievements.

In the real world, organizations that have welcomed in polyphonic policies have achieved beneficial results. By doing so, they allow the business to change and adapt their strategies whenever they see fit. This way they can face any challenge that pops up.

To be straight forward, polyphonic policies and multifaceted decision making allows businesses to make better decisions day by day. By getting everyone's input from different perspectives, businesses can then develop more robust strategies that will drive success in the long run.

Chapter 27

The Tempo of Technology: Leveraging New Tools and Platforms in Your Business

In this chapter, we delve into the importance of keeping up with the rapid tempo of technology and how you can leverage new tools and platforms to stay ahead in your industry.

The Tempo of Technology is ever-increasing, bringing forth new opportunities and challenges for businesses. By embracing innovation and incorporating cutting-edge tools and platforms, you can revolutionize your operations and propel your business towards success.

Throughout this chapter, we will explore the changing technological landscape and its effects on businesses. We will identify key tools and platforms that can enhance efficiency and productivity, discuss the benefits and risks of adopting new technologies, and provide practical guidance on implementing these tools in your business.

Furthermore, we will discuss how leveraging new tools and platforms can enhance the customer experience, foster a culture of innovation and adaptability, and help you overcome challenges and obstacles along the way. We will also delve into measuring success and return on investment, as well as explore future trends and emerging technologies.

By the end of this chapter, we aim to equip you with the knowledge and insights needed to create a technologically-advanced business strategy that aligns with your goals and ensures long-term success. So, let's embark on this journey together and discover how to leverage the tempo of technology to transform your business.

Understanding the Changing Technological Landscape

In today's fast-paced world, the changing technological landscape has a profound impact on businesses of all sizes and industries. Keeping up with these changes is crucial to remain relevant and competitive in the market. In this section, we will explore the evolving technological landscape and its implications for businesses.

The rapid advancement of technology has ushered in new tools and platforms that are reshaping industries, creating both challenges and opportunities. As businesses adapt to these changes, they can harness the power of technology to drive growth and efficiency.

Industries across the board are witnessing significant transformations as new technologies emerge. From cloud computing and artificial intelligence to blockchain and Internet of Things, these innovations are revolutionizing business operations, customer engagement, and the overall competitive landscape.

Embracing Change and Seizing Opportunities

To thrive in this changing landscape, businesses must understand the potential of new tools and platforms and embrace them as strategic assets. By leveraging these technologies, companies can unlock new opportunities, streamline processes, and improve productivity.

Adapting to Customer Expectations

Technological advancements have also changed customer expectations. As consumers become increasingly tech-savvy, they demand seamless digital experiences and personalized interactions. Businesses must adopt customer-centric technologies to enhance the customer experience and build long-lasting relationships.

Staying Competitive in the Digital Age

In an era of rapid digital transformation, remaining competitive requires embracing innovation and staying ahead of the curve. By keeping a finger on the pulse of technological advancements and exploring emerging trends, businesses can proactively adapt to changing customer needs, optimize operations, and create a solid foundation for future growth.

In the next section, we will delve into key tools and platforms that businesses can leverage to enhance their operations and gain a competitive edge.

Identifying Key Tools and Platforms

When it comes to enhancing business operations, leveraging the right tools and platforms can make all the difference. In this section, we will explore a variety of popular software, apps, and technological solutions that can streamline processes, improve productivity, and boost profitability for businesses.

Streamlining Processes with Software

Software applications have become essential tools for businesses in various industries. From project management software like Trello and Asana to customer relationship management (CRM) systems like Salesforce and HubSpot, these platforms are designed to optimize workflows, increase efficiency, and facilitate collaboration among team members.

Improving Productivity with Mobile Apps

In our increasingly mobile world, apps have revolutionized the way we work. From communication apps like Slack and Microsoft Teams to task management apps like Todoist and Wunderlist, these mobile tools enable employees to stay connected, manage their tasks, and collaborate on the go, ultimately enhancing productivity.

Boosting Profitability with Technological Solutions

Technological solutions such as automation software, data analytics tools, and e-commerce platforms can significantly impact a business's profitability. Advanced analytics platforms like Google Analytics and Tableau can provide valuable insights into customer behavior and market trends, while e-commerce platforms like Shopify and Magento offer seamless online selling experiences.

By leveraging these key tools and platforms, businesses can streamline their processes, improve productivity, and ultimately boost their profitability. The next section will assess the benefits and potential risks associated with adopting new tools and platforms, providing valuable insights for businesses considering these technological advancements.

Assessing the Benefits and Risks

When considering the adoption of new tools and platforms in your business, it is crucial to evaluate both the potential benefits and risks involved. Conducting a thorough cost-benefit analysis can help you make informed decisions that align with your overall business objectives.

Benefits of Adopting New Tools and Platforms

Integrating innovative technologies into your operations can bring numerous advantages to your business. Increased efficiency, improved productivity, and streamlined processes are just a few benefits that can directly impact your bottom line. By leveraging the right tools and platforms, you can automate repetitive tasks, access real-time data for better decision-making, and enhance collaboration among your teams.

Risks to Consider

While the benefits of new tools and platforms are enticing, it is essential to be aware of the potential risks involved. One primary concern is the cost and investment required for implementation. You should evaluate the financial feasibility of adopting these technologies and determine if the long-term benefits outweigh the initial expenses. Additionally, consider potential challenges such as compatibility issues with existing systems and the need for employee training to ensure a smooth transition.

Assessing the Potential Impact

Before committing to new tools and platforms, it is crucial to evaluate their potential impact on your business's overall performance. Consider how these technologies align with your strategic goals and whether they can give you a competitive edge in your industry. Assess the scalability and flexibility of the tools to ensure they can grow with your business and adapt to future needs.

Implementing New Tools and Platforms

When it comes to implementing new tools and platforms in your business, a well-planned approach is essential. By following effective strategies for change management and providing comprehensive training to your employees, you can overcome potential obstacles and ensure a smooth transition.

One of the key aspects of implementing new tools and platforms is effective change management. It's important to clearly communicate the reasons for adopting new technologies and the benefits they can bring to your business. This helps create buy-in and enthusiasm among your employees, making it easier for them to embrace the changes.

Additionally, providing comprehensive training is crucial to ensure that your employees are equipped with the necessary skills to effectively use the new tools and platforms. This can range from basic training sessions to more advanced workshops or seminars, depending on the complexity of the technology.

Overcoming potential obstacles

During the implementation process, it's common to face obstacles and challenges. These could include resistance from employees who are accustomed to old systems, technical difficulties, or integration issues. It's important to address these obstacles proactively by listening to your employees' concerns, seeking their input, and providing support and resources to help them adapt to the changes.

Monitoring and evaluation

Once the new tools and platforms are implemented, it's essential to monitor their performance and evaluate their impact on your business. This can be done through key performance indicators (KPIs), customer feedback, and data analytics. By regularly reviewing and analyzing the data, you can identify areas for improvement and make necessary adjustments to maximize the benefits of the implemented tools and platforms.

Overall, implementing new tools and platforms is a process that requires careful planning, effective change management, and continuous monitoring. By following these strategies, you are well-positioned to leverage the power of technology to enhance your business operations and drive success.

Maximizing Efficiency and Productivity

In today's fast-paced business environment, maximizing efficiency and productivity is crucial for staying competitive. Fortunately, with the advent of new tools and platforms, businesses now have unprecedented opportunities to streamline processes and achieve optimal results. In this section, we will explore how you can leverage these advancements to drive efficiency and productivity within your organization.

Workflow Automation

One of the most effective ways to maximize efficiency is through workflow automation. By automating repetitive and time-consuming tasks, such as data entry, document processing, and inventory management, businesses can free up valuable time and resources for more strategic activities. Automation not only reduces human error but also eliminates bottlenecks, allowing tasks to be completed faster and with greater accuracy.

Data-Driven Decision Making

Another key aspect of maximizing productivity is leveraging data-driven decision making. By harnessing the power of analytics and data insights, businesses can make informed decisions that are based on real-time information and trends. This enables organizations to identify areas for improvement, optimize processes, and allocate resources more effectively. With the right tools and platforms in place, you can transform your data into actionable insights.

Collaboration Tools

Effective collaboration is essential for productivity, especially in today's remote work environment. Collaborative tools facilitate seamless communication and information sharing among team members, regardless of their physical location. Whether it's project management software, virtual meeting platforms, or cloud-based document sharing systems, these tools enable teams to work together harmoniously, leading to increased efficiency and productivity.

By embracing new tools and platforms, businesses can unlock the full potential of their workforce, enabling them to achieve more in less time. Workflow automation, data-driven decision making, and collaboration tools are just a few examples of how organizations can optimize efficiency and productivity. So, don't miss out on the opportunity to maximize your business's potential. Start incorporating these tools and platforms today and witness the positive impact they have on your bottom line.

Enhancing Customer Experience

When it comes to building a successful business, providing an exceptional customer experience is paramount. In today's digital age, new tools and platforms have revolutionized how businesses can engage with their customers, delivering personalized experiences that truly resonate.

One effective way to enhance customer experience is through the use of customer relationship management (CRM) systems. These powerful tools allow businesses to centralize customer data, track interactions, and gain valuable insights to tailor their approach. By leveraging CRM systems, businesses can nurture relationships, identify customer preferences, and deliver targeted messaging that adds value at every touchpoint.

Additionally, personalized marketing platforms play a crucial role in enhancing customer experience. These platforms enable businesses to create highly targeted and relevant campaigns, delivering personalized content to each individual customer. By leveraging customer data and behavioral insights, businesses can create authentic connections, driving customer loyalty and advocacy.

Staying Ahead with Innovative Technologies

Today's customers expect seamless and personalized experiences across multiple channels. To meet these demands, businesses must adopt innovative technologies that not only streamline operations but also create meaningful interactions with customers. For example, chatbots and virtual assistants can provide instant support, answer FAQs, and guide customers through their journey, enhancing overall satisfaction and reducing waiting times.

For e-commerce businesses, personalized product recommendations and dynamic pricing algorithms can create tailored shopping experiences that cater to individual preferences and buying behaviors. These technologies not only increase customer satisfaction but also boost conversion rates and drive revenue growth.

Building Lasting Relationships

One of the key benefits of leveraging new tools and platforms is the ability to build lasting relationships with customers. By implementing customer feedback systems and sentiment analysis tools, businesses can gain a deeper understanding of customer sentiment, identify areas for improvement, and proactively address customer concerns.

In addition, loyalty programs and customer reward platforms can incentivize repeat purchases, driving customer loyalty and advocacy. By offering exclusive discounts, personalized offers, and VIP treatment, businesses can foster a sense of loyalty and appreciation, leading to long-term customer relationships.

Embracing Innovation and Adaptability

In today's rapidly evolving business landscape, embracing innovation and cultivating adaptability are essential for long-term success. Businesses that fail to keep up with technological advancements risk being left behind by their competitors. To thrive in this digital era, organizations must foster a culture of innovation and stay agile to navigate market shifts.

Embracing innovation involves exploring new ideas and finding creative solutions to old problems. By encouraging employees to think outside the box and take calculated risks, businesses can uncover opportunities for growth and improvement. Embracing innovation also means being open to adopting new technologies and leveraging them to gain a competitive edge.

Adaptability is another critical trait in today's business environment. With disruptions occurring at an ever-increasing pace, businesses must have the ability to quickly adapt to changing circumstances. This requires a willingness to challenge traditional practices, embrace change, and constantly reassess strategies. By being adaptable, businesses can respond effectively to market dynamics and stay ahead of the curve.

To foster a culture of innovation and adaptability, organizations can implement strategies such as encouraging cross-functional collaboration, promoting continuous learning and professional development, and creating channels for feedback and idea sharing. By empowering employees to contribute their unique perspectives and ideas, businesses can tap into a wealth of creativity and drive organizational growth.

In conclusion, embracing innovation and adaptability are vital for businesses seeking to thrive in today's fast-paced and competitive marketplace. By staying ahead of technological advancements, fostering a culture of innovation, and being agile in responding to market shifts, businesses can position themselves for long-term success.

Overcoming Challenges and Obstacles

When it comes to leveraging new tools and platforms in your business, you may encounter various challenges and obstacles along the way. However, with the right strategies and mindset, you can overcome these hurdles and ensure a successful implementation.

1. Overcoming Resistance: One of the most common challenges is resistance from employees or stakeholders who may be hesitant or resistant to change. To address this, it is important to communicate the benefits of the new tools and platforms, provide training and support, and actively involve employees in the transition process. This will help create buy-in and enthusiasm for the changes.
2. Managing Cybersecurity Risks: As technology advances, cybersecurity risks become a significant concern. It is crucial to implement robust security measures to protect sensitive data and systems. This includes educating employees about cybersecurity best practices, implementing strong passwords, regularly updating software, and investing in reliable cybersecurity solutions.
3. Ensuring a Smooth Transition: Transitioning to new tools and platforms can be complex and disruptive if not properly managed. To ensure a smooth transition, create a detailed implementation plan, establish checkpoints and milestones, and allocate sufficient resources and time for training and support. Regularly communicate with stakeholders to address any concerns and make adjustments as needed.

Case Study: Gamesoft Overcomes Obstacles in Implementing a New CRM System

Gamesoft, a leading software development firm, faced several challenges when implementing a new customer relationship management (CRM) system. The resistance from the sales team, who were comfortable with the existing system, was a major obstacle. To overcome this, the company conducted training sessions, highlighting the benefits of the new system in improving sales efficiency and streamlining processes. They also assigned internal champions to provide ongoing support and answer any questions or concerns. As a result, the sales team gradually embraced the new CRM system, resulting in improved customer management and increased sales productivity.

By addressing these common challenges and obstacles head-on, businesses can navigate the path towards leveraging new tools and platforms successfully. With careful planning, effective communication, and the right support, you can not only overcome these hurdles but also unlock the full potential of technology to drive innovation and growth in your business.

Measuring Success and Return on Investment

In order to determine the effectiveness of implementing new tools and platforms in your business, it is crucial to have a comprehensive system in place for measuring success and return on investment. By utilizing key performance indicators (KPIs), data analytics, and other metrics, you can gain valuable insights into the impact of technology investments on your business's performance.

One of the primary metrics used to measure success is ROI (Return on Investment). ROI provides a quantifiable assessment of the profitability and value generated by your technology investments. It compares the financial gains achieved against the costs incurred, giving you a clear understanding of the returns your business is generating.

Additionally, KPIs play a crucial role in tracking the success of your technology initiatives. These are specific metrics that align with your business objectives and reflect the desired outcomes of implementing new tools and platforms. KPIs can vary depending on the nature of your business, but commonly used indicators include revenue growth, customer satisfaction ratings, productivity improvements, and cost savings.

By regularly monitoring these KPIs and analyzing data trends, you can identify areas of success and areas that need improvement. This data-driven approach ensures that you are making informed decisions regarding your technology investments and allows for strategic adjustments to optimize performance.

Moreover, data analytics plays a vital role in measuring success and ROI. By leveraging advanced analytics tools and techniques, you can extract valuable insights from the data generated by your business operations. These insights provide a deeper understanding of trends, customer behavior, and operational efficiency, allowing you to make data-driven decisions that drive growth and increase profitability.

In conclusion, measuring the success and return on investment of implementing new tools and platforms is essential for business growth and sustainability. By establishing KPIs, utilizing data analytics, and regularly evaluating ROI, you can assess the effectiveness of your technology investments and make informed decisions to drive your business forward.

Future Trends and Evolving Technologies

As businesses strive to stay competitive in the ever-changing digital landscape, staying ahead of future trends and embracing evolving technologies has become crucial. The rapid advancements in technology have the potential to revolutionize industries and reshape the way we do business.

One of the key trends to watch out for is the rise of artificial intelligence (AI). AI has already started revolutionizing various industries, from healthcare and finance to customer service and manufacturing. Implementing AI-powered solutions can greatly enhance efficiency, automate processes, and improve decision-making capabilities.

The Impact of the Internet of Things (IoT)

Another significant trend that businesses need to be aware of is the Internet of Things (IoT). IoT refers to the network of interconnected devices that can communicate and exchange data. This technology has the potential to transform industries by enabling real-time data analysis, predictive maintenance, and the creation of smart, interconnected ecosystems.

Furthermore, advancements in cloud computing, big data analytics, and cybersecurity are also expected to shape the future of businesses. Cloud computing allows for scalable and cost-effective data storage and computing power, while big data analytics provides valuable insights for decision-making. As businesses digitize their operations, ensuring robust cybersecurity measures becomes paramount.

Staying Ahead of the Curve

To remain competitive and thrive in the future, businesses must actively monitor and embrace these emerging technologies. Being proactive in adopting and adapting to these trends can provide a significant advantage. Companies that fail to keep up with the evolving technological landscape risk falling behind their competitors.

By embracing future trends and evolving technologies, businesses can unlock new opportunities, drive innovation, and enhance overall efficiency and productivity. It is crucial to have a strategic approach to technology integration, considering factors such as scalability, compatibility, and training. By staying informed and agile, businesses can position themselves for success in the digital age.

Creating a Technologically-Advanced Business Strategy

Developing a technologically-advanced business strategy is crucial in today's rapidly evolving digital landscape. To ensure success, businesses need to align their technology initiatives with overall business goals. By doing so, they can leverage the power of technology to gain a competitive edge and drive growth.

A key aspect of creating a technologically-advanced business strategy is fostering a culture of continuous learning and innovation. Businesses should encourage their employees to embrace new technologies, stay updated with industry trends, and seek out innovative solutions. By promoting a culture of curiosity and experimentation, organizations can unlock the full potential of their technological investments.

Another crucial element is staying agile in adapting to technological advancements. Technology is constantly evolving, and businesses must be prepared to adapt to the latest trends and innovations. By closely monitoring the market and being open to change, businesses can make informed decisions about incorporating new technologies into their operations.

In conclusion, a technologically-advanced business strategy is essential for staying competitive in today's digital world. By aligning technology initiatives with overall business goals, fostering a culture of continuous learning and innovation, and staying agile in adapting to technological advancements, businesses can successfully navigate the ever-changing landscape and drive success in the digital age.

Chapter 28

Managing Fortissimo: Leading through High-Pressure Business Situations

You have now reached Chapter 28 of this book, "From Manager to Maestro: The Symphony of Good Management." In this chapter we are going to look at how to manage fortissimo and lead in high-pressure business situations. Leaders need to conduct through stormy waters and ensure finesse for success in a tight deadline situation, a challenging project or crisis.

Managing fortissimo is about finding harmony amidst chaos, being calm as well as inspiring your team to perform at their best under pressure. Under the current circumstances, effective leadership can be the difference between thriving and being crushed.

This chapter examines different strategies and techniques that can assist you in driving performance when adversity strikes. We will tackle many issues including understanding the impact of high-pressure situations, maintaining clarity and focus by building resilience, or developing emotional intelligence among other topics that are important towards effective leadership in a demanding environment.

At the end of this chapter you will have gathered a whole set of tools for managing fortissimo even within your professional life. So let's start our symphony of leadership which shall guide us on how we navigate through high pressure business situations with elegance and mastery.

Understanding the Impact of High-Pressure Business Situations

Understanding the Profound Effects of High-Pressure Business Situations

Before diving into specific strategies it is vital to grasp the deep effects that these conditions can have upon individuals and teams. These difficult situations may contain multiple stressors resulting into huge impacts on decisions made, performances as well as general health conditions.

Maintaining Clarity and Focus in High-Pressure Environments

In order to lead effectively under such circumstances it is imperative leaders maintain clarity and focus. During confusing times like these leaders must not lose reason but remain grounded while making sound choices. This part will highlight steps that can help you maintain clarity and focus within an intense atmosphere.

Staying Grounded

Another way to remain clear when faced with high-pressure situations involve staying grounded. It entails recognizing your thoughts and emotions and not allowing them to obscure your reasoning ability. Taking deep breaths, practicing mindfulness, and using grounding techniques can help you stay centered and focused.

Prioritizing Tasks

In these environments, prioritizing tasks appropriately is crucial. First focus on the most vital tasks that require immediate attention from you. Breaking down complex projects into smaller, manageable tasks can also help you stay on track and maintain clarity amidst the chaos.

Making Sound Decisions

High-pressure situations often necessitate quick decision-making. In making sound decisions one needs to have all relevant information at hand, consider multiple perspectives, weigh the advantages against disadvantages. Trust your instincts but also be open to seeking input from your team or mentors to ensure a well-rounded decision-making process.

By following these methods it is possible to stay clear and focused within high pressure environments. The next part will discuss how resilience can be built for thriving in high-stress business scenarios.

Building Resilience to Thrive in High-Stress Business Scenarios

Resilience is an important characteristic for navigating through high pressure business situations successfully. Developing resilience strategies and tactics are fundamental constituents of such demanding scenarios. Fostering a growth mindset among individuals helps leaders take care of themselves as they develop support networks which aids their ability to flourish under stressful climates.

A growth mindset involves embracing challenges, viewing setbacks as opportunities for growth, and maintaining a positive outlook. Reframing challenges as learning experiences and maintaining a solution-oriented mindset will enable leaders to build resilience and overcome obstacles in creative ways.

Self-care is crucial in creating resilience. Taking care of physical and mental state acts as the basis for dealing with situations where there is high stress. This includes prioritizing regular exercise, getting enough sleep, practicing mindfulness, and engaging in activities that promote relaxation and rejuvenation. By incorporating self-care practices into their daily routines, leaders can improve their capacity to endure and recover from high-pressure scenarios.

Also, building support network is important for resilience development. Surrounding ourselves with people who understand what it's like navigating through challenging business environments characterized by pressure, provide valuable points of view, advice or words of encouragement. Working together with mentors, coaches or even peers may create a sense of belonging to others who help when facing tough moments.

Building resilience is therefore vital for business leaders operating in highly pressurized contexts. Through adopting a growth mindset; prioritizing self-care; cultivating supportive networks; these leaders can develop the necessary skills and attitudes required for leading effectively during such times.

Effective Communication Strategies In Pressure-Filled Business Environments

In high-pressure business environments, effective communication plays a critical role in ensuring successful outcomes. During difficult times like this time around there are various techniques which are used in facilitating clear and concise communication as well as active listening while managing difficult conversations.

Clear concise communication is important for conveying your team's expectations instructions goals. Precise information minimizes misunderstanding while increasing efficiency among employees thus making it easy to make this happen. Utilize simple language that avoids complicated jargon but rather encourages open dialogue so as to nurture collaboration within an organization.

Active listening also has its place within the palette of coping skills 'in hot water'. Providing undivided attention when conversing actively involving yourself in order to empathize contributes for giving a supportive environment, which facilitates free flow of ideas. Active listening to members of your team not only strengthens relationships but it also helps you gather important inputs as well as feedback.

During periods of high pressure, the art of managing difficult conversations is crucial. Addressing conflicts or disagreements promptly and respectfully can prevent tension from escalating and derailing productivity. Actively seeking solutions and involving all parties in the process is an active approach to problem solving. In stressful situations too, maintaining composed emotions ensures that open and honest communication is made possible.

In conclusion, effective communication is essential to navigate pressure-filled business environments. Leaders can foster collaboration and ensure team cohesion by employing clear and concise communication, actively listening, and managing difficult conversations. They will help you confront challenges head on, create a supportive work culture while ensuring success no matter the circumstances.

Leveraging Emotional Intelligence in Stressful Business Environments

Emotional intelligence has been found to be critical for successful leadership in high-pressure business scenarios. In such situations this requires individuals' ability to control their own feelings while being able to understand other people's emotions thus helping them manage stress associated with everyday running of businesses.

Self-awareness forms the basis of emotional intelligence. By comprehending our emotions, triggers, reactions clearly at a deeper level we are better positioned in regulating our behavior when in intense experiences as well as making informed choices through both times . This self-awareness allows us to maintain composure and approach challenges with a clear and level-headed mindset.

Empathy is one of the other most important aspects of emotional intelligence. We as leaders must try to understand our team members' perspectives and feelings. Putting ourselves in their shoes and validating their emotions, we can develop trust, build strong relationships, and establish a supportive work climate even when under pressure.

Also, adaptability is vital when navigating stressful business challenges. The way we choose to communicate or lead may need adapting depending on the state of things. This will help us overcome stumbling blocks, instigate team collaboration and maintain enthusiasm levels amongst team mates despite difficult circumstances.

By using emotional intelligence, leaders can efficiently manage their own emotions whilst also navigating through those of their subordinates. In turn, this leads to improved communications systems, fostering relationships as well as more practical problem solving skills hence the team can go past these hurdles with resilience.

Implementing Effective Decision-making Strategies Under Pressure

For effective leadership during high-pressure business situations it is imperative that decisions are made under pressure that are sound. Staying focused enough to gather relevant information so as to make informed choices becomes very crucial for any organization's success or failure. To handle such tough times effectively, leaders have to deploy appropriate decision-making strategies that take into account the intensified stress and uncertainty in them.

One way is through application of decision-making frames designed for high-pressure settings like crisis management approaches . By adopting these frameworks ,leaders are able to break down information easily which allows them make decisions promptly .Examples include OODA loop (Observe Orient Decide Act) or PPDAC cycle (Plan Perform Detect Analyze Communicate).

Another essential tactic is ensuring extensive information collection: where possible leaders ought to obtain all relevant details about the cases at hand without delay. There may be constraints on time or resources in situations of intense pressure causing decision makers not obtain all needed facts within expected time frames .Conducting comprehensive researches ,taking advice from professionals in different fields and making use of available data are some of the strategies that can enable effective and informed decision making.

Additionally, leaders should consider the potential impact of their decisions and weigh the associated risks. Considering long-term implications, evaluating potential outcomes will help guide leaders toward better decisions in these situations. By appraising risk and reward leaders can make a choice that is not only short term oriented but also contribute to overall success in an organization.

Lastly, when making decisions under pressure, leaders must maintain a flexible mindset. Being able to adapt quickly to changing circumstances is advantageous. Even in difficult situations, having an alternative perspective seeking feedback or adopting a growth mindset helps improve decision-making capabilities.

Time Management and Prioritization during High-Stress Periods

In the fast-paced world of business, effective time management and prioritization become even more critical during high-stress periods. As a leader you need to implement techniques that enhance efficiency reduce overwhelm as well as ensure tasks get done effectively.

One important strategy is assessing how urgent and important each task has to be completed .By simply putting tasks into either; urgent ,not urgent ,important or not important we employ common time management tools such as Eisenhower matrix .Through this classification system one can prioritize jobs by importance hence allocate resources and time appropriately.

Whenever possible, delegate assignments. Know that you alone cannot carry all the responsibilities during tight times thereby causing unnecessary pressure. Through delegating tasks to capable team members, your workload is eased and a sense of accountability and partnership is instilled. Efficient delegation allows one to deal with significant matters instead.

To enhance time management, establish clear goals and deadlines for yourself as well as your team. Break down large tasks into smaller units that can be done within specific durations. The employment of project management methodologies such as Agile approach may help to ease workflows, manage deadlines and keep everyone on board.

Another important component of time management is protecting it. Distractions are common during stressful periods which could reduce your productivity levels. Create focused work blocks in order to minimize distractions by turning off notifications and setting boundaries. Focusing more in less time is essential through effective time blocking techniques like Pomodoro Technique.

Moreover, think about using technology and automation to improve your time management skills. One can use project management tools such as Trello or Asana to track the progress, deadlines, and activities happening in a particular task while calendar apps like Google Calendar or Microsoft Outlook can assist in scheduling appointments, meetings and managing deadlines.

Remember that efficient time management during high-pressure situations entails more than just finishing tasks but also maintaining a healthy work-life balance. Make self-care a priority by taking adequate rest breaks, exercise moments among other things that will give back energy thus increasing self-awareness as you maintain your wellbeing at such critical periods. This is crucial for sustaining productivity under intense business demands.

Preventing Burnout and Promoting Well-Being in High-Pressure Environments

Burnout concerns remain valid worries when working under high-pressure business environments because it takes a toll on individuals both mentally and physically considering its relentless demands and stress factors therefore ensuring long-term success requires efforts aimed at eliminating burnout risks while encouraging well-being.

Creating a Healthy Work-Life Balance

Developing of a healthy work-life balance is one of the major factors that can help prevent burnout. Encourage workers to practice self-care and set boundaries between their personal lives and work. To reduce the pressures associated with high pressure roles, it is important to encourage holidays and breaks where individuals can relax and rejuvenate.

Stress Management Techniques

Mitigating burnout necessitates effective stress management. Provide individuals with resources and support needed in developing strategies for dealing with stress such as mindfulness meditation, relaxation exercises or physical exercise. This will help in reducing stress levels leading to better well-being.

Fostering a Supportive Work Environment

A supportive work environment is critical to promoting well-being and preventing burnout. Encourage an open communication culture where employees are free to discuss their challenges ad seek support when necessary through fostering collaboration among workers thereby resulting into teamwork spirit which reduces the loneliness emanating from high-pressure situations.

Recognizing and Appreciating Achievements

It is easy for people working under intense environments not to be recognized for what they do. Regularly appreciate both small and big achievements so as to motivate your team while increasing morale at the workplace. Celebrating achievements therefore helps alleviate individuals' feelings of disvalorisation hence curbing burnout risk.

By adopting these approaches and prioritizing well-being within high-stress conditions, it will be possible for commanders to effectively contain burnout while promoting a healthier and more sustainable working culture. Being proactive about supporting the well being of employees improves individual satisfaction, productivity and fosters an environment that is resilient and successful.

Leading by Example: Inspiring Resilience in the Face of Pressure

During times of high-pressure as a leader, your behavior is what sets the pace for your team. It is important to realize that your actions and reactions are going to have great influence on how your team deals with stress. You can stir up resilience by leading through example even when under pressure resulting into optimistic support at work.

Conclusion

In summary, leading during high-pressure business situations calls for multifaceted tactics. Additionally, leaders can ably maneuver their teams through stressful periods successfully if they understand how these situations affect them and stay focused on where they are headed. To manage challenges in such settings resilience building and exploiting emotional intelligence are significant. Productivity and collaboration can only be ensured by effective communication, decision making complemented by efficient time management techniques embraced by the individual. What's more leading through example promotes well-being; thus creating a positive work environment aimed at inspiring resilience in this kind of scenario hence fostering success even when one is faced with pressure.

Ultimately, leadership through high-pressure business situations is not just about managing the external challenges but also about cultivating inner strength and resilience. By giving themselves an arsenal of strategies, leaders can lead their teams through testing times with confidence hence growth will take place which will lead to attaining desired results. Consequently as leaders think strategically communicate effectively or prioritize their time they can not only survive but prosper amidst high pressure situations.

Through "From Manager to Maestro: The Symphony of Good Management" chapter we have seen various methods in which leaders could navigate successfully throughout those moments in their businesses that are full of stressors . These are the practices and methods that leaders can apply to lead boldly, flexibly, and adaptively in a way that guides their team and organization toward greater growth and accomplishment.

Chapter 29

Allegro to Adagio: Adjusting Pace to Encourage Work-Life Harmony in Business

In this chapter, we will be exploring the significance of adjusting pace to promote a better work-life harmony in your company. Striking a balance between work and personal life is vital for increased productivity, employee satisfaction, and overall success.

Work-life harmony is not just a buzzword; it's an engine that propels engaged and motivated employees. When individuals feel supported enough to pursue their private lives while they meet job requirements, they become more likely to thrive both professionally and personally. This chapter will take you through the process of adjusting the pace in your business enterprise beginning from understanding different approaches through identifying advantages and implementing strategies towards achieving work-life harmony.

Thus, come with us as we embark on this Allegro to Adagio journey. Let us now look at how one can adjust pace to encourage work-life balance in your organization thereby creating a positive fulfilling work environment for all staff members.

Understanding The Allegro Approach

When it comes to business, what mostly matters under Allegro approach are short-term results. This means that decisions within the company should be made quickly without wasting much time. This method may produce impressive results when it comes to productivity and innovation but there is also need for companies to understand its risks and disadvantages.

The stress-filled world of Allegro approach

Sometimes, though, the speedy nature of this model can lead to high-intensity workplaces. In this case, employees may feel like the constant demand for fast results does not allow them any rest since they have always got deadlines right on their heads; which may result into fatigue of some sort as well as interfere with other aspects of their lives such as well-being or life-work-satisfaction among others (King & Cooper 1992). Every successful person needs rest (Norton et al., 2001).

While speed and agility are fundamental aspects of the Allegro model, there should also be concerns about how workers are feeling which would ensure healthier relationships at home among employees. The organizational environment has to be creative and apply the Allegro model in a way that it is able to strike this balance by ensuring that on one hand, the objectives of the organization are met with and on the other hand, all workers in it are able to enjoy a good work life harmony so as to enhance their productivity (Hochschild 2003).

Balancing speed with well-being

Balance is thus what can help keep dangers associated with Allegro approach at bay; though fastness and agility are important, employee welfare should also be taken into account in order for organizations thereunder to maintain a healthy workplace atmosphere. Understanding how this is done can assist businesses in creating policies that will achieve equilibrium thereby increasing production as well as enhancing general happiness among their working populations.

The Impact on Work-Life Balance

When companies employ the Allegro mode of operation, this can dramatically influence work-life balance. Indeed, many employees often get caught up within fast moving environments leaving them with no time or energy for other areas of life (Gardenswartz & Rowe 2007).

This kind of pursuit therefore tends to affect people's health negatively. In most cases, individuals experience increased stress levels, burnout problems together with various mental health disorders since they are always seeking ways through which they may succeed within an extremely short period (Cooper et al., 1994). Indeed, some positive effects of having enough leisure time may include better mental health.

Moreover, out-of-work relationships often suffer from this imbalance. Consequently, family members or friends start feeling ignored leading to lack of attachment and isolation when these occur between friends or loved ones; thereby eroding overall satisfaction or happiness (Greenhaus et al., 2010).

Recognizing the impact of an imbalanced work-life dynamic is crucial for both employees and employers. It hence becomes critical for companies at times like these when they discover several harmful effects including loss of commitment among their workers, unhappiness as well as challenges in relationships, to begin implementing strategies that will enable them restore the situation and focus on their employees' overall needs (Wood et al., 2004).

Recognizing the Importance of Adagio

In fast-paced business environments, it is crucial to acknowledge the importance of Adagio approach as a counterbalance to Allegro. Now while Allegro emphasizes rapidity and dynamism at work, Adagio focuses on a slower pace for fostering work-life balance.

By recognizing the importance of Adagio, businesses can benefit from balancing work and life. When people go slow, they have a chance to recharge themselves, lessening their stress and improving on their well-being. This can be an opportunity for personal developments in one's personal life such as having time with family, hanging out with friends or just relaxing.

Contrary to popular belief, embracing Adagio does not restrict productivity. It may even increase productivity over time. Having time off enables workers to come back to work with new eyes and revived strength which is associated with increased levels of innovation, problem solving and engagements in general.

Additionally, recognizing its significance promotes a healthier working environment where everyone gets what he deserves. Instructing employees about this tells them that their health matters a lot. This fosters commitment & loyalty thus creating engagement within the employees.

Added to this is the relevance of Adagio in helping businesses balance the fast paced nature of Allegro approach and need for work-life harmony. Leaders and managers need to create an environment that allows for flexibility regarding working hours for staff members as well as leave days when necessary.

Conclusion: Recognizing the importance of Adagio in business is a crucial step toward promoting work-life harmony. Slowing down and focusing on employee welfare can make organizations thrive more compared to what they are now doing. Now it's time both approaches combined together so as create a balanced fulfilling job experiences between Allegro Approach and Adagio Approach.

Creating a Culture of Balance

In today's fast-paced, demanding work world, establishing a culture of balance is essential for enhancing employee well-being and performance at the workplace While every company may take proactive measures towards ensuring work-life balance through positive work culture that considers overall wellbeing of workers.

One method of achieving a wholesome lifestyle includes offering flexible schedules at workplaces . Companies should allow employees manage their own lives by determining how who decides when they leave office or report back. In this case, there will be less stress and the workers would support the establishment leading to loyalty and increased outputs.

Alternatively, businesses can consider introducing remote working opportunities. By embracing remote work, organizations provide employees with freedom to work from home or any other suitable place.

This way they are able to balance their professional and private life, eliminate travel-related stress and make workplaces more consistent.

Further on, time off is an essential element in combining the two cultures above mentioned.Letting workers occasionally take breaks enables them not only to avoid fatigue but also to strike a balance between work and personal life thus making them healthier. This break allows one to concentrate on his or her job again when it recommences since it provides sufficient room for recharging of energy level and generation of new ideas.

Finally, creating wellness opportunities at the workplace helps cultivate a balanced culture. Corporations may organize activities like yoga lessons, meditation sessions & health workshops that support physical & mental health of employees. Moreover, promoting fitness through exercise programs, healthy eating habits as well as enough sleep aids in enhancing productivity while striking a balanced workforce.

Furthermore, developing open communication channels and supportive leaders play crucial roles in cultivating a culture of balance Communication has to be there where it must be held with open mind among employees concerning issues on balancing their lives alongside their jobs. Inclusive safe places are required so that particular needs are addressed while promoting harmony between personal interests and business requirements within an organization itself which fosters individual growth.

In conclusion, embracing measures such as flexible scheduling, remote work options, promoting time off and supporting employee well-being can create a culture of balance that acknowledges the significance of work-life harmony. Prioritizing work-life balance results in happier, healthier and more involved employees who ultimately contribute to the long-term success of an organization.

Setting Realistic Expectations

In today's fast-paced world of work, it is important to set realistic expectations for fostering a healthy work-life balance. By setting achievable goals and managing expectations both employers and their staff can avoid burnout and create an environment that values work-life harmony.

For employers realistic expectations means understanding what their employees are capable of doing and what they cannot do. It is necessary for them to communicate clear objectives and deadlines while considering factors like workload and resources. Thus by giving realistic targets employers can lower anxiety levels as well as creating a workplace that is more effective with satisfied workers.

Employees equally have a part to play when it comes to setting realistic expectations for themselves. The point is not taking on too much or overcommitment but rather assessing one's abilities as well as workload realistically. Therefore setting achievable goals together with prioritizing tasks contributes towards maintaining a good work-life balance avoiding overwhelm.

To achieve this kind of life, open communication between employer and employee is paramount. Regular check-ins regarding workload, deadlines or even expectations allows everyone to understand each other hence reducing unnecessary stress.

However it should be noted that having realistic expectations does not mean settling for mediocrity. In essence it is all about striking the right balance between ambition and feasibility. Employees can keep motivated with self-assuredness when they establish attainable goals thus experiencing increased job satisfaction that leads to overall wellbeing.

In conclusion, developing office cultures that encourage social lives at works requires making sure there are reasonable anticipations about completion amounts by way of goal alignment. Thus alignment objectives among employees help prevent burnout while establishing environments where well-being coupled with productivity is appreciated.

Redefining Success

In today's fast-paced business world, there is a growing need to redefine success. It can no longer be defined in terms of financial achievements and professional milestones only. Let us therefore shift our understanding towards attaining a healthy work-life balance which we ought to perceive as real success. Conventional ideas concerning success tend to value work more than anything else and this leads to burnout, strained relationships and overall dissatisfaction. Thus, by redefining success, we can embrace a more sustainable and harmonious approach for both our careers and personal lives.

Thinking beyond career climbs or wealth accumulation would mean rethinking how we understand achievement as finding equilibrium that allows people to flourish in their careers as well as private lives. It entails taking care of yourself first, building relationships second and engaging in other interests apart from the job you do.

A culture that supports work-life balance creates happier and more committed employees who achieve a healthier balance between work and their personal life become motivated, productive and dedicated to their organizations.

It's time thus that the outmoded way of defining success which focuses on happiness be replaced by another one that emphasizes wellness or meaning instead. Hence when we redefine success to include the concept of work-life balance then it becomes possible for everyone to approach both life & work sustainably.

Implementing Work-Life Integration Strategies

Lifestyle balance requires that work and personal life be integrated. In this section we'll look at some practical strategies which can help you achieve work-life integration and improve overall well-being.

1. Time blocking

One effective way through which people can integrate their work and personal lives is by using time blocking. This entails setting aside specific chunks of time for different activities including job duties, personal engagements, and leisure times. With these demarcations in place you will have the assurance that no area will be left out.

2. Prioritization

Another important part of incorporating work-life balance is prioritization. Take time to identify your most important tasks and responsibilities both at work and in your personal life. By focusing on what really matters, you can manage your time better hence striking a balance between commitments at work and home.

3. Setting boundaries

To ensure continuity of blending a person's professional life with his or her private one it entails creating clear boundaries between the two worlds i.e., At least communicate to colleagues or superiors about the limits one has set regarding his/her private schedules; this must include particular free times for instance weekends and evenings as well as daytime breaks during official working hours; Thus no works should invade ones private time thus maintaining healthy work-life balance.

4. Utilizing technology

The use of technological resources in order to streamline our lives has become increasingly popular both at home and at the workplace due to its efficiency gains; thereby easing our overall workload either professional or otherwise—it must involve both working hours as well as non-working periods while it may reduce stress associated with such career demands.

5. Seek support

You don't have to go through all the challenges brought by integrating your personal life with your profession alone—after all there are friends, family members who standby us even when we are struggling professionally; Therefore this implies that when facing those difficulties opening up about them while seeking suggestions from others would be beneficial since they are affected as well.

By using these work-life integration strategies, you can create a more balanced and happier everyday life. Achieving a synergistic connection between professional and personal commitments is a vital step towards achieving lasting joy and accomplishment.

Supporting Employee Well-being

Supporting employee well-being is an important part of maintaining a healthy work-life balance in any organization. This requires companies to prioritize the physical and mental health of their workforce hence making them be productive with happiness at work leading to satisfaction in general.

Wellness Programs

Implementing wellness programs can significantly contribute to supporting employee well-being. Such initiatives can include fitness classes, dietary counseling or advice, mindfulness classes among others. For organizations this means that they would provide opportunities for their employees to do things that promote their health and prosperity daily lives thus creating healthier environment within which employees' wellbeing would further improve because of self-care based procedures.

Mental Health Support

Businesses need to recognize the importance of mental health in their employees by investing in mental welfare support initiatives. This may involve offering confidential counseling services; they must establish an atmosphere where one can express his/her feelings without fear; while at the same time providing information on what it takes to identify various mental illnesses; Thus promoting understanding around stress levels as well as how it affects people's overall quality of life; In order that staffs feel comfortable about this Organizations should focus on such counseling needs that help maintain good relations with each other so less stress occurs due their own health status being taken care off accordingly by such business establishments.

Stress Management Initiatives

Employee wellness is greatly affected by work-related stress. Consequently, organizations can introduce different stress management initiatives through which employees will be able to handle this condition better thereby improving individual productivity levels within specific institutions dealing with such cases like this one (Kessler et al., 2003). Among other ways businesses may pursue measures aimed at implementing better approaches for managing pressure including training workshops designed specifically at coping skills or other similar mechanisms that support work-life balance.

By supporting employee well-being through wellness programs, mental health support, and stress management initiatives, businesses not only demonstrate a commitment to their employees' health and happiness but also create an environment that fosters productivity and success.

Leadership's Role in Promoting Work-Life Harmony

Effective leadership plays a crucial role in creating a work environment that values work-life harmony. Managers and executives have the power to lead by example and create a supportive culture that prioritizes the well-being of their employees.

One of the main opportunities for leaders to foster work-life harmony is through promoting healthy work-life balance among their team members. It involves setting achievable goals, encouraging flexible timetables, as well as building chances for people to get days off when needed.

The role of leaders is also very critical in making the culture of open communication and transparent decision-making. Leaders can thus contribute towards inclusive and supportive workplaces by actively listening to workers concerns. This helps employees feel heard and understood, reducing the potential for undue stress or burnout.

Moreover, policies enforced by leaders can assist in integrating professional life with personal life. These may involve remote work resources for instance; wellness programs could be promoted as well where different benefits packages are flexible covering many needs within employees' ranks.

Reliable management ought to portray empathy alongside understanding when dealing with issues affecting personnel's families or schedules at home. By so doing, they will engender trust plus respect within their respective teams thereby promoting cohesion which brings forth great results (Source).

In conclusion, leadership plays a vital role in promoting work-life harmony within organizations. By leading by example, creating a supportive culture, and implementing policies that prioritize the well-being of employees, leaders can foster an environment that encourages individuals to achieve a healthy work-life balance.

The Benefits of Work-Life Harmony

There are numerous benefits associated with achieving this balance both individually and institutionally (Hoffman 2016). Having recognized this fact from at least two angles, it becomes more pertinent for this study to evaluate the employees' perspective as well. To begin with, work-life balance fosters a healthy internal environment within a firm (Hoffman 2016). This is because employees tend to be satisfied with their jobs when they find it possible to attend to their personal matters (Hoffman 2016).

Increased Productivity

It is easier for people who live balanced lives between work and family to remain focused on their tasks than those who do not. They therefore bring out the best in them that leads to higher productivity and efficiency at workplaces. By having low levels of stress and clear minds, staff can think creatively while performing their duties hence contributing towards growth and development of businesses.

Enhanced Employee Satisfaction

Work-life harmony plays a significant role in the satisfaction and well-being of employees. When individuals are able to maintain a healthy balance between being workers and family members or friends, there is improved job satisfaction among them. In such context, workers feel worthy plus supported by employers leading to increased loyalty thereby commitment within organizations? A happy employee works in an atmosphere with high morale where all feel united as one big family.

Improved Work-Life Integration

Work-life harmony encourages a seamless integration of work and personal life, allowing individuals to better manage their time and responsibilities.When businesses promote arrangements like remote working or flexible schedules; they enable employees form better interface between professional life & other preoccupations (Source). This means less pressure on them since they can allocate enough time on both private matters alongside accomplishing their organization's goals without any strains experienced by these professionals.

Attracting and Retaining Top Talent

In the industry, organizations that prioritize work-life balance attract and retain the top talent. Employers' lives are believed by job applicants to be of value, in addition to providing a supportive workplace. In this way, businesses can become attractive employers who place their employees' welfare as important through promoting work-life balance and displaying harmony benefits. As a result, hiring becomes stronger and turnover slows down, which leads to more stable high performing workforce.

In conclusion, there are several advantages for individuals and businesses when they attain work-life harmony. A balanced approach also entails an improved integration between life at work and personal life as well as being able to attract skilled employees.

Conclusion

Maintaining one's overall well-being and productivity is crucial in today's demanding business environment for people juggling professional and personal responsibilities. It is about adjusting speed so that it encourages business/work-life harmony.

Throughout this section we have touched on the concept of adjusting pace within the workplace as well as its impact on finding work/life balance.Like this Allegro quick paced method can lead to negative consequences such as dissatisfaction among employees.

However if Adagio systems (work at a moderate pace ad keep up with your private life) that involve slow pacing towards achieving a good balance between work and private life are understood by businesses; then flexible hours, setting realistic goals should be implemented.

By putting emphasis on smooth working conditions both individuals would feel much satisfied when doing their tasks while organizations will enjoy higher performance indices due to enhanced productivity levels of their workers together with higher rates of employee retention. So, let us prioritize our well-being and embrace a balanced approach to work and personal life, adjusting the pace to encourage work-life harmony in business.

Part V:
Beyond the Concert Hall

Chapter 30

The Global Stage: Cross-Cultural Management and Diversity

What if Anna, a skilled project manager, welcomed an opportunity to work on a multinational project with different team players? She looked forward to collaborating with coworkers who had diverse backgrounds and thought that their varied opinions would lead to creative ideas. However, Anna ran into some difficulties during the implementation of the project.

Her teammates used different styles of communication sometimes creating misunderstanding and causing delays. Cultural distinctions also influenced decision-making processes; therefore friction stemmed from this and slowed down the progress. By embracing diversity and managing cultural differences, businesses can unlock numerous benefits such as improved communication, enhanced teamwork, increased creativity and higher employee satisfaction.

In conclusion, the implementation of Cross-Cultural Management practices in business organizations has many benefits that lead to increased creativity and innovation in overall business performance. Consequently, companies can thrive in today's globalized and multicultural business landscape through embracing diversity and leveraging cultural differences.

Challenges Encountered In Cross-Cultural Management

Apart from numerous advantages that accompany Cross-cultural management in Business, it also poses some challenges for organizations. These challenges are mainly cultural differences, language barriers, communication styles and different work ethics. Thus in this era of globalization characterized by international commerce there is need to understand these obstacles and overcome them if the company is to excel globally.

Language Barriers

For any enterprise to succeed there has to be effective communication at its foundation. However, when working with diverse cultural groups, language barriers may hinder clear and concise communication. As a result misunderstandings occur interfering with collaboration as well as productivity. Organizations must therefore come up with strategies such as providing language training, making use of translators or interpreters and promoting language learning among workforce members to address this gap.

Communication Styles

Every society has its own way of communicating based on historical formation and tradition which makes them unique to other communities. In cross-cultural management these dissimilarities can be problematic as different individuals from diverse backgrounds expect anything starting from the manner of speaking they communicate with other people up to methods used for reaching agreements during negotiations. Hence developing cross-culture intellectuality plus enhancing open dialogue within an organization can help it manage these situations effectively and further promote intercultural communication.

Differing Work Ethics

Different cultures have varying ideas about what constitutes ethical behavior at work. This affects individuals' performances both as a team or individually; how decisions are made; what everyone expects concerning productivity amongst others matters regarding civilization at workplaces across borders vary greatly (Saee 2009). Thereby these variations may give rise to conflicts; misinterpretations plus difficulties experienced while managing teams consisting of people from various nations. Hence, companies should be pro-active towards embracing and reconciling these diverse work ethics for the purpose of building cohesive and high performing multicultural teams.

Cultural Biases

In cross-cultural management, cultural biases and stereotypes cause interpersonal problems, hinder sound decision-making processes as well as impair overall organizational dynamics. This means that it may be difficult for some individuals in an organization to collaborate effectively because they have preconceived ideas about others. It can be argued that cultural bias is a great obstacle to the effective function of organizations (Majid 2010). In this regard, organizations need to stimulate economic development by enhancing cultural awareness; creating inclusive environments and challenging biases so that diversity can be leveraged as a competitive advantage.

Overcoming these challenges in Cross-Cultural Management requires organizations to invest in cultural intelligence training, promote open and inclusive communication, and implement strategies that acknowledge and respect cultural differences. By taking on these challenges head-on, businesses will benefit from cultures with different perspectives which lead to innovation among other things.

Strategies for Effective Cross-Cultural Management

Today's business environment necessitates effective management of cross-cultural groups and organizations. In order for harmony and increased productivity during collaboration enterprises must therefore adopt strategies as well as best practices that enhance cultural understanding inclusiveness.

1. Intercultural Communication: Communication is a critical aspect of managing across cultures. Encourage open channels of communication that value diversity in thought. Promote active listening, empathy, and respect to bridge gaps between cultures thereby promoting cooperation resulting into valuable collaborations.
2. Cultural Awareness Training: Implement comprehensive cultural programs aimed at raising awareness on differences in culture such as norms, values and behaviors among workers. This enables individuals adapt sufficiently in different cross-cultural interactions.
3. Creating an Inclusive Work Environment: Establish policies promoting fairness within the organization where all employees are treated equally regardless of their backgrounds or characteristics such sex or gender.
4. Another approach is to have team building activities that inspire cross-cultural interaction and collaboration. Also, you need to make an environment whereby the members can find it easy to learn from each other through sharing their stories that would enlighten them in different aspects.
5. Cultural Intelligence: Leaders and employees should be developed and encouraged towards having cultural intelligence. One way of developing cultural intelligence is understanding cultural differences and adapting management approaches accordingly.
6. Trust Building: Trust is a foundation for effective cross-cultural management. To build trust among team members, encourage honest dialogue, promote interpersonal relationship, demonstrate fairness and respectfulness in all your interactions.

In doing so, organizations are able to deal with the issue of culture barriers among themselves; they also enhance teamwork in order to boost their business success within the international arena.

The Influence of Cross-Cultural Management on Global Business Success

Cross-Cultural Management has a significant role to play thus determine whether an organization will be successful or not in today's global business environment. Having knowledge about cultural diversity, therefore managing it effectively becomes crucial for those businesses operating on the global platform. Cultural intelligence assist company's managers in adapting to various cultures' norms and practices which is essential for sustainable growth as well as meaningful competitive advantage.However businesses can develop strong relationships with customers, partners and employees globally by embracing diverse views or adapting local customs.

Global companies that prioritize Cross-Cultural Management strategies create inclusive work environments where employees feel valued and empowered. This promotes co-operation between teams leading into invention since teams are composed individuals from different cultures who contribute different ideas based on their experiences.

Moreover effective Cross-Cultural Management enhances communication while minimizing misunderstandings. Accordingly organizations may recognize any potential language hurdles such as communication styles plus prejudice arising from cultural inclinations thus promoting clear channels of effective communication that results into successful collaborations among separate units within the same company.

By investing in Cross-Cultural Management, firms situate themselves for survival and success in today's highly globalized business landscape. Understanding and appreciating cultural differences helps businesses navigate the complexities of international markets, make informed decisions, and tailor their products and services to meet the diverse needs and preferences of customers worldwide.

To sum up, Cross-Cultural Management is no longer an elective skill but rather a must have for organizations to survive in today's business world. Thus, organisations who are culturally intelligent will be able to build strong relationships that foster innovation thereby taking advantage of vast opportunities offered by global business environment.

Leveraging Diversity in Cross-Cultural Management

Cross-cultural management plays a crucial role towards success in the modern global market. The importance of leveraging diversity is one aspect that firms need to understand and embrace. It goes beyond those differences on race, gender or even ethnicity; it covers various perspectives, experiences as well as backgrounds brought about by different people.

Managing diversity entails recognizing and valuing individual strengths and insights based upon their own cultural background. This variety can then be harnessed by organizations through embracing its power thereby unlocking several innovations as well as creativity.

One major advantage related with managing diversity refers to the many ways through which challenges could be approached thus making problem-solving easier. Different cultures come up with new ideas on how they can find solutions in alternative ways. Organizations can leverage this rich diversity when they encourage open discussions among team members hence promoting creative thinking and innovations.

For effective utilization of diversity, inclusive work culture is very essential. This means creating an environment where individuals feel valued, respected and empowered to express their ideas. When workers are included and recognized they tend to offer different views and thoughts which help in raising the level of employee commitment and efficiency.

Diversity management in Cross-Cultural Management also offers better understanding from various markets and customer segments. Information on cultural quirks, preferences, and mindsets that shape products as well as services for a given target audience can be obtained by organizations. Such knowledge of culture will result in market expansion while at the same time improving quality of services offered to customers.

To leverage diversity effectively in Cross-Cultural Management, organizations need to invest in cultural awareness training and provide opportunities for individuals to learn from one another. By encouraging cross-cultural interactions and collaborations knowledge is enriched which ensures strong teams are built.

Finally, leveraging diversity does not just mean reaching certain quotas or ticking boxes but it also involves embracing unique strengths brought forth by each individual. Organizations that promote innovation foster growth through creation of an inclusive workplace valuing diversity within a highly diverse interconnected global business environment.

Implementation of Cross-Cultural Management Practices

It is a must for all businesses operating within today's globalized world to implement cross-cultural management practices. In order to manage cultural differences effectively as well as encourage diversity, practical strategies have to be put on board by these companies thus creating a culture that fosters inclusion. Below are some key practices:

Cross-cultural Training Programmes

Providing staff with training programs aimed at enhancing their culture intelligence is one major step taken towards implementation of Cross-Cultural Management (CCM). These could include intercultural communication skills development sessions; workshops on cultural awareness; or even teaching negotiation across cultures among other things. Through such training organizations can develop employees' abilities necessary for effective collaboration despite their cultural backgrounds.

Strategies for Recruitment Diversity

Proactive approaches to recruitment foster building up a diverse and equal workforce. This calls for widening recruitment channels; engaging with different communities; and accepting a broad range of hiring approaches. Organizations can therefore benefit from having people with different perspectives, backgrounds and skills as their staff by attracting and retaining employees with diverse social-cultural backgrounds.

Creation of an Inclusive Culture

It is necessary for organizations to have a culture that appreciates diversity and promotes inclusivity. It implies giving equal opportunities to all, open dialogues as well as creating safe working environment among others. By embracing the diversities in beliefs, cultures and views, companies can fully utilize its workers thereby causing innovation.

Through implementation of these practices in Cross-Cultural Management (CCM), harmonious work environments can be created where people of varied cultural backgrounds can collaborate effectively. Enhancing creative thinking as well as better communication among other things lead to better performance at the workplace.

Case Study 2: Bridging Cultural Divides in International Collaboration

Company: Gamesoft Corporation

Aforementioned is a case of Gamesoft Corporation, a major software company which had great challenges in managing cross-cultural teams during its international collaboration projects. They implemented a Cross-Cultural Management program which covered cultural awareness training, communication strategies for effective understanding and a work together environment. The Gamesoft Corporation by embracing cultural diversity and leveraging the strengths of their multinational workforce successfully bridged cultural divides and accomplished their project objectives thus improving productivity and customer satisfaction.

Case Study 2: Cultural Adaptation and Market Expansion

Company: Avon Cosmetics

Avon Cosmetics, a well-known beauty brand that sought to expand into the Asian market. To be able to navigate through the cultures of the Asian populations as desired by their clients in these regions, they practiced Cross-Cultural Management ideology. To conform to Asia's demographic expectations however, the firm undertook thorough market research as well as local consultant associations with a view to tailoring their product offerings, marketing strategies and customer service practices. This made them appear very culturally sensitive leading to strong footing in the region consequently attracting huge revenue shares attained through brand loyalty.

Case Study 3: Global Leadership and Multicultural Team Development

Company: Unilever Pharmaceuticals

Unilever Pharmaceuticals is one such company that has this challenge given that it is operating globally as a pharmaceutical industry. They have set up a comprehensive leadership training program on cross cultural management focusing on cultural intelligence, adaptability and team work orientation for leaders across all levels within the organization. Cultural differences may be navigated by teaching people how to think differently when they are dealing with others from different backgrounds hence improving communication among members of different teams working in diverse parts of the world thus enhancing partnerships between different industries as was observed in Unilever Pharmaceuticals where various stakeholders aimed at enhancing wellbeing via cooperation (Todd & Wintle 12).

These case studies illustrate how much Cross-Cultural Management can contribute towards companies achieving success in the international business context; thus underlining why diversity is important in the workplace. Here, it is about embracing differences and embedding cultural understanding so as to create an open working environment where everyone feels valued and respected. By using such strategies, organizations are able to navigate through culture complexities, leverage diversity and finally attain a competitive advantage in the turbulent international business environment.

Looking Ahead: The Future of Cross-Cultural Management

Sprinkled with technological advancements globalization and demographical changes around the world, global business environment keeps on changing at a very fast pace. In this respect therefore, cross cultural management is highly relevant in business. Essentially, companies that embrace diversity and acquire abilities necessary for handling cross-cultural issues have better chances of success in the present globalized world.

Looking ahead there are some major emerging trends that will shape Cross-Cultural Management globally. One such trend is that virtual teams are being increasingly employed as well as remote work: A case of digital natives from different cultures coming together in one platform with a common objective (Hofstede 19). Hence every organization should redesign its leadership style for successful collaboration in this new era characterized by virtual cross-cultural teams.

Another crucial point that firms need to take into account is the increasing significance attached to cultural intelligence (CI). As companies go international, they encounter different markets and clients thus they require their employees who possess an orientation towards learning from others' cultures so as to understand or adapt themselves with these norms. Thus adapting cultural intelligence training will be essential for businesses competing on global scale.

Chapter **31**

Eco-Symphonies: Sustainable Practices in Management

Eco-Sustainable Solutions was a small company in Christchurch who were known to be grounded on environmental sustainability. Emily, the creator of Eco-Sustainable Solutions, has always held the view that businesses should get into harmony with nature for a greener future.

Emily grew up in an environment full of thick forests, clear lakes and variations of animals. As she started getting involved in business matters, it was difficult for her to ignore how badly the ecosystem was treated by many companies. In this case, Emily wanted to form a company which would excel in its operation and reinforce sustainable development.

Emily and her team adopted many eco-friendly measures throughout their operations at Eco-Sustainable Solutions. They led by example through everything such as reducing waste and energy consumption and supporting sustainable innovation along with staff involvement.

She knew that running a business sustainably did not involve merely ticking boxes or following trends; it was like creating a symphony where all instruments spoke the language of sustainability together. Each practice orchestrated itself to create a harmonious and enduring melody towards sustainability similar to musical instruments in an orchestra.

With other companies looking up to them requesting guidance, they became pioneers of sustainable management within the corporate world because this realization meant that going green is also good for business, not just the planet.

This chapter examines why integrating sustainable practices into management is vital. We will see how companies can become sustainable by having every note sounding out a greener future symphony.

Understanding Sustainable Management

This section will discuss principles and importance of sustainable management. Sustainable management integrates environmental, social, and economic considerations into designing more sustainable ways of operating enterprises.

Organizations adopting such practices enable them to exert less pressure on the environment as well as contribute to social welfare while remaining profitable over time. This holistic approach recognizes the relationship between environmental stewardship, social accountability and financial solvency.

Sustainable management involves making informed decisions that avoid negative long term implications of business activities. In this case, resource conservation, waste minimization, renewable power adoption and ethical practices across the supply chain are some of the strategies and policies that have to be implemented.

Furthermore, sustainable management also advocates for stakeholder involvement while fostering cooperation and openness with employees, customers and societies within which they operate. Engaging stakeholders in decision making processes ensures that an organization's moves resonate with societal values and expectations at large.

Sustainable management also considers the interests of future generations beyond short term profit maximization. It encourages creative thinking as well as continuous improvement so that businesses can come up with more environmentally friendly ways of doing things alongside being socially responsible.

All in all, understanding sustainable management is essential for businesses to operate in a fast changing world. By adopting sustainable practices such as reducing their ecological footprint, firms may build a better brand reputation while attracting conscious consumers; thus eventually contributing to a sustainable world for everyone.

Pros of Eco-friendly Practices

There are a variety of benefits that go beyond the environment if companies adopt eco-friendly practices as part of their management. These methods also help in creating a sustainable economy and ensure prosperity for many businesses. Let us look at some of them:

Cost Savings

Eco-friendly practices can help organizations reduce costs significantly. Businesses can reduce their utility bills and operational expenses by consuming less energy, utilizing resources efficiently, and implementing waste reduction measures. Additionally, apart from cost reductions in the long-run, sustainability may as well lead to streamlining of operations and increased efficiency hence more productivity.

Enhanced Brand Reputation

In the current environmental world, customers prefer brands that are seen to be green. The use of sustainability in business processes helps develop brand names with positive connotation thus enhancing reputation. It is more likely for loyal clients to have trust in firms which observe environmental responsibility leading to market share improvement.

Positive Environmental Impact

The positive impact on the environment is one among the major advantages of eco-friendly practices. Organizations may cut down on greenhouse gas emissions, minimize waste generation or conserve natural resources by implementing sustainable management approaches. Such actions are important in mitigating climate change, ensuring biodiversity and having a healthier planet for future generations.

By adopting ecofriendly practices in management, an organization's efforts will not only contribute towards achieving a sustainable future but also bring savings on costs enhance its brand reputation as well as make a positive environmental impact though; it is a win-win situation for both sides.

Sustainable Supply Chain Management

Sustainable supply chain management has become critical for most organizations today because we live in an increasingly interconnected world that values the environment. This can mean minimizing any adverse effects on the environment when undertaking any activities along supply chains while sourcing materials ethically and maintaining transparency among others.

One way to manage this is by lowering carbon dioxide emissions towards sustainable supply chains through optimizing transport routes, greener modes of transportations and energy efficient warehouse techniques which greatly reduces their carbon footprint. This helps to protect the environment while improving efficiency of operations, leading to cost reductions.

the other hand, sustainable supply chain management involves ensuring that all materials and products are sourced from suppliers who adhere to fair labor practices, respect human rights, and prioritize environmental stewardship. Partnering with conscientious suppliers allows businesses to make a positive social impact while maintaining brand integrity.

In order for management to be regarded as sustainable throughout the supply chain, it needs transparency. Transparency in terms of product origin, process involved and socially responsible practices builds customer trust and stakeholder confidence. Such openness helps customers not only make choices but also aid them in supporting environmentally friendly brands.

Apart from this section's contribution towards a greener future; there are other benefits that organizations can get from incorporating sustainable supply chain management practices such as creating a positive brand image among those environmentally conscious consumers and driving long-term sustainability through minimizing environmental impact, ethical sourcing and encouraging transparency.

Green Initiatives for Energy Conservation

Organizations nowadays understand that energy saving is paramount if they want their operations to continue being viable amid these ever changing times. Therefore by embracing green initiatives companies reduce their energy consumption & help protect our planet against global warming. In this section we will explore different ways in which organizations can embrace ideas towards conserving energy.

Renewable Energy Sources

One way businesses can lower their carbon footprints and save energy is by using renewable energy. Organizations can choose solar, wind, or geothermal power to substantially reduce their reliance on traditional fossil fuels and in the long term, they could save much money spent on energy.

Energy Efficient Technologies

Another aspect of conserving energy is through adopting an efficient use of energy technologies. For example, by purchasing energy-saving appliances and installing LED lights and smart HVAC systems that optimize both cooling and heating processes, organizations may minimize wastage of electricity. Energy usage with intelligence can be executed by businesses adopting smart sensors as well as automation to ensure resources are effectively utilized.

Employee Engagement Programs

In any organization involving its employees in the efforts to conserve power significantly impacts its overall consumption rate. People can be trained on how to save electricity; hence reducing the amount of it at work places. A culture of environmentalism will therefore develop in offices where an employee's consistency in carrying out green practices are awarded or otherwise recognized.

Being a socially responsible company means implementing these conservation procedures for sustainability that not only help organizations to reduce their footprint but also enhance their image. Renewable sources, efficient devices and worker engagement programs are some of the things that organizations may employ for this purpose.

Waste Reduction Strategies

To help limit environmental impact, there are various critical steps businesses must take including effective methods that cut down waste levels within them. By adopting such strategies however, companies play a role towards a greener future while getting a range of benefits like saving costs and enhancing sustainability as it were shall discuss some key waste reduction strategies for companies herein below.

Recycling

Recycling is known globally as a means of reducing wastes whereby materials are transformed into new products rather than being disposed off completely. Business establishments could send most refuse possible away from landfills through comprehensive recycling plans which also protect valuable resources. These include paper, plastics, glasses metals recycling among others alongside implementing e-waste recycling programs for electronic devices.

Composting

Another effective waste reduction strategy is called composting which involves decomposition of organic waste such as food remains, grass clippings, into a substance known as humus that is full of plant nutrients. Such schemes ensure that no more organic matters go to landfill sites and therefore reducing the amount of green house gasses emitted while at the same time producing materials like compost which enriches gardens and agricultural lands.

Waste Management Techniques

For companies seeking to minimize their waste generation and improve overall waste management practices, it is important that they employ certain strategies. Thus includes conducting what audits in order to identify areas where wastages occur together with implementing waste reduction measures such as source minimization, employee training on appropriate collection and disposal methods among others. Besides, businesses may also have agreements with garbage disposal firms which offer services ranging from refuse recycling to segregation.

By implementing these policies on minimizing wastes corporations can be able to achieve a lot in terms of environmental conservation and promoting sustainable development on earth.

Sustainable Innovation & Product Development

During the contemporary fast changing world, the need for sustainable innovation and product development cannot be overemphasized by organizations that wish to have a positive impact on environment. Consequently businesses should make sure that they are environmentally friendly not just by making products but also researching on ways through which sustainability principles can be integrated into their existing models.

The use of energy-efficient technology and renewable materials is one of the major aspects of sustainable innovation. For example, companies are coming up with alternative sourcing for their products from bamboo or recycled plastics in order to cut back on the usage of non-renewable resources thereby reducing wastage that comes with them as well. Besides, production of products that consider energy consumption and greenhouse gas emissions volume helps in fostering a greener environment.

Another important issue to consider when developing sustainable products or services is the whole life cycle right from its packaging to disposal. To this end, companies are shifting towards circular economy principles that emphasize on making goods with ease of repair, reuse or recycling in mind. This way waste can be reduced thus enabling more sustainable product life cycles which help move businesses towards a circular economy and lower their total environmental footprints.

Case Study: Patagonia

Outdoor clothing company Patagonia is an outstanding example of sustainable innovation and product development. Throughout its supply chain and range of product line, it has always emphasized sustainability. Jackets made from recycled materials and clothes designed for longevity are among the various eco-friendly items produced by this firm. The company also encourages customers to extend the lives of their garments through repair services.

Patagonia's holistic approach to sustainability goes beyond just creating great outdoor gear; it entails environmental advocacy and grassroots support for environmental causes as well. This commitment to sustainability has helped build a strong brand reputation with loyal customers who share similar values.

Sustainable innovation and product development are critical for organizations seeking a more sustainable future especially through research and development processes that incorporate sustainability principles into business operations while meeting consumer demands for green products thus minimizing degradation caused to the environment by these companies such as using eco friendly raw materials, incorporating concepts such as clean technology within design & manufactuing processes among others.The use of renewable materials, adoption 0f energy efficient technologies alongside embracing circular economies will position businesses at the forefront f sustainable product innovations leading to a more sustainable planet.

Employee Engagement for Sustainability

Employee engagement is core to sustainability efforts in organizations. Once employees have been trained and involved in sustainable practices, they become agents of environmental responsibility thus fostering sustainability culture.

Various mechanisms can be devised by organizations to get their staff engaged in sustainability initiatives. For instance, through comprehensive training programs that enlighten and educate the employees on significance of their roles towards environmental conservation and what specific steps an individual can undertake for greener future.

Moreover, open communication platforms and collaborative spaces can be set up within the company where employee's ideas or suggestions about how to effectively apply sustainable practices could be shared. Organizations therefore need to involve their workforce in decision-making processes so as to give them sense of belonging besides empowering them towards taking active part in ecological conservation drives.

Recognizing Employee Contributions

Recognition is also a crucial element of employee engagement for sustainability because it plays a role in creating a positive work climate which also motivates further involvement.

To this end, they can initiate incentive campaigns aimed at celebrating stars who have demonstrated uncommon commitment towards attaining environmental sustainability objectives. These programs may range from award ceremonies including rewards/incentives that not only recognize employees' contributions but also motivate others into becoming more actively engaged participants towards conserving environment.

Creating a Culture of Environmental Responsibility

Sustainability must form part and parcel of an organization's core values as well as its mission so as to foster cultures characterized by environmental conscientiousness among other things. Through aligning with overall strategic objectives companies are able communicate commitment towards ecological sustainability thus sending clear messages about the company as far as environmental care goes.

In addition, organizations can also encourage staff's participation in sustainability initiatives by providing them with resources and tools that will enable them to get involved. This may involve setting up dedicated sustainability committees or employee-led green teams that not only drive sustainability projects but also provide opportunities for employees to develop leadership and teamwork skills.

Measuring Employee Engagement for Sustainability

Measuring and analyzing employee engagement for sustainability is critical in assessing the effectiveness of initiatives as well as spotting areas where they need improvement. To gather employees' insights regarding their level of engagement in sustainable practices, surveys and feedback mechanisms are used by organizations.

By tracking key performance indicators related to sustainability like employee participation rates in green initiatives, organisations can monitor progress towards targets and make data-driven decisions to improve their outcomes on these fronts. Regular communication of such measures can build transparency and responsibility among the workers hence fostering continuous involvement.

So to sum up, within a company, it is necessary to ensure that employees have high commitment level if business needs its operations to be eco friendly. Through educating, involving and acknowledging staffs about sustainable practices companies can foster environmental responsibility culture which can lead them into more sustainable future.

Green Marketing and Branding

Green marketing and branding have become crucial strategies for organizations wishing to position themselves as leaders in sustainability in today's environmentally conscious world . Green marketing involves promoting products and services that have minimal environmental impact while branding seeks to create a positive image or reputation around its sustainability pillar.

One important aspect of green marketing is effective communication of an organization's sustainable practices with consumers. For businesses it is imperative that they transparently depict their eco-friendly efforts such as use of renewable energy sources; reduction of carbon emissions through recycling programs .

These actions will help attract environmentally minded consumers who are increasingly seeking products that resonate with their values while at the same time positioning themselves as sustainable brands businesses aim at tapping into the growing market segment thereby gaining a competitive advantage.

Successful green branding must take into consideration environmental concerns while also considering the social and economic factors involved. Organisations need to show they are committed to sustainability at all touchpoints, from product design and packaging, through to advertising and customer service.

Moreover, companies that use green messaging within their brand identity can create a compelling narrative for consumers. By demonstrating their commitment to the environment, wellness of society and ethical practices, such organizations gain trust and loyalty from eco-conscious customers.

Additionally, green marketing and branding efforts can improve a company's reputation while mitigating risks related to environmental issues. Organizations can build positive image in relation long-term ecological stability by proactively responding to sustainability concerns while communicating openly about it.

To sum up this part on green marketing and branding is necessary because it plays an important role in today's business landscape. Companies therefore should effectively communicate sustainable practices as part of entering into a green brand image which will help them attract environmentally conscious consumers gain competitive advantages among others.

Responsible Stakeholder Management

In today's fast changing business environment responsible stakeholder management drives sustainable business practice. Companies are recognizing the importance of engaging with suppliers, customers and community in addressing social and environmental challenges.

Responsible stakeholder management entails fostering strong relationships with important stakeholders, ensuring their needs are met and actively involving them in sustainable initiatives. When organizations have interest of stakeholders at heart, win-win situations can be created which prioritize both business goals and societal well-being.

Collaboration between companies and their suppliers leads to responsible sourcing, ethical production practices and improved working conditions. This type of partnerships help reduce adverse environmental impacts on the supply chain as well as supporting local communities.

Engaging customers as stakeholders enables organizations to understand their preferences, values, and expectations regarding sustainability. By incorporating customer feedback and involving them in product development processes, businesses can create innovative and eco-friendly offerings that resonate with target audiences.

In addition to suppliers and customers, responsible stakeholder management extends to the wider community. Organizations can actively participate in community development projects, support local initiatives, and contribute to the overall well-being of society. These activities not only strengthen the organization's reputation but also foster goodwill and enhance brand loyalty.

The integration of responsible stakeholder management in sustainable practices creates a collaborative and holistic approach to addressing social and environmental challenges. By working together, organizations and stakeholders can achieve long-term success while driving positive impact for the planet and society as a whole.

Measuring and Reporting Sustainability Performance

In today's world, measuring and reporting sustainability performance has become a crucial aspect of responsible business practices. It allows organizations to assess their impact on the environment, society, and the economy, and take necessary steps towards a more sustainable future.

Measuring sustainability performance

Measuring sustainability performance involves the use of various tools and methodologies to track and evaluate key performance indicators (KPIs). These KPIs help organizations understand their progress towards sustainability goals and identify areas for improvement.

Sustainability reporting frameworks

Sustainability reporting frameworks provide organizations with a standardized approach to report their sustainability efforts. These frameworks, such as the Global Reporting Initiative (GRI) and the Sustainability Accounting Standards Board (SASB), guide organizations in disclosing relevant information and metrics to stakeholders.

Transparency and commitment

Transparency is paramount when reporting sustainability performance. By openly sharing their achievements, challenges, and future plans, organizations demonstrate their commitment to sustainability and build trust with stakeholders. Transparent reporting also allows benchmarking and sharing best practices across industries.

Benefits of measuring and reporting sustainability performance

Measuring and reporting sustainability performance brings several benefits. It helps organizations identify inefficiencies and implement strategies for resource optimization, leading to cost savings. It also enhances brand reputation, as stakeholders increasingly value socially and environmentally responsible businesses.

Furthermore, measuring sustainability performance provides valuable insights into the effectiveness of sustainability initiatives, enabling organizations to refine their practices and set ambitious targets for continuous improvement.

Overall, measuring and reporting sustainability performance is essential for organizations to showcase their dedication to environmental and social responsibility. By adopting robust measurement frameworks and transparent reporting practices, businesses can contribute to a more sustainable future for generations to come.

The Future of Sustainable Management

In an increasingly environmentally conscious world, the future of sustainable management is poised to play a significant role in shaping businesses and their impact on the planet. As organizations strive to adopt more sustainable practices, emerging trends are paving the way for a greener future.

One key aspect of the future of sustainable management lies in the utilization of new technologies. Innovations such as artificial intelligence, data analytics, and the Internet of Things (IoT) are revolutionizing how businesses operate. These technologies can be harnessed to optimize resource usage, reduce waste, and improve overall sustainability performance.

Moreover, policies and regulations will continue to drive the adoption of sustainable management practices. Governments around the world are implementing stricter environmental regulations and encouraging businesses to prioritize sustainability. In response, organizations will need to develop comprehensive sustainability strategies and integrate them into their core operations to remain competitive.

Looking ahead, the future of sustainable management also involves the development of innovative strategies. Concepts like circular economy, where waste is minimized and resources are reused, are gaining traction. Additionally, collaborations between businesses, nonprofits, and governments are fostering sustainability-focused initiatives and collective efforts towards a more environmentally friendly future.

Chapter 32

Philanthropy in Harmony: Corporate Social Responsibility

Imagine a busy city street, crowded with people of every creed. Among them stands Emma, a young girl whose eyes are filled with hope and curiosity. She dreams of a world where education is available to all children regardless of social-economic background.

Unbeknownst to Emma, just several blocks away from her location in the city, there is a head office where individuals similar to her work tirelessly towards helping to realize her dream.

This is the spirit of philanthropy in tandem with corporate social responsibility; an amalgam that companies enter into as they help solve social issues. It is what top firms around the globe adopt because they know that their success depends not only on revenue but also what it contributes to society.

In this journey through corporate social responsibility and philanthropy, we shall learn how companies can go beyond their financial goals and align their efforts with the needs of local communities. We will see how strategic giving, partnerships, employee engagement and sustainability practices have created change for good. And together we will unlock this unlimited possibility that business has in making Emma's life better or any other girl out there today.

Understanding Corporate Social Responsibility

Corporate Social Responsibility (CSR) plays an important role in fostering positive societal change and defines the relationship between businesses and society at large. It goes beyond conventional notion that corporations are purely profit-oriented institutions highlighting the significance of incorporating social and environmental considerations into business strategies.

In today's world, consumers increasingly value companies that demonstrate a commitment to social responsibility and sustainability. By practicing CSR related activities businesses can help improve society, make positive differences in people's lives or even conserve our environment.

At its core corporate social responsibility entails ethical actions that go beyond legal obligations for the benefit of stakeholders who include employees customers community as well as environment around them.It includes diverse initiatives such as charity works environmental conservation employee welfare programs community outreach among others.

Implementing CSR practices can bring immense benefits to businesses. These may range from improved reputation/brand image, talent attraction and retention, customer loyalty increase to long term success and profitability. Additionally businesses that acknowledge their social responsibility tend to enjoy a better relationship with regulators, investors among others key stakeholders.

Adopting CSR requires strategic planning where the company's goals are aligned with its wider social impact objectives. Through integrating CSR into their overall business management strategies, organizations can effectively tackle societal challenges, contribute towards sustainable development and create shared value for all stakeholders.

The Role of Philanthropy in Corporate Social Responsibility

Among the dimensions of corporate social responsibility (CSR), philanthropy plays a central role in driving meaningful change and making a positive impact in communities. Enterprises can be agents of change and mitigate critical social issues through leveraging their resources and influence.

CSR's cornerstone is philanthropy that involves strategic giving as well as charity initiatives focused on addressing societal needs. It transcends normal business practices by supporting causes that resonate with a firm's values or objectives for the betterment of society at large.

Business can contribute to society through philanthropy by investing in education, health care, environmental conservation and community development. Philanthropy is capable of uplifting communities and bringing about transformational change either through financial contribution, in-kind donation or volunteering programs.

Besides, altruism as a part of CSR provides a chance for businesses to exhibit their commitment to social responsibility hence presenting their image better and promoting stakeholder goodwill. Through practicing philanthropy in active terms firms are able to create stronger bonds with workers, customers as well as the wider public and this eventually enhances loyalty and brand affinity.

In addition, the corporate impact of philanthropy goes beyond just managing reputation. Firms can help create a better business environment which eventually affects economic growth positively among other factors such as employees' wellbeing that contributes to the general improvement of society. Thus, when integrated into the fabric of an organization's operations, philanthropy has long-term sustainable development effects.

To conclude, philanthropy is an indispensable component of Corporate Social Responsibility because it drives transformative changes that have positive impacts on communities. Businesses can play a crucial role in ensuring social responsibility is upheld while also contributing towards creating a better future by leveraging on their resources and aligning their charitable endeavors with their core values.

Aligning Business Goals with Social Impact

Aligning business goals with social impact forms an integral part of corporate social responsibility. This means embracing practices that contribute to sustainability both for business and society at large. In fact, blending together social impact into its basic operation makes companies more human- oriented hence adding value to society.

Strategies for Effective Corporate Philanthropy

When it comes to corporate philanthropy companies need be methodical so that they achieve meaningful results which will last long after they are gone. By adopting effective strategies businesses can maximize the positive change they bring to society. The following will discuss some key strategies which could help improve the effectiveness of companies' philanthropic activities.

1 Embrace strategic giving

Strategic giving involves aligning philanthropic efforts with a company's core values, mission, and expertise. Focusing on areas that are closely related to their business where they can make the biggest difference, companies will ensure that their charitable acts are aimed and have significance. This approach not only allows the most cost-effective use of resources but also enhances the corporate image and influence.

2 Support social initiatives

Effective corporate philanthropy goes beyond monetary donations. Companies may employ their resources, capabilities or even networks to support social initiatives which resonate with their values and directly impact communities being served. They can thus engage non-profit organizations through provision of pro bono services, mentorship programs or collaborations for driving change in a sustainable way.

3 Form partnerships and collaborations

Collaboration with other organizations such as NGOs government agencies or community based groups would help amplify the effects of corporate acts of charity in the society . Partnerships formed by a corporation can therefore create an opportunity to contribute towards complex social issues more effectively using collective competences, connections and wealth. Such relationships do not only increase efficiency of benevolent actions but also cultivate a sense of shared responsibility thereby generating room for emerging solutions.

4 Measure and evaluate impact

To ensure that resources are used efficiently and to find out areas of improvement, it is important to measure and evaluate the impact of philanthropic initiatives. Consequently, businesses can understand the impact they make by setting clear goals, defining key performance indicators and tracking their progress to help them make informed decisions in their next philanthropic endeavors. Transparent reporting and communication about the impact achieved also enhances credibility and builds trust with stakeholders.

These strategies enable companies to elevate their philanthropy efforts from mere charity into strategic, impactful, and sustainable actions. Effective philanthropy combined with strategic giving allows organizations to create positive change that contributes towards society's betterment while building its own brand and reputation.

Employee Engagement and Volunteering

Employee engagement together with volunteering plays an integral part in enabling a firm's corporate social responsibility (CSR) initiatives have a positive social impact. Not only does encouraging employees to actively participate in community involvement programs benefit the communities thus served but also improves morale among the involved employees enhancing company reputation at large.

The Employee engagement programs provide opportunities for individuals' skills time as well as resources being applied towards meaningful projects addressing social issues. Employees can involve themselves in activities leaded them towards positive change through volunteering such causes.Corporate partnerships with non-profits can also be established as well as volunteer days organized among other initiatives which assist businesses promote employee engagement with respect to various aspects of the society.Employees become more connected both with their communities served by joint employer's support or any other form of award given by a company because any initiative makes everyone feel purposeful within this organization.

Personal growth on personal level occurs when engaged employees willingly volunteer. Volunteering allows individuals to develop new skills, build networks, and gain a deeper understanding of social issues all which may affect their career path positively hence increase job satisfaction generally.

In addition employee volunteering programmes contribute greatly towards having a good brand name for the company. Sharing stories of successes emanating from an employee based idea can inspire others and also show that a company is committed to making a difference. It also helps attract like-minded individuals who share same values and goals as the organization.

A social responsibility culture that extends to broader society is created by companies through employee engagement plus volunteering. As employees develop a sense of pride in their company's philanthropic endeavors, their engagement and dedication to their work increase, benefiting both the company and the communities it serves.

Partnerships and Collaborations for Greater Impact

Collaboration is key in today's complicated world. With regards to corporate social responsibility, partnerships and collaborations are important ingredients towards greater collective impact on the issue at hand. The businesses are able to combine efforts with non-profit organizations, government agencies among other shareholders hence they are able to put into practice good work done through their vast skills that they have acquired over some years.

Therefore, pooling resources and knowledge among companies help realize more effective solutions which are sustainable. In many cases, collaborations bring together people with different backgrounds thus thinking producing innovation as well creativity when solving complex societal issues. Through these strategic alliances businesses may be able to extend their initiatives reach resulting into more profound lasting positive change.

Driving Collective Impact Through Cross-Sector Collaboration

Collaborations involving businesses, nonprofits, and government agencies are necessary for driving collective impact. These partnerships can deal more broadly with complex social problems by teaming up together and leveraging on one another's strengths. For example, such projects could not only create jobs for say local farmers but also foster eco-friendly farming practices contributing to increased food security and economic liberation within the region.

Collaborations also serve as knowledge exchange platforms and capacity building initiatives that promote long-term sustainability as well as self-reliance in communities. When firms unite with nonprofit organizations along with other stakeholders it creates a web or connected organizations working towards a shared goal which multiples their impact many times over.

To Conclude, Partnerships And Collaborations Are Powerful Vehicles To Make Social Impact More High-impactful Endeavors. Therefore through this collaborative approach business can make an impact on society beyond what they would do individually alone. It is through strategic partnering across sectors whereby we can see collective action in the making rather than just something hoped for.

Measuring and Reporting Social Impact

In the contemporary corporate world, measuring and reporting social impact has become indispensable among CSR-committed companies. Companies quantify and evaluate the effects of their actions to gain insights into their journey so far helping them make informed decisions that will result into positive change.

It involves assessing the outcomes of social initiatives on key stakeholders such as employees, communities or environment by organizations. This goes beyond a simple accounting of financial contributions to include the broader social and environmental outcomes being targeted.

Businesses can also use frameworks such as Social Return on Investment (SROI) and Global Reporting Initiative (GRI) that are structured methodologies for assessing and reporting social and environmental performance that allow corporations to assess their initiatives from an all-rounded perspective taking into account both the qualitative as well as quantitative aspects of their impact.

As a result, the public disclosure is very important because it boosts credibility while ensuring that trust is maintained amongst stakeholders. When firms openly disseminate the results or progress achieved through their projects, they are demonstrating their commitment towards being accountable for their activities as well as showing responsible conduct in business. Social reports are placed on company websites, distributed among shareholders and available for general public so as to show transparency of the firm.

Moreover technology has played a key role in aiding measurement and reporting of social impact. With automated data collection systems, real-time monitoring tools and interactive dashboards, businesses easily capture this information making it flow more smoothly through internal pipelines. Thanks to these technological advancements, companies are able to track how far they have come towards realizing objectives whilst displaying visually appealing information about their societal significance in ways which simplify complex ideas into readily understandable ones.

Businesses which measure and communicate about the social impact of their initiatives are not only able to understand how effective they have been, but also inspire others to embrace corporate social responsibility. By generating transparent communication and data-driven insights, these organizations act as agents of change thereby spurring innovation and breeding collective commitment towards a better world.

Beyond Philanthropy: Fusing Social Responsibility into Business Operations

Corporate social responsibility (CSR) in today's fast-changing business environment no longer encompasses philanthropy alone. They are embracing the need for more than just traditional acts of charity, instead incorporating social responsibility in the main operations. This includes integrating sustainable practices throughout the value chain whereby such firms create positive societal effect while reaping benefits from operational integration.

Social responsibility is linked to operational integration since companies should harmonize their strategic objectives with sustainable practices. Businesses are able to build a more sustainable future by encompassing social and environmental concerns in their day-to-day activities thus increasing overall efficiency of operation as well. The incorporation of such things as eco-friendly manufacturing processes or other fair labour strategies mean that this is advantageous both for business and society.

One way of incorporating social responsibility into operations is through sustainable practices across the entire value chain. This involves sourcing materials sustainably, minimizing waste and emissions, and promoting ethical supply chain management among others. This ensures that at every stage sustainability is given priority so that products and services can have a positive environmental as well as social impact.

Moreover, operational integration refers to making stakeholders participants at all levels. Thus involving employees, customers, suppliers among others will help set up an environment where everyone feels socially responsible. Non-profit organizations, employee volunteer programs or even community engagement initiatives can facilitate this process.

This goes beyond conventional philanthropy; when social responsibility gets integrated into businesses it has far-reaching consequences for a community. In addition to this being good for society at large it also improves brand reputation leading to customer loyalty. An instance where consumers nowadays are increasingly aware of the environmental and social influences of what they buy, it becomes a company's strategic concern rather than a matter of choice.

Case Studies: Outstanding Corporate Social Responsibility Initiatives

In this section, case studies of some leading companies that have featured distinguished initiatives as part of their corporate social responsibility will be examined. These case studies further illustrate the innovative strategies these organizations use and the positive societal impact they achieved.

Unilever: Empowering Women through Skills Training

The significance of gender equality and women's empowerment is acknowledged by Unilever. To deal with this problem, the company has put in place a comprehensive skills training programme that targets women from disadvantaged communities. Through this program, women are equipped with skills in entrepreneurship, leadership and financial literacy among other areas. Consequently, these women have developed capability and confidence to establish small businesses thereby making valuable contributions to local economies while becoming socially empowered.

Unilever is also aware of the impact on the environment of traditional packaging materials, which is why they have been proactive in tackling this problem. As a result, they have introduced innovative and sustainable packaging solutions made from recycled substances and other ones that disintegrate naturally. The adoption of such eco-friendly practices has reduced their carbon footprint as well as underscored their dedication to preserving the environment. This has also encouraged many other firms to be part of this initiative while reducing plastic pollution towards a greener future.

Google: Education for All

Education should be available universally, and Google is committed to this goal. They have worked with local schools and nonprofit organizations to develop educational programs and offer support services for underprivileged neighborhoods. By these means, they managed to establish community learning centers stocked with modern technology facilities and teaching aids. Now children that previously had no access to good quality education can finally learn, grow up or follow their dreams.

Tesla: Renewable Energy for a Sustainable Future

With an urgent need for clean and renewable energy sources in mind, Tesla has invested heavily in renewable energy projects. They have installed solar cells as well as wind turbines capable of generating green power thus lessening dependence on conventional fuels while minimising greenhouse gas emissions into the atmosphere. In essence, it has not only ensured a more sustainable future but encouraged other ventures and people to embrace renewables thereby making our planet greener and cleaner than ever before.

These case studies illustrate the immense social impact that firms can make through their corporate social responsibility (CSR) efforts. They serve as models for others by implementing creative approaches and addressing societal issues, thus inspiring collective pursuits towards change.

Key Challenges and Future Opportunities

Today's business environment is fast changing, with many challenges facing businesses when it comes to corporate social responsibility (CSR) implementation by companies. One of these primary challenges involves navigating complexities of integrating CSR into running businesses without forsaking financial performance. This calls for careful planning alongside strategic decision making in order to balance sustainability and profitability.

Moreover, there are challenges in terms of effective measurement and reporting of social impact for businesses. There are frameworks and tools available, but this can be a daunting task of selecting the most appropriate ones as well as gathering accurate data. However, this challenge must be addressed for stakeholders to see transparency and accountability.

The Challenges:

Sustaining long-term engagement with CSR initiatives poses yet another significant challenge. For some organizations, getting consistent staff involvement is not easy particularly if it may not be directly related to their daily occupation responsibilities. Overcoming this challenge requires creating a culture of socially responsible behavior within the organization while also promoting employee participation through meaningful engagements.

Additionally, businesses must investigate their complete value chain on its social or environmental impacts; through collaboration with suppliers enforcing ethical sourcing methods or reducing its general carbon footprint. But due to complicated global supply chains as well as potential costs associated with sustainable practices, these implementations may prove difficult.

Future Opportunities and Trends:

However, there are several opportunities that firms have in embracing CSR despite these challenges. In fact, smart companies today realize that embedding CSR into their core operations facilitates innovation; improves the brand reputation and more importantly helps in attracting top talent into an organization so as to remain competitive.\" By aligning sustainability goals with business objectives, they can create positive social impact while also achieving long-term growth and success.

Looking ahead technology has been cited as an important factor in the future of CSR. With artificial intelligence (AI), data analytics and blockchain companies are able to measure their social impact, track supply chain sustainability and engage stakeholders in a whole new way. These technological advancements present opportunities for companies to improve their CSR strategies, increase transparency and cause significant change.

Additionally, there are future trends pointing towards a more holistic approach to CSR. More companies will address larger societal problems such as income inequality, diversity and inclusion, climate change among others. Including these issues in their CSR strategies contribute not only to positive impacts but also the long-term sustainability of both business and society.

As mentioned earlier, difficulties faced by organizations regarding implementing corporate social responsibility provide platforms for growth and innovation as well. By directly confronting these challenges and embracing forthcoming tendencies corporations can make positive social impacts that would facilitate sustainable development thereby building a better life for mankind.

Conclusion

Businesses need philanthropy integrated with corporate social responsibility to create positive social impact. Prioritizing philanthropic initiatives allows companies to be part of the solution while improving the society around them.

Corporate social responsibility surpasses financial goals and encompasses incorporating sustainable practices, aligning corporate ambitions with societal change and involving employees in charitable activities (GEOS, 2015). By means of strategic giving, alliances and partnerships businesses can use their resources and knowledge to enhance social impact as well as to affect deep-rooted transformations. Measuring and reporting on social impact improves transparency and accountability hence assisting companies in monitoring their progress and effectively communicating the results of their initiatives. Furthermore, embedding the philosophy of corporate philanthropy into core operations and embracing social responsibility principles are some of the ways organizations can develop sustainable business practices within an ethical framework.

In addition to this, it is important for corporations to face up challenges while still being open to new prospects that may arise as they move forward through the ever changing landscape of corporate social responsibility (CSR) and philanthropy. Through maintaining a focus on CSR, organizations can not only fulfill their responsibilities towards society but also make positive contributions towards society thus making it better place for everyone (Bolnick et al., 2012).

Chapter 33

The Ethical Composer: Integrity in Leadership

Welcome to Chapter 33 of "From Manager to Maestro: The Symphony of Good Management." In this chapter, we delve into the world of ethical leadership and the vital role that integrity plays in business. From the maestros of the corporate world to the virtuosos of corporate governance, this chapter explores the harmonious relationship between leadership, integrity, and success.

Picture this: It's a busy Monday morning, and the bustling streets are filled with professionals rushing to their offices. Among them is Sarah, a talented and respected marketing executive who leads a team of ambitious individuals. Known for her unmatched creativity and strategic thinking, Sarah's name has become synonymous with success in her industry.

As Sarah walks into her office building, she notices a discarded envelope on the ground. Being the conscientious person she is, she picks it up and is surprised to find a stack of confidential documents inside. The envelope, it turns out, belongs to a competitor, and the contents could potentially give Sarah's company an unprecedented advantage in the market.

Sarah faces a momentous decision—should she use the information to propel her company forward, or should she uphold her integrity and discard the envelope, ensuring fair play in the industry?

Integrity is the ethical compass that guides leaders like Sarah in making the right choices, even when the temptation to compromise is strong. It is the foundation upon which a successful business is built, inspiring trust, shaping corporate culture, and fostering ethical practices.

Join us as we explore the importance of integrity in business leadership and corporate governance. Discover the characteristics of ethical leaders, learn how to build a moral compass, and explore case studies of leaders who have led with integrity. Together, let's uncover the symphony of ethical leadership and its transformative power in shaping the future of business.

Understanding Ethical Leadership

In today's complex and ever-evolving business landscape, ethical leadership plays a pivotal role in shaping the success and reputation of organizations. Ethical leadership embodies a set of principles and values that guide leaders in making decisions that prioritize not only organizational interests but also the well-being of stakeholders at large.

At its core, ethical leadership is grounded in the principles of business ethics, which encompass the moral and ethical standards that guide conduct in the business world. Leaders who embrace ethical leadership understand the importance of upholding these standards, not only for legal compliance but also to build trust, establish credibility, and foster a positive organizational culture.

Values-based leadership is instrumental in creating a foundation of integrity within an organization. Leaders who exemplify values-based leadership are guided by a strong sense of purpose and core values that align with ethical principles. They demonstrate authenticity, transparency, and accountability, inspiring others to do the same.

Why is ethical leadership essential?

Ethical leadership serves as a compass that navigates the complex ethical challenges that leaders and organizations face. By embracing ethical leadership, businesses can establish a corporate culture rooted in integrity, employee well-being, and responsible decision-making.

Furthermore, ethical leadership contributes to the long-term sustainability and success of organizations. Companies that prioritize ethical behavior and values-based leadership are more likely to attract and retain top talent, build stronger relationships with stakeholders, and maintain a positive reputation.

In the next section, we will delve into the importance of integrity in the business world and highlight how ethical practices can safeguard an organization's reputation and foster long-term success.

The Importance of Integrity in Business

In today's competitive business landscape, integrity is not just a buzzword; it is an essential foundation for success. Ethical business practices rooted in integrity have become paramount, not only for fostering trust among stakeholders but also for effective reputation management.

Integrity serves as a guiding principle for businesses, ensuring that all decisions and actions are aligned with ethical standards and values. By prioritizing integrity, organizations can build a solid reputation, enhance customer loyalty, and attract top talent.

When businesses operate with integrity, they establish themselves as trustworthy and reliable partners, gaining the confidence of customers and clients. This leads to increased customer loyalty and positive word-of-mouth recommendations, ultimately contributing to long-term growth and profitability.

Furthermore, ethical business practices that embody integrity are critical in reputation management. With the advent of social media and online platforms, maintaining a positive reputation has never been more crucial. Any misstep or unethical behavior can quickly go viral, damaging a company's image and eroding trust among stakeholders.

By emphasizing integrity in their business operations, organizations can effectively navigate ethical challenges and mitigate potential reputational risks. They can proactively build resilience and credibility, effectively safeguarding their reputation.

Integrity is not a mere slogan but a powerful tool for sustainable business success. It creates a transparent and accountable organizational culture where employees are motivated to uphold high ethical standards. Ultimately, integrity becomes ingrained in the DNA of the company, permeating every level of the organization.

In conclusion, the importance of integrity in business cannot be overstated. It forms the bedrock of ethical business practices, which, in turn, contribute to effective reputation management. By prioritizing integrity, organizations can build trust, enhance their reputation, and position themselves as leaders in their respective industries.

Characteristics of Ethical Leaders

When it comes to ethical leadership, certain traits are vital to maintaining integrity in business. Honesty, transparency, and accountability are key characteristics that ethical leaders embody, setting them apart as role models in their field.

Honesty is the foundation of ethical leadership. Ethical leaders are truthful and forthcoming in their interactions, earning the trust and respect of their teams and stakeholders. By upholding honesty, ethical leaders create an environment where open communication and integrity thrive.

Transparency is another crucial trait that ethical leaders possess. They are transparent in their decision-making processes, ensuring that their actions align with ethical principles and are accessible to everyone involved. With transparency, ethical leaders foster a culture of trust and empower their teams to do the same.

Accountability is essential for ethical leadership. Ethical leaders take responsibility for their actions and decisions, both successes and failures. They hold themselves and others accountable for upholding ethical standards and contribute to the overall integrity of the organization.

Leading by Example

Ethical leaders demonstrate these traits in their everyday actions, serving as role models for their teams. By embodying honesty, transparency, and accountability, ethical leaders inspire others to follow suit and contribute to a culture of integrity in business.

Building a Moral Compass

Developing a strong moral compass is essential for individuals and organizations to navigate the complex landscape of business ethics. By embracing core values and prioritizing ethical decision-making, leaders can establish a foundation of integrity that guides their actions and shapes the culture of their businesses.

At its core, a moral compass is a set of deeply held beliefs and values that serve as a guide for ethical conduct. It reflects the principles and ideals that individuals and organizations stand for, providing a framework for making morally sound decisions in even the most challenging situations.

Defining and refining core values is a crucial component of building a moral compass. Core values are the fundamental principles that guide behavior and shape the culture of an organization. By clearly articulating and consistently living these values, leaders foster a culture of integrity that permeates all levels of the business.

Furthermore, ethical decision-making is a foundational aspect of building a moral compass. Leaders must demonstrate the ability to analyze complex situations, evaluate the potential impact of their choices, and make decisions that align with their core values. This process requires both critical thinking skills and a deep commitment to ethical principles.

By building a moral compass based on core values and ethical decision-making, individuals and organizations can navigate the ever-evolving ethical landscape with confidence and integrity. This serves as a powerful tool for establishing trust, fostering a positive reputation, and ultimately creating a culture that upholds the highest standards of ethics.

Nurturing Integrity in Corporate Culture

Creating a corporate culture that prioritizes ethics and fosters an ethical work environment is essential for nurturing integrity among employees and leaders. When an organization values integrity, it sets the tone for ethical decision-making and behavior throughout all levels of the company.

One key aspect of nurturing integrity in corporate culture is establishing clear expectations of ethical conduct. By defining and promoting a set of core values and ethical standards, organizations can create a foundation for employees to make ethically sound choices in their daily work.

A transparent and inclusive communication flow is also crucial in maintaining an ethical work environment. When employees feel heard and respected, they are more likely to speak up about unethical practices or concerns, ultimately contributing to the preservation of integrity.

H3: Leading by Example

Leadership plays a significant role in fostering integrity in corporate culture. Leaders who exemplify integrity through their actions and decisions set the standard for ethical conduct within the organization. When leaders align their words with their actions, they inspire trust and create an atmosphere where integrity is valued and celebrated.

H3: Encouraging Ethical Behavior

In addition to leading by example, organizations can encourage ethical behavior by establishing mechanisms and processes that promote integrity. This can include whistleblower protection policies, ethics training programs, and regular assessments of ethical practices. By providing resources and support, organizations empower employees to make ethical choices and reinforce the importance of integrity.

H3: Recognizing and Rewarding Integrity

Recognizing and rewarding individuals who demonstrate integrity can further reinforce its importance in corporate culture. By acknowledging employees who consistently make ethical decisions and act with integrity, organizations not only motivate and inspire others but also send a powerful message that upholding ethical principles is valued and recognized.

In summary, nurturing integrity in corporate culture is crucial for fostering an ethical work environment. By setting clear expectations, promoting transparent communication, leading by example, encouraging ethical behavior, and recognizing integrity, organizations can build a strong ethical foundation that supports the growth and success of both employees and the company as a whole.

Leading with Integrity: Case Studies

In this section, we delve into real-life case studies that highlight leaders who have demonstrated exceptional integrity in their business practices. These examples provide valuable insights and lessons for ethical leadership and serve as inspiration for fostering integrity in today's corporate world.

One notable case study is Patricia Williams, CEO of Global Solutions Inc. Despite facing pressure to cut corners and compromise on ethical standards in order to maximize profits, Williams remained steadfast in her commitment to integrity. She implemented transparency measures, ensuring that all business decisions were made with the utmost honesty and accountability. As a result, Global Solutions Inc. gained a reputation for ethical business practices and became a trusted industry leader.

Another inspiring example is Michael Johnson, founder of CleanTech Innovations. Johnson recognized the environmental impact of his company's operations and took decisive action to address it. He spearheaded initiatives to reduce carbon emissions and implement sustainable practices, demonstrating that ethical leadership goes beyond financial success and encompasses social and environmental responsibility.

These case studies demonstrate that leaders who prioritize integrity can achieve long-term success, build trust with stakeholders, and make a positive impact on society. By following their examples, aspiring leaders can navigate complex ethical challenges and create a culture of integrity within their organizations.

The Role of Ethics Training

In today's complex and fast-paced business landscape, the importance of ethics training cannot be overstated. Ethics training plays a crucial role in developing and enhancing the integrity of business leaders, equipping them with the necessary knowledge and skills to make ethical decisions in various professional situations.

Integrity education is the backbone of ethics training, as it provides individuals with a comprehensive understanding of moral values, principles, and standards that guide ethical behavior. Through integrity education, business leaders gain a deep appreciation for the significance of integrity in fostering trust, respect, and credibility within their organizations.

Ethical decision-making skills are another critical aspect of ethics training. With the rapid advancements in technology, globalization, and diverse stakeholder interests, leaders often face complex ethical dilemmas. By honing their ethical decision-making skills, leaders become better equipped to navigate challenging situations, identify potential risks, and choose the ethical course of action that upholds the highest standards of integrity.

Furthermore, ethics training provides a platform for leaders to engage in meaningful discussions and case studies that highlight real-world ethical challenges. By analyzing these scenarios, leaders develop a deeper understanding of the consequences of their actions and the impact they have on stakeholders and the overall reputation of the organization.

Ultimately, ethics training serves as a crucial foundation for fostering ethical cultures within organizations. It helps establish clear expectations for ethical behavior, promotes transparency, and provides ongoing support for leaders to uphold integrity in their daily operations and decision-making processes.

Overcoming Ethical Dilemmas

Addressing ethical dilemmas can be a daunting task for business leaders. These challenges require navigating the complex landscape of moral choices and making decisions that uphold ethical values and principles. In this section, we will explore strategies and approaches for overcoming ethical dilemmas and discuss the importance of moral courage in making ethically sound decisions.

Understanding Ethical Dilemmas

An ethical dilemma arises when a person is faced with a situation where two or more morally conflicting choices need to be made. These dilemmas may arise from conflicts between personal values, organizational policies, or societal expectations. Navigating such challenges requires a deep understanding of the ethical implications and the ability to balance competing interests.

Strategies for Overcoming Ethical Dilemmas

When confronted with an ethical dilemma, it is essential to approach the situation with clarity and a strong ethical framework. Here are some strategies that can aid in overcoming ethical dilemmas:

Seeking Guidance and Advice: Consulting mentors, colleagues, or ethical advisors can provide valuable insights and perspectives in navigating ethical challenges.

Analyzing Consequences: Assessing the potential outcomes and consequences of different decisions can help determine the most ethically responsible course of action.

Applying Ethical Decision-Making Models: Utilizing established ethical decision-making frameworks, such as the Utilitarian or Deontological approach, can provide structure and guidance in complex situations.

Considering Stakeholder Impact: Evaluating the interests and perspectives of all stakeholders involved can assist in making decisions that uphold fairness and promote ethical behavior.

Reflecting on Core Values: Reflecting on personal and organizational core values can serve as a compass in navigating ethical dilemmas and making choices aligned with these values.

The Importance of Moral Courage.

Moral courage is the strength and determination to act ethically and make difficult decisions even in the face of adversity or potential negative consequences. It involves standing up for what is right and staying committed to ethical principles, even when it might be easier to compromise integrity. Developing moral courage is essential for leaders to overcome ethical dilemmas and uphold their moral compass.

By adopting these strategies and embracing moral courage, business leaders can navigate ethical challenges with integrity and make decisions that align with their core values. Overcoming ethical dilemmas is a vital step towards fostering a culture of ethical conduct and building a foundation of trust and respect within organizations.

Regaining Trust: Restoring Integrity

After a breach of integrity, rebuilding trust is a challenging yet essential task for businesses. Restoring integrity requires a strategic approach that addresses the damage caused and implements effective reputation management strategies.

One of the key steps in trust rebuilding is acknowledging the wrongdoing and accepting responsibility. This demonstrates transparency and a genuine commitment to restoring integrity. By openly addressing the breach, businesses have the opportunity to regain trust and rebuild their reputation.

Alongside acknowledging the issue, it is critical to take immediate corrective actions. Implementing measures to prevent similar breaches in the future shows a commitment to doing right by customers, employees, and stakeholders. Transparency, accountability, and corrective actions are all crucial components in restoring integrity.

Additionally, businesses can rebuild trust by prioritizing open and honest communication. Transparently sharing the steps taken to rectify the breach and actively engaging with stakeholders promotes trust and assures them that the organization is dedicated to maintaining integrity.

Reputation Management Strategies

Effective reputation management strategies play a pivotal role in rebuilding trust. While the specific approach may vary depending on the circumstances, there are several key strategies to consider:

Develop a proactive communication plan: This includes crafting messages that effectively communicate the organization's commitment to integrity and outlining the steps taken to rectify the breach.

Engage with stakeholders: Actively seek feedback and address concerns from customers, employees, and external partners. This demonstrates a willingness to listen and learn from past mistakes.

Monitor and respond to online reputation: Maintain a vigilant approach to monitoring digital platforms and promptly address any negative comments or reviews.

Invest in ongoing training: Provide employees with training programs that emphasize ethical decision-making and reinforce the importance of integrity in the organization.

Showcase positive actions: Highlight initiatives that reflect the organization's commitment to integrity, such as participation in community service or partnerships with ethical organizations.

By implementing these reputation management strategies and actively working towards restoring integrity, businesses can regain the trust of their stakeholders, rebuild their reputation, and pave the way for a more ethical and sustainable future.

Building Sustainable Ethics Programs

In today's ever-evolving business landscape, organizations must prioritize sustainable ethics to ensure long-term integrity and maintain a positive reputation. By developing and implementing ethical programs, companies can establish a strong foundation built on ethical principles and practices.

One key aspect of building sustainable ethics programs is the integration of sustainable practices into everyday operations. This includes promoting environmentally friendly initiatives, such as reducing waste and carbon emissions, and supporting fair trade and social responsibility.

Another crucial element is the establishment of clear ethical guidelines and codes of conduct. These guidelines outline the expected behaviors and ethical standards for all employees, from top-level executives to entry-level staff. By clearly defining expectations, organizations can promote a culture of integrity and accountability.

Furthermore, regular ethics training and education play a vital role in maintaining sustainable ethics within an organization. By providing ongoing training sessions, workshops, and resources that address relevant ethical dilemmas and decision-making, companies can foster a deep understanding of ethical principles and equip employees with the necessary tools to navigate complex situations.

Implementing a system of continuous monitoring and evaluation is essential for the long-term success of ethics programs. This allows organizations to identify potential areas of improvement, address any unethical practices or behaviors promptly, and reinforce the importance of ethical conduct.

Lastly, it is crucial for organizations to promote transparency and accountability throughout all levels of the company. This can be achieved through regular communication channels, open-door policies, and anonymous reporting mechanisms. By encouraging employees to speak up about ethical concerns without fear of retaliation, organizations can foster a culture that values integrity and upholds ethical standards.

In conclusion, building sustainable ethics programs is essential for organizations committed to long-term integrity. By integrating sustainable practices, establishing ethical guidelines, providing ongoing training, and promoting transparency and accountability, companies can cultivate a culture of ethics and ensure their continued success in today's ethical business landscape.

Conclusion and Reflections

Throughout this chapter, we have explored the concept of integrity in leadership and its crucial role in shaping successful businesses. Our discussions have focused on ethical leadership, the importance of integrity in business, the characteristics of ethical leaders, and the process of building a moral compass.

Integrity serves as a guiding principle that fosters trust, transparency, and accountability within an organization. Ethical leaders, through their honesty and commitment to ethical values, inspire others to uphold the highest standards of integrity in their actions and decision-making.

Reflection on the various case studies presented has further emphasized the powerful impact integrity can have on an organization's reputation and long-term success. Whether it is navigating ethical dilemmas, regaining trust after a breach, or developing sustainable ethics programs, the unwavering commitment to integrity remains a cornerstone of effective leadership.

In conclusion, integrity plays a fundamental role in establishing a culture of ethical behavior, respect, and trust within organizations. By embodying integrity in leadership, businesses can create an environment that cultivates ethical decision-making, fosters employee engagement, and upholds the highest standards of corporate governance.

Chapter **34**

The Rhapsody of Risks: Risk Management and Mitigation in Business

Picture a busy city street, alive with life's beat and the melodies of multitudinous voices and diverse dreams resonating in harmony. In the same way that every note in an orchestra contributes critically to a masterpiece, uncertainties and dangers are inherent in the business environment. They are unchecked chords which can either lift companies to great heights or throw them down like discordant refrains.

In this chapter, we analyze the absorbing "Rhapsody of Risks," an exploration into how risk management is conducted as both art and science in today's business world. We find out strategies that help companies overcome complexities of risks resulting into opportunities for growth as well as success.

From identifying and assessing risks to implementing proactive measures and employing reactive approaches, we uncover the evolving symphony of risk management practices. By integrating modern technology with sectorial insights, firms may blend a melodious composition harmonizing between hazard and return.

Join us on this musical journey as we unravel the secrets behind the symphony of risk management and mitigation, unlocking the melody that resonates with long-term sustainability and triumph in the ever-changing business world.

Understanding Risk Management in Business

For businesses wishing to prosper amid uncertainty, it is important they comprehend how risk management operates within their organizations. Risk management involves processes aimed at identifying potential risks associated with activities or operations carried out by an organization; assessing these risks; determining acceptable risks levels; making informed decisions on such risks; monitoring identified risks; designing appropriate internal control systems; taking corrective actions where necessary; reviewing results achieved from undertaken strategies against organizational goals on periodical basis (Harrington & Otieno 2012).

Within the realm of risk management, businesses must first strive to gain a comprehensive understanding of the risks they face. These can be characterized by internal factors such as financial risks or market volatility while external factors include regulatory changes or technological advancements among others (Ling 2013).

Once these have been identified, firms should then assess them in terms of their likelihood and potential impact. By doing so, it will be possible to know the seriousness of each risk and this allows firms to prioritize on the mitigation process (Levine 2013). This prioritization enables businesses to allocate their resources towards the most important areas thereby limiting vulnerabilities that may arise while at the same time minimizing negative outcomes.

For instance, businesses must plan for risks by developing procedures that will mitigate these challenges, identify early warning indicators for these risks, put control measures in place to limit impacts of such events as well as come up with crisis intervention plans (Malmi & Brown 2008). Proactive enterprises can detect risks before they get out of hand through actions like this saving their reputation alongside financial status.

Additionally, business risk management is a continuous process which must be regularly evaluated so as to ensure its effectiveness within changing organizational environments. This attitude ensures a constant update of existing strategies depending on altering market patterns hence remaining dynamic (Ehring 2012).

To sum up, understanding risk management in business is vital for companies working in uncertain conditions and aiming at long-term excellence. Through assessing and identifying these elements business can address them beforehand thus reducing any negative influence while maximizing on the opportunities available. Thereby using sound risk management strategies and frequently monitoring and adjusting them will help keep organizations resilient and ahead in an unpredictable business environment.

The Importance Of Risk Mitigation

For successful and sustainable businesses, risk mitigation is very crucial. Minimizing the chances and effects of possible risks that may threaten smooth operations as well as profit making depends on effective implementation of various risk mitigation measures.

Risk mitigation entails recognizing, assessing and acting proactively on these challenges before they become significant problems. Businesses can safeguard their assets, reputation and financial well-being through a proactive approach to risk management.

One of the key reasons why it is important for firms to engage in risk mitigation is because if this risks are not addressed there can be huge consequences. Such may include financial losses, legal liabilities, damage on brand reputation and even close down of business.

In this regard, companies can also reduce the level or magnitude of potential threats by introducing certain strategies aimed at mitigating it. This includes creating or establishing wide-ranging risk management plans that target the peculiar hazards faced by a corporation.

Some of these strategies include;

Diversification: Allocating investments to different markets/industries so that an entity does not heavily rely on only one source

Insurance:

1. Transferring certain risks associated with finance to insurance companies through policies covering specified types like property destructions, liability claims or cyber attacks.
2. Contingency Planning: Developing contingency plans so that quick decisions can be made when facing potential risks. They outline steps to be taken whenever any danger occurs reducing impact on normal business activities.
3. Regular Training and Education: Continuous training programs for personnel to enhance their consciousness about perils such as those associated with employment contracts or data secrecy laws.

Businesses should adopt strategies for identifying potential hazards in a bid to ensure they remain relevant among dynamically changing situations involving commerce enterprises together with emerging threats.Risk management protocols ought to be constantly updated hence staying relevant in business landscape."By continuously evaluate and update their risk management plans'' Consequently, firms can ably maneuver through impending dangers while availing opportunities for growth purposes.

Summary

Assessing Risks in Business

In the risky world of business, thorough evaluation is essential when it comes to managing risks. Informed decisions can be made by businesses on their mitigation strategies by understanding and evaluating potential risks.

There are several approaches and models used to assess the level of risk within a business organization. One popular way is quantitative based analysis where numerical values are assigned to different threats in relation to their probabilities and impact. This enables prioritization of risks and allocation of resources accordingly.

On the other hand, qualitative methods rely more on personal judgment as inputs for determining risks, which consider factors such as experience and knowledge levels among other things. They generally provide a holistic view about hazards and may be useful especially where accurate figures about them cannot be found easily.

The choice between these two approaches is not so important but what matters most is conducting comprehensive risk assessments. Since this helps identify potential threats, areas of weaknesses as well as possible improvements. Consequently, an entity will develop a comprehensive risk management strategy that will help address all its specific needs in operations.

Moreover, risk assessments are important in informing decision-making processes. Businesses can weigh the potential rewards against the possible negative outcomes by understanding the potential risks associated with a particular course of action which helps make strategic decisions that align with the organization's risk appetite and long-term objectives.

All in all, one of the most important steps in any risk management process is assessing business risks. It assists businesses to anticipate potential challenges, minimize uncertainties and retain competitiveness within today's dynamic business environment.

Proactive strategies for Risk Management

Companies striving for sustained success must therefore develop proactive strategies for managing risk in the ever – changing fast paced business environment. By identifying potential risks early on and combating them head on through preventive actions, organizations can minimize their impact while maximizing growth opportunities.

An integral part of proactive risk management is developing an understanding and defining risk appetite. Risk appetite refers to how much risk an organization is willing to take in order to achieve its strategic objectives. When organizations define their boundaries for tolerable losses, they can align their enterprise wide risk management (ERM) strategy with overall goals thus ensuring that right balance between reward and risk is struck when making informed decisions.

Another proactive measure for managing risks entails conducting regular assessment of such perils. Proactive identification may involve continuously evaluating uncertain or emerging situations that might have an effect on the company's operations (O'Connell & Cuthbertson 2006). As a result, entities are able to outperform competition because there exists a critical focus on dealing with vulnerabilities that may hinder progress.

Scenario planning

Scenario planning is another way through which companies can be proactive regarding handling various kinds of risks encountered along the way. This implies that groups create hypothetical situations based on different variables then analyze what these might mean if they were applied to their enterprises or industry as such; this provides scenarios for thought whereby leaders identify inherent dangers (Nieuwenhuizen, Rossouw & Barkhuizen 2008). Thus, they can engage in effective risk management by developing alternative plans and countering unforeseen events.

Effective internal control systems are also key in proactive risk management. Organizations can avoid risks by putting into place clear policies and procedures to minimize the probability of risks occurring as well as correct any departures from established frameworks immediately. Regular monitoring, review, and assessment of these essentials bring out any gaps or weakness that may have been overlooked thus allowing for preventive action.

Finally, the creation of a risk aware culture within the organization is important to ensure proactive risk management. Employee empowerment through open communication channels will aid in disseminating comprehensive training materials involving identification and reporting on hazards (Daft 2009). This means that when everyone knows what his/her part is in relation to risk handling hereafter, the whole entity becomes more adaptable to potential problems hence less susceptible to possible risks.

Therefore a business with a growth mindset should take proactive strategies towards risk management. These strategies enable firms anticipate and deal with probable dangers thus building long-term success foundation in present day's dynamic corporate environment.

Reactive Approaches to Risk Management

This calls for reactive approaches aimed at minimizing the impact of such unexpected events once they occur. Contingency planning and crisis management therefore become imperative aspects during this period so as to reduce consequences while maintaining continuous operations.

Contingency planning refers to recognizing possible risks and coming up with predetermined action plans that are to be used in their effective management. This way, an organization can minimize disruptions caused by different scenarios hence ensuring that its operations continue even during a tough time.

Crisis management is also an important part of reactive risk management. So, when something unexpected happens, well-defined crisis management strategies enable organizations to react quickly and efficiently. Amongst others, these include mobilization of resources, communication with stakeholders and implementing measures to protect the reputation of the organization.

The use of reactive approaches to risk management helps firms navigate through challenges more effectively, safeguard their assets as well as reduce potential negative impacts on their operations and stakeholders. Meanwhile a combination of both proactive and reactive strategies leads to a comprehensive framework for risk management thus guaranteeing business resilience and long-term success.

Technology in Risk Management

Technological advancements empower businesses in managing risks more effectively. This implies that companies now have access to streamlined processes for carrying out risk assessment exercises including monitoring as well as response.

One key advantage of technology in risk management is providing real-time data & analytics. By so doing, it enables businesses make sound decisions based on accurate information hence embracing proactive risk management strategies.

There are different software solutions specifically designed for addressing risk requirements. Allowing them undertake such functions like assessing probability or ranking allows organizations identify which issues need attention most among others.

Risk Communication and Data Visualization

Technology also assists in facilitating the communication about risks within an enterprise setting. For instance, using data visualization tools assists managers portray hard-to-understand information meaningfully therefore allowing stakeholder understand better potential implications those might bring about if not properly addressed.

Similarly, it helps automate tracking and reporting indicators of exposure at peril level electronically. In this case whereby certain thresholds are surpassed notifications can be triggered thereby giving rise to quick decision making with regards to new threats being realized across entities' environment.

To sum up, technology is a key enabler of effective risk management and mitigation in business. This is why today's organizations can digitize their risk assessment, improve risk communication and act to potential threats with great agility. For the long-term success and resilience, businesses have to adopt technology in their risk management strategies as they continue to face changing risks.

10.Risk Management in Specific Business Sectors

Every business sector has its unique challenges when it comes to risk management. To effectively handle them, businesses need an understanding of these industry-specific risks so that highly tailored approaches can be developed. Let us see how various sectors utilize varying approaches to risk management.

11.Risk Management in The Financial Services Industry

Risk management in the financial services industry is critical for stability maintenance and asset preservation. Market volatility, credit defaults, regulatory compliance issues and cyber security are some of them. Financial institutions employ comprehensive methodologies for identifying, analyzing and mitigating these specific risks.

12.Managing Operational Risks in Manufacturing

In manufacturing industry there is a wide range of operational risks from supply chain disruptions to equipment failure, quality control issues like workplace safety crises. Robust contingency plans implementation, preventive maintenance protocols establishment, product quality control guaranteeing together with strict safety standards observance are only a few features of efficient risk management in this sphere.

13.Addressing Regulatory and Legal Risks in Healthcare

The healthcare sector operates in a high regulated environment, which make regulatory compliance and legal risks major concerns. Health care providers are obligated to follow complicated rules, secure patient information, and mitigate against possible malpractices. Risk management in this industry focuses on the development of robust compliance programs, robust cyber security measures and consistent documentation.

Risk Mitigation in Technology Sector

The fast-paced and ever-changing technology sector is exposed to dangers such as data breaches, patent thefts, disruptive innovations and rapidly changing markets conditions. Risk mitigation practices for the technology industry include adoption of advanced cyber security measures; conducting regular vulnerability assessments; and remaining agile in anticipation of new threats or opportunities.

Managing Environmental Risks in Energy Industry

Among some environmental risks that energy sector faces include natural calamities, climate change and emissions regulations as well as sustainability requirements. In this context risk management involves implementing stringent safety protocols; diversifying energy sources; investing into renewable types of energy; monitoring and responding to potential environmental impacts.

As companies operate within their respective sectors they should not forget that risk management strategies are part of their overall business approach hence an integral component. Companies can navigate these challenges effectively by understanding industry-specific hazards. Therefore it is important for firms to properly identify relevant industry risks so that mitigation strategies can be better tailored for greater resilience going forward.

Implementing Monitoring Risk Management Plans

Once a comprehensive risk management plan has been developed the next most crucial step is its implementation as well as monitoring. This ensures that it is effectively put into action while responding to any emerging risks through regular evaluation procedures. The process of implementing risk management plans includes various strategic steps designed to minimize potential threats while maximizing opportunities for successful business transactions.

Implementing Risk Management Plans

Implementing risk management plans requires a systematic approach involving collaboration at all organizational levels. Typically this process involves:

Assign responsibilities: Designate individuals or groups responsible for specific risk management strategies/tactics.

Allocate resources: Provide the necessary resources including funding, technology and personnel to effectively execute risk management plans.

Communicate the plan: Ensure stakeholders are aware of the risk management plan and understand their responsibilities regarding its implementation.

Training and awareness: Undertake training programs as well as awareness campaigns so that employees are educated about the value of risk management and what specific actions they should take.

Embedding risk management within processes: incorporating risk control into existing business systems such as project management, procurement or decision making frameworks.

Implementing risk management plans will help companies gain more resilience while minimizing possibilities of risks occurring and their impacts. However, these strategies can only be effective if continuously monitored and assessed.

Monitoring Risk Management Plans

Monitoring risk management plans involves regular evaluation and review to ensure their ongoing effectiveness. This process includes:

Evaluate indicators of risks: Monitor key risk indicators that show whether possible risks are being managed efficiently and identify if there is any new one that emerged.

Review action items: Review the progress on mitigation actions proposed in the plan for adequacy purposes.

Periodic assessments:: Conduct periodic assessments to identify shifts in the risk landscape with a view to adjusting accordingly the RM plan

Stakeholder engagement: stokeholders should participate in monitoring for feedback gathering , gaps identification , etc which would ensure compliance with organizational objectives .

Documenting lessons learned : Documenting and analyzing lessons learned from previous risks/incidents in order to consistently improve on RM strategies .

Businesses can only remain ahead of risks by consistently monitoring and reviewing their risk management plans. They will be able to make informed decisions that will mitigate potential risks.

Future Perspectives in Risk Management within Business World

The future of risk management is extremely significant given the complexities associated with business operations like those mentioned above. Therefore, reacting to and adopting new ways of assessment as well as mitigation are going to be necessary.

Technology is one of the key drivers that influence the future of risk management. Modernized software and tools are helping streamline risk identification process thus enabling businesses to survey and respond on real-time basis. From data analytics platforms to artificial intelligence-powered risk modeling, technology has brought about a revolution in the field of managing risks.

Moreover, in the days to come, a more proactive and forward-looking approach will be needed for effective control over potential threats. Businesses should proactively seek out & anticipate danger. This will require holistic risk management frameworks that assess risks across the entire organizational landscape.

Another key aspect of the future of risk management is the integration of risk management into strategic decision-making processes. Astute businesses will view risk management as a strategic advantage, incorporating risk considerations into every aspect of their operations, from new product development to market expansion. By doing so, they can not only enhance their ability to navigate uncertainties but also identify new opportunities for growth.

Chapter **35**

Presto Change-o: Agile Management and the Ability to Pivot

Chapter 35 of "From Manager to Maestro: The Symphony of Good Management" welcomes you. We shall be exploring agile management in this chapter and how good managers can pivot in today's dynamic business environment. To start off, let me tell you a story that shows the importance of being able to adapt and change when faced with uncertainties.

Imagine it is a sunny day and you are on your way to the beach with your family. Your car is packed full with snacks, shades, and beach towels. This trip has been something you had waited for weeks, and nothing could ruin your mood. However, as you sing along with your favorite songs while driving on the highway suddenly there comes a loud thud which makes you startled because it is then that you realize that one of the tires has gone flat.

Disappointment and frustration come over you like a flood as your heart sinks down. Rather than wallowing in the setback however, I take a deep breath before springing into action. You reach out for your phone and make a call requesting roadside assistance even as you drive safely towards the side of the road whereupon while waiting for help to arrive; it dawns on you that everything has suddenly changed hence necessitating adaptation.

This incident compares well with many other everyday businesses challenges wherein companies go on certain paths equipped with plans and strategies just like yours was a planned trip to the beach. Success does not always manifest itself smoothly though; what separates between greatness an ordinary achievement is what we do when confronted by unforeseen circumstances...pivot—quickly but effectively.

That is where Agile Management comes into play; Organizations can create adaptability, innovation and resilience through embracing agility principles. Agility allows businesses to be more nimble: reacting faster more accurately in case of market shifts or customer needs change (Cadle et al., 2010). Agile management allows businesses to respond quickly to changes in markets and customer preferences better than ever before. Agile management is like a presto change-o that turns challenges to growth opportunities.

The next sections will delve into detail regarding agile management, the art of pivoting and its numerous benefits. This chapter will provide you with details on how to implement agile strategies and develop a mindset for pivoting besides overcoming difficulties to help you steer your business towards success.

So, are you ready for the power of "presto change-o" and realize the magic behind Agile Management? Let's get started!

Understanding Agile Management

Traditional management approaches may no longer work in today's fast-paced, dynamic business environment. It is here that agile management steps in. Agile management is an innovative approach which emphasizes flexibility, collaboration and innovation to enable businesses thrive in rapidly changing environment.

Unlike traditional management that usually follows rigid hierarchical structures and linear processes, agile management espouses flexibility and continuous improvement. This creates an enabling environment where teams can react swiftly upon market shifts or any demand from customers hence nurturing creativity within them as well as proactive problem solving culture.

The central principles of agility are iterative development, frequent communication and decentralized decision-making. Cross functional teams are formed where people with diverse specialties can collaborate together providing holistic solutions over problems as well as generating new ideas since there are different perspectives brought together through such diversity (Cadle et al., 2010).

Agile's adaptability is one of the most important merits that it has. It means using evaluation and reflection on a regular basis to cause changes in tactics and strategies by teams. This repetitive nature enables businesses to remain agile in dynamic markets reducing chances of being overtaken.

Another strength of an agile management style is its concentration on novelty. Agile management promotes experimentation and learning at all levels so as to stimulate new ideas and solutions from teams. Continuous feedback loops facilitate quick learning, iteration, and improvement that leads to high-quality products and services

To sum up, in terms of business administration, agility offers refreshing insights into the philosophy which gives priority to adaptability, cooperation as well as innovation. By adopting agile principles, companies can position themselves for success given the ever-changing business landscape.

Embracing Change: The Art of Pivoting

The ability to pivot is critical for success in today's fast-paced and fluid world of business. As markets change and customer needs evolve rapidly, businesses must be able to respond quickly.

In order not only to embrace change but also have flexibility when it comes to pivoting in times that demand it, agile business management will require one's involvement with early warning systems.This involves being proactive, responsive, open-minded while constantly scanning the environment making strategic decisions geared towards addressing emerging challenges as well taking advantage of the available opportunities.

Pivoting requires having a culture within an organization that fosters innovation and leaning toward change.Pivot means reviewing what you have done critically such as strategy process or product adjustments if necessary.

To stay nimble enough for different things like launching new products or services or trying out new markets or even reimagining the entire model upon which your company operates.Agility is key here since it allows managers to keep an eye on their target market always while daring some extraordinary moves occasionally.

By embracing change through the art of pivoting, businesses get ahead. They are swift in responding to emerging trends, adapt their strategies to fit customer needs and stay ahead of competitors.

In this section, we will provide several advantages that relate to agile management as well as pivot to businesses. They are crucial for long-term success in today's ever changing business world that can be summarized as enhanced innovation and making better decisions.

The Benefits of Agile Management and Pivoting

Agile management along with the ability to pivot are essential requirements for organizations operating in today's fast-paced competitive business environment. The numerous benefits associated with the adoption of these practices forms a major part in the success of any organization in the long run.

Improved Decision-Making

Collaborative and iterative approach is encouraged by agile management towards decision-making. By involving various departments within an organization as well as other experts, diverse ideas can be explored thus coming up with better decisions. Hence better outcomes can be achieved thus increasing the likelihoods of achieving strategic objectives.

Enhanced Productivity

Some methodologies such as Scrum or Kanban emphasize on flexible methods, efficiency and continuous improvement by which they manage them.Agile teams break down project tasks into small iterations and utilize visual management tools so that workflows become streamlined, bottlenecks eliminated while productivity goes up. This enables organizations deliver products and services more efficiently improving on quality.

Fostered Innovation

Creativity, adaptability, learning from failures are all necessary elements for fostering a culture of innovation that supports employees' taking risks so they can come up with new ideas.Companies use creative ideas given by development team members to produce innovative products/services.This drives product innovations leading companies into industry leadership.

Adaptability to Change

Business environments are ever changing and therefore organizations must be able to respond quickly in order to stay competitive. In the face of changing market dynamics, customer needs and emerging trends, agile management and the ability to pivot give businesses both the tools and mindset they need to respond effectively. By being flexible and embracing change, they can seize opportunities while mitigating any potential threats.

Long-Term Business Success

Ultimately, there are many benefits of agile management and pivoting which contribute to long-term business success. Organizations could build a sustainable competitive advantage by making better decisions that increase their efficiency, innovation attractiveness and adaptability. This helps them navigate through dynamic business landscapes retaining customer loyalty; attracting top talent as well as achieving strategic goals.

Implementing Agile Management Strategies

Furthermore, in this rapidly evolving business environment adopting agile management strategies is essential for organizations that want to remain competitive despite changing market behavior. It ensures businesses operate with agility and adaptability hence fostering innovation over time leading to long term success.

To have an effective agile management strategy, cross-functional teams should be created where each team member brings different skills sets. These collaborative teams consist of members with varied backgrounds thus helping instill creativity culture as well as promoting holistic problem-solving approach. When market changes happen these teams can respond swiftly together with delivering value across their shared efforts.

Another crucial aspect is implementing iterative processes whereby projects are broken down into smaller manageable tasks called sprints. The principle of iterative development is emphasized in agile management where projects are divided into small sprints. This allows for regular feedback loops enabling early identification of problems, incremental improvements or refinements thereby enhancing continuous learning within a team based on real-time insights.

Continuous feedback loops form an integral part when implementing agile management strategies. Regular communication channels will enable teams share information so that they can identify bottlenecks while making informed decisions based on data collected. It promotes collaboration culture between employees thus increasing transparency among staff working towards common purpose.

There has to be a change in mindset within the organization when implementing agile management strategies. It means that people must be willing to embrace changes and exercise experimentation as well as learning. In this regard, leaders should create an environment that fosters innovation by instilling ownership spirit within the employees.

By utilizing agile management strategies, businesses can navigate the challenges of today's volatile business landscape. This encourages adaptability, promotes innovation and ensures organizations are ready to take up opportunities in times of uncertainty.

Developing a Pivoting Mindset

Pivoting and adapting are important for success in today's fast-paced business world. For leaders as well as employees it is important to develop a pivoting mindset which allows them to accept uncertainties, embrace change and take new opportunities. Organizations can thrive amidst evolving challenges if they develop some key traits while fostering resilience culture and embracing experiments.

The Importance of Embracing Change

Embracing change is the most paramount aspect when developing a pivoting mindset. In business change is inevitable hence those who try to resist experience setbacks eventually. On the other hand, individuals who proactively embrace such changes will always be ahead of market curve by anticipating shifts and responding accordingly. Therefore, instead of fearing it, recognizing change becomes an agent of growth and innovation.

Cultivating Resilience

A resilient person is also an essential quality of a changeable mindset. It consists of the capacity to rebound from disappointments, soldier on in the midst of problems, and maintain an optimistic viewpoint. By having resilience, both individuals and organizations can better navigate through uncertain times and evolve to fit into new circumstances. Leaders are able to lead with confidence due to resilience while teams remain motivated even when they face adversity.

Promote Experimentation and Learning Culture

On the other hand, a flexible attitude entails embracing experimentalism and lifelong learning. Accordingly, staff members should be encouraged to take calculated risks while generating novel ideas that have been learned from successes as well as failures. By developing a work environment where innovation is highly appreciated and learning is well rewarded, organizations can create a more agile workforce which adapts easily to changes. As such, this experimentation culture allows firms quickly iterate their strategies resulting in better decision making process as well as increased competition.

Developing a pivoting mindset never ends; instead it becomes an on-going process that requires leaders themselves to be at the forefront by providing support systems for people or groups within them who would embrace those changes develop resilience and craft cultures that promote experimentalism and knowledge sharing. Organizations that possess strong pivoting mindsets have high degrees of self-confidence enabling them steer through dynamic business environments suspending vagueness.

Overcoming Challenges in Agile Management and Pivoting

For companies implementing agile management practices coupled with successful business pivot points may present several challenges Nonetheless there are ways in which these hurdles can be overcome hence leading seamlessly towards agile businesses transformations.

Resistance to Change Is One of the Major Challenges In Agile Management

One major opposition faced by agile management is resistance to change Some organisations are used to traditional approaches in management thus may not be willing to adopt a more dynamic approach This hindrance could however be eliminated if proper change management techniques were applied including efficient communication networks affiliate relations outlining benefits of being Agile business model as well as a Pivot that may secure the approval of concerned parties.

Resistance to change is one of the major challenges in agile management. Several organizations are comfortable with traditional managing techniques and may be reluctant to adapt a more flexible approach. To address this issue, suitable change management methods should be implemented including effective communication and engagement with stakeholders. By specifying the benefits of agile management and pivoting, firms can provide incentives for buying in and promote smoother implementation.

The other obstacle is organizational structure and processes Traditional hierarchal structures might hinder the agility which is required in agile management For proper implementation there will be need for breaking down silos while fostering cross-functional collaboration Besides, streamlining their operations by eliminating unnecessary steps, adopting modern technology facilitating knowledge sharing are important considerations that companies need to look at so as to have flexible systems

Also, because of how fast-paced business landscape usually presents itself keeping alignment as well as prioritization may be challenging This requires a strong project management framework where priorities are set out clearly, goals identified while resources allocated effectively In addition, frequent communication among team members can help identify any roadblocks or misunderstandings that could exist.

Additionally, businesses often find it hard to respond promptly to market changes and customer preferences. To pivot successfully therefore entails thorough understanding of the target market, competitor analysis on a continuous basis as well as monitoring industry trends These old strategies must be abandoned by firms who should also dare embrace new opportunities even if they involve calculated risks.

In conclusion adversity is part of life but overcoming it during agile management and pivoting is what makes businesses competitive. By addressing resistance to change; restructuring organizational processes; maintaining alignment; embracing market dynamics organizations can go through these impediments unlocking flexibility; innovation resilience in their business operations.

Case Studies: Agile Management and Successful Pivots

This section will examine real life examples of organizations that have adopted the principles of agile management and made strategic pivots that were successful. We can gain useful insights from these case studies which can be applied to different business settings.

Case Study 1: Apple Inc.

Apple Inc. is famous for its use of agile management strategies to effect successful changes in direction. A good example is the company's shift from being a computer manufacturer to becoming a world leader in consumer electronics. Adopting an agile approach, Apple was able to identify the growth in demand for portable gadgets and make rapid changes to the product mix by introducing iconic products like iPhone and iPad.

Case Study 2: Netflix

Netflix, a game-changer in entertainment industry, also provides another powerful case study. Their agile management practices made them realize the change in consumer preferences towards streaming services and they strategically pivoted by moving away from DVD rental business into a leading streaming platform. By so doing, Netflix enhanced its ability to exploit the ever changing digital landscape and grabbed hold of its position as an entertainment industry giant.

Case Study 3: Amazon

Amazon is yet another success story that owes much of its achievements to Agile Management Strategies and successful strategic pivots. Beginning as online bookshop, Amazon has continuously changed its business model to include e-commerce, cloud computing and digital content streaming among others according market volatility through adaptation of Agile principles . Currently it has become one of the most valuable companies globally due to their ability to embrace adaptive organizational principles that are implemented based on emerging trends .

These case studies demonstrate how businesses can grow by adopting agile management practices which involves calculated risk taking through deliberate strategic shifts . They show why adaptability, responsiveness as well as readiness for market pressures ,are important virtues for any company which needs survival . And finally these examples are meant not only guide but also release creative abilities within organizations with regard opening up new opportunities for innovation ,growth , and long term success .

The Future of Agile Management and Pivoting

In today's fast paced and rapidly changing business environment, the future of agile management and pivoting has become more vital than ever. It is those organizations that can react swiftly to emerging trends and grab new opportunities who succeed in the competition.

Looking forward, a bright future is anticipated for agile management. As technology continues to advance, agile methodologies will evolve and become even more sophisticated. With growing application of data analytics as well as artificial intelligence , organizations will benefit from improved decision making processes which are also enhanced by process automation techniques.

Moreover, a culture of innovation that embraces continuous learning will be essential in determining how successfully we pivot towards the future. Therefore, companies that emphasize experimentation and creativity have an advantage because they quickly sense customer demands and market changes . Being able to pivot strategically yet swiftly ,enables firms stay ahead of time save them away from redundancy within this dynamic corporate landscape .

It is clear that going forward; agility together with pivoting will be crucial determinants of success in business. Only those organizations that are adaptable, innovative and can respond quickly to market shifts shall possess an upper hand for survival in the long run. Such companies are able to lead change thus promoting growth while remaining resilient when dealing with uncertainties.

Part VI:
The Maestro's
Personal Symphony

Chapter 36

Self-Composing: Personal Development for Business Leaders

In this chapter we investigate self-composing as a transformative concept and its powerful influence on an individual's personal development that will enhance your leadership skills and success in the ever changing business world.

Think of yourself standing on an empty stage, with your built-in talents and imagination. The spotlight falls on you highlighting the vast potential that lies in you, untapped. This is where self-composing comes in.

This chapter examines self-composing which gives leaders like you greater control over their personal growth and development. It is introspection; the baton wielded by conductors to take them through the symphony of their career paths.

Chapter 36 provides a roadmap for improving your leadership skills and forging your own path to success. We will equip you with tools for understanding who you truly are and what it takes to triumph in different spheres of life including self-awareness, emotional intelligence, resilience, adaptability among others.

Let us plunge into the realms of effective communication, high performing teams, innovation at work place and sustaining growth. Every part of this chapter is aimed at unlocking one's true potential so as to lead excellently.

Let there be curtains up for your journey into self-composing; let this be a moment when you can find personal growth within yourself again: discover a leader within you!

What Is Self-Composing?

To fully uncover the possibilities presented by personal development one needs to comprehend what exactly is meant by self-composing. In this part we delve into its meaning while emphasizing how it empowers business leaders towards determining their own paths of growth and expansion.

Developing Self-Awareness

Self-awareness forms one of the basic aspects of developing oneself personally within business leadership. These include understanding oneself more deeply such as knowing our strengths weaknesses or areas that need improvement. Leaders' ability to make conscious choices about things they do allows them make right decisions for themselves during tough times thereby maximizing their potentials.

Why Self-Awareness Matters for Personal Development

For personal development, self-awareness is a guide. Through this, leaders in business can pick up some patterns by becoming cognizant of our feelings thoughts and behaviors hence enhancing their leadership skills when necessary. Furthermore, it creates room for trust building within the team members creating an atmosphere of cooperation and collaboration.

Strategies for Enhancing Self-Awareness

There are several powerful strategies and techniques that business leaders can employ to enhance their self-awareness:

Reflecting: It is important for leaders to take time and reflect on their thoughts, actions as well as outcomes since it provides insight into their decision-making process and areas they need improvement in.

Requesting feedback: By actively seeking comments from co-workers, mentors or team members makes one get different perspectives which gives insight on how your actions impact them.

Writing a diary: In this case, leaders jot down the way they feel about various issues; capturing ideas at different points during life's journey.

Mindfulness: Mindfulness practices such as meditation or deep breathing exercises help leaders develop present-moment awareness and foster a deeper connection with themselves.

Benefits of Self-Aware Leaders

Developing self-awareness has numerous benefits to business leaders such as:

Better Decision-Making – Being aware of one's values, preferences and goals allows self-aware leaders to make more informed decisions that result in greater effectiveness.

Greater Emotional Intelligence – Self-awareness is closely related to emotional intelligence because it enables individuals navigate the stormy waters of human relationships with much empathy and resilience.

Leaders who are self-aware are better able to communicate their thoughts, expectations, and feedback, thereby fostering open and honest communication within their teams.

Self-awareness is the foundation of continuous learning and development. It enables leaders to focus on areas for personal growth based on an understanding of their strengths and weaknesses, which they can then exploit to achieve long-term success.

Cultivating self-awareness is an empowering journey that allows business leaders to unlock their full potentials so as to have a positive change in the way they affect their organizations. Leaders who choose self-reflection along with effective strategies can enhance personal development and become more effective while acting in influential capacities.

Developing Emotional Intelligence

Emotional intelligence is an essential characteristic for business leaders who desire personal growth and success in their roles. It includes recognizing emotions within oneself as well as others' feelings like managing them appropriately. Developing emotional intelligence helps in maneuvering complex interpersonal dynamics and creating strong collaborative relationships within organizations.

One of the most effective ways of enhancing emotional intelligence is through self-reflection as well as self-awareness. By reflecting on one's own emotions, triggers, and reactions over time, a leader can notice his/her emotional patterns more deeply resulting into better control of these emotions. This is where empathy begins growing from.

The Power of Empathy

Empathy – sharing another person's feelings – is basic to emotional intelligence. It assists leaders in bonding with team members at a deeper level hence building trust among them thus creates a supportive working environment. To grow empathy among themselves; leaders can attentively listen or sympathize with the feelings showed by workers without necessarily discouraging them.

Additionally, good conflict resolution skills may enable a leader cultivate his or her emotional intelligence too. Workplaces always have conflicts however good EI will help leaders address such issues constructively by concentrating on win-win solutions that foster wholesome team relationships.

To this end; unlearning ones emotion should be part of developing emotional intelligence. Consequently, business managers may acquire books, workshops and trainings that have a message on emotional self-awareness, empathy and effective communication to mention but a few. Through personal growth as well as emotional intelligence investment, leadership skills are improved while the team gets an enabling environment.

Harnessing Resilience and Adaptability

For leaders in business, resilience and adaptability are very important attributes particularly when they face uncertainty or adversity due to changing business environments. In this section, we will explore some of the most effective ways in which businesses can develop resilient ad adaptable leaders.

Resilience is the ability to bounce back from challenges and keep on despite setbacks. This involves having a mindset that views hurdles as opportunities for growth and learning. Leaders who harness resilience maintain focus, motivation and determination even in the toughest circumstances.

On the other hand; adaptability means adjusting well to changes in situations. It involves embracing change as it comes by seeking new ideas proactively so as to come up with innovative solutions within businesses. By fostering adaptability, leaders can navigate their teams through transition periods of change into a shifting business world effectively.

Practical techniques of developing resilience and adaptability will be looked at in this section. These include stress management, building a growth mindset, and decision-making flexibility. We also focus on the importance of self-reflection and self-care for resilience and adaptability.

With resilience and adaptability, business managers can overcome their own challenges while inspiring their teams to do the same. These qualities enhance individual development and enable leaders to effectively handle complex situations with confidence and agility. Discover with us some winning strategies for harnessing resilience and adaptability in the modern world of business.

Effective Communication Strategies

Business leaders have to develop strong communication skills as they develop personally. Different strategies that can make your communication skills better enabling you communicate your vision effectively, inspire your staffs, encourage teamwork will be explored in this part.

1. Active Listening: One of the most important aspects about good communication is active listening. Being fully attentive during conversations, keenly observing verbal cues as well as non-verbal signals while empathizing with others' perspective could significantly raise one's communication potential.
2. Clear and Concise Messaging: In a fast-moving corporate environment, clear and concise messaging is necessary. Putting across complicated ideas using few words helps you attract audience attention better so that they get the point you want to make quickly.
3. Non-Verbal Communication: Non-verbal cues such as body language, facial expression or gestures are key elements used in communicating messages. Being conscious on how you present yourself through nonverbal means coupled with interpreting others messages can lead to an overall effective communication process.

4.Empathy and Emotional Intelligence:

Empathy combined with emotional intelligence are powerful tools of communication that promote understanding with colleagues of different levels of complexity within an organization. It allows one to understand other people emotions or perspectives hence responding emotionally while building trust among themselves.

Active Feedback: Providing feedback is extremely important; therefore it should not be neglected in any way possible if we want our communication to be effective. Regularly seeking input from your team and actively providing constructive feedback can foster a culture of open communication and continuous improvement.

Cross-Cultural Communication: In the current globalized world, business managers often deal with people from different cultures. Developing effective cross-cultural communication skills, such as understanding cultural diversity, adapting to different ways of communicating and respecting cultural standards will enable one to effectively communicate across countries.

Keep in mind that effective communication is an active skill that must be practiced constantly. These strategies integrated into your personal development journey will make you a more influential communicator as a business leader.

Building and Leading High-Performing Teams

Building and leading high-performing teams are must-have skills for business leaders. This becomes crucial when organizations aspire towards success while aiming at growing better by cultivating an excellence-oriented culture. The following section identifies strategies that have been tried and tested thereby enabling business managers to build high-performance teams through personal development processes.

Effective leadership entails facilitating cooperation among team members so that they work towards achieving a common goal and motivating them to reach their full potential. Business owners who develop themselves personally can obtain the necessary expertise needed for forming consolidated structures of highly performing teams.

One key component of creating high performance teams is recognizing individual strengths, talents, or abilities. For instance, there are several frameworks used by leaders in promoting strengths-based leadership which enhances individual's unique potentials hence improving overall team performance.

Besides, effective communication is important in forming teams and leadership. Leaders with good communication skills can voice out their thoughts clearly and make sure that their team members are on the same page, hence creating unity among them.

Additionally, trust building and fostering a collaborative environment are crucial in developing high-performing teams. For business leaders to create an environment where members of their teams can take responsibility for their work, collaborate efficiently as well as innovate together it will require establishing a basis of trust and encouraging collaboration.

Finally, continuous personal growth and development are necessary for business leaders to cope with the ever-changing market dynamics and effectively lead their teams. The focus on personal improvement by these seniors is a standard because it also shows their team members the value of ongoing training in such areas as adaptability, resilience and other life skills.

Through amalgamation of personal development with efficient methods of team building leaders in organizations can make environments promoting high performance, collaboration and innovation. Investing in high-performance teams not only drives organizational success but also instills fulfillment as well as accomplishment within team members themselves including leaders.

Nurturing Innovation and Creativity

The modern competitive business climate means that business leaders must be innovators who employ creativity.

Building an innovative culture begins with active strategic steps at organization level. Business leaders need to create an atmosphere where employees are encouraged to think outside the box and generate new ideas. Companies can anticipate market trends, stay ahead of competition or find very unique solutions by being innovative.

One way to stimulate creativity among team members is through offering personal development opportunities. This may include encouraging employees to enroll for training programs; attending workshops or even participating in cross-functional projects that could bring new light on something.

Harnessing diversity is another key factor that leads innovation and creativity. When people come together from different backgrounds, experiences or skill sets there will be great exchange of ideas thus generating ground-breaking solutions.

Moreover, embracing a continuous improvement mindset helps nurture innovation within an organization. Openness to suggestions and ideas from all employees across the organization creates an environment of collaboration and idea generation within companies. This enables companies to adapt quickly to changing market conditions and customer demands.

Ultimately, fostering innovation and creativity requires continuous experimentation and willingness to take risks. Leaders should give their workers a safe space in which they can try new things without fear of making mistakes. A company culture that appreciates innovation will motivate the employees to go beyond the set limits and seek for more growth opportunities.

Business leaders can drive positive change, lead their teams to new heights, and position their organizations as industry trailblazers by embracing innovation and creativity.

Balancing Work and Life Demands

The success of business leaders depends on them leading a healthy work-life balance. Although this may be difficult due to workloads, employing certain strategies would help manage the workload while at the same time having personal health issues prioritized by these executive staff members.

One way to do this is by clearly defining the boundaries of work and personal life. Setting aside time for relaxation, hobbies and spending quality time with loved ones will help balance things out. It is important to communicate such limits with colleagues or team members so that they can appreciate your private moments.

Another effective strategy is prioritizing yourself through self-care and personal development. Maintaining equilibrium and preventing burnout necessitates taking care of your physical as well as mental health. Additionally, allocate periods for exercising, eating healthy food, and having enough sleep. Besides that, involve yourself in activities aimed at self-improvement like reading books, attending workshops or having other hobbies apart from your work.

Delegate tasks to co-workers and other people on the team so that you reduce everyone's workload. While effectively delegating duties is one way of reducing stress, it also promotes trust among members within an organization. This offers avenues for growth both personally as well as professionally of the team members when others are empowered to share responsibilities with them.

Use technology and efficient work systems to make operations more streamlined hence boosting productivity. Automating ordinary tasks; organizing workflow can save time thereby reducing unnecessary pressure on employees' shoulders. Some other valuable tips include embracing productivity tools like Pomodoro Technique timers or adopting some useful techniques for time management to stay focused on any given task thus leaving ample room for personal engagements.

Remember that achieving a balanced life requires periodic assessment and change process since it is a journey rather than destination (Cascio 2012). As a business leader you need to constantly re-asses your top priority in order to make necessary changes aligning it with your personal and professional goals (Schein 2010). When leaders consistently support work-life balance they not only maximize employee well-being but also generate productive workforce capable of long-term future achievements.

Growth Maintenance

Personal Development: The Inner Journey of A Leader And Business Owner

To sustain growth and development, it is important for leaders to be open to learning and change as part of their professional journey.

Another key approach to enhancing growth entails regular personal and professional development investments. Through seminars, workshops & conferences; new perspectives, insights and skills can be learnt by the managers. This not only keeps them ahead of the game in terms of trends, innovations and best practices but also connects them with other professionals who can help them do better in their fields.

Moreover, fostering a culture of growth within the company is crucial. Employee engagement in personal growth and provision of resources to facilitate this will benefit both employees and the entire organization (Goleman et al., 2002). In order to develop collaborative environments that are motivated through development and expansion of team members; leaders should give priority on growing their staffs.

Lastly, sustainable growth requires embracing change and remaining innovative. Change readiness is a major factor affecting all organizations due to the rapidly evolving business environment (Carr et al., 2010). Leaders should constantly challenge themselves as well as their teams through encouraging new ideas which foster creativity leading to innovations within an organization.

Chapter 37

The Solo Retreat: The Importance of Reflection and Solitude in Business

Imagine this: Sarah, a triumphant businesswoman feels swamped by endless requests from her company. Her timetable is crammed with continuous meetings, everlasting decision-making, and infinite cobwebs of emails and notifications. She has begun to lose touch with herself and can barely see what her true purpose is.

One day, however, Sarah decides that she needs to escape the chaos. She books a snug cabin nestled in the mountains far away from the frenzy of city life. It will serve as a serene background for her solo retreat that promises time for self-reflection, solitude and self-discovery.

During these days on retreat she immerses herself in nature, taking long walks through the forest or just sitting quietly near a calm lake enjoying peaceful aloneness. She unplugs from technology and reconnects with herself.

As she reflects in silence, Sarah finds consoling peace of mind. She starts seeing things anew recognizing various patterns hidden behind noise of her busy life like strengths, weaknesses. She rediscovers all those passions, values which have been lost since childhood till today.

Through deeply reflecting upon it all, Sarah realizes how powerful it is to step away from daily grind to introspectively grow as a person. This way she understands that making time for reflection & solitude helps one grow personally by unleashing untapped potential inside.

Returning from this retreat one more time gave Sarah an increased sense of purpose towards her business and clearer vision for its future prospects. With a completely new perspective on things and better understanding about herself than ever before she energizes her team; makes strategically informed decisions; creates an environment where people's thoughts can be reflected upon; allows others' personal growth as well as own development.

This is what solo retreats are about-reflecting alone within yourself in relation to your business interests! The next section discusses all about this matter – understanding solo retreats; creating an environment conducive for deep thinking; planning inner thinking and reflection; reaping benefits of reflection in business.

Knowing the Solo Retreat

A solo retreat is a special occasion for those who are busy with their careers to engage themselves into deep thoughts and self-examination. It is an opportunity to take a break from usual everyday life, be alone, get your head clear up and gain some insight. People who take part in such retreats usually disconnect themselves from surrounding noise and distractions to move towards the inner world for self-analysis of thoughts, feelings and ambitions.

One of the main reasons people go on a solo retreat is that they can stop for a while and reconsider what they do as professionals in wider context. For an entrepreneur, executive or even freelancer, moments of silence at these facilities can serve as spaces conducive for self-discovery, brainstorming ideas or coming up with strategies.

The length of time spent on this meditation depends on personal preference as well as circumstances. It may range from several days to weeks with long periods left for soul searching. Moreover, choosing an appropriate site is important when planning a solitary journey. Could be anywhere – isolated log cabin in the forest or beachfront villa or quiet spiritual centers among trees – actually anything which brings tranquility and room for rumination.

In selecting isolation for introspection, individuals can delve into their inner thoughts and feelings thereby attaining valuable insights and clarity. In this way, through this process, one can understand oneself better, his/her goals, and how they relate to what one does as a career. Solo retreats become life changing journeys that help people make good decisions; set meaningful goals and bring changes at personal and professional levels.

While on a solo retreat there are reflective activities an individual may indulge in such as journaling or meditation or just sitting out in nature. Through these practices; self-awareness is enhanced leading to creative thinking and better problem solving abilities. The aloneness found within the retreat gives a greater attention that it provides space in which people think deeply about what is happening in business with fresh eyes.

Solo Retreat Environment

The Next Section

Creating the Right Atmosphere

When you decide to go for a solo retreat, you have to consider the type of environment that should be present for it to have any real meaning. It helps in creating a serene atmosphere thus providing quiet space necessary for deeper reflection and soul seeking.

One consideration when choosing your perfect retreat environment is finding a location with ideal conditions for this purpose. Look out for calm settings such as peaceful cabin in the woods, warm cottage next to the sea-beach or quite mountain resort where you will not be affected by city life noises. Nature is very helpful when looking forward to avoid regular hustles of everyday world hence immersing yourself can help create your desired environment of having an amazing time during that session.

Also keep away from anything that will distract you during your time away from everyone else. Find an area where you know nothing will disturb you throughout your entire stay at the place of choice; maybe somewhere with no noise or disturbances like closed doors would do best.

Your designated place must have some elements conducive enough for deep meditation. Consider surrounding it with things including soft lighting fixtures enhancing the reflective mood and a few comfortable seats. For deep thinking and self-examination, the place ought to be tranquil, with soft lightings and furniture conducive for meditations.

To help you create the right environment, think of bringing things that are important for your solitude and reflection. In such case, carry with you resourceful materials like journals or books, loose clothing as well as meditation aids that promote this kind of thinking. This will make sure that not only are you comfortable but also able to have a deeper introspection.

By carefully curating the retreat environment to prioritize retreat environment, solitude space, and a reflective atmosphere, you can ensure that your solo retreat becomes a transformative experience filled with profound self-discovery and personal growth.

Planning for Reflection

Thoughtful planning is necessary in order to create an environment where one can deeply reflect about oneself on a personal level during such time alone. Engaging in different exercises of thoughtfulness or self-reflection can trigger change within someone's life at both their social and professional levels.

One way to encourage self-reflection is through journaling. Through putting down your thoughts, feelings and even aspirations onto paper in your own privacy may serve as one form of journaling. By writing without any limitation it helps explore deepest feelings thus making clear our ambitions and dreams.

Introspection can be promoted using meditation which is a very powerful tool. Dedicate specific time for sitting still and silent, thereby giving an opportunity for the mind to calm down and thoughts to rise gently. Consequently, this activity will foster self-realization besides allowing one to observe his or her feelings without being biased.

Planning such a retreat often involves setting goals for introspection. The process of setting these goals helps in developing a framework for contemplation as well as enabling individuals to have aspirations on their personal and professional growth. In other words, the aims that are easily set off help someone become more purposeful and directed during their experience.

This will also be important in organizing your days such that they enhance reflection and self-discovery. This means that you should have different activities accomplished at particular intervals; like meditating throughout morning hours then journaling afternoons towards goal setting in the evenings.This systematic arrangement confirms that each day has some valuable reflective practices.

Therefore, the planning phase is vital in determining how your solo retreat turns out.Once you do it with reflection planning, it will mean becoming involved in introvert-related activities including self-reflection exercises hence paving way for a transformative journey of self- discovery and growth.

Why Reflect in Business

Reflection is a powerful tool with numerous benefits applicable to businesses. When individuals reflect on their experiences and actions, they get insights about who they are within the organization's context. This knowledge improves decision-making abilities leading into better interpersonal relationships, higher level of creativity among staff members among others.

Business professionals can gain insights into their own strengths , weaknesses and areas of improvements by engaging in self-reflection (Silk et al., 2008). This awareness allows them to make more informed decisions aligning with their personal and professional objectives thus benefiting the whole organization eventually.

Moreover, professionals engage their creative thinking through reflection since it provides them with opportunities to think widely and differently about things.Professionals who step back to reflect on a problem or challenge can use their imaginative abilities and innovative mindset thus developing new ideas and approaches that foster business performance in general.

Equally important, reflection enhances the level of self-understanding thus improving relationships within the work place. In their quest for comprehending their emotions, thoughts and actions workplace participants are encouraged to focus inwardly. This increased understanding of others progressed by an individual's enhanced empathy results in efficient communication and collaboration among colleagues hence making the working environment positive and productive.

Tangible benefits resulting from reflection in businesses can be illustrated through real-life examples as well as case studies. For example, firms that have put policies in place to encourage employee introspection reported increased job satisfaction, reduced stress levels and overall improved performance of staff. These organizations recognize that investing in reflection not only benefits individuals but also contributes to the growth and success of the business as a whole.

To sum up, it is clear that reflection has many applications in business because it promotes self-awareness, improves decision- making skills, leads to creativity thereby boosting interpersonal relationships among employees. With this perspective continuously reflected upon by businesses there is always progress being made leading to sustainable growth.

Surmounting Challenges Alone

Solitary retreats offer an opportunity for one person to experience profound personal reflections for growth. However, it is normal for challenges to arise along this path that may deter people from achieving seclusion which is necessary for such meditations. In this part we will look at some of these difficulties faced by individuals during a solitary retreat and how they can be overcome.

Dealing with Loneliness in Reflection

It is a quiet time that requires being by oneself if one is to reflect deeply and this at times creates feelings of loneliness. However, it is important to note that there is a difference between solitude and loneliness. Loneliness emanates from disconnection and unavailability while self-reflection through being alone gives room for one's own personal discovery. To overcome loneliness during the retreat, people can:

Stay connected with loved ones through regular check-ins and virtual communication.

Engage in activities that facilitate self-connection such as journaling, creative arts or practicing meditation/mindfulness. Take breaks walking around the town or nature to connect with other humans and change scenes.

Coping with Distractions During the Retreat

Distractions can be problematic when trying to focus on the retreat fully. The following strategies can be used to address distractions:

Have a separate place of retreat free from external disturbances including turning off notifications on electronic gadgets.

Have a daily timetable or routine which will help organize the retreat, thus reducing chances of distraction.

Do some mindfulness techniques as they will enable you not to drift away from your purpose.

Install tools and apps meant for productivity as well as time management so that all essential tasks can be handled efficiently.

Through these methods, individuals can handle isolation's challenges creating an atmosphere for deep reflection and self-improvement. During this precious moment, staying motivated, engaged and focused on why one is here should never be forgotten.

Integrating Retreat Insights into Business Strategy

The actual value after going on solo retreats comes from translating what has been learnt into actionable steps for business growth: just reflecting upon events does not suffice because application of reflection is key for measurable outcomes in business operations.

One approach would be reflecting on common ideas or patterns when looking back at your reflections. These themes are helpful indicators for general decision making within different areas of the firm.

Moreover, bridging individual growth with company goals is an essential part of a holistic approach to business strategy. Personal accomplishments and areas needing improvement can help people see how their own growth relates to the company's wider objectives. This ensures that efforts for self-development have a direct impact on the success of an enterprise.

Also important is the creation of a culture that values and supports individual introspection. When leaders and managers prioritize and encourage reflection, employees feel empowered to take the time for self-reflection and utilize their retreat insights in their day-to-day activities. A helping ground where growth and innovation are nurtured comes up as a result.

Reflection in business strategy goes beyond one's personal development. This involves actively searching for opportunities where what was learnt during solo retreats can be applied in practice. These may include setting up new procedures, adjusting current strategies or exploring new markets/endeavors.

Organizations can use reflection in retreats for their strategic planning by adopting insights from them thereby promoting innovative thinking, better decision-making processes, as well as business expansion. Applying the lessons from this silent retreat guarantees that personal reflection translates into significant results for the whole organization at large.

Sustaining Reflection Practices

After undergoing a transformative reflection experience during your retreat alone, you must maintain these practices over the long haul. Sustained reflection is important for personal and professional development and changed their life forever. Below are some ideas on how to incorporate reflection into your day and help create an environment of continuous growth:

1. Make Reflection a Habit

Include time for self-reflection in your daily routine. You can set apart a few minutes in the morning or before going to bed when you think about your thoughts, experiences, and goals. This may involve writing a journal, meditating or just thinking about something deeply.

2. Growth-oriented Goals

For instance, continuously strive towards holistic development by setting targets that align with both personal and professional aspirations. Reflect on what you have done so far to achieve those aims as well as the extent achieved annually. Use reflective processes to identify areas to improve upon (a critical self-examination), learn from successes (celebration), and make necessary changes while still pursuing success (self-directedness).

3. Promote Lifelong Learning

Be committed to lifelong learning by adopting a mindset of continuous improvement. For example, read books, attend training sessions or go for conferences that will provide additional knowledge on subjects related to your business endeavor(s). In this way, you will be able to apply what you have learnt which enhances better aptitude in carrying out your role.

4. Get Feedback and Support From Others

Surround yourself with mentors, colleagues and advisers who can offer valuable insights through feedbacks given constructively concerning your work whether at individual level or organizational level. They should give reflections regularly for reviewing purposes so that they can help one evaluate his/her practices against others' opinions as well as place their advice within a context of justification.

5. Cultivate A Reflection Culture

If you happen to be in charge of such an entity then it will be essential promoting reflection across the organization's culture via several ways. For example, be a role model and share your reflections of how it has positively influenced your own development. This can include conducting group discussions where the members are encouraged to reflect on their experiences and dedicated reflection sessions.

By continuing with the practice of reflection beyond the solo retreat, you will support a continuous self-improvement journey in future. Therefore, make reflection a habit, set goals for further growth, have a learning mindset, seek feedback and assistance and finally create an environment that encourages critical thinking. All these practices will ensure that benefits from reflective practices continue to enhance personal growth and development as well as professional advancement.

Conclusion

Reflection is essential to business growth; hence it requires solitude. In this section we have attempted to explain why taking a time off for oneself helps in both personal and professional outcomes positively. As such, individuals can build self-awareness and foster creativity while making informed choices through solitary deliberation which is facilitated by retreats alone aimed at promoting reflection.

There is something special about being alone that makes us think deeply about ourselves. Some of the knowledge we gain from journaling, meditation or goal setting can be helpful when developing our own strategies in business world. Therefore such insights help us align our personal growth with organizational objectives which aid us in better decision-making and building sustainable relationships within an institution since they provide opportunities for personal improvement too like writing down reflections etcetera. And so here we see why reflection is very powerful indeed!

Despite the difficulties which can occur while maintaining solitude in a business context, such as desolation feelings and distractions, we will be able to overcome them by using appropriate strategies and motivation. This is achievable through maintaining reflection practices beyond the solo retreat, and making regular self-reflection part of our day-to-day activities that help us develop a mindset where we perpetually learn about ourselves for continuous self-improvement resulting in long-term growth both in our personal and professional lives.

To sum up, when incorporated into corporate culture would result in discovering oneself completely. So when we embrace this form of getting to know who we are better then we can keep on growing thus transforming our businesses into success stories. The isolation and introspection are not merely some luxury but rather a necessity for those individuals who want to achieve their objectives as well as leaving legacy in entrepreneurship world.

Chapter **38**

The Health of the Maestro: Physical and Mental Wellness - Managing Your Self in Business

Think about the applause gradually dying, the spotlight dimming and the stage empty. Daniel, an accomplished conductor of an orchestra also known as the Maestro, was alone in the silence.

Conducting for many years had taken its toll on his body and mind. His demanding career had seen him neglect his health both inside and out. Rehearsing for long hours, touring, and continuous pressure began to manifest themselves in weakened leadership.

However, as he stood before the barren auditorium filled with emptiness Daniel realized that even for him to keep making these exceptional symphonies he needed to consider himself first. At this point in time it was appropriate for Maestro to come into accord with his life by finding a middle ground between chasing success and taking care of himself.

In this chapter of "From Manager to Maestro: The Symphony of Good Management," we delve into the importance of physical and mental wellness for successful business leaders. Come along as we learn some strategies and tips one can use to make their career journey more enjoyable just like what happened with our own maestro.

Understanding The Importance Of Physical Health

Physical health is key when it comes to attaining success in any organization. The importance of good physical health on overall well-being is underrated; thereby, influencing corporate output significantly due poor fitness levels leading to poor work results or personal problems being manifested outwardly at work place. Exercise is one way that helps maintain a healthy balance between work commitments while at same time ensuring effective leadership capacity within organizations today.

It's through exercise you improve your physical fitness and boost cognitive function clarity within your mind too. When you engage in exercises your body releases endorphins – hormones responsible good moods- henceforth reducing stress levels together boosting overall mood enhancement.

Additionally, getting adequate nutrition is important for maintaining optimum energy levels; staying focused throughout your busy day at workplace so that you will be able achieve more tasks without tiring easily unlike situation when you could feed on any junk food. Consuming whole foods fuels the body by supporting brain functionality and maintaining physical stamina.

Prioritizing your physical health increases your ability to make good decisions, lead with confidence, and stay strong in difficult times. The integration of wellness practices into your everyday routine empowers you to be at your best while securing a work-life balance that is sustainable.

Your investments in physical well-being are critical to successful business leadership. Recognizing how physical health affects overall well-being provides a basis for personal as well as professional development.

Nurturing Mental Wellness in Business

In pursuit of success within the commercial sector, mental wellness is non-negotiable. The way you manage daily stresses in corporate set up goes hand in hand with positive mindset creating space for better management skills hence effective leadership.

One of the ways of nurturing mental wellness involves effectively managing stress. In this case, running businesses at pace may result to high levels of anxiety which further undermines one's wellbeing or performance at the place of work. When applied density exercises deep breathing techniques together time planning strategies relieve job stressors leading a more flexible state of mind.

Boosting Resilience

Furthermore, apart from managing stress, nurturing resilience is a pivotal part of promoting mental wellness. Developing resilience gives you a chance to bounce back from disappointments and challenges to cultivate strength and adaptability. Resilience can be nurtured through practices such as self-reflection, seeking mentorship or coaching and developing a growth mindset that enables you to keep moving forward despite the highs and lows of your career journey.

Another important aspect of mental wellness is the positive mindset. Emphasis should be put on optimism; these are things like gratitude, self- belief and others. Seeing challenges as opportunities for growth while maintaining good mental health requires reframing everyday problems into positive ones with daily affirmations and realistic goal settings.

What's more, paying attention to your mental well-being not only improves your personal life but also makes you an efficient business leader. By adopting strategies that promote well-being and showing adequate care for one's own mental wellness, you will gain more clarity, focus and become more resilient leading the way to long-term success.

Becoming a Maestro in Achieving Work-Life Balance

Without balance between work responsibilities and personal life activities sustainable success cannot be achieved in both areas. In order for you as a maestro in business to have good health then it requires that you strike a balance between these two aspects of life. This includes prioritizing tasks through effective time management setting boundaries between work-life integration.

To achieve work-life balance, it's important to develop effective time management techniques. This includes prioritizing tasks, setting realistic deadlines, and delegating responsibilities when necessary. By managing your schedule so that there is time allocated for both work-related matters as well as personal ones this will save your day since either side does not dominate the other significantly.

In addition, defining boundaries is another strategy that can help people achieve work-life balance since it helps create some orderliness besides preventing burnout risks. For instance this may involve having fixed working hours or dedicated time for personal activities and refraining from being constantly connected to work through technology.

Another important aspect of achieving work-life balance is harmonious integration of your professional and personal domains. You should strive to merge these two areas in terms of interests, values and passions. This merging can promote a sense of fulfillment by ensuring that both aspects of life contribute positively to the overall well-being.

By finding work-life balance you will be able to keep up with performance in your job but still take care of your relationships and well-being. The ability to prioritize work-life balance enables one to be more present, focused, and efficient in both areas hence leading greater overall satisfaction and success.

Prioritizing Self-Care: A Maestro's Guide

For business leaders it is easy to forget oneself in all the requirements at the workplace. However, self-care is necessary as it increases resilience during challenging periods while maintaining peak performance. Through self-discipline, one can experience rewarding mental peace via simple practices that revitalize body, mind, soul.

Mindfulness is one of the primary components of self-care. Being fully present in moments throughout the day can decrease anxiety and improve your overall well-being. Do things that make you happy such as going for a walk in the woods, reading a book or indulging in a hobby. These mindfulness breaks are empowering and refocus you to perform better in the business arena.

Self-Care Essential: Mindfulness Plus

Aside from mindfulness, relaxation techniques are also valuable aspects of self-care. Find what works for you best whether it's deep breathing exercises, meditating or listening to calming sounds. By making these practices part of your daily routine, you can cope with stress better thus leading to calmness and enhanced decision-making.

Reflection as a Key Self-Care Tool

Another tool that is very effective when prioritizing self-care is reflection. Evaluate what you want, what drives you and how much you can withstand personally? This contemplation helps to bring together your behaviours and decisions with who you really are as an individual thereby giving you more satisfaction and sense of direction along your career path.

Self-Care Is Not Selfish; It's Necessary for Well-Being and Success as a Business Leader

You should not think that caring about yourself is selfishness since it plays an important role towards enhancing your general health while at work as business leader. By identifying this importance of prioritizing oneself by carrying out these activities daily will enable someone develop resilience important for leadership hence becoming successful even within tough business management situations.

Healthy Habits: Nutrition and Exercise

For optimal performance both at work and at home, unlocking one's potential requires establishing good nutrition habits coupled with regular exercise routines. What we eat affects our energy levels, cognitive abilities besides influencing our lives.

The Role of Good Nutrition in Our Lives

Our bodies need to be fueled properly through eating nutritious food so that they can function optimally. A well-balanced diet full fruits, vegetables, lean proteins, and whole grains gives the body all required vitamins and minerals to keep one energized throughout the day. They should avoid processed foods, excessive sugar, unhealthy fats, as these can cause tiredness, lack of concentration and weak immune system.

The Importance of Water

Drinking a lot of water is something that people should never underrate any time they think about nutrition. Proper hydration ensures that all our systems are working correctly, we are able to concentrate well as well staying healthy. You should aim at drinking 8 glasses minimum of water daily but cut down on sweetened drinks.

Exercise: The Key to Physical Well-Being, Mental Balance

Physical exercise has a positive impact on our mental health in addition to being important for physical fitness. Even if you do not want to go jogging or swimming every day just walk instead because doing exercise on a regular basis releases endorphins which make us happy and lower stress levels. It increases blood circulation while also improving concentration enabling you perform better mentally.

Finding Your Perfect Exercise Routine

When it comes to exercise, finding activities that you enjoy is crucial for long-term adherence. Whether it's running, swimming, yoga or lifting weights, make sure you move your body every day for various health benefits. Try to do moderate-intensity exercises for at least 150 minutes each week or vigorous-intensity ones for 75 minutes at least per week.

The Economic Importance of Early Childhood Education

Healthy habits can be included in your daily life with a little planning and self-control; however, the advantages they offer are well worth the effort. You can fuel your body with nutritious food and exercise regularly to have sustainable energy levels, improved cognitive performance, and overall well-being that make you excel in all spheres of life.

Stress Management and Building Resilience

Stress is inevitable within corporate settings but how we handle it makes all the difference in our general well-being as well as success. Thriving in any business environment necessitates developing effective stress management techniques and building resilience.

When addressing stress management, it is important to identify its sources and adopt healthy coping strategies. One approach could be engaging in self-care activities that don't only promote relaxation but rejuvenate the mind-body balance. This may entail hobbies, spending quality time with loved ones or taking a moment to recharge batteries.

Mindfulness is another important technique of dealing with stress. We can manage our minds by practicing mindfulness which encourages us to focus on our present moments hence creating calmness within oneself. Some of these activities include meditation, deep breathing exercises or just paying attention to our thoughts and sensations without judgment. Building resiliency is also key while navigating through the challenges of the business world.

It Makes Us Bounce Back From Setbacks And Have A Positive Mindset And Adapt To Change One Way Of Building Resilience Is By Cultivating A Growth Mindset That Enables Us See Challenges As Opportunities For Learning And Personal Development When we reframe setbacks as learning experiences, we develop a resilient mindset that empowers us to overcome obstacles on our way to success.

Moreover, having strong support system plays significant role towards building resilience. Being surrounded by caring individuals who are always there for us helps tackle stressors better than doing it alone.

We can achieve greater personal well-being, maintain work-life balance and lead with confidence within the corporate world by managing stress effectively and building resilience.

The Importance of Sleep in Maestro's Wellness

Sleep remains a crucial element for supporting good health and wellbeing. As a business maestro, ensuring that I have quality sleep is critical in maintaining a fresh mind and an optimal cognitive function. Quality sleep helps to revive the body, support immune system functioning and lead to overall wellness. It allows the brain to rest and revitalize, thereby boosting such cognitive abilities as problem-solving, memory retention as well as creativity. A well-rested mind performs better in a fast-paced professional environment with various pressures and deadlines. In order to increase the quality of sleep one can adopt healthy sleeping habits. Formulate a regular bed time schedule that gives you enough time for full night's rest. Establishing routines such as reading before going to bed or taking warm baths are effective methods of relaxing your body making it ready for some sleep. Sleep-inducing atmosphere is also key here. Buy yourself a comfortable mattress that supports your back while lying on it and firm pillows. Make sure you're always cool in your bedroom because high temperatures can affect your sleep negatively thus leading to bad mood throughout the day; moreover it should be dark so that light won't wake you up when someone goes into your room unexpectedly since there are no curtains blocking sunshine from pouring through windows – trust me, this is not appropriate! If falling asleep proves challenging or staying asleep becomes impossible then try relaxation techniques like deep breathing exercises or listening to soft music.

Do not engage in any stimulating activities close to bedtime; switch off any electronic devices used by individuals who find it difficult catching some sleep; avoid coffee late at night because these things disrupt natural cyclical patterns associated with resting period which every human being requires if they want their bodies functioning properly during daylight hours ahead

Remember, sound sleep has an important role in self-care and maintaining a clear mind. Prioritize good sleep like successful people do!

Looking for Professional Help: Therapy versus Coaching

For optimum mental wellness, it is essential to acknowledge the importance of seeking professional help. Therapy and coaching are immensely helpful tools that can offer insights, strategies and support needed to navigate the challenges of life and maintain a healthy mental state.

Therapy provides a secure environment where one is allowed to share their thoughts, feelings or actions without being judged by anyone else. It helps you understand yourself better, deal with your past traumas and develop effective strategies for coping with life's issues. Through therapy sessions, individuals can get rid of the causes leading to their mental illness hence having a capacity to overcome other obstacles like those at work place.

On the contrary, coaching emphasizes on goal setting as well as personal development in career advancement perspective. For instance, an adept coach will be able to provide guidance, support and accountability while you work towards your career objectives. They will assist you in identifying your strong areas as well as combating self-imposed limitations by having a continuous strategy for success in whatever field they may find themselves in: thus making every effort count more than if there were left alone without any assistance outside their comfort zones – this makes real difference! With coaching, one gets to learn more about oneself through increased self-awareness; knows what his/her values are; understands own priorities thereby encompassing the entire consciences inside him together so that he becomes much more than just ordinary human being but rather extraordinary leader too!

Advantages of Professional Support for Mental Wellness

Several gains come from getting external help from therapists or coaches:

Enhanced Self-Awareness: Through therapy and coaching one gets to know what he/she believes in more deeply – getting deeper into our minds makes it easier spotting negative patterns which hinder us by pulling us backwards instead of allowing successful future moves forward.

Effective Coping Mechanisms: Talking with experts can give someone useful tips on how he must deal with anxiety or stress when they come across different types of situations surrounding them every day within small groups formed by different colleagues or/and families. It's essential finding helpful ways that will enable an individual to go through hardships in life, control emotions and remain optimistic during difficult times – this is quite challenging for many people worldwide today!

Personal growth and development: There are therapists and trainers who offer valuable insights and guidance, which helps you to grow personally as well as professionally. They encourage self-reflection, promote personal accountability, and give one the confidence to make substantial life changes.

Problem-solving and decision-making: Professional support aids in developing problem-solving and decision-making skills, helping one overcome hurdles, make informed choices, and be clear and confident in reaching their goals.

Support during transitions: During periods of change like career shifts or major life events therapy or coaching can come in handy. It is a safe place for you to navigate through uncertainty as well as gain clarity about the choice that you need to make so that you can seize upon it.

Remember; seeking professional help is a sign of strength not weakness. This demonstrates an individual's commitment towards mental health hence he or she invests into his own personal growth both at work place or outside. One can choose therapy alone or combine it with coaching because they provide helpful resources for business leaders that enable them thrive while taking care of their physical wellbeing.

Creating a Supportive Work Environment

To foster your well-being along with your team members' well-being it is important to have a supportive work environment. Through prioritizing employee's collaboration approachability at workplace will be embedded resulting into success-happiness driven culture.

Collaboration forms part of this kind of work environment. Encouraging team building and open-talk conditions facilitate creativity that enhances productivity among staff within any organization. Make employees understand why working together towards common goals matters by providing platforms that enable efficient collaboration such as project management software, communication apps, virtual meeting platforms etc.

Promoting Employee Well-Being

An organization that cares about its employees' well-being creates an atmosphere where people feel valued, supported, and motivated. By making available resources which target various aspects of employee wellness including mental health counseling services or even flexible working hours teams can achieve top performance leading healthy lifestyles.

Ensure that employees have access to wellness programs and initiatives that cater for different facets of their well-being. These are things like fitness classes, mindfulness workshops, mental health counseling services or even flexible work arrangements. Investing in your employees' wellbeing creates loyalty and dedication among them leading to satisfaction in what they do and high productivity.

Cultivating a positive workplace culture is also vital for creating a supportive work environment. By nurturing open discussions, recognizing milestones and belonging together everyone grows mentally. When you care about your team members wellbeing as a business leader you help create positivity within the company therefore success is inevitable.

Maestro's Mental Wellness: Mindfulness and Meditation

Mental wellness is important for sustainable success as well as general welfare. In the business world, however, it may be very easy to lose oneself in the rush of tasks, deadlines and duties. Nevertheless, practicing mindfulness regularly through meditation practice can greatly contribute towards one's soundness of mind.

Mindfulness involves intentionally paying attention to what is happening at present without any judgmental attitude (Bakhshi & Allameh 2014). This way we can look inside ourselves and see how our thoughts interact with each other physically causing us feelings on certain occasions.

In contrast, meditation helps quieten minds thus achieving inner peace. This may involve focusing on one thing; guided imagery; repeating mantras among others (Roeser et al., 2012). Stress reduction; increased self-awareness; improved cognitive functioning are realized through meditating.

Regular mindfulness meditation training deepens our awareness of the present. It teaches us how to live in the present moment by giving up concerns about the past and fears for the future (as we exist in the actuality of now). This awareness of now helps us make better decisions, succeed with stress and improve focus.

Furthermore, mindfulness and meditation have been shown to enhance emotional intelligence – the ability to recognize, understand, and manage our own emotions and those of others. By engaging in these practices, we become more empathetic, compassionate, and connected to our own inner wisdom and the needs of those around us.

So, how can you incorporate mindfulness and meditation into your daily life? Start by setting aside a few minutes each day for formal practice. Find a quiet space where you can sit comfortably and focus on your breath or follow a guided meditation app or video. As you become more accustomed to these practices, you can also incorporate mindfulness into your everyday activities – paying attention to the sensation of water on your skin during a shower or fully savoring each bite of a meal.

Remember, mental wellness is an ongoing journey. By integrating mindfulness and meditation into your routine, you can cultivate a sense of calm, clarity, and resilience that will support your well-being as a Maestro in the business world.

Sustaining Maestro's Wellness: Long-Term Strategies

As a business leader, prioritizing and sustaining wellness is crucial for long-term success in the dynamic world of management. It involves an ongoing commitment to physical and mental well-being, allowing you to continuously grow and thrive as a Maestro.

One of the key long-term strategies for sustaining wellness is to create a holistic approach to self-care. This involves incorporating daily practices that promote physical fitness, such as regular exercise and nutritious eating habits. Additionally, nurturing your mental well-being through mindfulness and self-reflection can enhance resilience and maintain a balanced mindset.

Continuous growth also requires effective stress management. By implementing stress-reducing techniques, such as deep breathing exercises and time management strategies, you can cultivate a sense of calmness even in high-pressure situations. Building resilience and adapting to change are essential skills that will serve you well in the long run.

To sustain wellness in the long term, it's important to establish a supportive network. Surround yourself with mentors, coaches, and peers who foster a positive work environment and provide guidance and resources for personal and professional growth. Collaboration and employee well-being are the building blocks of a thriving organization.

Chapter 39

Balancing the Scales: Work-Life Integration

Work-life integration is a concept that many of us strive to achieve. We want to find a harmonious balance between our ambitious career goals and our personal well-being. But how exactly do we strike that delicate balance? Let's dive into the world of work-life integration and explore effective strategies that can help us navigate this journey.

Imagine this: You're sitting at your desk, engrossed in your work, filled with a sense of accomplishment and purpose. But as the hours fly by, you suddenly realize that you've missed yet another family gathering, where laughter and love were shared. You begin to wonder if there's a way to pursue your career ambitions without sacrificing those precious personal moments.

That's where work-life integration comes in. It's not just about clocking in and out of the office or striving for a perfect work-life balance. It's about finding strategies that allow us to seamlessly blend our professional aspirations with the flexibility to nurture our personal lives.

Whether you're a working professional, an aspiring entrepreneur, or a passionate individual with big dreams, work-life integration can be your guiding light. It helps us prioritize our goals, establish boundaries, and create a supportive network. It paves the way for a more fulfilling and holistic approach to both our personal and professional lives.

So, are you ready to embark on this journey towards work-life integration? Join us as we delve into the depths of this concept, uncovering practical strategies, and embracing a harmonious existence where career and personal well-being coexist in perfect harmony.

Understanding Work-Life Integration

In today's fast-paced world, achieving a harmonious balance between work and personal life has become increasingly challenging. It is time to understand what work-life integration truly means, its definition, and the challenges it presents.

Work-life integration refers to the seamless blending of professional and personal activities, allowing individuals to fulfill their career ambitions while prioritizing their overall well-being. Unlike the traditional concept of work-life balance, which implies a strict separation of work and personal life, work-life integration emphasizes the integration of both aspects to create a more fulfilling and sustainable lifestyle.

However, work-life integration comes with its own set of challenges. Constant connectivity, technological advancements, and the pressure to achieve career success often lead to blurred boundaries between work and personal life. This can result in increased stress, burnout, and a decreased quality of life.

Nevertheless, understanding the definition of work-life integration and the challenges it presents is crucial for individuals seeking a more balanced and fulfilling lifestyle. By doing so, we can explore effective strategies and techniques to overcome these challenges and integrate work and personal life in a way that promotes well-being and success.

Assessing Priorities

When it comes to achieving work-life integration, one of the essential steps is assessing your priorities. By understanding what truly matters to you, you can set meaningful goals that align with your career ambitions and personal well-being.

Start by evaluating different aspects of your life, such as your professional aspirations, relationships, health, and personal interests. Take the time to reflect on what brings you joy, fulfillment, and a sense of purpose. Consider the values that guide your decisions and shape your priorities.

Once you have a clear understanding of your priorities, it becomes easier to make choices that support your work-life integration. You can allocate your time, energy, and resources more effectively, focusing on the things that truly matter to you.

Goal setting plays a crucial role in this process. By setting specific, measurable, achievable, relevant, and time-bound (SMART) goals, you can create a roadmap that aligns your priorities with your actions. Break down your goals into smaller milestones to track your progress and stay motivated along the way.

Techniques for Assessing Priorities

There are various techniques you can use to assess your priorities and gain clarity on what truly matters to you:

Journaling: Writing down your thoughts, feelings, and aspirations can help you gain insight into your deepest desires and priorities.

Meditation: Taking moments of stillness and mindfulness can provide clarity by quieting the noise and distractions of everyday life.

Seeking guidance: Talking to a trusted mentor, coach, or therapist can provide valuable insights and help you navigate the process of assessing your priorities.

Self-reflection: Carving out dedicated time for self-reflection allows you to explore your values, passions, and purpose.

Remember, work-life integration is a dynamic process that requires ongoing assessment and adjustment. As your priorities evolve over time, it's essential to revisit and reassess them periodically to ensure your goals and actions remain aligned with your personal and professional aspirations.

Establishing Boundaries

Creating and maintaining strong boundaries is vital in achieving a healthy work-life integration. By effectively managing your time and setting clear boundaries between your work commitments and personal time, you can avoid feeling overwhelmed and prevent burnout.

One strategy to establish boundaries is to designate specific hours for work-related tasks and personal activities. This helps create a sense of structure and allows you to allocate dedicated time for both aspects of your life.

It's also important to communicate your boundaries to your colleagues and employers, ensuring they understand your availability and personal commitments. By setting expectations and managing others' expectations, you can strike a balance between your professional responsibilities and personal life.

Another effective technique is to create physical boundaries by demarcating a workspace in your home or setting clear guidelines for when and where work-related activities occur. This allows you to mentally switch between work and personal life, reducing the chances of work encroaching on your personal time.

Remember that setting boundaries is not just about protecting your personal time—it also enhances your productivity and focus during work hours. By creating a clear separation between work and personal life, you can optimize your performance and truly be present in both domains.

Flexible Work Arrangements

Work-life integration is all about finding harmony between your professional commitments and personal life. One way to achieve this balance is through flexible work arrangements that promote flexibility, freedom, and a better work-life integration.

Remote work, for example, allows individuals to work from anywhere, eliminating the need for a daily commute and providing the freedom to choose where and when to work. This flexibility can greatly enhance work-life integration, as it allows for more control over one's schedule and the ability to prioritize personal commitments.

Another flexible work option is flextime, which enables employees to have more control over their daily working hours. This means being able to start and end work at different times, as long as the required number of hours is fulfilled. Flextime can be especially helpful for individuals who have personal responsibilities or prefer to work during their most productive hours.

In addition to remote work and flextime, there are various other flexible work arrangements available, such as compressed workweeks or job sharing. These options provide individuals with the opportunity to design their work schedule in a way that best suits their work-life integration needs.

By embracing flexible work arrangements, individuals can enjoy the benefits of a better work-life balance. They can prioritize their personal well-being, manage family responsibilities more effectively, and pursue personal interests without compromising their professional growth. Work-life integration ultimately leads to greater satisfaction and fulfillment in all aspects of life.

Building Support Systems

In the pursuit of work-life integration, it's essential to have a strong support system that understands and supports your goals. Building a supportive work culture and connecting with like-minded individuals can greatly enhance your work-life integration journey.

Nurturing relationships with colleagues and mentors who share your values and aspirations can provide the encouragement and guidance you need. Seek out mentors who have successfully achieved work-life integration and learn from their experiences. Their insights can help you navigate the challenges and make the most of the opportunities.

Building a network of individuals who understand the importance of work-life integration can provide a sense of belonging and solidarity. By connecting with others who share similar goals, you can exchange ideas, share strategies, and support each other along the way.

Additionally, fostering a supportive work culture is crucial for work-life integration. Encourage open communication and promote a healthy work-life balance within your organization. Advocate for flexible work arrangements, such as remote work or flexible schedules, that prioritize personal well-being alongside professional productivity.

Remember, a strong support system and a nurturing work culture can make all the difference in achieving a harmonious work-life integration. By surrounding yourself with individuals who understand and support your goals, you'll have the encouragement and guidance to thrive both personally and professionally.

Managing Stress and Burnout

Work-life integration can often be a challenging endeavor, as the demands of both career and personal life can create a high level of stress. However, with effective stress management techniques and burnout prevention strategies, you can maintain a healthy work-life balance and prioritize self-care.

One crucial aspect of managing stress and preventing burnout is prioritizing self-care. Taking care of your physical, mental, and emotional well-being is essential for long-term success and work-life integration. Incorporate self-care activities into your daily routine, such as exercise, meditation, or engaging in hobbies that bring you joy.

To further reduce stress levels, it's vital to incorporate stress-reduction techniques into your day-to-day life. These can include deep breathing exercises, practicing mindfulness, or taking short breaks throughout the day to relax and recharge.

Remember, prevent burnout by setting boundaries and avoiding overcommitting yourself. Learn to say no when necessary and delegate responsibilities whenever possible. Prioritize tasks and focus on the most critical ones to ensure you're not overwhelmed by an excessive workload.

Creating a supportive work environment and seeking help when needed is also essential. Connect with your colleagues and foster positive relationships that can provide emotional and professional support.

By implementing effective stress management techniques, preventing burnout, and prioritizing self-care, you can successfully navigate the challenges of work-life integration and maintain overall well-being.

Productivity and Time Management

When it comes to work-life integration, productivity and effective time management play a crucial role in maintaining a healthy balance. By implementing the right techniques and strategies, you can optimize your efficiency, minimize distractions, and achieve a better integration between your work and personal life.

Tips for Improving Productivity

To enhance your productivity, start by prioritizing your tasks and creating a realistic schedule. Identify the most important and urgent tasks, and allocate dedicated time slots for them. Utilize to-do lists or productivity apps to stay organized and focused. Break down complex tasks into smaller, manageable steps to make them less overwhelming.

Minimizing distractions is key to staying productive. Find a quiet and conducive workspace, free from noise and interruptions. Practice techniques such as time blocking, where you allocate specific blocks of time for focused work, and utilize the Pomodoro Technique, which involves working in short bursts with regular breaks to maintain concentration.

Effective Time Management Strategies

Time management is essential for achieving an optimal work-life integration. Start by analyzing how you currently spend your time and identify areas where you can make improvements. Set clear goals and establish specific deadlines to keep yourself accountable.

Learn to delegate tasks and avoid micromanaging. Prioritize your tasks based on their importance and urgency, and eliminate or delegate tasks that do not align with your goals or core responsibilities.

Use technology to your advantage by utilizing time management apps, calendar tools, and project management software. These tools can help you streamline your tasks, stay organized, and ensure you meet your deadlines.

Achieving a Better Work-Life Integration

By improving your productivity and time management skills, you can create more space and time for your personal life while still excelling in your professional endeavors. Remember, work-life integration is about finding harmony rather than separating the two worlds.

Efficiently managing your time allows you to allocate dedicated periods for family, hobbies, self-care, and other personal aspects that add fulfillment to your life. It's about recognizing that productivity and personal well-being go hand in hand.

Start implementing these strategies today to enhance your productivity, effectively manage your time, and achieve a better work-life integration. With the right balance, you can thrive both personally and professionally, leading to a more fulfilling and harmonious life.

Nurturing Relationships

When it comes to work-life integration, nurturing relationships is a vital aspect of maintaining a healthy balance. Investing time and energy into your family, friends, and social connections can greatly contribute to your overall well-being and happiness.

Family plays a fundamental role in our lives, providing love, support, and a sense of belonging. Despite professional commitments, it is important to prioritize spending quality time with your loved ones. Create opportunities for shared experiences, such as family outings or regular family dinners, to strengthen bonds and foster a sense of unity.

Friendships also play a significant role in our work-life integration journey. Cultivate meaningful connections with friends who understand and support your goals. Make an effort to schedule regular catch-ups or outings to maintain these relationships. Whether it's grabbing a cup of coffee or participating in a shared hobby, these moments of connection can provide much-needed social support and rejuvenation.

Building a Supportive Social Life

In addition to family and friends, nurturing a fulfilling social life outside of work is essential. Engage in activities and hobbies that bring you joy and allow you to meet like-minded individuals. Join interest-based groups or clubs that align with your passions and interests, as this can lead to meaningful connections and the cultivation of a support system beyond the workplace.

Furthermore, networking events or professional organizations can provide valuable opportunities to expand your social and professional circles. Connect with individuals who share similar career aspirations or interests, as these connections can provide valuable insights, advice, and even potential career opportunities.

Remember, work-life integration encompasses more than just achieving professional success. It involves finding fulfillment and happiness in all areas of your life, including the relationships you form and nurture. By investing time and energy into building and maintaining connections, you can create a harmonious work-life integration that enhances your personal and professional well-being.

Embracing Work-Life Integration

Work-life integration is not just a trendy concept; it is a path to a more fulfilling and harmonious life. By embracing the idea of work-life integration, you can achieve a sense of balance and satisfaction both personally and professionally.

Work-life integration encourages you to align your career ambitions with your personal well-being, allowing you to pursue success without sacrificing other important aspects of your life. It goes beyond simply balancing work and personal life; it aims to harmonize them in a way that brings you joy and fulfillment.

When you fully embrace work-life integration, you open yourself up to countless benefits and rewards. You can experience a greater sense of purpose, as you are no longer compartmentalizing your life but rather integrating all elements into a unified whole. This integration allows you to pursue your passion while nurturing relationships, taking care of your well-being, and finding time for personal growth.

To embrace work-life integration, start by assessing your priorities and setting meaningful goals. Establish clear boundaries between work and personal life to maintain a sense of balance. Seek out flexible work arrangements and build a strong support system that understands and supports your journey. Prioritize self-care, manage stress, and enhance productivity through effective time management. Lastly, nurture relationships and invest time in your social life to create a well-rounded and fulfilling lifestyle.

Chapter 40

The Art of Letting Go: Succession Planning and Departing Gracefully in Business

One can imagine a busy office, with the energy of a group towards one goal. The center of this activity is David, an inspired CEO who has brought remarkable success to the company. This business has become his passion and livelihood but now after years of dedication he finds himself at the crossroads and it is time to pass on the torch.

As reality dawns on him, David's mind becomes clouded with inquiries and worries. What should he do to make sure that the company remains successful? How can he exit in a way that leaves behind good memories? These answers are found in succession planning and departing gracefully.

Succession planning entails preparing for leadership transitions in an organization. It involves identifying potential successors, developing their skills and competencies, and creating a roadmap for a smooth transition. But it goes beyond just finding somebody else; it implies encapsulating company values as well as leaving indelible footprints.

Departing gracefully means letting go with dignity and finesse, while going out as a true success story deserving respect. It means successfully journeying through emotions of surrendering authority while allowing room for continuity and sustainability of operations of the organization.

In this section we will look at how companies effectively use succession planning and depart from business smoothly. We will explore important elements of succession plans together with techniques used when assessing leadership candidates as well as examination into succession pools creation. Lastly we will handle challenges encountered during changes in transition process plus provide tips for making graceful exits from positions held by leaders.

Come along with us on this journey where we shall unearth secret ingredients needed for successful transitioning which encompasses letting go off old ways in business world today.

Understanding Succession Planning

Smooth leadership transitions are guaranteed by effective Succession Planning processes within organizations to ensure continuity (Lepak & Gowan 2009). Succession Planning is about identifying individuals within an organization who have potential to take up future key management positions (Schwartz & Kipp 2000). With proper planning, companies will not experience disruptions and maintain their status quo during leadership changes (Lepak & Gowan 2009).

There are several advantages of implementing a well-executed succession plan to a business. First, it protects the company against sudden vacancies in key management positions which can adversely affect organizational performance and stability (Schwartz & Kipp 2000). Having potential successors in place saves the firm time and energy when recruiting for crucial vacancies.

Furthermore, such an approach assists organizations in developing necessary skills and competencies among their future leaders. By identifying high-potential employees and offering them requisite training as well as development prospects, businesses can ensure that they mould leaders capable of addressing tomorrow's issues.

Additionally, firms with robust succession plans foster transparency within themselves by encouraging trustworthiness. Employees of such companies are more likely to feel appreciated and motivated when career paths become clearer and contributions are recognized. Consequently this aspect may enhance retention rates besides increasing employee engagement levels.

It goes without saying that succession planning is not just about getting ready for the departure of current leaders only but also ensuring that there is sustainable growth in the organization. In addition to investing in the development of future managers, creating an environment where leadership perpetuation is treasured by all stakeholders helps to guarantee longevity amidst constantly shifting business dynamics for firms operating within diverse industry sectors.

Key Components of Succession Planning

To ensure that a leadership transition goes on smoothly, it is mandatory to have a well-structured succession plan. What elements make up an effective succession plan and what strategies can be employed to successfully implement one?

Identifying Potential Successors

One of the fundamental aspects of succession planning is recognizing individuals who have the ability to take over senior positions. This entails evaluating their competences, experience and future potential for leading. By identifying and nurturing them, organizations can identify talented successors who are prepared for leadership.

Developing Leadership Competencies

Developing their leadership competencies is crucial if potential successors are to succeed in their future roles. They can be trained through training programs, mentoring as well as practical leadership experiences. Organizations investing on their development will ensure they are equipped with necessary information that will enable them lead effectively.

Creating a Talent Development Pipeline

Succession planning requires development of pipeline for talent. This includes identification of high potential employees and providing them with growth opportunities and challenging assignments. By growing talent from inside the organization, organizations always have ready leaders for tomorrow.

Managing Knowledge Transfer

Knowledge transfer between outgoing leaders and those taking over is important in succession planning. It requires documenting critical information, processes, best practices among others so as to facilitate smooth transitioning process. Through effective knowledge transfer organizations can minimize disruptions and ensure continuity.

Preparing the Organization for Change

Another key component of succession planning is getting the organization ready for change. Involves communicating the succession plan to stakeholders such as shareholders or investors so that they know why it was done this way or objectives behind it all are met fully understood by stakeholders involved; hence employees' morale will remain high during this period because they were consulted before making decisions about transition through addressing any concerns raised by employees which would act as support during these trying times assuring them about their place within new setup or structure thereby providing an opportunity where whole staff would feel ownership towards changes implemented rather than being imposed upon since they were part of decision making process, thus management will be able to run business smoothly without facing resistance in form of strikes or go slows from workers who would otherwise think that their interests were neglected considering that they did not participate in such important undertakings.

It is by identifying people who have the proper blend of skills, characteristics and signs of potential that organizations can effectively groom future leaders. This proactive approach ensures a smooth transition and a strong leadership pipeline for long-term success.

Succession Candidates Development

To ensure continuity within an organization and effect a smooth change in its leadership, it is imperative to develop potential successors. Developing succession candidates involves a strategic approach that includes leadership development programs, mentoring, and coaching.

Grooming individuals for future leadership roles heavily depends on leadership development programs. Through such programs, these individuals are provided with a ready framework to improve their leadership skills as well as extend their knowledge base towards developing the necessary competencies required for leading positions.

Additionally; the development of succession candidates also involves mentoring and coaching. The guidance provided through experienced leaders play an important role in shaping potential successors' abilities. Mentors and coaches offer valuable feedbacks as well as guiding them through one-on-one interactions for growth opportunities.

There is also creation of talent pipeline through investing in development of succession candidates. High-potential persons need to be identified so that they can be mentored into managerial position whenever there will be any position vacancy. It not only entails continuity in the governance but it also provides for some sort of defensive mechanism against any instances when there would have been vacuum in top management.

Another critical aspect of developing succession candidates is providing continuous learning and growth opportunities. Providing ongoing training sessions, workshops or educational programs keeps potential successors engaged and motivated helping them acquire new skills broaden their perspective on things happening around their industries thereby keeping up with industry trends.

Organizations can achieve this by investing in the development of succession candidates creating culture that fosters continuous learning and development. That shows willingness to support employee's growth while improving employee morale thus attracting talented people who prefer working at places where they are encouraged grow all the time.

The section following looks at transparent communication in relation to the importance of involving key stakeholders in the succession planning process.

Transparent Communication of the Succession Plan

Any succession plan's success largely depends on clear communication. By effectively communicating the succession plan, businesses can ensure that all key stakeholders, including employees, are on board and understand the rationale and objectives behind the plan. This level of transparency fosters trust, minimizes uncertainty, and strengthens the overall transition process.

Engaging employees in a succession planning process is important. Organizations should engage them early enough and invite their input to address their concerns gain insightful ideas from them as well as making them have a sense of belongingness. This collaborative approach not only helps ensure a smoother transition but also boosts employee morale and confidence in the leadership's decision-making.

It is important to proactively manage issues that may raise concerns among employees during transitions by addressing those fears. Anxiety levels are reduced by giving consistent progress updates through open honest communication keeping work environment healthy. Company-wide meetings, town halls news letters or even private feedback sessions can help achieve this.

This is all about being transparent in succession planning, which also means disclosing progress and milestones of the plan. Informing everyone about the process, timeline and landmark makes them feel inclusive and well-informed. On top of that, making regular updates ensures your workers that you are not just sitting back on the matter.

Besides verbal communication, other written materials such as summaries of succession plans or FAQ may be useful to clarify doubts. These resources should be kept within reach.

Good communication during this time is more than just giving information; it involves listening to employees' feedback and concerns. Thus firms can obtain useful ideas, identify any barriers and solve out any arising issues by creating a culture for open talks.

To summarize, a transparent effective communication method is an important foundation for successful succession planning strategy. This can be achieved using stakeholder participation approach while addressing fears through open discussions relating to these changes during transition period.

Putting Succession Plan into Practice

Having established a proper structure for your succession plan's design, the next most significant thing will be its implementation within your organization effectively. Therefore there must be comprehensive planning plus coordination together with clear communication so as to have a smooth leadership takeover.

Firstly , you need to make sure that the objectives of the organization are in line with those of your planned transition e.g., goals . Assess how best the plan would support our missions , visions , long-term goals . Through this way therefore we can guarantee that our success plan has been linked with future successes plus sustainability within your entity.

Additionally, specific responsibilities should be assigned for each stakeholder. In terms of seeing who will take over from whom? , who will assess replacements? and how does they manage staff training?

This means following up what is happening in order to see effectiveness gaps or challenges encountered along the way so that adjustments can be done accordingly. Set some milestones and performance indicators which would help tracking implementation progress as well as ensuring accountability of all stakeholders.

Meeting Challenges and Barriers

The implementation of succession plan may face some difficulties. The most common ones include resistance to change, lack of stakeholder buy-in, and limited resources or time constraints. It is important to anticipate these challenges and develop strategies to overcome them.

One way of dealing with this is by ensuring that there is open and transparent communication during the entire process of implementing the succession plan. During this time, concerns can be handled, questions answered including constant updates on how far the plan has gone for employees and stakeholders by engaging with them. This will help build trust, manage expectations, and maintain motivation throughout the transition.

Additionally consider training employees involved in executing the plan. They need professional development programs as well as resources that can get them prepared for complexities in succession plans . These are tools that should be availed through investing in your team's skills development.

Bear in mind that succession planning is not something that happens once; it requires continuous assessment and refinement. By being proactive and adaptable to changing conditions while utilizing organizational knowledge , successful execution of a planned transitions within your business can be achieved thereby securing its future prosperity.

Managing Change in the Process of Succession

For organizations, leading through transitions can be a challenging task. The whole organization may be affected by leadership change. Therefore, it is crucial to manage this transition properly to make it smooth and maintain productivity and morale.

One main approach towards managing change is effective communication during succession. Employees' concerns can be reduced by openly communicating the reasons for the changes as well as vision of the future. Employee worries may also be allayed by regular notifications or meetings that promote openness.

Addressing resistance to change is also important besides communication. For example, individuals are likely to feel anxious about an unknown area especially during times of transition like these ones above. Acknowledgment and addressing of fears eliminates resistance while creating a supportive environment for all stakeholders.

Another critical aspect of managing change during succession is supporting employees through uncertain times. By helping them navigate their roles and responsibilities within the new leadership structure—through resources, training, guidance—organizations can always provide support when most needed without hindering workflow and easing transition.

Additionally, maintaining productivity and morale is important all through the transitional period. Motivating employees at this time should not be taken lightly by an organization. For instance, recognition programs that foster positive work environments and enable staff members grow personally have been known to lead in productivity improvement.

Effective handling of succession requires careful planning and action steps ahead of time. Organizations can make use of effective communication strategies, overcoming resistance, employee support mechanisms, and ensuring consistent productivity levels if they are to undergo these changes with ease into the future and succeed in their long term goals.

Exiting Gracefully from a Leadership Role

The art of exiting gracefully from a leadership role requires careful planning prior to execution since it's more than just handing over responsibility but also maintaining relationships on a good note.

To ensure smooth transition one strategy would be gradually passing over tasks upon your successor; which allows knowledge transfer as well as providing room for growth into new roles. Open and candid conversation through the process helps in managing expectations and building trust among team members.

During this transition period, it is important that you remain connected to colleagues, subordinates and other stakeholders. By recognizing their contributions and thanking them for their support, a positive impression can be left behind. This will also enable these relationships to survive by maintaining open lines of communication even after stepping down while still being available for guidance.

The emotional side of letting go should not be underestimated. There will naturally be mixed feelings including pride and nostalgia but perhaps even some sense of loss as well. Take care of yourself during this time of change. Engage in self-care activities; seek support from friends and family; focus on new opportunities in front.

Remember the importance of leaving a positive legacy as you transit out of a leadership role. Reflect upon your achievements within the organization as well as how you influenced its success. Therefore, documenting best practices, lessons learned and successes are valuable future leadership resources.

As a final point, gracefully leaving a leadership position requires careful and courteous departure. Transfer duties, keep contacts and prioritize personal wellness for an affirmative impact as well as the smooth handover to new management. Graciously embrace this chance of handing over the mantle, so as to prepare the ground for eventual triumphs.

Conclusion

In conclusion, the art of letting go through effective succession planning and departing gracefully is crucial for the long-term success of businesses. Throughout this section, we have explored the key components of succession planning, including assessing leadership potential, developing succession candidates, communicating the plan, implementing the plan, managing change, and exiting a leadership role with grace. By embracing these strategies, organizations can ensure a smooth transition and maintain continuity in leadership.

It is important for readers to take action and start implementing these strategies within their own organizations. By proactively planning for leadership transitions, businesses can avoid disruptions and maintain productivity. By investing in the development of potential successors, organizations can nurture a strong pipeline of future leaders. By communicating the succession plan transparently, businesses can address concerns and maintain morale. By managing change effectively, organizations can navigate the transition process successfully. And by exiting a leadership role with grace, individuals can leave a positive legacy.

Let us remember that succession planning is an ongoing process that requires continuous monitoring, evaluation, and adjustment. By prioritizing continuity and sustainability, businesses can ensure their long-term success. By embracing the art of letting go and departing gracefully, leaders can pave the way for a smooth transition and create a legacy they can be proud of. It is time to take action and embark on the journey of effective succession planning.

Part VII:
Encore - The Conductor's Legacy

Chapter **41**

Cultural Crescendos: Building a Legacy through Organizational Culture

Imagine this: It's a chilly Monday morning, and you're walking into your office, a bustling hive of activity. As you navigate through the cubicles, you notice an energy in the air – a vibrant hum of collaboration, innovation, and camaraderie. Smiling faces greet you at every turn, as colleagues engage in lively discussions and share ideas.

This isn't just any workplace; it's a place where the organizational culture fosters growth, success, and a lasting legacy. It's a place where employees are motivated, empowered, and united in a shared vision. It's a place where Cultural Crescendos resonate, shaping the very fabric of the organization and building a legacy that will endure for years to come.

In this chapter, we delve into the concept of Cultural Crescendos and explore how they contribute to building an impactful organizational legacy. We'll uncover the strategies and techniques to cultivate a strong organizational culture that not only inspires but also allows your company to thrive. So, buckle up and get ready to embark on a journey of discovery and transformation as we explore the power of building a legacy through organizational culture.

Understanding Cultural Crescendos

Are you curious about the concept of cultural crescendos and how they shape an organization's legacy? Look no further. In this section, we will delve into the meaning and significance of cultural crescendos in building a lasting organizational legacy.

So, what exactly are cultural crescendos? They are the defining moments, values, and behaviors that define an organization's identity and success. Cultural elements, such as shared values, norms, and traditions, play a crucial role in shaping employee attitudes and behaviors, ultimately contributing to the organizational legacy.

When an organization fosters a strong cultural crescendo, it creates a sense of belonging and purpose among its employees. This shared identity helps align individual efforts towards a common goal, driving innovation, collaboration, and organizational success.

Understanding the significance of cultural crescendos is key to harnessing their power. By cultivating a positive and inclusive culture, organizations can attract top talent, retain employees, and build a legacy that transcends the test of time.

Creating a Visionary Organizational Culture

Creating a visionary organizational culture is essential for building a legacy that stands the test of time. When your company's culture is aligned with its mission and values, it becomes a driving force for innovation, adaptability, and long-term success.

To develop a visionary organizational culture, start by clearly defining your company's vision and strategic goals. This will serve as a compass, guiding your organization towards the future you envision. Communicate this vision to all employees, ensuring everyone understands and embraces it.

One effective strategy for creating a visionary culture is to encourage and value innovation. Foster an environment where employees are empowered to think creatively, challenge the status quo, and explore new ideas. Encourage cross-functional collaboration and provide resources for experimentation and prototyping.

Another important element of a visionary organizational culture is adaptability. In today's fast-paced and ever-changing business landscape, the ability to adapt is crucial for long-term success. Encourage a culture that embraces change, welcomes new challenges, and encourages learning from failures.

Empowering Employees

Empowering employees is a key aspect of creating a visionary organizational culture. When employees feel empowered, they are more likely to take ownership of their work, be proactive, and contribute their best ideas and efforts. Provide opportunities for growth and development, and encourage autonomy and decision-making at all levels of the organization.

Furthermore, foster a culture of transparency and open communication. Encourage feedback, listen to ideas, and involve employees in decision-making processes. This creates a sense of ownership and shared responsibility, fueling a collective drive towards achieving the company's vision.

A visionary organizational culture should also promote a strong sense of purpose and meaning. Connect the work employees do to a larger, inspiring purpose beyond individual tasks. Highlight the impact each person's contributions have on the organization's overall mission and vision.

By creating a visionary organizational culture, you are not only building a legacy but also ensuring the long-term success and relevance of your company. When employees are inspired, empowered, and aligned with a shared vision, they become catalysts for growth and innovation, driving the organization towards new heights.

Building Strong Leadership Foundations

Leadership is a vital component in shaping the organizational culture of any company. Strong leadership sets the tone, values, and expectations within an organization, influencing the behaviors and attitudes of its members. By cultivating strong leadership foundations, organizations can create a culture of trust, respect, and open communication, laying the groundwork for success.

The Role of Leadership in Culture

Leadership acts as a guide, steering the organization towards its goals and shaping the values and beliefs that define its culture. When leaders embody the principles they wish to see reflected in their organization, they inspire and motivate others to follow suit. This alignment between leadership and culture is essential for creating a harmonious and productive work environment.

Developing Strong Leadership Skills

Strong leadership skills are key to fostering a culture that promotes growth, innovation, and collaboration. Leaders must possess the ability to effectively communicate organizational values, set clear expectations, and provide guidance and support. By investing in leadership development programs, organizations can empower their leaders with the tools and knowledge needed to drive cultural transformation.

Fostering a Culture of Trust and Respect

Trust and respect are foundational elements of a healthy organizational culture. Strong leaders create an atmosphere of psychological safety, where team members feel comfortable expressing their ideas, challenging the status quo, and taking calculated risks. By promoting a culture of trust and respect, leaders foster a sense of belonging and empower employees to fully contribute to the organization's success.

Open Communication as a Catalyst for Cultural Development

Open communication is crucial in building strong leadership foundations. Leaders must actively listen to their team members, value their input, and provide regular feedback. Transparent and inclusive communication channels promote collaboration, problem-solving, and the exchange of innovative ideas, driving the development of a vibrant organizational culture.

Fostering Collaboration and Teamwork

Collaboration and teamwork are essential components of a strong organizational culture. When employees work together towards a shared goal, they can achieve remarkable results and drive collective success.

In a collaborative environment, individuals bring their unique perspectives, skills, and expertise to the table. This diversity of thought fosters creativity and innovation, allowing teams to come up with fresh ideas and solutions to complex problems.

Effective collaboration also promotes effective problem-solving. By pooling their knowledge and experiences, teams can tackle challenges more efficiently and develop robust strategies that address the root causes of the issues they face.

Moreover, collaboration and teamwork contribute to building a supportive and positive work environment. When employees feel that their voices are heard and valued, they are more motivated, engaged, and loyal to the organization. This sense of belonging fosters a strong sense of camaraderie and unity within the team.

Strategies for fostering collaboration and teamwork

To foster collaboration and teamwork, organizations can implement the following strategies:

Encourage open communication and active listening: Create a culture where individuals feel comfortable expressing their ideas and opinions. Promote active listening to ensure that everyone's perspectives are heard and respected.

Build cross-functional teams: Assemble teams with members from different departments or areas of expertise to encourage diversity of thought and maximize collaboration opportunities.

Provide collaboration tools and technology: Equip teams with the necessary tools and technology to facilitate seamless communication and collaboration, whether they are working in the office or remotely.

Recognize and reward collaborative efforts: Acknowledge and celebrate instances of successful collaboration, both on an individual and team level. This recognition reinforces the importance of collaboration and encourages others to follow suit.

Promote a culture of trust and psychological safety: Create an environment where individuals feel safe to take risks, share their ideas, and offer constructive feedback. Trust is essential for effective collaboration and teamwork.

By fostering collaboration and teamwork, organizations can cultivate a thriving organizational culture that inspires creativity, solves complex challenges, and achieves collective success.

Encouraging Employee Engagement and Empowerment

Employee engagement and empowerment are key ingredients for fostering a thriving organizational culture. When employees feel engaged and empowered, they become more invested in their work, leading to increased productivity, innovation, and overall job satisfaction.

Creating a culture that values and leverages the skills, talents, and ideas of all employees is essential for long-term success. It starts with creating an environment where employees feel heard, respected, and included. Open lines of communication and regular feedback can go a long way in making employees feel empowered and valued.

Additionally, providing opportunities for growth and development is crucial in fostering employee engagement. By investing in their professional development and offering training programs, employees feel empowered to take ownership of their careers and contribute meaningfully to the organization.

Collaboration also plays a vital role in employee engagement and empowerment. Encouraging teamwork and creating cross-functional projects and initiatives enable employees to connect, collaborate, and learn from one another. This not only strengthens their engagement with their work but also empowers them to contribute to the organization's success.

By unlocking the potential of employees through engagement and empowerment, organizations can create a culture that attracts and retains top talent, fosters innovation, and drives long-term growth. Investing in employee engagement and empowerment is an investment in the organization's future success.

Embracing Diversity and Inclusion

Embracing diversity and inclusion is crucial in fostering a thriving organizational culture. By celebrating diversity and creating an inclusive workplace, organizations can reap numerous benefits.

Diversity brings together individuals with different backgrounds, perspectives, and experiences. It fuels innovation, creativity, and problem-solving by introducing a variety of ideas and approaches. Embracing diversity allows organizations to tap into a rich pool of talents, leading to better decision-making and improved business outcomes.

Inclusion is the act of creating an equitable environment where everyone feels valued, respected, and supported. It goes beyond diversity by actively involving individuals from diverse backgrounds in decision-making processes, providing equal opportunities for growth and advancement, and fostering a sense of belonging.

Organizations that prioritize diversity and inclusion in their organizational culture cultivate a workplace that attracts and retains top talent. This, in turn, enhances employee engagement, productivity, and overall satisfaction. A diverse and inclusive culture also helps organizations better serve diverse customer bases and connect with a wider range of stakeholders.

Strategies for Creating an Inclusive and Equitable Workplace

Creating an inclusive and equitable workplace requires intentional efforts from leadership and every member of the organization. Here are some strategies to consider:

Promote diversity in recruitment and hiring processes, ensuring diverse candidate pools and equitable selection criteria.

Provide diversity and inclusion training to all employees, raising awareness and promoting empathy.

Foster an inclusive culture through open dialogue, active listening, and addressing biases and stereotypes.

Create employee resource groups or affinity networks that provide support and representation for underrepresented groups.

Establish inclusive policies and practices, such as flexible work arrangements, to accommodate diverse needs and promote work-life balance.

Regularly assess and measure diversity and inclusion efforts to identify areas for improvement and track progress.

By embracing diversity and inclusion, organizations can foster a culture where every individual feels valued, respected, and empowered to contribute their unique perspectives and talents. This not only strengthens the organization but also contributes to a more inclusive society as a whole.

Nurturing a Culture of Continuous Learning

Continuous learning plays a vital role in building an impactful organizational culture. By fostering a culture of ongoing growth and development, companies can stay ahead of the curve and adapt to the ever-changing business landscape.

One technique for nurturing a culture of continuous learning is to encourage employees to embrace a learning mindset. This involves promoting a curiosity-driven approach to work and providing opportunities for knowledge sharing and exploration. Encouraging employees to ask questions, seek out new learning experiences, and challenge the status quo can lead to innovative ideas and breakthrough solutions.

Another strategy is to provide development opportunities that empower employees to enhance their skill sets and expand their knowledge. This can include offering training programs, workshops, conferences, and mentoring opportunities. By investing in their employees' growth, organizations not only foster a culture of continuous learning but also demonstrate their commitment to their workforce's professional development.

Furthermore, organizations can encourage continuous learning by creating channels for knowledge sharing and collaboration. This can involve setting up internal platforms for employees to share articles, insights, or best practices related to their respective fields. By embracing a culture of collective learning, organizations can tap into the collective wisdom and expertise of their employees, accelerating growth and fostering innovation.

Lastly, it is essential for leaders to lead by example and prioritize their own continuous learning journeys. When leaders show a genuine commitment to learning and development, it sends a powerful message to the rest of the organization. By modeling the behavior they wish to see, leaders create an environment where continuous learning is valued and embraced by all.

In conclusion, nurturing a culture of continuous learning is crucial for building an impactful organizational culture. By fostering a learning mindset, providing development opportunities, promoting knowledge sharing, and leading by example, companies can create an environment that thrives on growth, innovation, and long-term success.

Sustaining Cultural Crescendos for the Future

In order to maintain a strong organizational culture in the long term, it is vital to sustain and nurture the cultural crescendos that have been established. These cultural crescendos are the powerful moments, values, and traditions that shape the essence of an organization. They create a sense of identity and purpose, and contribute to building a lasting legacy.

One strategy for sustaining cultural crescendos is to continuously reinforce the values and behaviors that align with the desired culture. Regularly communicate and celebrate the core principles that define your organizational culture. This can be done through internal communication platforms, such as newsletters, town hall meetings, and recognition programs, to ensure that the cultural crescendos remain at the forefront of employees' minds.

Another important aspect of sustaining cultural crescendos is adapting to changing times. As organizations evolve and face new challenges, it is essential to review and refine cultural elements to ensure they remain relevant and meaningful. Embracing innovation and fostering a culture of continuous learning can help organizations stay agile and responsive, allowing them to sustain their cultural crescendos while embracing necessary adaptations.

Lastly, sustaining cultural crescendos requires strong leadership commitment and involvement. Leaders play a crucial role in championing the organizational culture and modeling the desired behaviors. By consistently demonstrating and reinforcing the cultural crescendos, leaders can inspire and motivate employees to uphold the cultural legacy of the organization.

Chapter **42**

Virtuoso Values: Embedding Values in Everyday Business Practices

Imagine a small coffee shop nestled in the heart of a bustling city. Day in and day out, the aroma of freshly brewed coffee fills the air, enticing weary travelers and regulars alike. But what sets this particular coffee shop apart is not just the quality of their drinks, but the values that guide every aspect of their business.

Virtuoso Values.

From the fair trade beans they source to the eco-friendly packaging they use, this coffee shop is a shining example of how embedding values in everyday business practices can create a truly exceptional experience for both customers and employees.

In this chapter, we will explore the concept of Virtuoso Values and how they can be integrated into your own company's operations. By infusing your core ethics into every decision and action, you can lay the groundwork for a business that not only thrives financially but also makes a positive impact on the world.

Understanding Virtuoso Values

Before delving into the practical aspects of embedding values in everyday business practices, it is crucial to grasp the concept of Virtuoso Values. These values are not merely a set of guidelines; they represent the core ethics that underpin a company's operations and shape its identity.

By embracing virtuoso values, businesses can establish an ethical framework that guides decision-making, fosters a positive work culture, and builds trust among stakeholders. It goes beyond compliance with regulations; it involves a genuine commitment to ethical business practices.

While the specific values may differ from one organization to another, some common examples include integrity, transparency, accountability, and social responsibility. These values form the foundation for ethical behavior in the workplace and contribute to the development of a sustainable business.

Understanding the importance of core ethics allows businesses to create an environment that encourages ethical decision-making at all levels. By aligning actions with virtuoso values, companies can build a reputation for integrity, attract top talent, and foster strong relationships with customers and clients.

The Benefits of Virtuoso Values

Embracing Virtuoso Values and embedding them in your company's daily operations can have a multitude of benefits for your business's long-term success. These values, based on core ethics and ethical business practices, create a strong foundation that goes beyond financial gains.

One of the key benefits of embracing Virtuoso Values is the establishment of trust with stakeholders. By consistently demonstrating ethical behavior and transparency, your company builds a reputation for integrity and reliability. This trust can lead to stronger relationships with customers, investors, and partners, opening doors to new opportunities and collaborations.

Moreover, Virtuoso Values can differentiate your business from competitors in the market. In an era where consumers increasingly value sustainability and social responsibility, companies that prioritize ethical practices are more likely to attract and retain customers. By aligning your business with these values, you can build a loyal customer base and establish a competitive advantage.

Additionally, embedding Virtuoso Values into your company's culture can have a positive effect on employee satisfaction and engagement. Your values become a guiding force that employees can rally behind, leading to a stronger sense of purpose and a more cohesive workforce. This, in turn, fosters a positive work environment and enhances productivity and innovation.

Furthermore, ethical business practices can attract and retain top talent. In today's workforce, many individuals seek employers with strong values and a commitment to making a positive impact. By clearly demonstrating your company's dedication to Virtuoso Values, you can attract like-minded individuals who are passionate about contributing to a purpose-driven organization.

Lastly, embracing Virtuoso Values can contribute to long-lasting success by ensuring sustainability and adaptability. Companies that prioritize ethical business practices are more likely to navigate challenges effectively, embrace change, and stay ahead in an ever-evolving business landscape.

In summary, the benefits of embracing Virtuoso Values are vast. By incorporating these values into your company's everyday practices, you can build trust, differentiate your business, engage employees, attract top talent, and ensure long-lasting success in a rapidly changing world.

Developing a Values-Driven Culture

Creating a values-driven culture is essential for effectively embedding Virtuoso Values into your everyday business practices. A values-driven culture sets the stage for a cohesive and purposeful company culture, aligning with your core ethics and engaging employees at every level.

A values-driven culture is rooted in strong leadership and a clear articulation of the organization's values and principles. It requires intentional effort to integrate these values into all aspects of the business, including decision-making, communication, and employee behavior.

One key strategy for developing a values-driven culture is establishing communication channels that foster transparency and openness. This allows employees to understand and align with the values that guide the company's operations. Engaging employees in regular dialogues about the importance of these values encourages them to embrace and apply them in their daily work.

Another crucial aspect of developing a values-driven culture is fostering employee engagement. Engaged employees are more likely to connect with the company's values and contribute to their integration. This can be accomplished through employee recognition programs, opportunities for growth and development, and creating a positive work environment where employees feel valued and empowered.

A values-driven culture also requires support and reinforcement from leadership. When leaders consistently demonstrate and promote the organization's values, employees are more likely to embrace them as well. Leaders should lead by example, demonstrating ethical behavior and making decisions that align with the company's values.

Nurturing a Commitment to Virtuoso Values

To foster a values-driven culture, it is essential to create opportunities for ongoing education and training on the organization's values. This helps employees understand how they can embody these values in their day-to-day work and interactions with colleagues, customers, and other stakeholders.

Providing regular feedback and recognition for employees who exemplify the values helps reinforce their importance and encourages others to follow suit. This can be done through performance evaluations, team meetings, or other forms of recognition and celebration.

Ultimately, developing a values-driven culture is an ongoing process that requires continuous improvement and reinforcement. It goes far beyond simply stating the company's values; it involves integrating them into the fabric of the organization and creating an environment where they are lived and breathed by every employee.

A values-driven culture not only enhances employee engagement and satisfaction but also attracts top talent who are aligned with the company's principles. It fosters a sense of shared purpose and drives long-term success for the organization.

Communicating Values Effectively

Simply having Virtuoso Values is not enough; you need to effectively communicate them both internally and externally. Clear and consistent communication plays a crucial role in ensuring alignment and transparency throughout your organization.

Internally, it is essential to communicate your company's values to employees in a way that inspires and motivates them. This can be achieved through regular communication channels such as team meetings, email updates, and company-wide announcements. By highlighting the importance of the values and providing examples of how they can be incorporated into daily work, you can encourage employees to embrace and live out these values in their roles.

External communication plays a key role in portraying your company's values to customers, partners, and other stakeholders. Your website, social media platforms, and marketing materials should clearly and authentically communicate your core ethics, demonstrating how your organization aligns with those values. This can help attract and retain customers who share similar beliefs and create a sense of trust and loyalty among your stakeholders.

Internal Communication

When it comes to internal communication, consider using various channels to reinforce your company's values. Regularly share success stories that exemplify how employees have integrated the values into their work, encouraging others to do the same. Foster an open and transparent environment where employees feel comfortable discussing and raising concerns related to the values. By involving employees in the process and providing opportunities for feedback and discussion, you can ensure that the values are understood, embraced, and consistently practiced throughout the organization.

External Communication

Externally, your communication should reflect the authenticity and sincerity of your values. Develop a strong brand messaging strategy that revolves around your values, making them prominent in your marketing campaigns and customer interactions. Highlight the ways in which your organization is making a positive impact on society or the environment, ensuring that these actions align with your stated values. This can create a strong emotional connection with your target audience, establishing trust and loyalty.

Remember, effective communication is a continuous process. Regularly evaluate and adjust your communication strategies to ensure they remain relevant and impactful. By consistently and authentically communicating your Virtuoso Values, both internally and externally, you can create a strong, values-driven culture that sets your organization apart.

Aligning Values with Business Goals

For a company to thrive and achieve long-term success, it is crucial to align its values with its business goals. By integrating Virtuoso Values into the strategic planning process, organizations can ensure that their core ethics and principles guide every decision and action. This alignment between values and business objectives creates a powerful synergy that drives growth, fosters employee engagement, and enhances the company's overall reputation.

Strategic planning serves as the roadmap for achieving organizational goals. It involves setting measurable objectives, identifying key performance indicators, and determining the strategies and tactics needed to achieve those objectives. However, for strategic planning to be truly effective, it must incorporate the company's values as guiding principles and strategic drivers.

When aligning values with business goals, it is essential to consider the broader impact of the organization's actions on its stakeholders, including employees, customers, communities, and the environment. By integrating Virtuoso Values into the strategic planning process, companies can ensure that their actions are not only profitable but also ethical and sustainable.

To align values with business goals effectively, organizations should:

Define organizational values: Clearly articulate the core values that represent the company's ethical principles and beliefs.

Align values with mission and vision: Ensure that the organization's values are in harmony with its mission and vision statements, providing a unified framework for decision-making.

Integrate values into goal-setting: Incorporate Virtuoso Values into the establishment of strategic objectives, ensuring that they are consistent with the company's ethical guidelines.

Communicate and train: Effectively communicate the organization's values to all employees, and provide training programs to ensure understanding and alignment.

Evaluate and measure: Establish metrics and performance indicators that assess the implementation and impact of Virtuoso Values on business goals.

By aligning values with business goals, organizations can create a strong ethical foundation while also promoting financial success and sustainable growth. This alignment fosters a positive company culture, enhances employee satisfaction and loyalty, builds trust with customers and stakeholders, and ultimately leads to long-term success and a positive impact on society.

Integrating Values into Hiring and Onboarding

Embedding Virtuoso Values into your company's culture starts from the very first step of the employee journey - the hiring and onboarding process. By incorporating values-based hiring practices, you can ensure that new employees align with your company's core ethics and contribute to a positive workplace environment.

Values-based hiring goes beyond simply assessing qualifications and skills. It focuses on finding candidates who demonstrate a strong cultural fit and share the same values as your organization. This approach helps create a cohesive team that is committed to upholding the ethical standards of your business.

During the onboarding process, it is essential to emphasize your company's Virtuoso Values and their importance. This can be done through interactive orientation sessions, training programs, and mentorship opportunities. By providing new employees with a clear understanding of your organization's values, you can set expectations and enable them to make decisions that align with your core ethics.

An effective onboarding process also includes integrating new hires into your company's culture through team-building activities, introductions to key stakeholders, and opportunities to engage with existing employees. This allows new team members to build relationships, adapt quickly, and feel a sense of belonging within your company.

By embedding Virtuoso Values into the hiring and onboarding process, you can foster a strong ethical foundation within your organization. This commitment to values-based practices not only attracts employees who are aligned with your core ethics but also strengthens your company's culture and enhances overall employee satisfaction.

Implementing Values in Performance Management

Embedding values into everyday business practices requires a comprehensive approach that extends to performance management systems. By integrating values-based performance management, employee evaluations, feedback processes, and performance metrics, organizations can reinforce ethical behavior and foster a culture of integrity.

Values-based performance management goes beyond assessing individual job performance; it incorporates a holistic evaluation of employees based on their adherence to the organization's core values. This approach recognizes that an employee's behavior and actions are equally important indicators of their contributions.

During employee evaluations, managers should assess not only performance outcomes but also how well employees demonstrate the organization's values in their daily work. This evaluation should involve specific examples and observations that highlight the alignment between an employee's actions and the organization's ethical standards.

Providing feedback is another crucial element of values-based performance management. Managers should offer constructive feedback that acknowledges and reinforces ethical behavior while also addressing areas for improvement. This feedback should be fair, transparent, and focused on promoting a values-driven culture.

Additionally, performance metrics should reflect the organization's values and ethical expectations. By setting standards that align with the desired behaviors and outcomes, organizations can incentivize employees to embody the organization's core values in their work.

Integrating values into performance management requires ongoing communication and training. Managers should be equipped with the skills to effectively evaluate employee alignment with values and provide constructive feedback. Furthermore, employees should have a clear understanding of how their performance is measured against the organization's values.

Through values-based performance management, organizations can cultivate a workforce that not only achieves business goals but also upholds the organization's ethical principles. By aligning performance evaluations, feedback processes, and performance metrics with the organization's values, companies can create a culture that promotes integrity, accountability, and long-term success.

Engaging Employees in Values Integration

Employee engagement is a crucial factor in successfully embedding Virtuoso Values into your organization's everyday business practices. When employees are actively committed to your company's values, they become strong ambassadors for ethical behavior and contribute to a positive and productive work environment.

To foster employee commitment to your organization's values, it is important to create opportunities for meaningful participation and involvement. By involving employees in the values integration process, you empower them to take ownership of the company's ethical framework and contribute their unique insights. This not only enhances their sense of belonging and fulfillment but also strengthens the overall alignment between individual and organizational values.

Creating a Sense of Purpose

One effective strategy for fostering employee commitment is to clearly communicate the purpose behind your organization's Virtuoso Values. When employees understand the why behind their work and the values driving it, they are more likely to feel a sense of purpose and be motivated to align their actions accordingly.

Regularly communicate the impact of their contributions towards upholding these values and emphasize how their work directly contributes to the larger organizational goals. By connecting their daily tasks to the broader ethical framework, employees will see the value and importance of their efforts, further strengthening their commitment to the company's values.

Providing Opportunities for Growth and Development

Investing in employee growth and development is another powerful way to engage them in the values integration process. By providing access to training and development programs that align with your organization's Virtuoso Values, you are not only enhancing their skills but also reinforcing the importance of those values in their professional growth.

Recognize and reward employees who demonstrate exemplary commitment to the company's values. This can be done through promotions, special assignments, or formal recognition programs. By highlighting and celebrating their adherence to Virtuoso Values, you reinforce the significance of ethical behavior and inspire others to follow suit.

Building a Supportive and Inclusive Culture

Create a supportive and inclusive work culture that encourages open dialogue and active participation. Foster an environment where employees feel safe to share their perspectives, ask questions, and raise concerns related to the organization's values.

Encourage collaboration and teamwork by providing opportunities for cross-functional projects and initiatives centered around the Virtuoso Values. By involving employees from different departments and levels, you promote a sense of camaraderie and shared responsibility for upholding the company's ethical framework.

Regularly communicate updates and progress on values integration initiatives, such as improvements in company policies and practices that further support Virtuoso Values. This demonstrates transparency and reinforces employees' trust and confidence in the organization's commitment to ethical behavior.

By engaging your employees in the values integration process, you foster a culture of committed individuals who actively contribute to the successful implementation of Virtuoso Values in everyday business practices. Their dedication and alignment with the company's core ethics will not only strengthen your organization's reputation but also create a positive and fulfilling work environment for all.

Overcoming Challenges in Values Integration

While embedding Virtuoso Values in everyday business practices brings numerous benefits, it is not without its challenges. Organizations often face resistance to change and struggle to achieve organizational alignment when integrating values into their operations. Overcoming these challenges is essential to ensure the successful integration and sustained impact of Virtuoso Values.

Resistance to Change:

One of the primary challenges in values integration is the resistance to change from employees and other stakeholders. People naturally tend to resist significant changes in their routines and established ways of working. To address this, organizations must focus on effective change management strategies that emphasize the purpose and benefits of the values integration effort. Clear communication, engagement, and ongoing support are crucial in overcoming resistance and fostering a positive attitude towards change.

Organizational Alignment:

Another challenge is achieving organizational alignment when integrating values into everyday business practices. This involves ensuring that all departments, teams, and individuals are aligned with the core ethics and behaviors associated with Virtuoso Values. It requires a comprehensive analysis of existing processes, structures, and systems to identify any misalignments. By prioritizing values alignment in strategic planning and decision-making, organizations can create a cohesive culture that supports and reinforces the desired ethical behaviors.

Strategies for Overcoming Challenges:

To successfully overcome the challenges in values integration, organizations can implement the following strategies:

Clear and consistent communication: Communicate the purpose, benefits, and expected outcomes of values integration throughout the organization. Engage employees in open dialogue and address any concerns or misconceptions they may have.

Leadership commitment: Leadership plays a crucial role in driving values integration. Leaders should actively demonstrate and promote the desired values, acting as role models for the rest of the organization.

Education and training: Provide necessary education and training to employees to help them understand and embrace the embedded values. This includes workshops, seminars, and ongoing learning opportunities.

Recognition and rewards: Recognize and reward individuals and teams who exemplify the desired values in their work. This highlights the importance of values integration and motivates others to align their behaviors accordingly.

Continuous monitoring and feedback: Regularly assess the progress of values integration efforts through feedback mechanisms and performance evaluations. Use this feedback to identify areas for improvement and make necessary adjustments.

By implementing these strategies, organizations can overcome the challenges in values integration, foster a culture of ethical behavior, and achieve long-lasting organizational alignment.

Sustaining Virtuoso Values for the Future

As businesses navigate an ever-changing landscape, sustaining virtuoso values becomes paramount for long-term success. Embedding these core ethics into everyday business practices sets the foundation for creating a company culture that embraces continuous improvement and evolving values.

Continuous improvement is essential to sustain virtuoso values. By regularly evaluating and refining your business practices, you can ensure that your values remain relevant and aligned with the evolving needs of your stakeholders. This commitment to growth and adaptation fosters a culture of innovation and drives positive change within the organization.

Evolving values are a natural part of any dynamic business environment. As societal expectations shift, it is crucial to have the flexibility to revise and update your values while staying true to your ethical principles. This adaptability allows your company to remain relevant and responsive to the changing needs of your customers, employees, and the wider community.

Ultimately, sustaining virtuoso values requires an ongoing commitment to an ethical business mindset. By integrating these values into your decision-making processes, communication channels, and employee engagement initiatives, you create a holistic approach that aligns your business practices with your core ethics. This commitment not only strengthens your organization's reputation but also attracts like-minded employees, investors, and partners who are essential for long-term growth and success.

Chapter 43

A Standing Ovation: Recognition and Reward Systems in Business Management

Imagine you're walking into an office and the atmosphere is charged with electricity as employees exchange smiles, and work output skyrockets. All this has been attributed to a culture in a workplace that knows the strength of acknowledgment and rewards in propelling motivation and engagement.

In today's competitive business environment, companies are realizing the need to have effective recognition and reward systems to keep their best workers and also create a positive working environment.

This chapter focuses on the role played by recognition and reward systems as tools for running firms. From understanding why workplace recognition matters, through different awards programs, designing pay structures that work, measuring their effects, we reveal the tactics as well as good practices that can make your company become a hub of motivation and triumph.

Let us take you through this journey of unearthing your employee's potentiality by awarding them with meaningful recognitions.

Significance of Recognition at Work

Workplace recognition plays an important role in creating an encouraging work place; this is especially so due to present day dynamic business setting. When employees feel valued for the effort they put into their works, it boosts not only their morale but also increases their level of motivation hence optimal performance.

However, appreciating workers' input goes beyond mere patting on the back; it is about acknowledging what they have done so far which shows how much what they do actually matters within that organization. In essence it creates appreciation culture within an organization where people are seen for who they are or even recognized when they excel collectively or individually.

Recognition at work helps employees gain purposefulness which leads to increased job satisfaction resulting from a strong sense of belongingness among other factors such as loyalty towards ones employer. Similarly appreciated workers tend to give more than what is required of them at their workplaces resulting into higher productivity levels (Hermes & Lenssen 2015).

Moreover, one can argue that recognizing one's colleagues in this way will foster an environment where everyone feels valued and supported. Such a positive culture not only improves employee wellbeing but also boosts collaboration, team working, and camaraderie amongst staff members. It creates a virtuous cycle where employees are motivated to support one another, resulting in a more harmonious and effective working environment.

Ultimately organizations can use recognition as an effective tool towards enhancing motivation of their employees, increasing productivity at the workplace and creating a conducive work environment among others. By utilizing various tools that feature effective rewards programs for instance, businesses will be able to encourage such human capital by appreciating them which consequently leads to higher levels of stakeholders' engagement.

Recognition Programs

When it comes to recognizing or appreciating outstanding workers, there are many types of recognition programs available for companies. In addition, these programs highly encourage employees' appreciation and engagement apart from just awarding those who are excelling at their work places. This portion therefore looks into some common forms of recognition programs together with their advantages and how best they can be implemented.

Employee of the month

Employee of the Month is one example of conventional reward program designed for high performing workers who have made significant contributions. As an organization this initiative does not only motivate the exceptional performance but also raises performance standards. This will enable different firms highlight on specific achievements that may lead to increased morale as well as motivation besides strengthening their commitment towards rewarding remarkable effort demonstrated by chosen personnel.

Peer Recognition

Employees themselves have the power to appreciate and acknowledge their colleagues' hard work in peer recognition plans. This way of acknowledging is intended to create a good working environment where individuals are inspired to support each other. Organizations can help develop a sense of teamwork and companionship by enabling employees to acknowledge their colleagues' achievements, leading ultimately to improved employee satisfaction and involvement.

The Team Approach

An effective way of fostering cooperation and team work is recognizing and rewarding teams for their collective contributions. The program of rewards that is team-based recognizes how collective efforts resulted in successful outcomes, thus motivating employees towards common goals. By honoring group accomplishments businesses are able to foster unity, stimulus and pride across the workforce.

To implement such recognition programs there should be proper planning, organization procedures need to be transparently laid down so that no one feels neglected on grounds of favoritism within selection process. Moreover, companies must clearly articulate the value of these programs so that workers can willingly participate in them with enthusiasm. On the other hand, an atmosphere of appreciation can be created within organizations by embracing this type of recognition through developing a sense purpose hence improve employee engagement.

Designing Effective Reward Systems

Effective reward systems play a vital role in motivating employees as well as driving high performance among workers. Through aligning these systems with your company's objectives you can create an environment that not only acknowledges but also incentivizes top performing employees.

In order for it to become effective, setting clear goals is always recommended before designing this system. Employees are able to realize what they should achieve at any given time since they understand what specific targets have been set for them on which basis compensation may depend later on. In any case whether it concerns attaining sales quotas or completing project stages, goals must abide by criteria based on SMART (specific, measurable, achievable, relevant & time-bound).

Choosing appropriate incentives also plays a significant part in boosting employee morale; monetary motivators although effective are best complemented with non-financial incentives. For example, personalized rewards like extended holiday time, flexible working hours and chances at professional growth could be considered among them. When it comes to rewarding employees, personalizing such incentives will give them a sense of being valued.

Establishing Fair and Transparent Processes

Just as when designing reward systems, this also applies in establishing fair and transparent processes. Employees need to know how their performance is evaluated for purposes of determining reward; otherwise they would feel unfairly treated. This creates transparency that strengthens trust within the organization and ensures fairness of the system.

In addition, involve employees in the process by soliciting their input and feedback. They will then have a sense of ownership and confidence in the system. Regularly update on progress towards goals and criteria so that the process remains open for everyone to see.

To sum up, designing effective reward systems entails setting clear goals, selecting meaningful incentives, establishing fair and transparent processes. By aligning these systems with your business objectives while leveraging employee preferences you can create an environment that is exciting enough thereby serving as a motivating factor towards your workforce.

The Role of Leadership in Recognizing Employees

Leadership has a major say in shaping an organizational culture where recognition is important. Positive work environments are created by supervisors who acknowledge their subordinates' inputs to team projects or tasks assigned to them respectively . By respecting colleagues' accomplishments leaders set examples to others making it possible for success stories to continue happening.

Qualities of Effective Employee Recognition Leaders

Visibility – This aspect is seen when the leader engages the employees, regularly acknowledges their efforts and recognizes exceptional work done.

Empathy – In this case, the leader must understand individual members of his team on a personal level so as to know how to appreciate them differently.

Authenticity – Moreover, authenticity in accepting territorial realities gives rise to trust between superiors and subordinates.

Additionally, effective leaders prioritize employee recognition and integrate it into daily operations. For instance, by embedding these rewards into performance appraisals, team discussions or day-to-day interactions they underscore how important employee appreciation is throughout an organization.

Leaders also have the opportunity to empower their team members by involving them in recognition processes. Employee involvement may involve peer-to-peer recognition programs as well as providing avenues where employees can nominate other fellow workers for special commendations.

To summarize, leadership plays a crucial role in acknowledging employees. By exhibiting factors such as visibility, empathy and authenticity among others; effective leaders contribute towards developing the culture of recognition within their organizations that enhance motivation at work and overall success..

Measuring Impact of Recognition and Rewards

Impact: Effective recognition and reward programs have a significant impact on employee engagement and overall performance. However, businesses need different methods of measuring the effectiveness of these initiatives. Organizations should use techniques like specific analysis approaches as well as studying key indicators which will inform them about whether their programs are working or not.

Employee engagement is another important metric to consider. Measuring engagement allows us to obtain an overview of how much satisfaction or motivation we get from our organizational rewards system. A survey can be conducted among the workers while at work or even after work which would enable them rate their involvement with regard to how engaged they are with what is happening around them.

Also organizational metrics such productivity measures, performance ratings and retention rates can be used for evaluating the effect that rewarding has had on employees' careers over time. These metrics can then be compared before and after implementation to see if there has been positive shift in employee outcomes.

Again, a qualitative research method such as focus groups or interviews with employees can be used to gather information about how recognition and rewards affect their engagement and commitment levels. These insights help organizations understand how well these programs are perceived by their workforce and inform some of the possible ways for making them better.

Measurement using technology

With new technological advances, organizations use technology to measure the impact of recognition and reward programs. The software that is available in the market today can track engagement surveys, award distribution and feedback from employees. These tools offer comprehensive reporting and analytics thereby allowing businesses acquire up-to-the-minute details on the efficacy of their initiatives.

It should also be noted that measuring impact of recognition and rewards does not happen just once. Firms should consistently evaluate their programs to ensure they are still effective enough. This will enable recognition and reward systems to remain relevant both from an employee's standpoint as well as towards business objectives.

Measuring impact of recognition and reward programs helps in optimizing employee engagement and overall performance. By blending qualitative with quantitative research approaches, firms learn a lot from this exercise which informs them when making future decisions thereby promoting learning culture..

Overcoming challenges in implementing Recognition & Reward Systems

The issue of recognition and reward systems' implementation in an organization can be complex and challenging. In this section, we discuss several obstacles that companies generally face and provide strategies for overcoming them.

For example, ensuring that the reward and recognition system aligns with the company's goals, values and objectives is a major challenge. Systems should represent not only mission and values of the company but also strike a chord with employees. Companies are able to adapt their programs for rewards and appreciation to make it part of belongingness by understanding relationship between their cultures.

Additionally, establishing a supportive work culture where workers participate actively in the management process can be difficult. Recognition or rewards should not exist as individual efforts; they should become part of organizational culture. Leaders play a pivotal role in driving a culture of recognition by setting examples. With leaders actively promoting employee recognition programs, fostering positive working environment where appreciation will form part of daily communication.

Addressing Resistance and Change Management

Resistance to change is one factor that may impede the implementation of reward and recognition programs. Employees may resist new procedures or question whether these schemes are effective at all. It is important for firms to explain why they have implemented these initiatives highlighting advantages as well as addressing queries or misconceptions. Trust can therefore be cultivated on organizational level after involving employees in decision making process as well as allowing them an opportunity to express their thoughts.

In addition, clear communication plays an integral role in ensuring successful execution of reward and recognition schemes. For example, employees should understand what constitutes criteria or processes underlying certain rewards programs such as "employee of the month." Such platforms like team meetings, email newsletters or intranet updates can help disseminate information across employees during implementation stage so as keep them engaged.

Measuring Success and Continuous Improvement

Finally measuring the impact or success of these systems poses its own set of difficulties. Firms need to establish appropriate performance metrics together with evaluation models used to gauge effectiveness of these initiatives. As an example, employee feedback may be collected from employees, key performance indicators tracked or even surveys and focus groups conducted. By analyzing and evaluating data on a regular basis, companies are able to identify areas for improvement as well as make informed decisions.

In conclusion, challenges in implementing recognition and reward systems will occur but they can be mitigated by using the right approaches and fostering a supportive work environment. Businesses that want to succeed should promote their values through rewards and recognition programs or address resistance accordingly. This creates an atmosphere where workers feel appreciated and valued by aligning the firm's values with its reward structure.

Case Studies: Successful Recognition and Reward Programs

This section offers real-life case studies that illustrate how effective recognition and reward programs drive employee engagement and performance. These practical examples provide invaluable lessons on how organizations have used such programs to create vibrant workplaces.

Case Study 1: Acorn Corporation

Acorn Corporation, a technology leader in the market, has come up with an incentive program known as "Star Performers." Such program enabled employees to nominate their colleagues for outstanding contributions and achievements. The nominees would then be given a special badge and a personalized note from their CEO acknowledging their exemplary performance. This small but symbolic gesture had an immediate impact on employee morale and motivation and resulted in a 20% increase in productivity after only six months.

Case Study 2: Dell Enterprises

Dell Enterprises, an international consulting company introduced "Empower and Excel," which was an all-encompassing reward system. These rewards ranged from extra paid leave, exclusive training courses, global assignments among others. By making rewards more personal, Dell Enterprises greatly increased its levels of staff satisfaction leading to a 15% drop in turnover rates; followed by a corresponding 30% rise in customer loyalty scores.

Case Study 3: Green Inc.

Green Inc., a company that has long been one of the largest retailers around, has created something unique titled "Employee Appreciation Store." Thus, they were given points based upon performance that could be used for purchases within the organization or its partners. This approach did not just encourage competition within departments but also led to significant sales growth as well as improved customer satisfaction thus enhancing the firm's competitive position and revenue base.

These three cases demonstrate how recognition and reward programmes can transform workplace dynamics culminating into organisational prosperity. By developing customised programmes aligned with organisational values and employees' desires businesses can create positive work environments that foster cultures of excellence.

Best Practices for Implementing Recognition and Reward Systems

In order to make recognition and reward systems work effectively over time in your organization, it is very crucial that you follow some of the best practices. The following are key considerations along with strategies for implementation that can help you develop a culture of appreciation thereby motivating your workers.

Firstly, aligning recognition systems with organizational goals and values is very important. Once you define the specific behaviours or accomplishments that you wish to acknowledge, it is possible to ensure that your programs have meaningful impact on employee motivation and performance. Regularly communicate such expectations to your employees for fostering transparency and the shared understanding of what matters.

Secondly, this will also involve exploring different types of recognition. These may be in the form of cash rewards or non-monetary types such as certificates or extra time off work. It is advisable, therefore, to link recognition with corporate customs as well as individual achievements.

Finally, regular assessment and improvement are key ingredients for continuous success with such programs. Assessing employee engagement levels and productivity among other key metrics can be useful ways of identifying program effectiveness. Moreover, gather feedback from staff members concerning these systems and their suggestions on how they could be enhanced. Such data should then be used to refine the systems so that they can continue appealing to employees hence driving desirable outcomes.

Chapter 44

Ongoing Overtures: Looking to the Future of Business Management

In this chapter of "From Manager to Maestro: The Symphony of Good Management," we paint a vibrant picture of the future, exploring the concept of ongoing overtures and how they shape the business landscape. So, sit back, relax, and let us take you on a journey into the realms of business management.

Imagine a bustling city, teeming with diverse businesses, each playing its part in the grand symphony. In this metropolis, leaders are like conductors, guiding their teams through the harmonious interplay of strategy, innovation, and adaptability. They understand that business management is not a static art but an ongoing composition.

Meet Emma, a visionary entrepreneur who runs a successful start-up in the heart of the city. With an unwavering passion for her craft, Emma has built a business that thrives on embracing change and staying ahead of the curve. She constantly seeks new ways to improve her management style and harnesses the power of ongoing overtures.

Like Emma, forward-thinking leaders recognize that business management is not about reaching a final crescendo but rather about constantly fine-tuning their skills and strategies. They understand that the key to success lies in anticipating emerging trends, embracing innovation, and navigating through disruptions with agility.

As we journey through this chapter, we will explore the evolving face of leadership, the power of innovation, digital transformation, navigating disruption and uncertainty, building agile and adaptive teams, embracing diversity and inclusion, the role of purpose and ethics in business, as well as the future trends that will shape the world of business management.

So, join us as we unravel the mysteries of ongoing overtures and discover the symphony of good management that propels businesses into a harmonious future.

The Evolution of Leadership

In today's fast-paced and ever-changing business landscape, the role of leadership has undergone a significant evolution. Gone are the days of top-down hierarchy and authoritative decision-making. The modern leader must possess a unique set of qualities and adapt their approach to inspire and motivate teams for long-term success.

Successful leaders recognize that leadership is no longer about domination and control, but rather about collaboration and empowerment. They understand that fostering a culture of inclusivity and embracing diverse perspectives leads to innovation and better decision-making. These leaders prioritize building strong relationships with their teams, fostering trust and open communication.

The evolution of leadership also involves being adaptable and agile in the face of constant change. Today's leaders must be comfortable navigating ambiguity and uncertainty, making thoughtful decisions based on data and insights.

Furthermore, effective leaders recognize the importance of continuous learning and personal growth. They invest in their own development, staying abreast of the latest trends and best practices in leadership. They encourage a culture of continuous learning within their teams, providing opportunities for skill development and growth.

In conclusion, the evolution of leadership can be attributed to the changing dynamics of the business world. Successful leaders embrace collaboration, adaptability, inclusivity, and continuous learning. By embodying these qualities, leaders can navigate the complexities of the modern business environment and inspire their teams to achieve long-term success.

The Power of Innovation

In today's rapidly evolving business landscape, innovation has become a driving force behind growth and staying competitive. Businesses are harnessing the power of innovation to not only meet the needs of their customers but also to disrupt traditional industries and create new opportunities.

At the heart of innovation lies the ability to think and act creatively, to challenge the status quo, and to embrace change. It's about tapping into the collective intelligence of your team and empowering them to explore new ideas and solutions.

Technology plays a crucial role in enabling innovation. From AI-powered systems that automate processes to data analytics tools that uncover valuable insights, technology provides a foundation for transformative innovation. Businesses are leveraging these technological advancements to streamline operations, enhance customer experience, and drive future success.

But innovation is not just about technology. It's also about fostering a culture of creativity and out-of-the-box thinking. Organizations that encourage their employees to experiment, take risks, and learn from failures are more likely to bring innovative ideas to the table.

Moreover, innovation is about understanding the needs and desires of customers and finding novel ways to meet those demands. By actively listening to customers, gathering feedback, and identifying unmet needs, businesses can develop innovative products and services that stand out in the market.

Ultimately, the power of innovation lies in its ability to fuel business growth, drive competitive advantage, and create lasting impact. By embracing innovation, organizations can navigate the ever-changing business landscape with agility and resilience.

Embracing Digital Transformation

Digital transformation has become a buzzword in today's business landscape, and for good reason. It refers to the integration of digital technology into various aspects of a business, fundamentally changing how organizations operate and deliver value to their customers. From automating manual processes to leveraging data analytics and adopting cloud computing, digital transformation has the power to revolutionize businesses of all sizes.

One of the key areas where digital transformation has a profound impact is streamlining operations. By digitizing and automating processes, organizations can increase efficiency, reduce costs, and improve productivity. This allows employees to focus on higher-value tasks, while repetitive and time-consuming tasks are handled by intelligent systems.

In addition to operational efficiency, digital transformation also presents opportunities for enhancing the customer experience. Through the use of data analytics and artificial intelligence, businesses can gain valuable insights into customer preferences and behavior, enabling them to deliver personalized and targeted experiences. This not only increases customer satisfaction but also drives customer loyalty and repeat business.

The ever-evolving digital landscape requires organizations to adapt and stay ahead. Digital transformation enables businesses to be agile and responsive to market changes, enabling them to make data-driven decisions and seize new opportunities. By embracing digital transformation, organizations can future-proof their operations and remain competitive in an increasingly digital world.

Embracing digital transformation is not just a choice, but a necessity for businesses that want to thrive in the digital age. It requires a holistic approach, combining technology adoption with organizational change and a culture of innovation. By leveraging digital solutions and staying abreast of emerging technologies, organizations can unlock new ways of doing business, drive growth, and create a sustainable future.

Navigating Disruption and Uncertainty

In today's rapidly evolving business landscape, leaders face numerous challenges posed by disruptive forces and uncertain market conditions. The ever-present need to adapt and stay ahead requires a strategic approach to navigating disruption and uncertainty.

While disruption can be unsettling, it also presents unique opportunities for growth and innovation. Organizations that embrace change and proactively address disruptive forces are better equipped to thrive in turbulent times.

One key strategy for navigating disruption is to embrace a mindset of agility and resilience. This involves staying informed about market trends, consumer behavior, and emerging technologies. By continuously monitoring the landscape, leaders can identify potential disruptions and develop strategies to mitigate risks.

Another crucial aspect of navigating uncertainty is fostering a culture of innovation and experimentation. Encouraging teams to think creatively and explore new ideas can lead to transformative solutions that not only address disruptions but also drive long-term success.

Moreover, effective leadership plays a critical role in navigating disruption and uncertainty. Leaders must inspire and motivate their teams, providing clear direction and guidance during times of change. By fostering open communication and creating a supportive work environment, leaders can empower their teams to navigate disruption with confidence.

Ultimately, navigating disruption and uncertainty requires a proactive approach and a willingness to embrace change. By anticipating potential disruptions, fostering innovation, and providing strong leadership, organizations can turn challenges into opportunities for growth and resilience.

Building Agile and Adaptive Teams

As the business landscape continues to rapidly evolve, organizations must adapt and embrace agility and adaptability within their teams. Building agile and adaptive teams is essential for navigating the complex and ever-changing environment with confidence and resilience.

To create agile teams, it is crucial to foster a culture of continuous learning. Encourage team members to embrace new knowledge and skills, staying updated on industry trends and best practices. By investing in their professional development, teams can stay ahead of the curve and respond effectively to new challenges.

Collaboration is another key aspect of building agile teams. Encourage open communication and the sharing of ideas among team members. By working together and leveraging the diverse perspectives and expertise within the team, innovative solutions can be generated and implemented quickly.

Innovation is a fundamental characteristic of adaptive teams. Encourage a mindset of experimentation and risk-taking. Embrace failure as a learning opportunity and encourage team members to explore new approaches and ideas. By fostering an environment that rewards creativity and innovation, teams can adapt to changes more effectively and seize new opportunities.

Building agile and adaptive teams also requires a focus on inclusivity and diversity. Embrace the unique strengths and perspectives of each team member and create an environment where everyone feels valued and included. By harnessing the power of diversity, teams can tap into a wide range of ideas and insights, leading to better decision-making and problem-solving.

Adopting agile and adaptive practices is not a one-time effort but an ongoing journey. Regularly assess and refine team processes and structures to ensure their effectiveness in the face of changing business dynamics. Encourage a continuous improvement mindset and embrace feedback as a tool for growth and development.

By building agile and adaptive teams, organizations can navigate the challenges and uncertainties of the business landscape with confidence. Cultivating a culture of continuous learning, collaboration, and innovation is key to building teams that can thrive in today's fast-paced and ever-changing world.

Embracing Diversity and Inclusion

Understanding the significance of diversity and inclusion is crucial for driving innovation and enhancing organizational performance. Embracing diversity means valuing and welcoming individuals from different backgrounds, cultures, and perspectives. Inclusion, on the other hand, entails creating an environment that encourages participation and respects the contributions of all employees, regardless of their differences.

Companies that prioritize diversity and inclusion experience numerous benefits. A diverse workforce brings together a variety of skills, knowledge, and experiences, fostering creativity and innovation. By embracing diversity, organizations can tap into a wider talent pool and attract top talent from different demographics.

To foster a diverse and inclusive work environment, organizations can implement several strategies. Firstly, they can prioritize diversity in their recruitment and hiring practices, ensuring that job opportunities are accessible to individuals from all backgrounds. Secondly, organizations can provide training programs and workshops to promote cultural competency and unconscious bias awareness among employees.

An inclusive work culture should be built on trust, respect, and equal opportunities. Encouraging open communication channels and empowering employees at all levels can foster a sense of belonging and engagement. Additionally, supporting employee resource groups and affinity networks can create spaces for underrepresented groups to connect, share experiences, and advocate for change.

Nurturing a Diverse Workforce

Nurturing a diverse workforce involves creating an environment where individuals feel valued, heard, and empowered. To achieve this, organizations can implement mentorship and sponsorship programs that enable diverse employees to access opportunities for growth and advancement.

Furthermore, organizations should prioritize diversity in leadership positions. When employees see leaders who look like them, they are more likely to feel motivated and believe that their contributions are valued. Creating a diverse leadership team can also bring diverse perspectives and enhance decision-making processes.

Finally, organizations should regularly assess their progress in fostering diversity and inclusion. Conducting anonymous employee surveys, tracking key performance indicators related to diversity and inclusion, and establishing accountability measures can help organizations identify areas for improvement and drive meaningful change.

The Role of Purpose and Ethics in Business

As businesses evolve and adapt to changing societal expectations, the role of purpose and ethics in business has become increasingly paramount. Purpose-driven organizations that prioritize ethical practices not only contribute to a better world but also reap long-term benefits in terms of success, employee engagement, and customer loyalty.

Integrating purpose into a company's strategy goes beyond just defining a mission statement. It involves aligning every aspect of the business with a greater purpose that goes beyond profits. By clearly communicating and living out their purpose, organizations foster a sense of meaning and direction for their employees, resulting in heightened motivation and a stronger sense of unity.

Ethical business practices, on the other hand, are vital for establishing trust and credibility with employees, customers, and partners. Transparent operations, fair treatment of employees, responsible sourcing, and environmental sustainability are all key components of sound ethical practices.

By prioritizing purpose and ethics, businesses can tap into a growing consumer base that values companies with a strong moral compass. Consumers are increasingly seeking out brands that align with their own values and beliefs, making purpose-driven and ethical companies more likely to attract and retain loyal customers.

Moreover, purpose and ethics can act as guiding principles that help businesses navigate complex decisions and ethically ambiguous situations. By establishing a firm ethical foundation, leaders can ensure that their organizations make choices that are not only profitable but also responsible and sustainable in the long run.

Overall, the role of purpose and ethics in business goes beyond mere compliance and becomes a catalyst for positive change. When purpose and ethics are at the core of a business, it creates a virtuous cycle of success, employee fulfillment, and customer loyalty, ensuring a brighter future for both the organization and society as a whole.

Future Trends in Business Management

As the business landscape continues to evolve, it is crucial for organizations to stay ahead of the curve and embrace the emerging trends that will shape the future of business management. From leveraging artificial intelligence (AI) and automation to prioritizing sustainability and social responsibility, the way businesses operate and lead is undergoing a significant transformation.

One of the key future trends in business management is the integration of AI and automation into various aspects of operations. AI-powered technologies can optimize processes, enhance decision-making, and improve overall efficiency. Automation, on the other hand, can streamline workflows, reduce human error, and free up valuable time for employees to focus on higher-value tasks.

In addition to technological advancements, sustainability and social responsibility are emerging as essential considerations in business management. With growing concerns about climate change and environmental impact, organizations are increasingly adopting sustainable practices to minimize their carbon footprint and contribute to a more sustainable future. Moreover, consumers are placing greater emphasis on supporting companies that prioritize social responsibility and ethical practices, making it crucial for businesses to align their values with those of their target audience.

Looking ahead, future trends in business management will require leaders to embrace innovation, adapt to disruptive forces, and foster diversity and inclusion within their organizations. By staying abreast of these trends and effectively navigating the changing landscape, businesses can position themselves for long-term success and maintain a competitive edge.

Chapter 45

Maestro's Coda: Reflections and Final Thoughts for the Aspiring Conductor-manager

As we reach the final chapter of "From Manager to Maestro: The Symphony of Good Management," it's time to reflect on the incredible journey we've embarked on together. But before we dive into our key insights and final thoughts, let me share a relatable story that sets the stage for what's to come.

Picture this: a young manager named Sarah, passionate about both music and business, found herself torn between her two loves. She often wondered if there was a way to combine her artistic spirit and managerial prowess into one harmonious symphony.

One fateful evening, as Sarah attended a captivating orchestral performance, she was struck by the conductor's magnetic presence. Not only did he guide the musicians with impeccable precision, but he also effortlessly commanded the audience's attention, evoking a sea of emotions through the music.

Inspired by this conductor's ability to lead and inspire, Sarah had a realization. The world of business management and orchestra conducting were not as dissimilar as she had once thought. Both roles required a delicate balance of artistry, teamwork, and strategic decision-making.

Driven by this newfound insight, Sarah delved deep into the world of conductor-managers. She studied their methods, dissected their leadership styles, and drew parallels between the maestro's baton and the manager's responsibilities.

Throughout her journey, Sarah discovered that being a successful conductor-manager meant more than just managing a team; it meant orchestrating a symphony of collaboration, communication, innovation, and emotional intelligence.

And now, dear reader, as we approach the finale of our series, it's time for you to step into Sarah's shoes. Join us as we explore the final thoughts, insights, and wisdom that will guide you on your path to becoming a conductor-manager extraordinaire in the world of business management.

Embracing the Conductor-Manager Role

As an aspiring conductor-manager, you are entering a role that requires full embrace of its unique responsibilities and challenges. A conductor-manager is not only a leader but also a navigator, guiding a diverse orchestra of employees while managing the complexities of running a business.

Operating at the intersection of artistry and business acumen, the conductor-manager must strike a harmonious balance. This role demands the ability to seamlessly blend creative vision with strategic decision-making to drive organizational success.

In the realm of business management, the conductor-manager's main task is to orchestrate the different facets of the organization, ensuring that each component works in harmony towards a common goal. By leveraging their expertise and understanding of business dynamics, conductor-managers can effectively steer their teams towards optimal performance and achievement.

One of the significant challenges conductor-managers face is leading in a diverse and dynamic workforce. With employees of varying backgrounds, skills, and perspectives, it is essential to be inclusive and foster an environment where everyone feels valued and motivated to contribute their best.

As a conductor-manager, you must become adept at navigating the complexities of the business landscape. This includes understanding market trends, identifying opportunities for growth, and making strategic decisions that align with the organization's vision. By honing your business management skills, you can create a solid foundation for success.

Embracing the role of a conductor-manager is a commitment to continuous growth and learning. It requires ongoing professional development, an open mind to embrace new ideas and approaches, and a willingness to adapt to the ever-evolving challenges of the business world.

By fully embracing the conductor-manager role, you have the opportunity to create a symphony of success, leading your team towards greatness and achieving extraordinary results in the field of business management.

Mastering the Art of Collaboration

Collaboration is a cornerstone of successful conductor-managers. In today's fast-paced business landscape, teamwork and collaboration have become essential for driving innovation and achieving organizational goals. As a conductor-manager, mastering the art of collaboration is crucial to create a harmonious and productive work environment.

Effective collaboration involves creating a culture that values diverse perspectives and encourages open communication. By fostering a collaborative environment, conductor-managers can leverage the collective knowledge, skills, and expertise of their team members, resulting in enhanced problem-solving capabilities and increased creativity.

To foster collaboration, conductor-managers can implement strategies such as:

1. Establishing Shared Goals and Objectives:

By setting clear and shared goals, conductor-managers provide a common purpose that unites the team and aligns their efforts. This clarity helps team members understand how their individual contributions fit into the bigger picture, fostering a sense of ownership and collaboration.

2. Promoting Open Communication:

Encouraging open and honest communication among team members creates an environment where ideas and feedback can be freely shared. Regular team meetings, brainstorming sessions, and one-on-one conversations can facilitate effective communication and foster a culture of collaboration.

3. Building Trust and Psychological Safety:

Trust is the foundation of effective collaboration. Conductor-managers can cultivate trust by promoting transparency, respecting diverse opinions, and encouraging risk-taking without fear of judgment. Creating a psychologically safe environment where team members feel comfortable taking risks and expressing their ideas fosters collaboration and innovation.

Collaboration is not limited to internal teams; it also extends to partnerships and collaborations with external stakeholders such as clients, vendors, and industry experts. By nurturing these relationships, conductor-managers can tap into additional resources, knowledge, and opportunities.

By mastering the art of collaboration, conductor-managers can harness the power of teamwork and unlock the full potential of their team members. Collaboration not only enhances productivity and innovation but also cultivates a sense of belonging and engagement among team members, ultimately leading to long-term success.

Orchestrating Effective Communication

Effective communication is the cornerstone of successful conductor-managers. It bridges the gap between team members, fosters collaboration, and ensures alignment with organizational objectives. To excel in this role, conductor-managers must master essential communication techniques that facilitate understanding, promote transparency, and inspire their teams towards success.

One crucial aspect of effective communication is active listening. By attentively listening to employees' perspectives, concerns, and ideas, conductor-managers can demonstrate empathy and create an open dialogue. This promotes a culture of trust and encourages team members to contribute their unique insights, leading to improved decision-making and innovative solutions.

Furthermore, clear and concise verbal and written communication is vital for conveying expectations, goals, and feedback. By articulating instructions and objectives in a straightforward manner, conductor-managers can ensure everyone is on the same page, minimizing misunderstandings and enhancing productivity.

Additionally, non-verbal communication plays a significant role in effective communication. As conductor-managers, being aware of body language, facial expressions, and tone of voice can help convey messages with clarity and authenticity. This awareness can foster positive relationships, strengthen team dynamics, and create an environment where open and honest communication thrives.

Another critical aspect is communication technology. Leveraging modern communication tools such as video conferencing, project management software, and instant messaging facilitates timely and efficient communication, especially in remote or globally dispersed teams. Conducting virtual meetings, sharing updates, and providing feedback become seamless, contributing to enhanced team collaboration and efficiency.

On a broader scale, effective communication also involves stakeholder management. Conductor-managers need to communicate with various stakeholders, including clients, partners, and executives, to ensure a shared understanding and alignment of strategic goals. By effectively communicating the organization's vision, values, and progress, conductor-managers can cultivate strong partnerships and secure support for their initiatives.

In summary, effective communication is paramount for conductor-managers in orchestrating success. By actively listening, utilizing clear and concise communication, being mindful of non-verbal cues, leveraging communication technology, and managing stakeholders, conductor-managers can build strong relationships, foster collaboration, and guide their teams towards achieving organizational objectives.

Setting the Tempo for Innovation

Innovation is the lifeblood of business growth and success. As conductor-managers, it is your responsibility to foster a culture of innovation within your organization. By fostering an environment that encourages creativity, embracing change, and inspiring fresh ideas, you can set the tempo for innovation and drive your team towards new levels of excellence.

Effective leadership is crucial in creating an atmosphere that promotes innovation. By displaying a clear vision and supporting your team's ideas, you can empower them to think outside the box and push boundaries. Encouraging collaboration and providing resources for experimentation allows for the generation of groundbreaking ideas and solutions.

Embracing change is another critical aspect of fostering innovation. As a conductor-manager, you must be willing to adapt to new technologies, market trends, and customer preferences. By embracing change, you can create an environment where experimentation and continuous improvement thrive.

Furthermore, innovation requires an environment that inspires and motivates individuals to contribute their creative ideas. By recognizing and rewarding innovation, you can cultivate a culture where employees feel valued and encouraged to think innovatively.

Ultimately, a conductor-manager who sets the tempo for innovation is a catalyst for growth and success. By leading with vision, embracing change, and inspiring creativity, you can create a culture of innovation that propels your organization forward.

Conducting Performance Management

Effective performance management is a critical aspect of optimizing employee output and maximizing organizational success. By implementing strategies that focus on setting goals, providing constructive feedback, and motivating individuals, conductor-managers can help their team members reach their full potential.

Setting Clear Goals: A key responsibility of the conductor-manager is to establish clear and achievable goals for each team member. By setting specific, measurable, attainable, relevant, and time-bound (SMART) goals, employees have a clear understanding of expectations and can work towards achieving them.

Providing Constructive Feedback: Regular and constructive feedback is essential for fostering growth and improvement. Conductor-managers should provide timely feedback that highlights both strengths and areas for development. This feedback should be specific, actionable, and delivered in a supportive manner.

Motivating for Excellence: Motivation plays a crucial role in employee performance. Conductor-managers can inspire their team members by recognizing their achievements, offering opportunities for growth and development, and creating a positive work environment that values and rewards excellence.

The Impact of Performance Management on Employee Performance

Effective performance management can significantly impact employee performance and overall organizational productivity. When team members have clear goals, receive regular feedback, and feel motivated to excel, they are more likely to be engaged, productive, and committed to achieving exceptional results.

In conclusion, conducting performance management is a vital responsibility for conductor-managers who aim to optimize employee performance. By setting clear goals, providing constructive feedback, and nurturing motivation, they can inspire their team members to reach new heights of success.

Leading with Emotional Intelligence

intelligence is a critical trait for conductor-managers who strive for effective leadership and success in business management. By developing their emotional intelligence, conductor-managers can create a positive work environment, build strong relationships, and inspire their teams to achieve greatness.

Emotional intelligence encompasses the ability to understand and manage one's own emotions while also empathizing with others. It involves being aware of emotional cues, regulating emotions, and effectively communicating with team members.

Conductor-managers with strong emotional intelligence are adept at recognizing the needs and concerns of their employees. They can empathize with their team members and provide the support and guidance needed to navigate challenges.

Furthermore, emotional intelligence enables conductor-managers to motivate and inspire their teams. By understanding the unique strengths and motivations of each individual, they can provide tailored feedback, recognition, and opportunities for growth. This not only enhances employee engagement but also fosters a sense of belonging and loyalty within the team.

Leaders who possess emotional intelligence are also skilled at managing conflict and resolving interpersonal issues. They can navigate difficult conversations and create a harmonious work environment where collaboration thrives.

Developing emotional intelligence is a lifelong journey. Conductor-managers can enhance their emotional intelligence by practicing self-awareness, actively listening to others, seeking feedback, and continuously learning and growing.

By leading with emotional intelligence, conductor-managers can build successful, high-performing teams and create a culture of trust, collaboration, and innovation.

Balancing Artistry and Business Acumen

As a conductor-manager, it is essential to find harmony between your artistic vision and the practicality of making sound business decisions. This delicate balance allows you to create outstanding artistic performances while driving organizational success.

Artistry is the essence of your work, guiding the interpretation and expression of the music. It is what sets you apart and captivates audiences. Your unique artistic sensibilities enable you to bring out the very best in your musicians and create transformative experiences for your audience.

However, business acumen is equally important to ensure sustainable success. You must possess an understanding of financial management, budgeting, marketing, and strategic planning that align with your artistic aspirations. This knowledge empowers you to make informed decisions that optimize resources, attract sponsorship, and expand your organization's reach.

Finding Common Ground

Artistry and business acumen should never exist in isolation. Instead, they should coexist and complement each other to achieve a harmonious partnership. By leveraging your artistic vision and aligning it with sound business strategies, you can create a thriving organization that both captivates audiences and achieves financial stability.

A successful conductor-manager artfully navigates the complexities of the business world while fostering an environment conducive to artistic excellence. This requires a deep understanding of the unique challenges faced by artists and musicians and developing innovative approaches to overcome them.

Cultivating Your Leadership Style

Striking a balance between artistry and business acumen necessitates effective leadership skills. An exceptional conductor-manager inspires, motivates, and empowers their team members to contribute their best work. By understanding the needs and aspirations of your musicians, you can provide the guidance, support, and resources necessary for their artistic growth.

At the same time, your business acumen enables you to manage finances, negotiate contracts, and collaborate with stakeholders effectively. Leading with confidence, transparency, and integrity, you ensure the sustainability and success of your organization while allowing your artistic vision to flourish.

In conclusion, mastering the art of balancing artistry and business acumen is crucial for conductor-managers. By combining your unique artistic sensibilities with strategic decision-making, you can lead your organization to new heights while captivating audiences and nurturing artistic excellence.

Conducting Change Management

In today's fast-paced business environment, change is inevitable. As a conductor-manager, it is crucial to possess the skills and strategies to effectively lead and navigate organizational change. Change management involves implementing structured approaches to support individuals and teams as they transition from current practices to new ones.

Organizational change can encompass various initiatives, such as implementing new technologies, restructuring teams, or adapting to market shifts. Regardless of the nature of the change, successful change management requires a thoughtful and systematic approach.

One key aspect of change management is ensuring smooth transitions and fostering employee buy-in. Organizational change can often create uncertainty and resistance among team members. It is essential for conductor-managers to communicate openly, addressing employees' concerns, and actively involving them in the change process. By promoting transparency and sharing the rationale for change, conductor-managers can build trust, encourage engagement, and facilitate a smoother transition.

Change management strategies can also include creating a clear roadmap that outlines the steps, timelines, and expectations associated with the change. This helps provide clarity and minimize disruption within the organization. Moreover, conductor-managers can play a vital role in identifying and mitigating potential risks and challenges that may arise during the change process.

It is important to understand that change management is an ongoing effort. Even after the initial implementation, conductor-managers should continue to monitor and evaluate the effectiveness of the change, making necessary adjustments to ensure its success.

Embracing change management as a conductor-manager not only helps organizations adapt and thrive, but it also demonstrates strong leadership capabilities. By effectively conducting change management initiatives, conductor-managers can position their teams and organizations for long-term success in today's ever-evolving business landscape.

Striving for Continuous Growth and Learning

The journey to becoming a conductor-manager is a lifelong pursuit of continuous growth and learning. In this dynamic role, it is essential to stay updated with the latest industry trends, hone your leadership skills, and expand your knowledge base to effectively lead your team and drive organizational success.

Embracing a mindset of continuous growth involves seeking out opportunities for professional development and actively pursuing learning experiences that will enhance your capabilities as a conductor-manager. This can include attending workshops and conferences, enrolling in relevant courses or certifications, and engaging in self-study through reading books and articles.

As you strive for continuous growth, it is also important to prioritize personal development. Cultivate emotional intelligence, resilience, and self-awareness, as these qualities will enhance your ability to navigate the challenges and complexities of the conductor-manager role.

One effective way to foster continuous growth and learning is by seeking mentorship and guidance from experienced professionals in your field. By learning from their experiences and insights, you can gain valuable perspectives and accelerate your own development as a conductor-manager.

Additionally, don't underestimate the power of networking and building relationships within your industry. Connect with like-minded individuals, join professional associations, and engage in meaningful conversations to exchange ideas and learn from others' experiences.

Continuous growth and learning are not only beneficial for your own development as a conductor-manager but also for the success of your team and organization. By staying current with industry trends, acquiring new knowledge and skills, and fostering a culture of curiosity and learning within your team, you can promote innovation, increase productivity, and create a dynamic and engaging work environment.

Orchestrating Work-Life Harmony

Maintaining a healthy work-life balance is essential for your overall well-being and productivity as a conductor-manager. The demands of your role may sometimes feel overwhelming, but finding harmony between your personal and professional life is achievable. Here are some effective techniques and strategies to help you create work-life harmony:

1. Prioritize and Delegate

Identify your core responsibilities and prioritize tasks based on their importance and urgency. Delegate tasks whenever possible to lighten your workload and free up time for personal activities.

2. Set Boundaries

Establish clear boundaries between your work and personal life. Designate specific hours for work and non-work activities. Respect these boundaries by avoiding work-related tasks during your personal time.

3. Schedule Self-Care

Make self-care a priority by scheduling regular time for activities that recharge your energy and promote well-being. This could include exercise, leisure activities, spending quality time with loved ones, or pursuing hobbies.

4. Practice Mindfulness

Adopt mindfulness practices to help you stay present and focused in both your personal and professional life. This can enhance your overall sense of balance and reduce stress levels.

5. Utilize Technology Wisely

Use technology tools to streamline your work processes and increase efficiency. However, be mindful of excessive use of technology that may encroach upon your personal time.

6. Seek Support

Don't hesitate to seek support from your colleagues, friends, or family when needed. Delegate tasks, share responsibilities, and rely on your support network to help you maintain work-life harmony.

7. Plan Regular Breaks

Take regular breaks throughout the day to recharge and refresh your mind. This allows you to maintain focus and productivity while preventing burnout.

8. Communicate and Negotiate

Have open and honest conversations with your team, supervisor, or clients about your workload and commitments. Negotiate flexible working arrangements or adjustments when necessary to accommodate personal obligations.

By implementing these techniques into your daily routine, you can orchestrate a harmonious balance between your professional aspirations and personal well-being as a conductor-manager.

Embodying Leadership Excellence

Leadership is at the core of conductor-manager roles, driving teams towards success in the dynamic realm of business management. Aspiring conductor-managers must aim for leadership excellence to inspire and empower their teams, creating an environment that fosters growth and innovation.

To embody leadership excellence, it is crucial to develop and nurture essential qualities and skills. Effective communication, both verbal and non-verbal, is key to building strong relationships and ensuring clarity in organizational objectives. By actively listening, providing constructive feedback, and encouraging open dialogue, conductor-managers can establish trust and create a collaborative atmosphere.

Furthermore, a leader who demonstrates emotional intelligence has the ability to empathize, motivate, and inspire their teams. By recognizing and managing their own emotions while understanding and responding to the emotions of others, conductor-managers can cultivate a positive and inclusive work culture.

Strategies and best practices can also elevate leadership excellence. Conductors-managers should embrace a growth mindset and actively seek opportunities for continuous learning and professional development. Additionally, they must strike a balance between artistic sensibilities and business acumen to make sound strategic decisions that drive organizational success.

"Just as the complex business world dances, music balances novelty and tradition, innovation and strategy, rhythm and expansion. This means that achievement is not about playing notes alone but the way they strike a chord with listeners. In music as in business, it's the harmonious juxtaposition of various components that makes a masterpiece which can influence transformation, propel development and charm audiences everywhere."

Appendix
References and Additional Reading

Books:

Good to Great: Why Some Companies Make the Leap...And Others Don't by Jim Collins - Discusses strategies for effective leadership and management practices that can help organizations achieve sustained success.

The Innovator's Dilemma by Clayton Christensen - Explains how disruptive innovation and technologies can impact businesses and offers strategies for adapting to change.

The Five Dysfunctions of a Team by Patrick Lencioni - Focuses on building cohesive and high-performing teams through overcoming common issues.

Leading Change by John Kotter - Provides a framework for leading organizational change effectively through various stages.

Journal Articles:

"Developing Leadership Talent" by David Berke (Harvard Business Review) - Discusses strategies for identifying and cultivating leadership potential within companies.

"Time Management in the Age of New Work" by Laura Vanderkam (Harvard Business Review) - Explores effective time management and productivity techniques in today's work environment.

"Leading Change: Why Transformation Efforts Fail" by John Kotter (Harvard Business Review) - Analyzes reasons why organizational change initiatives fail and offers a framework for successful transformation.

Websites/Reports:

The Society for Human Resource Management - Resources on topics like performance management, leadership development, and change management.

McKinsey Quarterly Reports - Market insight and case studies on various business management topics including leadership, strategy, and innovation.

Gallup Articles/Reports - Research-based content on measuring and enhancing employee and customer engagement.

www.ingramcontent.com/pod-product-compliance
Lightning Source LLC
Chambersburg PA
CBHW080849120626
46546CB00008B/2750

* 9 7 8 1 9 6 3 9 7 2 0 9 2 *